BIBLIOGRAPHY OF STATISTICAL LITERATURE
1940-1949

BIBLIOGRAPHY OF STATISTICAL LITERATURE

1940-1949

MAURICE G. KENDALL, M.A., Sc.D.

MANAGING DIRECTOR, C.E.I.R. LTD.

AND

ALISON G. DOIG, B.Sc., M.A.

SENIOR LECTURER IN STATISTICS, UNIVERSITY OF MELBOURNE

OLIVER AND BOYD

EDINBURGH AND LONDON

OLIVER AND BOYD LTD
Tweeddale Court
Edinburgh 1

39a Welbeck Street
London W.1

FIRST PUBLISHED 1965

PRINTED IN GREAT BRITAIN BY OLIVER AND BOYD LTD., EDINBURGH

PREFACE

THE WAY in which this bibliography has been constructed was described in the preface to the first volume relating to the years 1950 to 1958. That volume contained some 10,000 references, this one contains about 6500. The final volume, relating to the years prior to 1940, is in active preparation and is now passing through the press.

As might have been expected, a number of references have come to light which should have been included in the first volume. We wish to acknowledge the assistance of many colleagues in advising us of errors and omissions. In particular, our thanks are due to Professor H. O. Lancaster of the University of Sydney who compared the proofs of this volume with his own extensive card index. Any other omissions from this volume and from the first part of the bibliography will be included as a supplement in the final volume. We should be grateful if our readers would bring any gaps of which they are aware to our notice, since the final responsibility for the selection of material to be included and for the completeness of this selection rests with the editors.

We are greatly indebted to the Nuffield Foundation and to the London School of Economics and Political Science for financial support in the preparation of the second and third volumes. The detailed work involved in searching the literature and checking the references makes heavy demands on staff time which could not have been afforded without this generous assistance.

It may be of interest to record that Dr. M. J. R. Healy of the Rothamsted Experimental Research Station has classified the references in volume 1 by subject. The data have been punched on cards and transferred to magnetic tape for analysis on an Orion computer. His work is described in the *Journal of the Royal Statistical Society* for 1963, Series A, vol. 126, pages 270-5.

We should like to record our thanks to the publishers, Oliver & Boyd, Ltd., for their patience and skill in the setting and correction of some rather tedious manuscript.

January 1965

M. G. K.
A. G. D.

ACKNOWLEDGMENTS

THIS VOLUME has been prepared under the supervision of M. G. Kendall and Alison G. Doig in the Research Techniques Division of the London School of Economics and Political Science. The following participated in the work:

> MR. S. S. AHMAD
> MR. J. A. BEAVAN
> MR. A. C. JHAVARY
> MRS. L. A. KINGSMAN

CYRILLIC ALPHABET

Transliteration of the Cyrillic alphabet. " British " system in B.S. 2979 (British Standards Institution) with accents and diacritics omitted in accordance with note 1 on page 7 of B.S. 2979.

А	A	К	K	Х	KH
Б	B	Л	L	Ц	TS
В	V	М	M	Ч	CH
Г	G	Н	N	Ш	SH
Д	D	О	O	Щ	SHCH
Е	E	П	P	Ъ	”
Ё	E	Р	R	Ь	’
Ж	ZH	С	S	Ы	Y
З	Z	Т	T	Э	E
И	I	У	U	Ю	YU
Й	I	Ф	F	Я	YA

BIBLIOGRAPHY OF STATISTICAL LITERATURE

A.N.A. 1949.   1
Improvement of official crop-forecasts in India. *Bull. Calcutta Statist. Ass.*, **2**, 53-64.

Abbot, C. G. 1940.   2
On periodicities in the Smithsonian solar-constant values. *Bull. Amer. Met. Soc.*, **21**, 156-7.

Acton, F. S. & Olds, E. G. 1948.   3
Tolerances—additive or Pythagorean? *Industr. Qual. Contr.*, **5** (3), 6-12.

Adam, A. 1948.   4
Statistische Fundamentalgrössen. *Statist. Vierteljschr.*, **1**, 57-76.

Adam, A. 1949.   5
Randbemerkungen zum Varianzbegriff. *Statist. Vierteljschr.*, **2**, 113-16.

Adam, W. B. 1948.   5a
The use of statistical methods in research on food canning; the application of statistical methods to food problems. *Analyst*, **73**, 7-11.

Adcock, C. J. 1946.   6
Simplified factor analysis. *Occup. Psychol., London*, **20**, 188-98.

Adelman, M. A. 1946.   7
Correlations and forecasting. *Amer. Econ. Rev.*, **36**, 645-50.

Adkins, D. 1949.   8
Note on the computation of product-moment correlation coefficients. *Psychometrika*, **14**, 69-73.

Adler, H. A. & Miller, K. W. 1946.   9
A new approach to probability problems in electrical engineering. *Trans. Amer. Inst. Elect. Engrs.*, **65**, 630-2.

Afzal, M., Nanda, D. N. & Abbas, M. 1943.   10
Studies on the cotton jassid (*Empoasca devastans* Distant) in the Punjab. IV. A note on the statistical study of jassid population. *Indian J. Agric. Sci.*, **13**, 634-8.

Agnew, R. P. & Kac, M. 1941.   11
Translated functions and statistical independence. *Bull. Amer. Math. Soc.*, **47**, 148-54.

Aguado Smolinski, J. 1947.   12
An example of the application of mathematical statistics to forest yield. (Spanish.) *Bol. Inst. Invest. Exper. Agron. For., Madrid*, no. 18, 55 pp.

Aitken, A. C. 1940.   13
On the independence of linear and quadratic forms in samples of normally distributed variates. *Proc. Roy. Soc. Edin.*, **60**, 40-6 (correction: *A*, **62**, 277).

Aitken, A. C. 1945.   14
Studies in practical mathematics. IV. On linear approximation by least squares. *Proc. Roy. Soc. Edin. A*, **62**, 138-46.

Aitken, A. C. 1948.   15
On a problem in correlated errors. *Proc. Roy. Soc. Edin. A*, **62**, 273-7.

Aitken, A. C. 1948.   16
On the estimation of many statistical parameters. *Proc. Roy. Soc. Edin. A*, **62**, 369-77.

Aitken, A. C. 1949.   17
A note on the " problème des rencontres ". *Edin. Math. Notes*, **37**, 9-12.

Aitken, A. C. 1949.   18
On the Wishart distribution in statistics. *Biometrika*, **36**, 59-62.

Aitken, A. C. & Silverstone, H. 1942.   19
On the estimation of statistical parameters. *Proc. Roy. Soc. Edin. A*, **61**, 56-62; 186-94 (correction: *A*, **62**, 377).

Aiyer, S. J. 1945.   20
On the arithmetic and the geometric means from a Type III population. *Math. Student*, **13**, 11-15.

Aizsilnieks, A. P. 1949.   21
Nya vindor i den sovjetryska statistiken. (New views in Soviet Russia concerning the theory and methods of statistics.) (Swedish.) *Ekon. Tidskr.*, **51**, 19-26.

Akhieser, N. I. & Krein, M. 1940.   22
Some remarks about three papers of M. S. Verblunsky. (Russian.) *Gos. Univ. Kharkov, Zap. Inst. Mat. Mekh.*, (4) **16**, 129-34.

Alanís Patiñó, E. 1943.   23
Esquema de los métodos estadísticos. V. Correlación. *Irrig. Méx.*, **24**, 199-214.

Alarcão, J. 1948.   24
Alguns princípios da investigação quantitativa em ciências sociais; inferência e estimação estatística. *Rev. Economia, Lisbon*, **1**, 92-8.

Albert, A. A. 1944.   25
The matrices of factor analysis. *Proc. Nat. Acad. Sci. U.S.A.*, **30**, 90-5.

Albert, A. A. 1944.   26
The minimum rank of a correlation matrix. *Proc. Nat. Acad. Sci. U.S.A.*, **30**, 144-6.

Albert, G. E. 1947.   27
A note on the fundamental identity of sequential analysis. *Ann. Math. Statist.*, **18**, 593-6 (correction: **19**, 426-7).

Alcarez, E. 1949.   28
Genética cuántica. *Agricultura, Madrid*, **18**, 551-4.

Alchian, A. A. 1949.   29
Note on some errors in " The evidence of periodicity in short time series ". *J. Amer. Statist. Ass.*, **44**, 559-65.

Aldanondo, I. 1942.   30
On a probability distribution. (Spanish.) *Rev. Mat. Hisp.-Amer.*, (4) **2**, 232-41.

Aldanondo, I. 1943.   31
A probability distribution. (Spanish.) *Rev. Mat. Hisp.-Amer.*, (4) **3**, 62-72.

Alexander, H. W. 1946.   32
A general test for trend. *Psychol. Bull.*, **43**, 533-57.

1

Alexander, H. W. 1947. 33
The estimation of reliability when several trials are available. *Psychometrika*, **12**, 79-99.

Alexander, L., Klug, H. P. & Kummer, E. 34
1948. Statistical factors affecting the intensity of X-rays diffracted by crystalline powders *J. Appl. Phys.*, **19**, 742-53.

Alfrén, H. 1947. 35
Magneto-hydrodynamic waves and sunspots. III. *Ark. Mat., Astr. Fys.*, **34A** (23), 20 pp.

Alger, P. L. 1941. 35ᵃ
The importance of the statistical viewpoint in high production manufacturing. *J. Amer. Statist. Ass.*, **36**, 50-2.

Alger, P. L. 1946. 35ᵇ
Statistical control through product testing. *Elect. Engng., New York*, **65**, 11-12.

Alger, P. L. & Stokley, J. 1944. 35ᶜ
Progress in engineering knowledge during 1943. Design engineering: quality control. *Gen. Elect. Rev.*, **47** (2), 18-19.

Allard, G. 1947. 36
Détermination de la valeur la plus probable des grandeurs statistiques. I. Généralités. II. La vie moyenne des éléments radioactifs. *J. Phys. Radium*, (8) **8**, 212-14; 262-9.

Allen, N. N. 1944. 37
A standard for evaluation of dairy sires proved in dairy herd improvement associations. *J. Dairy Sci.*, **27**, 835-47.

Allen, P. & Walder, P. S. 1945. 38
Accuracy of mineral frequency analysis of sediments. *Nature*, **155**, 173-4.

Allen, P., Pearce, S. C. & Gaddum, J. H. 39
1945. Lognormal distributions. *Nature*, **156**, 746-7.

Allinson, V. A. & Bates, C. D. 1944. 40
The basis of the C.S.M. test—Charts and methods of calculation. *U.K. Min. Supply Advisory Service Statist. Method & Qual. Contr. Tech. Rep. Ser. R*, no. QC/R/17, 10 March 1944, 11 pp.

Almeida, A. 1942. 41
Estatística e biologia. *Rev. Brasil. Estatíst.*, **3**, 65-76.

Almendras, D. 1946. 42
Funciones ortogonales y sus aplicaciones a la estadística. (Spanish.) *Estadíst. Chilena, Santiago*, **19**, 681-6.

Almendras, D. 1947. 43
La distribucion de Poisson y sus aplicacions a la estadística. *Estadíst. Chilena, Santiago*, **20**, 195-6.

Almendras, D. 1947. 44
Ajuste de las curvas de Gompertz y logistica. *Estadíst. Chilena, Santiago*, **20**, 363-5.

Alpatov, W. W. 1944. 45
A basic principle governing the changes in organisms under the action of external factors. *Nature,* **154**, 54-5.

Alt, F. L. 1942. 45ᵃ
Distributed lags. *Econometrica*, **10**, 113-28.

Altman, O. & Goor, G. 1946. 46
Actuarial analysis of the operating life of B-29 aircraft engines. *J. Amer. Statist. Ass.*, **41**, 190-203.

Amaral, E. 1947. 47
Fundamentos da análise da variaçao. *Rev. Brasil. Estatíst.*, **8**, 869-74.

Amato, V. 1947. 48
Sulla differenza media. *Statistica, Milano*, **7**, 31-7.

Amato, V. 1947. 49
Sulla formula di de Moivre-Stirling e sua applicazione al calcolo della probabilità di un dato scarto. *Ann. Ist. Statist. Bari*, **23**, 40-53.

Amato, V. 1947. 50
Generalizzazione della formula di Baily. *Ann. Ist. Statist. Bari*, **23**, 54-8.

Amato, V. 1947. 51
Sulle matrici caratteristiche di alcuni metodi di interpolazione statistica. *G. Economisti*, **6**, 646-60.

Amato, V. 1948. 52
Sulla misura della concentrazione dei redditi. *Riv. Ital. Econ. Demogr. Statist.*, **2**, 504-29.

Amato, V. 1949. 53
Di un indice di concentrazione. *Statistica, Milano*, **9**, 83-92.

Amato, V. 1949. 54
Indice di concentrazione temporale. *Atti 9ma Riun. Soc. Ital. Demogr. Statist.*, 1947, pp. 240-8.

Amato, V. 1949. 55
Su un procedimento di calcolo per l'applicazione dei metodi interpolatori a matrici di Vandermonde. *Statistica, Milano*, **9**, 205-17.

Amato, V. 1949. 56
Su un procedimento di calcolo per l'applicazione del metodo dei minimi quadrati. *G. Economisti*, **8**, 416-24.

Amato, V. 1949. 57
Sulla rappresentazione analitica delle curve di concentrazione dei redditi col metodo delle trasformate euleriane di prima specie. *Riv. Ital. Econ. Demogr. Statist.*, **3** (1-2), 60-70.

Amato, V. 1949. 58
Sulla formula di Poisson. *Riv. Ital. Econ. Demogr. Statist.*, **3** (3-4), 219-22.

Ambarzumian, G. A. 1940. 59
A study of a special case of a continuous stochastic process. (Russian.) *Uch. Zap. Leningrad Gos. Univ., Ser. Mat.*, **10**, 120-38.

Ambarzumian, G. A. 1946. 60
Stochastic processes with two parameters giving in infinity the normal correlation. (Russian. Armenian and English summaries.) *Dokl. Akad. Nauk Armyan. SSR*, **5**, 65-70.

Ambrose, W. 1940. 61
On measurable stochastic processes. *Trans. Amer. Math. Soc.*, **47**, 66-79.

Ames, E. 1943. 62
A method for estimating the size distribution of a given aggregate income. *Rev. Econ. Statist.*, **25**, 184-9.

Ames, E. 1948. 63
A theoretical and statistical dilemma—the contributions of Burns, Mitchell, and Frickey to business-cycle theory. *Econometrica*, **16**, 347-69.

Ammeter, H. 1942.   64
Das Zufallsrisiko bei kleinen Versicherungsbeständen. *Mitt. Ver. Schweiz. Versich.-Math.*, **42**, 155-82.

Ammeter, H. 1945.   65
Untersuchungen über die jährlichen Sterblichkeitsschwankungen in einem Versicherungsbestand. *Mitt. Ver. Schweiz. Versich-Math.*, **45**, 323-60.

Ammeter, H. 1946.   66
Das Maximum des Selbstbehaltes in der Lebensversicherung unter Berücksichtigung der Rückversicherungskosten. *Mitt. Ver. Schweiz. Versich.-Math.*, **46**, 187-213.

Ammeter, H. 1948.   67
A generalization of the collective theory of risk in regard to fluctuating basic-probabilities. *Skand. Aktuartidskr.*, **31**, 171-98.

Ammeter, H. 1949.   68
Die Elemente der kollektiven Risikotheorie von festen und zufallsartig schwankenden Grundwahrscheinlichkeiten. *Mitt. Ver. Schweiz. Versich.-Math.*, **49**, 35-95.

Amoroso, L. 1949.   69
Scala propria e scala naturale nella equazione paretiana dei redditi. *Ann. Fac. Econ. Com. Palermo*, **3** (1), 1-7.

Amy, L. 1940.   70
Étude statistique de l'expression

$$\frac{p_1}{q_1} = \frac{p_2}{q_2} = \dots = \frac{p_i}{q_i} = \dots = c^{te}$$

Première application à l'étude de la fréquence des formules digitales. *J. Soc. Statist. Paris*, **81**, 39-47.

Amy, L. 1949.   71
La statistique des images. *J. Soc. Statist. Paris*, **90**, 92-120.

Ananthachar, V. S. 1947.   72
A modified definition of probability. *Current Science*, **16**, 18-19.

Andersen, E. S. 1949.   73
On the number of positive sums of random variables. *Skand. Aktuartidskr.*, **32**, 27-36.

Andersen, N. E. 1941.   74
De la durée moyenne d'une série de prestations en capitaux arbitraires en fonction du taux instantané d'intérêt et des demi-invariants de la répartition. (German, Italian and English summaries.) *Trans. 12th. Int. Congr. Actuar., Lucerne*, 1940, **3**, 437-57.

Anderson, H. W. 1947.   75
Soil freezing and thawing as related to some vegetation, climatic and soil variables. *J. Forestry*, **45**, 94-101.

Anderson, J. A. 1945.   76
The role of statistics in technical papers. *Trans. Amer. Ass. Cereal Chemists*, **3**, 69-73.

Anderson, O. 1947.   77
Zum Problem der Wahrscheinlichkeit a posteriori in der Statistik. *Schweiz. Zeit. Volkwirtsch. Statist.*, **83**, 489-518.

Anderson, O. 1948.   78
Zur Frage der Umkehrung des Theorems von Bernoulli; eine Erwiderung. *Schweiz. Zeit. Volkwirtsch. Statist.*, **84**, 178-80 (addendum (1949): **85**, 70).

Anderson, O. 1949.   79
Um Aufklärung wird gebeten, zum Problem des "Wärmetodes". *Mitt. Math. Statist.*, **1**, 131-49.

Anderson, O. 1949.   80
Die Begründung des Gesetzes der grossen Zahlen und die Umkehrung des Theorems von Bernoulli. *Dialectica*, **3**, 65-77.

Anderson, O. 1949.   81
Die Grundprobleme der Stichprobenmethode. I, II. *Mitt. Math. Statist.*, **1**, 37-52; 81-9.

Anderson, O. 1949.   82
Mehr Vorsicht mit Indexzahlen! *Allg. Statist. Arch.*, **33**, 472-85.

Anderson, P. H. 1942.   83
Distributions in stratified sampling. *Ann. Math. Statist.*, **13**, 42-52.

Anderson, R. D. 1942.   84
On the application of quantum mechanics to mortality tables. *J. Inst. Actuar.*, **71**, 228-58.

Anderson, R. L. 1942.   85
Distribution of the serial correlation coefficient. *Ann. Math. Statist.*, **13**, 1-13.

Anderson, R. L. 1946.   86
Missing plot techniques. *Biometrics Bull.*, **2**, 41-7.

Anderson, R. L. 1947.   87
Use of variance components in the analysis of hog prices in two markets. *J. Amer. Statist. Ass.*, **42**, 612-34 (correction: **43**, 242).

Anderson, R. L. 1949.   88
The use of regression techniques with economic data. *Proc. Auburn Conf. Statist. Appl. Res. Social Sci., Plant Sci. and Animal Sci.*, 1948, pp. 3-14.

Anderson, R. L. & Houseman, E. E. 1942.   89
Tables of orthogonal polynomial values extended to $n = 104$. *Iowa Agric. Exper. Sta. Res. Bull.*, **297**, 593-672.

Anderson, R. L. & Manning, H. L. 1948.   90
An experimental design used to estimate the optimum planting date of cotton. *Biometrics*, **4**, 171-96.

Anderson, T. W. 1943.   91
On card matching. *Ann. Math. Statist.*, **14**, 426-35.

Anderson, T. W. 1946.   92
The non-central Wishart distribution and certain problems of multivariate statistics. *Ann. Math. Statist.*, **17**, 409-31.

Anderson, T. W. 1947.   93
A note on a maximum-likelihood estimate. *Econometrica*, **15**, 241-4.

Anderson, T. W. 1948.   94
The asymptotic distributions of the roots of certain determinantal equations. *J. R. Statist. Soc. B*, **10**, 132-9.

Anderson, T. W. 1948.   95
On the theory of testing serial correlation. *Skand. Aktuartidskr.*, **31**, 88-116.

Anderson, T. W. & Darling, D. A. 1949.   96
Some statistical problems connected with stochastic processes. *RAND Corp., Res. Memo.*, 11 November 1949, RM-284, 12 pp.

Anderson, T. W. & Girshick, M. A. 1944.　　97
Some extensions of the Wishart distribution. *Ann. Math. Statist.*, **15**, 345-57.

Anderson, T. W. & Hurwicz, L. 1949.　　98
Errors and shocks in economic relationships. *Econometrica Suppl.*, **17**, 23-5.

Anderson, T. W. & Rubin, H. 1949.　　99
Estimation of the parameters of a single equation in a complete system of stochastic equations. *Ann. Math. Statist.*, **20**, 46-63.

Andersson, E. & Tedin, O. 1944.　　100
The effect upon the mean and variability of the dependent variate of a selection according to the independent. *Hereditas, Lund*, **30**, 249-53.

Andersson, W. 1940.　　101
A general formula for the normal mean errors of the coefficients in parabolic least squares graduation. *Skand. Aktuartidskr.*, **23**, 44-53.

Andersson, W. 1941.　　102
The binomial type of Gram's series. *Skand. Aktuartidskr.*, **24**, 203-13.

Andersson, W. 1942.　　103
On the Gram series on Pearson's system of frequency functions. *Skand. Aktuartidskr.*, **25**, 141-9.

Andersson, W. 1944.　　104
Short notes on Charlier's method for expansion of frequency functions in series. *Skand. Aktuartidskr.*, **27**, 16-31.

Andreoli, G. 1940.　　105
Sull'analisi statistica di fatti economici ed in generale di fenomeni di scambio. *R.C. Accad. Napoli*, (4) **10**, 128-36.

Andreoli, G. 1940.　　106
Statistica degli aggregati in una collettività e concentrazione rispetto a due caratteri. *R.C. Accad. Napoli*, (4) **10**, 160-72.

Andreoli, G. 1940.　　107
Schema statistico di evoluzione e di selezione in una collettivita a monoibridismo mendeliano. *R.C. Accad. Napoli*, (4) **10**, 260-80.

Andreoli, G. 1941.　　108
Statistica di configurazioni. (Ricerche su coppie di variabili casuali in correlazione.) *R.C. Accad. Napoli*, (4) **11**, 150-8.

Andreoli, G. 1942.　　109
Interpretazione probabilistica di teorie logiche e matematiche relative a fenomeni concreti. *R.C. Accad. Napoli Sci. Fis. Mat.* (4) **12**, 245-50.

Andreoli, G. 1943.　　110
Interpretazione probabilistica di teorie logiche e matematiche relative a fenomeni concreti. *Atti 5ta. Riun. Sci., Soc. Ital. Statist.*, pp. 226-31.

Andrews, T. G. 1943-8.　　111
Statistical studies in allergy. I. A correlation analysis. II. A factorial analysis. *J. Allergy*, **14**, 322-8; **19**, 43-6.

Andrews, W. B. 1940.　　112
The elimination of differences in investment in the evaluation of fertilizer analyses. *J. Amer. Soc. Agron.*, **32**, 495-502.

Angelo, E. & Potter, G. F. 1940.　　113
The error of sampling in studying distribution of the root systems of tung trees by means of the Viehmeyer soil tube. *Proc. Amer. Soc. Hort. Sci.*, **37**, 518-20.

Anonymous. 1940.　　114
1837-1937: A retrospect of vital statistics. *Brit. Med. J.*, **2** (1), 574.

Anonymous. 1945.　　115
Facilities for statistical study offered at various centres in India. *Math. Student*, **13**, 117-23.

Anonymous. 1947.　　116
New statistical method of predicting sunspots. *Current Science*, **16**, 306.

Anonymous. 1948.　　117
Enige beschouwingen over steekproeven. (Some considerations on sampling.) (Dutch. English summary.) *Statist. Econ. Onderzoek.*, **3**, 94-101.

Anós, A. 1944.　　118
Present state of the theory of testing statistical hypotheses. *Bol. Inst. Invest. Exper. Agron. For., Madrid*, **10**, 93-135.

Anós, A. 1945.　　119
A graphical method for determining the number of replications necessary in comparative experiments. *Bol. Inst. Invest. Exper. Agron. For., Madrid*, **13**, 1-16.

Ansari, M. A. A. & Sant, G. K. 1943.　　120
A study of soil heterogeneity in relation to size and shape of plots in wheat field at Raya (Muttra District). *Indian J. Agric. Sci.*, **13**, 652-6.

Ansbacher, H. L. & Mather, K. 1945.　　121
Group differences in size estimation. *Psychometrika*, **10**, 37-56.

Anscombe, F. J. 1946.　　122
Linear sequential rectifying inspection for controlling fraction defective. *J. R. Statist. Soc. Suppl.*, **8**, 216-22.

Anscombe, F. J. 1948.　　123
On estimating the populations of aphids in a potato field. *Ann. Appl. Biol.*, **35**, 567-71.

Anscombe, F. J. 1948.　　124
The transformation of Poisson, binomial and negative-binomial data. *Biometrika*, **35**, 246-54.

Anscombe, F. J. 1948.　　125
Validity of comparative experiments. *J. R. Statist. Soc. A*, **111**, 181-211.

Anscombe, F. J. 1949.　　126
Large-sample theory of sequential estimation. *Biometrika*, **36**, 455-8.

Anscombe, F. J. 1949.　　127
Note on a problem in probit analysis. *Ann. Appl. Biol.*, **36**, 203-5.

Anscombe, F. J. 1949.　　128
The statistical analysis of insect counts based on the negative binomial distribution. *Biometrics*, **5**, 165-73.

Anscombe, F. J. 1949.　　129
Tables of sequential inspection schemes to control fraction defective. *J. R. Statist. Soc. A*, **112**, 180-206.

Anscombe, F. J., Godwin, H. J. & Plackett, R. L. 130
1947. Methods of deferred sentencing in testing the fraction defective of a continuous output. *J. R. Statist. Soc. Suppl.*, **9**, 198-217.

Anzai, H. 1949. 131
A remark on spectral measures of the flow of Brownian motion. *Osaka Math. J.*, **1**, 95-7.

Arbey, L. 1949. 132
Les erreurs d'observations considérées comme liées. *Bull. Astr.*, (2) **14**, 75-144.

Archibald, E. E. A. 1948. 133
Plant populations. I. A new application of Neyman's contagious distribution. *Ann. Bot.*, **12**, 221-35.

Argañaraz, C. J. M. 1947. 134
New methods in the calculation of a ballistic pattern. (*Spanish.*) *An. Soc. Cient. Argent.*, **143**, 49-82.

Arley, N. 1940. 135
On the distribution of relative errors from a normal population of errors. A discussion of some problems in the theory of errors. *Danske Vid. Selsk. Math.-Fys. Medd.*, **18** (3), 1-61.

Arley, N. 1944. 136
On the elementary, time-homogeneous, discontinuous, stochastically definite process. *Skand. Aktuartidskr.*, **27**, 172-6.

Arley, N. 1949. 137
On the " birth-and-death " process. *Skand. Aktuartidskr.*, **32**, 21-6.

Arley, N. & Borchsenius, V. 1945. 138
On the theory of infinite systems of differential equations and their application to the theory of stochastic processes and the perturbation theory of quantum mechanics. *Acta Math.*, **76**, 261-322.

Armellini, G. 1945. 139
Fondamenti e risultati della statistica stellare. *Atti 6ta. Riun. Sci., Soc. Ital. Statist.*, pp. 5-22.

Armitage, P. 1944. 140
A go not-go sequential *t*-test. *U.K. Min. Supply Advisory Service Statist. Method & Qual. Contr. Tech. Rep. Ser. R*, no. QC/R/20, 22 Nov. 1944, 11 pp.

Armitage, P. 1947. 141
Comparison of stratified with unrestricted random sampling from a finite population. *Biometrika*, **34**, 273-80.

Armitage, P. 1947. 142
Some sequential tests of Student's hypothesis. *J. R. Statist. Soc. Suppl.*, **9**, 250-63.

Armitage, P. 1949. 143
An overlap problem arising in particle counting. *Biometrika*, **36**, 357-66.

Armitage, P., Baines, A. H. J. & Lindley, D. V. 144
1944. On some properties of binomial sequences. *U.K. Min. Supply Advisory Service Statist. Method & Qual. Contr. Tech. Rep. Ser. R*, no. QC/R/28, 1 Nov. 1944, 14 pp.

Armstrong, C. E. 1949. 145
Moving averages. *Amer. Statistician*, **3** (4), 10.

Armstrong, D. T. 1947. 145[a]
Quality control aid supervisors. I. Fundamentals and purposes. II. Quality control and inspection. III. Interpretation of chart data. IV. Measure of variation. *Amer. Machinist*, **91**, 241-5; 314-18; 355-8; 452-5.

Armstrong, G. R. & Clarke, P. C. 1946. 146
Frequency distribution vs. acceptance tables. *Industr. Qual. Contr.*, **3** (2), 22-7.

Armstrong, W. M. 1946. 146[a]
Foundry applications of quality control. *Industr. Qual. Contr.*, **2** (6), 12-16.

Armstrong, W. M. 1946. 146[b]
Statistical control in manufacturing steel strips and Tin plate. *Iron & Steel Engng.*, **23** (7), 69-77.

Arnold, E. H. 1944. 147
Médecine et statistique. *J. Méd. Leysin.*, **22**, 393-400.

Arnous, E. 1947. 148
Méthodes d'approximation: La condition d'extremum

$$\delta \frac{\int \bar{\psi} H \psi \, d\tau}{\int \bar{\psi} \psi \, d\tau} = 0$$

et l'écart type de la loi de probabilité de *H*. *C. R. Acad. Sci., Paris*, **225**, 449-51.

Arnous, E. & Massignon, D. 1948. 149
Grandeurs observables et fonctions aléatoires. *C. R. Acad. Sci., Paris*, **226**, 318-20.

Arnous, E. & Massignon, D. 1948. 150
Les principales familles de fonctions aléatoires et leurs propriétés. *C. R. Acad. Sci., Paris*, **226**, 785-7.

Arnous, E. & Massignon, D. 1948. 151
Équations d'évolution des lois de probabilité et théorie du transfert pour les fonctions aléatoires du second ordre. *C. R. Acad. Sci., Paris*, **226**, 1127-9.

Arnous, E., Bass, J. & Massignon, D. 1948. 152
Sur les relations fonctionelles vérifiées par les fonctions caractéristiques des fonctions aléatoires dérivables en moyenne quadratique. *C. R. Acad. Sci., Paris*, **226**, 627-9.

Aroian, L. A. 1941. 153
Continued fractions for the incomplete Beta function. *Ann. Math. Statist.*, **12**, 218-23.

Aroian, L. A. 1941. 154
A study of R. A. Fisher's *z*-distribution and the related *F*-distribution. *Ann. Math. Statist.*, **12**, 429-48.

Aroian, L. A. 1943. 155
A new approximation to the levels of significance of the chi-square distribution. *Ann. Math. Statist.*, **14**, 93-5.

Aroian, L. A. 1944. 156
Some methods for the evaluation of a sum. *J. Amer. Statist. Ass.*, **39**, 511-15.

Aroian, L. A. 1947. 157
Note on the cumulants of Fisher's *z*-distribution. *Biometrika*, **34**, 359-60.

Aroian, L. A. 1947. 158
The probability function of the product of two normally distributed variables. *Ann. Math. Statist.*, **18**, 265-71.

Aroian, L. A. 1948. 159
The fourth degree exponential distribution function. *Ann. Math. Statist.*, **19**, 589-92.

Arrow, K. J., Blackwell, D. & Girshick, M. A. 160
1949. Bayes and minimax solutions of sequential decision problems. *Econometrica*, **17**, 213-44.

Arscott, D. P. 1946. 161
Quality control. *O. A. C. Rev.*, **59** (1), 14ff.

Ascoli, G. 1947. 162
Sopra una valutazione asintotica che si presenta nella teoria probabilistica dei contatori di corpuscoli. *Ric. Sci.*, **17**, 611-16.

Ashby, E. 1948. 162ᵃ
Statistical ecology. II. A reassessment. *Botanical Rev.*, **14**, 222-34.

Ashcroft, A. G. 1941. 162ᵇ
An outline of organization for quality control. *Taylor Soc. Bull.*, **16**, 81-2.

Ashcroft, A. G. 1944. 162ᶜ
The interpretation of laboratory tests as quality indices in textiles. *Bull. Amer. Soc. Test. Mat.*, **131**, 27-31. (Also: *Amer. Dyestuff Reporter*, **33**, 486-91.)

Ashley, J. W. 1945. 162ᵈ
The construction of nomograms. *Mech. World*, **117**, 488-92, 531-5.

Aspin, A. A. 1948. 163
An examination and further development of a formula arising in the problem of comparing two mean values. *Biometrika*, **35**, 88-96.

Aspin, A. A. 1949. 164
Tables for use in comparisons whose accuracy involves two variances, separately estimated. *Biometrika*, **36**, 290-3.

Atherton, A. L. 1942. 164ᵃ
Quality control in bomb fuse manufacture. *Steel*, **110**, 58-61.

Atherton, A. L. 1943. 164ᵇ
Wind tunnel test specifications for quality control of bomb fuses. *Product Engng.*, **14**, 95-8.

Atherton, A. L. 1945. 164ᶜ
Curbing defective work. *Mill & Factory*, **37**, 111-13.

Attneave, F. 1949. 165
A method of graded dichotomies for the scaling of judgments. *Psychol. Rev.*, **56**, 334-40.

Atwood, K. C. & Norman, A. 1949. 166
On the interpretation of multi-hit survival curves. *Proc. N.Y. Acad. Sci.*, **35**, 696-709.

Auer, C. 1946. 167
Statistical investigation of the early growth of larches of different provenance in the instructional forest of the Swiss Federal Technical College. (German.) *Schweiz. Zeit. Forstwesen*, **97**, 224-43.

Austen, A. E. W. & Pelzer, H. 1946. 168
Linear " curves of best fit ". *Nature*, **157**, 693-4.

Ayyangar, A. A. K. 1940. 169
Random lines—a statistical study. *Sankhyā*, **5**, 307-12.

Ayyangar, A. A. K. 1941. 170
The triangular distribution. *Math. Student*, **9**, 85-7.

Ayyangar, A. A. K. 1943. 171
Statistical formulae. *Current Science*, **12**, 145.

Ayyangar, A. A. K. 1945. 172
Interaction formulae in analysis of variance. *Current Science*, **14**, 35.

Ayyangar, A. A. K. 1945. 173
On test criteria for statistical hypotheses. *Math. Student*, **13**, 166.

Azevedo, A. M. 1947. 174
Estatística aplicada. *Rev. Brasil. Estatíst.*, **7**, 557-9.

B

Baas Becking, L. G. M. 1946. 175
On the analysis of sigmoid curves. *Acta Biotheor. A*, **8**, 42-59.

Babington Smith, B. *See* **Smith, B. Babington.**

Babitz, M. & Keys, N. 1940. 176
A method for approximating the average intercorrelation coefficient by correlating the parts with the sum of the parts. *Psychometrika*, **5**, 283-8.

Bacharach, A. L. 1945. 176ᵃ
Biological assay and chemical analysis. *Analyst*, **70**, 394-403.

Bacharach, A. L. & Chance, M. R. A. 1945. 177
Inter-litter variability as a source of error in gonadotrophin assay. *Quart. J. Pharm.*, **18**, 10-14.

Bachelier, L. 1941. 178
Probabilités des oscillations maxima. *C. R. Acad. Sci., Paris*, **212**, 836-8 (erratum: **213**, 220).

Bachi, R. 1947. 179
Statistical analysis of data; based upon: " The attraction of mosquitoes by human beings." by G. Mer, D. Birnbaum and A. Aioub. *Parasitology*, **38**, 5-9.

Bachmann, W. K. 1940. 180
L'ellipsoïde d'erreur. *Schweiz. Zeit. Vermess.*, **28**, 181-97; 201-8; 213-6.

Bachmann, W. K. 1945. 181
Théorie des erreurs de l'observation des variables secondaires. *Schweiz. Zeit. Vermess.*, **43**, 21-7; 45-51.

Bacon, H. M. 1948. 182
A matrix arising in correlation theory. *Ann. Math. Statist.*, **19**, 422-4.

Bacon, R. H. 1946. 183
Practical statistics for practical physicists. *Amer. J. Phys.*, **14**, 84-98.

Badger, E. H. M. 1946. 183ᵃ
Some statistical methods in refractory testing. *Brit. Ceram. Soc. Trans.*, **45**, 33-44.

Baer, R. 1945. 184
Sampling from a changing population. *Ann. Math. Statist.*, **16**, 348-61.

Bailey, A. L. 1942-3. 185
Sampling theory in casualty insurance. *Proc. Casualty Actuar. Soc.*, **29**, 50-79; **30**, 31-65.

Bailey, A. L. 1945. 186
A generalized theory of credibility. *Proc. Casualty Actuar. Soc.*, **32**, 13-20.

Bailey, B. 1940. 187
Diameter relationships of wool fibres from five breeds of sheep raised in South Dakota. *J. Agric. Res.*, **60**, 415-26.

Bailey, B. 1941. 188
A study of sampling in cross-section measurements of wool fibre. *J. Agric. Res.*, **63**, 407-15.

Bailey, N. T. J. 1949. 189
A method of allowing for differential viability in estimating linkage from backcross matings in coupling only or repulsion only. *Heredity*, **3**, 225-8.

Bailey, W. G. & Haycocks, H. W. 1947. 190
A synthesis of methods of deriving measures of decrement from observed data. *J. Inst. Actuar.*, **73**, 179-212.

Baillie, D. C. 1946. 191
On testing the significance of mortality ratios by the use of χ^2. *Trans. Actuar. Soc. Amer.*, **47**, 326-44.

Bainbridge, J. R. 1947. 192
The teaching of statistics. *Engineering, London*, **164**, 448; 38.

Baines, A. H. J. 1943. 193
On the allocation of observations in certain types of factorial experiment when the number of observations is limited. *U.K. Min. Supply Advisory Service Statist. Method & Qual. Contr. Tech. Rep. Ser. R*, no. QC/R/4, 25 June 1943, 13 pp.

Baines, A. H. J. 1944. 194
Methods of detecting non-randomness in a given series of observations. *U.K. Min. Supply Advisory Service Statist. Method & Qual. Contr. Tech. Rep. Ser. R*, no. QC/R/12, 5 February 1944, 13 pp.

Baines, A. H. J. 1944. 195
On the economical design of statistical experiments. *U.K. Min. Supply Advisory Service Statist. Method & Qual. Contr. Tech. Rep. Ser. R*, no. QC/R/15, 20 July 1944, 22 pp.

Baker, G. A. 1940. 196
Comparison of Pearsonian approximations with exact sampling distributions of means and variances in samples from populations composed of the sums of normal populations. *Ann. Math. Statist.*, **11**, 219-24.

Baker, G. A. 1940. 197
Maximum likelihood estimation of the ratio of the components of non-homogeneous populations. *Tôhoku Math. J.*, **47**, 304-8.

Baker, G. A. 1941. 198
Linear regression when the standard deviations of arrays are not all equal. *J. Amer. Statist. Ass.*, **36**, 500-6.

Baker, G. A. 1941. 199
Tests of homogeneity for normal populations. *Ann. Math. Statist.*, **12**, 233-6.

Baker, G. A. 1942. 200
Correlations between functions of variables. *J. Amer. Statist. Ass.*, **37**, 537-9.

Baker, G. A. 1942. 201
Mathematical model of embryo abortion in Philips Cling peaches. *J. Agric. Res.*, **64**, 173-8.

Baker, G. A. 1943. 202
Length-growth curves for the razor clam. *Growth*, **7**, 439-43.

Baker, G. A. 1944. 203
Weight-growth curves. *Poultry Sci.*, **23**, 83-90.

Baker, G. A. 1945. 204
Graduation of human growth curves. *Growth*, **9**, 299-302.

Baker, G. A. 1945. 205
Test of the significance of the differences of per cents of emergence of seedlings in multiple field trials. *J. Amer. Statist. Ass.*, **40**, 93-7.

Baker, G. A. 1946. 206
Distribution of the ratio of sample range to sample standard deviation for normal and combinations of normal distributions. *Ann. Math. Statist.*, **17**, 366-9.

Baker, G. A. 1949. 207
The variance of the proportions of samples falling within a fixed interval for a normal population. *Ann. Math. Statist.*, **20**, 123-4.

Baker, G. A. & Briggs, F. N. 1945. 208
Wheat-bunt field trials. *J. Amer. Soc. Agron.*, **37**, 127-33.

Baker, G. A. & Briggs, F. N. 1949. 209
Wheat-bunt field trials, II. *Proc. Berkeley Symp. Math. Statist. and Probab.*, 1945-6, pp. 485-91.

Baker, G. A. & Guilbert, H. R. 1942. 210
Non-randomness of variations in daily weights of cattle. *J. Animal Sci.*, **1**, 293-9.

Baker, G. A. & Kleiber, M. 1944. 211
Characteristics of the daily weights of sexually mature rats on a constant diet. *Growth*, **8**, 159-67.

Baker, G. A. & Mead, S. W. 1942. 211[a]
The oscillatory character of the variations in the weights of dairy heifers. *J. Dairy Sci.*, **30**, 967-74.

Baker, H. J. 1941. 211[b]
The fetish of statistics. *J. Educ. Res.*, **34**, 458-9.

Baker, J. W. 1944. 211[c]
Post-war control of quality of commercial products. *Engng. Insp.*, **9** (4), 39-40.

Baker, M. L., Hazel, L. N. & Reinmiller, C. F. 212
1943. The relative importance of heredity and environment in the growth of pigs at different ages. *J. Animal Sci.*, **2**, 3-13.

Baldi, E. 1943. 213
Numero stazionario di una popolazione naturale confinata. *Atti Soc. Ital. Sci. Mat.*, **82**, 309-17.

Baldi, E. & Pirocchi, L. 1947. 214
Ulteriori ricerche sulla distribuzione spaziale del mesoplancton pelagico in un grande lago oligotrofo. *Mem. Ist. Ital. Idrobiol.*, **3**, 123-45.

Baldwin, A. L. 1942. 215
Personal structure analysis: a statistical method for investigating the single personality. *J. Abnorm. & Soc. Psychol.*, **37**, 163-83.

Baldwin, E. M. 1946. 216
Table of percentage points of the *t*-distribution. *Biometrika*, **33**, 362.

Ballarin, S. 1948. 217
Espressione rigorosa dello scarto mediano nel problema delle prove ripetute nello schema di Bernoulli. *Mem. Soc. Astr. Ital.*, **19**, 63-5.

Baltensperger, P. 1941. 218
Über die Vorausberechnung der Sterblichkeit der Schweizerischen Bevölkerung. *Mitt. Ver. Schweiz. Versich.-Math.*, **41**, 109-61.

Banachiewicz, T. 1942. 219
An outline of the Cracovian algorithm of the method of least squares. *Astr. J.*, **50**, 38-41.

Banachiewicz, T. 1945. 220
On the accuracy of least squares solution. *Ark. Mat., Astr. Fys.*, **31 B** (8), 3 pp.

Bancroft, G. 1940. 221
Consistency of information from records and interviews. *J. Amer. Statist. Ass.*, **35**, 377-81.

Bancroft, T. A. 1944. 222
On biases in estimation due to the use of preliminary tests of significance. *Ann. Math. Statist.*, **15**, 190-204.

Bancroft, T. A. 1945. 223
Note on an identity in the incomplete Beta function. *Ann. Math. Statist.*, **16**, 98-9.

Bancroft, T. A. 1949. 224
Some recurrence formulae in the incomplete Beta function ratio. *Ann. Math. Statist.*, **20**, 451-5.

Banerjee, D. P. 1941. 225
Note on the limit of correlation and regression coefficients in mingled records. *Math. Student*, **9**, 155-7.

Banerjee, D. P. 1948. 226
On the cumulants of β_3. *Bull. Calcutta Math. Soc.*, **40**, 76.

Banerjee, D. P. 1949. 227
On percentage points of incomplete beta-functions and χ^2 distribution. *Bull. Calcutta Math. Soc.*, **41**, 53-4.

Banerjee, K. S. 1948. 228
On the design of experiments for weighing and making other types of measurements. *Science & Culture*, **13**, 344.

Banerjee, K. S. 1948. 229
Weighing designs and balanced incomplete blocks. *Ann. Math. Statist.*, **19**, 394-9.

Banerjee, K. S. 1949. 230
On certain aspects of spring balance designs. *Sankhyā*, **9**, 367-76.

Banerjee, K. S. 1949. 230[a]
On the construction of Hadamard matrices. *Science & Culture*, **14**, 434-5.

Banerjee, K. S. 1949. 231
A note on weighing design. *Ann. Math. Statist.*, **20**, 300-4.

Banerjee, K. S. 1949. 232
On variance factors in weighing designs. *Bull. Calcutta Statist. Ass.*, **2**, 38-42.

Banerjee, P. K. 1948. 233
Setting tolerance limits. *Bull. Calcutta Statist. Ass.*, **1**, 161-70.

Banks, C. 1948. 234
Primary personality factors in woman: a re-analysis. *Brit. J. Psychol. (Statist. Sec.)*, **1**, 204-18.

Baptist, J. H. 1941. 235
Le calcul des probabilités dans le domaine de l'assurance. (German, Italian and English summaries.) *Trans. 12th. Int. Congr. Actuar., Lucerne*, 1940, **1**, 117-36.

Baptist, J. H. 1945. 236
Étude de la dépendance stochastique. *Bull. Ass. Actuair. Belg.*, **50**, 15-36.

Baptist, J. H. 1949. 237
Le raisonnement probabilitaire. *Dialectica*, **3**, 93-103.

Barankin, E. W. 1945. 238
Bounds for the characteristic roots of a matrix. *Bull. Amer. Math. Soc.*, **51**, 767-70.

Barankin, E. W. 1949. 239
Extension of the Romanovsky-Bartlett-Scheffé test. *Proc. Berkeley Symp. Math. Statist. and Probab.*, 1945-6, pp. 433-49.

Barankin, E. W. 1949. 240
Locally best unbiased estimates. *Ann. Math. Statist.*, **20**, 477-501.

Barberi, B. 1948. 241
Alcune considerazioni sulla construzione dei numeri indici. *Ann. Statist., Rome*, **8** (2), 1-31.

Bardwell, J. & Winkler, C. A. 1949. 242
The formation and properties of three-dimensional polymers. I. Statistics of network polymers. II. Network formation. III. The effect of network structure on elastic properties. *Canadian J. Res.*, **27** (B), 116-27; 128-38; 139-50.

Barit, I. Ya. & Podgoretskii, M. I. 1949. 243
Some statistical relations connected with the observation of wide atmospheric showers. (Russian.) *Dokl. Akad. Nauk SSSR*, **68**, 23-6.

Barkalaia, A. 1944. 244
Sur des chaînes de Markoff. (Russian. French summary.) *Uch. Zap. Moskov. Gos. Univ., Ser. Mat.*, **73**, 33-6.

Barkworth, H. 1941. 245
Lay-out of experiments. *Proc. Soc. Agric. Bact.*, 1941, 50ff.

Barkworth, H. & Irwin, J. O. 1943. 246
Comparative detection of coliform organisms in milk and water by the presumptive coliform test, with an appendix on the possible bactericidal effect of bile salt. *J. Hyg., Camb.*, **43**, 129-35.

Barnard, G. A. 1943. 247
The use of the median in place of the mean in quality control charts. *U.K. Min. Supply Advisory Service Statist. Method & Qual. Contr. Tech. Rep. Ser. R*, no. QC/R/2, 19 April 1943, 2 pp.

Barnard, G. A. 1943. 248
Statistical methods applied to assembly processes. *U.K. Min. Supply Advisory Service Statist. Method & Qual. Contr. Tech. Rep. Ser. R*, no. QC/R/3(I), 1 May 1943, 10 pp.

Barnard, G. A. 1944. 249
Economy in sampling with special reference to engineering experimentation. *U.K. Min. Supply Advisory Service Statist. Method & Qual. Contr. Tech. Rep. Ser. R*, no. QC/R/7(I), 1 January 1944, 29 pp. (Also: *N.R.D.C. Appl. Math. Panel, Memo.* no. 30, 2; *Columbia Univ. Statist. Res. Group*, no. 182.)

Barnard, G. A. 1944. 250
An analogue of Tchebycheff's inequality in terms of range. *U.K. Min. Supply Advisory Service Statist. Method & Qual. Contr. Tech. Rep. Ser. R*, no. QC/R/11, 5 February 1944, 2 pp.

Barnard, G. A. 1944. 250ª
A new method of quality control of measured items. *U.K. Min. Supply Advisory Service Statist. Method & Qual. Contr. Tech. Rep. Ser. R*, no. QC/R/14, 21 February 1944, 13 pp.

Barnard, G. A. 1944. 250ᵇ
A test for homogeneity of Poisson series. *U.K. Min. Supply Advisory Service Statist. Method & Qual. Contr. Tech. Rep. Ser. R*, no. QC/R/18, 10 March 1944, 4 pp.

Barnard, G. A. 1945. 251
A new test for 2×2 tables. *Nature*, **156**, 177; 783.

Barnard, G. A. 1945. 252
Economy in sampling. *Nature*, **156**, 208.

Barnard, G. A. 1946. 253
Sequential tests in industrial statistics. *J. R. Statist. Soc. Suppl.*, **8**, 1-26.

Barnard, G. A. 1947. 254
Significance tests for 2×2 tables. *Biometrika*, **34**, 123-38.

Barnard, G. A. 1947. 255
2×2 tables. A note on E. S. Pearson's paper. *Biometrika*, **34**, 168-9.

Barnard, G. A. 1947. 256
The meaning of a significance level. *Biometrika*, **34**, 179-82.

Barnard, G. A. 1949. 257
Statistical inference. *J. R. Statist. Soc. B*, **11**, 115-49.

Barnard, G. A. & Godwin, H. J. 1944. 257ª
Statistical methods applied to assembly processes—selective assembly. *U.K. Min. Supply Advisory Service Statist. Method & Qual. Contr. Tech. Rep. Ser. R*, no. QC/R/3 (III), 4 April 1944, 11 pp.

Barnard, G. A. & Plackett, R. L. 1943. 257ᵇ
Appendix to " The use of the median in place of the mean in quality control charts ". *U.K. Min. Supply Advisory Service Statist. Method & Qual. Contr. Tech. Rep. Ser. R*, no. QC/R/2, 19 April 1943, 6 pp.

Barracco, E. 1941. 258
Modificazioni di una formula per il calcolo dei corso teorici dei titoli a reddito fisso, nel caso in cui si tenga conto delle imposte e tasse. *G. Ist. Ital. Attuari*, **12**, 43-52.

Barrett, L. R. 1945. 258ª
Quality must be built—all along the line. *Wings*, **4**, 1665-7.

Barricelli, N. A. 1943. 259
Les plus grands et les plus petits maxima ou minima annuels d'une variable climatique. *Arch. Math. Naturv.*, **46** (6), 155-94.

Barricelli, N.A. 1947. 259ª
L'intégrale relative d'une fonctionnelle et ses applications dans la théorie de la distribution de probabilité d'une courbe. *Arch. Math. Naturv. B*, **11** (3), 1-83.

Bartels, J. 1943. 260
Gesetz und Zufall in der Geophysik. *Naturwiss.*, **31**, 427-35.

Bartels, J. 1943. 261
Statistik in der Geophysik. *Ann. Hydrogr.*, Berlin, **71**, 107-14.

Bartholomaei, H. A. 1944. 261ª
Records keep everybody quality conscious. *Wings*, **3**, 1313-18.

Bartky, W. 1943. 262
Multiple sampling with constant probability. *Ann. Math. Statist.*, **14**, 363-77.

Bartlett, M. S. 1940. 263
A note on the interpretation of quasi-sufficiency. *Biometrika*, **31**, 391-2.

Bartlett, M. S. 1940. 264
The present position of mathematical statistics. *J. R. Statist. Soc.*, **103**, 1-29.

Bartlett, M. S. 1941. 265
Statistical significance of canonical correlations. *Biometrika*, **32**, 29-37.

Bartlett, M. S. 1945. 266
Negative probability. *Proc. Camb. Phil. Soc.*, **41**, 71-3.

Bartlett, M. S. 1946. 267
A general class of confidence interval. *Nature*, **158**, 521.

Bartlett, M. S. 1946. 268
The large-sample theory of sequential tests. *Proc. Camb. Phil. Soc.*, **42**, 239-44.

Bartlett, M. S. 1946. 269
On the theoretical specification and sampling properties of autocorrelated time-series. *J. R. Statist. Soc. Suppl.*, **8**, 27-41; 85-97 (corrigenda (1948): **10**).

Bartlett, M. S. 1946. 270
A modified probit technique for small probabilities. *J. R. Statist. Soc. Suppl.*, **8**, 113-17.

Bartlett, M. S. 1947. 271
The general canonical correlation distribution. *Ann. Math. Statist.*, **18**, 1-17.

Bartlett, M. S. 1947. 272
Multivariate analysis. *J. R. Statist. Soc. Suppl.*, **9**, 176-97.

Bartlett, M. S. 1947. 273
The use of transformations. *Biometrics Bull.*, **3**, 39-52.

Bartlett, M. S. 1948. 274
Internal and external factor analysis. *Brit. J. Psychol.* (*Statist. Sec.*), **1**, 73-81.

Bartlett, M. S. 1948. 275
A note on the statistical estimation of supply and demand relations from time series. *Econometrica*, **16**, 323-9.

Bartlett, M. S. 1948. 276
Smoothing periodograms from time series with continuous spectra. *Nature*, **161**, 686-7.

Bartlett, M. S. 1949. 277
Some evolutionary stochastic processes. *J. R. Statist. Soc. B*, **11**, 211-29; 265-82.

Bartlett, M. S. 1949. 278
Fitting a straight line when both variables are subject to error. *Biometrics*, **5**, 207-12.

Bartlett, M. S. 1949. 279
Probability in logic, mathematics and science. *Dialectica*, **3**, 104-13.

Bartlett, M. S. & Kendall, D. G. 1946.   280
The statistical analysis of variance-heterogeneity and the logarithmic transformation. *J. R. Statist. Soc. Suppl.*, **8**, 128-38.

Bartlett, M. S. & Moyal, J. E. 1949.   281
The exact transition probabilities of quantum-mechanical oscillators calculated by the phase-space method. *Proc. Camb. Phil. Soc.*, **45**, 545-53.

Bartlett, N. R. 1946.   282
A punched-card technique for computing means, standard deviations and the product moment correlation coefficient and for listing scattergrams. *Science*, **104**, 374-5.

Barton, W. W. & Stott, C. B. 1946.   283
Simplified guide to intensity of cruise. *J. Forestry*, **44**, 750-4.

Bass, J. 1945.   284
Les fonctions aléatoires et leur interprétation mécanique. *Rev. Sci., Paris*, **83**, 3-20.

Bass, J. 1945.   285
Sur la structure des fonctions aléatoires. *C. R. Acad. Sci., Paris*, **220**, 190-2.

Bass, J. 1945.   286
Quelques conséquences mécaniques de l'équation de structure d'un corpuscle aléatoire. *C. R. Acad. Sci., Paris*, **220**, 272-4.

Bass, J. 1945.   287
Sur les rapports entre la mécanique ondulatoire et la théorie des fonctions aléatoires. *C. R. Acad. Sci., Paris*, **221**, 46-9.

Bass, J. 1946.   288
Quelques remarques sur la signification du théorème des probabilités composées dans la formalisme de la mécanique quantique. *C. R. Acad. Sci., Paris*, **222**, 1372-4.

Bass, J. 1947.   289
Sur le corpuscle aléatoire à masse aléatoire. *C. R. Acad. Sci., Paris*, **225**, 38-40.

Bass, J. 1948.   290
Les bases d'une théorie statistique de la turbulence. *Proc. 7th. Int. Congr. Appl. Math.*, **2**, 212-26.

Bass, J. 1948.   291
Sur les propriétés des relations fonctionnelles vérifiées par les lois de probabilité des fonctions aléatoires dérivables. *C. R. Acad. Sci., Paris*, **226**, 1120-2.

Bass, J. 1948.   292
Application aux mélanges de la théorie du transfert des grandeurs aléatoires. *C. R. Acad. Sci., Paris*, **226**, 1351-3.

Bass, J. 1948.   293
Sur les moyennes et les lois de probabilité en mécanique ondulatoire. *C. R. Acad. Sci., Paris*, **227**, 112-14.

Bass, J. 1949.   294
Sur les bases mathématiques de la théorie de la turbulence d'Heisenberg. *C. R. Acad. Sci., Paris*, **228**, 228-9.

Bass, J. & LeCam, L. 1948.   295
Sur certaines classes de fonctions aléatoires. *C. R. Acad. Sci., Paris*, **227**, 1206-8.

Bass, J., Dedebant, G. & Wehrlé, P. 1945.   296
Sur la connexion aléatoire d'un fluide. Application à la turbulence. *C. R. Acad. Sci., Paris*, **220**, 165-7.

Bass, J., Dedebant, G. & Wehrlé, P. 1945.   297
Les équations différentielles aléatoires. *C. R. Acad. Sci., Paris*, **221**, 168-71.

Bassali, W. 1949.   298
Probability in problems in nuclear chemistry. II. *Proc. Roy. Irish. Acad. A*, **52**, 191-201.

Batchelor, G. K. 1947.   299
Kolmogoroff's theory of locally isotropic turbulence. *Proc. Camb. Phil. Soc.*, **43**, 533-59.

Batchelor, G. K. 1948.   300
Recent developments on turbulence research. *Proc. 7th. Int. Congr. Appl. Mech. London*, pp. 27-56.

Bateman, A. J. 1947.   301
Contamination of seed crops. I. Insect pollination. II. Wind pollination. III. Relation with isolation distance. *J. Genet.*, **48**, 257 ff. *Heredity*, **1**, 235-46; 303-36.

Bateman, A. J. 1947.   301[a]
Number of *S*-Alleles in a population. *Nature*, **160**, 337.

Bateman, G. I. 1948.   302
On the power function of the longest run as a test for randomness in a sequence of alternatives. *Biometrika*, **35**, 97-112.

Bateman, G. I. 1949.   303
The characteristic function of a weighted sum of non-central squares of normal variates subject to *s* linear restraints. *Biometrika*, **36**, 460-2.

Baten, W. D. 1940.   304
A solution of normal equations giving the standard errors of the constants. *J. Agric. Res.*, **61**, 237-40.

Baten, W. D. 1941.   305
A comparison of annual and biennial inflorescences of *Daucus carota* (wild carrot). *Biometrika*, **32**, 82-7.

Baten, W. D. 1941.   306
How to determine which of two variables is better for predicting a third variable. *J. Amer. Soc. Agron.*, **33**, 695-9.

Baten, W. D. 1943.   307
The discriminant functions applied to score measurements. *Mich. Acad. Sci.*, **29**, 3-7.

Baten, W. D. 1945.   308
Analyzing degrees of freedom into comparisons when the " classes " do not contain the same number of items. *Nat. Math. Mag.*, **19**, 221-8.

Baten, W. D. 1946.   309
Analysis of scores from smelling tests. *Biometrics Bull.*, **2**, 11-14.

Baten, W. D. 1946.   310
Organoleptic tests pertaining to apples and pears. *Food Res.*, **11**, 89-94.

Baten, W. D. & Dewitt, C. C. 1944.   311
Use of the discriminant function in the comparison of proximate coal analyses. *Industr. Engng. Chem.*, **16**, 32-4.

Baten, W. D. & Hatcher, H. M. 1944.   312
Distinguishing method differences by use of discriminant functions. *J. Exper. Educ.*, **12**, 184-6.

Baten, W. D. & Henderson, E. W. 1941. 312[a]
A method of handling ratios by the analysis of variance. *Poultry Sci.*, **20**, 227-31.

Baten, W. D. & Trout, G. M. 1946. 313
A critical study of the summation-of-difference-in-rank method of determining proficiency in judging dairy products. *Biometrics Bull.*, **2**, 67-9.

Baten, W. D., Northam, J. I. & Yeager, A. F. 1941. 313[a]
Grouping of strains or varieties by use of a Latin square. *J. Amer. Soc. Agron.*, **33**, 616-22.

Baticle, E. 1940. 314
Sur la composition des probabilités de densités constantes. *C. R. Acad. Sci., Paris*, **211**, 420-2.

Baticle, E. 1946. 315
Le problème des stocks. *J. Soc. Statist., Paris*, **87**, 100-9. (Also: *C. R. Acad. Sci., Paris*, **222**, 355-7.)

Baticle, E. 1948. 316
Sur une loi de probabilité à priori des paramètres d'une loi laplacienne. *C. R. Acad. Sci., Paris*, **226**, 55-7.

Baticle, E. 1949. 317
Sur une loi de probabilité à priori pour l'interprétation des résultats de tirages dans une urne. *C. R. Acad. Sci., Paris*, **228**, 902-4.

Batrawi, A. & Morant, G. M. 1947. 318
A study of a first dynasty series of Egyptian skulls from Sakkara and of an eleventh dynasty series from Thebes. *Biometrika*, **34**, 18-27.

Batson, E. 1944. 319
The use of random sampling in sociographical research. *South Africa J. Econ.*, **12**, 46-56.

Battara, P. 1948. 320
Sul concetto di concentrazione. *Riv. Ital. Demogr. Statist.*, **2**, 107-25.

Battin, I. L. 1942. 321
On the problem of multiple matching. *Ann. Math. Statist.*, **13**, 294-305.

Bauer, M. 1946. 322
Statistika a desetinné třídění. (Statistique et classification décimale.) (Czech. Russian, English & French summaries.) *Statist. Obzor.*, **26**, 410-27.

Baumgart, E. L. M. 1948. 323
The quantic and statistical bases of visual excitation. *J. Gen. Physiol.*, **31** (3), 269-90.

Baur, F. 1944. 324
Über die grundsätzliche Möglichkeit langfristiger Witternungs vorhersagen. *Ann. Hydrogr., Berlin*, **72**, 15-21.

Baxter, B. 1940. 325
The application of factorial design to a psychological problem. *Psychol. Rev.*, **47**, 494-500.

Baxter, B. 1941. 325[a]
Problems in the planning of psychological experiments. *Amer. J. Psychol.*, **54**, 270-80.

Baxter, B. 1943. 326
The problem of reliability in relation to factorial design. *J. Gen. Psychol.*, **29**, 157-61.

Bayley, G. V. & Hammersley, J. M. 1946. 327
The " effective " number of independent observations in an autocorrelated time-series. *J. R. Statist. Soc. Suppl.*, **8**, 184-97.

Bazalar, T. N. 1945. 327[a]
On the law of large numbers of the theory of probability. *Rev. Cienc. Lima*, **47**, 601-45.

Beale, F. S. 1941. 328
On a certain class of orthogonal polynomials. *Ann. Math. Statist.*, **12**, 97-103.

Beall, G. 1940. 329
The fit and significance of contagious distributions when applied to observations on larval insects. *Ecology*, **21**, 460-74.

Beall, G. 1940. 329[a]
The technique of randomization in field work. *Canadian Ent.*, **72**, 45-8.

Beall, G. 1941. 330
Method of estimating the population of an agricultural pest over areas of many square miles. *Canadian J. Res. D.*, **19**, 167-77.

Beall, G. 1942. 331
The transformation of data from entomological field experiments so that the analysis of variance becomes applicable. *Biometrika*, **32**, 243-62.

Beall, G. 1945. 332
Approximate methods in calculating discriminant functions. *Psychometrika*, **10**, 205-17.

Beall, G. 1947. 333
Quantitative treatment of density distribution pattern on photographic paper as produced by the disturbance of a spotlight galvanometer. *Paper Tr. J.*, **124**, 35-7; *Paper Industry*, **28**, 1801-2.

Beard, R. E. 1947. 334
Statistical problems of naval aircraft provisioning. *J. Inst. Actuar. Students' Soc.*, **6**, 144-8.

Beard, R. E. 1947. 335
The standard deviation of the distribution of sickness. *J. Inst. Actuar. Students' Soc.*, **7**, 23-8.

Beard, R. E. & Perks, W. 1949. 336
The relation between the distribution of sickness and the effect of duplicates on the distribution of deaths. *J. Inst. Actuar.*, **75**, 75-86.

Bebutov, M. 1941. 337
Markoff chains with a compact state space. *C. R. (Dokl.) Acad. Sci. URSS*, **30**, 482-3.

Bebutov, M. 1942. 338
Markoff chains with a compact state space. (English. Russian summary.) *Mat. Sbornik*, **10** (52), 213-38.

Beckenbach, E. F. 1942. 339
Convexity properties of generalized mean value functions. *Ann. Math. Statist.*, **13**, 88-90.

Becknell, E. A. 1940. 340
Probability: a function of ideology. *Amer. J. Psychol.*, **53**, 604-9.

Beckwith, O. P. 1944. 341
A fresh approach to quality control. *Textile World*, **94**, 79-81.

Beckwith, O. P. 1944. 342
The quality control chart technique in applied textile research. *Textile Res.*, **14**, 319-25.

Beebe-Center, J. G. & Beebe-Center, R. 1946. 343
Measurement of affective power in terms of ratios of partial ϵ^2s. *Amer. J. Psychol.*, **59**, 290-5.

Beer, A., Drummond, A. J. & Fürth, R. 1946.   344
Sequences of wet and dry months and the theory of
probability. *Quart. J. R. Met. Soc.*, **72**, 74-86.

Beers, H. S. 1944-5.   345
Six-term formulas for routine actuarial interpolation.
Rec. Amer. Inst. Actuar., **33**, 245-60; **34**, 35-61.

Beers, H. S. 1945.   346
Modified-interpolation formulas that minimise fourth
differences. *Rec. Amer. Inst. Actuar.*, **34**, 14-20;
184-7.

Beers, H. S. 1947.   347
Premium interpolation. *Trans. Actuar. Soc. Amer.*,
48, 53-75.

Behrens, F. 1941.   348
Die statistische Masse. (Czech and French summaries.) *Statist. Obzor*, **22**, 223-30.

Behrens, F. 1941-2.   349
Zusammenhang zwischen betriebswirtschaftlicher und
volkswirtschaftlicher Statistik. *Allg. Statist. Arch.*, **30**,
246-63.

Behrens, F. 1942.   350
Sinn und Unterschied der Indexformeln Laspeyres
und Paasche's. *Statist. Obzor*, **23**, 109-20.

Behrens, F. 1942.   351
Zur Theorie des Lohnvergleiches. *Statist. Obzor*, **23**,
11-25.

Belgique, Office Centr. Statist. 1946.   352
Application des théories statistiques aux vérifications
d'instruments présentés en série. *Bull. Statist. Office
Centr. Statist., Belgique*, **32** (2), 188-90.

Bell, G. E. 1949.   353
Operational research into air traffic control. *J. Roy.
Aero. Soc.*, **53**, 965-78.

Bellinghausen, A. P. 1946.   353a
Sampling a lot, and life tests. *Metal Prog.*, **50** (16),
1205-6.

Bellinson, H. R. 1940.   354
The distribution of the estimate of standard deviation
obtained by the method of successive differences.
Aberdeen Proving Ground Md. Ballistic Res. Lab. Rep.
no. 200, 20 pp.

Bellman, R. E. 1949.   355
A note on the Monte Carlo method and the potential
equation. *RAND Corp., Res. Memo.*, 1 September
1949, RM-234, 3 pp.

Bellman, R. & Blackwell, D. 1949.   356
Some two-person games involving bluffing. *Proc.
Nat. Acad. Sci. U.S.A.*, **35**, 600-5.

Bellman, R. & Harris, T. E. 1948.   357
On the theory of age-dependent stochastic branching processes. *Proc. Nat. Acad. Sci. U.S.A.*, **34**,
601-4.

Bellman, R. E. & Harris, T. E. 1949.   358
Occurrence of improbable states in a modified Ehren-
fest model. I. *RAND Corp., Res. Memo.*, 17 November 1949, RM-289, 13 pp.

Bellman, R. E. & LaSalle, J. P. 1949.   359
On non-zero-sum games and stochastic processes.
RAND Corp., Res. Memo., 19 August 1949, RM-212,
12 pp.

Below, F. 1948.   360
Dimensionswertung in der Statistik, ein Beitrag
zur Theorie der statistischen Massenerscheinungen.
Statist. Praxis, **3**, 107-8.

Belz, M. H. 1947.   361
Note on the Liapounoff inequality for absolute
moments. *Ann. Math. Statist.*, **18**, 604-5.

Bendersky, L. 1948.   362
Sur quelques problèmes concernant les épreuves
répétées. *Bull. Sci. Math.*, (2) **72**, 99-107.

Benedikt, E. T. 1949.   363
Errors in second-order measuring instruments. *Rev.
Sci. Instru.*, **20**, 229-33.

Benini, R. 1948.   363a
Le interpolazioni della Cantica dell' inferno alla luce
della statistica. *Riv. Ital. Demogr. Statist.*, **2**, 3-77.

Benjamin, B. 1943.   364
Height and weight measurements of school children.
J. Hyg., Camb., **43**, 55-68.

Benjamin, K. 1945.   365
An I.B.M. technique for the computation of ΣX^2 and
ΣXY. *Psychometrika*, **10**, 61-7.

Bennett, G. K. & Doppelt, J. E. 1948.   366
The evaluation of pairs of tests for guidance use.
Educ. and Psychol. Measurement, **8**, 319-25.

Bennett, W. A. & Rodgers, J. W. 1943.   366a
Practical application of quality control. *Machinery,
London*, **63**, 701-6.

Bennett, W. A. & Rodgers, J. W. 1943.   366b
Quality control—recording the results of multidimensional inspection. *Aircraft Production*, **5**, 172-5.

Bennett, W. A. & Rodgers, J. W. 1943.   366c
The recording of results of multi-dimensional inspection in connection with quality control. *Engng. Insp.*,
8 (3), 16-21.

Bennett, W. R. 1948.   367
Distribution of the sum of randomly phased components. *Quart. Appl. Math.*, **5**, 385-93.

Bennett, W. R. 1948.   368
Spectra of quantized signals. *Bell Syst. Tech. J.*,
27, 446-72.

Benson, C. B. & Kimball, B. F. 1945.   369
Mortality characteristics of physical property based
upon location life table and re-use ratios. *Econometrica*, **13**, 214-24.

Benson, F. 1949.   370
A note on the estimation of mean and standard deviation from quantiles. *J. R. Statist. Soc. B*, **11**, 91-100.

Bentzel, R. & Wold, H. 1946.   371
On statistical demand analysis from the viewpoint of
simultaneous equations. *Skand. Aktuartidskr.*, **29**,
95-114.

Beretta, L. 1941.   372
A proposito del lemma di Bienaymé. *G. Ist. Ital.
Attuari*, **12**, 122-6.

Berg, W. F. 1945.   373
Aggregates in one- and two-dimensional random
distributions (developability of silver specks of known
dimensions and the size of photographic sensitivity
specks). *Phil. Mag.*, (7) **36**, 337-46.

Berg, W. N. 1941. 374
The law of small numbers as applied to virulence measurement. *Amer. Rev. Tuberc.*, **43**, 685-91.

Berg, W. N. 1945. 375
Blood cell counts. Their statistical interpretation. *Amer. Rev. Tuberc.*, **52**, 179-220.

Berger, A. 1941. 376
Welche Hypothesen liegen der Versicherungsmathematik zugrunde und wie kann die Anwendung der Wahrscheinlichkeitstheorie und der Risikotheorie im Versicherungswesen begründet werden? (French, Italian and English summaries.) *Trans. 12th. Int. Congr. Actuar., Lucerne*, 1940, **4**, 9-26.

Berger, A. & Wald, A. 1949. 377
On distinct hypotheses. *Ann. Math. Statist.*, **20**, 104-9.

Bergmann, G. 1941. 378
The logic of probability. *Amer. J. Phys.*, **9**, 263-72.

Bergmann, G. 1943. 379
Outline of an empiricist philosophy of physics. *Amer. J. Phys.*, **11**, 248-58; 335-42.

Bergmann, G. 1945. 380
Frequencies, probabilities and positivism. (English. Spanish summary.) *Phil. Phenom. Res.*, **6**, 26-44.

Bergmann, G. 1945. 381
The logic of quanta. *Amer. J. Phys.*, **15**, 397-408; 497-508.

Bergmann, G. 1946. 382
Some comments on Carnap's logic of induction. *Philos. Sci.*, **13**, 71-8.

Bergson, A. 1947. 383
A problem in Soviet statistics. *Rev. Econ. Statist.*, **29**, 234-42.

Bergström, H. 1944. 384
On the central limit theorem. *Skand. Aktuartidskr.*, **27**, 139-53.

Bergström, H. 1945. 385
On the central limit theorem in the space R_k, $k > 1$. *Skand. Aktuartidskr.*, **28**, 106-27.

Bergström, H. 1949. 386
On the central limit theorem in the case of not equally distributed random variables. *Skand. Aktuartidskr.*, **32**, 37-62.

Berjman, E. 1941-2. 387
A solution of the problem of least square adjustment by Gauss polynomials, using the computation and tabulation of the parametric coefficients of parabolic functions from the first to the fifth order for series having up to one hundred elements. *An. Soc. Cient. Argent.*, **132**, 34-48, 104-17, 212-17; **133**, 208-15, 442-5.

Berkson, J. 1940. 388
A note on the chi-square test, the Poisson and the binomial. *J. Amer. Statist. Ass.*, **35**, 362-7.

Berkson, J. 1941. 389
A punch card designed to contain written data and coding. *J. Amer. Statist. Ass.*, **36**, 535-8.

Berkson, J. 1942. 390
Tests of significance considered as evidence. *J. Amer. Statist. Ass.*, **37**, 325-35.

Berkson, J. 1943. 391
Experience with tests of significance: A reply to Professor R. A. Fisher. *J. Amer. Statist. Ass.*, **38**, 242-6.

Berkson, J. 1944. 392
Application of the logistic function to bio-assay. *J. Amer. Statist. Ass.*, **39**, 357-65.

Berkson, J. 1946. 393
Approximation of chi-square by " probits " and " logits ". *J. Amer. Statist. Ass.*, **41**, 70-4.

Berkson, J. 1946. 394
Limitations of the application of fourfold table analysis to hospital data. *Biometrics Bull.*, **2**, 47-53.

Berkson, J. 1947. 395
" Cost-Utility " as a measure of the efficiency of a test. *J. Amer. Statist. Ass.*, **42**, 246-55.

Berkson, J. 1949. 396
Minimum χ^2 and maximum likelihood solution in terms of a linear transform with particular reference to bio-assay. *J. Amer. Statist. Ass.*, **44**, 273-8.

Berkson, J. & Geary, R. C. 1941. 396a
Comments on Dr. Madow's " Note on tests of departure from normality " with some remarks concerning tests of significance. *J. Amer. Statist. Ass.*, **36**, 539-43.

Berkson, J., Magath, T. B. & Hurn, M. 1940. 397
The error of estimate of the blood cell count as made with the hemocytometer. *Amer. J. Physiol.*, **128**, 309-23.

Berlovich, E. 1946. 398
Statistics of misses in Geiger-Müller counters. (Russian. English summary.) *Zh. Eksper. Teor. Fiz. Akad. Nauk SSSR*, **16**, 543-6.

Berlovich, E. 1946. 399
The theory of misses in an electromagnetic numerator at the output of a dividing scheme with a Geiger-Müller counter. (Russian. English summary.) *Zh. Eksper. Teor. Fiz. Akad. Nauk SSSR*, **16**, 547-52.

Bernadelli, H. 1941. 400
Population waves. *J. Burma Res. Soc.*, **31**, 1-18.

Bernadelli, H. 1944. 401
The stability of the income distribution. *Sankhyā*, **6**, 351-62.

Bernstein, M. M. & Burks, B. S. 1942. 402
The incidence and Mendelian transmission of mid-digital hair in man. *J. Heredity*, **33**, 45-53.

Bernstein, P. 1941. 403
How many automatics should a man run? *Fact. Magmt.*, **99**, 85-164.

Bernstein, S. N. 1940. 404
Nouvelles applications des grandeurs aléatoires presqu'indépendantes. (Russian. French summary.) *Izv. Akad. Nauk SSSR, Ser. Mat.*, **4**, 137-50.

Bernstein, S. N. 1940. 405
The Petersburg school of the theory of probability. (Russian.) *Uch. Zap. Leningrad Gos. Univ., Ser. Mat.*, **10**, 3-11.

Bernstein, S. N. 1940. 406
Sur un problème du schéma des urnes à composition variable. *C. R. (Dokl.) Acad. Sci. URSS*, **28**, 5-7.

Bernstein, S. N. 1941. 407
On "fiducial" probabilities of Fisher. (Russian. English summary.) *Izv. Akad. Nauk SSSR, Ser. Mat.*, **5**, 85-94.

Bernstein, S. N. 1941. 408
Sur une propriété caractéristique de le loi de Gauss. (Russian. French summary.) *Trudy Leningrad Polytechnic Inst.*, **3**, 21-2.

Bernstein, S. N. 1941. 409
Sur les sommes de grandeurs aléatoires liées de classes (A, N) et (B, N). *C. R. (Dokl.) Acad. Sci. URSS*, **32**, 303-7.

Bernstein, S. N. 1942. 410
Solution of a mathematical problem connected with the theory of heredity. *Ann. Math. Statist.*, **13**, 53-61. (Translated by **E. Lehmer** from (1924) *Ann. Sci. Ukrain.*, **1**, 83-114.)
1, 83-114.)

Bernstein, S. N. 1943. 411
Retour au problème de l'évaluation de l'approximation de la formule limite de Laplace. (Russian. French summary.) *Izv. Akad. Nauk SSSR, Ser. Mat.*, **7**, 3-16.

Bernstein, S. N. 1944. 412
An extension of the distribution theorem of probability theory to the sum of dependent variables. (Russian.) *Usp. Mat. Nauk* (10), 65-114.

Bernstein, S. N. 1945. 413
On P. L. Chebyshev's researches in the theory of probability. *The Scientific Legacy of P. L. Chebyshev*, **1**, pp. 43-68. (Published by Akad. Nauk SSSR, Moscow-Leningrad.)

Bernstein, S. N. 1946. 414
Sur le théorème limite de la théorie des probabilités. (Russian. French summary.) *Izv. Nauch. Issled. Inst. Mat. Mekh. Gos. Univ. Tomsk*, **3**, 174-90.

Bernstein, V. 1941. 415
Signal fluctuations. *Zh. Tekh. Fiz.*, **11**, 302-4.

Bernyer, G. 1943. 416
L'estimation des facteurs psychologiques par la regression. *L'Année Psychol.*, **43-4**, 299-322.

Berry, A. C. 1941. 417
The accuracy of the Gaussian approximation to the sum of independent variates. *Trans. Amer. Math. Soc.*, **49**, 122-36.

Berry, C. E. 1945. 418
A criterion of convergence for the classical iterative method of solving linear simultaneous equations. *Ann. Math. Statist.*, **16**, 398-400.

Berry, D. S. & Green, F. H. 1948. 419
Techniques for measuring overall speed in urban areas. *Proc. 29th. Annu. Meeting, Highway Res. Bd.*, **29**, 311ff.

Berry, J. C. 1945. 420
Reliability of averages of different numbers of lactation records for comparing dairy cows. *J. Dairy Sci.*, **28**, 355-66.

Bertrand, I. & Quivy, D. 1945. 421
Distribution statistique de coefficient exponentiel *a* de Fisher. *C. R. Soc. Biol., Paris*, **139**, 603-5.

Beyer, P. & Tremolières, J. 1944. 422
Study on maternity and its relation to certain living conditions in Paris in 1942-3. *Rec. Trav. Inst. Nat. Hyg., Paris*, **1** (3), 57-147.

Bhargava, R. P. 1946. 423
Test of significance for intra-class correlation when family sizes are not equal. *Sankhyā*, **7**, 435-8.

Bhatia, C. M. 1943. 424
An analysis of the High School examination marks in English of the U.P. Board. *Sankhyā*, **6**, 325-6.

Bhattacharya, K. N. 1943. 425
A note on twofold triple systems. *Sankhyā*, **6**, 313-14.

Bhattacharya, K. N. 1944. 426
A new balanced incomplete block design. *Science & Culture*, **9**, 508.

Bhattacharya, K. N. 1944. 427
On a new symmetrical balanced incomplete block design. *Bull. Calcutta Math. Soc.*, **36**, 91-6.

Bhattacharya, K. N. 1946. 428
A new solution in symmetrical balanced incomplete block designs $(v = b = 31, \ r = k = 10, \ \lambda = 3)$. *Sankhyā*, **7**, 423-4.

Bhattacharyya, A. 1942. 429
A note on Ramamurti's problem of maximal sets. *Sankhyā*, **6**, 189-92.

Bhattacharyya, A. 1943. 430
On a measure of divergence between two statistical populations defined by their probability distributions. *Bull. Calcutta Math. Soc.*, **35**, 99-109.

Bhattacharyya, A. 1944. 431
On some sets of sufficient conditions leading to the normal bivariate distribution. *Sankhyā*, **6**, 399-406.

Bhattacharyya, A. 1945. 432
A note on the distribution of the sum of chi-squares. *Sankhyā*, **7**, 27-8.

Bhattacharyya, A. 1946. 433
On a measure of divergence between two multinomial populations. *Sankhyā*, **7**, 401-6.

Bhattacharyya, A. 1946-8. 434
On some analogues of the amount of information and their use in statistical estimation. *Sankhyā*, **8**, 1-14, 201-18, 315-28.

Bhattacharyya, B. C. 1941. 435
An alternative method of the distribution of Mahalanobis's D^2-statistic. *Bull. Calcutta Math. Soc.*, **33**, 87-92.

Bhattacharyya, B. C. 1942. 436
A note on the tractrix and the cycloid as statistical distribution curves. *Bull. Calcutta Math. Soc.*, **34**, 105-8.

Bhattacharyya, B. C. 1942. 437
The use of McKay's Bessel function curves for graduating frequency distributions. *Sankhyā*, **6**, 175-82.

Bhattacharyya, B. C. 1943. 438
A note on the health examination of school boys in the municipal town of Rajshàhi. *Sankhyā*, **6**, 323-4.

Bhattacharyya, B. C. 1944. 439
On an aspect of Pearsonian system of curves and a few analogies. *Sankhyā*, **6**, 415-18.

Bhattacharyya, D. P. & Narayan, R. D. 1941. **440**
Moments of the D^2-statistic for populations with unequal dispersions. *Sankhyā*, **5**, 401-12.

Bickerstaff, A. 1947. **441**
One fifth acre versus one tenth acre plots in sampling immature stands. *Dominion Forest Service, Canada, Silvicultural Res. Note* no. 83.

Bickerstaff, A. 1947. **442**
The measurement of growth on forest areas by means of recurrent line plot surveys. *For. Chron.*, **23**, 36-43.

Bickerstaff, A. 1947. **443**
Sampling efficiency of line plot survey on Riding Mountain research area. *Dominion Forest Service, Canada, Silivicultural Res. Note* no. 84.

Bicking, C. A. 1948. **444**
Industrial statistics; their place in the manufacture of pulp and paper. *Pulp and Paper*, **49**, 181-8.

Bicking, C. A. & Wernimont, G. 1947. **445**
Quality control in the chemical industry. I. How statistics contributes to quality control in the chemical industry. II. Statistical quality control in the chemical laboratory. III. Statistical techniques for the production control and plant scale experimentation. *Industr. Qual. Contr.*, **3** (4), 17-20; (6), 5-11; 11-14.

Bidlack, W., Close, E. R. & Warren, J. C. 1945. **446**
Applications of quality control at Bausch and Lomb Optical Company. *Industr. Qual. Contr.*, **2** (1), 3-9.

Biehler, W. & Wohlschnitt, H. 1941. **447**
Beitrag zur statistischen Beurteilung biologischer Wirkungen. *Arch. Exper. Path. Pharmak.*, **198**, 278-91.

Biesheuvel, S. & White, M. 1949. **448**
The human factor in flying accidents. *J. South African Air Force*, **1**, 2ff.

Bignardi, F. 1947. **449**
Sulle generalizzazioni della diseguaglianza di Bienaymé-Tchebychef nello studio della distribuzioni di frequenze. *Ann Fac. Econ. Com. Palermo*, **1**, 41-72.

Bignardi, F. 1947. **450**
Di alcuni criteri di applicazione delle diseguaglianze di Bienaymé-Tchebychef e di Vinci nelle studio delle distribuzioni di frequenze. *Ann. Fac. Econ. Com. Palermo*, **1**, 84-108.

Bignardi, F. 1947. **451**
Intorno ad una nuova diseguaglianza per lo studio delle distribuzioni di frequenze. *Statistica, Milano*, **7**, 237-51.

Bignardi, F. 1948. **452**
Di una distribuzione statistica deducibile da un principio degli errori di proporzione. *Ann. Fac. Econ. Com. Palermo*, **2**, 148-71.

Billings, W. D. 1941. **453**
Quantitative correlations between vegetational changes and soil development. *Ecology*, **22**, 448-56.

Bingham, M. D. 1941. **454**
A new method for obtaining the inverse matrix. *J. Amer. Statist. Ass.*, **36**, 530-4.

Bingham, W. V. 1949. **455**
Great expectations. *Personnel Psychol.*, **2**, 397-404.

Biondo, G. 1947. **456**
Gli schemi teorici del Polya. *Ann. Fac. Econ. Com. Palermo*, **1**, 62-83.

Birch, L. C. 1944. **457**
The effect of temperature and dryness on the survival of the eggs of *calandra oryzae L.* (small strain), and *Rhizopertha dominica Fab.* (Coleoptera). *Aust. J. Exper. Biol. Med. Sci.*, **22**, 265-9.

Birch, L. C. 1944. **458**
Two strains of *calandra oryzae L.* (Coleoptera). *Aust. J. Exper. Biol. Med. Sci.*, **22**, 271-5.

Birch, L. C. 1944. **459**
An improved method for determining the influence of temperature on the rate of development of insect eggs (using eggs of the small strain of *calandra oryzae L*, (Coleoptera)). *Aust. J. Exper. Biol. Med. Sci.*, **22**, 277-83.

Bird, S. 1945. **460**
Measuring roundness of breast in live turkeys. *U.S. Egg Poultry Mag.*, **51**, 206-9, 235.

Birge, R. T. 1947. **461**
Least squares fitting of data by means of polynomials. *Rev. Mod. Phys.*, **19**, 298-360.

Birkhoff, G. D. 1942. **461a**
What is the ergodic theorem? *Amer. Math. Monthly*, **49**, 222-6.

Birnbaum, Z. W. 1942. **462**
An inequality for Mills' ratio. *Ann. Math. Statist.*, **13**, 245-6.

Birnbaum, Z. W. 1948. **463**
On random variables with comparable peakedness. *Ann. Math. Statist.*, **19**, 76-81.

Birnbaum, Z. W. & Andrews, F. C. 1949. **463a**
On sums of symmetrically truncated normal random variables. *Ann. Math. Statist.*, **20**, 458-61.

Birnbaum, Z. W. & Zuckerman, H. S. 1940. **464**
On the properties of a collective. *Amer. J. Math.*, **62**, 787-91.

Birnbaum, Z. W. & Zuckerman, H. S. 1944. **465**
An inequality due to H. Hornich. *Ann. Math. Statist.*, **15**, 328-9.

Birnbaum, Z. W. & Zuckerman, H. S. 1948. **466**
On the determination of the dependence of a disease, especially cancer, on age. *Univ. Washington Publ. Math.*, **3**.

Birnbaum, Z. W. & Zuckerman, H. S. 1949. **467**
A graphical determination of sample size for Wilks' tolerance limits. *Ann. Math. Statist.*, **20**, 313-16.

Birnbaum, Z. W., Raymond, J. & Zuckerman, H. S. 1947. **468**
A generalization of Tchebycheff's inequality to two dimensions. *Ann. Math. Statist.*, **18**, 70-9.

Bisbee, R. F. 1941. **468a**
All-out for quality. *Fact. Mgmt.*, **99**, 57-64.

Bishop, D. J. 1942. **469**
The renewal of aircraft. *Ministry of Aircraft Production Aero Res. Com. Rep. & Memo.* no. 1907 (6342), 12 pp.

Bistrup, C. 1944. **470**
Approximate calculation of the standard deviation. *Dansk. Skovforen. Tidsskr.*, **29**, 166-8.

Bitancourt, A. A. 1945. 471
A probit scale for slide rules. *Biometrics Bull.*, **1**, 46-53.

Bitter, F. 1949. 471a
The mathematical formulation of strategic problems. *Proc. Berkeley Symp. Math. Statist. and Probab.*, 1945-6, pp. 223-8.

Bitterlich, W. 1948. 472
Die Winkelzählprobe. *Allg. Forst-Holywirtschaft. Zeit.*, **59**, 4-5.

Bittner, R. H. & Wilder, C. E. 1946. 473
Expectancy tables: a method of interpreting correlation coefficients. *J. Exper. Educ.*, **14**, 245-52.

Bityutskov, V. I. 1948. 474
A local limit theorem for sequences of events forming a compound chain of the second order. (Russian.) *Izv. Akad. Nauk SSSR, Ser. Mat.*, **12**, 101-10.

Bizley, M. T. L. 1947. 475
On Waring's *B*-formula. *J. Inst. Actuar. Students' Soc.*, **6**, 123-34.

Bjerke, B. 1940. 476
Wahrscheinlichkeit auf Grund von Stichproben. (Norwegian.) *Nordisk. Mat. Tidskr.*, **22**, 64-9.

Blachman, N. M. 1948. 477
A theoretical study of the demodulation of a frequency-modulated carrier and random noise by an FM receiver. *Harvard Univ. Cruft Lab. Tech. Rep.* no. 31.

Black, D. 1948. 478
The decisions of a committee using a special majority. *Econometrica*, **16**, 245-61.

Black, D. 1948. 479
The elasticity of committee decisions with an altering size of majority. *Econometrica*, **16**, 262-70.

Black, M. 1947. 479a
Professor Broad on the limit theorems of probability. *Mind*, **56**, 148-50.

Blackman, M. & Michiels, J. L. 1948. 480
Efficiency of counting systems. *Proc. Phys. Soc.*, **60**, 549-61.

Blackwell, D. 1942. 481
Idempotent Markoff chains. *Ann. Math.*, (2) **43**, 560-7.

Blackwell, D. 1945. 482
The existence of anormal chains. *Bull. Amer. Math. Soc.*, **51**, 465-8.

Blackwell, D. 1945. 483
Finite non-homogeneous chains. *Ann. Math.*, (2) **46**, 594-9.

Blackwell, D. 1946. 484
On an equation of Wald. *Ann. Math. Statist.*, **17**, 84-7.

Blackwell, D. 1947. 485
Conditional expectation and unbiased sequential estimation. *Ann. Math. Statist.*, **18**, 105-10.

Blackwell, D. 1948. 486
A renewal theorem. *Duke Math. J.*, **15**, 145-50.

Blackwell, D. & Girschick, M. A. 1946. 487
On functions of sequences of independent chance vectors with applications to the problem of the " random walk " in *k* dimensions. *Ann. Math. Statist.*, **17**, 310-17.

Blackwell, D. & Girschick, M. A. 1947. 488
A lower bound for the variance of some unbiased sequential estimates. *Ann. Math. Statist.*, **18**, 277-80.

Blair, G. W. Scott & Coppen, F. M. V. 1943. 489
The estimation of firmness in soft materials. *Amer. J. Psychol.*, **56**, 234-46.

Blake, A. 1946. 490
Criteria for the reality of apparent periodicities and other regularities. *Publ. Bur. Central Séismologique Int. A*, **16**, 5 pp.

Blakeley, L. 1949. 491
The Lindisfarne s/ð problem. *Studia Neophilogica*, **22**, 15-47.

Blakey, R. 1940. 492
A re-analysis of a test of the theory of two factors. *Psychometrika*, **5**, 121-36.

Blanche, E. E. 1946. 493
The mathematics of gambling. *Sch. Sci. Math.*, **46**, 217-27.

Blanc-Lapierre, A. 1943. 494
Sur les fluctuations produites par l'effet de grenaille dans les amplificateurs. *C. R. Acad. Sci., Paris*, **217**, 73-4.

Blanc-Lapierre, A. 1943. 495
Fluctuations dues à l'émission thermo-électronique de la couche photoélectrique dans un amplificateur en lumière modulée. *C. R. Acad. Sci., Paris*, **218**, 42-4.

Blanc-Lapierre, A. 1944. 496
Sur certaines fonctions aléatoires introduites par un problème d'électricité. *C. R. Acad. Sci., Paris*, **218**, 924-5.

Blanc-Lapierre, A. 1944. 497
Sur quelques propriétés ergodiques de certaines fonctions aléatoires. *C. R. Acad. Sci., Paris*, **218**, 985-6.

Blanc-Lapierre, A. 1945. 498
Effet Schottky. Fluctuations dans les amplificateurs linéaires et dans les détecteurs. *Bull. Soc. Française Électriciens*, (6) **5**, 343-51.

Blanc-Lapierre, A. 1945. 499
Les fonctions aléatoires stationnaires laplaciennes. *C. R. Acad. Sci., Paris*, **220**, 378-80.

Blanc-Lapierre, A. 1945. 500
Sur l'effet de scintillation. *C. R. Acad. Sci., Paris*, **221**, 375-7.

Blanc-Lapierre, A. 1946. 501
Étude des fluctuations produites par l'effet de grenaille dans les amplificateurs. *Rev. Sci., Paris*, **84**, 75-94.

Blanc-Lapierre, A. 1947. 502
Remarques sur l'analyse harmonique des fonctions aléatoires. *Rev. Sci., Paris*, **85**, 1027-40.

Blanc-Lapierre, A. 1947. 503
Remarques sur les propriétés énergetiques des fonctions aléatoires. *C. R. Acad. Sci., Paris*, **225**, 982-4.

Blanc-Lapierre, A. 1947. 504
Sur quelques problèmes poses par la detérmination des spectres de puissance ou d'énergie des grandeurs aléatoires. *C. R. Acad. Sci., Paris*, **225**, 1264-6.

Blanc-Lapierre, A. 1948. 505
Remarques sur certaines fonctions aléatoires. *C. R. Acad. Sci., Paris*, **227**, 1333-5.

Blanc-Lapierre, A. 1949. 506
Considérations sur l'analyse harmonique des fonctions aléatoires. *Le calcul des probabilités et ses applications. Colloq. Int. Centre Nat. Rech. Sci., Paris,* **13**, 61-6.

Blanc-Lapierre, A. 1949. 507
Analyse harmonique des fonctions aléatoires stationnaires. *Analyse Harmonique. Colloq. Int. Centre Nat. Rech. Sci., Paris,* **15**, 121-32.

Blanc-Lapierre, A. & Brard, R. 1945. 508
La loi forte des grands nombres pour les fonctions aléatoires stationnaires continues. *C. R. Acad. Sci., Paris,* **220**, 134-6.

Blanc-Lapierre, A. & Brard, R. 1946. 509
Les fonctions aléatoires stationnaires et la loi des grands nombres. *Bull. Soc. Math. France,* **74**, 102-15.

Blanc-Lapierre, A. & Fortet, R. 1946. 510
Sur la décomposition spéctrale des fonctions aléatoires stationnaires d'ordre deux. *C. R. Acad. Sci., Paris,* **222**, 467-8.

Blanc-Lapierre, A. & Fortet, R. 1946. 511
Résultats sur la décomposition spectrale des fonctions aléatoires stationnaires d'ordre 2. *C. R. Acad. Sci., Paris,* **222**, 713-14.

Blanc-Lapierre, A. & Fortet, R. 1946. 512
Sur la structure des fonctions aléatoires strictement stationnaires à spectre totalement discontinu. *C. R. Acad. Sci., Paris,* **222**, 1155-7.

Blanc-Lapierre, A. & Fortet, R. 1946. 513
Extension de la méthode des filtres à des fonctions aléatoires non stationnaires. *C. R. Acad. Sci., Paris,* **222**, 1270-1.

Blanc-Lapierre, A. & Fortet, R. 1947. 514
Les fonctions aléatoires stationnaires de plusieurs variables. *Rev. Sci., Paris,* **85**, 419-22.

Blanc-Lapierre, A. & Fortet, R. 1947. 515
Sur une propriété fondamentale des fonctions de corrélation. *C. R. Acad. Sci., Paris,* **224**, 786-8.

Blanc-Lapierre, A. & Fortet, R. 1947. 516
Analyse harmonique des fonctions aléatoires et caractère stationnaire. *C. R. Acad. Sci., Paris,* **225**, 1119-20.

Blanc-Lapierre, A. & Lapostolle, P. 1946. 517
Fluctuations dans les grandeurs physiques quasi-sinusoïdales. *C. R. Acad. Sci., Paris,* **222**, 1324-5.

Blanc-Lapierre, A. & Lapostolle, P. 1946. 518
Fluctuations dans les grandeurs physiques quasi-sinusoïdales. *J. Phys. Radium,* (8) **7**, 153-64.

Blanc-Lapierre, A. & Lapostolle, P. 1946. 519
Propagation d'une perturbation à spectre peu étendu dans un milieu dispersif non absorbant. *Rev. Sci., Paris,* **84**, 579-95.

Blaxter, K. L. 1948. 520
The evaluation of the nutritive value of animal feeding-stuffs: the application of statistical methods to food problems. *Analyst,* **73**, 11-15.

Bleeker, W. 1946. 521
The verification of weather forecasts. *Meded. Verhandelingen B, Deel,* **1** (2), 23ff.

Bleick, W. E. 1940. 522
A least squares accumulation theorem. *Ann. Math. Statist.,* **11**, 225-6.

Blind, A. 1949. 523
Der Anwendungsbereich der logarithmischen Kurve in der Statistik. *Allg. Statist. Arch.,* **33**, 338-66.

Bliss, C. I. 1940. 524
Factorial design and covariance in biological assay of Vitamin D. *J. Amer. Statist. Ass.,* **35**, 498-506.

Bliss, C. I. 1940. 525
Quantitative aspects of biological assay. *J. Amer. Pharm. Ass.,* **29**, 465-75.

Bliss, C. I. 1941. 526
Biometry in the service of biological assay. *Industr. Engng. Chem.,* **13**, 84-8.

Bliss, C. I. 1941. 527
Statistical problems in estimating populations of Japanese beetle larvae. *J. Econ. Ent.,* **34**, 221-31.

Bliss, C. I. 1944. 528
A chart of the chi square distribution. *J. Amer. Statist. Ass.,* **39**, 246-8.

Bliss, C. I. 1944. 529
A simplified calculation of the potency of penicillin and other drugs assayed biologically with a graded response. *J. Amer. Statist. Ass.,* **39**, 479-87.

Bliss, C. I. 1944. 530
The U.S.P. collaborative cat assays for digitalis. *J. Amer. Pharm. Ass.,* **33**, 225-45.

Bliss, C. I. 1945. 531
The combined slope in comparative tests of tibia and toe ash in the chick assay for vitamin D. *Poultry Sci.,* **24**, 534-41.

Bliss, C. I. 1945. 532
Confidence limits for biological assays. *Biometrics Bull.,* **1**, 57-64.

Bliss, C. I. 1946. 533
An experimental design for slope-ratio assays. *Ann. Math. Statist.,* **17**, 232-7.

Bliss, C. I. 1946. 534
A revised cylinder-plate assay for penicillin. *J. Amer. Pharm. Ass.,* **35**, 6-12.

Bliss, C. I. 1947. 535
2×2 factorial experiments in incomplete groups for use in biological assays. *Biometrics Bull.,* **3**, 69-88.

Bliss, C. I. 1948. 536
Estimation of the mean and its error from incomplete Poisson distributions. *Connecticut Agric. Exper. Sta. Bull.,* **513**, 12 pp.

Bliss, C. I. & Allmark, M. G. 1944. 537
The digitalis cat assay in relation to rate of injection. *J. Pharmacol.,* **81**, 378-89.

Bliss, C. I. & Cattell, M. 1943. 538
Biological assay. *Ann. Rev. Physiol.,* **5**, 479-539.

Bliss, C. I. & Dearborn, R. B. 1942. 539
The efficiency of lattice squares in corn selection tests in New England and Pennsylvania. *Proc. Amer. Soc. Hort. Sci.,* **41**, 324-42.

Bliss, C. I. & Packard, C. 1941. 540
Stability of the standard dosage-effect curve for radiation. *Amer. J. Roentgenol.,* **46**, 400-4.

Bliss, C. I. & Tose, C. L. 1940.   541
The assay of parathyroid extract from the serum
calcium of dogs. *Amer. J. Hyg. A*, **31**, 79-98.

Bliss, C. I., Anderson, E. D. & Marland, R. E.   542
1943. A technique for testing consumer preferences
with special reference to the constituents of ice cream.
Storrs Agric. Exper. Sta. Bull., **251**, 20 pp.

Blom, G. 1949.   543
A generalization of Wald's fundamental identity.
Ann. Math. Statist., **20**, 439-44.

Blommers, P. 1945.   544
Statistical theory. Some recent developments. *Rev.
Educ. Res.*, **15**, 423-40.

Blondel, F. 1949.   545
Note sur la répartition géographique de la production
minérale. *J. Soc. Statist. Paris*, **90**, 372-82.

Bloodworth, W. H. 1946.   545a
How the designer can tie in with statistical quality
control. *Elect. Mfg.*, **37**, 102-5.

Bloom, B. S. 1942.   545b
Test reliability for what? *J. Educ. Psychol.*, **33**, 517-26.

Bloom, B. S. & Lubin, A. 1942.   546
Use of the test scoring machine and the graphic item-
counter for statistical work. *Psychometrika*, **7**,
233-41.

Bloomers, P. & Lindquist, E. F. 1942.   546a
Experimental and statistical studies on the application
of newer statistical techniques. *Rev. Educ. Res.*, **12**,
501-20.

Blum, H. F. 1943.   547
Accuracy and reproducibility in the induction of
tumours with ultra-violet radiation. *J. Nat. Cancer
Inst.*, **4**, 75-9.

Blum, H. F., Grady, H. G. & Kirby-Smith, J. S.   548
1942. Limits of accuracy in experimental carcino-
genesis as exemplified by tumor induction with ultra-
violet radiation. *J. Nat. Cancer Inst.*, **3**, 83-9.

Blumenstock, G. 1942.   548a
Drought in the United States analyzed by means of
the theory of probability. *U.S. Dept. Agric. Tech.
Bull.*, no. 819, 1-63.

Blunn, C. T. & Grandstaff, J. O. 1945.   549
Comparison of the yields of side samples from weanling
and yearling sheep. *J. Animal Sci.*, **4**, 122-7.

Blythe, R. H., Jr. 1945.   550
The economics of sample size applied to the scaling of
sawlogs. *Biometrics Bull.*, **1**, 67-70.

Boag, J. W. 1948.   551
The presentation and analysis of the results of radio-
therapy. I, II. *Brit. J. Radiol.*, **21**, 128-38; 189-203.

Boag, J. W. 1949.   552
Maximum likelihood estimates of the proportion of
patients cured by cancer therapy. *J. R. Statist. Soc. B*,
11, 15-53.

Boaga, G. 1948.   553
Interpretazione géometrica del coefficiente di correlazione. *Riv. Ital. Demogr. Statist.*, **2**, 471-4.

Boas, R. P., Jr. 1941.   554
A general moment problem. *Amer. J. Math.*, **63**,
361-70.

Boas, R. P., Jr. 1949.   554a
The Charlier *B*-series. *Trans. Amer. Math. Soc.*,
67, 206-16.

Boas, R. P., Jr. 1949.   555
Representation of probability distributions by Charlier
series. *Ann. Math. Statist.*, **20**, 376-92.

Bobroff, A. A. 1945.   556
Conditions of applicability of the strong law of large
numbers. *Duke Math. J.*, **12**, 43-6.

Bobrov, A. A. 1947.   557
A simplified proof of a theorem of A. N. Kolmogorov
on the strong law of large numbers. (Russian.)
Usp. Mat. Nauk (N.S.), **2** 3(19), 194-6.

Bobrov, A. A. 1949.   558
On the relative stability of sums of positive random
quantities. (Russian.) *Uch. Zap. Moskov. Gos.
Univ.* **146**, *Ser. Fiz. Mat.* **3**, 92-107.

Bochner, S. 1946.   559
Finitely additive set functions and stochastic processes.
Proc. Nat. Acad. Sci. U.S.A., **32**, 259-61.

Bochner, S. 1947.   560
Stochastic processes. *Ann. Math.*, (2) **48**, 1014-61.

Bochner, S. 1949.   561
Diffusion equation and stochastic processes. *Proc.
Nat. Acad. Sci. U.S.A.*, **35**, 368-70.

Boggs, M. M. & Hanson, H. L. 1949.   562
Analysis of foods by sensory difference tests. *Advanc.
Food Res.*, **2**, 219-58.

Bogolyubov, N. N. 1945.   563
On certain limiting distributions for sums depending
on arbitrary phases. (Russian.) *Uch. Zap. Moskov.
Gos. Univ., Fiz.*, **77**, 43-50.

Bogolyubov, N. N. 1945.   564
On the influence of a random force on a harmonic
oscillator. (Russian.) *Uch. Zap. Moskov. Gos. Univ.,
Fiz.*, **77**, 51-73.

Bogolyubov, N. N. & Khachet, B. I. 1949.   565
On some mathematical problems of the theory of
statistical equilibrium. (Russian.) *Dokl. Akad. Nauk
SSSR*, **66**, 321-4.

Böhm, F. 1941.   566
Über eine Aufgabe aus der Theorie der Momente.
Bla. Versich.-math., **5**, 245-9.

Bohr, H. 1940.   567
Om det matematiske grundlag for sandsynlighedsreg-
ningen. (On the mathematical foundation for
probability calculus.) *Mat. Tidsskr. A*, **1940**,
1-29.

Bok, S. T. 1946.   568
De gedachtengang van de statistica. (Statistical
reasoning.) *Étud. Inst. Med. Prev.*, **3**.

Bok, S. T. 1946-7.   569
Statistica. *Statistica Neerlandica*, **1**, 45-6.

Bolant, R. 1949.   570
Recherche des débits admissibles dans les canalisations
par le calcul des probabilités. *Houille Blanche*, **4**,
315-30. (English summary, 228-9.)

Boldrini, M. 1940.   571
La media aritmetica subbiettiva tipica. *G. Economisti*
2, 348-65.

Boldrini, M. 1941.   572
Sulla dispersione dei caratteri Mendeliani. *Statistica, Ferrara*, **1**, 61-76. (Also: Acta Pontif. Acad. Sci., **5**, 85-101.)

Boldrini, M. 1941.   573
La statistica e le scienze naturali. *Statistica, Ferrara*, **1**, 281-302.

Boldrini, M. 1946.   574
Sulla teoria della media tipica. *Pontif. Acad. Sci. Comment.*, **10**, 1-41 (also (1948) *Contr. Lab. Statist., Milano*, **21**, 83-111).

Boldrini, M. 1948.   575
Ultima replica sulla media aritmetica tipica. *Riv. Ital. Econ. Demogr. Statist.*, **2**, 196-8.

Boldrini, M. 1948.   576
Le statistiche letterarie e i fonemi elementari nella poesia. I-IV. (Italian. French and English summaries.) *Contrib. Lab. Statist., Univ. Milano*, **21**, 1-15; 16-65; 66-75; 75-9.

Bolz, R. W. 1945.   576ª
Statistical control—The yardstick of performance. *Machine Design*, **17** (7), 135-8.

Bolza, H. 1942-3.   577
Bemerkungen zur Logistica-Kurve. *Allg. Statist. Arch.*, **31**, 369-71.

Bond, T. E. T. 1947.   578
Some Ceylon examples of the logarithmic series and the index of diversity of plant and animal population. *Ceylon J. Sci.*, **12** (A), 195-202.

Bonet, P. 1942.   579
Méthodes statistiques de titrage des ultravirus. *Ann. Inst. Pasteur*, **68**, 491-4.

Bonferroni, C. E. 1940.   580
Sulle condizioni necessarie e sufficienti affinché un centro ponderato sia un valor medio. *Suppl. Statist. Nuovi Problemi Pol. Istoria Econ., Ferrara*, **6** (1), 16-23.

Bonferroni, C. E. 1940.   581
Relazione fra curve di frequenza e di concentrazione. *Riun. Firenze Soc. Demogr. Statist.*

Bonferroni, C. E. 1941.   582
Ancora sulle condizioni necessarie e sufficienti affinché un centro ponderato sia un valor medio. *Statistica, Ferrara*, **1**, 111-19.

Bonferroni, C. E. 1941.   583
Corrélation et interpolation. *J. Soc. Hongr. Statist., Budapest*, **19** (3-4), 175-85.

Bonferroni, C. E. 1942.   584
Nuovi indici di connessione fra variabili statistiche. *Studi sulla correlazione e sulla connessione, Vol. I*, pp. 57-100.

Bonferroni, C. E. 1942.   585
Di un coefficiente di correlazione simultanea. *Atti 2do Congr. Mat. Ital., Bologna*, 1940, pp. 707-14.

Bonferroni, C. E. 1942.   586
Sulla correlazione e sulla connessione. *Publ. Ist. Statist. Univ. Commerciale, Milano, Florence.*

Bonferroni, C. E. 1942.   587
Di un indice di miglioramento d'interpolazione. *G. Economisti*, **4**, 246-56; 351-7.

Bonferroni, C. E. 1942.   588
Un indice quadratico di concentrazione. *Atti 2do Congr. Mat. Ital., Bologna*, 1940, pp. 700-6.

Bonferroni, C. E. 1948.   589
Sulle medie multiple di potenze. *Atti Congr. Un. Mat. Ital., Pisa.*

Bonifacio, G. 1947.   589ª
Analisi stagionalità della produzione nell' assicurazione vita. *Statistica, Milano*, **7**, 9-30.

Bonifacio, G. 1948.   590
Sulla correlazione fra reddito e taluni consumi alimentari. *Riv. Ital. Demogr. Statist.*, **2**, 550-61.

Bonnier, G. 1942.   591
The fourfold table and the heterogeneity test. *Science*, **96**, 13-14.

Bonnier, G. 1942.   592
The χ^2 linkage test. *Hereditas, Lund*, **28**, 230-2.

Bonnier, G. 1946.   593
The sire index. *Acta Agric. Suec., Stockh.*, **1**, 321-34.

Bonnier, G. & Lüning, K. G. 1949.   594
Studies on X-ray mutations in the white and forked loci of *Drosophila Melanogaster*. I. A statistical analysis of mutation frequencies. *Hereditas, Lund*, **35**, 163-89.

Bonnier, G., Hansson, A. & During, T. 1946.   595
The efficiency of the (uniovular) twin method in experimental research. *Kon. Landtbr. Akad. Handl., Stockh.*, **85**, 455-67.

Bonnier, G., Hansson, A. & Jarl, F. 1946.   596
Studies in the variations of the calory content of milk. *Acta Agric. Suec., Stockh.*, **2**, 159-69.

Boonstra, A. E. H. R. 1943.   597
Correlation in practice. *Landbouwk. Tijdschr. Wageningen*, **55**, 639-59.

Borden, R. J. 1943.   598
Replication: The safeguard for uncontrolled variation. *Hawaii Plant Rec.*, **47**, 135-53.

Borden, R. J. 1943.   599
Yield variations with special reference to border effects in field tests. *Hawaii Plant. Rec.*, **47**, 195-203.

Bordin, E. S. 1941.   600
Factor analysis—art or science? *Psychol. Bull.*, **38**, 520-1.

Borel, É. 1940.   601
Une objection à la définition empirique de la probabilité. *C. R. Acad. Sci., Paris*, **211**, 312-13.

Borel, É. 1941.   602
Applications du calcul des probabilités aux problèmes concernant les nombres premiers. Théorème de Goldbach. *C. R. Acad. Sci., Paris*, **212**, 317-20 (erratum: 520).

Borel, É. 1941.   603
Théorie de l'hérédité: définitions et problèmes. *C. R. Acad. Sci., Paris*, **212**, 777-80.

Borel, É. 1941.   604
Sur certains problèmes d'hérédité connexes au problème de la ruine des joueurs. *C. R. Acad. Sci., Paris*, **212**, 821-5.

Borel, É. 1942.   605
Sur l'emploi du théorème de Bernoulli pour faciliter le calcul d'un infinité de coefficients. Application au problème de l'attente à un guichet. *C. R. Acad. Sci., Paris*, **214**, 452-6.

Borel, É. 1947.   606
Sur les probabilités dénombrables et le pari de Pascal. *C. R. Acad. Sci., Paris*, **224**, 77-8.

Borel, É. 1947.   607
Sur les développements unitaires normaux. *C. R. Acad. Sci., Paris*, **225**, 772.

Borel, É. 1948.   608
Sur les développements unitaires normaux. *Ann. Soc. Polon. Math.*, **21**, 74-9.

Borel, É. 1948.   609
Sur les séquences en météorologie. *Annu. Bureau Longitudes*, **1948**, A.1-A.18.

Borel, É. 1948.   610
Sur les sondages de l'opinion publique. *C. R. Acad. Sci., Paris*, **227**, 993-5.

Borel, É. 1949.   611
Remarques sur les notes de MM. Baticle et Dumas. *C. R. Acad. Sci., Paris*, **228**, 906.

Borel, É. 1949.   612
Le paradoxe de Saint-Pétersbourg. *C. R. Acad. Sci., Paris*, **229**, 404-5.

Borel, É. 1949.   613
Sur une propriété singulière de la limite d'une espérance mathématique. *C. R. Acad. Sci., Paris*, **229**, 429-31.

Borel, É. 1949.   614
Sur une martingale mineure. *C. R. Acad. Sci., Paris*, **229**, 1181-3.

Borel, É. & Cheron, A. 1940.   615
Théorie mathématique du bridge à la portée de tous. 134 tableaux de probabilités avec leurs modes d'emploi. Formules simples. Applications. Environ 4000 probabilités. *Monographies des probabilités*, V., xx+392 pp. (Gauthier-Villars, Paris).

Boring, E. G. 1941.   616
Statistical frequencies as dynamic equilibria. *Psychol. Rev.*, **48**, 279-300.

Bortolotti, G. 1945-6.   617
Procedimento grafico per la interpolazione delle curve di frequenza. *Statistica, Milano*, **5-6**, 50-74.

Boschan, P. 1941.   618
Some considerations concerning probability in actuarial science and the foundation of the extended life table. (German, French and Italian summaries.) *Trans. 12th. Int. Congr. Actuar., Lucerne*, 1940, **1**, 159-69.

Bose, A. N. 1941.   619
Some problems of field operations in labour enquiries. *Sankhyā*, **5**, 229-30.

Bose, C. 1942.   620
The variance of the forecasted mean values subjecting to two-way fluctuations. *Science & Culture*, **7**, 514 (correction: *Sankhyā*, **6**, 330).

Bose, C. 1943.   621
Note on the sampling error in the method of double sampling. *Sankhyā*, **6**, 329-30.

Bose, C. 1945.   622
Standardization and quality control. *Science & Culture*, **11**, 171.

Bose, C. & Gayen, A. K. 1946.   623
Note on the expected discrepancy in the estimation (by double sampling) of a variate in terms of a concomitant variate when there exists a non-linear regression between the two variates. *Sankhyā*, **8**, 73-4.

Bose, P. K. 1941.   624
On the reduction formulae for the incomplete probability integral of the multiple correlation coefficient of the second kind. *Science & Culture*, **7**, 171-2.

Bose, P. K. 1942.   625
On the exact distribution of the ratio of two means belonging to samples drawn from a given correlated bivariate normal population. *Bull. Calcutta Math. Soc.*, **34**, 139-41.

Bose, P. K. 1942.   626
Certain moment calculations connected with multivariate normal populations. *Science & Culture*, **7**, 411-12.

Bose, P. K. 1944.   627
On confluent hypergeometric series. *Sankhyā*, **6**, 407-12.

Bose, P. K. 1947.   628
Mental tests. *Bull. Calcutta Statist. Ass.*, **1**, 22.

Bose, P. K. 1947.   629
Parametric relations in multivariate distributions. *Sankhyā*, **8**, 167-71.

Bose, P. K. 1947.   630
On recursion formulae, tables and Bessel function populations associated with the distribution of classical D^2-statistic. *Sankhyā*, **8**, 235-48 (correction: **11**, 96).

Bose, P. K. 1948.   631
Crop estimation and its relation to agricultural meteorology. *Bull. Calcutta Statist. Ass.*, **1**, 114-19.

Bose, P. K. 1949.   632
Incomplete probability integral tables connected with studentised D^2-statistic. *Bull. Calcutta Statist. Ass.*, **2**, 131-7.

Bose, P. K. & Rao, S. R. 1944.   633
On the limiting forms of statistical distributions. *Science & Culture*, **9**, 402-3.

Bose, R. C. 1941.   634
Discussion of the mathematical theory of design of experiments. *Sankhyā*, **5**, 169-74.

Bose, R. C. 1942.   635
A note on two combinatorial problems having applications in the theory of design of experiments. *Science & Culture*, **8**, 192-3.

Bose, R. C. 1942.   636
Some new series of balanced incomplete block designs. *Bull. Calcutta Math. Soc.*, **34**, 17-31.

Bose, R. C. 1942.   637
A note on two series of balanced incomplete block designs. *Bull. Calcutta Math. Soc.*, **34**, 129-30.

Bose, R. C. 1942.   638
A note on the resolvability of balanced incomplete block designs. *Sankhyā*, **6**, 105-10.

Bose, R. C. 1945. 639
Minimum functions in Galois fields. *Proc. Nat. Acad. Sci., India,* **14**, 191.

Bose, R. C. 1946. 640
The patch number problem. *Science & Culture,* **12**, 199-200.

Bose, R. C. 1947. 641
Mathematical theory of the symmetrical factorial design. *Sankhyā,* **8**, 107-66.

Bose, R. C. 1947. 642
Recent work on incomplete block designs in India. *Biometrics,* **3**, 176-8.

Bose, R. C. 1947. 643
On a resolvable series of balanced incomplete block designs. *Sankhyā,* **8**, 249-56.

Bose, R. C. 1947. 644
The design of experiments. *Proc. Indian Sci. Congr.,* **34** (II), 1-25.

Bose, R. C. 1949. 645
Least squares aspects of analysis of variance. *North Carolina Inst. Statist., Mimeo Ser.,* no. 9.

Bose, R. C. 1949. 646
A note on Fisher's inequality for balanced incomplete block designs. *Ann. Math. Statist.,* **20**, 619-20.

Bose, R. C. & Kishen, K. 1940. 647
On the problem of confounding in the general symmetrical factorial design. *Sankyhā,* **5**, 21-36.

Bose, R. C. & Nair, K. R. 1941. 648
On complete sets of Latin squares. *Sankhyā,* **5**, 361-82.

Bose, R. C., Chowla, S. & Rao, C. R. 1945. 649
On the roots of a well known congruence. *Proc. Nat. Acad. Sci., India,* **14**, 193.

Bose, S. S. 1940. 650
A study of forty-three years of rainfall in Calcutta, 1893-1935. *Sankhyā,* **4**, 559-62.

Bosworth, R. C. L. 1944. 651
Bessel's formula in relation to the calculation of the probable error from a small number of observations. *Proc. Roy. Soc. N.S.W.,* **78**, 81-3.

Bottema, O. 1949. 652
A probability computation of Emanuel Lasker. (Dutch.) *Simon Stevin,* **27**, 1-5.

Bottema, O. & van Veen, S. C. 1943-6. 653
Calculation of probabilities in the game of billiards. I, II. (Dutch.) *Nieuw Arch. Wisk.,* (2) **22**, 15-33; 123-58.

Bouzitat, J. 1947. 654
Note sur un problème de sondage. *Office Nat. Études Rech. Aero. Publ.* no. 1, iv+57 pp.

Bowen, E. G. 1948. 655
Operational research into the air traffic problem. *J. Inst. Navig.,* **1**, 338-41.

Bowen, E. G. & Pearcey, T. 1948. 656
Delays in air traffic flow. *J. Roy. Aero. Soc.,* **52**, 251-8.

Bowen, I. G. 1945. 657
The strength of riveted joints: The results of a statistical analysis of test data. *Aircraft Engng.,* **17**, 83-7.

Bowen, M. F. 1947. 658
Population distribution of the beet leafhopper relation to experimental field-plot layout. *J. Agric. Res.,* **75**, 259-78.

Bowers, D. A. 1947. 659
Progressive timing for traffic signals. *Proc. Inst. Traffic Engng., Strathcona Hall, New Haven* 11, Conn., U.S.A., pp. 93-100.

Bowie, O. L. 1947. 660
A least-square application to relaxation methods. *J. Appl. Phys.,* **18**, 830-3.

Bowker, A. H. 1944. 661
Note on consistency of a proposed test for the problem of two samples. *Ann. Math. Statist.,* **15**, 98-101.

Bowker, A. H. 1946. 662
Computation of factors for tolerance limits on a normal distribution when the sample is large. *Ann. Math. Statist.,* **17**, 238-40.

Bowker, A. H. 1947. 663
On the norm of a matrix. *Ann. Math. Statist.,* **18**, 285-8.

Bowker, A. H. 1948. 664
A test for symmetry in contingency tables. *J. Amer. Statist. Ass.,* **43**, 572-4.

Box, G. E. P. 1949. 665
A general distribution theory for a class of likelihood criteria. *Biometrika,* **36**, 317-46.

Box, G. E. P. & Collumbine, H. 1947. 666
The relationship between survival time and dosage with certain toxic agents. *Brit. J. Pharm. Chemotherap.,* **2**, 27-37.

Box, K. & Thomas, G. 1944. 667
Wartime Social Survey. *J. R. Statist. Soc.,* **107**, 151-89.

Boyarskii, A. Ya. 1941. 668
Sur la corrélation géométrique. (Russian. French summary.) *Izv. Akad. Nauk SSSR, Ser. Mat.,* **5**, 159-64.

Boyce, S. W. 1945. 669
Statistical studies on New Zealand wheat trials. I. The efficiency of lattice design. II. The analysis of lattice trials with incomplete data. *New Zealand J. Sci. Tech. A,* **27**, 270-5; 276-80.

Boyd, D. A. & Mathison, I. 1947. 670
Fertilizer application. Findings of the survey of fertilizer practice. *Agriculture,* **54**, 325-8.

Boyer, C. B. 1947. 671
Note on an early graph of statistical data. (Huygens, 1669.) *Isis,* **37**, 148-9.

Braconnier, J. 1948. 672
Spectres d'espaces et de groupes topologiques. *Portug. Math.,* **1**, 93-111.

Bradford Hill, A. *See* **Hill, A. Bradford.**

Brambilla, F. 1940. 673
La teoria statistica della correlazione e della connessione. " *Studi sulla correlazione e sulla connessione* ". *Ist. Statist. Univ. Bocconi, Milano,* **I** (A).

Brambilla, F. 1942. 674
Alcune considerazioni sull'attrazione matrimoniale. *Atti 3za Riun. Sci., Soc. Ital. Statist.,* pp. 76-85.

Brambilla, F. 1942. 675
Rappresentazione matematica della curva cumulativa di frequenza. *Atti 3za Riun. Sci., Soc. Ital. Statist.*, pp. 40-59.

Brambilla, F. 1943. 676
Per la compilazione di un glossario statistico. *Atti 4ta Riun. Sci., Soc. Ital. Statist.*, pp. 5-7.

Brambilla, F. 1947. 677
Nuovi metodi statistici per lo studio delle produzione industriali. *Industria, Milano*, 1, 165-94.

Brambilla, F. 1948. 678
Modelli stocastici in econometrica. *Industria, Milano*, 2, 148-76.

Brambilla, F. 1949. 679
Applicazione del metodo del campione nel campo delle statistiche agrarie. *Riv. Ital. Demogr. Statist.*, 3 (1-2), 143-53.

Brambilla, F. 1949. 680
Il metodo del campione come nuova tecnica di rilevazione delle statistiche periodiche. *Rassegna Statist. Lavoro*, 1, 254-62.

Brambilla, F. 1949. 681
La teoria statistica degli effetti cumulativi. *Atti 9na Riun. Sci., Soc. Ital. Statist.*, pp. 198-239.

Brandt, A. E. 1940. 682
Practical difficulties met in the use of experimental designs. *J. Amer. Statist. Ass.*, 35, 101-6.

Brandt, A. E. 1941. 683
The relation between the design of an experiment and the analysis of variance. *J. Amer. Statist. Ass.*, 36, 283-92.

Bransby, E. R., Daubney, C. G. & King, J. 1948. 684
Comparison of results obtained by different methods of individual dietary survey. *Brit. J. Nutrit.*, 2, 89-110.

Brard, R. 1944. 685
Interdépendance du tourbillon moyen local et de la vitesse moyenne locale d'agitation dans les mouvements turbulents. *C. R. Acad. Sci., Paris*, 218, 144-6.

Brard, R. 1944. 686
Sur la répartition du tourbillon dans un écoulement turbulent statistiquement permanent. *C. R. Acad. Sci., Paris*, 219, 604-5.

Brasnett, N. V. 1946. 687
The efficiency of enumerations: A review. *Emp. For. Rev.*, 25, 42-6.

Brayer, E. F. 1940. 688
Can safety be handled statistically? *J. Amer. Statist. Ass.*, 35, 382-5.

Breiger, F. G. 1946. 689
Unilateral and bilateral limits in statistical analysis. *Bragantia, Sao Paulo*, 6, 479-545.

Brennan, J. F. 1949. 690
Evaluation of parameters in the Gompertz and Makeham equations. *J. Amer. Statist. Ass.*, 44, 116-21.

Bresciani-Turroni, C. 1949. 691
Recherches inductives sur la prévision des prix. *Metroeconomica*, 1, 5-29.

Brethouwer, D. H. G. 1948. 692
Hyperbolische foutenwet. (Dutch. English summary.) *Statistica Neerlandica*, 2, 55-73.

Brethouwer, D. H. G. 1949. 693
Critiek op de " Hyperbolische foutenwet ". (Criticisms against the " hyperbolic error distribution ".) (Dutch. English summary.) *Statistica Neerlandica*, 3, 133-40.

Brewbaker, H. E. & Bush, H. L. 1942. 694
Pre-harvest estimate of yield and sugar percentage based on random sampling technique. *Ann. Amer. Soc. Sugar Beet Technol.*

Breyer, R. F. 1946. 695
Some preliminary problems of sample design for a survey of retail trade flow. *J. Marketing*, 10, 343-53.

Bridgman, P. W. 1945. 696
Some general principles of operational analysis. *Psychol. Rev.*, 52, 246-9.

Brieger, F. G. 1940. 697
The χ^2 test. *J. Agron., Sao Paulo*, 3, 103-10.

Brieger, F. G. 1945. 698
As distribuições do acaso. (English summary.) *An. Ex. Sup. Agric. Luiz de Queiroz*, 2, 322-91.

Brieger, F. G. 1946. 699
Limites unilaterais e bilaterais na análise statistica. (English summary.) *Bragantia, Sao Paulo*, 6, 479-545.

Brier, G. W. 1944. 700
Verification of a forecaster's confidence and the use of probability statements in weather forecasting. *U.S. Weather Bureau, Dept. Commerce, Washington D.C.*, 10 pp.

Brier, G. W., Schoot, R. G. & Simmons, V. L. 701
1940. The discriminant function applied to quality rating in sheep. *Proc. Amer. Soc. Animal Prod.*, 1, 153-60.

Briquet, R., Jr. & Lush, J. L. 1947. 702
Heritability of amount of spotting in Holstein-Friesian cattle. *J. Heredity*, 38, 99-105.

British Medical Research Council. 1948. 703
Streptomycin treatment of pulmonary tuberculosis. *Brit. Med. J.*, 2, 769-83.

Britzelmayr, W. 1941-2. 704
Über die Methoden der Stellarstatistik. *Allg. Statist. Arch.*, 30, 241-6.

Broad, C. D. 1944. 705
Hr. von Wright on the logic of induction. I, II, III. *Mind*, 53, 1-24; 97-119; 193-214.

Broadhurst, S. W. & Harmston, A. T. 1949. 706
An electronic traffic analyser. *Post Office Elect. Engrs. J.*, 42, 181-7.

Brockmeyer, E. 1949. 707
The application of the theory of probability to telephony. (Danish.) " *Larebog in telefonteknik* ", Chap. 9, pp. 144-87.

Brockmeyer, E., Halstrøm, H. L. & Jensen, A. 708
1948. The life and works of A. K. Erlang. *Trans. Danish Acad. Sci.*, no. 2, 277 pp. (Also published by the Copenhagen Telephone Company.)

Broderick, T. S. & Schrödinger, E. 1940. 709
Boolean algebra and probability theory. *Proc. Roy. Irish Acad. A*, 46, 103-12.

Brodman, E., Pheulpin, F. J. & 710
Deutschberger, J. 1947.
Some statistical methods useful to medical librarians.
Bull. Med. Libr. Ass., **35**, 7-57.

Brogden, H. E. 1944. 711
On the estimation of the changes in correlation and
regression constants due to selection on a single given
variable. *J. Educ. Psychol.*, **35**, 484-92.

Brogden, H. E. 1946. 712
An approach to the problem of differential prediction.
Psychometrika, **11**, 139-54.

Brogden, H. E. 1946. 713
The effect of bias due to difficulty factors in product-
moment item intercorrelations on the accuracy of
estimation of reliability by the Kuder-Richardson
formula number 20. *Educ. and Psychol. Measurement*,
6, 517-20.

Brogden, H. E. 1946. 714
On the interpretation of the correlation coefficient as
a measure of predictive efficiency. *J. Educ. Psychol.*,
37, 65-76.

Brogden, H. E. 1946. 715
Variation in test validity with variation in the distribution of item difficulties, number of items, and degree
of their intercorrelation. *Psychometrika*, **11**, 197-
214.

Brogden, H. E. 1949. 716
A new coefficient: Application to biserial correlation
and to estimation of selective efficiency. *Psychometrika*,
14, 169-82.

Broman, D., Dahlberg, D. & Lichtenstein, A. 1942. 717
Height and weight during growth. *Acta Pediatr.,
Uppsala*, **30**.

Bronfenbrenner, J. 1949. 718
Extent of least squares bias in estimating a single
stochastic equation in a complete system. *Cowles
Comm. Discussion Paper Mimeo. Statistics*, no. 330,
5 pp.

Bronfenbrenner, U. 1943. 719
A constant frame of reference to sociometric research.
Sociometry, **6**, 363-97. (Reprinted (1945) " The
measurement of sociometric status, structure and
development ". *Sociometry Monogr.* no. 6.)

Bronowski, J. 1949. 720
Some uses of statistics in the building industry:
An investigation into the erection times of nine types
of non-traditional house. *J. R. Statist. Soc. A*, **112**,
287-308.

Bronowski, J. & Neyman, J. 1945. 721
The variance of the measure of a two dimensional
random set. *Ann. Math. Statist.*, **16**, 330-41.

Brookes, B. C. 1947. 722
The incorporation of statistics into a school course.
Math. Gaz., **31**, 211-18.

Brookner, R. J. 1941. 723
A note on the mean as a poor estimate of central
tendency. *J. Amer. Statist. Ass.*, **36**, 410-12.

Brookner, R. J. 1945. 724
Choice of one among several statistical hypotheses.
Ann. Math. Statist., **16**, 221-42.

Brooks, E. M. & Senf, C. 1949. 725
A report on the general enumerative surveys. *Agric.
Econ. Res.*, **1**, 37-48, 105-28.

Brosek, J. M. & Alexander, H. 1947. 726
Components of variation and the consistency of
repeated measurements. *Res. Quart. Amer. Ass.
Hlth. phys. Educ. & Recreation*, **18** (2), 152-66.

Brossman, J. R. 1941. 727
Laboratory control of incoming materials. *Purchasing*,
11, 59-61.

Broster, E. J. 1942. 728
Correlation analysis by margins. *J. Amer. Statist.
Ass.*, **37**, 359-66.

Brouwer, E. 1945. 729
On high correlations and their biological significance.
Landbouwk. Tijdschr., Wageningen, **56**, 504-7.

Brouwer, E. 1946. 730
Complex indices for butter. *Acta Brev. Neerl. Physiol.*,
13, 74-7.

Brown, A. W. 1940. 731
A note on the use of a Pearson type III function in
renewal theory. *Ann. Math. Statist.*, **11**, 448-53.

Brown, B. 1944. 732
A design for sampling Iowa families. *Proc. Iowa Acad.
Sci.*, **51**, 335-9.

Brown, B. B. 1948, 733
Tests of the randomness of digits. *RAND Corp. Res.
Memo*, 17 May 1948, RM-38, 13 pp. (Also *RAND
Corp. Paper* RAOP-44, 19 Oct. 1948, 15 pp.)

Brown, B. H. 1941. 734
Simple examples of limiting processes in probability.
Amer. Math. Monthly, **48**, 98-102.

Brown, D. F. 1944. 735
Growth of a quality control department in a Canadian
ammunition plant. *Industr. Qual. Contr.*, **1** (3), 5-9.

Brown, G. H. 1947. 736
A comparison of sampling methods. *J. Marketing*,
11, 331-7. (Also: *U.S. Quartermaster Corps Comm.
Food Res. Conf. Food Acceptance Res.*, 1946, pp.
46-51.)

Brown, G. W. 1940. 737
Reduction of a certain class of composite statistical
hypotheses. *Ann. Math. Statist.*, **11**, 254-70.

Brown, G. W. 1947. 738
Discriminant functions. *Ann. Math. Statist.*, **18**,
514-28.

Brown, G. W. 1947. 739
On small-sample estimation. *Ann. Math. Statist.*, **18**,
582-5.

Brown, G. W. 1949. 740
Estimation of mortality parameters. *RAND Corp.
Res. Memo.*, 8 April 1949, RM-135, 3 pp.

Brown, G. W. & Flood, M. M. 1947. 741
Tumbler mortality. *J. Amer. Statist. Ass.*, **42**, 562-74.

Brown, G. W. & Mood, A. M. 1948. 742
Homogeneity of several samples. *Amer. Statistician*,
2 (3), 22.

Brown, G. W. & Tukey, J. W. 1946. 743
Some distributions of sample means. *Ann. Math.
Statist.*, **17**, 1-12.

Brown, L. M. 1944. 744
Some parameters of sampling distributions simply obtained. *Edin. Math. Notes*, **34**, 8-11.

Brown, T. H. 1942. 745
Scientific sampling in business. *Harvard Busin. Rev.*, **20**, 358-68.

Brown, T. H., Franzen, R. & Robinson, D. E. 746
1946. Design, size, and validation of sample for market research. *J. Marketing*, **10**, 221-33.

Brown, W. M. 1948. 747
Measuring physical inventories. *J. Amer. Statist. Ass.*, **43**, 377-90.

Browning, W. H. 1943. 748
Mold fungi in the etiology of respiratory allergic diseases. II. Mold extracts—a statistical study. *J. Allergy*, **14**, 231-43.

Brownlee, K. A. & Loraine, P. K. 1948. 749
The relationship between finite groups and completely orthogonal squares, cubes, and hyper-cubes. *Biometrika*, **35**, 277-82.

Brownlee, K. A., Kelly, B. L. & Loraine, P. K. 750
1948. Fractional replication arrangements for factorial experiments with factors at two levels. *Biometrika*, **35**, 268-76.

Brownlee, O. H. & Gainer, W. 1949. 751
Farmers' price anticipations and the role of uncertainty in farm planning. *J. Farm Econ.*, **31**, 266-75.

Bruening, M. E. 1940. 752
How are progressive signals timed? *Proc. Inst. Traffic Engrs. Strathcona Hall, New Haven* 11, *Conn.*, pp. 79-91.

Bruges, W. E. 1948. 753
The curve of error in which the maximum error is defined. *Phil. Mag.*, (7) **39**, 394-9.

Brumbaugh, M. A. 1945. 754
The analysis of sampling plans in receiving inspection. *Industr. Qual. Contr.*, **1** (4), 6-9, 15.

Brumbaugh, M. A. 1945. 755
Use of a table of areas of the normal curve in quality control work. *Industr. Qual. Contr.*, **1** (6), 15-16.

Brumbaugh, M. A. 1945. 755[a]
A report on pre-war quality. *Industr. Qual. Contr.*, **2** (2), 11-12.

Brumbaugh, M. A. (Editor). 1946. 755[b]
Industry's use of quality control. (Report of a symposium.) *Industr. Qual. Contr.*, **2** (4a), 4-19.

Brumbaugh, M. A. 1946. 755[c]
Quality reports for management. *Elect. Engng.*, **65**, 391-3.

Brumbaugh, M. A. 1947. 755[d]
Demonstrating and reporting quality control. *Tool & Die J.*, **12**, 88-92.

Bruner, N. 1947. 756
Note on the Doolittle solution. *Econometrica*, **15**, 43-4.

Bruni, L. 1947. 757
Generalità su un nuovo metodo statistico per lo studio dei problemi della nutrizione. *G. Economisti*, **6**, 372-8.

Brunk, H. D. 1948. 758
The strong law of large numbers. *Duke Math. J.*, **15**, 181-95.

Brunswik, E. 1949. 759
Systematic and representative design of psychological experiments with results in physical and social perception. *Proc. Berkeley Symp. Math. Statist. and Probab.*, 1945-6, pp. 143-202.

Bruyere, P. T., Bruyere, M. C. & Gleeson, G. A. 760
1946. The use of $2 \times n$ chi square in the analysis of change in age distributions. *Amer. J. Publ. Health*, **36**, 510-14.

Buch, K. R. 1945. 761
Et mindstevaerdispørgsmål i det abstrakt rum. (The minimum problem in the abstract space.) *Mat. Tidsskr.*, **3**, 30-4.

Buch, K. R. 1947. 762
Remarques sur les mesures dans les espaces abstraits et sur la théorie de la probabilité. *Proc. 10th. Skand. Mat. Kongr., København*, 1946, pp. 264-9.

Buchanan-Wollaston, H. J. 1941. 763
On tests of the significance of differences in degree of pollution by coliform bacteria and the estimation of such differences. *J. Hyg., Camb.*, **41**, 139-68.

Buchanan-Wollaston, H. J. 1945. 764
On statistical treatment of the results of parallel trials with specific reference to fishery research. *Freshwater Biol. Ass. Brit. Emp., Sci. Publ.* no. 10, 55 pp.

Bucher, O., Debrunner, H. & Stadeli, H. 1947. 765
Die Wirkung von Penicillin auf menschliche Leukocyten *in vitro*, zugleich ein Beitrag zur statistischen Auswertung biologischer Untersuchungsresultate. *Schweiz. Med. Wschr.*, **77**, 332-5.

Buchholz, J. T. & Kaeiser, M. 1940. 766
A statistical study of two variables in the Sequoias pollen grain size and cotyledon number. *Amer. Nat.*, **74**, 279-83.

Buckatzsch, E. J. 1947. 767
The influence of social conditions on mortality rates. *Population Stud.*, **1**, 229-48.

Bugelski, B. R. 1949. 768
A note on Grant's discussion of the Latin square principle in the design and analysis of psychological experiments. *Psychol. Bull.*, **46**, 49-50.

Buist, J. M. & Davies, O. L. 1947. 768[a]
Statistical evaluations of variations in rubber processes and correlation in physical properties. *Rubber Chem. & Technol.*, **20**, 288-300.

Bukhman, F. N. 1942. 769
Problems of congestion in telephony. (Russian. English summary.) *Zh. Prikl. Mat. Mekh. Akad. Nauk SSSR*, **6**, 247-56.

Bukhman, F. N. 1947. 770
The problem of waiting times. (Russian. English summary.) *Zh. Prikl. Mat. Mekh. Akad. Nauk SSSR*, **11**, 475-84.

Bula, C. A. 1940. 771
Theory and evaluation of central moments in two dimensions. Sheppard's corrections. The simpler method of Mitropolsky. (Spanish.) *Rev. Union Mat. Argent.*, **5**, 1-97. (Also: *Union Mat. Argent. Publ.*, no. 9, 97 pp.)

Bula, C. A. 1940.   772
Calculation of frequency surfaces. Experimental verification and comparison of the method of marginal functions with that of the 15 constants of Karl Pearson. (Spanish. French summary.) *Rev. Union Mat. Argent.*, **6**, 109 pp. (Also: *Union Mat. Argent. Publ.*, no. 10, 109 pp.)

Bunický, E. 1949.   773
Remarque sur le critère de l'indépendance des caractères. *Aktuárské Vědy*, **8** (2), 53-60.

Bunimovich, V. I. 1946.   774
Effect of the fluctuations and signal voltages on a non-linear system. (English.) *Zh. Fiz. Akad. Nauk SSSR* (English edition), **10**, 35-48.

Bunimovich, V. I. 1949.   775
The fluctuation process as an oscillation with random amplitude and phase. (Russian.) *Zh. Tekh. Fiz. Akad. Nauk SSSR*, **19**, 1231-59. (Translated by M. D. Friedman, Newtonville, Mass., 1956, 41 pp.)

Bunimovich, V. I. 1949.   776
Spectral response of a quadratic device to non-Gaussian noise. *J. Appl. Phys.*, **25**, 1357-65.

Bunimovich, V. I. & Leontovich, M. A. 1946.   777
On the distribution of the number of large deviations in electric fluctuations. *C. R. (Dokl.) Acad. Sci. URSS*, **53**, 21-3.

Bunle, H. 1947.   777ᵃ
Sur le calcul d'un taux mensuel de mortalité infantile. *Proc. 25th. Session Int. Statist. Inst. Conf., Washington, D.C.*, 1947 (Publ. 1951), **3B**, 794-804.

Burgers, J. M. 1948.   778
A mathematical model illustrating the theory of turbulence. *Advances in Appl. Mech.* (ed. von Mises, R. & von Kármán, T.) pp. 171-99. (Academic Press, New York.)

Burgers, J. M. 1948.   779
Spectral analysis of an irregular function. *Proc. Kon. Ned. Akad. Wetensch.*, **51**, 1073-6; 1222-31.

Burkhardt, F. 1941.   780
Über Stand und Wandlungen von bevölkerungs- und versicherungsstatistischen Personengesamtheiten. *Blä. Versich.-math.*, **5**, 212-17.

Burkhardt, F. 1941.   781
Über Umkehrung und Verknüpfung von statistischen Beziehungen. *Arch. Math. Wirtsch.*, **7**, 1-8.

Burman, J. P. 1946.   782
Sequential sampling formulae for a binomial population. *J. R. Statist. Soc. Suppl.*, **8**, 98-103.

Burman, J. P. & Plackett, R. L. 1944.   782ᵃ
A contribution to the theory of maximum precision in industrial experimentation. I, II. *U.K. Min. Supply Advisory Service Statist. Method & Qual. Contr. Tech. Rep. Ser. R*, no. QC/R/27, 26 September 1944, 27 pp.

Burnens, E. 1947.   783
Die Erfahrungsnachwirkung bei Wahrscheinlichkeiten. *Mitt. Ver. Schweiz. Versich.-Math.*, **47**, 329-52.

Burns, A. F. 1944.   784
Frickey on the decomposition of time series. *Rev. Econ. Statist.*, **26**, 136-47.

Buros, O. K. 1945-7.   785
Statistical methodology index. A quarterly guide to current literature. *J. Amer. Statist. Ass.*, **40**, 417-23; 539-52; **41**, 144-54; 270-4; 415-20; 625-35; **42**, 203-8; 353-5; 491-6; 668-81.

Burr, I. W. 1942.   786
Cumulative frequency functions. *Ann. Math. Statist.*, **13**, 215-32.

Burrau, Ø. 1943.   787
Middelfejlen som usikkerhedsmål. (The mean error as a measure of uncertainty.) (Danish.) *Mat. Tidsskr. B*, **1943**, 9-16.

Burrau, Ø. 1945.   788
Om bestemmelse af meddelfejl. (On the determination of the mean error.) (Danish.) *Mat. Tidsskr. B*, **1945**, 97-109.

Burt, C. 1943.   789
Ability and income. *Brit. J. Educ. Psychol.*, **13**, 83-98.

Burt, C. 1943.   790
Validating tests for personnel selection. *Brit. J. Psychol.*, **34**, 1-19.

Burt, C. 1944.   791
The factorial study of physical types. *Man*, **44**, 82-6.

Burt, C. 1944.   792
Mental abilities and mental factors. *Brit. J. Educ. Psychol.*, **14**, 85-94.

Burt, C. 1944.   793
Statistical problems in the evaluation of army tests. *Psychometrika*, **9**, 219-35.

Burt, C. 1945.   794
The reliability of teachers' assessments of their pupils. *Brit. J. Educ. Psychol.*, **15**, 80-92.

Burt, C. 1945.   795
The assessment of personality. *Brit. J. Educ. Psychol.*, **15**, 107-21.

Burt, C. 1945.   796
Use of stereographic projection for statistical problems. *Nature*, **156**, 338.

Burt, C. 1947.   797
L'analyse factorielle dans la psychologie anglaise. *Biotypologie*, **9**, 7-44.

Burt, C. 1947.   798
A comparison of factor analysis and analysis of variance. *Brit. J. Psychol. (Statist. Sec.)*, **1**, 3-26.

Burt, C. 1947.   799
Factor analysis and physical types. *Psychometrika*, **12**, 171-88.

Burt, C. 1947.   800
Family size, intelligence and social class. *Population Stud.*, **1**, 177-86.

Burt, C. 1948.   801
Factor analysis and canonical correlations. *Brit. J. Psychol. (Statist. Sec.)*, **1**, 95-106.

Burt, C. 1948.   801ᵃ
The factorial study of temperamental traits. *Brit. J. Psychol. (Statist. Sec.)*, **1**, 178-203.

Burt, C. 1949.   802
Subdivided factors. *Brit. J. Psychol. (Statist. Sec.)*, **2**, 41-63.

Burt, C. 1949. 803
Pearson's method modified to allow for non-significant factors. *Brit. J. Psychol.* (*Statist. Sec.*), **2**, 65-6.

Burt, C. 1949. 804
Alternative methods of factor analysis. *Brit. J. Psychol.* (*Statist. Sec.*), **2**, 98-121.

Burt, C. 1949. 805
The two factor theory. *Brit. J. Psychol.* (*Statist. Sec.*), **2**, 151-79.

Burt, C. 1949. 806
The structure of the mind: A review of the results of factor analysis. *Brit. J. Educ. Psychol.*, **19**, 100-11; 176-99.

Burt, C. & Banks, C. 1947. 807
A factor analysis of body measurements for British adult males. *Ann. Eugen.*, **13**, 238-56.

Burt, C. & Grieve, J. 1945. 808
Defective colour vision in relation to pigmentation and hair. *Man*, **45**, 81-3.

Burt, C. & John, E. 1942. 809
A factorial analysis of Terman Binet Test. *Brit. J. Educ. Psychol.*, **12**, 117-27; 156-61.

Bush, H. L. 1942. 810
Further studies in newer designs for large scale variety tests. *Proc. Amer. Soc. Sugar Beet Technol.*, 1942, pp. 365-72.

Busk, Th. 1943. 811
Some remarks on the computation of the mean error for values graduated by the method of least squares. (Danish.) *Festskr. J. F. Steffensen*, pp. 40-4.

Busk, Th. 1946. 812
Dot and scatter diagrams made by means of a typewriter. *J. R. Statist. Soc.*, **109**, 451-6.

Busk, Th. 1948. 813
Some observations on heredity in breast cancer and leukemia. *Ann. Eugen.*, **14**, 213-29.

Butler, J. B. 1945. 813a
Some conclusions regarding resistance welding and statistical quality control. *Welding J.*, **24**, 909-14.

Butler, J. M. 1942. 814
A ratio for estimating the reliability of test scores. *J. Educ. Psychol.*, **33**, 391-5.

Butler, W. 1945. 815
Fatality rate of measles: study of its trend in time. *J. R. Statist. Soc.*, **108**, 259-85.

Butterbaugh, G. I. 1944. 816
Statistical quality control—a new tool of production. *Western Metals*, **2**, 56-8.

Butterbaugh, G. I. 1946. 817
A bibliography of statistical quality control. *Bur. Bus. Res. Coll. Econ. & Bus., Univ. of Washington*, 1946, viii+114 pp.

Buzzati-Traverso, A. & Cavalli, L. L. 1945. 818
Fenotipi e costituzione genetica di una popolazione di *Drosophila melanogaster*. *Mem. Ist. Ital. Idrobiol.*, " *Dott. Marco de Marchi* ", **2**, 219-51.

Buzzati-Traverso, A., Cavalli, L. L. & 819
di Modrone, N. V. 1947.
Volume d'urto nelle fasi S. e R. di *Escherichia coli*. *Riv. Radiol.*, **2**, 43-53.

C

Calabrese, D. M. *See* **Miani-Calabrese, D.**

Calabrese, G. 1947. 820
Generating reserve capacity determined by the probability method. *Trans. Amer. Inst. Elect. Engrs.*, **66**, 1439-50.

Calandra, A. 1941. 821
Scoring formulas and probability considerations. *Psychometrika*, **6**, 1-9.

Camacho, B. L. 1946. 822
Sobre métodos estadísticos para la determinación del éxito en series de observaciones. *Rev. Sanid. Hig. Publ., Madrid*, **20**, 818-31.

Cameron, R. H. & Martin, W. T. 1944. 823
Transformations of Wiener integrals under translations. *Ann. Math.*, (2) **45**, 389-96.

Cameron, R. H. & Martin, W. T. 1944. 824
The Wiener measure of Hilbert neighbourhoods in the space of real continuous functions. *J. Math. Phys.*, **23**, 195-209.

Cameron, R. H. & Martin, W. T. 1945. 825
Evaluation of various Wiener integrals by use of certain Sturm-Liouville differential equations. *Bull. Amer. Math. Soc.*, **51**, 73-90.

Cameron, R. H. & Martin, W. T. 1945. 826
Transformations of Wiener integrals under a general class of linear transformations. *Trans. Amer. Math. Soc.*, **58**, 184-219.

Cameron, R. H. & Martin, W. T. 1947. 827
The behavior of measure and measurability under change of scale in Wiener space. *Bull. Amer. Math. Soc.*, **53**, 130-7.

Cameron, R. H. & Martin, W. T. 1947. 828
Fourier-Wiener transforms of functionals belonging to L_2 over the space C. *Duke Math. J.*, **14**, 99-107.

Cameron, R. H. & Martin, W. T. 1947. 829
The orthogonal development of non-linear functionals in series of Fourier-Hermite functionals. *Ann. Math.*, (2) **48**, 385-92.

Camp, B. H. 1940. 830
Further comments on Berkson's problem. *J. Amer. Statist. Ass.*, **35**, 368-76.

Camp, B. H. 1942. 831
Some recent advances in mathematical statistics. I. *Ann. Math. Statist.*, **13**, 62-73.

Camp, B. H. 1946. 832
The effect on a distribution function of small changes in the population function. *Ann. Math. Statist.*, **17**, 226-31.

Camp, B. H. 1948. 833
Generalization to N dimensions of inequalities of the Tchebycheff type. *Ann. Math. Statist.*, **19**, 568-74.

Campagne, C. 1943. 834
De Stelling van Hattendorf en haar algemeene geldigheid door de stelling van Cantelli. (The theorem of Hattendorf and its general validity by the theorem of Cantelli.) (Dutch.) *Verzekerings-archief*, **24**, 121-44.

Campbell, G. C. 1945.   835
A study of the variance of the observed death-rate when the exposure is estimated from a sample. *Trans. Actuar. Soc. Amer.*, **46**, 59-68.

Campbell, G. C. 1948.   836
Problems with sampling procedures for reserve valuations. *J. Amer. Statist. Ass.*, **43**, 413-27.

Campbell, J. A. & Emslie, A. R. G. 1945-7.   837
Studies on the chick assay for vitamin D. III. The variability of chicks and the estimation of error from replicated group data. IV. The reproducibility of five criteria of calcification. V. A comparison of A.O.A.C. and B.S.I. diets and feeding periods. VI. Sources of variation in the response of replicate groups with time. *Poultry Sci.*, **24**, 296-304; **26**, 255-61; 568-72.

Campbell, J. A. & Emslie, A. R. G. 1947.   838
Variability in chick growth data. *Poultry Sci.*, **26**, 573-5.

Campbell, J. A., Migicovsky, B. B. &   839
Emslie, A. R. G. 1945.
Studies on the chick assay for vitamin D. I. Precision of tibia and toe ash as criteria of response. II. A comparison of four criteria of calcification. *Poultry Sci.*, **24**, 3-7; 72-80.

Campbell, N. R. 1941.   840
The replacement of perishable members of a continually operating system. *J. R. Statist. Soc. Suppl.*, **7**, 110-30.

Campbell, N. R. 1946.   840[a]
Experiment and theory in statistics. *Nature*, **158**, 521.

Campbell, N. R. & Francis, V. J. 1946.   841
Random fluctuations in a cathode ray oscillograph. *Phil. Mag.*, (7) **37**, 289-310.

Campbell, W. E. 1942.   841[a]
Use of statistical control in corrosion and contact resistance studies. (English. Spanish summary.) *Trans. Electrochem. Soc.*, **81**, 377-90.

Campeao, R. 1947.   841[b]
Sur des limites pour les probabilités des décès, en fonction des données empiriques. *Bol. Inst. Actuár. Port.*, **2**, 45-62.

Canfield, R. H. 1941.   842
Application of the line interception method in sampling range vegetation. *J. Forestry*, **39**, 388-94.

Cansado Maceda, E. 1944.   843
Variables aleatorias. *Bol. Estadíst. Dir. Gen. Estadíst.*, Madrid, **23**, 239-54.

Cansado Maceda, E. 1946.   844
Integral de Stieltjes-Lebesgue y sus applicaciones a la Estadística. (Stieltjes-Lebesgue integral and its applications to statistics.) *Mem. Mat. Inst. " Jorge Juan "*, **3**, 66 pp.

Cansado Maceda, E. 1947.   845
Cumulants of Fisher's *z*. (Spanish.) *Rev. Mat. Hisp.-Amer.*, (4) **7**, 87-9.

Cansado Maceda, E. 1947.   846
Sobre la función característica factorial. *Rev. Mat. Hisp.-Amer.*, (4) **7**, 159-64.

Cansado Maceda, E. 1947-8.   847
Funciones cáracterísticas de las distribuciones de Pearson. I, II. (Spanish.) *Rev. Mat. Hisp.-Amer.*, (4) **7**, 117-27; (4) **8**, 203-25.

Cansado Maceda, E. 1948.   848
On the compound and generalized Poisson distributions. *Ann. Math. Statist.*, **19**, 414-16.

Cantelli, F. P. 1940.   849
Le moderne vedute sulla teoria della probabilità nei suoi rapporti con l'analisi. *Atti Riun. Soc. Ital. Prog. Sci.*

Cantelli, F. P. 1940.   850
Osservazioni sulla nota " Su una teoria astratta del calcolo delle probabilità e sulla sua applicazione al teorema detto ' delle probabilità zero e uno ' ". *G. Ist. Ital. Attuari*, **11**, 101-6.

Cantelli, F. P. 1940.   851
Osservazioni sulla formula di Hattendorff. *G. Ist. Ital. Attuari*, **11**, 261-9.

Cantelli, F. P. 1942.   852
Sulla costruzione delle tavole di mortalita. *Atti 3za Riun. Sci., Soc. Ital. Statist.*, pp. 17-24.

Cantelli, F. P. 1942.   853
I fondamenti matematici della tecnica delle assicurazioni. *G. Ist. Ital. Attuari*, **13**, 1-27.

Cantelli, F. P. 1943.   854
Sull'adattamento delle curve ad una serie di misure o de osservazioni. *Atti 5ta Riun. Sci., Soc. Ital. Statist.*, pp. 417-26.

Cantelli, F. P. 1945.   855
Sulle difficoltà della deduzione delle leggi di frequenza da considerazioni di probabilità. *Atti 6ta Riun. Sci., Soc. Ital. Statist.*, pp. 74-83.

Cantelli, F. P. 1945.   856
Le variabili casuali nella assicurazione incendi. *Atti 7ma Riun. Sci., Soc. Ital. Statist.*, pp. 723-40.

Cantelli, F. P. 1949.   857
Sulle probabilità di Karup. *R. C. Accad. Lincei, Sci. Fis. Mat. Nat.*, (8) **6**, 397-402.

Cantelli, F. P. 1949.   858
Considerazioni sulla legge uniforme dei grandi numeri. I. *R. C. Accad. Lincei, Sci. Fis. Mat. Nat.*, (8) **6**, 550-5.

Cantelli, F. P., Insolera, F. &   859
Bonferroni, C. E. 1942.
Sui fondamenti della matematica finanziaria. *G. Mat. Finanz.*, (2) **11**, 1-8, 9-23, 29-43, 44-55.

Capó, B. G. 1944.   860
A method of interpreting the results of field trials. *J. Agric., Univ. Puerto Rico*, **28**, 7-21.

Capó, B. G. 1944.   861
A new method of performing field trials. *J. Agric., Univ. Puerto Rico*, **28**, 22-34.

Capoccia, O. 1948.   861[a]
Un indice bilaterale di correlazione. *Statistica, Milano*, **8**, 66-7.

Capt, J. C. and others. 1945.   862
A chapter in population sampling. *Washington D.C., United States Dept. of Commerce, Bureau of Census.*

Caradog Jones, D. *See* **Jones, D. Caradog.**

Carasone, U. 1941. 863
Una osservazione sul calculo approssimato del premio per assicurazioni in caso di morte a capitale variabile ed alcune applicazioni pratiche. (English, French and German summaries.) *Trans. 12th. Int. Congr. Actuar. Lucerne*, 1940, **3**, 519-28.

Card, D. G. 1943. 864
Graphic methods of presenting multiple correlation analysis. *J. Farm Econ.*, **25**, 881-9.

Carlander, K. D. & Lewis, W. M. 1948. 865
Some precautions in estimating fish population. *Progr. Fish Cult.*, **10**, 134-7.

Carleton, J. 1945. 866
Non-random accident distributions and the Poisson series. *Proc. Casualty Actuar. Soc. Amer.*, **32**, 21-6.

Carlinfanti, E. 1945-6. 866[a]
La valutazione statistica degli effetti delle vaccinazioni, con particolare riguardo alle cause d'errore. *Statistica, Milano*, **5-6**, 75-111.

Carlinfanti, E. & Cavalli, L. L. 1945. 867
Studi quantitativi sull'immunità. *Boll. Ist. Sieroterap., Milano*, **24**, 215-32.

Carlson, H. B. 1945. 868
A simple orthogonal multiple factor approximation procedure. *Psychometrika*, **10**, 283-301.

Carlton, A. G. 1946. 869
Estimating the parameters of a rectangular distribution. *Ann. Math. Statist.*, **17**, 355-8.

Carnap, R. 1945. 870
On inductive logic. *Philos. Sci.*, **12**, 72-97.

Carnap, R. 1945. 871
The two concepts of probability. I. (English. Spanish summary.) *Phil. & Phenom. Res.*, **5**, 513-32.

Carnap, R. 1946. 872
Remarks on induction and truth. *Phil. & Phenom. Res.*, **6**, 590-602.

Carnap, R. 1946. 873
Theory and prediction in science. *Science*, **104**, 520-1.

Carnap, R. 1947. 874
On the application of inductive logic. (English. Spanish summary.) *Phil. & Phenom. Res.*, **8**, 133-48; 461-2.

Carnap, R. 1947. 874[a]
Probability as a guide in life. *J. Philos.*, **44**, 141-8.

Carpenter, A. 1940. 875
Short cuts in working out intercorrelations. *Res. Quart. Amer. Ass. Hlth. phys. Educ.*, **11**, 32-7.

Carpenter, H. C. H. 1945. 876
Statistical quality control. *J. Inst. Actuar. Students' Soc.*, **5**, 207-17.

Carrier, N. H. 1947. 876[a]
Experimental data and " sufficient " accuracy. *Nature*, **159**, 167.

Carroll, J. B. 1945. 877
The effect of difficulty and chance success on correlations between items or between tests. *Psychometrika*, **10**, 1-19.

Carruthers, N. 1949. 878
Accuracy of mean of *n* temperature observations. *Met. Mag., London*, **78**, 65-8.

Carter, A. H. 1947. 879
Approximation to percentage points of the z-distribution. *Biometrika*, **34**, 352-8.

Carter, A. H. 1949. 880
The estimation and comparison of residual regression where there are two or more related sets of observations. *Biometrika*, **36**, 26-46.

Carter, L. F. 1947. 881
An experiment on the design of tables and graphs used for presenting numerical data. *J. Appl. Psychol.*, **31**, 640-50.

Carter, L. F. 1947. 882
The relative effectiveness of presenting numerical data by the use of tables and graphs. *Psychol. Res. Equipment Design, Washington D.C.*, pp. 65-72.

Cartwright, W. & Festinger, L. 1943. 883
A quantitative theory of decision. *Psychol. Rev.*, **50**, 595-621.

Casal, P. 1948. 884
Statistique d'un champ homogène de vecteurs aléatoires de divergence nulle. Application à la turbulence homogène. *C. R. Acad. Sci., Paris*, **226**, 870-2.

Casanova, T. 1940. 885
Corrections to correlation coefficients on account of homogeneity in one variable. *J. Exper. Educ.*, **8**, 341-5.

Casanova, T. 1941. 886
Analysis of the effect upon the reliability coefficient of changes in variables involved in the estimation of test reliability. *J. Exper. Educ.*, **9**, 219-28.

Casanova, T. 1944. 886[a]
The use of the method of runs for testing the randomness of the order of examination items. *J. Exper. Educ.*, **12**, 165-8.

Casasus, N. 1947. 887
Über die quantitativen Beziehungen der lagebestimmten Mittelwerte zueinander und zu den errechneten Mittelwerten. *Festgabe für Dr. Hans Schorer, Berne*, pp. 193-205.

Case, R. A. M. 1945. 887[a]
Inverse binomial sampling. *Nature*, **156**, 115.

Cashen, R. O. 1947. 888
The influence of rainfall on the yield and botanical composition of permanent grass at Rothamsted. *J. Agric. Sci.*, **37**, 1-10.

Cassady, R., Jr. 1945. 889
Statistical sampling techniques and marketing research. *J. Marketing*, **9**, 317-41.

Castellano, V. 1948. 890
Osservazioni su alcune medie continue. *Statistica, Bologna*, **8**, 3-6.

Castellano, V. 1948. 891
Il principio della media aritmetica e gli errori accidentali. *Riv. Ital. Demogr. Statist.*, **2**, 582-5.

Castellano, V. 1949. 892
Sulle mutue relazioni tra i vari metodi per la determinazione della frequenza dei deni nei gruppi sanguigni. *Metron*, **15**, 375-401.

Castellano, V. 1949. 893
Vecchi e nuovi problemi nello studio delle distribuzioni dei redditi. *G. Economisti*, **8**, 379-89.

Castellano, V. & de Vergottini, M. 1948.   894
Sul valore divisorio. *Riv. Ital. Demogr. Statist.*,
2, 427-32.

Castore, G. F. & Dye, W. S., III. 1949.   895
A simplified punch card method of determining sums
of squares and sums of products. *Psychometrika*, **14**,
243-50.

Catcheside, D. G. 1945.   896
Effect of ionizing radiation on chromosomes. *Biol.
Rev. Camb. Phil. Soc.*, **20**, 14-28.

Catlin, J. B. 1944.   896[a]
Process control of quality by statistical method. *Paper
Ind. & Paper World*, **26**, 717-20.

Cattaneo, P. 1941.   897
Sul problema delle concordanze. *Ist. R. Veneto, Sci.
Mat. Nat.*, II, **101**, 89-104.

Cattaneo, P. 1941.   898
Tre problemi sulle concordanze. *Atti Mem. Accad.
Sci. Padova Mem. Cl. Sci. Fis.-Mat.*, (N.S.) **57**, 139-48.

Cattaneo, P. 1944.   899
Sul problema delle concordanze generalizzato. *Ist.
R. Veneto, Sci. Mat. Nat.*, II, **103**, 439-56.

Cattell, R. B. 1943.   899[a]
The description of personality. I. Foundation of
trait measurement. II. Basic traits resolved into
clusters. *Psychol. Rev.*, **50**, 559-94; *J. Abnorm.
Soc. Psychol.*, **38**, 476-506.

Cattell, R. B. 1944.   900
A note on correlation clusters and cluster search
methods. *Psychometrika*, **9**, 169-84.

Cattell, R. B. 1944.   901
" Parallel proportional profiles " and other principles
for determining the choice of factors by rotation.
Psychometrika, **9**, 267-83.

Cattell, R. B. 1945.   902
The description of personality. III. Principles and findings in a factor analysis. *Amer. J. Psychol.*, **58**, 69-90.

Cattell, R. B. 1946.   903
Simple structure in relation to some alternative
factorizations of the personality sphere. *J. Gen.
Psychol.*, **35**, 225-38.

Cattell, R. B. 1948.   904
Primary personality factors in the realm of objective
tests. *J. Personality*, **16**, 459-87.

Cattell, R. B. 1949.   905
A note on factor invariance and the identification of
factors. *Brit. J. Psychol. (Statist. Sec.)*, **2**, 134-9.

Cattell, R. B., Cattell, A. K. S. &   906
Rhymer, R. M. 1947.
P-technique demonstrated in determining psycho-
physiological source traits in a normal individual.
Psychometrika, **12**, 267-88.

Cauer, W. 1940.   907
Das Poissonsche Integral und seine Anwendungen auf
die Theorie der linearer Wechselstromschaltungen
(Netzwerke). *Elektr. Nachr. Tech.*, **17**, 17-30.

Cavailles, J. 1940.   908
Du collectif au part. À propos de quelques théories
récentes sur les probabilités. *Rev. Métaphys. Moral.*,
47, 139-63.

Cavalli, L. L. 1945.   909
Alcuni problemi della analisi biometrica di popolazi-
oni naturali. *Mem. Ist. Idrobiol. " Dott. Marco de
Marchi "*, **2**, 301-23.

Cavalli, L. L. 1947.   909[a]
Analisi della varianza ponderata ed applicazioni
all' analisi del χ^2 di eterogeneitá. *Mem. Ist. Ital.
Idrobiol.*, **3**, 146-9.

Cavalli, L. L. 1949.   910
Sulla correlazione media fra più caratteri in relazione
alla biometria. *Metron*, **15**, 173-88.

Cavalli, L. L. & Magni, G. 1947.   911
Methods of analysing the virulence of bacteria and
viruses for genetical purposes. *Heredity*, **1**, 127-32.

Cave, R. C. 1943.   912
Variations in expenditures where families of wage-
earners and clerical workers are classified by economic
level. *J. Amer. Statist. Ass.*, **38**, 445-52.

Cawley, R. H., Waterhouse, J. A. H.   913
& Hogben, H. 1949.
Studies on puberty. II. The pattern of differential
growth. *Brit. J. Soc. Med.*, **3**, 157-82.

Cernuschi, F. 1949.   914
A noncontradictory formulation of the collective of
von Mises. (Spanish.) *Ciencia e Investigación*, **5**,
258-60.

Cernuschi, F. & Castagnetto, L. 1946.   915
Chains of rare events. *Ann. Math. Statist.*, **17**, 53-61.

Cernuschi, F. & Castagnetto, L. 1947.   916
Probability schemes with contagion in space and time.
Ann. Math. Statist., **18**, 122-7.

Cernuschi, F. & Saleme, E. 1944.   917
A new scheme of contagion in probability. (Spanish.)
An. Soc. Cient. Argent., **138**, 201-13.

Cervinka, V. 1948.   918
Factor analysis. *Statist. Obzor*, **28**, 145-62.

Chakrabarti, M. C. 1946.   919
A note on skewness and kurtosis. *Bull. Calcutta
Math. Soc.*, **38**, 133-6.

Chakrabarti, M. C. 1946.   920
The moments and seminvariants of the mean square
successive difference. *Bull. Calcutta Math. Soc.*, **38**,
185-9.

Chakrabarti, M. C. 1947.   921
On a special case of the distribution law of the mean
square successive difference. *Bull. Calcutta Math.
Soc.*, **39**, 15-18.

Chakrabarti, M. C. 1947.   922
On the inadequacy of measuring the peakedness of a
distribution curve by the standardised fourth moment.
Bull. Calcutta Math. Soc., **39**, 154-6.

Chakrabarti, M. C. 1948.   923
On the ratio of mean deviation to standard deviation.
Bull. Calcutta Statist. Ass., **1**, 187-90.

Chakrabarti, M. C. 1949.   924
On the moments of non-central χ^2. *Bull. Calcutta
Math. Soc.*, **41**, 208-10.

Chalkly, H., Cornfield, J. & Park, H. 1949.   925
A method for estimating volume-surface ratios.
Science, **110**, 295-7.

Chamberlin, T. C. 1944. 926
The method of multiple working hypotheses. *Scientific Monthly*, **59**, 357-62.

Chambers, E. G. 1943. 927
Statistics in psychology and limitations of the test methods. *Brit. J. Psychol.*, **33**, 189-99.

Chambers, E. G. 1946. 928
Statistical techniques in applied psychology. *Biometrika*, **33**, 269-73.

Chambers, E. G. & Yule, G. U. 1941. 929
Theory and observation in the investigation of accident causation. *J. R. Statist. Soc. Suppl.*, **7**, 89-109.

Champernowne, D. G. 1948. 930
Sampling theory applied to autoregressive sequences. *J. R. Statist. Soc. B*, **10**, 204-42.

Chand, U. 1949. 931
Formulas for the percentage points of distribution of the arithmetic mean in random samples, from certain symmetrical universes. *J. Res. Nat. Bur. Stand.*, **43**, 79-80.

Chandra Sekar, C. 1942. 932
A note on the inverse sine transformation. *Sankhyā*, **6**, 195-8.

Chandra Sekar, C. 1944. 933
Distribution of Fisher's g_1 for samples of three from a continuous rectangular distribution. *Current Science*, **13**, 10-11.

Chandra Sekar, C. & Deming, W. E. 1949. 934
On a method of estimating birth and death rates and the extent of registration. *J. Amer. Statist. Ass.*, **44**, 101-15.

Chandra Sekar, C. & Francis, M. G. 1941. 935
A method to get the significance limit of a type of test criteria. *Sankhyā*, **5**, 165-8.

Chandrasekhar, S. 1941. 936
A statistical theory of stellar encounters. *Astrophys. J.*, **94**, 511-24.

Chandrasekhar, S. 1943. 937
Stochastic problems in physics and astronomy. *Rev. Mod. Phys.*, **15**, 1-89. (Translated into Russian (1947). Reprinted in "Selected Papers on Noise and Stochastic Processes," New York, Dover, 1954.)

Chandrasekhar, S. 1944. 937[a]
The statistics of the gravitation field arising from a random distribution of stars. III. The correlations in the forces acting at two points separated by a finite distance. IV. The stochastic variation of the force acting on a star. *Astrophys. J.*, **99**, 25-46; 47-53.

Chandrasekhar, S. 1944. 937[b]
On the stability of binary systems. *Astrophys. J.*, **99**, 54-8.

Chandrasekhar, S. 1949. 938
Brownian motion, dynamical friction, and stellar dynamics. *Rev. Mod. Phys.*, **21**, 383-8. (Also: *Dialectica*, **3**, 114-26.)

Chandrasekhar, S. 1949. 939
On a class of probability distributions. *Proc. Camb. Phil. Soc.*, **45**, 219-24.

Chandrasekhar, S. & von Neumann, J. 1942-3. 940
The statistics of the gravitational field arising from a random distribution of stars. I. The speed of fluctuations. II. The speed of fluctuations; dynamic friction; spatial correlations. *Astrophys. J.*, **95**, 489-531; **97**, 1-27.

Chapanis, A. 1941. 941
Notes on the rapid calculation of item validities. *J. Educ. Psychol.*, **32**, 297-304.

Chapin, F. S. 1943. 942
Some problems in field interviews, when using the control group technique in studies in the community. *Amer. Sociol. Rev.*, **8**, 63-8.

Chapman, D. G. 1948. 943
A mathematical study of confidence limits of salmon populations calculated from sample tag ratios. *Bull. Int. Pacific Salmon Fish. Comm.*, **1948** (2), 69-85.

Chapman, W. H. 1945. 943[a]
Skeleton tables derived from the experience of the continuous mortality investigation. *J. Inst. Actuar.*, **72**, 234-9.

Chapple, E. D. 1942. 944
The measurement of interpersonal behaviour. *Trans. N.Y. Acad. Sci.*, **4**, 222-3.

Charnley, F. 1941. 945
Some properties of a composite, bivariate distribution in which the means of the component normal distributions are linearly related. *Canadian J. Res. A*, **19**, 139-51.

Charnley, F. 1942. 946
The variances of the means and the variance of the slope of the line of relation of a linear, composite bivariate distribution. *Canadian J. Res. A*, **20**, 6-9.

Chase, H. 1944. 946[a]
Bell puts teeth into quality control. *Wings*, **3**, 1181-6.

Chase, H. 1944. 947
Planned inspection improves quality control. *Wings*, **3**, 1276-8.

Chassan, J. B. 1948. 948
The autocorrelation approach to the analysis of the incidence of communicable diseases. *Hum. Biol.*, **20** 90-108.

Chassan, J. B. 1948. 949
On a statistical approximation to the infection interval. *Biometrics*, **5**, 243-9.

Chatterjee, T. P. 1947. 950
On the general law of demand for raw jute. *Sankhyā*, **8**, 271-4.

Chatterjee, T. P. & Sinha, A. R. 1941. 951
A statistical study of the demand for raw jute. *Sankhyā*, **5**, 433-8.

Chattopadhyay, K. P. 1942. 952
Application of statistical methods to anthropological research. *Sankhyā*, **6**, 99-104.

Chattopadhyay, K. P. 1949. 953
Comparability of measurements. *Sankhyā*, **9**, 399-402.

Chaturvedi, H. K. & Bhattacharyya, S. 1948. 954
On the change of standard of living of the jute mill workers of Jagaddal between the years 1941-5. *Sankhyā*, **8**, 360-71.

Chein, I. 1947.   955
A note on the alleged equality of standard deviational units. *J. Gen. Psychol.*, **36**, 233-6.

Cheng, C. 1942.   956
On the fecundity of some gammerids. *J. Mar. Biol. Ass. U.K.*, **25**, 467-74.

Cheng, T.-T. 1943.   957
On the combination of statistical elements. *Coll. Papers Sci. Engng. Nat. Univ. Amoy*, **1**, 73-82.

Cheng, T.-T. 1943.   958
A simplified formula for mean difference. *Coll. papers Sci. Engng. Nat. Univ. Amoy*, **1**, 69-72. (Also: (1944) *J. Amer. Statist. Ass.*, **39**, 240-2.)

Cheng, T.-T. 1944.   959
A new probability function and its properties. *J. Amer. Statist. Ass.*, **39**, 243-5.

Cheng, T.-T. 1949.   960
The normal approximation to the Poisson distribution and a proof of a conjecture of Ramanujan. *Bull. Amer. Math. Soc.*, **55**, 396-401.

Cheriyan, K. C. 1941.   961
A bivariate correlated gamma-type distribution function. *J. Indian Math. Soc.*, **5**, 133-44.

Cheriyan, K. C. 1945.   962
Distribution of certain frequency constants in samples from non-normal populations. *Sankhyā*, **7**, 159-66.

Cheriyan, K. C. 1949.   963
Estimation of consumption requirements. *Bull. Calcutta Statist. Ass.*, **2**, 29-32. (Also: *Proc. Indian Sci. Congr.*, 1947.)

Chern, S.-S. 1945.   964
On Grassman and differential rings and their relations to the theory of multiple integrals. *Sankhyā*, **7**, 2-8.

Chernoff, H. 1949.   965
Asymptotic Studentization in testing of hypotheses. *Ann. Math. Statist.*, **20**, 268-78.

Chester, K. S. 1941.   966
The probability law in cotton seedling disease. *Phytopath.*, **31**, 1078-88.

Chevallier, A. 1946.   967
L'application de la méthode statistique aux données médicales. *Sem. Hôp. Paris*, **22**, 1756-7.

Chevry, G. 1949.   968
Control of a general census by means of an area sampling method. *J. Amer. Statist. Ass.*, **44**, 373-9.

Chiassino, G. 1948.   969
Il teorema dell' invarianzia dei birapporto e sua applicazione al calcolo dei parametri di talune curve interpolanti. *Riv. Ital. Econ. Demogr. Statist.*, **2**, 177-83.

Chiassino, G. 1949.   970
Considerazioni sull'interpolazione statistica. *Ann. Ist. Statist. Bari*, **23**, 59-66.

Child, I. L. 1946.   971
A note on Grant's " New statistical criteria for learning and problem solution ". *Psychol. Bull.*, **43**, 558-61.

Chimenti, A. 1947.   972
Disuguaglianze tra medie associative. *Statistica, Milano*, **7**, 38-47.

Choudhary, N. A. 1947.   973
A generalization of binomial, Lexian and Poisson distributions. *Math. Student*, **15**, 8.

Chow, K. Y. 1946.   974
A comparative study of the structure and chemical composition of tension wood and normal wood in beech. *Forestry*, **20**, 62-77.

Chowla, S. 1944.   975
Contribution to the theory of the construction of balanced incomplete block designs used in the statistical tables of Fisher and Yates. *Proc. Lahore Phil. Soc.*, **6**, 10-12.

Chowla, S. 1944.   976
A new case and another case of " complete 1-m-n configuration ". *Proc. Lahore Phil. Soc.*, **6**, 13-14.

Chowla, S. 1944.   977
Contributions to the theory of the construction of balanced incomplete block designs. *Proc. Lahore Phil. Soc.*, **6**, 17-23.

Chowla, S. 1945.   978
A contribution to the theory of the construction of balanced incomplete block designs. *Proc. Lahore Phil. Soc.*, **7**, 3 pp.

Chrétien, C. D. 1943.   978[a]
The quantitative method for determining linguistic relationships. Interpretation of results and tests of significance. *Univ. Calif. Publ. Linguistics*, **1**, 11-20.

Chrétien, C. D. 1945.   978[b]
Culture element distributions. XXV. Reliability of statistical procedures and results. *Anthrop. Rec., Univ. Calif.*, **8**, 469-90.

Christensen, J. R. 1948.   979
Determinación de parcelas experimentales para viñas. *Experimenta, Mendoza*, **1**, 20-5.

Chrzaszcz, R. 1943.   980
Ein Problem der Bestimmung und Eliminierung von systematischen Beobachtungsfehlern. *Samml. wissen. Arbeiten Schweiz internierten Polen*, **1** (3), 23-6.

Chulanovskii, I. V. 1949.   981
On cycles in Markov chains. (Russian.) *Dokl. Akad. Nauk SSSR*, **69**, 301-4.

Chung, K. L. 1940.   982
Sur un théorème de M. Gumbel. *C. R. Acad. Sci., Paris*, **210**, 620-1.

Chung, K. L. 1941.   983
On the probability of the occurrence of at least m events among n arbitrary events. *Ann. Math. Statist.*, **12**, 328-38.

Chung, K. L. 1942.   984
On mutually favourable events. *Ann. Math. Statist.*, **13**, 338-49.

Chung, K. L. 1943.   985
Generalization of Poincaré's formula in the theory of probability. *Ann. Math. Statist.*, **14**, 63-5.

Chung, K. L. 1943.   986
On fundamental systems of probabilities of a finite number of events. *Ann. Math. Statist.*, **14**, 123-33.

Chung, K. L. 1943.   987
Further results on probabilities of a finite number of events. *Ann. Math. Statist.*, **14**, 234-7.

Chung, K. L. 1946. 988
The approximate distribution of Student's statistic. *Ann. Math. Statist.*, **17**, 447-65.

Chung, K. L. 1947. 989
On the maximum partial sum of independent random variables. *Proc. Nat. Acad. Sci. U.S.A.*, **33**, 132-6.

Chung, K. L. 1947. 990
Note on some strong laws of large numbers. *Amer. J Math.*, **69**, 189-92.

Chung, K. L. 1948. 991
Asymptotic distribution of the maximum cumulative sum of independent random variables. *Bull. Amer. Math. Soc.*, **54**, 1162-70.

Chung, K. L. 1948. 992
On a lemma by Kolmogoroff. *Ann. Math. Statist.*, **19**, 88-91.

Chung, K. L. 1948. 993
On the maximum partial sums of sequences of independent random variables. *Trans. Amer. Math. Soc.*, **64**, 205-33; 596.

Chung, K. L. 1949. 994
An estimate concerning the Kolmogoroff limit distribution. *Trans. Amer. Math. Soc.*, **67**, 36-50.

Chung, K. L. & Erdös, P. 1947. 995
On the lower limit of sums of independent random variables. *Ann. Math.*, (2) **48**, 1003-13.

Chung, K. L. & Feller, W. 1949. 996
On fluctuations in coin tossing. *Proc. Nat. Acad. Sci. U.S.A.*, **35**, 605-8.

Chung, K. L. & Hsu, L. C. 1945. 997
A combinatorial formula and its application to the theory of probability of arbitrary events. *Ann. Math. Statist.*, **16**, 91-5.

Chung, K. L. & Hunt, G. A. 1949. 998

On the zeros of $\sum_1^N \pm 1$. *Ann. Math.*, (2) **50**, 385-400.

Church, A. 1940. 999
On the concept of a random sequence. *Bull. Amer. Math. Soc.*, **46**, 130-5.

Churchill, E. 1946. 1000
Information given by odd moments. *Ann. Math. Statist.*, **17**, 244-6.

Churchill, H. V. 1946. 1001
A system of laboratory evaluation. *Industr. Engng. Chem. (Anal. Ed.)*, **18**, 66.

Churchill, H. V. & Churchill, J. R. 1945. 1002
Evaluation of spectographic analytical data. *Industr. Engng. Chem. (Anal. Ed.)*, **17**, 751-4.

Churchman, C. W. 1945. 1003
Probability theory. *Philos. Sci.*, **12**, 147-73.

Churchman, C. W. 1946. 1003[a]
Carnap's " On inductive logic ". *Philos. Sci.*, **13**, 339-42.

Churchman, C. W. 1946. 1004
Most economic sampling for chemical analysis. *Industr. Engng. Chem.*, **18**, 267-8.

Churchman C. W. 1946. 1005
Philosophical aspects of statistical theory. *Phil. Rev.*, **55** (1), 81-7.

Churchman, C. W. 1947. 1006
Much ado about probability. *Philos. Sci.*, **14**, 176-8.

Churchman, C. W. 1948. 1007
Statistics, pragmatics, induction. *Philos. Sci.*, **15**, 249-68.

Churchman, C. W. & Epstein, B. 1946. 1008
Tests of increased severity. *J. Amer. Statist. Ass.*, **41**, 567-624.

Cioranescu, N. 1945. 1009
Serii de frecvente ce comporta interpretari geometrice spatiale. (Interprétation géométrique de séries de fréquence.) *An. Inst. Statist. Rômin.*, **2**, 23-7.

Clancey, V. J. 1947. 1010
Statistical methods in chemical analysis. *Nature*, **159**, 339-40.

Clark, C. & Dyne, R. E. 1946. 1011
Applications and extensions of the Karmel formula for reproductivity. *Econ. Record*, **22**, 23-39.

Clark, C. E. 1949. 1012
The statistical theory of the dead time losses of a counter. *Rev. Sci. Instru.*, **20**, 51-2.

Clark, E. & Fishman, L. 1947. 1013
Appraisal of methods for estimating the size distribution of a given aggregate income. *Rev. Econ. Statist.*, **29**, 43-6.

Clark, E. L. 1949. 1014
Methods of splitting vs. samples as sources of instability in test-reliability coefficients. *Harvard Educ. Rev.*, **19**, 178-82.

Clarke, B. L., Smith, G. F., Youden, W. J. and others. 1947. 1014[a]
Symposium on statistical methods in experimental and industrial chemistry. *Industr. and Engng. Chem. (Anal. Ed.)*, **19**, 943-60.

Clarke, R. D. 1946. 1015
An application of the Poisson distribution. *J. Inst. Actuar.*, **72**, 481.

Clayton, A. J. H. 1941. 1016
Road traffic calculations. *J. Inst. Civ. Engrs.*, **16**, 247-84.

Clifford, P. C. 1947. 1016[a]
Acceptance sampling inspection by variables. *Industr. Qual. Contr.*, **3** (5), 12-15.

Clos, C. 1948. 1017
An aspect of the dialling behaviour of subscribers and its effect on the trunk plant. *Bell Syst. Tech. J.*, **27**, 424-45.

Clough, H. W. 1942. 1018
A note on methods of correlation. *Bull. Amer. Met. Soc.*, **23**, 410.

Coates, R. P. & Cody, D. D. 1946. 1019
Observations on exposure sampling procedure. *Trans. Actuar. Soc. Amer.*, **47**, 116, 311-25, 528-40.

Cobb, C. W. 1943. 1020
A regression. *Econometrica*, **11**, 265-7.

Cobb, P. W. 1940. 1021
The limit of usefulness of accident rate as a measure of accident proneness. *J. Appl. Psychol.*, **24**, 154-9.

Cochran, W. G. 1940.   1022
Analysis of a lattice and triple lattice experiments. II. Mathematical theory. *Iowa Agric. Exper. Sta. Res. Bull.*, **281**, 64-5.

Cochran, W. G. 1940.   1023
The estimation of the yields of cereal experiments by sampling for the ratio of grain to total produce. *J. Agric. Sci.*, **30**, 262-75.

Cochran, W. G. 1940.   1024
Note on an approximate formula for the significance levels of *z. Ann. Math. Statist.*, **11**, 93-5.

Cochran, W. G. 1940.   1025
The analysis of variance when experimental errors follow the Poisson or binomial laws. *Ann. Math. Statist.*, **11**, 335-47.

Cochran, W. G. 1941.   1026
The distribution of the largest of a set of estimated variances as a fraction of their total. *Ann. Eugen.*, **11**, 47-52.

Cochran, W. G. 1941.   1027
An examination of the accuracy of lattice and lattice square experiments on corn. *Iowa Agric. Exper. Sta. Res. Bull.*, **289**, 397-415.

Cochran, W. G. 1941.   1028
Lattice designs for wheat variety trials. *J. Amer. Soc. Agron.*, **33**, 351-60.

Cochran, W. G. 1942.   1029
The χ^2 correction for continuity. *Iowa State Coll. J. Sci.*, **16**, 421-36.

Cochran, W. G. 1942.   1030
Sampling theory when the sampling-units are of unequal sizes. *J. Amer. Statist. Ass.*, **37**, 199-212.

Cochran, W. G. 1943.   1031
Some additional lattice square designs. *Iowa Agric. Exper. Sta. Res. Bull.*, **318**, 731-48.

Cochran, W. G. 1943.   1032
Analysis of variance for percentages based on unequal numbers. *J. Amer. Statist. Ass.*, **38**, 287-301.

Cochran, W. G. 1943.   1033
The comparison of different scales of measurement for experimental results. *Ann. Math. Statist.*, **14**, 205-16.

Cochran, W. G. 1943.   1034
Some developments in statistics. *Chronica Botanica*, **7**, 383-6.

Cochran, W. G. 1943.   1035
Sampling techniques when the sampling units differ in size. *Statist. J., City College, New York*, **6**, 18-24.

Cochran, W. G. 1946.   1036
Graduate training in statistics. *Amer. Math. Monthly*, **53**, 193-9.

Cochran, W. G. 1946.   1037
Relative accuracy of systematic and stratified random samples for a certain class of populations. *Ann. Math. Statist.*, **17**, 164-77.

Cochran, W. G. 1946.   1038
Use of the I.B.M. equipment in an investigation of the truncated normal problem. *Proc. Res. Forum, I.B.M. Corp., New York*, 26-30 August 1946, pp. 40-4.

Cochran, W. G. 1947.   1039
Some consequences when the assumptions for the analysis of variance are not satisfied. *Biometrics Bull.*, **3**, 22-38.

Cochran, W. G. 1947.   1040
Recent developments in sampling theory in the United States. *Proc. 25th. Session Int. Statist. Inst. Conf., Washington, D.C.*, 1947 (Publ. 1951), **3A**, 40-66.

Cochran, W. G. 1947.   1041
Analysis of covariance. *North Carolina Inst. Statist., Mimeo Ser.*, no. 2.

Cochran, W. G. 1948.   1042
A critical examination of the Beevers-Lipson method of Fourier series summation. *Acta Cryst.*, **1**, 54-6.

Cochran, W. G. 1948.   1043
Sample survey techniques. *North Carolina Inst. Statist., Mimeo Series*, no. 7, 154 pp.

Cochran, W. G. 1949.   1044
The present status of biometry. *Bull. Int. Statist. Inst.*, **32** (2), 132-50.

Cochran, W. G. & Bliss, C. I. 1948.   1045
Discriminant functions with covariance. *Ann. Math. Statist.*, **19**, 151-76.

Cochran, W. G., Autrey, K. M. & Cannon, C. Y.   1046
1941. A double change-over design for dairy cattle feeding experiments. *J. Dairy Sci.*, **24**, 937-51.

Cochrane, D. 1949.   1047
Measurement of economic relationships. *Econ. Record*, **25**, 7-23.

Cochrane, D. & Orcutt, G. H. 1949.   1048
Application of least squares regression to relationships containing auto-correlated error terms. *J. Amer. Statist. Ass.*, **44**, 32-61.

Cockayne, E. A. 1940.   1049
Transposition of the visceral and other reversals of symmetry in monozygotic twins. *Biometrika*, **31**, 287-94.

Cody, D. D. 1941.   1050
The standard deviation in the rate of mortality by amounts. *Trans. Actuar. Soc. Amer.*, **42**, 69-73.

Cody, D. D. 1948.   1051
Sampling errors in mortality and other statistics in life insurance. *Trans. Amer. Statist. Ass.*, **43**, 442-50.

Cohan, G. M. 1947.   1051a
New uses for the average range. *Industr. Qual. Contr.*, **3** (6), 17-19.

Coheen, H. W. & Kayruck, S. 1948.   1052
A work-sheet for tetrachoric *r* and standard error of tetrachoric *r* using Hayes diagrams and tables. *Psychometrika*, **13**, 279-80.

Cohen, A. C., Jr. 1940.   1053
The numerical computation of the product of conjugate imaginary gamma functions. *Ann. Math. Statist.*, **11**, 213-18.

Cohen, A. C., Jr. 1949.   1054
On estimating the mean and standard deviation of truncated normal distributions. *J. Amer. Statist. Ass.*, **44**, 518-25.

Cohen, A. C., Jr. 1949. 1055
A note on truncated distributions. *Industr. Qual. Contr.*, **6** (3), 22.

Cole, L. C. 1945. 1056
A simple test of the hypothesis that alternative events are equally probable. *Ecology*, **26**, 202-5.

Cole, L. C. 1946. 1056a
A study of the cryptozoa of an Illinois woodland. *Ecological Monogr.*, **16**, 49-86.

Cole, L. C. 1946. 1057
A theory for analysing contagiously distributed populations. *Ecology*, **27**, 329-41.

Cole, L. C. 1949. 1058
The measurement of interspecific association. *Ecology*, **30**, 411-24.

Cole, R. 1948. 1059
An item-analysis of the Terman-Merrill revision of the Binet tests. *Brit. J. Psychol. (Statist. Sec.)*, **1**, 137-51.

Cole, R. H. 1944. 1060
Associated frequency distributions in biometry. *Amer. Math. Monthly*, **51**, 252-61.

Cole, R. H. 1946. 1061
The theory of small samples. *Proc. 1st Canadian Math. Congr., Montreal, Symp. Statist.*, no. 4, pp. 33-6.

Cole, R. H. 1949. 1062
An *R*-ply range estimation of mean and standard deviation. *Princeton Univ. Statist. Res. Group, Mimeo. Rep.* no. 20.

Collatz, L. 1942. 1063
Fehlerabschatzung für das Iterationsverfahren zur Auflösung linearer Gleichungssysteme. *Zeit. angew. Math. Mech.*, **22**, 357-61.

Collatz, L. & Zurmühl, R. 1944. 1064
Glätten und Vertafeln empirischer Funktionen mittels Differenzen. *Zeit. Ver. Dtsch. Ing.*, **88**, 511-15.

Colley, R. H. 1946. 1065
How to determine the size of a survey sample. *Printers' Ink, New York*, **216** (10), 35.

Colley, R. H. 1949. 1066
Some practical applications of precision sampling. *J. Marketing*, **14**, 437-41.

Collias, N. E. 1943. 1067
Statistical analysis of factors which make for success in initial encounters between hens. *Amer. Nat.*, **77**, 519-38.

Collings, S. N. 1944. 1068
A sampling scheme for testing and eliminating defects from batches to any desired quality level. *U.K. Min. Supply Advisory Service Statist. Method & Qual. Contr. Tech. Rep. Ser. R*, no. QC/R/16, 10 March 1944, 6 pp.

Colombo, G. 1947. 1069
Recenti sviluppi delle indagini campionarie. *Riv. Ital. Demogr. Statist.*, **1**, 53-9.

Combes, B. 1947. 1070
Le principe de Bayes et le problème de l'ajustement. *Bull. Trim. Inst. Actuair. Français*, **58**, 1-72.

Comrie, L. J. 1946. 1071
The application of commercial calculating machines to scientific computing. *Math. Tab., Wash.*, **2**, 149-59.

Comrie, L. J. & Hartley, H. O. 1941. 1071a
Tables of percentage points of the incomplete beta-function: Description of the calculation. *Biometrika*, **32**, 154-61.

Comrie, L. J. & Hartley, H. O. 1941. 1072
Table of Lagrangian coefficients for harmonic interpolation in certain tables of percentage points. *Biometrika*, **32**, 183-6.

Comstock, R. E. 1943. 1073
Overestimation of mean squares by the method of expected numbers. *J. Amer. Statist. Ass.*, **38**, 335-40.

Comstock, R. E. 1949. 1074
Statistics in animal breeding research. *Proc. Auburn Conf. Statist. Appl. Res. Social Sci., Plant Sci. and Animal Sci.*, 1948, pp. 74-6.

Comstock, R. E. & Robinson, H. F. 1948. 1075
The components of genetic variance in populations of biparental progenies and their use in estimating the average degree of dominance. *Biometrics*, **4**, 254-66.

Comstock, R. E. & Winters, L. M. 1942. 1076
Design of experimental comparisons between lines of breeding in livestock. *J. Agric. Res.*, **64**, 523-32.

Comstock, R. E., Peterson, W. J. & 1077
Steward, H. A. 1948.
An application of the balanced lattice design in a feeding trial with swine. *J. Animal Sci.*, **7**, 320-31.

Conagin, A. 1947. 1078
Some statistical notions. *Rev. Agric. Sao Paulo*, **22**, 119-34.

Conagin, A. 1947. 1079
Use of statistical tests in agricultural experimentation. *Rev. Agric. Sao Paulo*, **22**, 340-56.

Condon, E. U. 1943. 1079a
Statistical handling of laboratory data. *Product Engng.*, **14**, 615-17.

Connelly, G. M. 1945. 1080
Now let's look at the real problem: Validity. *Public Opinion Quart.*, **7**, 51-60.

Conrad, H. S. 1945. 1081
A statistical evaluation of the basic classification test battery (Form I) O.S.R.D. Rep. 4346. *Washington, D.C., Appl. Psychol. Panel, N.D.R.C.*, 93 pp.

Conrad, H. S. & Jones, H. E. 1940. 1082
Environmental and genetic implications of parent, child and sibling correlations. *Yearbook Nat. Soc. Stud. Educ.*, **39** (2), 97-141.

Consael, R. 1941. 1083
Sur une généralisation des formules d'ajustement de E. T. Whittaker. *Mitt. Ver. Schweiz. Versich.-Math.*, **41**, 95-107.

Consael, R. 1948. 1084
Sur une généralisation du processus de Pólya. *Bull. Acad. Roy. Belg. Cl. Sci.*, (5) **34**, 863-76.

Consael, R. 1949. 1085
Sur quelques processus stochastiques discontinus à deux variables aléatoires. I, II. *Bull. Acad. Roy. Belg. Cl. Sci.*, (5) **35**, 399-416; 743-55.

Consael, R. 1949. 1086
Sur le schéma de Pólya-Eggenberger à deux variables aléatoires. *Bull. Ass. Actuair. Belg.*, **55**, 11-23.

Consoli, T. 1940. 1087
Généralisation d'un théorème sur la probabilité de la somme d'un nombre infini de variables aléatoires. (French. Turkish summary.) *Rev. Fac. Sci. Univ. Istanbul A*, **5**, 1-17.

Cook, R. L., Millar, C. E. & Robertson, L. S. 1088
1946. A crop rotation field layout with an illustration of the statistics involved in combining several years data. *Proc. Soil Sci. Soc. Amer.*, **10**, 213-18.

Coombs, C. H. 1941. 1089
A criterion for significant common factor variance. *Psychometrika*, **6**, 267-72.

Coombs, C. H. 1948. 1090
Some hypotheses for the analysis of qualitative variables. *Psychol. Rev.*, **55**, 167-74.

Coombs, C. H. 1948. 1091
A rationale for the measurement of traits in individuals. *Psychometrika*, **13**, 59-68.

Coombs, C. H. 1948. 1092
The role of correlation in analysis of variance. *Psychometrika*, **13**, 233-43.

Copeland, A. H. 1941. 1093
Fundamental concepts of the theory of probability. *Amer. Math. Monthly*, **48**, 522-30.

Copeland, A. H. 1941. 1094
Postulates for the theory of probability. *Amer. J. Math.*, **63**, 741-62.

Copeland, A. H. 1944. 1095
The teaching of the calculus of probability. *Notre Dame Univ. Indiana, Math. Lectures* no. 4, pp. 31-43.

Copeland, A. H. 1949. 1096
A postulational characterization of statistics. *Proc. Berkeley Symp. Math. Statist. and Probab.*, 1945-6, pp. 51-61.

Copeland, P. L. 1945. 1097
Accuracy of constants in exponential decay as obtained from finite samples. A review. *Amer. J. Phys.*, **13**, 215-22.

Coppini, M. A. 1949. 1097a
Tecnica " approssimata " dei fondi pensione. *Atti 10ma Riun. Sci., Soc. Ital. Demogr. Statist.*, 104-33.

Corbett, R. A. 1941. 1098
Uniform annual reports for artificial breeding associations, including standardized methods of calculating conception rates. *J. Dairy Sci.*, **24**, 490-1.

Cornell, F. G. 1947. 1099
Sample plan for a survey of higher education enrollment. *J. Exper. Educ.*, **15**, 213-18.

Cornell, F. G. 1947. 1100
A stratified-random sample of a small finite population. *J. Amer. Statist. Ass.*, **42**, 523-32.

Cornfield, J. 1942. 1101
On certain biases in samples of human populations. *J. Amer. Statist. Ass.*, **37**, 63-8.

Cornfield, J. 1944. 1102
On samples from finite populations. *J. Amer. Statist. Ass.*, **39**, 236-9.

Cornish, E. A. 1940. 1103
The estimation of missing values in incomplete randomized block experiments. *Ann. Eugen.*, **10**, 112-18.

Cornish, E. A. 1940. 1104
The estimation of missing values in quasi-factorial designs. *Ann. Eugen.*, **10**, 137-43.

Cornish, E. A. 1940. 1105
The analysis of covariance in quasi-factorial designs. *Ann. Eugen.*, **10**, 269-79.

Cornish, E. A. 1940-1. 1106
The analysis of quasi-factorial designs with incomplete data. *J. Aust. Inst. Agric. Sci.*, **6**, 31-9; **7**, 19-26.

Cornish, E. A. 1943-4. 1107
The recovery of inter-block information in quasi-factorial designs with incomplete data. I. Square, triple and cubic lattices. II. Lattice squares. *Bull. C.S.I.R., Aust.*, no. 158, 22 pp.; no. 175, 19 pp.

Cornish, E. A. 1949. 1108
Yield trends in the wheat belt of South Australia during 1896-1941. *Aust. J. Sci. Res. B*, **2**, 83-137.

Cornish, E. A., Belz, M. H. & Stewart, A. L. 1109
1943. The application of statistical methods to the quality control of materials and manufactured products. *Trans. Inst. Engrs. Aust.*, **24**, 53-62.

Corson, J. J. 1944. 1110
The use of statistics in management. *Advanced Mgmt.*, **9**, 74-8.

Cortes, R. T. & Hambanada, P. 1947. 1111
Fiber length of Anilau (*Columbia serratifolia*) Hinlaumo (*Mallotus ricinoides*) and Kupang (*Parkia javanica*). *Philipp. J. Forestry*, **5**, 50-70.

Cottam, G. & Curtis, J. T. 1949. 1111a
A method for making rapid surveys of woodlands by means of pairs of randomly selected trees. *Ecology*, **30**, 101-4.

Cotterman, C. W. 1942. 1112
The biometrical approach in human genetics. *Amer. Nat.*, **76**, 144-55.

Cotterman, C. W. 1947. 1113
A weighting system for the evaluation of gene frequencies from family records. *Univ. Mich., Contr. Lab. Vertebr. Biol.*, **33**.

Cotton, H. R. 1943. 1114
Housing scales for rural Pennsylvania. *J. Amer. Statist. Ass.*, **38**, 406-16.

Coulson, C. A. 1947. 1115
Note on the random-walk problem. *Proc. Camb. Phil. Soc.*, **43**, 583-6.

Count, E. W. 1942. 1116
A quantitative analysis of growth in certain human skull dimensions. *Hum. Biol.*, **14**, 143-65.

Count, E. W. 1943. 1117
Growth patterns of the human physique: An approach to kinetic anthropometry. I. *Hum. Biol.*, **15**, 1-32.

Court, A. 1949. 1118
Separating frequency distributions into two normal components. *Science*, **110**, 500-1.

Court, L. M. 1944. 1119
A reciprocity principle for the Neyman-Pearson theory of testing statistical hypotheses. *Ann. Math. Statist.*, **15**, 326-7.

Cousin, G. 1948.   1120
Sur les formules permettant l'estimation exacte de la variation des types structuraux dans l'espèce. *C. R. Acad. Sci., Paris*, **226**, 1039-41.

Coward, K. H. 1941.   1120a
The accuracy of the spectrophotometric determination of vitamin B. *Quart. J. Pharm.*, **14**, 329-34.

Coward, L. E. 1949.   1121
The distribution of sickness. *J. Inst. Actuar.*, **75**, 12-38.

Cowden, D. J. 1943.   1122
Correlation concepts and the Doolittle method. *J. Amer. Statist. Ass.*, **38**, 327-34.

Cowden, D. J. 1946.   1123
An application of sequential sampling to testing students. *J. Amer. Statist. Ass.*, **41**, 547-56.

Cowden, D. J. 1947.   1124
Simplified methods of fitting certain types of growth curves. *J. Amer. Statist. Ass.*, **42**, 585-90.

Cowden, D. J. & Connor, W. S. 1945.   1124a
The use of statistical methods for economic control of quality in industry. *Southern Econ. J.*, **12**, 115-29.

Cowgill, D. O. 1949.   1124b
The theory of population growth cycles. *Amer. J. Sociol.*, **55**, 163-70.

Cowie, G. A. 1945   1124c
Study of the effects of fertilizers and rainfall on yields of crops grown in rotation. *J. Agric. Sci.*, **35**, 197-206.

Cox, D. R. 1946.   1125
The derivation of significance tests for the differences between accident rates. *R. Aircraft Est., Farnborough*, RAE Rep. no. SME 3367, 25 pp.

Cox, D. R. 1948.   1126
A note on the asymptotic distribution of range. *Biometrika*, **35**, 310-15.

Cox, D. R. 1949.   1127
Use of range in sequential analysis. *J. R. Statist. Soc. B*, **11**, 101-14.

Cox, D. R. & Townsend, M. W. 1948.   1128
The use of the correlogram in measuring yarn irregularity. *Proc. Int. Wool Textile Org.*, **2**, 28-34.

Cox, G. J. & Matuschak, M. C. 1941.   1129
An abbreviation of the method of least squares. *J. Phys. Chem.*, **45**, 362-9.

Cox, G. M. 1940.   1130
Enumeration and construction of balanced incomplete block configurations. *Ann. Math. Statist.*, **11**, 72-85.

Cox, G. M. 1944.   1131
Statistics as a tool for research. *J. Home Econ.*, **36**, 575-80.

Cox, G. M. 1949.   1132
A proposed statistical plan for the Southeastern States. *Proc. Auburn Conf. Statist. Appl. Res. Social Sci., Plant. Sci. and Animal Sci.*, 1948, pp. 26-36.

Cox, G. M. & Cochran, W. G. 1946.   1133
Designs of greenhouse experiments for statistical analysis. *Soil Sci.*, **62**, 87-98.

Cox, G. M. & McKay, H. 1942.   1134
Length of the observation period as a factor in variability in calcium retentions. *J. Home Econ.*, **34**, 679-81.

Cox, G. M., Eckhardt, R. C. & Cochran, W. G.   1135
1940. The analysis of lattice and triple lattice experiments in corn varietal tests. *Iowa Agric. Exper. Sta. Res. Bull.*, **281**, 1-66.

Cox, R. T. 1946.   1136
Probability, frequency and reasonable expectation. *Amer. J. Phys.*, **14**, 1-13.

Craig, A. T. 1943.   1137
A note on the best linear estimate. *Ann. Math. Statist.*, **14**, 88-90.

Craig, A. T. 1943.   1138
Note on the independence of certain quadratic forms. *Ann. Math. Statist.*, **14**, 195-7.

Craig, A. T. 1947.   1139
Bilinear forms in normally correlated variables. *Ann. Math. Statist.*, **18**, 565-73.

Craig, C. C. 1940.   1140
The product semi-invariants of the mean and a central moment in samples. *Ann. Math. Statist.*, **11**, 177-85.

Craig, C. C. 1941.   1141
Note on the distribution of non-central t with an application. *Ann. Math. Statist.*, **12**, 224-8.

Craig, C. C. 1941.   1142
A note on Sheppard's corrections. *Ann. Math. Statist.*, **12**, 339-45.

Craig, C. C. 1942.   1143
On frequency distributions of the quotient and of the product of two statistical variables. *Amer. Math. Monthly*, **49**, 24-32.

Craig, C. C. 1942.   1144
Recent advances in mathematical statistics. II. *Ann. Math. Statist.*, **13**, 74-85.

Craig, C. C. 1947.   1144a
Control charts versus the analysis of variance in process control by variables. *Industr. Qual. Contr.*, **3** (4), 14-16.

Cramer, G. F. 1948.   1145
An approximation to the binomial summation. *Ann. Math. Statist.*, **19**, 592-4.

Cramér, H. 1940.   1146
On the theory of stationary random processes. *Ann. Math.*, (2) **41**, 215-30.

Cramér, H. 1941.   1147
Deux conférences sur la théorie des probabilités. *Skand. Aktuartidskr.*, **24**, 34-69.

Cramér, H. 1942.   1148
On harmonic analysis in certain functional spaces. *Ark. Mat. Astr. Fys.*, **28B** (12), 17 pp.

Cramér, H. 1946.   1149
A contribution to the theory of statistical estimation. *Skand. Aktuartidskr.*, **29**, 85-94.

Cramér, H. 1946.   1150
Lundberg's risk theory and the theory of stochastic processes. (Swedish.) *Förs.mat. Stud. Filip Lundberg*, pp. 25-31.

Cramér, H. 1947.   1151
Problems in probability theory. *Ann. Math. Statist.*, **18**, 165-93.

Cramér, H. 1947.   1152
On the theory of stochastic processes. *Proc. 10th. Congr. Math. Scand.*, 1946, pp. 28-39.

Cramér, H. 1949. 1153
On the factorization of certain probability distributions. *Ark. Mat.*, **1** (7), 61-5.

Crampton, E. W. 1942. 1154
The design of animal husbandry experiments. *J. Animal Sci.*, **1**, 263-76.

Crawford, J. R. 1944. 1154a
Mathematics of quality control. *Aero Digest*, **46**, 112-13.

Crew, F. A. E. 1945. 1154b
The role of statistics in the furtherance of medical research. *J. Fac. Actuar. Edin.*, **17**, 270-83.

Crisswell, J. H. 1946. 1155
Foundations of sociometric measurement. *Sociometry*, **9**, 7-13.

Crist, J. W. 1940. 1156
Correlation from ranks for horticultural research. *Proc. Amer. Soc. Hort. Sci.*, **38**, 593-5.

Crist, J. W. 1942. 1157
Tetrachoric correlation for horticultural research. *Proc. Amer. Soc. Hort. Sci.*, **40**, 549-51.

Crist, J. W. 1943. 1158
The coefficient of contingency for horticultural research. *Proc. Amer. Soc. Hort. Sci.*, **42**, 484-6.

Crist, J. W. & Seaton, H. L. 1941. 1158a
Reliability of organoleptic tests. *Food Res.*, **6**, 529-36.

Cronbach, L. J. 1943. 1159
On estimates of test reliability. *J. Educ. Psychol.*, **34**, 485-94.

Cronbach, L. J. 1943. 1160
Note on the reliability of ratio scores. *Educ. and Psychol. Measurement*, **3**, 67-70.

Cronbach, L. J. 1946. 1160a
A case study of the split-half reliability coefficient. *J. Educ. Psychol.*, **37**, 473-80.

Cronbach, L. J. 1947. 1161
Test "reliability". Its meaning and determination. *Psychometrika*, **12**, 1-16.

Cronbach, L. J. 1949. 1161a
Statistical methods applied to Rorschach scores: A review. *Psychol. Bull.*, **46**, 393-429.

Crossley, A. M. 1941. 1162
Theory and application of representative sampling as applied to marketing. *J. Marketing*, **5**, 456-61.

Crout, P. D. 1941. 1163
A short method of evaluating determinants and solving systems of linear equations with real or complex coefficients. *Trans. Amer. Inst. Elect. Engrs.*, **60**, 1235-41.

Crow, J. F. 1945. 1164
A chart of the χ^2 and t distributions. *J. Amer. Statist. Ass.*, **40**, 376.

Crowther, F. & Cochran, W. G. 1942. 1165
Rotation experiments with cotton in the Sudan Gezira. *J. Agric. Sci.*, **32**, 390-405.

Croxton, F. E. 1941. 1166
Toward standardized symbols for basic statistical concepts. *J. Amer. Statist. Ass.*, **36**, 426-8.

Croxton, F. E. & Cowden, D. J. 1946. 1167
Tables to facilitate computation of sampling limits of "s" and fiducial limits of sigma. *Industr. Qual. Contr.*, **3** (1), 18-21.

Crump, S. L. 1946. 1168
The estimation of variance components in analysis of variance. *Biometrics Bull.*, **2**, 7-11.

Crutchfield, R. S. & Tolman, E. C. 1940. 1169
Multiple-variable design for experiments involving interaction of behaviour. *Psychol. Rev.*, **47**, 38-42.

Cunningham, L. B. C. & Hynd, W. R. B. 1946. 1170
Random processes in problems of air warfare. *J. R. Statist. Soc. Suppl.*, **8**, 62-97.

Cupr, K. 1942. 1171
Matematické základy nauky o logisticke krivcé. (Die mathematischen Grundlagen der Lehre von der logarithmischen Linie.) (Czech and German.) *Statist. Obzor*, **23**, 35-44.

Curtis, J. M., Umberger, E. J. & Knudsen, L. F. 1947. 1172
The interpretation of estrogenic assays. *Endocrinology*, **40**, 831-40.

Curtiss, J. H. 1941. 1173
On the distribution of the quotient of two chance variables. *Ann. Math. Statist.*, **12**, 409-21.

Curtiss, J. H. 1941. 1174
Generating functions in the theory of statistics. *Amer. Math. Monthly*, **48**, 374-86.

Curtiss, J. H. 1942. 1175
A note on the theory of moment generating functions. *Ann. Math. Statist.*, **13**, 430-3.

Curtiss, J. H. 1943. 1176
Convergent sequences of probability distributions. *Amer. Math. Monthly*, **50**, 94-105.

Curtiss, J. H. 1943. 1177
On transformations used in the analysis of variance. *Ann. Math. Statist.*, **14**, 107-22.

Curtiss, J. H. 1946. 1178
A note on some single sampling plans requiring the inspection of a small number of items. *Ann. Math. Statist.*, **17**, 62-70.

Curtiss, J. H. 1946. 1178a
Statistical inference applied to naval engineering. *J. Amer. Soc. Naval Engrs.*, **58**, 335-98.

Curtiss, J. H. 1947. 1179
Acceptance sampling by variables, with special reference to the case in which quality is measured by average or dispersion. *J. Res. Nat. Bur. Stand.*, **39**, 271-90.

Curtiss, J. H. 1947. 1179a
The application of statistical theory to the preparation of industrial specifications. *Proc. 25th. Session Int. Statist. Inst. Conf., Washington, D.C., 1947* (Publ. 1951), **3A**, 351-7.

Curtiss, J. H. 1949. 1180
Sampling methods applied to differential and difference equations. *Proc. Seminar Sci. Computation, I.B.M. Corp., New York.*

Cusimano, G. 1948. 1181
Sull'analisi della varianza. *Ann. Fac. Econ. Com. Palermo*, **2**, 49-91.

Cutter, G. O. 1945. 1181ᵃ
A simplified approach to quality control. *Iron Age*, **155**, 70-4.

D

da Cruz, E. G. 1940. 1182
Ligeiras consideracoes sobre a probabilidade de provas repetidas e o teorema de Bernoulli. (Portuguese.) *Bol. Minist. Trabalho, Insdutr. e Com., Rio de Janeiro*, **7** (76), 267-74.

D'Addario, R. 1940. 1183
Un metodo per la rappresentazione analitica della distribuzioni statistiche. *Atti Ist. Naz. Assicuraz.*, **12**, 93-121.

Dagobert, E. B. 1946. 1184
Mathematical probabilities in games of chance: The game of sevens. *Math. Teach.*, **39**, 155-8.

Dahlberg, G. 1942. 1185
Methodik zur Unterscheidung von Erblichkeits- und Milieuvariationen mit Hilfe von Zwillingen. *Hereditas, Lund*, **28**, 409-28.

Dahlberg, G. 1943. 1186
Mathematische Erblichkeitsanalyse von Populationen. *Acta Med. Scand. Suppl.*, **148**, 1-219.

Dahlberg, G. 1949. 1187
Bloodsinking reaction from a statistical viewpoint in normal men and women. *Acta Genet.*, **1**, 267.

Dahlberg, G. 1949. 1188
A new method of determining the mutation frequency in man. *Proc. 8th. Int. Congr. Genetics, Hereditas*, **35**, *Suppl.*, 555-6.

Dalenius, T. 1949. 1189
Den nyare utvecklingen inom teorin och metodiken för stickprovsundersökningar. *Forhandl. Nordisk. Statist., Helsingfors*, 13-14 June 1949, pp. 46-74.

Dalenius, T. 1949. 1190
Problem vid företagssampling. (Problèmes relatifs aux enquêtes représentatives sur les entreprises.) (Swedish. French and English summaries.) *Sociala meddelander.*, **59**, 251-61.

Dalla Valle, J. M. 1941. 1191
Note on the " most probable number " index as used in bacteriology. *Publ. Health Rep.*, **56**, 229-34.

Dalmulder, J. J. J. 1948. 1192
De functie van de econometrie bijhet bedrijfsbeheer. *Statistica, Rijswijk*, **2**, 2-18.

Daly, J. F. 1940. 1193
On the unbiased character of likelihood-ratio tests for independence in normal systems. *Ann. Math. Statist.*, **11**, 1-32.

Daly, J. F. 1941. 1194
A problem in estimation. *Ann. Math. Statist.*, **12**, 459-61.

Daly, J. F. 1946. 1195
On the use of the sample range in an analogue of Student's *t*-test. *Ann. Math. Statist.*, **17**, 71-4.

Damon, A. 1942. 1196
A note on the estimation of dysplasia in human physiques: Sheldon's method and the analysis of variance. *Hum. Biol.*, **14**, 110-12.

D'Amore, F. 1948. 1197
Variazioni dinamiche del grado di liquidità nel sistema industriale. *Riv. Ital. Demogr. Statist.*, **2**, 562-81.

Daniel, C. 1940. 1198
Statistically significant differences in observed per cents. *J. Appl. Psychol.*, **24**, 826-30.

Daniels, H. E. 1941. 1199
A method of improving certain routine measurements. *J. R. Statist. Soc. Suppl.*, **7**, 146-50.

Daniels, H. E. 1941. 1200
The probability distribution of the extent of a random chain. *Proc. Camb. Phil. Soc.*, **37**, 244-51.

Daniels, H. E. 1941. 1201
A property of the distribution of extremes. *Biometrika*, **32**, 194-5.

Daniels, H. E. 1944. 1202
The relation between measures of correlation in the universe of sample permutations. *Biometrika*, **33**, 129-35.

Daniels, H. E. 1945. 1203
The statistical theory of the strength of bundles of threads. I. *Proc. Roy. Soc. A*, **183**, 405-35.

Daniels, H. E. 1947. 1204
Grouping corrections for high autocorrelations. *J. R. Statist. Soc. Suppl.*, **9**, 245-9.

Daniels, H. E. 1948. 1205
A property of rank correlations. *Biometrika*, **35**, 416-17.

Daniels, H. E. & Kendall, M. G. 1947. 1206
Significance of rank correlation where parental correlation exists. *Biometrika*, **34**, 197-208.

Dantzig, G. B. 1940. 1207
On the non-existence of tests of " Student's " hypothesis having power functions independent of σ. *Ann. Math. Statist.*, **11**, 186-92.

Dantzig, G. B. 1948. 1208
Programming of interdependent activities. II. Mathematical model. *Econometrica*, **17**, 200-11.

Dapples, E. C. & Rominger, J. F. 1945. 1209
Orientation analysis of fine-grained clastic sediments: a report of progress. *J. Geology*, **53**, 246-61.

Darling, D. A. 1949. 1210
The problem of Cunningham and Hynd. *RAND Corp. Res. Memo.*, 8 Aug. 1949, RM-195, 20 pp.

Darlington, C. D. & Mather, K. 1944. 1211
Chromosome balance and interaction in *hyacinthus*. *J. Genet.*, **46**, 52-61.

Darmois, G. 1940. 1212
Les mathématiques de la psychologie. *Mém. Sci. Math.*, **98**, 51 pp.

Darmois, G. 1945. 1213
Sur les limites de la dispersion de certaines estimationes. *Rev. Int. Statist. Inst.*, **13**, 9-15.

Darmois, G. 1946. 1214
Sur certaines lois de probabilité. *C. R. Acad. Sci., Paris*, **222**, 164-5.

Darmois, G. 1946. 1215
Résumés exhaustifs et problème du Nil. *C. R. Acad. Sci., Paris*, **222**, 266-8.

Darmois, G. 1947. 1216
Analyse des liaisons de probabilité. *Proc. 25th Session Int. Statist. Inst. Conf., Washington D.C.*, 1947, (Publ. 1951), **3** (A), 231-40.

Darmois, G. 1947. 1217
Sur les regressions linéaires et paraboliquès. *Conf. Ass. Français Avan. Sci.*, October 1945, pp. 121-3. (*Intermédiare des Recherches Maths.*, January 1947.)

Darmois, G. 1949. 1218
Sur certaines formes de liaison de probabilité. *Le calcul des probabilités et ses applications, Colloq. Int. Centre Nat. Rech. Sci., Paris*, **13**, 19-21.

Darwin, C. G. 1942. 1219
Statistical control of production. *Nature*, **149**, 573-5.

Das, A. C. 1948. 1220
A note on the D^2-statistic when the variances and the covariances are known. *Sankhyā*, **8**, 372-4.

Das, A. C. 1949. 1221
Two-dimensional systematic sampling. *Science & Culture*, **15**, 157-8.

da Silva Rodrigues, M. *See* **Rodrigues, M. da S.**

Daudin, J. 1947. 1222
Calcul des observations de grandes gerbes. *J. Phys. Radium*, (8) **8**, 301-5.

Davenport, C. B. 1940. 1223
Analysis of variance applied to human genetics. *Proc. Nat. Acad. Sci. U.S.A.*, **26**, 1-3.

Davey, R. 1942. 1224
The number of sample trees required for determining volumes of woods with various degrees of accuracy. *Forestry*, **16**, 52-5.

David, F. N. 1947. 1225
A χ^2 ' smooth ' test for goodness of fit. *Biometrika*, **34**, 299-310.

David, F. N. 1947. 1226
A power function for tests of randomness in a sequence of alternatives. *Biometrika*, **34**, 335-9.

David, F. N. 1948. 1227
Correlations between χ^2 cells. *Biometrika*, **35**, 418-22.

David, F. N. 1949. 1228
Note on the application of Fisher's k-statistics. *Biometrika*, **36**, 383-93.

David, F. N. 1949. 1229
Moments of the z and F distribution. *Biometrika*, **36**, 394-403.

David, F. N. & Johnson, N. L. 1948. 1230
The probability integral transformation when parameters are estimated from the sample. *Biometrika*, **35**, 182-90.

David, F. N. & Kendall, M. G. 1949. 1231
Tables of symmetric functions. I. *Biometrika*, **36**, 431-49.

David, H. T. 1949. 1232
A note on random walk. *Ann. Math. Statist.*, **20**, 603-8.

Davidson, Å. 1946. 1233
On the problem of ruin in the collective risk theory under the assumption of variable safety loading. (Swedish.) *Förs.mat. Stud. Filip Lundberg*, pp. 32-47.

Davidson, W. M. & Carroll, J. B. 1945. 1234
Speed and level components in time-limit scores: a factor analysis. *Educ. and Psychol. Measurement*, **5**, 411-27.

Davies, G. R. & Bruner, N. 1943. 1235
A second moment correction for grouping. *J. Amer. Statist. Ass.*, **38**, 63-8.

Davies, G. R. & Smith, R. H. 1941. 1236
Probabilities in logarithmic skewed distributions. *J. Amer. Statist. Ass.*, **36**, 493-99.

Davies, J. A. 1947. 1237
Life test predictions by statistical methods to expedite radio tube shipments. *Industr. Qual. Contr.*, **4** (1), 12-17.

Davies, J. A. 1949. 1238
Quality control in radio tube manufacture. *Proc. Inst. Radio Engrs.*, **37**, 548-56.

Davies, O. L. 1947. 1239
Statistical evaluation of growth curves. *Proc. Soc. Exper. Biol.*, **66**, 567-8.

Davis, A. L. 1946. 1240
The quality control organization. *Industr. Qual. Contr.*, **2** (3), 12-16.

Davis, D. J. & Howard, W. J. 1948. 1241
Examination of some models of failure of equipment during operation. *RAND Corp. Res. Memo.*, 26 Oct. 1949, RM-87, 27 pp.

Davis, F. B. 1945. 1242
The reliability of component scores. *Psychometrika*, **10**, 57-60 (erratum, 163).

Davis, F. B. 1947. 1243
The interpretation of principal axis factors. *J. Educ. Psychol.*, **38**, 471-81.

Davis, H. T. 1941. 1244
The statistics of time series. *Northwestern Univ. Stud. Math. Phys. Sci.*, I. *Math. Monogr.*, **1**, 45-85.

Davis, J. F. 1940. 1245
The relationship between leaf area and yield of the field bean with a statistical study of methods for determining leaf area. *J. Amer. Soc. Agron.*, **32**, 323-9.

Davis, J. F. 1945. 1246
A method of estimating the weight of roots of green manure crops. *J. Amer. Soc. Agron.*, **37**, 661-2.

Davis, J. F., Baten, W. D. & Cook, R. L. 1247
1946. The effect of time of application and levels of nitrogen, phosphorus and potash on the growth of sugar beets with a detailed statistical procedure of confounding in a $3 \times 3 \times 3$ design. *Michigan Agric. Exper. Sta. Tech. Bull.*, **203**, 40 pp.

Davis, J. F., Cook, R. L. & Baten, W. D. 1248
1942. A method of statistical analysis of a factorial experiment involving influence of fertilizer analyses and placement of fertilizer on stand and yield of cannery peas. *J. Amer. Soc. Agron.*, **34**, 521-32.

Davis, R. J. 1946.   1248ª
How to use statistical methods in quality control.
Chem. Engng., **53**, 115-17.

Davis, S. C. 1943.   1249
Coordinating production for war. *J. Amer. Statist.
Ass.*, **38**, 417-24.

Daw, R. H. 1946.   1250
On the validity of statistical tests of the graduation of
a mortality table. *J. Inst. Actuar.*, **72**, 174-202.

Dawson, E. H., Duehring, M.   1251
& Parks, V. E. 1947.
Addition of ground egg shell to dried egg for use in
cooking. *Food Res.*, **12**, 288-97.

Day, B. B. 1949.   1252
Application of statistical methods to research and
development in engineering. *Rev. Int. Statist. Inst.*,
17, 129-55.

Day, B. B. & Sandomire, M. M. 1942.   1253
Use of the discriminant function for more than two
groups. *J. Amer. Statist. Ass.*, **37**, 461-72.

Day, W. R. 1946.   1254
On the effect of changes in elevation aspect, slope and
depth of free-rooting material on the growth of
European larch, Japanese larch, Sitka spruce, and
Scots pine in Mynydd Dhu Forest. *Forestry*, **20**, 7-20.

Dayre, J. 1945.   1255
Essai sur le foisonnement des stocks dans l'économie
concurrentielle. *J. Soc. Statist. Paris*, **86**, 122-30.

de Abreu, L. S. 1949.   1256
Sondagens no dominio do rendimento nacional
rendimento e o imposto. *Rev. Economia, Lisboa*, **2**,
217-51.

De Almeida, D. M. 1947.   1257
A função do erro. *Agronomia, Rio de Janeiro*, **1** (6),
39-41.

Dean, J. & James, R. W. 1943.   1258
The long-run behavior of costs in a chain of shoe
stores. A statistical analysis. *Univ. Chicago, Stud.
Business Admin.*, **12** (3), 54 pp.

de Bach, P. & Smith, H. S. 1941.   1259
Are population oscillations inherent in the host-parasite
relation? *Ecology*, **22**, 363-9.

De Beer, E. J. 1945.   1260
The calculation of biological assay results by graphic
methods. The all-or-none type of response. *J.
Pharmacol & Exper. Therap.*, **85**, 1-13.

De Beer, E. J. & Sherwood, M. B. 1945.   1261
The paper-disc agar-plate method for the assay of
antibiotic substances. *J. Bact.*, **50**, 459-67.

De Broglie, L. 1946.   1262
Sur l'application du théorème des probabilités com-
posées en mécanique ondulatoire. *C. R. Acad. Sci.,
Paris*, **223**, 874-7.

De Broglie, L. 1948.   1263
Sur la statistique des cas purs en mécanique ondulatoire. *C. R. Acad. Sci., Paris*, **226**, 1056-8.

de Carvalho, P. E. 1940.   1264
Distribuicao efetiva e distribucao normal de um
fenômeno. Sua comparacao pelo metodo de Risser.
(Portuguese.) *Rev. Brasil. Estatíst.*, **1**, 486-8.

de Carvalho, P. E. 1940.   1265
O problema das provas repetidas. *Rev. Brasil.
Estatíst.*, **1**, 694-6.

Dedebant, G. 1947.   1266
Sur le calcul aléatoire. *An. Fac. Ci. Porto*, **32**, 5-48,
65-112, 129-76, 193-216.

Dedebant, G. & Wehrlé, P. 1940.   1267
La mécanique des fluides turbulents fondée sur des
concepts statistiques. *Thalès*, **4**, 151-67.

Dedebant, G. & Wehrlé, P. 1944-5.   1268
Mécanique aléatoire. I. Le calcul aléatoire. II.
Applications physiques. *Portug. Phys.*, **1**, 95-149;
179-296.

Dedebant, G., Moyal, J. & Wehrlé, P. 1940.   1269
Sur les équations aux dérivées partielles que vérifient
les fonctions de distribution d'un champ aléatoire.
C. R. Acad. Sci., Paris, **210**, 243-5 (errata, 352).

Dedebant, G., Moyal, J. & Wehrlé, P. 1940.   1270
Sur l'équivalent hydrodynamique d'un corpuscule
aléatoire. Application à l'établissement des équations
aux valeurs probables d'un fluide turbulent. *C. R.
Acad. Sci., Paris*, **210**, 332-4.

Deemer, W. L. 1940.   1270ª
A numerical example illustrating the generalized
formula for testing significance of experimental
treatments. *Harvard Educ. Rev.*, **10**, 75-81.

Deemer, W. L. 1942.   1271
A method of estimating accuracy of test scoring.
Psychometrika, **7**, 65-73.

Deemer, W. L., Jr. 1947.   1272
The power of the *t* test and the estimation of required
sample size. *J. Educ. Psychol.*, **38**, 329-42.

Deemer, W. L., Jr. (editor). 1947.   1273
Records, analysis and test procedures. *Army Air
Force Aviation Psychol. Program, Res. Rep.* no. 18.

Deevey, E. S., Jr. 1947.   1274
Life tables for natural populations of animals. *Quart.
Rev. Biol.*, **22**, 283-314.

de Fériet, J. K. *See* **Kampé de Fériet, J.**

De Fina, A. L. 1943.   1275
A graphical and numerical index for determining the
degree of efficiency of agricultural varieties. *Rev.
Fac. Agron. La Plata*, **25**, 21-54.

de Finetti, B. 1940.   1276
Indici statistici e " teoria delle strutture ". *Atti 1ma
Riun. Sci., Soc. Ital. Statist.*, pp. 1-4.

de Finetti, B. 1940.   1277
Il problema die " Pieni ". *G. Ist. Ital. Attuari*, **11**,
1-88.

de Finetti, B. 1941.   1278
Il calcolo delle probabilità nel dominion dell'assicurazione. (German, French and English summaries.)
Trans. 12th Int. Congr. Actuar., Lucerne, 1940, **1**,
253-61.

de Finetti, B. 1943.   1279
La matematica nelle concezioni e nelle applicazioni
statistiche. *Statistica, Milano*, **3**, 89-112.

de Finetti, B. 1947.   1280
La prévision, ses lois logiques, ses sources subjectives.
Ann. Inst. H. Poincaré, **7**, 1-68.

de Finetti, B. 1949. 1281
La " logica del plausibile " secondo la concezione di Polya. *Atti 42da Riun. Soc. Ital. Prog. Sci.*, **1**, 227ff.

de Finetti, B. 1949. 1282
A proposito dell'articolo " Probabilità ". *Period Mat.*, (4) **27**, 140-8.

de Finetti, B. 1949. 1283
Le vrai et le probable. *Dialectica*, **3**, 78-92.

De Floriani, W. 1948. 1284
Applicazioni della media esponenziale in matematica finanziaria e in demografia. *Statistica, Milano*, **8**, 68-77.

De Floriani, W. 1948. 1284ª
Il potenziale di procreazione. *Riv. Ital. Demogr. Statist.*, **2**, 541-9.

De Fraga Torrejon, E. 1949. 1285
Die wahrscheinlichste Gerade für ein System von nicht kollinearen Punkten. (Spanish.) *Gac. Mat. Madrid*, **1** (1), 135-8.

de Freitas Bueno, L. 1945. 1286
Funçôes de freqüência e os momentos. (Portuguese.) *Rev. Brasil. Estatíst.*, **6**, 17-28.

de Freitas Filho, L. 1942. 1287
O clinico e a bio-estatística. (Estudos e sugestòes.) *Rev. Brasil. Estatíst.*, **3**, 153-74.

de Froe, A., Huizinga, J. & van Gool, J. 1947. 1288
Variation and correlation coefficient. *Proc. Kon. Ned. Akad. Wetensch.*, **50**, 807-15.

Degan, J. W. 1948. 1289
A note on the effects of selection in factor analysis. *Psychometrika*, **13**, 87-9.

De Gusmâo, A. A. C. 1945. 1290
A psicologia na estatística. *Rev. Brasil. Estatíst.*, **6** 35-48

Dehalu, M. 1942. 1290ª
Sur la démonstration de la formule de K. Pearson dans le cas du schéma simple des urnes. *Bull. Soc. Roy. Sci., Liège* **11**, 146-51.

Dehalu, M. 1949. 1291
Confrontation des méthodes de Pearson et Charlier à propos d'une expérience d'Arne Fisher. *Bull. Soc. Roy. Sci., Liège*, **18**, 239-49.

de Jong, A. J. 1947. 1292
Het monsternemen als probleem in het bedrijf. (Sampling as a problem in industry.) (Dutch. English summary.) *Statistica Neerlandica*, **1**, 293-303.

de Jongh, B. H. 1941. 1293
General minimum-probability theorem. (Dutch. German summary.) *Proc. Kon. Ned. Akad. Wetensch.*, **44**, 738-43.

de Jongh, S. E., Lens, S. & Spanhoff, R. W. 1294
1947. On the standardization of insulin by means of the rabbit test. *Arch. Int. Pharmacodyn.*, **74**, 63-82.

Delaporte, P. 1945. 1295
Vérification de l'efficacité d'une méthode d'analyse factorielle. *C. R. Acad. Sci., Paris*, **220**, 212-14.

Delaporte, P. 1946. 1296
Sur l'estimation des corrélations des caractères avec le facteur général et les facteurs de groupe et sur l'écart-type de cette estimation, en analyse factorielle. *C. R. Acad. Sci., Paris*, **222**, 525-7.

Delaporte, P. 1947. 1297
Une nouvelle méthode d'analyse factorielle. *Proc. 25th. Session Int. Statist. Inst. Conf., Washington D.C.*, 1947 (Publ. 1951), **3A**, 241-57.

Delaporte, P. 1947. 1298
Prolongement de la méthode d'analyse factorielle de Spearman en utilisant la statistique mathématique. *Biotypologie*, **9**, 45-59.

Delaporte, P. 1949. 1299
Une condition nécessaire que les observations doivent remplir pour être réprésentables par un schéma d'analyse factorielle de Spearman. *C. R. Acad. Sci., Paris*, **229**, 973-5.

Delaporte, P. 1949. 1300
Sur une utilisation systématique de la statistique mathématique en analyse factorielle. *Le calcul des probabilités et ses applications, Colloq. Int. Centre Nat. Rech. Sci., Paris*, no. 13, pp. 101-4.

Delbrück, M. 1940. 1301
Statistical fluctuations in autocatalytic reactions. *J. Chem. Phys.*, **8**, 120-4.

Delbrück, M. 1944. 1302
A statistical problem. *J. Tennessee Acad. Sci.*, **19**, 177-8.

Delbrück, M. 1945. 1303
Spontaneous mutations of bacteria. *Ann. Missouri Bot. Gdn.*, **32**, 223-33.

Del Chiaro, A. 1940. 1304
Sulla teoria formale della popolazione. *G. Ist. Ital. Attuari*, **11**, 214-32.

Del Chiaro, A. 1941. 1305
Sui tassi centrali di mortalità. *G. Ist. Ital. Attuari*, **12**, 208-20.

de Leeuw, Th. A. 1948. 1306
Een noodzakelijke correctie van de overschrijdings-grenzen voor steekproefgemiddelden bij toepassing van stratified sampling. (A necessary correction of the control chart limits for averages of samples in the case of stratified sampling.) (Dutch. English summary.) *Statistica Neerlandica*, **2**, 40-54.

de Leeuw, Th. A. 1948. 1306ª
Enkele opmerkingen over de mogelijkheid van toepassing van mathematisch-statistische methoden bij tijdstudieprobleem en in het bijzonder bij het Bedaux-systeem. (Some remarks on the possibility of applying mathematical-statistical methods to time-study problems and in particular to the Bedaux system.) (Dutch. English summary.) *Statistica Neerlandica*, **2**, 235-41.

Delgleize, A. 1942. 1307
Sur la fonction de Makeham. *Bull. Soc. Roy. Sci., Liège*, **11**, 163-6.

Delgleize, A. 1942. 1308
Sur le schéma simple des urnes. *Bull. Soc. Roy. Sci., Liège*, **11**, 398-403.

Delgleize, A. 1943. 1309
Sur les courbes de fréquence. *Bull. Soc. Roy. Sci., Liège*, **12**, 264-76.

Delgleize, A. 1949. 1310
Sur la détermination de $\bar{a}_x$. *Bull. Soc. Roy. Sci., Liège*, **18**, 391-4.

D'Elia, E. 1947. 1311
Alcuni metodi per la misura delle correlazioni statistiche. *Riv. Ital. Econ. Demogr. Statist.*, **1**, 175-99.

de Lury, D. B. 1946. 1312
The analysis of Latin squares when some observations are missing. *J. Amer. Statist. Ass.*, **41**, 370-89.

de Lury, D. B. 1947. 1313
On the estimation of biological populations. *Biometrics Bull.*, **3**, 145-67.

de Lury, D. B. 1948. 1314
The analysis of covariance. *Biometrics*, **4**, 153-70.

de Macedo Soares, J. C. 1945. 1315
Estatistica geografia recenseamento. *Rev. Brasil. Estatíst.*, **6**, 349-62.

de Menezes, O. B. 1944. 1316
Genetic studies of the pigeon pea (*Cajanus indicus*). Spacing and competition in varieties. *Rev. Agric. Piracicaba*, **19**, 399-412.

de Meo, G. 1940. 1317
Sulle nascite dei promogeniti in Italia. *Metron*, **14**, 79-158.

de Meo, G. 1948-9. 1318
Efficacia della selezione e tavole selazionate di mortalità nell' assicurazione vita. *Riv. Ital. Demogr. Statist.*, **2**, 352-78; **3**, 172-9.

Deming, G. W. & Coleman, O. H. 1942. 1319
Comparative efficiency of lattice and random-block designs for a sugarbeet variety test. *Proc. Amer. Soc. Sugar Beet Technol.*, 1942, pp. 181-3.

Deming, W. E. 1940. 1320
Sampling problems of the 1940 census. *Cowles Commission Res. Econ. Rep. 6th. Ann. Res. Conf. Econ. and Statist., Colorado Springs*, pp. 39-53.

Deming, W. E. 1941. 1321
Some thoughts on statistical inference. *J. Wash. Acad. Sci.*, **31**, 85-93.

Deming, W. E. 1942. 1322
On a classification of the problems of statistical inference. *J. Amer. Statist. Ass.*, **37**, 173-85.

Deming, W. E. 1943. 1323
Opportunities in mathematical statistics, with special reference to sampling and quality control. *Science*, **97**, 209-14.

Deming, W. E. 1943. 1323a
Sampling and quality control. *J. Amer. Soc. Naval Engrs.*, **55**, 573-9.

Deming, W. E. 1944. 1324
On errors in surveys. *Amer. Sociol. Rev.*, **9**, 359-69. (Spanish version (1948-9): *Estadística*, **6**, 493-504; **7**, 84-91.)

Deming, W. E. 1944. 1324a
A view of the statistical method. *Accounting Rev.*, **19**, 254-60.

Deming, W. E. 1945. 1325
Aspectos del metodo estadístico. (English summary.) *Estadística*, **3**, 576-84.

Deming, W. E. 1945. 1325a
The gamma and beta functions: notes and problems designed for use in mathematical statistics and mathematical physics. *U.S. Dept. Agric., Washington D.C., Grad. School*, ii+37 pp.

Deming, W. E. 1945. 1326
On training in sampling. *J. Amer. Statist. Ass.*, **40**, 307-16.

Deming, W. E. 1947. 1327
Some criteria for judging the quality of surveys. *J. Marketing*, **12**, 145-57.

Deming, W. E. 1948. 1328
A brief statement on the uses of sampling in censuses of population, agriculture, public health and commerce. *United Nations Statist. Commission, Lake Success, New York*, 15 pp. (Chinese version: *Stat. monthly* (133/134), 2-11. Italian version: *Riv. Econ. Agric.*, **3**, 212-25.)

Deming, W. E. & Geoffrey, L. 1941. 1329
On sample inspection in the processing of census returns. *J. Amer. Statist. Ass.*, **36**, 351-60.

Deming, W. E. & Simmons, W. 1946. 1330
On the design of a sample for dealers' inventories. *J. Amer. Statist. Ass.*, **41**, 16-33.

Deming, W. E. & Stephan, F. F. 1940. 1331
On a least squares adjustment of a sampled frequency table when the expected marginal totals are known. *Ann. Math. Statist.*, **11**, 427-44.

Deming, W. E. & Stephan, F. F. 1941. 1332
On the interpretation of censuses as samples. *J. Amer. Statist. Ass.*, **36**, 45-9.

Deming, W. E., Tepping, B. J. & Geoffrey, L. 1333
1942. Errors in card punching. *J. Amer. Statist. Ass.*, **37**, 525-36.

de Moraes, O. 1948. 1334
Posiçao, fundamento e aplicaçao de amostragem por seleçao ao acaso no campo da estatística administrativa. (Basis and application of sampling for random selection from administrative statistics.) (Portuguese.) *Rev. Brasil. Estatíst.*, **9**, 627-36.

Dempster, E. R. & Lerner, I. M. 1949. 1334a
Selection problems in animal breeding. *Proc. Berkeley Symp. Math. Statist. and Probab.*, 1945-6, pp. 481-3.

Denney, H. R. & Remmers, H. H. 1940. 1335
Reliability of multiple-choice measuring instruments as a function of the Spearman-Brown prophecy formula. II. *J. Educ. Psychol.*, **31**, 699-704.

Dennis, A. E. 1945. 1335a
Quality control by statistical methods. *Rayon Textile Monthly*, **26**, 397-9.

Dennukat, G. 1948. 1336
Das Wetter in der statistischen Diagnose. *Statist. Praxis*, **3**, 21-2.

Dennukat, G. 1949. 1337
Statistik und Wirklichkeit. *Statist. Praxis*, **4**, 25-6.

Densen, P. M. 1947. 1338
The development and use of statistical practices in hospital work. *Biometrics Bull.*, **3**, 109-17.

Denton, J. E. & Beecher, H. K. 1949. 1338a
New analgesics. *J. Amer. Med. Ass.*, **141**, 1051-7.

de Oliveira, A. J. 1945. 1339
Uniformity trials. A preliminary study with *lupinus luteus* L. at Sacavém. *Agron. Lusitana*, **7**, 207-44.

de Oliveira, A. J. 1949. 1340
Eficiência relativa dos diversos delineamentos estatis-
ticas. Usados na comparação de grande número de
variedades. *Agron. Lusitana*, **8**.

Depoid, P. 1949. 1341
Le degré de précision des statistiques démographiques.
Bull. Int. Statist. Inst., **32** (2), 339-49.

Dereymaeker, R. 1948. 1342
Étude statistique mathématique sur l'indice des prix de
détail. *Bull. Statist. Inst. Nat. Statist. Belg.*, **34**,
1487-90.

Derksen, J. B. D. 1940. 1343
Long cycles in residential building: an explanation.
Econometrica, **8**, 97-116.

Derksen, J. B. D. 1941. 1344
Einige Anwendungen der mathematischen Statistik auf
versicherungswissenschaftlichem Gebiet. (Dutch.)
Verzekerings-archief, **22**, 385-414.

Derksen, J. B. D. 1941. 1345
Probability-theoretical foundations of " regression-
analysis ". (Dutch.) *Ned. Tijdschr. Natuurk.*, **8**, 37-54.

Derksen, J. B. D. 1942. 1346
De berekening der sterftekansen bij de samenstelling
van sterftetafels; een mathematisch-statistische studie.
Verzekerings-archief, **23**, 15-29.

Derksen, J. B. D. 1943. 1347
De berekeningsmethode der periodieke sterftetafels
voor Nederland. (La Méthode de calcul des tables
périodiques de mortalité de Pays-Bas.) (Dutch.) *De
Verzekeringsbode, Utrecht*, **62**, 117-19.

Derksen, J. B. D. 1943. 1348
De berekening der periodieke sterftekansen; een
repliek. (Le calcul des quotients périodiques de
mortalité. Une réplique.) (Dutch.) *Verzekerings-
archief*, **24**, 232-7.

Derksen, J. B. D. 1944. 1349
Statistische berekeningen over de veideling dez
gezinsinkomens. (Dutch.) *Maandschr. Centr. Bur.
Statist's Gravenhage*, **39**, 287-96.

Derksen, J. B. D. 1948. 1350
The calculation of mortality-rates in the construction of
life tables. A mathematical statistical study. *Population Stud.*, **1**, 457-70.

Derksen, J. B. D. 1949. 1351
Statistics of the distribution of family incomes by size.
Milbank Mem. Fund Quart., **27**, 329-31.

de Rudder, B. 1943. 1352
Allgemeinbiologisches zur Phänogenese statistischer
Krankheitsgipfel. *Klin. Wschr.*, **22**, 453-7.

de Sampaio Ferraz, J. 1947. 1353
Notas sôbre a conveniencia da expansao da climatologia
fundamental. (Estatistica climatologica.) *Rev. Brasil.
Estatíst.*, **8**, 285-302.

de Sornay, A. 1942. 1354
Estimation of cane yields by means of random rows
and stools. *Rev. Agric. Ile Maurice*, **21**, 107-13.

de Toledo Piza, A. P. 1946. 1354a
Representative values of a distribution: Indices of
dispersion. (Portuguese). *An. Acad. Brasil. Cienc.*,
28, 209-35.

de Toledo Piza, A. P. 1947. 1355
On the factor of elimination $p\,(t,\lambda)$ and its applications
to the study of the movement of a population. (Portuguese.) *São Paulo*, 9 pp.

de Toledo Piza, A. P. 1947. 1356
On an integral equation of interest in the theory of
the movement of a population. (Portuguese.) *São
Paulo*, 4 pp.

de Toledo Piza, A. P. 1947. 1357
The notion of density of distinct values per interval
unit. (Portuguese.) *São Paulo*, 24 pp.

de Toledo Piza, A. P. 1947-8. 1358
Series estatísticas. *Rev. Brasil. Estatíst.*, **8**, 11-42;
9, 3-19.

de Toledo Piza, A. P. 1948. 1358a
Teoria matemática elementar do tráfego (caso parti-
cular do tráfego rodiviario). (Portuguese.) *Rev.
Brasil. Estatíst.*, **9**, 192-9.

Deutsch, A. J. 1945. 1359
The probability distribution around a fix in celestial
navigation. *Amer. J. Phys.*, **13**, 379-83.

de Varennes e Mendonça, P. 1942. 1360
Orthogonality and analysis of variance. *Portug.
Math.*, **3**, 234-52.

de Vergottini, M. 1940. 1361
Sul significato di alcuni indici di concentrazione.
G. Economisti, **2**, 317-47.

de Vergottini, M. 1941. 1362
Sulla relazione tra il rapporto di correlazione e il
coefficiente di correlazione. *G. Economisti*, **3**,
308-18.

de Vergottini, M. 1947. 1363
Sulla relazione tra gli indici Alfa e Delta. *G. Economisti*, **6**, 56-60.

de Vergottini, M. 1948. 1364
Medie, indici di variatibilità e di relazione. *Ann.
Statist., Roma*, **8** (2), 33-48.

de Vergottini, M. 1948. 1365
Sul metodo della popolazione tipo. *Ann. Semin.
Giur., Catania* (*N.S.*), **2**, 195-210.

de Vergottini, M. 1948. 1366
Sul valore mediale. *Riv. Ital. Demogr. Statist.*, **2**,
79-89.

de Vergottini, M. 1949. 1367
Sull'asimmetria. *Statistica, Milano*, **9**, 505-21.

de Vergottini, M. 1949. 1367a
Sugli indici di relazione. *Atti 9ma Riun. Soc. Ital.
Demogr. Statist.*, pp. 167-72.

De Wit, G. W. 1949. 1368
Stochastische Probleme in der Versicherungsmathematik. (Dutch.) *Verzekerings-archief*, **28**, 19-45.

de Wolff, P. 1948. 1368a
Statistische kwaliteitscontrôle. (Dutch.) *Tijdschr.
Effic. Docum.*, **18**, 228-34.

Diananda, P. H. 1949. 1369
Note on some properties of maximum likelihood
estimates. *Proc. Camb. Phil. Soc.*, **45**, 536-44.

Dice, L. R. 1945. 1370
Measures of the amount of ecologic association
between species. *Ecology*, **26**, 297-302.

Dice, L. R. 1948. 1371
Application of statistical methods, to the analysis of ecologic association between species of birds. *Amer. Midland Nat.*, **39**, 174-8.

Dick, I. D. 1947. 1372
A note on the correlation of products. *New Zealand J. Sci. Tech. A*, **29**, 75.

Dickerson, G. E. 1942. 1373
Experimental design for testing inbred lines of swine. *J. Animal Sci.*, **1**, 326-41.

Dickerson, P. M. 1945. 1373[a]
A new gaging method for quality control. *Tool & Die J.*, **10** (12), 132-4 (also: *Steel*, **116** (22), 105; 146).

Dickey, H. C. & Labarthe, P. 1945. 1374
Predicting the transmitting ability of young dairy sires for milk production, butterfat test and butterfat production. *J. Dairy Sci.*, **28**, 893-900.

Dietz, A. A. 1946. 1375
Composition of normal bone marrow in rabbits. *J. Biol. Chem.*, **165**, 505-11.

Dieudonné, J. 1947-8. 1376
Sur le théorème de Lebesgue-Nicodym. III. *Ann. Univ. Grenoble*, **23**, 25.

Dieulefait, C. E. 1940. 1377
On Thiele's semi-invariants and the conjugate Fourier function. (Spanish.) *An. Soc. Cient. Argent.*, **129**, 208-11.

Dieulefait, C. E. 1940. 1378
On a result of Prof. Beppo Levi and its relation to the problem of frequency surfaces. (Spanish.) *An. Soc. Cient. Argent.*, **129**, 249-53.

Dieulefait, C. E. 1941. 1379
Some new derivations of limiting probability functions. (Spanish.) *Rev. Cienc. Tucumán A*, **2**, 25-30.

Dieulefait, C. E. 1942. 1380
Note on a method of sampling. *Ann. Math. Statist.*, **13**, 94-7.

Dieulefait, C. E. 1942. 1381
On Slutsky's sinusoidal limit law, derived from a new sequence of random variables. (Spanish.) *An. Soc. Cient. Argent.*, **134**, 257-85.

Dieulefait, C. E. 1943. 1382
The multidimensional Gaussian distribution and its generalization. (Spanish.) *An. Soc. Cient. Argent.*, **136**, 193-215.

Dieulefait, C. E. 1944. 1383
Sobre la teoria de las muestras. *Rev. Fac. Cienc. Econ. Com. Pol.*, (4), **3** (1), 181-223.

Dieulefait, C. E. 1948. 1384
Sobre la inversion de limites y el prolongamiento analitico. *An. Soc. Cient. Argent.*, **146**, 379-90.

Dieulefait, C. E. 1949. 1385
Análisis estadístico de la significación de las diferencias entre dos o mas muestras que provienen de un universo gaussiano. *Rosario Fac. Cienc. Econ. Com. Pol. Inst. Estadíst.*, 24 pp.

Dieulefait, C. E. 1949. 1385[a]
Sobre el metodo de los momentos y su aplicacion al analisis de las series de tiempo. *Rev. Fac. Cienc. Econ.*, *Com. Pol.*, no. 57, 11 pp.

Dilger, J. 1940. 1386
Das Gauss'sche Streuungsgesetz in der praktischen Psychologie. *Industr. Psychol.*, **17**, 1-20.

Dilworth, R. P. 1949. 1387
Note on the strong law of large numbers. *Amer. Math. Monthly*, **56**, 249-50.

Dimond, A. E., Horsfall, A. G., Heuberger, J. W. 1388
& Stoddard, E. M. 1941.
Role of the dosage-response curve in the evaluation of fungicides. *Conn. Agric. Exper. Statist. Bull.*, **451**.

DiPaola, P. P. 1945. 1388[a]
Statistical quality control program. *Aero. Digest*, **50**, 107-13; 166-8.

DiPaola, P. P. 1945. 1389
Use of correlation in quality control. *Industr. Qual. Contr.*, **2** (1), 10-14.

Di Prima, S. 1948. 1390
Principate calcoli statistici ed applicazioni per le ricerche nel campo agrario. (Italian. English summary.) *Ann. Sper. Agr. N.S.*, **2** (5), 1-82.

Divatia, V. V. 1949. 1391
A note on sequential exponential tests. *J. Indian Soc. Agric. Statist.*, **2**, 86-93.

Divisia, F. 1940. 1392
A propos d'une étude statistique des contaminations tuberculeuses. (English summary.) *Rev. Int. Statist. Inst.*, **8**, 113-27.

Divisia, F. 1943. 1393
Essai de théorie statistique de la contagion et de la contamination donnant un critère de classification des maladies microbiennes au point de vue social et au point de vue individuel et, éventuellement, quelques directives pour l'étude scientifique de ces maladies. *Rev. Int. Statist. Inst.*, **11**, 150-69.

Divisia, F. 1949. 1394
Aspects de la technique des sondages statistiques dans le domaine social. *Bull. Int. Statist. Inst.*, **32** (2), 240-4.

Dixon, W. J. 1940. 1395
A criterion for testing the hypothesis that two samples are from the same population. *Ann. Math. Statist.*, **11**, 199-204.

Dixon, W. J. 1944. 1396
Further contributions to the problem of serial correlation. *Ann. Math. Statist.*, **15**, 119-44.

Dixon, W. J. 1948. 1397
Table of normal probabilities for intervals of various lengths and locations. *Ann. Math. Statist.*, **19**, 424-7.

Dixon, W. J. & Mood, A. M. 1946. 1398
The statistical sign test. *J. Amer. Statist. Ass.*, **41**, 557-66.

Dixon, W. J. & Mood, A. M. 1948. 1399
A method for obtaining and analyzing sensitivity data. *J. Amer. Statist. Ass.*, **43**, 109-26.

Dmitriev, N. A. & Dynkin, E. B. 1945. 1400
On the characteristic numbers of a stochastic matrix. *C. R. (Dokl.) Acad. Sci. URSS*, **49**, 159-62.

Dmitriev, N. & Dynkin, E. 1946. 1401
On characteristic roots of stochastic matrices. (Russian. English summary.) *Izv. Akad. Nauk SSSR, Ser. Mat.*, **10**, 167-84.

Doblin, V.   *See also* **Doeblin, W.**
Doblin, V.   1940.   1402
Éléments d'une théorie générale des chaînes simples constantes de Markoff. *Ann. Sci. Éc. Norm. Sup., Paris*, (3) **57**, 61-111.
Doblin, V.   1940.   1403
Sur des mouvements mixtes. *C. R. Acad. Sci., Paris,* **210**, 690-2.
Dobzhansky, T.   1945.   1404
Directly observable genetic changes in population of *Drosophila pseudoobscura*. *Biometrics Bull.*, **1**, 7-8.
Dobzhansky, T. & Levene, H.   1948.   1405
Genetics of natural populations. XVII. Proof of operation of natural selection in wild populations of *Drosophila pseudoobscura*. *Genetics*, **33**, 537-47.
Dobzhansky, T. & Wright, S.   1941.   1406
Genetics of natural populations. V. Relations between mutation rate and accumulation of lethals in populations of *Drosophila pseudoobscura*. *Genetics*, **26**, 23-51.
Dobzhansky, T. & Wright, S.   1943.   1407
Genetics of natural populations. X. Dispersion rates in *Drosophila pseudoobscura*. *Genetics*, **28**, 304-40.
Dodd, E. L.   1940.   1408
The substitutive mean and certain subclasses of this general mean. *Ann. Math. Statist.*, **11**, 163-76.
Dodd, E. L.   1941.   1409
The cyclic effects of linear graduations persisting in the differences of the graduated values. *Ann. Math. Statist.*, **12**, 127-36.
Dodd, E. L.   1941.   1410
Some generalizations of the logarithmic mean and of similar means of two variates which become indeterminate when the two variates are equal. *Ann. Math. Statist.*, **12**, 422-8.
Dodd, E. L.   1941.   1411
The problem of assigning a length to the cycle to be found in a simple moving average and in a double moving average of chance data. *Econometrica*, **9**, 25-37.
Dodd, E. L.   1942.   1412
Certain tests for randomness applied to data grouped into small sets. *Econometrica*, **10**, 249-57.
Dodd, E. L.   1942.   1413
A transformation of Tippett random sampling numbers into numbers normally distributed. *Bol. Mat. Buenos Aires*, **15**, 73-7.
Dodd, N. G.   1945.   1413a
Quality control and spot welding; application and value of statistical methods. *Aircraft Production*, **7**, 563-4.
Dodd, S. C.   1940.   1414
Analyses of the interelation matrix by its surface and structure. *Sociometry*, **3**, 133-43.
Dodd, S. C.   1949.   1415
On measuring languages. *J. Amer. Statist. Ass.*, **44**, 77-88.
Dodge, H. F.   1942.   1415a
Quality control. *Mech. Engng.*, **64**, 678.

Dodge, H. F.   1943.   1416
A sampling inspection plan for continuous production. *Ann. Math. Statist.*, **14**, 264-79 (also (1944): *Trans. Amer. Soc. Mech. Engrs.*, **66**, 127-33).
Dodge, H. F.   1947.   1417
Sampling plans for continuous production. *Industr. Qual. Contr.*, **4** (3), 5-9.
Dodge, H. F. & Romig, H. G.   1941.   1418
Single sampling and double sampling inspection tables. *Bell Syst. Tech. J.*, **20**, 1-61.
Doeblin, W.   *See also* **Doblin, V.**
Doeblin, W.   1940.   1419
Sur l'ensemble de puissances d'une loi de probabilité. (French. Ukrainian summary.) *Studia Math.*, **9**, 71-96. (Also (1947): *Ann. Sci. Éc. Norm. Sup., Paris*, (3) **63**, 317-50.)
Doeblin, W.   1940.   1420
Sur l'équation matricielle $A^{(t)+(s)} = [A^{(t)}A^{(s)}]$ et ses applications au calcul des probabilités. *Bull. Sci. Math.*, **64**, 35-7.
Doeblin, W.   1940.   1421
Sur l'équation de Kolmogoroff. *C. R. Acad. Sci., Paris*, **210**, 365-7.
Doeblin, W.   1940.   1422
Remarques sur la théorie métrique des fractions continues. *Compos. Math. Groningen*, **7**, 353-71.
Doeblin, W.   1942.   1423
Sur deux problèmes de M. Kolmogorov concernant les chaînes dénombrables. *Bull. Soc. Math. France*, **52**, 37-67.
Doi, T.   1948.   1424
A stochastic method for estimation of the survival rate. *Bull. Jap. Soc. Sci. Fish.*, **14**, 91-104.
Domb, C.   1946-7.   1425
The resultant of a large number of events of random phase. I, II. *Proc. Camb. Phil. Soc.*, **42**, 245-9; **43**, 587-9.
Domb, C.   1947.   1426
The problem of random intervals on a line. *Proc. Camb. Phil. Soc.*, **43**, 329-41.
Domb, C.   1948.   1427
Some probability distributions connected with recording apparatus. I. *Proc. Camb. Phil. Soc.*, **44**, 335-41.
Domb, C.   1949.   1428
Order-disorder statistics. I, II. *Proc. Roy. Soc. A*, **196**, 36-50; **199**, 199-221.
Dominguez, L. M.   1944.   1429
Comentarios sobre nuevas aplicaciones de la tecnica de las muestras. (English summary.) *Estadística*, **2**, 353-7.
Doob, J. L.   1940.   1430
The law of large numbers for continuous stochastic processes. *Duke Math. J.*, **6**, 290-306.
Doob, J. L.   1940.   1431
Regularity properties of certain families of chance variables. *Trans. Amer. Math. Soc.*, **47**, 455-86.
Doob, J. L.   1941.   1432
Probability as measure. *Ann. Math. Statist.*, **12**, 206-14; 215-17.

Doob, J. L. 1942. 1433
The Brownian movement and stochastic equations. *Ann. Math.*, (2) **43**, 351-69.

Doob, J. L. 1942. 1434
What is a stochastic process? *Amer. Math. Monthly*, **49**, 648-53.

Doob, J. L. 1942. 1435
Topics in the theory of Markoff chains. *Trans. Amer. Math. Soc.*, **52**, 37-64.

Doob, J. L. 1944. 1436
The elementary Gaussian processes. *Ann. Math. Statist.*, **15**, 229-82.

Doob, J. L. 1945. 1437
Markoff chains—denumerable case. *Trans. Amer. Math. Soc.*, **58**, 455-73.

Doob, J. L. 1947. 1438
Probability in function space. *Bull. Amer. Math. Soc.*, **53**, 15-30.

Doob, J. L. 1948. 1439
Asymptotic properties of Markoff transition probabilities. *Trans. Amer. Math. Soc.*, **63**, 393-421.

Doob, J. L. 1948. 1440
Renewal theory from the point of view of the theory of probability. *Trans. Amer. Math. Soc.*, **63**, 422-38.

Doob, J. L. 1949. 1441
Application of the theory of martingales. *Le calcul des probabilités et ses applications. Colloq. Int. Centre Nat. Rech. Sci.*, Paris, no. 13, 23-7.

Doob, J. L. 1949. 1442
Heuristic approach to the Kolmogorov-Smirnov theorems. *Ann. Math. Statist.*, **20**, 393-403.

Doob, J. L. 1949. 1443
Time series and harmonic analysis. *Proc. Berkeley Symp. Math. Statist. and Probab.*, 1945-6, pp. 303-43.

Doob, J. L. 1949. 1444
The transition from stochastic difference to stochastic differential equations. *Econometrica*, **17**, 68-70.

Doob, J. L. & Ambrose, W. 1940. 1445
On two formulations of the theory of stochastic processes depending upon a continuous parameter. *Ann. Math.*, (2) **41**, 737-45.

Doob, J. L. & Leibler, R. A. 1943. 1445a
On the spectral analysis of a certain transformation. *Amer. J. Math.*, **65**, 263-72.

Dor, L. 1943. 1445b
Sur la fonction caractéristique des schémas de Poisson et de Lexis. *Mém. Soc. Roy. Sci. Liège*, **1**, 211-49.

Dor, L. 1944. 1446
Quelques remarques sur les variables aléatoires combinées xy, $\sqrt{\alpha^2 x^2 + \beta^2 y^2}$. *Bull. Soc. Roy. Sci., Liège*, **13**, 203-9.

Dor, L. 1948. 1447
Analyse des phénomènes logistiques à l'aide de la courbe normale intégrale. *Bull. Inst. Rech. Écon. Soc.*, **14**, 597-621.

Dor, L. 1948. 1448
Économie et probabilité. *Bull. Tech. Soc. Roy. Belge Ing. Industr. A*, no. 5, 261-7.

Dore, P. 1940. 1449
Sulla valutazione degli errori accidentali di una livellazione di precisione. *R. C. Accad. Sci. Ist. Bologna*, **44**, 31-6.

Dorfman, R. 1943. 1450
The detection of defective members of large populations. *Ann. Math. Statist.*, **14**, 436-40.

Dorfman, R. I. & Rubin, B. L. 1947. 1451
Studies on the bio-assay of hormones: The assay of chorionic gonadotrophin from human pregnancy urine and serum. *Endocrinology*, **41**, 456-63.

Dorph-Petersen, K. 1942. 1452
Am Anlaeg Opgørelse af Markforsøg. (On the design and analysis of agricultural experiments.) *Ogeskrift Landmaend.*, **36 & 37**, 589-94, 605-8.

Dorph-Petersen, K. 1942. 1453
Fejlberegning på Forsøg med systematisk Parcelfordeling. (On the determination of mean errors for experiments with systematic arrangement of plots.) *Nord. Jordbr.Forskn.*, **24**, 140-50.

Dorph-Petersen, K. 1943. 1454
Some statistical investigations of the variation in the productivity of the soil. *K. Vet. Landb. Aarsskr.*, 1943, pp. 129-48.

Dorph-Petersen, K. 1944. 1455
Usikkerhenden på Jordbundsanalyser i Markforsøg. (On the determination of mean errors of soil-analysis in agricultural experiments.) *Tidskr. Plant.*, **48**, 358-66.

Dorph-Petersen, K. 1949. 1456
Parcelfordeling i Markforsøg. (Arrangements of plots in agricultural experiments.) *Tidskr. Plant.*, **52**, 111-75.

Doss, S. 1948. 1457
Sur la moyenne d'un élément aléatoire abstrait. *C. R. Acad. Sci., Paris*, **226**, 1418-19.

Doss, S. 1949. 1458
Sur la moyenne d'un élément aléatoire dans un espace distancié. *Bull. Sci. Math.*, **73** (2), 48-72.

Dos Santos Fernandes, L. 1949. 1459
Introdução na demografia de alguns conceitos de geometria das massas. *Bol. Inst. Atuár. Port.*, **4**, 7-13.

Douw, G. G. 1948. 1460
Verband tussen het aantal eindkiezers en het aantal verloren oproepen per maand. (Relation between the number of final selectors and the monthly number of lost calls.) *Het. P.T.T.Bedrijf*, **2**, 46-52.

Dove, W. F. 1943. 1461
The relative nature of human preference: with an example in the palatibility of different varieties of sweet corn. *J. Comp. Psychol.*, **35**, 219-26.

Dowdeswell, W. H., Fisher, R. A. & Ford, E. B. 1940. 1462
The quantitative study of populations in the Lepidoptera. 1. *Polyommatus icarus* Rott. *Ann. Eugen.*, **10**, 123-36.

Dowdeswell, W. H., Fisher, R. A. & Ford, E. B. 1949. 1463
The quantitative study of populations in the Lepidoptera. 2. *Maniola jurtina* L. *Heredity*, **3**, 67-84.

Dowell, A. A. & Engelman, G. 1949.   1464
Research into the problems involved in marketing slaughter livestock by carcass weight and grade. *J. Farm Econ.*, **31**, 343-69.

Dowker, Y. N. 1947.   1465
Invariant measure and the ergodic theorems. *Duke Math. J.*, **14**, 1051-61.

Down, E. E. & Thayer, J. W. 1942.   1466
Plot technic studies with navy beans. *J. Amer. Soc. Agron.*, **34**, 919-22.

Dozier, H. L. 1948.   1467
Estimating muskrat populations by house counts. *Trans. 13th North Amer. Wildlife Conf.*, **13**, 372-92.

Dresch, F. W. 1949.   1468
Continuous index numbers and quantitative study of the general economy. *Proc. Berkeley Symp. Math. Statist. and Probab.*, 1945-6, pp. 203-21.

Dressel, P. L. 1940.   1469
Some remarks on the Kuder-Richardson reliability coefficient. *Psychometrika*, **5**, 305-10.

Dressel, P. L. 1940.   1470
Statistical semi-invariants and their estimates with particular emphasis on their relation to algebraic invariants. *Ann. Math. Statist.*, **11**, 33-57.

Dressel, P. L. 1941.   1471
A symmetric method for obtaining unbiased estimates and expected values. *Ann. Math. Statist.*, **12**, 84-90.

Driscoll, R. L., Hodge, M. W. & Ruark, A. E.   1472
1940. An interval meter and its application to studies of Geiger counter statistics. *Rev. Sci. Instru.*, **11**, 241-50.

Dryden, H. L. 1943.   1473
A review of the statistical theory of turbulence. *Quart. Appl. Math.*, **1**, 7-42.

Du Bois, P. H. 1941.   1474
Some statistical operations on the counting sorter. *Psychometrika*, **6**, 383-90.

Du Bois, P. H. 1942.   1475
A note on the computation of biserial *r* in item validation. *Psychometrika*, **7**, 143-6.

Dubourdieu, J. 1947.   1476
Sur une généralisation d'un théorème de M. B. de Finetti et son application à la théorie collective du risque. *C. R. Acad. Sci., Paris*, **224**, 514-16.

Dubrovskii, V. M. 1940.   1477
Sur un problème limite de la théorie des probabilités. (Russian. French summary.) *Izv. Akad. Nauk SSSR, Ser. Mat.*, **4**, 411-16.

Dubrovskii, V. M. 1944.   1478
Investigation of purely discontinuous random processes by means of integro-differential equations. (Russian. English summary.) *Izv. Akad. Nauk SSSR, Ser. Mat.*, **8**, 107-28.

Dubrovskii, V. M. 1945.   1479
On purely discontinuous random processes with residual effect. *C. R. (Dokl.) Acad. Sci. URSS*, **47**, 79-81.

Dubrovskii, V. M. 1945.   1480
On a problem connected with purely discontinuous random processes. *C. R. (Dokl.) Acad. Sci. URSS*, **47**, 459-61.

Ducasse, C. J. 1941.   1481
Some observations concerning the nature of probability. *J. Philos.*, **38**, 393-403.

Dudding, B. P. 1942.   1482
Quality control in manufacture. *Nature*, **149**, 555.

Dudding, B. P. 1942.   1482ª
Sampling inspection; methods of applying statistical analysis for quality control. *Army Ordnance*, **32**, 109-13.

Dudding, B. P. 1942.   1482ᵇ
Sampling inspection and quality control. *J. Inst. Production Engrs.*, **21**, 13-62.

Dudding, B. P. 1944.   1482ᶜ
Statistical methods and the function of inspection in manufacturing industry. *Engng. Insp.*, **9** (4), 4-8.

Dudding, B. P. & Jennett, W. J. 1940.   1482ᵈ
Statistics and engineering practice. *J. Inst. Elect. Engrs*, **87**, 1-21 (also: *Gen. Elect. Co. J.*, **11** (3); *Machinery, London*, **55**, 696-701; **56**, 51-60).

Dudding, B. P. & Jennett, W. J. 1942.   1483
The application of statistical methods to quality control. *Brit. Stand. Inst.*, no. 600 R: 1942, 77 pp.

Dudding, B. P. & Jennett, W. J. 1942.   1484
Quality control charts. *Brit. Stand. Inst.*, B.S. 600R. 89 pp.

Dudding, B. P. & Jennett, W. J. 1942.   1484ª
Statistical control of repetition work. *Engineering, London*, **153**, 332-3; 433-4.

Dudding, B. P. & Jennett, W. J. 1944.   1484ᵇ
Quality Control chart technique when manufacturing to a specification: with special reference to articles machined to dimensional tolerances. *Gen. Elect. Co. Ltd., London*, iii+74 pp. (Also: *Gen. Elect. Co. J.*, **13**, 60-4.)

Dudding, B. P. & Jennett, W. J. 1945.   1484ᶜ
Quality control: Use of statistical methods in metallurgical industry. *Metal Ind.*, **66**, 130-3; 146-9.

Dudding, B. P. & Keen, J. 1949.   1485
Statistical methods and specifications. *Bull. Int. Statist. Inst.*, **32** (2), 39-47.

Dufrénoy, J. 1947   1485ª
Représentation rectilinéaire de distributions logarithmiques. *J. Soc. Statist. Paris*, **88**, 47-52.

Dufrénoy, J. & Dufrénoy, M.-L. 1948.   1486
La distribution des biens et des aptitudes. *J. Soc. Statist. Paris*, **89**, 321-33.

Dufrénoy, J. & Goyan, F. M. 1947.   1487
A graphical calculator for statistical analysis. *J. Amer. Pharm. Ass.*, **36**, 309-14.

Dugué, D. 1941.   1488
Sur quelques exemples de factorisation de variables aléatoires. *C. R. Acad. Sci., Paris*, **212**, 838-40.

Dugué, D. 1941.   1489
Sur un nouveau type de courbe de fréquence. *C. R. Acad. Sci., Paris*, **213**, 634-5.

Dugué, D. 1941.   1490
Sur certaines composantes des lois de Cauchy. *C. R. Acad. Sci., Paris*, **213**, 718-19.

Dugué, D. 1946.   1491
Un théorème de théorie des fonctions obtenu à partir de résultats de calcul des probabilités. *C. R. Acad. Sci., Paris,* **223,** 845.

Dumas, M. 1947.   1492
Le groupage des observations et les corrections qu'il nécessite dans le calcul des moments. *J. Soc. Statist. Paris,* **88,** 175-89.

Dumas, M. 1947.   1493
Sur une loi de probabilité à priori conduisant aux arguments fiduciaires de Fisher. *Rev. Sci., Paris,* **85,** 3-18.

Dumas, M. 1948.   1494
Sur les courbes de fréquence de K. Pearson. *Biometrika,* **35,** 113-17.

Dumas, M. 1948.   1495
L'introduction des probabilités dans les sciences concrètes. *J. Soc. Statist. Paris,* **89,** 435-43.

Dumas, M. 1949.   1496
Interprétation de résultats de tirages exhaustifs. *C. R. Acad. Sci., Paris,* **228,** 904-6 (erratum, 1264).

Dumas, M. 1949.   1496[a]
Interprétation statistique des épreuves sur prélèvement effectués dans l'industrie. *J. Soc. Statist. Paris,* **90,** 133-40.

Dumas, M. 1949.   1497
Rapport sur l'état des applications industrielles de la statistique en France. *Bull. Int. Statist. Inst.,* (Publ. 1950) **32** (2), 58-73.

Dumas, M. & Maheu, P. 1948.   1498
Les méthodes statistiques et leurs applications dans le domaine des techniques industrielles. *Mém. Artill. française,* **22,** 413-80; 837-967.

Dumitriu, A. 1942.   1499
Hasard et science. *Scientia,* **72** (9-10), 65-71.

Dumon, A. G. 1940.   1500
Correlatiestudie en genetisch onderzook bij kippen (Correlation studies and genetical investigations on chickens.) *Nat. Wetensch. Tijdschr.,* **21,** 393-9.

Dumontier, J. 1949.   1501
La comptabilité nationale et les corrélations. *Rev. Écon. Pol.,* **59,** 479-96.

Duncan, A. J. 1948.   1502
Detection of non-random variation when size of sample varies. *Industr. Qual. Contr.,* **4** (4), 9-12.

Duncan, W. J. 1944.   1503
Some devices for the solution of large sets of simultaneous linear equations. *Phil. Mag.,* (7) **35,** 660-70

Dunlap, J. W. 1940.   1504
Note on the computation of tetrachoric correlation. *Psychometrika,* **5,** 137-40.

Dunlap, J. W. 1941.   1505
Recent advances in statistical theory and applications. *Amer. J. Psychol.,* **54,** 583-601.

Dunn, C. G. 1944.   1506
Probability method applied to the analysis of recrystallization data. *Phys. Rev.,* (2) **66,** 215-20.

Dunn, H. K. & White, S. D. 1940.   1507
Statistical measurements on conversational speech. *J. Acoust. Soc. Amer.,* **11,** 278-88.

Dunn, J. W. 1942.   1507[a]
Quality control in Curtiss-Wright plants. *Aircraft Engng.,* **14,** 181.

Dunn, L. C. 1947.   1508
The effects of isolates on the frequency of a rare human gene. *Proc. Nat. Acad. Sci. U.S.A.,* **33,** 359-63.

Dunn, M. S., Murphy, E. A. & Rockland, L. B.   1509
1947. Optimal growth of the rat. *Physiol. Rev.,* **27,** 72-94.

Durand, D. 1943.   1510
A simple method for estimating the size distribution of a given aggregate income. *Rev. Econ. Statist.,* **25,** 227-30.

Durand, D. 1948.   1511
An appraisal of the errors involved in estimating the size distribution of a given aggregate income. *Rev. Econ. Statist.,* **30,** 63-8.

Durant, J. & Goldman, J. 1945.   1512
The distribution of working-class savings. *Bull. Oxford Inst. Statist.,* **7,** 1-7.

Durante, D. 1946.   1512[a]
Coordination of principles useful for estimating crop yields: Quantitative agroscopy. *Int. Rev. Agric.,* **37,** 33T-48T; 61T-74T.

Dütschler, H. 1945.   1513
Eine statistische Verifikation der Bernoullischen Hypothese über die Grenznutzenfunktion des Geldes. *Schweiz. Zeit. Volkswirtsch. Statist.,* **81,** 175-84.

Dvoretzky, A. 1949.   1514
On the strong stability of a sequence of events. *Ann. Math. Statist.,* **20,** 296-9.

Dvoretsky, A. & Motzkin, T. 1947.   1515
The asymptotic density of certain sets of real numbers. *Duke Math. J.,* **14,** 315-21.

Dvoretsky, A. & Motzkin, T. 1947.   1516
A problem of arrangements. *Duke Math. J.,* **14,** 305-13.

Dwight, T. W. 1943.   1516[a]
The statistical control of quality: The use of statistical methods in forestry. *Engng. J., Canada,* **26,** 400-1.

Dwinas, S. 1947.   1517
Una aplicación de la teoria de las muestras aleatorieas a la teoria de la integral. *Rev. Mat. Hisp.-Amer.,* (4) **7,** 234-8.

Dwinas, S. 1948.   1518
Una deducción de la ley de errores de Laplace-Gauss. *Rev. Mat. Hisp.-Amer.,* (4) **8,** 12-18.

Dwinas, S. 1948.   1519
Über gewisse Determinanten, die in der Statistik gebraucht werden. (Spanish.) *Mat. Elem., Madrid,* **8** (4), 79-80.

Dwyer, P. S. 1940.   1520
The calculation of correlation coefficients from ungrouped data with modern calculating machines. *J. Amer. Statist. Ass.,* **35,** 671-3.

Dwyer, P. S. 1940.   1521
The cumulative numbers and their polynomials. *Ann. Math. Statist.,* **11,** 66-71.

Dwyer, P. S. 1940. 1522
Combinatorial formulas for the rth standard moment of the sample sum, of the sample mean, and of the normal curve. *Ann. Math. Statist.*, **11**, 353-5.

Dwyer, P. S. 1940. 1523
The evaluation of multiple and partial correlation coefficients from the factorial matrix. *Psychometrika*, **5**, 211-32.

Dwyer, P. S. 1940. 1524
Summary of problems in the computation of statistical constants with sorting and tabulating machines. *Proc. Educ. Res. Forum*, 26-31 August 1940, *I.B.M. Corp., New York*.

Dwyer, P. S. 1941. 1525
The solution of simultaneous equations. *Psychometrika*, **6**, 101-29.

Dwyer, P. S. 1941. 1526
The evaluation of determinants. *Psychometrika*, **6**, 191-204.

Dwyer, P. S. 1941. 1527
The implicit evaluation of linear forms and the solution of simple matrix equations. *Psychometrika*, **6**, 355-65.

Dwyer, P. S. 1941. 1528
The skewness of the residuals in linear regression theory. *Ann. Math. Statist.*, **12**, 104-10.

Dwyer, P. S. 1941. 1529
The Doolittle technique. *Ann. Math. Statist.*, **12**, 449-58.

Dwyer, P. S. 1942. 1530
Grouping methods. *Ann. Math. Statist.*, **13**, 138-55.

Dwyer, P. S. 1942. 1531
Recent developments in correlation technique. *J. Amer. Statist. Ass.*, **37**, 441-60.

Dwyer, P. S. 1944. 1532
A matrix presentation of least squares and correlation theory with matrix justification of improved methods of solution. *Ann. Math. Statist.*, **15**, 82-9.

Dwyer, P. S. 1945. 1533
The square root method and its use in correlation and regression. *J. Amer. Statist. Ass.*, **40**, 493-503.

Dwyer, P. S. 1946. 1534
Simultaneous computation of correlation coefficient with missing variates. *Proc. Res. Forum, I.B.M. Corp., New York*, pp. 20-7.

Dwyer, P. S. 1949. 1535
Pearsonian correlation coefficients associated with least squares theory. *Ann. Math. Statist.*, **20**, 404-16.

Dwyer, P. S. & MacPhail, M. S. 1948. 1536
Symbolic matrix derivatives. *Ann. Math. Statist.*, **19**, 517-34.

Dynkin, E. B. 1949. 1537
On a problem of the theory of probability. (Russian.) *Usp. Mat. Nauk*, **4**, 5(33), 183-97.

Dyson, F. J. 1943. 1538
Note on kurtosis. *J. R. Statist. Soc.*, **106**, 360-1.

E

Eaton, H. C. 1947. 1538a
Machine accuracy analysis. *Industr. Qual. Contr.*, **3** (5), 10-12.

Ebel, R. L. 1947. 1538b
The frequency of errors in the classification of individuals on the basis of fallible test scores. *Educ. and Psychol. Measurement*, **7**, 725-34.

Eckler, A. R. & Staudt, E. P. 1943. 1539
Marketing and sampling uses of population and housing data. *J. Amer. Statist. Ass.*, **38**, 87-92.

Eddington, A. S. 1940. 1540
The correction of statistics for accidental error. *Monthly Not. Roy. Astr. Soc.*, **100**, 354-61.

Edelberg, V. 1940. 1541
Flexibility of the yield of taxation—some econometric investigations. *J. R. Statist. Soc.*, **103**, 153-90.

Edgerton, H. A. & Thomson, K. F. 1942. 1542
Test scores examined with Lexis ratio. *Psychometrika*, **7**, 281-8.

Edwards, A. L. 1946. 1543
A critique of " neutral " items in attitude scales constructed by the method of equal appearing intervals. *Psychol. Rev.*, **53**, 159-69.

Edwards, A. L. 1948. 1544
Note on the " correction for continuity " in testing the significance of the difference between correlated proportions. *Psychometrika*, **13**, 185-7.

Edwards, A. L. & Kenney, K. C. 1946. 1545
A comparison of the Thurstone and Lickert techniques of attitude scale construction. *J. Appl. Psychol.*, **30**, 72-83.

Edwards, A. L. & Kilpatrick, F. P. 1948. 1546
Scale analysis and the measurement of social attitudes. *Psychometrika*, **13**, 99-114.

Edwards, D. S. 1948. 1547
The constant frame of reference problem in sociometry. *Sociometry*, **11**, 372-9.

Edwards, G. D. 1942. 1547a
Quality control of munitions. The modern ounce of prevention applied to ordnance. *Army Ordnance*, **23**, 482-5.

Edwards, G. D. 1942. 1547b
Quality control procedures in ordnance inspection. *Mech. Engng.*, **64**, 673-5 (also (1943): *Engng. Insp.*, **8** (2), 29-33).

Edwards, G. D. 1946. 1547c
Post-war quality control. *Industr. Qual. Contr.*, **2** (4a), 2-3.

Edwards, J. C. & Bennett, W. A. 1943. 1548
Inspection efficiency. *Engng. Insp.*, **8** (4), 12-21 (also (1945): *Proc. Inst. Mech. Engrs.*, **152**, 69-75).

Edwards, L. 1948. 1549
The use of normal significance limits when the parent population is of Laplace form. *J. Inst. Actuar. Students' Soc.*, **8**, 87-99.

Edwards, T. I. 1942. 1550
The coding and tabulation of medical and research data for statistical analysis. *Public Health Rep.*, **57**, 7-21.

Egermayer, F. 1941. 1551
Dve kriteria k zjisteni systematickych odchylek v biometrickych souborech. (Deux critères pour l'établissement des déviations systématiques dans des ensembles biométriques.) *Statist. Obzor*, **22**, 23-46.

Egermayer, F. 1941. 1552
Náhodny vyber v representativní metode. (La sélection fortuite dans la méthode représentative.) (Czech. French and German summaries.) *Statist. Obzor*, **22**, 424-35.

Egermayer, F. 1943. 1553
Vliv odhadu hodnot na rozdělení četností. (Der Einfluss der Abschätzungen von Werten auf der Häufigkeitsverteilung.) *Statist. Obzor*, **24**, 85-98.

Egermayer, F. 1946. 1554
Zhodnocení roentgenových snímků. (Utilization of radiography.) *Statist. Obzor*, **26**, 121-9.

Egermayer, F. 1947. 1555
Rozpad krivek cetnosti. (Partage des courbes de fréquence.) (Czech. French, English and Russian summaries.) *Statist. Obzor*, **27**, 25-47.

Egermayer, F. 1949. 1556
Statisticky odhad. (L'estimation statistique.) (Czech. Russian, English and French summaries.) *Statist. Obzor*, **29**, 20-56.

Eggleton, P. & Kermack, W. O. 1944. 1557
A problem in the random distribution of particles. *Proc. Roy. Soc. Edin. A*, **62**, 103-15.

Egler, F. E. 1944. 1558
Some statistics of *Achras zapota* leaves, British Honduras. *Bull. Torrey Bot. Club*, **71**, 235-45.

Egudin, G. I. 1945. 1559
Parameters of distribution of a random variable invariant under translations, and algebraic semi-invariants. *C. R. (Dokl.) Acad. Sci. URSS*, **48**, 615-17.

Egudin, G. I. 1946. 1560
On an effective method of calculation of the mathematical expectations of central sample moments. *C. R. (Dokl.) Acad. Sci. URSS*, **53**, 487-90.

Egudin, G. I. 1947. 1561
On the stability of some very general classes of statistics. (Russian.) *Dokl. Akad. Nauk SSSR*, **57**, 115-17.

Egudin, G. I. 1947. 1562
Certain relations between the moments of the distribution of extreme values in random samples. (Russian.) *Dokl. Akad. Nauk SSSR*, **58**, 1581-4.

Eisenhart, C. 1947. 1563
The assumptions underlying the analysis of variance. *Biometrics*, **3**, 1-21.

Eisenhart, C. 1948. 1564
Some inventory problems. *Nat. Bur. Stand., Techn. Statist. Inference*, Rep. A2-2, 6 January 1948, 14 pp.

Eisenhart, C. 1949. 1565
Operational aspects of instrument design. *Science*, **110**, 343-6.

Eisenhart, C. 1949. 1566
Probability centerlines for standard deviation and range charts. *Industr. Qual. Contr.*, **6** (1), 24-6.

Eisenhart, C. & Wilson, P. W. 1943. 1567
Statistical methods and control in bacteriology. *Bact. Rev.*, **7**, 57-137.

Eisenhart, M. H. 1945. 1567[a]
Top management views quality control. *Industr. Qual. Contr.*, **1** (5), 3-5, 14.

Eisenschitz, R. 1944. 1568
Matrix theory of correlations in a lattice. I, II. *Proc. Roy. Soc. A*, **182**, 244-59; 260-9.

Eklund, B. 1942. 1569
A study of variations in annual growth rings at Malingsbo. *Svenska SkogsvFören. Tidsskr.*, **40**, 233-310.

Elderton, W. 1945. 1570
Cricket scores and some skew correlation distributions (an arithmetical study). *J. R. Statist. Soc.*, **108**, 1-11; 22-40.

Elderton, W. 1949. 1571
A few statistics on the length of English words. *J. R. Statist. Soc. A*, **112**, 436-45.

Elderton, W. & Ogborn, M. E. 1943. 1572
The mortality of adult males since the middle of the eighteenth century as shown by the experience of Life Assurance Companies. *J. R. Statist. Soc.*, **106**, 1-31.

Eldridge, H. T. & Siegel, J. S. 1946. 1573
The changing sex ratio in the United States. *Amer. J. Sociol.*, **52**, 224-34.

Elfving, G. 1946. 1574
On compound binomial processes. *Förs.mat. Stud. Filip Lundberg*, pp. 48-78.

Elfving, G. 1946. 1575
Contributions to the theory of integer-valued Markoff processes. *Skand. Aktuartidskr.*, **29**, 175-205.

Elfving, G. 1947. 1576
The asymptotical distribution of range in samples from a normal population. *Biometrika*, **34**, 111-19.

Elfving, G. 1947. 1577
On a class of elementary Markoff processes. *Proc. 10th Skand. Mat. Kongr. København*, 1946, pp. 149-59.

Elfving, G. 1947. 1578
The concept of mathematical probability. (Swedish.) *Elementa, Stockh.*, **30**, 19-33.

Elfving, G. 1947. 1579
A simple method of deducing certain distributions connected with multivariate sampling. *Skand. Aktuartidskr.*, **30**, 56-74.

Ellis, M. E. & Riopelle, A. J. 1948. 1580
An efficient punched card method of computing ΣX, ΣX^2, ΣXY and higher moments. *Psychometrika*, **13**, 79-85.

Ellson, D. G. 1940. 1581
A criticism of Dr. Pratt's use of Chapman's " Statistics of the method of correct matchings " in the evaluation of ESP in drawings. *J. Parapsychol.*, **4**, 329-36.

Elsdon-Dew, R. 1947. 1582
Statistical errors in counting blood cells. *Amer. J. Clin. Path.*, **17**, 575-9.

Emanuelli, F. 1949. 1582[a]
La ricerca " dell'optimum " nella distribuzione dei benefici delle assicurazioni sociali. *Riv. Ital. Demogr. Statist.*, **3**, (3-4), 93-7.

Emik, L. O. 1947. 1583
Statistical treatment of counts of trichostrongylid eggs. *Biometrics*, **3**, 89-93.

Emmens, C. W. 1940. 1584
The dose response relation for certain principles of the pituitary gland, and of the serum and urine of pregnancy. *J. Endocrinol.*, **2**, 194-225.

Emmert, E. M. 1939-40. 1585
Partial elimination of experimental error from data by the use of significance tests. *Proc. Amer. Soc. Hort. Sci.*, **37**, 272-8.

Emmett, W. G. 1949. 1586
Evidence of a space factor at 11+ and earlier. *Brit. J. Psychol. (Statist. Sec.)*, **2**, 3-16.

Emmett, W. G. 1949. 1587
Factor analysis by Lawley's method of maximum likelihood. *Brit. J. Psychol. (Statist. Sec.)*, **2**, 90-7.

Enders, T. & Stern, C. 1948. 1588
The frequencies of twins, relative to age of mothers, in American populations. *Genetics*, **33**, 263-72.

Engelfriet, J. 1943. 1589
Quelques formules actuarielles relatives à l'invalidité totale ou partielle par suite d'accident. (Dutch.) *Verzekerings-archief*, **24**, 145-61.

Engelhart, M. D. 1941. 1590
The analysis of variance and covariance techniques in relation to the conventional formulas for the standard error of a difference. *Psychometrika*, **6**, 221-33.

Enrick, N. L. 1945. 1590a
Operating characteristics of reject limits for measurements. *Industr. Qual. Contr.*, **2** (2), 9-10.

Enrick, N. L. 1947. 1591
Installing a quality control program. *Materials & Methods, New York*, **25** (3), 90-4.

Ensminger, M. E., Phillips, R. W., Schott, R. G. & Parsons, C. H. 1943. 1592
Measuring performance of progeny of rams in a small flock. *J. Animal Sci.*, **2**, 157-65.

Enters, J. H. 1948. 1592a
Mogelijkheden en moeilijkheden bij het toepassen van de sequentietest. (Possibilities and difficulties in applying sequential sampling.) (Dutch. English summary.) *Statistica Neerlandica*, **2**, 138-54.

Enters, J. H. 1948. 1593
De omvang van steekproef bij een enkel voudig steekproefsysteem. (Sample size for a single sampling scheme.) (Dutch. English summary.) *Statistica Neerlandica*, **2**, 228-34.

Enters, J. H. 1948. 1593a
De toepassing van statistische methoden bij kwaliteitsbeheersing en kwaliteits-contrôle. *Tijdschr. Effic. Docum.*, **18**, 262-6.

Epstein, A. 1947. 1594
Statistical analysis with hand-punched and sorted cards. *Amer. Statistician*, **1** (2), 6-7.

Epstein, B. 1944. 1594a
Quality control, a field for the mathematician. *J. Engng. Educ.*, **34**, 492-4.

Epstein, B. 1945. 1594b
Statistical control of assemblies eliminates selective fitting. *Amer. Machinist*, **89**, 126-7.

Epstein, B. 1947. 1595
The mathematical description of certain breakage mechanisms leading to the logarithmico-normal distribution. *J. Franklin Inst.*, **244**, 471-7.

Epstein, B. 1948. 1596
Some applications of the Mellin transform in statistics. *Ann. Math. Statist.*, **19**, 370-9.

Epstein, B. 1948. 1597
Application of the theory of extreme values in fracture problems. *J. Amer. Statist. Ass.*, **43**, 403-12.

Epstein, B. 1948. 1598
Estimates of mean life based on the rth smallest value in a sample of size n drawn from an exponential distribution. *Wayne Univ. Detroit, Mich., Dept. Math. Mimeo. Rep.* (Office of Naval Research Contract Nonr-451 (00) (NR) 042-017.)

Epstein, B. 1948. 1599
Statistical aspects of fracture problems. *J. Appl. Phys.*, **19**, 140-7.

Epstein, B. 1949. 1600
A modified extreme value problem. *Ann. Math. Statist.*, **20**, 99-103.

Epstein, B. 1949. 1601
The distribution of extreme values in samples whose members are subject to a Markoff chain condition. *Ann. Math. Statist.*, **20** 590-4 (correction: **22**, 133-4).

Epstein, B. & Brooks, H. 1948. 1602
The theory of extreme values and its implications in the study of the dielectric strength of paper capacitors. *J. Appl. Phys.*, **19**, 544-50.

Epstein, B. & Churchman, C. W. 1944. 1603
On the statistics of sensitivity data. *Ann. Math. Statist.*, **15**, 90-6.

Erdélyi, A. 1948. 1604
Transformations of hypergeometric functions of two variables. *Proc. Roy. Soc. Edin. A*, **62**, 378-85.

Erdös, P. 1942. 1605
On the law of the iterated logarithm. *Ann. Math.*, (2) **43**, 419-36.

Erdös, P. 1945. 1606
On a lemma of Littlewood and Offord. *Bull. Amer. Math. Soc.*, **51**, 898-902.

Erdös, P. 1949. 1607
On the strong law of large numbers. *Trans. Amer. Math. Soc.*, **67**, 51-6.

Erdös, P. 1949. 1608
On a theorem of Hsu and Robbins. *Ann. Math. Statist.*, **20**, 286-91 (addendum: **21**, 138).

Erdös, P. & Kac, M. 1940. 1609
The Gaussian law of errors in the theory of additive number theoretic functions. *Amer. J. Math.*, **62**, 738-42.

Erdös, P. & Kac, M. 1946. 1610
On certain limit theorems of the theory of probability. *Bull. Amer. Math. Soc.*, **52**, 292-302.

Erdös, P. & Kac, M. 1947. 1611
On the number of positive sums of independent random variables. *Bull. Amer. Math. Soc.*, **53**, 1011-20.

Erdös, P. & Kaplansky, J. 1946. 1611ª
The asymptotic number of Latin rectangles. *Amer. J. Math.*, **68**, 230-6.

Erdös, P., Feller, W. & Pollard, H. 1949. 1612
A property of power series with positive coefficients. *Bull. Amer. Math. Soc.*, **55**, 201-4.

Erickson, R. O. & Stehn, J. B. 1945. 1613
A technique for analysis of population density data. *Amer. Midland Nat.*, **33**, 781-7.

Erlee, T. J. D. 1943. 1614
Two problems in statistical variation based on 203 blank experiments, harvested in 1931, on sugar cane in Java. *Landbouwk. Tidjdschr., Wageningen*, **55**, 660-8.

Esnault-Pelterie, R. 1947. 1615
Remarques sur une formule usuelle. *C. R. Acad. Sci., Paris*, **224**, 1404-7; 1462-4.

Esnault-Pelterie, R. 1947. 1616
Sur la répartition des produits d'un ensemble de fécondations avec croisements libres. *C. R. Acad. Sci., Paris*, **224**, 1796-9; **225**, 14-16.

Esseen, C.-G. 1942. 1617
On the Liapounoff limit of error in the theory of probability. *Ark. Mat. Astr. Fys.*, **28A** (9), 19 pp.

Esseen, C.-G. 1943. 1618
Determination of the maximum deviation from the Gaussian law. *Ark. Mat. Astr. Fys.*, **29A**, (20), 10 pp.

Esseen, C.-G. 1945. 1619
Fourier analysis of distribution functions. A mathematical study of the Laplace-Gaussian law. *Acta Math., Stockh.*, **77**, 1-125.

Etherington, I. M. H. 1941. 1620
Non-associative algebra and the symbolism of genetics. *Proc. Roy. Soc. Edin. B*, **61**, 24-42.

Eudey, M. W. 1949. 1621
On the treatment of discontinuous random variables. *Univ. Calif. Berkeley Statist. Lab., ONR Project* NR-042-036, Tech. Rep. no. 13.

Eugene, S. A. 1943. 1622
New light on factor analysis. *J. Farm Econ.*, **25**, 477-86.

Evangelisti, G. 1942. 1623
Sopra le rappresentazioni statistiche dei regimi fluviali. *L'Energia Elettrica*, **19**, 57-66.

Evans, U. R. 1945. 1624
Statistical methods in deciding the efficacy of a modification in technical procedure. The use of the *t*-test to chemists and engineers. *Chemistry & Industry*, **1945** (14), 106-9.

Evans, W. D. 1940. 1625
Note on the moments of a binomially distributed variate. *Ann. Math. Statist.*, **11**, 106-7.

Evans, W. D. 1942. 1626
The standard error of percentiles. *J. Amer. Statist. Ass.*, **37**, 367-76.

Everett, C. J. & Ulam, S. 1948. 1627
Multiplicative systems. I, II, III. *Los Alamos Declassified Documents*, nos. 533, 534 (A.E.C.D. 2164, 2165) and 707. (Part I also in: *Proc. Nat. Acad. Sci. U.S.A.*, **34**, 403-5.)

Eyraud, H. 1941. 1628
Sur l'aléatoire fermée à une dimension. *Ann. Univ. Lyon A*, (3) **4**, 61-3.

Eysenck, H. J. & Crown, S. 1949. 1629
An experimental study in opinion-attitude methodology. *Int. J. Opinion & Attitude Res.*, **3**, 47-86.

Ezekiel, M. 1943. 1630
Choice of the dependent variable in regression analysis —comments. *J. Amer. Statist. Ass.*, **38**, 214-16.

Ezekiel, M. 1944. 1631
The statistical determination of the investment schedule. *Econometrica*, **12**, 89-90.

F

Faesi, M. 1940. 1632
Über die Glättung statistischer Verteilungsreihen. *Mitt. Ver. Schweiz. Versich.-Math.*, **40**, 61-84.

Fagerholt, G. & Hald, A. 1948. 1633
A few remarks on the application of statistical methods in industry. *Nord. Tidskr. Teknisk. Økonomi*, **37**, 83-8.

Fairfield, H. H. 1942. 1633ª
Statistical methods as aid to control of foundry operations. *Amer. Foundrymen's Ass.*, **50**, 611-36 (also: *Canad. Metals & Metall. Industr.*, **5**, 194-200).

Fairfield, H. H. 1943. 1634
Statistical analysis of inspection results. *Engng. J. Canada*, **26**, 492-501.

Fairfield, H. H. 1945. 1634ª
New management method for industrial processes: reducing defective material and inspection time by statistical quality control. *Canadian Metals & Metall. Industr.*, **8**, 32-6.

Fairfield, H. H. 1947. 1634ᵇ
An aid to revision of quality control chart limits. *Industr. Qual. Contr.*, **3** (4), 22-3.

Fairfield Smith, H. *See* **Smith, H. Fairfield.**

Falconer, D. S. 1947. 1635
Sensory thresholds for solutions of phenyl-thio-carbamide. Results of tests on a large sample made by R. A. Fisher. *Ann. Eugen.*, **13**, 211-22.

Faleschini, L. 1947. 1636
Sulla valutazione probabilistica delle diversità fra costanti statistiche. *G. Economisti.*, **6**, 379-418.

Faleschini, L. 1948. 1637
Alcuni criteri di normalità della distribuzioni statistiche. *G. Economisti*, **7**, 63-80.

Faleschini, L. 1948. 1638
Indici di connessione. (Italian. French and English summaries.) *Univ. Cattolica Milano, Contrib. Lab. Statist.*, **21**, 112-51.

Faleschini, L. 1948. 1639
Su alcune proprietà dei momenti impiegati nello studio della variabilità, asimmetria e curtosi. *Statistica, Milano*, **8**, 503-13.

Ky Fan. 1944. 1640
Sur l'approximation et l'intégration des fonctions aléatoires. *Bull. Soc. Math. France*, **72**, 97-117.

Ky Fan. 1944. 1641
Conditions d'existence de suites illimitées d'événements correspondant à certaines probabilités données. *Rev. Sci., Paris*, **82**, 235-40.

Ky Fan. 1944. 1642
Entfernung zweier zufälligen Grössen und die Konvergenz nach Wahrscheinlichkeit. *Math. Zeit.*, **49**, 681-3.

Ky Fan. 1944. 1643
Sur l'extension de la formule générale d'interpolation de M. Borel aux fonctions aléatoires. *C. R. Acad. Sci., Paris*, **218**, 260-2.

Ky Fan. 1944. 1644
Un théorème général sur les probabilités associées à un système d'événements dépendants. *C. R. Acad. Sci., Paris*, **218**, 380-2.

Ky Fan. 1944. 1645
Une définition descriptive de l'intégrale stochastique. *C. R. Acad. Sci., Paris*, **218**, 953-5.

Ky Fan. 1945. 1646
Généralisations du théorème de M. Khintchine sur la validité de la loi des grands nombres pour les suites stationnaires de variables aléatoires. *C. R. Acad. Sci., Paris*, **220**, 102-4.

Ky Fan. 1946. 1646[a]
On positive definite sequences. *Ann. Math.*, (2) **47**, 593-607.

Faragó, P. S. & Takács, L. 1949. 1647
The probability distribution of the number of secondary electrons. *Acta Phys. Acad. Sci. Hung.*, **1** (6), 43-52.

Farnell, A. B. 1944. 1648
Limits for the characteristic roots of a matrix. *Bull. Amer. Math. Soc.*, **50**, 789-94.

Farnsworth, P. R. 1945. 1649
Attitude scale construction and the method of equal appearing intervals. *J. Psychol.*, **20**, 245-8.

Fauré-Fremiet, E. 1944. 1650
Étude biométrique de quelques Trichodines. *Bull. Soc. Zool. France*, **68**, 158-69.

Faustino, D. G. 1947. 1651
Variation of the specific gravity of Bagtikan (*Parashora plicata*) from nine provinces of the Philippines. *Philipp. J. Forestry*, **5**, 7-21.

Fay, E. 1948. 1652
Grouping of observations for fitting regression curves. *U.S. Naval Ordnance Test Sta., Inyokern, Calif., Navord Rep.* 1057 (Nots 177), vi+30 pp.

Feather, N. 1943. 1653
On the statistics of random distributions of paired events, with applications to the results obtained in the use of the interval selector with particle counters. *Proc. Camb. Phil. Soc.*, **39**, 84-99.

Feather, N. 1949. 1654
The theory of counting experiments using pulsed sources: chance coincidences and counting-rate losses. *Proc. Camb. Phil. Soc.*, **45**, 648-59.

Feder, D. D. 1947. 1654[a]
Estimation of test item difficulty by averaging highest and lowest quarter performances compared with total population count. *Educ. and Psychol. Measurement*, **7**, 133-4.

Federer, W. T. 1949. 1655
The general theory of prime-power lattice designs. III. The analysis for p^3 varieties in blocks of p plots with more than 3 replicates. *Biometrics*, **5**, 144-61.

Federer, W. T. & Sprague, G. F. 1947. 1656
A comparison of variance components in corn yield trials: I. Error, tester×line, and line components in top-cross experiments. *J. Amer. Soc. Agron.*, **39**, 453-63.

Federici, N. 1945. 1657
Applicazioni pratiche dei vari metodi di eliminazione. *Atti 6ta. Riun. Sci., Soc. Ital. Statist.*, pp. 100-16.

Feibleman, J. 1945. 1657[a]
Pragmatism and inverse probability. *Phil. & Phenom. Res.*, **5**, 309-15.

Fejes Toth, L. & Hadwiger, H. 1947. 1658
Mittlere Trefferzahlen und geometrische Wahrscheinlichkeiten. *Experientia*, **3**, 366-9.

Feldheim, E. 1940. 1659
Sul rapporto fra la media dei quadrati di più errori e il quadrato della media dei loro valori assoluti. *Atti Accad. Sci. Torino, Cl.Sci. Fis. Mat. Nat.*, **75**, 296-305.

Feldheim, E. 1941. 1660
Nouvelle démonstration et généralisation d'un théorème du calcul des probabilités dû à Simmons. *J. Math. Pures Appl.*, (9) **20**, 1-16.

Feller, W. 1940. 1661
On the integro-differential equations of purely discontinuous Markoff processes. *Trans. Amer. Math. Soc.*, **48**, 488-515 (correction: **58**, 474).

Feller, W. 1940. 1662
On the logistic law of growth and its empirical verifications in biology. *Acta Biotheor. A*, **5**, 51-66.

Feller, W. 1940. 1663
Statistical aspects of ESP. *J. Parapsychol.*, **4**, 271-98.

Feller, W. 1940. 1664
On the time distribution of so-called random events. *Phys. Rev.*, (2) **57**, 906-8.

Feller, W. 1941. 1665
On the integral equation of renewal theory. *Ann. Math. Statist.*, **12**, 243-68.

Feller, W. 1943. 1666
On A. C. Aitken's method of interpolation. *Quart. Appl. Math.*, **1**, 86-7.

Feller, W. 1943. 1667
On a general class of "contagious" distributions. *Ann. Math. Statist.*, **14**, 389-400.

Feller, W. 1943. 1668
The general form of the so-called law of the iterated logarithm. *Trans. Amer. Math. Soc.*, **54**, 373-402.

Feller, W. 1943. 1669
Generalization of a probability limit theorem of Cramér. *Trans. Amer. Math. Soc.*, **54**, 361-72.

Feller, W. 1945. 1670
The fundamental limit theorems in probability. *Bull. Amer. Math. Soc.*, **51**, 800-32. (Spanish version (1948): *Rev. Mat. Hisp.-Amer.*, (4) **8**, 95-132.)

Feller, W. 1945. 1671
Note on the law of large numbers and "fair" games. *Ann. Math. Statist.*, **16**, 301-4.

Feller, W. 1945.   1672
On the normal approximation to the binomial distribu-
tion. *Ann. Math. Statist.*, **16**, 319-29 (correction: **21**,
301-2).

Feller, W. 1946.   1673
The law of the iterated logarithm for identically
distributed random variables. *Ann. Math.*, (2) **47**,
631-8.

Feller, W. 1946.   1674
A limit theorem for random variables with infinite
moments. *Amer. J. Math.*, **68**, 257-62.

Feller, W. 1948.   1675
On the Kolmogorov-Smirnov limit theorems for
empirical distributions. *Ann. Math. Statist.*, **19**,
177-89 (correction: **21**, 301-2).

Feller, W. 1948.   1676
On probability problems in the theory of counters.
Studies and Essays presented to R. Courant, pp.
105-15.

Feller, W. 1949.   1677
Fluctuation theory of recurrent events. *Trans. Amer.
Math. Soc.*, **67**, 98-119.

Feller, W. 1949.   1678
On the theory of stochastic processes, with particular
reference to applications. *Proc. Berkeley Symp.
Math. Statist. and Probab.*, 1945-6, pp. 403-32.

Fenwick, D. W. & Franklin, M. T. 1942.   1679
Identification of Heterodera species by larval length.
Technique for estimating the constants determining
the length variations within a given species. *J.
Helminthol.*, **20**, 67-114.

Féraud, L. 1941.   1680
Le renouvellement, quelques problèmes connexes et
les équations intégrales du cycle fermé. *Mitt. Ver.
Schweiz. Versich.-Math.*, **41**, 81-93.

Féraud, L. 1942.   1681
Critères statistiques applicables à un petit nombre
d'observations. *C. R. Séances Soc. Phys. Hist.
Nat., Genève*, **59**, 116-18.

Féraud, L. 1942.   1682
Problème d'analyse statistique à plusieurs variables.
Ann. Univ. Lyon A, (3) **5**, 42-53.

Féraud, L. 1943.   1683
Statistique mathématique: Distributions de produits
intérieurs. *C. R. Séances Soc. Phys. Hist. Nat.,
Genève*, **60**, 196-200, 296.

Féraud, L. 1945.   1684
Les notions de loi et d'hypothèse probabilistes. *Arch.
Sci. Phys. Nat., Genève*, **27**, 191-208.

Féraud, L. 1945.   1685
Paramètre ignorable dans une loi de probabilité.
C. R. Séances Soc. Phys. Hist. Nat., Genève, **62**,
58-61.

Féraud, L. 1946.   1686
Sur les distributions à projection indépendante du
paramètre. *C. R. Acad. Sci., Paris*, **222**, 1272-3.

Féraud, L. 1948.   1687
À propos de l'enquête internationale sur l'estima-
tion des paramètres. *J. Soc. Statist. Paris*, **89**,
506-7.

Féraud, L. 1949.   1688
Induction amplifiante et inférence statistique. *Dialec-
tica*, **3**, 127-52.

Féraud, L. 1949.   1689
Loi probabilitaire complètement formulée et familles
d'intervalles de confiance. *Schweiz. Zeit. Volkwirtsch.
Statist.*, **85**, 296-304.

Ferber, R. 1946.   1689[a]
The disproportionate method of market sampling.
J. Business, **19**, 67-75.

Ferguson, G. A. 1940.   1690
A bi-factor analysis of reliability coefficients. *Brit. J.
Psychol.*, **31**, 172-82.

Ferguson, G. A. 1941.   1691
The application of Sheppard's correction for grouping.
Psychometrika, **6**, 21-7.

Ferguson, G. A. 1941.   1692
The factorial interpretation of test difficulty. *Psycho-
metrika*, **6**, 323-9.

Ferguson, G. A. 1942.   1693
Item selection by the constant process. *Psychometrika*,
7, 19-29.

Ferguson, G. A. 1949.   1694
On the theory of test discrimination. *Psychometrika*,
14, 61-8.

Ferguson, L. W. 1940.   1694[a]
The measurement of primary social attitudes, *J.
Psychol.*, **10**, 199-205.

Ferguson, L. W. 1941.   1695
A study of the Likert technique of attitude scale
construction. *J. Soc. Psychol.*, **13**, 51-7.

Ferguson, L. W. & Lawrence, W. R. 1942.   1696
An appraisal of the validity of the factor loadings
employed in the construction of the Primary Social
Attitude scales. *Psychometrika*, **7**, 135-8.

Fernandez, B. O. 1946.   1697
Contribution to the study of Pearson's χ^2. *Rev. Mat.
Hisp.-Amer.*, (4) **6**, 66-83.

Féron, R. 1947.   1698
Mérites comparés des divers indices de corrélation.
J. Soc. Statist. Paris, **88**, 328-52.

Ferraby, J. G. 1945.   1699
Planning a mass observation investigation. *Amer. J.
Sociol.*, **51**, 1-6.

Ferrand, J. & Fortet, R. 1947.   1700
Sur des suites arithmétiques équiréparties. *C. R.
Acad. Sci., Paris*, **224**, 516-18.

Ferrari, E. 1940-1.   1701
On Bertrand's paradox. (Spanish.) *Rev. Union Mat.
Argent.*, **7**, 1-6; 74-80. (Also (1941): *Union Mat.
Argent. Publ.*, **19**, 15 pp.)

Ferrell, E. B. 1945.   1702
Statistical methods in the development of apparatus
life quality. *Trans. Amer. Inst. Elect. Engrs.*, **64**, 700-3.

Ferrell, E. B. 1946.   1702[a]
Life quality prediction by statistical methods. *Machine
Design*, **18**, 141-4.

Ferrieu, F. 1943.   1703
Étude sur les mesures liées des grandeurs; problème
des moyennes. *Rev. Sci., Paris*, **81**, 203-16.

Ferris, C. D., Grubbs, F. E. & Weaver, C. L.   1704
1946. Operating characteristics for the common statistical tests of significance. *Ann. Math. Statist.*, **17**, 178-97.

Festinger, L. 1943.   1705
An exact test of significance for means of samples drawn from populations with an exponential frequency distribution. *Psychometrika*, **8**, 153-60.

Festinger, L. 1943.   1706
A statistical test for means of samples from skew populations. *Psychometrika*, **8**, 205-10.

Festinger, L. 1943.   1707
Studies in decision. I. Decision-time, relative frequency of judgement and subjective confidence as related to physical stimulus difference. II. An empirical test of a quantitative theory of decision. *J. Exper. Psychol.*, **32**, 291-306; 411-23.

Festinger, L. 1946.   1708
The significance of difference between means without reference to the frequency distribution function. *Psychometrika*, **11**, 97-105.

Festinger, L. 1947.   1709
The treatment of qualitative data by " scale analysis ". *Psychol. Bull.*, **44**, 149-61.

Festinger, L. 1949.   1710
The analysis of sociograms using matrix algebra. *Human Relations*, **2**, 153-8.

Feynman, R. P. 1948.   1711
Space-time approach to non relativistic quantum mechanics. *Rev. Mod. Phys.*, **20**, 367-87.

Field, J. M. 1946.   1712
Machine utilization and economical assignment. *Fact. Mgmt.*, **104**, 288-96.

Fieller, E. C. 1940.   1713
The biological standardization of insulin. *J. R. Statist. Soc. Suppl.*, **7**, 1-64.

Fieller, E. C. 1944.   1714
A fundamental formula in the statistics of biological assay and some applications. *Quart. J. Pharm.*, **17**, 117-23.

Fieller, E. C. 1947.   1715
The general autoregressive series. *Boulton Paul Aircraft Ltd., Wolverhampton, Tech. Rep.* no. 50.

Fieller, E. C. 1947.   1716
Some remarks on the statistical background in bioassay. *Analyst*, **72**, 37-43.

Fierro del Rio, L. 1943.   1717
Calculo de la cifra media y de los valores limites normales du un grupo de mediciones biólogicas. *Rev. Esc. Med. Mil.*, **2**, 27-33.

File, Q. W. 1945.   1717[a]
A machine method for computing the critical ratio of the difference between means. *J. Educ. Psychol.*, **36**, 184-6.

Fine, N. J. & Niven, I. 1944.   1718
The probability that a determinant be congruent to a (mod m). *Bull. Amer. Math. Soc.*, **50**, 89-93.

Finkner, A. L., Morgan, J. J. & Monroe, R. J.   1719
1943. Methods of estimating farm employment from sample data in North Carolina. *North Carolina Agric. Exper. Sta. Tech. Bull.*, **75**, 35 pp.

Finney, D. J. 1940.   1720
The detection of linkage. I. *Ann. Eugen.*, **10**, 171-214.

Finney, D. J. 1941.   1721
The detection of linkage. II. Further mating types; scoring of Boyd's data. III. Incomplete parental testing. *Ann. Eugen.*, **11**, 10-30; 115-32.

Finney, D. J. 1941.   1722
On the distribution of a variate whose logarithm is normally distributed. *J. R. Statist. Soc. Suppl.*, **7**, 155-61.

Finney, D. J. 1941.   1723
The joint distribution of variance ratios based on a common error mean square. *Ann. Eugen.*, **11**, 136-40.

Finney, D. J. 1941.   1724
Wireworm populations and their effect on crops. *Ann. Appl. Biol.*, **28**, 282-95.

Finney, D. J. 1942.   1725
The analysis of toxicity tests on mixtures of poisons. *Ann. Appl. Biol.*, **29**, 82-94.

Finney, D. J. 1942.   1726
Examples of the planning and interpretation of toxicity tests involving more than one factor. *Ann. Appl. Biol.*, **29**, 330-2.

Finney, D. J. 1942.   1727
The detection of linkage. IV. Lack of parental records and the use of empirical estimates of information. *J. Heredity*, **33**, 157-60.

Finney, D. J. 1942.   1728
The detection of linkage. V. Supplementary tables. VI. The loss of information from incompleteness of parental records. *Ann. Eugen.*, **11**, 224-32; 233-44.

Finney, D. J. 1943.   1729
The detection of linkage. VII. Combination of data from matings of known and unknown phase. *Ann. Eugen.*, **12**, 31-43.

Finney, D. J. 1943.   1730
The statistical treatment of toxicological data relating to more than one dosage factor. *Ann. Appl. Biol.*, **30**, 71-9.

Finney, D. J. 1944.   1731
The application of probit analysis to the results of mental tests. *Psychometrika*, **9**, 31-40.

Finney, D. J. 1944.   1732
The application of the probit method to toxicity test data adjusted for mortality controls. *Ann. Appl. Biol.*, **31**, 68-74.

Finney, D. J. 1944.   1733
Mathematics of biological assay. *Nature*, **153**, 284.

Finney, D. J. 1945.   1734
The microbiological assay of vitamins: The estimate and its precision. *Quart. J. Pharm.*, **18**, 77-82.

Finney, D. J. 1945.   1735
Some orthogonal properties of the 4×4 and 6×6 Latin squares. *Ann. Eugen.*, **12**, 213-20.

Finney, D. J. 1945.   1736
The fractional replication of factorial arrangements. *Ann. Eugen.*, **12**, 291-301 (correction: **15**, 276).

Finney, D. J. 1946.   1737
The analysis of a factorial series of insecticidal tests. *Ann. Appl. Biol.*, **33**, 160-6.

Finney, D. J. 1946. 1738
Field sampling for the estimation of wireworm populations. *Biometrics Bull.*, **2**, 1-6.

Finney, D. J. 1946. 1739
The frequency distribution of deviates from means and regression lines in samples from a multivariate normal population. *Ann. Math. Statist.*, **17**, 344-9.

Finney, D. J. 1946. 1740
Latin squares of the sixth order. *Experientia*, **2**, 404-5.

Finney, D. J. 1946. 1741
Orthogonal partitions of the 5×5 Latin squares. *Ann. Eugen.*, **13**, 1-3.

Finney, D. J. 1946. 1742
Orthogonal partitions of the 6×6 Latin squares. *Ann. Eugen.*, **13**, 184-96.

Finney, D. J. 1946. 1743
Recent developments in the design of field experiments. I. Split-plot confounding. II. Unbalanced split-plot confounding. III. Fractional replication. *J. Agric. Sci.*, **36**, 56-62; 63-8; 184-91 (errata, III: *Ann. Eugen.*, **15**, 276).

Finney, D. J. 1946. 1744
Standard errors of yields adjusted for regression on an independent measurement. *Biometrics Bull.*, **2**, 53-5.

Finney, D. J. 1947. 1745
The adjustment of biological assay results for variation in concomitant observations. *J. Hyg., Camb.*, **45**, 397-406.

Finney, D. J. 1947. 1746
Application of statistical methods to food problems. *Nature*, **159**, 36-7.

Finney, D. J. 1947. 1747
The construction of confounding arrangements. *Emp. J. Exper. Agric.*, **15**, 107-12.

Finney, D. J. 1947. 1748
Errors of estimation in inverse sampling. *Nature*, **160**, 195-6.

Finney, D. J. 1947. 1749
The estimation from individual records of the relationship between dose and quantal response. *Biometrika*, **34**, 320-34.

Finney, D. J. 1947. 1750
The principles of biological assay. *J. R. Statist. Soc. Suppl.*, **9**, 46-91.

Finney, D. J. 1947. 1751
The significance of associations in a square point lattice. *J. R. Statist. Soc. Suppl.*, **9**, 99-103.

Finney, D. J. 1947. 1752
Statistical aspects of microbiological assays. *Biochem. J.*, **41**, 5-7.

Finney, D. J. 1947. 1753
Statistical science and agricultural research. *Math. Gaz.*, **31** (293), 21-30.

Finney, D. J. 1947. 1754
Volume estimation of standing timber by sampling. *Forestry*, **21**, 179-203.

Finney, D. J. 1948. 1755
The estimation of gene frequency from family records. I. Factors without dominance. II. Factors with dominance. *Heredity*, **2**, 199-218; 369-89.

Finney, D. J. 1948. 1756
The Fisher-Yates significance test in 2×2 contingency tables. *Biometrika*, **35**, 145-56.

Finney, D. J. 1948. 1757
The inevitability of statistics. *Analyst*, **73**, 2-6.

Finney, D. J. 1948. 1758
Main effects and interactions. *J. Amer. Statist. Ass.*, **43**, 566-71.

Finney, D. J. 1948. 1759
Random and systematic sampling in timber surveys. *Forestry*, **22**, 64-99.

Finney, D. J. 1948. 1760
Transformation of frequency distributions. *Nature*, **162**, 898.

Finney, D. J. 1949. 1761
The adjustment for a natural response rate in probit analysis. *Ann. Appl. Biol.*, **36**, 187-95.

Finney, D. J. 1949. 1762
The choice of a response metameter in bioassay. *Biometrics*, **5**, 261-72.

Finney, D. J. 1949. 1763
The efficiency of enumerations. I. Volume estimation of standing timber by sampling. II. Random and systematic sampling in timber surveys. *Dehra Dun, Indian Forest Res. Inst., Indian Forest Bull.*, no. 146, 61 pp.

Finney, D. J. 1949. 1764
The estimation of the frequency of recombinations. I. Matings of known phase. *J. Genet.*, **49**, 159-76.

Finney, D. J. 1949. 1765
A method of estimating frequencies. *Biometrika*, **36**, 233-4.

Finney, D. J. 1949. 1766
The estimation of the parameters of tolerance distributions. *Biometrika*, **36**, 239-56 (correction: **39**, 439).

Finney, D. J. 1949. 1767
The truncated binomial distribution. *Ann. Eugen.*, **14**, 319-28.

Finney, D. J. & Palca, H. 1949. 1768
The elimination of bias due to edge effects in forest sampling. *Forestry*, **23**, 31-47.

Finney, D. J. & Stevens, W. L. 1948. 1769
A table for the calculation of working probits and weights in probit analysis. *Biometrika*, **35**, 191-201.

Finney, K. F. & Yamazaki, W. T. 1946. 1770
Water retention capacity as an index of the loaf volume potentialities and protein quality of hard red winter wheat. *Cereal Chem.*, **23**, 416-27.

Finsler, P. 1945. 1771
Über die Wahrscheinlichkeit seltener Erscheinungen. *Experientia*, **1**, 56-7.

Finsler, P. 1947. 1772
Über die mathematische Wahrscheinlichkeit. *Elemente Math.*, **2**, 108-14.

Finucan, H. M. 1948. 1773
Sheppards' correction to the variance. *J. Inst. Actuar. Students' Soc.*, **8**, 100-3.

Fippin, E. O. 1941. 1774
The objectives and methods of field plot fertilizer tests and a proposed improvement of methods. *Proc. Amer. Soil Sci. Soc.*, **5**, 274-80.

Fischer, C. H. 1942.   1775
A sequence of discrete variables exhibiting correlation due to common elements. *Ann. Math. Statist.*, **13**, 97-101.

Fischer, E. 1942.   1776
Das Zinsfussproblem der Lebensversicherungsrechnung als Interpolationsaufgabe. *Mitt. Ver. Schweiz. Versich.-Math.*, **42**, 205-307.

Fischer, O. 1947.   1777
Nekteré vztahy mezi faktorovou analysou a theorii mnohonásobne a dilci korelace. (Quelques rapports entre l'analyse factorielle (factor analysis) et la théorie de la corrélation multiple et partielle.) (Czech. English, French and Russian summaries.) *Statist. Obzor*, **27**, 48-71.

Fischer, O. 1949.   1778
Diskriminační analysa a hodnocení zkoušek schopností. (Discriminatory analysis and the weighting of the results of psychological measurements.) *Statist. Obzor*, **29**, 106-29.

Fisher, I. 1941.   1779
Mathematical method in the social sciences. *Econometrica*, **9**, 185-97.

Fisher, J. C. & Holloman, J. H. 1947.   1780
A statistical theory of fracture. *Metals Technology*, **14**, 1-16.

Fisher, R. A. 1940.   1781
On the similarity of the distributions found for the test of significance in harmonic analysis, and in Stevens's problem in geometrical probability. *Ann. Eugen.*, **10**, 14-17.

Fisher, R. A. 1940.   1782
An examination of the different possible solutions of a problem in incomplete blocks. *Ann. Eugen.*, **10**, 52-75.

Fisher, R. A. 1940.   1783
The estimation of the proportion of recessives from tests carried out on a sample not wholly unrelated. *Ann. Eugen.*, **10**, 160-70.

Fisher, R. A. 1940.   1784
A note on fiducial inference. *Ann. Math. Statist.*, **10**, 383-8.

Fisher, R. A. 1940.   1785
The precision of discriminant functions. *Ann. Eugen.*, **10**, 422-9.

Fisher, R. A. 1941.   1786
The theoretical consequences of polyploid inheritance for the mid style form of *Lythrum Salicaria*. *Ann. Eugen.*, **11**, 31-8.

Fisher, R. A. 1941.   1787
Average excess and average effect of a gene substitution. *Ann. Eugen.*, **11**, 53-63.

Fisher, R. A. 1941.   1788
The asymptotic approach to Behrens's integral with further tables for the *d* test of significance. *Ann. Eugen.*, **11**, 141-72.

Fisher, R. A. 1941.   1789
The interpretation of experimental fourfold tables. *Science*, **94**, 210-11.

Fisher, R. A. 1941.   1790
The negative binomial distribution. *Ann. Eugen.*, **11**, 182-7.

Fisher, R. A. 1942.   1791
New cyclic solutions to problems in incomplete blocks. *Ann. Eugen.*, **11**, 290-9 (correction: Completely orthogonal 9×9 squares: a correction. **11**, 402-3).

Fisher, R. A. 1942.   1792
The likelihood solution of a problem in compounded probabilities. *Ann. Eugen.*, **11**, 306-7.

Fisher, R. A. 1942.   1793
The theory of confounding in factorial experiments in relation to the theory of groups. *Ann. Eugen.*, **11**, 341-53.

Fisher, R. A. 1942.   1794
Some combinatorial theorems and enumerations connected with the numbers of diagonal types of a Latin square. *Ann. Eugen.*, **11**, 395-401.

Fisher, R. A. 1943.   1795
Note on Dr. Berkson's criticism of tests of significance. *J. Amer. Statist. Ass.*, **38**, 103-4.

Fisher, R. A. 1943.   1796
Statistical analysis of initial and final weights. *Vet. Rec.*, **55**, 3-4.

Fisher, R. A. 1943.   1797
A theoretical distribution for the apparent abundance of different species. *J. Anim. Ecol.*, **12**, 54-8.

Fisher, R. A. 1944.   1798
Allowance for double reduction in the calculation of genotype frequencies with polysomic inheritance. *Ann. Eugen.*, **12**, 169-71.

Fisher, R. A. 1945.   1799
The logical inversion of the notion of the random variable. *Sankhyā*, **7**, 129-32.

Fisher, R. A. 1945.   1800
A new test for 2×2 tables. *Nature*, **156**, 388.

Fisher, R. A. 1945.   1800a
Recent progress in experimental design. *L'application du calcul des probabilités*, Colloquium held at Geneva, 12-15 July, 1939. (Inst. Int. de Coopération Intellectuelle.)

Fisher, R. A. 1945.   1801
A system of confounding for factors with more than two alternatives, giving completely orthogonal cubes and higher powers. *Ann. Eugen.*, **12**, 283-90.

Fisher, R. A. 1946.   1802
A system of scoring linkage data with special reference to the pied factors in mice. *Amer. Nat.*, **80**, 568-78.

Fisher, R. A. 1946.   1802a
Testing the difference between two means of observations of unequal precision. *Nature*, **158**, 713-14.

Fisher, R. A. 1946-7.   1803
The fitting of gene frequencies to data on rhesus reactions. *Ann. Eugen.*, **13**, 150-5; 223-4.

Fisher, R. A. 1947.   1804
The analysis of covariance method for the relation between a part and the whole. *Biometrics Bull.*, **3**, 65-8.

Fisher, R. A. 1947.   1805
Development of the theory of experimental design. *Proc. 25th. Session Int. Statist. Inst. Conf. Washington, D.C.,* 1947 (Publ. 1951), **3A**, 434-9.

Fisher, R. A. 1947.   1805[a]
Number of self-sterility alleles. *Nature,* **160**, 797-8.

Fisher, R. A. 1947.   1806
The Rhesus factor. *Amer. Scientist,* **35**, 95-103.

Fisher, R. A. 1947.   1807
The theory of linkage in polysomic inheritance. *Phil. Trans. Roy. Soc. B,* **233**, 55-82.

Fisher, R. A. 1948.   1808
Conclusions fiduciaires. *Ann. Inst. H. Poincaré,* **10**, 191-213.

Fisher, R. A. 1948.   1808[a]
Modern genetics. *Brit. Sci. News,* **1** (10), 2-4.

Fisher, R. A. 1948.   1809
A quantitative theory of genetic recombination and chiasma formation. *Biometrics,* **4**, 1-13.

Fisher, R. A. 1949.   1810
A biological assay of tuberculins. *Biometrics,* **5**, 300-11.

Fisher, R. A. 1949.   1810[a]
Note on the test of significance for differential viability in frequency data from a complete three point test. *Heredity,* **3**, 215-19.

Fisher, R. A. 1949.   1810[b]
A preliminary linkage test with *agouti* and *undulated* mice. I. The fifth linkage group. *Heredity,* **3**, 229-41.

Fisher, R. A. 1949.   1811
A theoretical system of selection for homostyle *primula. Sankhyā,* **9**, 325-42.

Fisher, R. A. & Dugué, D. 1948.   1812
Un résultat assez inattendu d'arithmétique des lois de probabilité. *C. R. Acad. Sci., Paris,* **227**, 1205-6.

Fisher, R. A. & Ford, E. B. 1947.   1813
The spread of a gene in natural conditions in a colony of the moth *Panaxia dominula* L. *Heredity,* **1**, 143-74.

Fisher, R. A. & Holt, S. B. 1944.   1813[a]
The experimental modification of dominance in Danforth's short-tailed mutant mice. *Ann. Eugen.,* **12**, 102-20.

Fisher, R. A. & Mather, K. 1943.   1814
The inheritance of style length in " *lythrum salicaria* ". *Ann. Eugen.,* **12**, 1-23.

Fisher, R. A. & Race, R. R. 1946.   1815
Rh gene frequencies in Britain. *Nature,* **157**, 48-9.

Fisher, R. A., Corbet, A. S. & Williams, C. B.   1816
1943. The relation between the number of species and the number of individuals in a random sample of an animal population. *J. Animal Ecol.,* **12**, 42-58.

Fisher, R. A., Lyon, M. F. & Owen, A. R. G.   1817
1947. The sex chromosome in the house-mouse. *Heredity,* **1**, 355-65.

Fiske, D. W. & Dunlap, J. W. 1945.   1818
A graphical test for the significance of differences between frequencies from different samples. *Psychometrika,* **10**, 225-9.

Fix, E. 1949.   1819
Distributions which lead to linear regressions. *Proc. Berkeley Symp. Math. Statist. and Probab.,* 1945-6, pp. 79-91.

Fix, E. 1949.   1820
Tables of noncentral χ^2. *Univ. Calif. Publ. Statist.,* **1** (2), 15-19.

Flanagan, J. C. 1941.   1821
Statistical methods related to test construction and evaluation. *Rev. Educ. Res.,* **11**, 109-30.

Flaskämper, P. 1943-4.   1822
Die Rolle der Schätzung in der Statistik. *Allg. Statist. Arch.,* **32**, 33-50.

Flavel, T. 1946.   1822[a]
Statistical methods in correspondence. *Chem. & Industr.,* **51**, 454.

Fleisch, A. & Posternak, J. 1943.   1823
Standard curves of dark adaptation and their evaluation. *Helvetica Phys. Acta,* **1**, 421-36.

Fleisch, A. & Tripod, J. 1942.   1824
Die Berechnung von Mittelwerten in der Biologie. *Arch. Exper. Path. Pharmak.,* **200**, 135-45.

Flood, M. M. 1940.   1825
A computational procedure for the method of principal components. *Psychometrika,* **5**, 169-72.

Flood, M. M. 1940.   1826
Recursive methods in business-cycle analysis. *Econometrica,* **8**, 333-53.

Foerster, R. E. & Ricker, W. E. 1941.   1827
The effect of reduction of predacious fish on survival of young sockeye salmon at Cultus Lake *J. Fish. Res. Bd. Canada,* **5**, 315-36.

Fog, D. 1948.   1828
The geometrical method in the theory of sampling. *Biometrika,* **35**, 46-54.

Fog, D. 1949.   1829
Om den Gaussiske Fejlkurve. (On the Gaussian frequency curve.) *Mat. Tidsskr. A,* **1949**, 25-34.

Fogh, I. F. 1943.   1830
Sampling methods in log scaling. *For. Chron.,* **19**, 127-38.

Földes, B. 1940.   1831
Statisztika és akaratszabadság. (Statistique et libre arbitre.) (Hungarian.) *Magyar Statist. Szemle,* **18** (6), 494-7.

Folsom, D. 1942.   1832
Sample size and reliability. *Amer. Potato J.,* **19**, 197-9.

Forsaith, C. C. 1943.   1833
Statistics for foresters. *Tech. Bull. N.Y. State Coll. For.,* **16**, 1-69.

Forster, C. I. K. 1947.   1834
An elementary introduction to the testing of statistical hypotheses. *J. Inst. Actuar. Students' Soc.,* **7**, 81-97.

Forsyth, E. & Katz, L. 1946.   1835
A matrix approach to the analysis of sociometric data: Preliminary report. *Sociometry,* **9**, 340-7.

Forsythe, G. E. 1943.   1836
Cesàro summability of independent random variables. *Duke Math. J.,* **10**, 397-428.

Forsythe, G. E. 1947.   1837
On Nörlund summability of random variables to zero. *Bull. Amer. Math. Soc.*, **53**, 302-13.

Fortet, R. 1940.   1838
Sur une suite également répartie. (French. Ukrainian summary.) *Studia Math.*, **9**, 54-70. (Also: *Rev. Sci., Paris*, **78**, 298-9.)

Fortet, R. 1941.   1839
Sur des fonctions aléatoires définies par leurs équations aux dérivées partielles. *C. R. Acad. Sci., Paris*, **212**, 325-6.

Fortet, R. 1941.   1840
Sur le calcul de certaines probabilités d'absorption. *C. R. Acad. Sci., Paris*, **212**, 1118-20.

Fortet, R. 1941.   1841
Sur la notion de fonction aléatoire. *Rev. Sci., Paris*, **79**, 135-9.

Fortet, R. 1941.   1842
Sur la résolution des équations paraboliques linéaires. *C. R. Acad. Sci., Paris*, **213**, 553-6.

Fortet, R. 1943.   1843
Les fonctions aléatoires du type de Markoff associées à certaines équations linéaires aux dérivées partielles du type parabolique. *J. Math. Pures Appl.*, (9) **22**, 177-243.

Fortet, R. 1944.   1844
Calcul des moments d'une fonction de répartition à partir de sa caractéristique. *Bull. Sci. Math.*, **68**, 117-31.

Fortet, R. 1948.   1845
Sur la probabilité de perte d'un appel téléphonique dans un group de *x* sélecteurs commandés par un orienteur unique. *C. R. Acad. Sci., Paris*, **226**, 159-61.

Fortet, R. 1948.   1846
Sur la probabilité de perte d'un appel téléphonique. *C. R. Acad. Sci., Paris*, **226**, 1502-4.

Fortet, R. 1949.   1847
Probabilité de perte d'un appel téléphonique, régime non stationnaire. Influence du temps d'orientation et due groupement des linges. *Le calcul des probabilités et ses applications. Colloq. Int. Centre Nat. Rech. Sci., Paris*, **13**, 105-13.

Fortet, R. 1949.   1848
Quelques travaux récents sur le mouvement brownien. *Ann. Inst. H. Poincaré*, **11**, 175-226.

Foster, A. A. 1940.   1849
A perception ratio statistic for ESP tests. *J. Parapsychol.*, **4**, 320-4.

Foster, G. A. R. 1946.   1850
Some instruments for the analysis of time-series and their application to textile research. *J. R. Statist. Soc. Suppl.*, **8**, 42-61; 85-97.

Fougstedt, G. 1947.   1851
Statistikens rationalisering. *Mercator. Helsingfors.*, **42** (11), 158-9.

Fourie, J. C. 1947.   1852
Sampling, graphical representation and block valuation. *J. Chem. Metall. Mining Soc., South Africa*, **48** (5), 129-48.

Fowler, F. J., Jr. & Caldwell, N. J. 1945.   1853
On fatigue failure under triaxial static and fluctuating stresses and a statistical explanation of size effect. *Trans. Amer. Soc. Mech. Engrs.*, **67**, 213-16.

Foy, T. D. 1946.   1853[a]
Applying quality control effectively. *Machine Design*, **18** (11), 127-30.

Foy, T. D. 1947.   1853[b]
Organization of quality control as a management tool. *Elect. Engng.*, **66**, 483-6.

Fracker, S. B. & Brischle, H. A. 1944.   1854
Measuring the local distribution of tribes. *Ecology*, **25**, 283-303.

Frame, J. S. 1945.   1855
Mean deviation of the binomial distribution. *Amer. Math. Monthly*, **52**, 377-9.

Franchetti, S. 1943.   1856
Probabilità di errore nelle distribuzioni di Poisson. *Comment. Pontif. Acad. Sci.*, **7**, 697-708.

Francis, V. J. 1946.   1857
On the distribution of the sum of *n* sample values drawn from a truncated normal population. *J. R. Statist. Soc., Suppl.*, **8**, 223-32.

Franck, R. E. 1944.   1857[a]
Controlling quality of resistance-thermometer bulbs. *Gen. Elect. Rev.*, **47**, 42-7.

Franckx, E. 1945.   1858
L'évolution des collectivités. *Mitt. Ver. Schweiz. Versich.-Math.*, **45**, 279-88. (Also (1949): *Bull. Ass. Actuair. Belg.*, **51**, 31-40.)

Franckx, E. 1949.   1859
Sur les probabilités d'arrivée des événements en nombre infini. *Skand. Aktuartidskr.*, **32**, 7-14.

Frankel, E. 1948.   1860
Novy spôsob vypocítania parabolickej trendovej ciary a korelácie. (A new method of mathematical treatment of parabolic trend lines and correlation.) Czech. English summary.) *Statist. Obzor*, **28**, 391-444.

Frankel, L. R. & Stock, J. S. 1942.   1861
On the sample survey of unemployment. *J. Amer. Statist. Ass.*, **37**, 77-80.

Fränz, K. 1940.   1862
Beiträge zur Berechnung des Verhältnisses von Signalspannung zu Rauschspannung am Ausgang von Empfängern. *Elekt. Nach. Technik*, **17**, 215-30.

Fränz, K. 1941.   1863
Die Übertragung von Rauschspannungen über den linearen Gleichrichter. *Zeit. Hoch. Elekt.*, **57**, 146-51.

Fraser, D. A. S. 1949.   1864
Generalized hit probabilities with a Gaussian target. *Princeton, New Jersey*, ii+62 pp.

Frear, D. E. H. 1945.   1865
Punched cards in correlation studies. *Chem. Engng. News*, **23**, 2077.

Fréchet, M. 1940.   1866
Comparaison des diverses mesures de la dispersion. (English summary.) *Rev. Int. Statist. Inst.*, **8**, 1-12.

Fréchet, M. 1940. 1867
Conditions d'existence de systèmes d'événements associés à certaines probabilités. *J. Math. Pures Appl.*, **19**, 51-62.

Fréchet, M. 1940. 1868
Sur quelques contributions aux fondements de la théorie des probabilités. *Scripta Math.*, **7**, 110-12.

Fréchet, M. 1940. 1869
Sur quelques idées modernes dans la théorie des probabilités. (French. Russian summary.) *Trudy Sred. Asia. Gos. Univ. Ser. V-a* **32**, 8 pp.

Fréchet, M. 1940. 1870
Sur une limitation très générale de la dispersion de la médiane. *J. Soc. Statist. Paris*, **81**, 67-78.

Fréchet, M. 1941. 1871
Sur la corréspondance entre certaines lois d'erreurs et certaines définitions de la distance. *Rev. Sci., Paris*, **79**, 3-14.

Fréchet, M. 1941. 1872
Sur une définition descriptive de la valeur moyenne et sur un mode nouveau d'introduction de l'intégrale de Stieltjes dans l'enseignement du calcul des probabilités. (English summary.) *Rev. Int. Statist. Inst.*, **9**, 113-21.

Fréchet, M. 1941. 1873
Les fonctions asymptotiquement presque périodiques. *Rev. Sci., Paris*, **79**, 337-40. (Also: *C.R.Acad. Sci., Paris*, **213**, 520-2.)

Fréchet, M. 1941. 1874
Une application des fonctions asymptotiquement presque périodiques à l'étude des familles de transformations ponctuelles et du problème ergodique. *Rev. Sci., Paris*, **79**, 341-54; 407-17.

Fréchet, M. 1941. 1875
Sur la loi de répartition de certaines grandeurs géographiques *J. Soc. Statist. Paris*, **82**, 115-23.

Fréchet, M. 1941. 1876
Sur une loi de probabilité considérée par J. F. Steffensen. *Skand. Aktuartidskr.*, **24**, 214-20.

Fréchet, M. 1941. 1877
Sur la théorème ergodique de Birkhoff. *C. R. Acad. Sci., Paris*, **212**, 607-9.

Fréchet, M. 1942. 1878
La médiane d'un petit nombre de variables aléatoires et sa dispersion. (English summary.) *Rev. Int. Statist. Inst.*, **10**, 139-51.

Fréchet, M. 1943. 1879
Sur une expression simple approchée de la loi de probabilité des erreurs d'observations. *J. Soc. Statist. Paris*, **84**, 52-70.

Fréchet, M. 1943. 1880
Sur l'extension de certaines évaluations statistiques au cas de petits échantillons. (English summary.) *Rev. Int. Statist. Inst.*, **11**, 182-205.

Fréchet, M. 1943. 1881
Valeurs moyennes attachées à un triangle aléatoire. *Rev. Sci., Paris*, **81**, 475-82.

Fréchet, M. 1944. 1882
L'intégrale abstraite d'une fonction abstraite d'une variable abstraite et son application à la moyenne d'un élément aléatoire de nature quelconque. *Rev. Sci., Paris*, **82**, 483-512.

Fréchet, M. 1944. 1883
Les systèmes d'événements et le jeu des recontres. *Rev. Mat. Hisp.-Amer.*, (4) **4**, 95-126.

Fréchet, M. 1945. 1884
Nouveaux essais d'explication de la répartition des revenus. (English summary.) *Rev. Int. Statist. Inst.*, **13**, 16-32.

Fréchet, M. 1946. 1885
Les définitions courantes de la probabilité. *Rev. Philos.*, **136**, 129-69.

Fréchet, M. 1946. 1886
Dégager les possibilités et les limites de l'application des sciences mathématiques (et en particulier du calcul des probabilités) à l'étude des phénomènes économiques et sociaux (première enquête scientifique). *Rev. Int. Statist. Inst.*, **14**, 16-51. (Also: *Proc. 25th. Session Int. Statist. Inst. Conf. Washington D.C.*, 1947, **3A**, 284-8.)

Fréchet, M. 1946. 1887
Fondements des méthodes statistiques d'estimation. *Portug. Math.*, **5**, 137-41.

Fréchet, M. 1946. 1888
Nouvelles définitions de la valeur moyenne et des valeurs équiprobables d'un nombre aléatoire. *Ann. Univ. Lyon A*, (3) **9**, 5-26.

Fréchet, M. 1946-8. 1889
A general method of constructing correlation indices. *Proc. Math. Phys. Soc. Egypt*, **3**, 13-20 (addendum: 73-4).

Fréchet, M. 1947. 1890
Anciens et nouveaux indices de corrélation. Leur application au calcul des retards économiques. *Econometrica*, **15**, 1-30 (errata: 374-5).

Fréchet, M. 1947. 1891
Definition of the probable deviation. *Ann. Math. Statist.*, **18**, 288-90.

Fréchet, M. 1947. 1892
The general relation between the mean and the mode for a discontinuous variate. *Ann. Math. Statist.*, **18**, 290-3.

Fréchet, M. 1947. 1893
Sur les expressions analytiques de la mortalité valables pour la vie entière. *J. Soc. Statist. Paris*, **88**, 261-85.

Fréchet, M. 1947. 1894
Les espaces abstraits et leur utilité en statistique théorique et même en statistique appliquée. *J. Soc. Statist. Paris*, **88**, 410-21.

Fréchet, M. 1947. 1895
Rapport sur une enquête internationale relative à l'estimation statistique des paramètres. *Proc. 25th. Session Int. Statist. Inst. Conf., Washington D.C.*, 1947 (Publ. 1951), **3A**, 363-422.

Fréchet, M. 1948. 1896
Le coefficient de connexion statistique de Gini-Salvemini. *Mathematica Timişoara*, **23**, 46-51.

Fréchet, M. 1948. 1897
Les éléments aléatoires de nature quelconque dans un espace distancié. *Ann. Inst. H. Poincaré*, **10**, 215-310.

Fréchet, M. 1948.   1898
Sur l'estimation statistique. *Ann. Soc. Polon. Mat.*, **21**, 207-13.

Fréchet, M. 1948.   1899
La notion de différentielle sur un groupe abélien. *Portug. Mat.*, **7**, 59-73.

Fréchet, M. 1948.   1900
Sur une nouvelle définition des positions typiques d'un element aléatoire abstrait *C. R. Acad. Sci., Paris*, **226**, 1419-20.

Fréchet, M. 1948.   1901
Positions typiques d'un élément aléatoire de nature quelconque. *Ann. Sci. Éc. Norm. Sup., Paris*, (3) **65**, 211-37.

Fréchet, M. 1948.   1902
On two new chapters of the calculus of probability. *Math. Mag.*, **22**, 1-12.

Fréchet, M. 1948.   1903
Les valeurs typiques d'ordre nul ou infini d'un nombre aléatoire. *Rev. Int. Statist. Inst.*, **16**, 1-22.

Fréchet, M. 1949.   1904
Avant-propos. *Le calcul des probabilités et ses applications. Colloq. Int. Centre Nat. Rech. Sci., Paris*, **13**, 5-10.

Fréchet, M. 1949.   1905
Sur l'estimation statistique. *Ann. Soc. Polon. Math.*, **21** (1948), 207-13.

Fréchet, M. 1949.   1906
Statistical self-renewing aggregates. (English. Arabic summary.) *Fouad I University Press, Cairo*, v+126+6 pp.

Fréchet, M. 1949.   1907
Les valeurs typiques d'order nul ou infini d'un nombre aléatoire et leur généralisation. *Le calcul des probabilités et ses applications. Colloq. Int. Centre Nat. Rech. Sci., Paris*, **13**, 47-51.

Freeman, H. 1944.   1908
Sequential analysis of statistical data: Applications. *Columbia Univ. Rep. Statist. Res. Group, Appl. Maths. Panel. Nat. Defence Res. Commun.*

Freeman, H. A. 1945.   1909
Sequential sampling inspection for attributes. *Industr. Qual. Contr.*, **2** (2), 3-7.

Frenkel, J. I. & Kontorova, T. A. 1943.   1910
A statistical theory of the brittle strength of real crystals. (English.) *Zh. Fiz. Akad. Nauk SSSR* (English edition), **7**, 108-14.

Frenkiel, F. N. 1946.   1911
Étude statistique de la turbulence: corrélation et spectres dans un écoulement homogène. *C. R. Acad. Sci., Paris*, **222**, 367-9.

Frenkiel, F. N. 1946.   1912
Études statistiques de la turbulence: corrélations et spectres dans un écoulement de turbulence homogène et isotrope. *C. R. Acad. Sci., Paris*, **222**, 473-5.

Frenkiel, F. N. 1946.   1913
Étude statistique de la turbulence; théorie de la mesure de la turbulence avec un seul fil chaud non compensé. *C. R. Acad. Sci., Paris*, **222**, 585-7.

Frenkiel, F. N. 1946.   1914
Étude statistique de la turbulence; théorie de la mesure de la corrélation avec deux fils chauds non compensés. *C. R. Acad. Sci., Paris*, **222**, 1377-8.

Frenkiel, F. N. 1946.   1915
Étude statistique de la turbulence: théorie de la mesure de l'intensité de la turbulence avec un fil chaud de longeur non négligeable. *C. R. Acad. Sci., Paris*, **222**, 1474-6.

Frenkiel, F. N. 1948.   1916
O.N.E.R.A. (Paris), Rep. Tech., 34.

Frenkiel, F. N. 1948.   1917
On the kinematics of turbulence. *J. Aero. Sci.*, **15**, 57-64.

Frenkiel, F. N. 1949.   1918
United States Naval Ordnance Lab., NOLR 1136, 67 pp.

Freudenberg, K. 1945-6.   1919
Zur Ausgleichung doppelt abgestufter Sterbetafeln. *Verzekerings-archief*, **26**, 69-100.

Freudenthal, A. M. 1946.   1920
The statistical aspect of fatigue of materials. *Proc. Roy. Soc. A*, **187**, 416-29.

Friede, G. & Münzner, H. 1948.   1921
Zur Maximalkorrelation. *Zeit. angew. Math. Mech.*, **28**, 158-60.

Friedman, B. 1949.   1922
A simple urn model. *Comm. Pure Appl. Math.*, **2**, 59-70.

Friedman, M. 1940.   1923
A comparison of alternative tests of significance for the problem of m rankings. *Ann. Math. Statist.*, **11**, 86-92.

Friedman, M. & Savage, L. J. 1948.   1924
The utility analysis of choices involving risk. *J. Polit. Econ.*, **56**, 279-304.

Frisch, R. 1947.   1925
The Neyman-Pearson theory of testing hypotheses. *Univ. Oslo, Inst. Socialøkon. Memo.*, 3 pp.

Frisch, R. 1948.   1926
Converging dyadic approximations by means of partially unknown elements. *Univ. Oslo, Inst. Socialøkon. Memo.*, 13 pp.

Frisch, R. 1949.   1927
On the zeros of homogeneous functions. *Econometrica*, **17**, 28-9.

Frisch, R. & Sverdrup, E. 1948.   1928
The cleavings of a univariate measurement into two factors. *Univ. Oslo, Inst. Socialøkon. Memo.*, 23 May 1948, 7 pp.

Fritzchel, F. 1942.   1929
Unfallstatistik der Einzelunternehmung. Wie verfolge ich meine Unfallkosten? *Hoch- und Tiefbau*, **25**, 211-12.

Frolow, V. 1941.   1930
Utilisation du coefficient de corrélation dans l'analyse harmonique. *C. R. Acad. Sci., Paris*, **213**, 56-7.

Fruchter, B. 1949.   1931
Note on the computation of the inverse of a triangular matrix. *Psychometrika*, **14**, 89-93.

Fry, F. E. J. 1949.   1932
Statistics of a lake trout fishery. *Biometrics*, **5**, 27-67.

Fry, T. C. 1942.   1933
Consistency of independent countings as a criterion for completeness. *Bell Tele. Syst. Monogr. B*-982.

Fry, T. C. 1945.   1934
Some numerical methods for locating roots of polynomials. *Quart. Appl. Math.*, **3**, 89-105.

Fryer, H. C. 1941.   1935
An analysis of group differences arising from a Poisson distribution of observations obtained from irradition experiments. *Iowa State Coll. J. Sci.*, **16**, 49-51.

Fulcher, J. S. & Zubin, J. 1942.   1936
The item analyzer: a mechanical device for treating the fourfold table in large samples. *J. Appl. Psychol.*, **26**, 511-23.

Furlan, L. V. 1946.   1937
Die statistiche Zahl als Kollektiv. *Schweiz. Zeit. Volkwirtsch. Statist.*, **82**, 1-21.

Furlan, L. V. 1946.   1938
Bemerkungen zum Petersburger Problem. *Schweiz. Zeit. Volkwirtsch. Statist.*, **82**, 444-8.

Furlan, L. V. 1949.   1939
Iterierte Konzentration. *Schweiz. Zeit. Volkswirtsch. Statist.*, **85**, 291-5.

Furry, W. H. & Hurwitz, H. 1945.   1940
Distribution of numbers and distribution of significant figures. *Nature*, **155**, 52-3.

Fürst, G. 1949.   1941
Mehr Vorsicht bei der Beurteilung behilfsmässiger Berechnungen. *Allg. Statist. Arch.*, **33**, 480-5.

Fürth, R. 1948.   1942
On the theory of electrical fluctuations. *Proc. Roy. Soc. A*, **192**, 593-615.

Fürth, R. & Macdonald, D. K. C. 1947. 1943
Statistical analysis of spontaneous electrical fluctuations. *Proc. Phys. Soc.*, **59**, 388-408.

G

Gabriel, F. 1942.   1944
Graphisch-rechnerisches Verfahren zur schnellen Ermittlung von Trefferprozenten unter einfachen und erschwerten Bedingungen " Trefferspinne ". *Luftfahrtforsch.*, **19**, 231-5.

Gabriel, F. 1948.   1945
Durch Höchstfehler begrenzte Fehlerverteilungen. *Zeit. angew. Math. Mech.*, **28**, 244-7.

Gabriel, F. 1948.   1946
Zur praktischen Anwendung der von Jordan angegebenen durch Höchstfehler begrenzten Fehler Verteilungen. *Zeit. angew. Math. Mech.*, **28**, 278-80.

Gaddum, J. H. 1943.   1947
The design of toxicity tests involving comparison with a standard preparation. *Quart. J. Pharm.*, **16**, 78-86.

Gaddum, J. H. 1945.   1948
Lognormal distributions. *Nature*, **156**, 463-6.

Gaede, K. 1942.   1949
Anwendung statistischer Untersuchungen auf die Prüfung von Baustoffen. *Bauingenieur*, **23**, 291-6.

Gaehr, P. F. 1947.   1950
Equations of straight lines. *Amer. J. Phys.*, **15**, 430.

Gafafer, W. M. 1942.   1951
The measurement and comparison of dental caries experience. *J. Dental Res.*, **21**, 443-53.

Gage, N. L. & Remmers, H. H. 1948.   1952
Opinion polling with mark-sensed punched cards. *J. Appl. Psychol.*, **32**, 88-91.

Gage, R. P. 1943.   1953
Contents of Tippett's " Random sampling numbers ". *J. Amer. Statist. Ass.*, **38**, 223-7.

Gage, R. P. 1946.   1953[a]
Statistics and medicine: the need for close cooperation between the physician and statistician in medical statistics. *Proc. Staff Mtgs. Mayo Clinic*, **21**, 130-6.

Gaillard, J. 1942.   1953[b]
Refined quality control. *Amer. Machinist*, **86**, 1430-2; 1498-1500.

Gaillard, J. 1943.   1953[c]
Refined quality control speeds up production. *Industr. Standardization*, **14**, 123-7; 155-8. (Also: *Elect. Commun.*, **22**, 3-10.)

Gaines, W. L. 1940.   1953[d]
Live weight and milk-energy yield in Holstein cows. *J. Dairy Sci.*, **23**, 259-65.

Gaines, W. L. 1940.   1953[e]
Milk-energy yield and the correlation between fat percentage and milk yield. *J. Dairy Sci.*, **23**, 337-42 (addendum (1941): **24**, 159-64).

Gaines, W. L. 1941.   1953[f]
Live weight of cow at various stages of lactation in relation to milk-energy yield. *J. Dairy Sci.*, **24**, 795-9.

Gaines, W. L. 1943.   1954
Feeding standard equations for cows and goats in milk. *J. Animal Sci.*, **2**, 304-13.

Gaines, W. L., Davis, H. P. & Morgan, R. F. 1954[a]
1941. Estimation of initial live weight at each lactation of dairy cows. *J. Dairy Sci.*, **24**, 983-92.

Gaines, W. L., Davis, H. P. & Morgan, R. F. 1955
1947. Within-cow regression of milk-energy yield on age and live weight. *J. Dairy Sci.*, **30**, 273-8.

Gaines, W. L., Rhode, C. S. & Cash, J. G. 1956
1940. Age, live weight and milk-energy yield in Illinois cows. *J. Dairy Sci.*, **23**, 1031-43. (Addendum (1942): **25**, 15-18.)

Gál, I. S. 1949.   1957
Sur l'ordre de grandeur des fonctions sommables. *C. R. Acad. Sci., Paris*, **228**, 636-8.

Galinat, W. C. & Everett, H. L. 1949. 1958
A technique for testing flavor in sweet corn. *Agron. J.*, **41**, 443-5.

Galvani, L. 1943.   1959
Ancora sul metodo della popolazione tipo al lume della logica. *Statistica, Ferrara*, **3**, 11-22.

Galvani, L. 1945.   1960
Insufficienza teorica del metodo della popolazione tipo. *Atti 6ta Riun. Sci., Soc. Ital. Statist.*, pp. 84-99.

Galvani, L. 1948.   1961
Di alcune definizioni insidiose e delle forme fonda-
mentali di una distribuzione statistica. *Riv. Ital.
Demogr. Statist.*, **2**, 334-51.

Galvani, L. 1948.   1962
Il problema delle file. *Statistica, Bologna*, **8**, 387-95.

Galvani, L. 1949.   1963
Del centro mediano di alcuni particolari sistemi di
punti. *Atti 8va Riun. Sci., Soc. Ital. Statist.* (Publ.
1951), pp. 51-62.

Galvani, L. 1949.   1964
Considerazioni sul metodo della popolazione tipo.
Statistica, Bologna, **9**, 309-22.

Galvani, L. 1949.   1965
Quelques remarques critiques sur la " méthode de la
population type ". *Bull. Int. Statist. Inst.*, **32** (2), 368-76.

Galvenius, I. & Wold, H. O. A. 1947.   1966
Statistical tests of H. Alfvén's theory of sunspots.
Ark. Mat. Astr. Fys., **34A** (24), 9 pp.

Ganguli, M. 1940-1.   1967
A method of estimating variance of sample grand-mean
and zone variances in unequal nested sampling. *Science
& Culture*, **6**, 724.

Ganguli, M. 1941.   1968
A note on nested sampling. *Sankhyā*, **5**, 449-52.

Gannett, D. K. 1940.   1969
Determination of the average life of vacuum tubes.
Bell Tele. Lab. Rec., **18**, 378-82.

García, G. 1945.   1970
On the integration of the equation of diffusion in the
case of a spherical shell. (Spanish.) *Actas Acad.
Cient., Lima*, **8**, 61-7.

Garcia-Mata, C. 1941.   1971
A practical method of smoothing statistical curves by
hand. *Bull. Pan-Amer. Un.*, **75**, 276-81.

Gårding, L. 1941.   1972
The distributions of the first and second order
moments, the partial correlation coefficients and the
multiple correlation coefficient in samples from a
normal multivariate population. *Skand. Aktuartidskr.*,
24, 185-202.

Garfath, H. L. 1946.   1973
A note on a formula of Newton and an extension
thereto. *J. Inst. Actuar. Students' Soc.*, **6**, 63-6.

Garfath, H. L. 1947.   1974
Tchebycheff's mean value theorem and some results
derivable therefrom. *J. Inst. Actuar. Students' Soc.*,
7, 70-80.

Garrett, H. E. 1940.   1975
Variability in learning under massed and spaced
practice. *J. Exper. Psychol.*, **26**, 547-67.

Garrett, H. E. 1942.   1976
The representativeness of a sample. *Amer. J. Psychol.*,
55, 580-1.

Garrett, H. E. 1943.   1977
The discriminant function and its use in psychology.
Psychometrika, **8**, 65-79.

Garrett, H. E. 1943.   1978
Mean differences and individual differences. *Hum.
Biol.*, **15**, 166-70.

Garrett, H. E. & Zubin, J. 1943.   1979
Analysis of variance in psychological research.
Psychol. Bull., **40**, 233-67.

Garti, Y. 1940.   1980
Les lois de probabilité pour les fonctions statistiques
(cas de collectifs à plusieurs dimensions). *Rev. Math.
Union Interbalkan*, **3**, 21-39.

Gartstein, B. N. 1948.   1981
On certain limit laws for the range. (Russian.) *Dokl.
Akad. Nauk SSSR*, **60**, 1119-21.

Garwood, F. 1940.   1982
Application of the theory of probability to the opera-
tion of vehicular-controlled traffic signals. *J. R. Statist.
Soc. Suppl.*, **7**, 65-77.

Garwood, F. 1941.   1983
The application of maximum likelihood to dosage
mortality curves. *Biometrika*, **32**, 46-58.

Garwood, F. 1947.   1984
The variance of the overlap of geometrical figures with
reference to a bombing problem. *Biometrika*, **34**, 1-17.

Gäumann, E. 1943.   1985
Über die Berechnung mittlerer Kurven. *Ber. Dtsch.
Bot. Ges.*, **61**, 111-14.

Gayen, A. K. 1948.   1986
Statistical estimate of time saving due to decimalization
of coins, weights and measures in India. *Science &
Culture*, **13**, 342.

Gayen, A. K. 1949.   1987
The distribution of Student's t in random samples
of any size drawn from non-normal universes. *Biometrika*, **36**, 353-69.

Geary, R. C. 1940.   1988
The mathematical expectation of the mean square
contingency when the attributes are mutually independent. *J. R. Statist. Soc.*, **103**, 90-1.

Geary, R. C. 1942.   1989
The estimation of many parameters. *J. R. Statist.
Soc.*, **105**, 213-17.

Geary, R. C. 1942.   1990
Inherent relations between random variables. *Proc.
Roy. Irish Acad. A*, **47**, 63-76.

Geary, R. C. 1943.   1991
Minimum range for quasi-normal distributions. *Bio-
metrika*, **33**, 100-3.

Geary, R. C. 1944.   1992
Comparison of the concepts of efficiency and closeness
for consistent estimates of a parameter. *Biometrika*,
33, 123-8.

Geary, R. C. 1944.   1993
Extension of a theorem by Harald Cramér on the
frequency distribution of the quotient of two variables.
J. R. Statist. Soc., **107**, 56-7.

Geary, R. C. 1944.   1994
Relations between statistics: the general and the
sampling problem when the samples are large. *Proc.
Roy. Irish. Acad. A*, **49**, 177-96.

Geary, R. C. 1947.   1995
The frequency distribution of $\sqrt{b_1}$ for samples of all
sizes drawn at random from a normal population.
Biometrika, **34**, 68-97.

Geary, R. C. 1947. 1996
Testing for normality. *Biometrika*, **34**, 209-42.

Geary, R. C. 1948. 1997
Studies in relations between economic time series. *J. R. Statist. Soc. B*, **10**, 140-58.

Geary, R. C. 1949. 1998
Determination of linear relations between systematic parts of variables with errors of observation the variances of which are unknown. *Econometrica*, **17**, 30-58.

Geary, R. C. 1949. 1999
Sampling aspects of the problem of relationship from the error-in-variable approach. *Econometrica Suppl.*, **17**, 26-8.

Geary, R. C. 1949. 2000
Sampling methods applied to Irish agricultural statistics. *Irish Trade J. & Statist. Bull.*, **24**, 140-5. (Also: *Tech. Series, Central Statistics Office, Dublin*, Sept. 1949.)

Geary, R. C. & Worlledge, J. P. G. 1947. 2001
On the computation of universal moments of tests of statistical normality derived from samples drawn at random from a normal universe. Application to the calculation of the seventh moment of b_2. *Biometrika*, **34**, 98-110 (correction: **37**, 189).

Gebelein, H. 1941. 2002
Das statistische Problem der Korrelation als Variations- und Eigenwertproblem und sein Zusammenhang mit der Ausgleichsrechung. *Zeit. angew. Math. Mech.*, **21**, 364-79.

Gebelein, H. 1942. 2003
Bemerkung über ein von W. Höffding vorgeschlagenes, maszstabsinvariantes Korrelationsmass. *Zeit. angew. Math. Mech.*, **22**, 171-3.

Gebelein, H. 1942. 2004
Verfahren zur Beurteilung einer sehr geringen Korrelation zwischen zwei statistischen Merkmalsreihen. *Zeit. angew. Math. Mech.*, **22**, 286-98; 553-92.

Geddes, A. 1943. 2005
Variability in rates of population change with reference to India, 1881 to 1931 and 1941: Some statistical considerations. *Indian J. Med. Res.*, **21**, 115-23.

Geiringer, H. 1940. 2006
Zu " Bemerkungen zur Hypothesenwahrscheinlichkeit ". *J. Unified Sci.*, **8**, 352-3.

Geiringer, H. 1940. 2007
A generalization of the law of large numbers. *Ann. Math. Statist.*, **11**, 393-401.

Geiringer, H. 1942. 2008
A new explanation of nonnormal dispersion in the Lexis theory. *Econometrica*, **10**, 53-60.

Geiringer, H. 1942. 2009
A note on the probability of arbitrary events. *Ann. Math. Statist.*, **13**, 238-45.

Geiringer, H. 1942. 2010
Observations on analysis of variance theory. *Ann. Math. Statist.*, **13**, 350-69.

Geiringer, H. 1944. 2011
On the probability theory of linkage in Mendelian heredity. *Ann. Math. Statist.*, **15**, 25-57.

Geiringer, H. 1945. 2012
Further remarks on linkage theory in Mendelian heredity. *Ann. Math. Statist.*, **16**, 390-3.

Geiringer, H. 1945. 2013
On the definition of distance in the theory of the gene. *Ann. Math. Statist.*, **16**, 393-8.

Geiringer, H. 1948. 2014
Contribution to the heredity theory of multivalents. *J. Math. Phys.*, **26**, 246-78.

Geiringer, H. 1948. 2015
On the mathematics of random mating in case of different recombination values for males and females. *Genetics*, **33**, 548-64.

Geiringer, H. 1949. 2016
Contribution to the linkage of autopolyploids. I, II. *Bull. Math. Biophys.*, **11**, 59-82; 197-219.

Geiringer, H. 1949. 2017
On some mathematical problems arising in the development of Mendelian genetics. *J. Amer. Statist. Ass.*, **44**, 526-47.

Geiss, W. 1947. 2017a
De statistische kwaliteitscontrôle als economisch probleem. (Dutch. English summary.) *Statistica Neerlandica*, **1**, 192-6.

Geiss, W. 1948. 2017b
Kwaliteitscontrôle op variabelen. *Tijdschr. Effic. Docum.*, **18**, 245-50.

Gelfond, A. O. 1949. 2018
On some common random distributions of the fractional parts of functions. (Russian.) *Dokl. Akad. Nauk SSSR*, **64**, 437-40.

Gellhorn, A., Krahl, M. E. & Fertig, J. W. 1946. 2018a
An evaluation of the rhodamine B method for the determination of antimony. *J. Pharm. & Exper. Therap.*, **87**, 159-68.

Gengerelli, J. A. 1948. 2019
A binomial method for analyzing psychological functions. *Psychometrika*, **13**, 69-77.

Gengerelli, J. A. 1948. 2020
A simplified method for approximating multiple regression coefficients. *Psychometrika*, **13**, 135-46.

Gennaro, A. 1942. 2021
Eventi subordinati linearmente dipendenti. *Atti Accad. Ital. Mem. Cl. Sci. Fis. Mat. Nat.*, **13**, 947-62.

Gentile, L. 1940. 2022
Nuovi contributi alla ricerca sperimentale sull'interpolazione di serie statistiche. *Atti 2da Ruin. Sci., Soc. Ital. Statist.*, pp. 25-35.

Gentile, L. 1942. 2023
Sulle maniere di colmare le lacune di una serie statistica. *Atti 3za Riun. Sci., Soc. Ital. Statist.*, pp. 86-8.

George, A. 1942. 2024
On the problem of interval estimation. *Sankhyā*, **6**, 111-20.

George, A. 1945. 2025
On the accuracy of the different approximations to the L_1-distribution. *Sankhyā*, **7**, 20-6.

Georgescu-Roegen, N. 1945.   2026
Probabilitatea privată de un statistician. (Le calcul des probabilités dans la statistique.) *An. Inst. Statist. României*, **2**, 11-21.

Georgescu-Roegen, N. 1949.   2027
Further contributions to the scatter analysis. *Econometrica* **17**, Suppl., 39-43. (Also: *Proc. 25th. Session Int. Statist. Inst. Conf., Washington D.C.*, 1947 (Publ. 1951), **5**, 39-43.)

Geppert, M.-P. 1940.   2028
Über die Alterskorrektur von Merkmalshäufigkeiten in der Erbstatistik. *Arch. Math. Wirtsch.*, **6**, 80-102.

Geppert, M.-P. 1940.   2029
Über eine Klasse von zweidimensionalen Verteilungen. *Zeit. angew. Math. Mech.*, **20**, 45-9.

Geppert, M.-P. 1942.   2030
Die Anwendung der Pascalschen Verteilung auf das Bayessche Rückschlussproblem. *Arch. Math. Wirtsch.*, **8**, 129-37.

Geppert, M.-P. 1942.   2031
Das Bayessche Rückschlussproblem. *Deutsche Math.*, **7**, 1-22.

Geppert, M.-P. 1944.   2032
Über den Vergleich zweier beobachteter Häufigkeiten. *Deutsche Math.*, **7**, 553-92.

Geppert, M.-P. 1945.   2033
Sul valore dei cosiddetti testi di significatività. *Atti 7ma Riun. Sci., Soc. Ital. Statist.*, pp. 315-23.

Geppert, M.-P. 1947.   2034
Mutungsgrenzen und Mutungswahrscheinlichkeit. *Zeit. angew. Math. Mech.*, **25-27**, 253-63.

Geppert, M.-P. 1948.   2035
Maximum-likelihood-Schätzung und Rückschlussverteilung. *Zeit. angew. Math. Mech.*, **28**, 85-91.

Geppert, M.-P. 1949.   2036
Die χ^2-Methode in der medizinischen Forschung. *Mitt. Math. Statist.*, **1**, 90-5.

Geppert, M.-P. 1949.   2037
Biologische Gesetze im Lichte der Mathematik. *Mitt. Math. Statist.*, **1**, 145-66.

Germond, H. H. 1948.   2038
A " semi-Poisson " distribution. *RAND Corp. Res. Memo.*, 26 May 1948, RM-40, 6 pp.

Germond, H. H. 1948.   2039
A circular probability grid. *RAND Corp. Res. Memo.*, 24 Aug. 1948, RM-309, 4 pp.

Germond, H. H. 1949.   2039[a]
Forecast of production time. *RAND Corp. Res. Memo.*, 20 *Jan.* 1949, RM-92, 7 pp.

Germond, H. H. 1949.   2040
Hermite polynomials of imaginary argument. *RAND Corp. Res. Memo.*, 1 February 1949, RM-97, 14 pp.

Germond, H. H. 1949.   2040[a]
Expected overlap. *RAND Corp. Res. Memo.*, 6 May 1949, RM-133, 7 pp.

Germond, H. H. 1949.   2040[b]
An approximate solution for a coverage problem. *RAND Corp. Res. Memo.*, 11 April 1949, RM-134, 7 pp.

Germond, H. H. 1949.   2041
An upper limit to cycle-length in a sequence of digit groups. *RAND Corp. Res. Memo.*, 7 July 1949, RM-181, 4 pp.

Germond, H. H. 1949.   2041[a]
Integral of the Gaussian distribution over an offset ellipse. *RAND Corp. Paper*, 28 July 1949, P-94, 13 pp.

Germond, H. H. & Himes, B. T. 1949.   2042
The potentialities of the photoelectric coverage machine. *RAND Corp. Res. Memo.*, 27 Sept. 1949, RM-251, 4 pp.

Gevorkiantz, S. R. 1944.   2043
Measuring stand normality. *J. Forestry*, **42**, 503-8.

Gevorkiantz, S. R. & Ochsner, H. E. 1943.   2044
A method of sample scaling. *J. Forestry*, **41**, 436-9.

Geyer, J. C. 1940.   2045
New curve-fitting method for analysis of flood-records. *Trans. Amer. Geophys. Un.*, **1940** (II), 660-8.

Geymonat, L. 1940.   2046
Il concetto di probabilità. *Saggiatore*, **1**, 320-30.

Ghering, L. G. 1944.   2047
Refined method of control of cordiness and workability of glass during production: statistical control charts of daily measurements of density. *J. Amer. Ceramic Soc.*, **27**, 373-87.

Ghidoli, G. B. 1949.   2048
Generalizzazione della legge sinusoidale. *Statistica, Milano*, **9**, 72-82.

Ghiselli, E. E. 1942.   2049
Estimating the minimal reliability of a total test from the inter-correlations among, and the standard deviations of, the component parts. *J. Appl. Psychol.*, **26**, 332-7.

Ghizzetti, A. 1942.   2050
Sui momenti di una funzione limitata. *Atti Accad. Sci. Torino*, **77**, 198-208.

Ghizzetti, A. 1943.   2051
Sui momenti di 2^0 ordine di una legge di probabilità in n dimensioni. *R. C. Mat. Univ. Roma*, **4** (5), 94-101.

Ghizzetti, A. 1945.   2052
Sul problema del collaudo di partite di numerosi oggetti. *Atti 7ma Riun. Sci., Soc. Ital. Statist.*, pp. 327-45. (Also: *Consiglio Naz. Ric. Publ. Ist. Appl. Calc.*, no. 164, 19 pp.)

Ghizzetti, A. 1948.   2053
Sul prodotto di due variabili casuali gaussiane. *R. C. Accad. Lincei, Cl. Sci. Fis. Mat. Nat.*, (8) **4**, 534-9.

Ghosh, B. 1941.   2054
On some methods of random sampling in a region having some known characteristic. *Science & Culture*, **7**, 117.

Ghosh, B. 1943.   2055
On the distribution of random distances in a rectangle. *Science & Culture*, **8**, 388.

Ghosh, B. 1943.   2056
On some artificial fields and their correlation function. *Science & Culture*, **8**, 424-5.

Ghosh, B. 1943.   2057
On random distances between two rectangles. *Science & Culture*, **8**, 464.

Ghosh, B. 1943. 2058
On two types of correlation function. *Science & Culture*, **9**, 46.

Ghosh, B. 1943. 2059
On sampling in unknown fields. *Science & Culture*, **9**, 129-30.

Ghosh, B. 1943. 2060
On the construction of some natural fields. *Science & Culture*, **9**, 213-14.

Ghosh, B. 1946. 2061
Measures of heterogeneity in agricultural and similar fields, and their interrelations. *Science & Culture*, **11**, 382-3.

Ghosh, B. 1947. 2062
Crop estimation in India; a brief review of the sampling methods. *Bull. Calcutta Statist. Ass.*, **1**, 5-12.

Ghosh, B. 1947. 2063
Bias introduced by changing the system of stratification. *Bull. Calcutta Statist. Ass.*, **1**, 43-5.

Ghosh, B. 1947. 2064
Double sampling with many auxiliary variates. *Bull. Calcutta Statist. Ass.*, **1**, 91-3.

Ghosh, B. 1949. 2065
Topographic variation in statistical fields. *Bull. Calcutta Statist. Ass.*, **2**, 11-28.

Ghosh, B. 1949. 2066
A query on double sampling. *Bull. Calcutta Statist. Ass.*, **2**, 34-7.

Ghosh, B. 1949. 2067
Topographic randomness and its statistical tests. *Bull. Calcutta Statist. Ass.*, **2**, 65-70.

Ghosh, B. 1949. 2068
Interpenetrating (networks of) samples. *Bull. Calcutta Statist. Ass.*, **2**, 108-19.

Ghosh, M. N. 1946. 2069
On the order of approximation involved in Laplace's central limit theorem in probability. *Sankhyā*, **7**, 323-6. (Also: *Proc. Indian Sci. Congr.*, 1945.)

Ghosh, M. N. 1947. 2070
Survey of public opinion. *Bull. Calcutta Statist. Ass.*, **1**, 13-18.

Ghosh, M. N. 1948. 2071
On the problem of similar regions. *Sankhyā*, **8**, 329-38. (Also: *Proc. Indian Sci. Congr.*, 1945.)

Ghosh, M. N. 1948. 2072
A test for field uniformity based on the space correlation method. *Sankhyā*, **9**, 39-46.

Ghosh, M. N. 1948. 2073
Tests of randomness. *Bull. Calcutta Statist. Ass.*, **1**, 135-7.

Ghosh, M. N. 1949. 2074
Expected travel among random points in a region. *Bull. Calcutta Statist. Ass.*, **2**, 83-7.

Ghosh, M. N. & Roy, S. N. 1947. 2075
On a statistical test of treatment on certain diseases. *Sankhyā*, **8**, 195-6.

Ghurye, S. G. 1948. 2076
A characteristic of species of 7×7 Latin squares. *Ann. Eugen.*, **14**, 133.

Ghurye, S. G. 1949. 2077
Transformations of a binomial variate for the analysis of variance. *J. Indian Soc. Agric. Statist.*, **2**, 94-109.

Ghurye, S. G. 1949. 2078
On the use of Student's t-test in an asymmetrical population. *Biometrika*, **36**, 426-30.

Giaccardi, F. 1948. 2079
Alcune considerazioni sulle " curve dei redditi " di Amoroso e di Gibrat. *Atti Accad. Sci. Torino. Cl. Sci. Fis. Mat. Nat.*, **81-2**, 67-74.

Giaccardi, F. 1949. 2080
Sulla " curva dei redditi ". *G. Economisti*, **8**, 115-21.

Gibb, C. A. 1942. 2081
Personality traits by factor analysis. *Aust. J. Psychol. Philos.*, **20**, 86-110.

Gibian, E. F. 1946. 2081[a]
Quality control by statistical methods applied to line production. *Industr. Qual. Contr.*, **3** (2), 7-12.

Gibson, G. D. 1947. 2082
On Gladwin's methods of correlation in tree-ring analysis. *Amer. Anthrop.*, **49**, 337-40.

Giese, A. 1942. 2083
Die stochastischen Abhängigkeiten im allgemeinen Wahrscheinlichkeitsproblem. Das problem der Teilschäden. *Arch. Math. Wirtsch.*, **8**, 13-20.

Gikhman, I. I. 1947. 2084
On a scheme of formation of random processes. (Russian.) *Dokl. Akad. Nauk SSSR*, **58**, 961-4.

Gilbert, S. M. 1945. 2085
The Coffee Research and Experiment Station, Tanganyika Territory: A brief survey of the first ten years' work. *Emp. J. Exper. Agric.*, **13**, 11-24.

Gilchrist, B. M. & Haldane, J. B. S. 1947. 2085[a]
Sex-linkage and sex determination in a mosquito, *Culex molestus*. *Hereditas, Lund.*, **33**, 175-90. (Also: (1946) *Experientia*, **2**, 372.)

Gildemeister, M. & van der Waerden, B. L. 2086
1944. Die Zulässigkeit des χ^2-Kriteriums für kleine Versuchzahlen. *Ber. Verh. Sächs. Akad. Wiss. Leipzig, Math.-Nat. Kl.*, **95**, 145-50.

Gill, F. 1943. 2086[a]
War production problems—the statistical control of quality. *Engng. J., Canada*, **26**, 11-17.

Gillett, H. W. 1944. 2087
Choosing the right material. V. Reliability and probability. *Machine Design*, **16**, 172-4.

Gillman, L. & Goode, H. H. 1946. 2088
An estimate of the correlation coefficient of a bivariate normal population when X is truncated and Y is dichotomized. *Harvard Educ. Rev.*, **16**, 52-5.

Gilmour, D., Waterhouse, D. F. 2089
& McIntyre, G. A. 1946.
An account of experiments undertaken to determine the natural population density of the sheep blowfly *Lucilia caprina wild. Bull. C.S.I.R., Aust.*, no. 195, 39 pp.

Giltay, J. 1943. 2090
A counter arrangement with constant resolving time. *Physica*, **10**, 725-34.

Gini, C. 1940. 2091
Nota all'articolo di C. E. Bonferroni: Sulle condizioni necessarie e sufficienti affinché un centro ponderato sia un valor medio. *Suppl. Statist. Nuovi Problemi Pol. Storia Econ.*, Ferrara, **6** (1).

Gini, C. 1940. 2092
Il principio della compensazione degli errori accidentali. *Suppl. Statist. Nuovi Problemi Pol. Storia Econ.*, Ferrara, **6** (1), 3-6. (Also: (1942) *Atti 2do. Congr. Un. Mat. Ital.*, pp. 673-6.)

Gini, C. 1940. 2093
The relative importance of hereditary and non-hereditary factors in determining the heterogeneity of a generation. *Ann. Eugen.*, **10**, 42-7.

Gini, C. 1940. 2094
Sur la théorie de la dispersion et sur la vérification des schémas théoriques. *Metron*, **14**, 1-29.

Gini, C. 1941. 2095
Alle basi del metodo statistico. Il principio della compensazione degli errori accidentali e la legge dei grandi numeri. *Metron*, **14**, 173-240.

Gini, C. 1941. 2096
Ancora sulle condizioni necessarie e sufficienti affinché un centro ponderato sai un valor medio. Replica al Prof. Bonferroni. *Statistica*, Ferrara, **1**, 120-4.

Gini, C. 1941. 2097
Degli indici sintetici di correlazione e delle loro relazioni con l'indice interno di correlazione (intraclass correlation coefficient) e con gli indici di correlazione tra serie di gruppi. *Metron*, **14**, 241-62.

Gini, C. 1941. 2098
Sur la mesure de la fécondité naturelle de la femme mariée. *Rev. Int. Statist. Inst.*, **9**, 1-20.

Gini, C. 1941. 2099
Di alcune questioni fondamentali per la metodologia statistica. *Atti 2do Riun. Sci., Soc. Ital. Statist.*, pp. 3-10.

Gini, C. 1941. 2100
Delle relazioni tra serie di gruppi. *Statistica*, Ferrara, **1**, 39-50.

Gini, C. 1942. 2101
Sul concetto di caso. *Atti 3za Riun. Sci., Soc. Ital. Statist.*, pp. 3-16.

Gini, C. 1942. 2102
Indici sintetici di correlazione. *Atti 3za Riun. Sci., Soc. Ital. Statist.*, pp. 60-1.

Gini, C. 1942. 2103
On the measure of fertility in women. *Rural Sociology*, **7**, 84-6.

Gini, C. 1943. 2104
Per la determinazione della probabilità di trans-variazione tra più gruppi. *Atti 5ta Riun. Sci., Soc. Ital. Statist.*, pp. 195-7.

Gini, C. 1943. 2105
Sull'uso delle curve integrali ai fini dell'interpolazione grafica. *Atti 5ta Riun. Sci., Soc. Ital. Statist.*, pp. 198-201.

Gini, C. 1943. 2106
Su la misura della dispersione e la sua relazione con l'indice di connessione. *Atti 5ta Riun. Sci., Soc. Ital. Statist.*, pp. 467-70.

Gini, C. 1945. 2107
A proposito dei " testi di significatività ". *Atti 6ta Riun. Sci., Soc. Ital. Statist.*, pp. 165-7.

Gini, C. 1945. 2108
I testi di significatività. *Atti 7ma Riun. Sci., Soc. Ital. Statist.*, pp. 241-79.

Gini, C. 1945. 2109
Sulla probabilità inversa nel caso di grandezze a distribuzione costante. *Atti 7ma Riun. Sci., Soc. Ital. Statist.*, pp. 283-99.

Gini, C. 1945. 2110
Osservazioni sulla communicazione della Dott. M. P. Geppert " Sul valore dei cosiddetti testi di significatività ". *Atti 7ma Riun. Sci., Soc. Ital. Statist.*, pp. 324-6.

Gini, C. 1945-6. 2111
Intorno alle basi logiche ed alla portata gnoseologica del metodo statistico. *Statistica*, Milano, **5-6**, 1-38. (Spanish version (1946) " Sobre las bases logicas del metodo estadístico ". *An. Inst. Actuar. Españ.*, **4-5**, 23-63. Portuguese version (1948) " Os fundamentos e o alcance do metodo estatístico ". *Rev. Brasil. Estatíst.*, **9**, 299-342.)

Gini, C. 1946. 2112
Gedanken zum theorem von Bernoulli. *Schweiz. Zeit. Volkswirtsch. Statist.*, **82**, 401-13. (Italian version (1949): Rileggendo Bernoulli. *Metron*, **15**, 117-32.)

Gini, C. 1947. 2113
The means of samples. *Proc. 25th. Session Int. Statist. Inst. Conf., Washington D.C.*, 1947 (Publ. 1951), **3A**, 258-71.

Gini, C. 1947. 2114
Sulla misura della variabilità dei caratteri biometrici. *Statistica*, Bologna, **7**, 1-8.

Gini, C. 1947. 2115
Intensità e precisione della connessione statistica. *Statistica*, Bologna, **7**, 127-37.

Gini, C. 1947. 2116
Statistical relations and their inversions. *Rev. Int. Statist. Inst.*, **15**, 24-42. (Also: *Proc. 25th. Session Int. Statist. Inst. Conf., Washington D.C.*, 1947 (Publ. 1951), **3B**, 759-62. German: " Über statistische Beziehungen und deren Inversion ". *Schweiz. Zeit. Volkswirtsch. Statist.*, **83**, 519-42.)

Gini, C. 1948. 2117
Über die Inversion der statistischen Beziehungen. *Schweiz. Zeit. Volkswirtsch. Statist.*, **84**, 379-81.

Gini, C. 1948. 2117[a]
The first steps of statistics. *Proc. Res. Forum, I.B.M. Corp., New York*, 26-30 August 1946, pp. 37-45.

Gini, C. 1949. 2118
Concept et mesure de la probabilité. *Dialectica*, **3** 36-54.

Gini, C. 1949. 2119
Le medie dei campioni. *Metron*, **15**, 13-28.

Gini, C. 1949. 2120
Considerazioni sulle probabilità a posteriori ed applicazioni al rapporto dei sessi nelle nascite umane. *Metron*, **15**, 133-71. (Reprinted from (1907): *Studi Econ. Giur. Univ. Cagliari*, **3**.)

Gini, C. 1949. 2121
Pregi ed inconvenienti delle rappresentazioni grafiche. *Bull. Int. Statist. Inst.*, **32** (2), 261-76.

Gini, C. 1949. 2122
Vecchie e nuove osservazioni sulle cause della natalità differenziale e sulla misura della fecondità naturale delle coniugate. *Metron*, **15**, 207-359.

Gini, C. & Livada, G. 1945. 2123
Transvariazione a più dimensioni. *Atti 6ta Riun. Sci., Soc. Ital. Statist.*, pp. 25-62.

Gini, C. & Livada, G. 1945. 2124
Sulla probabilità inversa nel caso di grandezze intensive ed in particolare sulle sue applicazioni a collaudi per masse a mezzo di campioni. *Atti 7ma Riun. Sci., Soc. Ital. Statist.*, pp. 300-6.

Gini, C. & Livada, G. 1945. 2125
Nuovi contributi alla teoria della transvariazione. *Atti 7ma Riun. Sci., Soc. Ital. Statist.*, pp. 346-71.

Ginzburg, G. M. 1940. 2126
Sur les lois limites des distributions dans les procédés stochastiques. (Russian. French summary.) *Zap. Inst. Mat. Mekh. Gos. Univ. Kharkov*, (4) **17**, 65-73.

Ginzburg, G. M. 1941. 2127
Sur les conditions suffisantes pour l'unicité des distributions limites. *C. R. (Dokl.) Acad. Sci. URSS*, **30**, 295-7.

Ginzburg, I. 1940. 2128
Divergence and probability in taxonomy. *Zoologica*, **25**, 15-31.

Giraldo, H. C. 1947. 2129
El analisis estadístico en la experimentación agrícola. *Agr. Trop.*, **3** (9), 54-6.

Girault, M. 1948. 2130
Sur la notion de facteur commun en analyse factorielle générale. *C. R. Acad. Sci., Paris*, **227**, 499-500.

Girshick, M. A. 1941. 2131
The distribution of the ellipticity statistic L_e when the hypothesis is false. *Statistica, Ferrara*, **2**, 157-62. (Also: *Terr. Magn. Atmos. Elect.*, **46**, 455-7.)

Girshick, M. A. 1942. 2132
The application of the theory of linear hypotheses to the coefficient of elasticity of demand. *J. Amer. Statist. Ass.*, **37**, 233-7.

Girshick, M. A. 1942. 2133
Note on the distribution of roots of a polynomial with random complex coefficients. *Ann. Math. Statist.*, **13**, 235-8 (correction: 447).

Girshick, M. A. 1946. 2134
Contributions to the theory of sequential analysis. I, II, III. *Ann. Math. Statist.*, **17**, 123-43: 282-98.

Girshick, M. A. 1948. 2134[a]
Sampling inspection plans for continuous production. *RAND Corp. Paper*, 10 May 1948, RAOP-17, 20 pp.

Girshick, M. A. & Haavelmo, T. 1947. 2135
Statistical analysis of the demand for food. Examples of simultaneous estimation of structural equations. *Econometrica*, **15**, 79-110.

Girshick, M. A., Mosteller, F. & Savage, L. J. 2136
1946. Unbiased estimates for certain binomial sampling problems with applications. *Ann. Math. Statist.*, **17**, 13-23.

Gjeddebaek, N. F. 1949. 2137
Contributions to the study of grouped observations. Application of the method of maximum likelihood in case of normally distributed observations. *Skand. Aktuartidskr.*, **32**, 135-59.

Gladwin, A. S. 1944-47. 2138
Energy distribution in the spectrum of a frequency modulated wave. I, II. *Phil. Mag.*, (7) **35**, 787-802; **38**, 229-51.

Glasgow, H. 1940. 2139
A plot arrangement for timing the applications in a control program. *J. Econ. Ent.*, **33**, 357-61.

Gleissberg, W. 1945. 2140
Eine Aufgabe der Kombinatorik und Wahrscheinlichkeitsrechnung. (German. Turkish summary.) *Univ. Istanbul Rev. Fac. Sci. A*, **10**, 25-35.

Gleissberg, W. 1945. 2141
Ein Kriterium für die Realität zyklischer Variationen. (German. Turkish summary.) *Univ. Istanbul, Rev. Fac. Sci. A*, **10**, 36-42.

Gleissberg, W. 1947. 2142
Bedingungen für die Anordnung zufälliger Fehler. (German. Turkish and English summaries.) *Univ. Istanbul, Rev. Fac. Sci. A*, **12**, 107-26.

Gleitze, B. 1947. 2143
Der Funktionswandel der Statistik. *Statist. Praxis*, **2**, 145-8.

Glock, W. S. 1941. 2144
Growth rings and climate. *Botanical Rev.*, **7**, 649-713.

Glock, W. S. 1942. 2145
A rapid method of correlation for continuous time series. *Amer. J. Sci.*, **240**, 437-42.

Gnambs, H. 1948. 2145[a]
Die Bevölkerungsstatistik bei den Klassikern der Wahrscheinlichkeitstheorie. *Statist. Viertel.schr.*, **1**, 129-44.

Gnedenko, B. V. 1940. 2146
Quelques théorèmes sur l'ensemble des puissances d'une loi de probabilité. (Russian. French summary.) *Uch. Zap. Moskov. Gos. Univ. Mat.*, **45**, 61-71.

Gnedenko, B. V. 1941. 2147
Limit theorems for the maximal term of a variational series. *C. R. (Dokl.) Acad. Sci. URSS*, **32**, 7-9.

Gnedenko, B. V. 1941. 2148
On the theory of Geiger-Müller counters. (Russian.) *Zh. Eksper. Teor. Fiz. Akad. Nauk SSSR*, **11**, 101-6.

Gnedenko, B. V. 1942. 2149
Locally stable distributions. (Russian. English summary.) *Izv. Akad. Nauk SSSR, Ser. Mat.*, **6**, 291-308.

Gnedenko, B. V. 1942. 2150
On locally stable probability distributions. *C. R. (Dokl.) Acad. Sci. URSS*, **35**, 263-6.

Gnedenko, B. V. 1942. 2151
Investigation of the growth of homogeneous random processes with independent increments. *C. R. (Dokl.) Acad. Sci. URSS*, **36**, 3-4.

Gnedenko, B. V. 1943. 2152
Sur la croissance des processus stochastiques homo-gènes à accroissements indépendants. (Russian. French summary.) *Izv. Akad. Nauk SSSR, Ser. Mat.,* 7, 89-110.

Gnedenko, B. V. 1943. 2153
Sur la distribution limite du terme maximum d'une série aléatoire. *Ann. Math.,* (2) 44, 423-53.

Gnedenko, B. V. 1943. 2154
On the growth of homogeneous random processes with independent single-type increments. *C. R. (Dokl.) Acad. Sci. URSS,* 40, 90-3.

Gnedenko, B. V. 1943. 2155
On the iterated logarithm law for homogeneous random processes with independent increments. *C. R. (Dokl.) Acad. Sci. URSS,* 40, 255-6.

Gnedenko, B. V. 1944. 2156
Limit theorems for sums of independent random variables. (Russian.) *Usp. Mat. Nauk* (10), 115-65. (Trans. 1951, *Amer. Math. Soc. Translation,* no. 45, 82 pp.)

Gnedenko, B. V. 1944. 2157
Elements of the theory of distribution functions of random vectors. (Russian.) *Usp. Mat. Nauk* (10), 230-44.

Gnedenko, B. V. 1948. 2158
On a local limit theorem of the theory of probability. (Russian.) *Usp. Mat. Nauk (N.S.),* 3, 3(25), 187-94.

Gnedenko, B. V. 1948. 2159
On a theorem of S. N. Bernstein. (Russian.) *Izv. Akad. Nauk SSSR, Ser. Mat.,* 12, 97-100.

Gnedenko, B. V. 1948. 2160
On the theory of growth of homogeneous random progresses with independent increments. (Ukrainian. Russian summary.) *Zb. Prak. Inst. Mat. Akad. Nauk Ukrain. RSR,* no. 10, 60-82.

Gnedenko, B. V. 1949. 2161
On a local limit theorem in case of infinite variance. *Trudy Inst. Mat. Akad. Nauk Ukrain. RSR,* 12, 22-30.

Gnedenko, B. V. 1949. 2162
On a local theorem for the region of normal attraction of stable laws. (Russian.) *Dokl. Akad. Nauk SSSR,* 66, 325-6.

Gnedenko, B. V. 1949. 2163
On some properties of limiting distributions for normed sums. (Russian.) *Ukrain. Mat. Zh.,* 1 (1), 3-8.

Gnedenko, B. V. 1949. 2164
On a local theorem for stable limit distributions. (Russian.) *Ukrain. Mat. Zh.,* 1 (4), 3-15.

Gobeil, R. 1940. 2165
Importance des statistiques dans les travaux forestiers. *Forêt Québéçoise,* 2, 31-48.

Goblet, Y. 1941. 2166
Géographie et statistique. *J. Soc. Statist. Paris,* 82, 155-9.

Godard, R. H. & Lindquist, E. F. 1940. 2167
An empirical study of the effect of heterogeneous within-groups variance upon certain F-tests of significance in analysis of variance. *Psychometrika,* 5, 263-74.

Goddard, L. S. 1945. 2168
The accumulation of chance effects and the Gaussian frequency distribution. *Phil. Mag.,* (7) 36, 428-33.

Goddess, E. 1945. 2168a
Quality control in tube manufacture. *Electronics,* 18, 122-5.

Goddess, E. 1946. 2168b
Probability and quality control. *Amer. Machinist,* 90, 110-11.

Goddess, E. 1946. 2168c
Sampling techniques applied to quality control. *Iron Age,* 158 (24), 70-5.

Goddess, E. 1946. 2168d
Using statistics to control mass production quality. *Fact. Mgmt.,* 104, 110-12.

Godwin, H. J. 1944. 2169
Incqualitics related to Tchebycheff's inequality. *U.K. Min. Supply Advisory Service Statist. Method & Qual. Contr., Tech. Rep .Ser. R,* no. QC/R/13, 14 February 1944, 7 pp.

Godwin, H. J. 1945. 2170
On the distribution of the estimate of mean deviation obtained from samples from a normal population. *Biometrika,* 33, 254-6.

Godwin, H. J. 1948. 2171
A further note on the mean deviation. *Biometrika,* 35, 304-9.

Godwin, H. J. 1949. 2172
On cartophily and motor cars. *Math. Gaz.,* 33, 169-71.

Godwin, H. J. 1949. 2173
On the estimation of dispersion by linear systematic statistics. *Biometrika,* 36, 92-100.

Godwin, H. J. 1949. 2174
A note on Kac's derivation of the distribution of the mean deviation. *Ann. Math. Statist.,* 20, 127-9.

Godwin, H. J. 1949. 2175
Some low moments of order statistics. *Ann. Math. Statist.,* 20, 279-99.

Goffman, C. 1945. 2175a
Statistics as an aid to engineering judgment in the manufacture of lightning-arrester blocks. *Elect. Engng., New York,* 64, 607-9.

Goffman, C. 1946. 2175b
The effect of a number of variables on a quality characteristic. *Industr. Qual. Contr.,* 2 (4), 3-5, 10.

Goffman, C. & Manuele, J. 1946. 2175c
The use of statistics in writing specifications. *Bull. Amer. Soc. Test. Mat.,* 139, 13-17.

Goldberg, H. & Levine, H. 1946. 2176
Approximate formulae for the percentage points and normalization of t and χ^2. *Ann. Math. Statist.,* 17, 216-25.

Goldberger, M. L. 1948. 2177
The interaction of high energy neutrons and heavy nuclei. *Phys. Rev.,* (2) 74, 1269-77.

Gomes, F. P. 1945. 2178
Os gráficos—como se fazem e para que servem. *Rev. Agric. Piracicaba,* 20, 261-8.

Gomes, F. P. & Malavolta, E. 1949. 2179
Aspestos matemáticos e estatísticos da lei de Mitscherlich. *An. Ex. Sup. Agric. Luiz de Queiroz*, **6**, 193-229.

Gompf, G. E. 1949. 2179a
Air battle theory: statistical survival analysis for close-controlled interceptors versus bombers. *RAND Corp. Res. Memo.*, 29 Aug. 1949, RM-239, 7 pp.

Gompf, G. E. 1949. 2179b
Basic survival-probability expressions for air combat models. *RAND Corp. Res. Memo.*, 22 Aug. 1949, RM-240, 4 pp.

Goncharov, V. L. 1942. 2180
Sur la distribution des cycles dans les permutations. *C. R. (Dokl.) Acad. Sci. URSS*, **35**, 267-9.

Goncharov, V. L. 1943. 2181
Sur la succession des événements dans une série d'épreuves indépendantes répondant au schème de Bernoulli. *C. R. (Dokl.) Acad. Sci. URSS*, **38**, 283-5.

Goncharov, V. L. 1944. 2182
Du domaine de l'analyse combinatoire. (Russian. French summary.) *Izv. Akad. Nauk SSSR, Ser. Mat.*, **8**, 3-48.

Goncharov, V. L. & Kolmogorov, A. N. 1940. 2183
Le soixantenaire de S. Bernstein. *Bull. Acad. Sci. URSS, Sér. Math.*, **4**, 249-60.

Gonin, H. T. 1944. 2184
Curve fitting by means of the orthogonal polynomials in binomial statistical distributions. *Trans. Roy. Soc. South Africa*, **30**, 207-15.

Good, I. J. 1949. 2185
The number of individuals in a cascade process. *Proc. Camb. Phil. Soc.*, **45**, 360-3.

Goodenough, F. 1947. 2186
Note on an unnecessary source of confusion in statistical terminology. *J. Educ. Psychol.*, **38**, 10-13; 443-5.

Goodfellow, L. D. 1940. 2187
The human element in probability. *J. Gen. Psychol.*, **23**, 201-5.

Goodman, A. A. 1946. 2187a
Tools and statistical quality control. *Tool Engng.*, **17**, 40-3.

Goodman, A. A. 1947. 2187b
A practical sequential sampling plan. *Industr. Qual. Contr.*, **4** (1), 5-7.

Goodman, C. N. & Morant, G. M. 1940. 2188
The human remains of the iron age and other periods from Maiden Castle, Dorset. *Biometrika*, **31**, 295-312.

Goodman, L. A. 1949. 2189
On the estimation of the number of classes in a population. *Ann. Math. Statist.*, **20**, 572-9.

Goodman, N. 1947. 2190
On infirmities of confirmation theory. *Phil. Phenom. Res.*, **8**, 149-51.

Goodman, R. 1947. 2191
Sampling for the 1947 survey of consumer finances. *J. Amer. Statist. Ass.*, **42**, 439-48.

Goodsell, W. D. 1942. 2192
Paired and group observations contrasted. *Illinois Univ. Dept. Agric. Econ. and Agric. Exper. Sta., Rep. AE-1837.*

Goodstein, R. L. 1940. 2193
On von Mises' theory of probability. *Mind*, **49**, 58-62.

Gordon, A. N. 1948. 2194
The restricted problem of the random walk. *Phil. Mag.*, (7) **39**, 572-5.

Gordon, R. A. 1941. 2195
Period and velocity as statistical concepts. *Quart. J. Econ.*, **55**, 306-13.

Gordon, R. D. 1941. 2196
The estimation of a quotient when the denominator is normally distributed. *Ann. Math. Statist.*, **12**, 115-18.

Gordon, R. D. 1941. 2197
Values of Mills' ratio of area to bounding ordinate and of the normal probability integral for large values of the argument. *Ann. Math. Statist.*, **12**, 364-6.

Gordon, S. 1941. 2198
A sampling technique for the determination of hunters' activities and the economics thereof. *J. Wildlife Mgmt.*, **5**, 260-78.

Göring, E. 1941. 2199
Eine Erweiterung der Mises'schen Kollektive und der entsprechende Ausbau der Theorie der Wahrscheinlichkeitsrechnung. (French, Italian and English summaries.) *Trans. 12th. Int. Congr. Actuar., Lucerne*, 1940, **1**, 329-48.

Göring, E. 1948. 2200
Definition und Bestimmung der Wahrscheinlichkeit durch des Kollektiv allgemeiner Art. *Mitt. Ver. Schweiz. Versich.-Math.*, **48**, 145-70.

Gottschalk, V. H. 1948. 2201
Symmetrical bi-modal frequency curves. *J. Franklin Inst.*, **245**, 245-52.

Gotusso, G. 1945. 2202
Probabilità de rottura di un filo. *Ist. Lombardo Sci. Lett. Rend. Cl. Sci. Mat. Nat.*, (3) **9** (78), 182-90.

Goudsmit, S. A. 1945. 2203
Random distribution of lines in a plane. *Rev. Mod. Phys.*, **17**, 321-2.

Goudsmit, S. A. & Furry, W. H. 1944. 2204
Significant figures of numbers in statistical tables. *Nature*, **154**, 800-1.

Goudsmit, S. A. & Saunderson, J. L. 1940. 2205
Multiple scattering of electrons. *Phys. Rev.*, (2) **52**, 24-9.

Goulden, C. H. 1944. 2206
Experimental design for cereal chemists. *Cereal Chem.*, **21**, 159-71.

Goulden, C. H. 1944. 2207
A uniform method of analysis for square lattice experiments. *Scientific Agric.*, **25**, 115-36.

Goulden, C. H. & Paull, A. E. 1946. 2208
Statistical methods in cereal chemistry. *Biometrics Bull.*, **2**, 26-9.

Goyan, F. M. & Dufrenoy, J. 1947. 2209
A graphical calculator for bio-assays. *J. Amer. Pharm. Ass.*, **36**, 305-8.

Grabill, W. H. 1945.   2210
Attrition life tables for the single population. *J. Amer. Statist. Ass.*, **40**, 364-75.

Grandstaff, J. O. & Blunn, C. T. 1945.   2211
Evaluating fleece quality of Navajo sheep from small samples. *J. Agric. Res.*, **71**, 183-92.

Grant, D. A. 1944.   2212
On the analysis of variance in psychological research. *Psychol. Bull.*, **41**, 158-66.

Grant, D. A. 1946.   2213
New statistical criteria for learning and problem solution in experiments involving repeated trials. *Psychol. Bull.*, **43**, 272-82.

Grant, D. A. 1947.   2213a
Additional tables of the probability of " runs " of correct responses in learning and problem-solving. *Psychol. Bull.*, **44**, 276-9.

Grant, D. A. 1948.   2214
The Latin square principle in the design and analysis of psychological experiments. *Psychol. Bull.*, **45**, 427-42.

Grant, E. L. 1940.   2215
The probability-viewpoint in hydrology. *Trans. Amer. Geophys. Un.*, **1940** (1), 7-12.

Grant, E. L. 1945.   2215a
Costs dropped, quality bettered, through statistical controls. *Wings*, **4**, 1716-19.

Grävell, W. 1940.   2216
Die Wirtschaftsstatistik als methodische und organisatorische Einheit. *Dtsch. Statist. Zbl.*, **32** (5-8), 25-48.

Gray, H. & Mahan, E. 1943.   2217
Prediction of heart weight in man. *Amer. J. Phys. Anthrop.*, **1**, 271-87.

Gray, P. 1941.   2218
A simplified method for computing the theoretical class frequencies of a binomial expansion. *Growth*, **5**, 267-71.

Gray, P. 1947.   2219
The effect of the death rate in biological experiments on the validity of observations, and on the " chi square " test for association. *Arch. Biochem.*, **13**, 461-74.

Grazia-Resi, B. 1948.   2220
Nuove ricerche sugli indici di cograduazione fra serie con termini uguali. *Statistica, Milano*, **8**, 409-26.

Greb, D. J. & Berrettoni, J. N. 1949.   2221
AOQL single sampling plans from a single chart and table. *J. Amer. Statist. Ass.*, **44**, 62-76.

Greenall, P. D. 1949.   2222
The concept of equivalent scores in similar tests. *Brit. J. Psychol. (Statist. Sec.)*, **2**, 30-40.

Greenshields, B. D. 1946.   2223
Applications of statistical sampling methods to traffic performance at urban intersections. *Proc. Hung. Res. Bd.*, **26**, 377-89.

Greenshields, B. D., Ericksen, E. L.   2224
& Schapiro, D. 1947.
Traffic performance at urban street intersections. *Yale Bureau of Highway Traffic, Tech. Rep. no. 1*, 152 pp.

Greenslade, R. M. & Pearce, S. C. 1940.   2225
Field sampling for the comparison of infestations of strawberry crops by the aphis *Capitophorus fragariae Theob. Pomology and Hort. Sci.*, **17**, 308-17.

Greenwood, J. A. 1940.   2226
A caution on the use of the method of correct matchings. *Amer. J. Psychol.*, **53**, 614-15.

Greenwood, J. A. 1940.   2227
The first four moments of a general matching problem. *Ann. Eugen.*, **10**, 290-2.

Greenwood, J. A. 1942.   2228
The role mathematics has played in E.S.P. research. *J. Parapsychol.*, **6**, 268-83.

Greenwood, J. A. 1943.   2229
On the evaluation of differences of success ratios from binomial populations. *J. Parapsychol.*, **7**, 277-80.

Greenwood, J. A. 1943.   2230
A preferential matching problem. *Psychometrika*, **8**, 185-91.

Greenwood, J. A. & Stuart, C. E. 1940.   2231
A review of Dr. Feller's critique. *J. Parapsychol.*, **4**, 299-319.

Greenwood, M. 1941-3.   2232
Medical statistics from Graunt to Farr. I-IX. *Biometrika*, **32**, 101-27; 203-25; **33**, 1-24.

Greenwood, M. 1946.   2233
The statistical study of infectious diseases. *J. R. Statist. Soc.*, **109**, 85-110.

Greenwood, M. 1948.   2234
The statistician and medical research. *Brit. Med. J.*, **2**, 467-8.

Greenwood, M. 1949.   2235
The infectiousness of measles. *Biometrika*, **36**, 1-8.

Greenwood, M. L. & Salerno, R. 1949.   2236
Palatability of kale in relation to cooking procedure and variety. *Food Res.*, **14**, 314-19.

Greenwood, R. E. 1949.   2237
Numerical integration for linear sums of exponential functions. *Ann. Math. Statist.*, **20**, 608-11.

Greiff. 1941.   2238
Eine neue Methode zur Berechnung der manifesten und latenten Zuckerkranken in einer Bevölkerung. *Münch. med. Wschr.*, **88** (13), 366-9.

Grenander, U. 1949.   2239
Stochastic processes and integral equations. *Ark. Mat.*, **1**, 67-70.

Grenet, G. & Bayard-Duclaux, F. 1945.   2240
Application des méthodes statistiques à la climatologie. *C. R. Acad. Sci., Paris*, **221**, 632-4.

Greville, T. N. E. 1941.   2241
The frequency distribution of a general matching problem. *Ann. Math. Statist.*, **12**, 350-4.

Greville, T. N. E. 1942-3.   2242
" Census " methods of constructing mortality tables and their relation to " insurance " methods. *Rec. Amer. Inst. Actuar.*, **31**, 367-73; **32**, 125-30.

Greville, T. N. E. 1943.   2243
Regularity of label-sequences under configuration transformations. *Trans. Amer. Math. Soc.*, **54**, 403-13.

Greville, T. N. E. 1943.   2244
Frequency distribution of ESP scores for certain selected call-patterns. *J. Parapsychol.*, 7, 272-6.

Greville, T. N. E. 1943.   2245
Short methods of constructing abridged life tables. *Rec. Amer. Inst. Actuar.*, 32, 29-43; 408-18.

Greville, T. N. E. 1944.   2246
The general theory of osculatory interpolation. *Trans. Actuar. Soc. Amer.*, 45, 83-101; 202-65.

Greville, T. N. E. 1944.   2247
A generalization of Waring's formula. *Ann. Math. Statist.*, 15, 218-19 (addendum: 18, 605-6).

Greville, T. N. E. 1944.   2248
On multiple matching with one variable deck. *Ann. Math. Statist.*, 15, 432-4.

Greville, T. N. E. 1945.   2249
Some extensions of Mr. Beers's method of interpolation. *Rec. Amer. Inst. Actuar.*, 34, 21-34; 188-93.

Greville, T. N. E. 1946.   2250
Subtabulaçâo por mínimos quadrados de difereñças finitas. *Bol. Inst. Brasil. Atuár.*, 2 (2), 7-34.

Greville, T. N. E. 1947.   2251
Adjusted average graduation formulas of maximum smoothness. *Rec. Amer. Inst. Actuar.*, 36, 249-64.

Greville, T. N. E. 1948.   2252
Recent developments in graduation and interpolation. *J. Amer. Statist. Ass.*, 43, 428-41.

Greville, T. N. E. 1949.   2253
On the derivation of discrete interpolation formulas. *Trans. Soc. Actuar., Chicago*, 1, 343-68.

Greville, T. N. E. 1949.   2254
Opinion polls and sample surveys. *Estadística*, 7, 92-3.

Gridgeman, N. T. 1943.   2255
The technique of the biological vitamin A assay. *Biochem. J.*, 37, 127-32.

Gridgeman, N. T. 1944.   2256
Mathematics of biological assay. *Nature*, 153, 461-2.

Gridgeman, N. T. 1945.   2257
Special designs for vitamin D assays. *Quart. J. Pharm.*, 18, 15-23.

Gridgeman, N. T. 1945.   2258
The potencies of vitamin D_2 and D_3. *Quart. J. Pharm.*, 18, 24-9.

Gridgeman, N. T. 1946.   2259
The transformation of biological responses with special reference to vitamin D assays. *Analyst*, 71, 376-9.

Griffith, A. L. 1947.   2260
The efficiency of enumerations. *Indian Forestry*, 73, 102-7. (Also: *Emp. Forestry Rev.*, 26, 105ff.)

Griffith, L. 1943.   2261
A theory of the size distribution of particles in a comminuted system. *Canadian J. Res. A*, 21, 57-64.

Grimminger, G. 1948.   2262
Probability that a meteorite will hit or penetrate a body situated in the vicinity of the earth. *J. Appl. Phys.*, 19, 947-56.

Grimsey, A. H. R. 1945.   2263
On the accumulation of chance effects and the Gaussian frequency distribution. *Phil. Mag.* (7) 36, 294-5.

Grimsey, A. H. R. 1946.   2264
Ultimate risks in sampling inspection. *J. R. Statist. Soc. Suppl.*, 8, 244-50.

Groebner, W. 1948.   2264a
Über die Konstruktion von Systemen orthogonaler Polynome in ein- und zwei-dimensionaler Bereich. *Monatshefte Math.*, 52, 38-54.

Grom, V. 1944.   2264b
Table of limits for charts for defects. *Industr. Qual. Contr.*, 1 (2), 11-13.

Grom, V. R. 1945.   2264c
Multiple characteristics as related to sampling. *Industr. Qual. Contr.*, 1 (5), 6-9.

Grootenhuis, J. A. & Post, J. J. 1946.   2265
The suitability of the Latin square for trials of a fairly simple character. *Meded. Dir. Tuinb.*, 1946, 173-5.

Grosch, H. R. J. 1946.   2266
Harmonic analysis by the use of progressive digiting. *Proc. Res. Forum I.B.M. Corp., New York*, 1946, pp. 81-4.

Groshev, A. 1941.   2267
Sur le domaine d'attraction de la loi de Poisson. (Russian. French summary.) *Izv. Akad. Nauk SSSR, Ser. Mat.*, 5, 165-72.

Gross, M. 1949.   2268
Leistungsvorrechnung bei mehr Maschinenbedienung. *Textil-Praxis*, 4, 113.

Grossman, D. 1944.   2269
Technique for weighting of choices and items on *I.B.M.* scoring machines. *Psychometrika*, 9, 101-4.

Grossman, D. 1947.   2270
Wesen, Berechnung und Anwendung das Trend. *Berliner Statist.*, 1, 169-75.

Grossnickle, L. T. 1942.   2271
The scaling of test scores by the method of paired comparisons. *Psychometrika*, 7, 43-64.

Grubbs, F. E. 1944.   2272
On the distribution of the radial standard deviation. *Ann. Math. Statist.*, 15, 75-81.

Grubbs, F. E. 1946.   2272a
The difference control chart with an example of its use. *Industr. Qual. Contr.*, 3 (1), 22-5.

Grubbs, F. E. 1948.   2273
On estimating precision of measuring instruments and product variability. *J. Amer. Statist. Ass.*, 43, 243-64 (correction: 564).

Grubbs, F. E. 1949.   2274
On designing single sampling inspection plans. *Ann. Math. Statist.*, 20, 242-56.

Grubbs, F. E. & Weaver, C. L. 1947.   2275
The best unbiased estimate of population standard deviation based on group ranges. *J. Amer. Statist. Ass.*, 42, 224-41.

Guerreiro, A. 1948.   2276
Números-indices de base fixa e de base movel. *Rev. Economia, Lisboa*, 1, 25-6.

Guerreiro, A. 1948.   2277
Amostras estatísticas: Métodos usados na sua escolha. *Rev. Economia, Lisboa*, 1, 221-4.

Guidotti, S. 1943. 2278
Su una interpretazione dell'indice di concentrazione δ. *Atti 5ta Riun. Sci., Soc. Ital. Statist.*, pp. 223-5.

Guidotti, S. 1945. 2279
Qualche considerazione sulla differenza media. *Atti 7ma Riun. Sci., Soc. Ital. Statist.*, pp. 372-84.

Guilbaud, G. T. 1949. 2280
La théorie des jeux. Contributions critiques à la théorie de la valeur. *Écon. Appl.*, 2, 275-319.

Guilbaud, G. T. 1949. 2281
Note sur l'économétrie des fluctuations. *Écon. Appl.*, 2, 429-95.

Guilford, J. P. 1941. 2282
The phi coefficient and chi square as indices of item validity. *Psychometrika*, 6, 11-19.

Guilford, J. P. 1948. 2283
Factor analysis in a test-development program. *Psychol. Rev.*, 55, 79-94.

Guilford, J. P. & Lyons, T. C. 1942. 2284
On determining the reliability and significance of a tetrachoric coefficient of correlation. *Psychometrika*, 7, 243-9.

Guilford, J. P. & Michael, W. B. 1948. 2285
Approaches to univocal factor scores. *Psychometrika*, 13, 1-22.

Guildford, J. P. & Michael, W. B. 1949. 2286
The prediction of categories from measurements. *Sheridan Supply Co., Beverley Hills, California.*

Gulliksen, H. 1942. 2287
An analysis of learning data which distinguishes between initial preference and learning ability. *Psychometrika*, 7, 171-94.

Gulliksen, H. 1944. 2288
Selection of test items by correlation with an external criterion, as applied to a mechanical comprehension test. *Washington, D.C., O.S.R.D. Publ. Bd. no. 13319.* (Also (1946): *U.S. Dept. Commerce Publ. no. 11.*)

Gulliksen, H. 1945. 2289
The relation of item difficulty and inter-item correlation to test variance and reliability. *Psychometrika*, 10, 79-91.

Gulliksen, H. 1946. 2290
Paired comparisons and the logic of measurement. *Psychol. Rev.*, 53, 199-213.

Gumbel, E. J. 1940. 2291
La dissection d'une répartition. *Trav. Inst. Math. et Inst. Sci. Financ. Assur., Lyon*, 89-94, 39-51. (Also (1940): *Ann. Univ. Lyon A*, (3), 2.)

Gumbel, E. J. 1940. 2292
La durée de retour des températures annuelles extrêmes. *C. R. Acad. Sci., Paris*, 210, 468-70.

Gumbel, E. J. 1941. 2293
The limiting form of Poisson's distribution. *Phys. Rev.*, (2) 60, 689-90.

Gumbel, E. J. 1941. 2294
Probablity-interpretation of the observed return-periods of floods. *Trans. Amer. Geophys. Un., 1941*, 836-50.

Gumbel, E. J. 1941. 2295
The return period of flood flows. *Ann. Math. Statist.*, 12, 163-89.

Gumbel, E. J. 1942. 2296
On the frequency distribution of extreme values in meteorological data. *Bull. Amer. Met. Soc.*, 23, 95-105.

Gumbel, E. J. 1942. 2297
Simple tests for given hypotheses. *Biometrika*, 32, 317-33 (errata: 33, 1).

Gumbel, E. J. 1942. 2298
Statistical control-curves for flood-discharges. *Trans. Amer. Geophys. Un.*, 23, 489-509.

Gumbel, E. J. 1943. 2299
La durée de retour. *La Météorologie, 1942*, 71-98.

Gumbel, E. J. 1943. 2299ᵃ
Exceedance or recurrence intervals in analysing flood discharges. *Civil Engng.*, 13, 438.

Gumbel, E. J. 1943. 2300
On the plotting of flood-discharges. *Trans. Amer. Geophys. Un.*, 24, 699-719.

Gumbel, E. J. 1943. 2301
Probable deviation. *New York City College J. Statist.*, 6, 25-6.

Gumbel, E. J. 1943. 2302
On serial numbers. *Ann. Math. Statist.*, 14, 163-78.

Gumbel, E. J. 1943. 2303
On the reliability of the classical chi-square test. *Ann. Math. Statist.*, 14, 253-63.

Gumbel, E. J. 1943. 2303ᵃ
Statistical analysis in hydrology. *Proc. Amer. Soc. Civil Engrs.*, 69, 995-1005.

Gumbel, E. J. 1944. 2304
Ranges and midranges. *Ann. Math. Statist.*, 15, 414-22.

Gumbel, E. J. 1945. 2305
Floods estimated by probability method. *Engng. New Rec.*, 134, 833-7.

Gumbel, E. J. 1945. 2306
Simplified plotting of statistical observations. *Trans. Amer. Geophys. Un.*, 26, 69-82.

Gumbel, E. J. 1945. 2306ᵃ
Studies on the extremes of statistical variates. *Yearbook Amer. Philos. Soc. 1944.*

Gumbel, E. J. 1946. 2307
Détermination commune des constantes dans les distributions des plus grandes valeurs. *C. R. Acad. Sci., Paris*, 222, 34-6.

Gumbel, E. J. 1946. 2308
On the independence of the extremes in a sample. *Ann. Math. Statist.*, 17, 78-81.

Gumbel, E. J. 1946. 2309
Probability of death and expectation of life. *Hum. Biol.*, 18, 238-40.

Gumbel, E. J. 1947. 2310
The distribution of the range. *Ann. Math. Statist.*, 18, 384-412.

Gumbel, E. J. 1948. 2310ᵃ
Ranges from large samples. *Amer. Statistician*, 2 (4), 23.

Gumbel, E. J. 1949. 2311
Probability tables for the range. *Biometrika*, **36**, 142-8.

Gumbel, E. J. 1949. 2312
The statistical forecast of floods. *Ohio Water Resources Board, Columbus, Ohio, Bull.* no. 15.

Gurgel, J. T. A. 1945. 2313
Análise estatística da distribuiçâo de Poisson. *An. Ex. Sup. Agric. Luiz de Queiroz*, **2**, 299-319.

Gurland, J. 1948. 2314
Inversion formulae for the distribution of ratios. *Ann. Math. Statist.*, **19**, 228-37.

Gutfeld, Dr. 1947. 2315
Vom Wesen der Statistik. *Statist. Praxis*, **2**, 25-6.

Gutfeld, Dr. 1947. 2316
Einiges zur statistischen Begriffs-bildung. *Statist. Praxis*, **2**, 57-8.

Gutfeld, Dr. 1948. 2317
Das Gesetz der grossen Zahl in der Statistik. *Statist. Praxis*, **3**, 9.

Gutfeld, Dr. 1948. 2318
Der Durchschnitt als statistische Aussage. *Statist. Praxis*, **3**, 25-6.

Guttman, L. 1940. 2319
Multiple rectilinear prediction and the resolution into components. *Psychometrika*, **5**, 75-99.

Guttman, L. 1941. 2320
Mathematical and tabulation techniques. (Including: An outline of the statistical theory of prediction.) *Bull. Soc. Sci. Res. Council*, no. 48, pp. 251-364.

Guttman, L. 1944. 2321
A basis for scaling qualitative data. *Amer. Sociol. Rev.*, **9**, 139-50.

Guttman, L. 1944. 2322
General theory and methods for matric factoring. *Psychometrika*, **9**, 1-16.

Guttman, L. 1945. 2323
A basis for analyzing test-retest reliability. *Psychometrika*, **10**, 255-82.

Guttman, L. 1945. 2324
Questions and answers about scale analysis. *Research Branch. Information and Education Division, U.S. Army Services Report*, D-2.

Guttman, L. 1946. 2325
An approach for quantifying paired comparisons and rank order. *Ann. Math. Statist.*, **17**, 144-63.

Guttman, L. 1946. 2326
Enlargement methods for computing the inverse matrix. *Ann. Math. Statist.*, **17**, 336-43.

Guttman, L. 1946. 2327
The test-retest reliability of qualitative data. *Psychometrika*, **11**, 81-95.

Guttman, L. 1947. 2328
The Cornell technique for scale and intensity analysis. *Educ. and Psychol. Measurement*, **7**, 247-79.

Guttman, L. 1947. 2329
On Festinger's evaluation of scale analysis. *Psychol. Bull.*, **44**, 451-65.

Guttman, L. 1948. 2330
An inequality for kurtosis. *Ann. Math. Statist.*, **19**, 277-8.

Guttman, L. 1948. 2331
A distribution-free confidence interval for the mean. *Ann. Math. Statist.*, **19**, 410-13.

Guttman, L. & Cohen, J. 1943. 2332
Multiple rectilinear prediction and the resolution into components. II. *Psychometrika*, **8**, 169-83.

Guttman, L. & Suchman, E. A. 1947. 2333
Intensity and a zero point for attitude analysis. *Amer. Sociol. Rev.*, **12**, 57-67.

Guyton, A. C. 1947. 2334
Analysis of respiratory patterns in laboratory animals. *Amer. J. Physiol.*, **150**, 78-83.

H

Haak, L. A. 1943. 2335
A new method of analysing the age and sex composition of a population. *Proc. Oklahoma Acad. Sci.*, **23**, 84-5.

Haavelmo, T. 1940. 2336
The inadequacy of testing dynamic theory by comparing theoretical solutions and observed cycles. *Econometrica*, **12**, *Suppl.*, viii+118 pp.

Haavelmo, T. 1941. 2337
A note on the variate difference method. *Econometrica*, **9**, 74-9.

Haavelmo, T. 1943. 2338
The statistical implications of a system of simultaneous equations. *Econometrica*, **11**, 1-12.

Haavelmo, T. 1943. 2339
Statistical testing of business-cycle theories. *Rev. Econ. Statist.*, **25**, 13-18.

Haavelmo, T. 1944. 2340
The probability approach in econometrics. *Econometrica*, **12**, *Suppl.*, viii + 118 pp.

Haavelmo, T. 1947. 2341
Methods of measuring the marginal propensity to consume. *J. Amer. Statist. Ass.*, **42**, 105-22.

Haden, H. G. 1947. 2342
A note on the distribution of the different orderings of *n* objects. *Proc. Camb. Phil. Soc.*, **43**, 1-9.

Hadwiger, H. 1940. 2343
Eine analytische Reproduktionsfunktion für biologische Gesamtheiten. *Skand. Aktuartidskr*, **23**, 101-13.

Hadwiger, H. 1940. 2344
Natürliche Ausscheidefunktionen für Gesamtheiten und die Lösung der Erneuerungsgleichung. *Mitt. Ver. Schweiz. Versich.-Math.*, **40**, 31-9.

Hadwiger, H. 1940. 2345
Bemerkung zum Problem des Ruins beim Spiele. *Mitt. Ver. Schweiz. Versich.-Math.*, **40**, 41-4.

Hadwiger, H. 1940. 2346
Über die Wahrscheinlichkeit des Ruins bei einer grossen Zahl von Geschäften. *Arch. Math. Wirtsch.*, **6**, 131-5.

Hadwiger, H. 1941. 2347
Eine Formel der mathematischen Bevölkerungstheorie. *Mitt. Ver. Schweiz. Versich.-Math.*, **41**, 67-73.

Hadwiger, H. 1941.   2348
Über eine Funktionalgleichung der Bevölkerungs-
theorie und eine spezielle Klasse analytischer Lösungen.
Bla. Versich.-math., **5**, 181-8.

Hadwiger, H. 1943.   2349
Über gleichwahrscheinliche Aufteilungen. *Zeit. angew.
Math. Mech.*, **22**, 226-32.

Hadwiger, H. 1943.   2350
Gruppierung mit Nebenbedingungen. *Mitt. Ver.
Schweiz. Versich.-Math.*, **43**, 113-22.

Hadwiger, H. 1945.   2351
Die Erfahrungsnachwirkung bei Wahrscheinlichkeiten.
Experientia, **1**, 87-9.

Hadwiger, H. 1945.   2352
Über Verteilungsgesetze vom Poissonschen Typus.
Mitt. Ver. Schweiz. Versich.-Math., **45**, 257-77.

Hadwiger, H. 1946.   2353
Eine Bemerkung über zufällige Anordnungen der
natürlichen Zahlen. *Mitt. Ver. Schweiz. Versich.-
Math.*, **46**, 105-9.

Hadwiger, H. 1948.   2354
An integral mean value for the Euler characteristic
for movable ovals. *Rev. Union Mat. Argent.*, **13**,
66-72.

Hadwiger, H. & Wegmüller, W. 1941.   2355
Entwicklung und Umschichtung von Personengesamtheiten. (French, Italian and English summaries.)
Trans. 12th. Int. Congr. Actuar., *Lucerne*, 1940, **3**,
369-86.

Haferl, E. 1941.   2356
Die Bestimmung der Selbstbehalte in der Lebensversicherung. (French, Italian and English summaries.)
Trans. 12th. Int. Congr. Actuar., *Lucerne*, 1940, **1**,
349-76.

Haferl, E. 1945.   2357
Betrachtungen über die Schwankungen der Sterblich-
keit in der Lebensversicherung. *Mitt. Ver. Schweiz.
Versich.-Math.*, **45**, 361-74.

Hafstad, L. R. 1940.   2358
On the Bartels technique for time-series analysis and
its relation to the analysis of variance. *J. Amer.
Statist. Ass.*, **35**, 347-61.

Hagood, M. J. 1943.   2359
Statistical methods for delineation of regions applied
to data on agriculture and population. *Social Forces*,
21, 287-97.

Hagood, M. J. 1947.   2360
Limitations and potentialities of the application of
the theory of experimental design in sociology. *Proc.
25th. Session Int. Statist. Inst. Conf. Washington, D.C.*,
1947 (Publ. 1951), **3A**, 453-7.

Hagood, M. J. 1947.   2361
Recent contributions of statistics to research methodology in sociology. *Social Forces*, **26**, 36-40.

Hagood, M. J. & Bernert, E. H. 1945.   2362
Component indexes as a basis for stratification in
sampling. *J. Amer. Statist. Ass.*, **40**, 330-41.

Hagstroem, K.-G. 1940.   2363
Stochastik, ein neues—und doch ein altes—Wort.
Skand. Aktuartidskr., **23**, 54-7.

Hagstroem, K.-G. 1941.   2364
Quelques réflexions sur le rôle de la théorie des
probabilités dans l'assurance practique. (German,
Italian and English summaries.) *Trans.* 12*th Int.
Congr. Actuar.*, *Lucerne*, 1940, **1**, 321-8.

Hagstroem, K.-G. 1942.   2365
Note sur l'incertitude de risque. *Skand. Aktuartidskr.*,
25, 150-68 (corrigenda: **26**, 276-7).

Hagstroem, K.-G. 1944.   2366
Private pensions and the Beveridge plan. *Skand.
Aktuartidskr.*, **27**, 43-68.

Hagstroem, K.-G. 1946.   2367
Un problème du calcul stochastique. *Förs.mat. Stud.
Filip Lundberg*, pp. 104-27.

Hájek, J. 1949.   2368
Užití komplexní methody a intervalu spolehlivosti
při važení. (An application of factorial design and
confidence intervals to weighing.) (Czech. English
and Russian summaries.) *Statist. Obzor*, **29**, 258-73.

Hajnal, J. 1947.   2369
The analysis of birth statistics in the light of the recent
international recovery of the birth rate. *Population
Stud.*, **1**, 137-64.

Hajnal, J. 1948.   2370
Some comments on Mr. Karmel's paper " The rela-
tions between male and female reproduction rates ".
Population Stud., **2**, 354-61.

Hajnal, J. 1948.   2371
The estimation of the family size of occupational
groups from the distribution of births by order and
duration of marriage. *Population Stud.*, **2**, 305-17.

Hajós, G. 1942.   2372
Grundzüge der Fehlerabschätzung. (Hungarian.
German summary.) *Mat. Lapok*, **49**, 84-122.

Hald, A. H. 1946.   2373
Den afstumpede normale Fordeling. (The truncated
normal distribution.) (Danish.) *Mat. Tidsskr. B*,
1946, 83-91.

Hald, A. 1947.   2374
The decomposition of a series of observations composed of a trend, a periodic movement and a stochastic
variable. *Nord. Tidskr. Teknisk. Økomomi*, **36**,
97-224. (Also published separately, Gads Forlag,
Copenhagen, 1948.)

Hald, A. 1949.   2375
Maximum likelihood estimation of the parameters of
a normal distribution which is truncated at a known
point. *Skand. Aktuartidskr.*, **32**, 119-34.

Hald, A. H. & Rasch, G. 1943.   2376
Nogle anvendelser af transformationsmetoden i den
normale fordelings teori. (Some applications of
transformation methods in normal distribution theory.)
(Danish.) *Festskr. J. F. Steffensen*, pp. 52-65.

Hald, A., Jersild, M. & Rasch, G. 1943.   2377
On the determination of the phagocytic power of
leucocytes. *Acta Path. Microbiol. Scand.*, **20**, 64-
85.

Haldane, J. B. S. 1940.   2378
The conflict between selection and mutation of harmful
recessive genes. *Ann. Eugen.*, **10**, 417-21.

Haldane, J. B. S. 1940. 2379
The estimation of recessive gene frequencies by inbreeding. *Proc. Indian Acad. Sci.*, **12**, 109-14.

Haldane, J. B. S. 1940. 2380
The mean and variance of χ^2 when used as a test of homogeneity, when expectations are small. *Biometrika*, **31**, 346-55.

Haldane, J. B. S. 1940. 2381
The cumulants and moments of the binomial distribution, and the cumulants of χ^2 for a $(n+2)$-fold table. *Biometrika*, **31**, 392-6.

Haldane, J. B. S. 1941. 2382
The cumulants of the distribution of the square of a variate. *Biometrika*, **32**, 199-200.

Haldane, J. B. S. 1941. 2383
The faking of genetical results. *Eureka*, **6**, 8-10.

Haldane, J. B. S. 1941. 2384
The fitting of binomial distributions. *Ann. Eugen.*, **11**, 179-81.

Haldane, J. B. S. 1941. 2385
The relative importance of principal and modifying genes in determining some human diseases. *J. Genet.*, **41**, 149-57.

Haldane, J. B. S. 1942. 2386
Moments of the distributions of powers and products of normal variates. *Biometrika*, **32**, 226-42.

Haldane, J. B. S. 1942. 2387
The mode and median of a nearly normal distribution with given cumulants. *Biometrika*, **32**, 294-9.

Haldane, J. B. S. 1942. 2388
Selection against heterozygosis in man. *Ann. Eugen.*, **11**, 333-40.

Haldane, J. B. S. 1943. 2389
Statistics of occupational mortality. *Camb. Univ. Med. Soc. Mag.*, **20**, 38-44.

Haldane, J. B. S. 1943. 2390
Variations in the weights of hatched and unhatched ducks' eggs. Appendix I. The coefficient of variation of egg volume. Appendix II. Interpretation of the greater variance of the unhatched eggs. *Biometrika*, **33**, 56-8.

Haldane, J. B. S. 1944. 2391
Mutation and the Rhesus reaction. *Nature*, **153**, 106.

Haldane, J. B. S. 1945. 2392
Chance effects and the Gaussian distribution. *Phil. Mag.*, (7) **36**, 184-5.

Haldane, J. B. S. 1945. 2393
A labour-saving method of sampling. *Nature*, **155**, 49-50.

Haldane, J. B. S. 1945. 2394
Inverse statistical variates. *Nature*, **155**, 453.

Haldane, J. B. S. 1945. 2395
On a method of estimating frequencies. *Biometrika*, **33**, 222-5.

Haldane, J. B. S. 1945. 2396
Moments of r and χ^2 for a fourfold table in the absence of association. *Biometrika*, **33**, 231-3.

Haldane, J. B. S. 1945. 2397
The use of χ^2 as a test of homogeneity in a $(n \times 2)$-fold table when expectations are small. *Biometrika*, **33**, 234-8.

Haldane, J. B. S. 1946. 2398
The cumulants of the distribution of Fisher's u_{11} and u_{31} scores used in the detection and estimation of linkage in man. *Ann. Eugen.*, **13**, 122-34.

Haldane, J. B. S. 1946. 2399
The interaction of nature and nurture. *Ann. Eugen.*, **13**, 197-205.

Haldane, J. B. S. 1947. 2400
The mutation rate of the gene for haemophilia, and its segregation ratios in males and females. *Ann. Eugen.*, **13**, 262-71.

Haldane, J. B. S. 1947. 2401
The dysgenic effect of induced recessive mutations. *Ann. Eugen.*, **14**, 35-43.

Haldane, J. B. S. 1948. 2402
Differences. *Mind*, **57**, 227-301.

Haldane, J. B. S. 1948. 2403
The formal genetics of man. *Proc. Roy. Soc. B*, **135**, 147-70.

Haldane, J. B. S. 1948. 2404
The precision of observed values of small frequencies. *Biometrika*, **35**, 297-300.

Haldane, J. B. S. 1948. 2405
Note on the median of a multivariate distribution. *Biometrika*, **35**, 414-15.

Haldane, J. B. S. 1948. 2406
The theory of a cline. *J. Genet.*, **48**, 277-84.

Haldane, J. B. S. 1948. 2407
The number of genotypes which can be formed with a given number of genes. *J. Genet.*, **49**, 117-19.

Haldane, J. B. S. 1949. 2408
A note on non-normal correlation. *Biometrika*, **36**, 467-8.

Haldane, J. B. S. 1949. 2409
Parental and fraternal correlations for fitness. *Ann. Eugen.*, **14**, 288-92.

Haldane, J. B. S. 1949. 2410
A test for homogeneity of records of familial abnormalities. *Ann. Eugen.*, **14**, 339-41.

Haldane, J. B. S. 1949. 2411
The rate of mutation of human genes. *Proc. 8th Int. Congr. Genetics. Hereditas*, **35**, *Suppl.*, 267-73.

Haldane, J. B. S. 1949. 2412
Statistical problems arising in genetics. *J. R. Statist. Soc. B*, **11**, 1-14.

Haldane, J. B. S. 1949. 2413
Suggestions as to quantitative measurement of rates of evolution. *Evolution*, **3**, 51-6.

Haldane, J. B. S. & Lea, D. E. 1947. 2414
A mathematical theory of chromosomal rearrangements. *J. Genet.*, **48**, 1-10.

Haldane, J. B. S. & Poole, R. 1942. 2415
A new pedigree of recurrent bullous eruption of the feet. *J. Heredity*, **33**, 17-18.

Haldane, J. B. S. & Smith, C. A. B. 1947. 2416
A new estimate of the linkage between the genes for colour-blindness and haemophilia in man. *Ann. Eugen.*, **14**, 10-31.

Haldane, J. B. S. & Smith, C. A. B. 1947.   2417
A simple exact test for birth-order effect. *Ann. Eugen.*, **14**, 117-24 (errata: 279).

Haldane, J. B. S. & Whitehouse, H. L. K.   2418
1946. Symmetrical and asymmetrical reduction in *Ascomycetes*. *J. Genet.*, **47**, 208-12.

Hale, W. T. 1947.   2419
A statistical sampling plan for refractory products with special reference to silica bricks. *British Ceramic Soc. Trans.*, **46**, 147-60.

Haley, T. J. 1947.   2420
An instrument for plotting ED_{50} curves. *Science (N.S.)*, **106**, 151.

Hall, D. M., Welker, E. L. & Crawford, I.   2421
1945. Factor analysis calculations by tabulating machines. *Psychometrika*, **10**, 93-125.

Hall, M. 1945.   2422
An existence theorem for Latin squares. *Bull. Amer. Math. Soc.*, **51**, 387-8.

Hall, M. 1948.   2423
Distinct representation of subsets. *Bull. Amer. Math. Soc.*, **54**, 922-6.

Hall, O. 1949.   2424
Use of sampling procedures and role of theory in sociological research. *Canad. J. Econ. Pol. Sci.*, **15**, 1-13.

Haller, B. 1945.   2424ᵃ
Verteilungsfunktionen und ihre Auszeichnung durch Funktionalgleichungen. *Mitt. Ver. Schweiz. Versich.-Math.*, **45**, 97-163. (Translated by **R. E. Kalaba**, *RAND Corp. Trans.*, 7 January 1953, T-27, 29 pp.)

Hallert, B. 1943.   2425
Über einige Verfahren zur Lösung von Normalgleichungen. *Zeit. Vermessungs.*, **72**, 238-44.

Hallonquist, T. 1946.   2426
Area sampling—en ny metod för intevjuernas fordelning. (Area-sampling—a new method for the distribution of persons interviewed.) *Affärsekonomi*, **19** (16), 1071-3; 1095.

Halmos, P. R. 1941.   2427
The decomposition of measures. *Duke Math. J.*, **8**, 386.

Halmos, P. R. 1941.   2428
Statistics, set functions, and spectra. (English. Russian summary.) *Mat. Sbornik*, **9** (51), 241-8.

Halmos, P. R. 1944.   2429
The foundations of probability. *Amer. Math. Monthly*, **51**, 493-510.

Halmos, P. R. 1944.   2430
Random alms. *Ann. Math. Statist.*, **15**, 182-9.

Halmos, P. R. 1946.   2431
The theory of unbiased estimation. *Ann. Math. Statist.*, **17**, 34-43.

Halmos, P. R. 1948.   2432
The range of a vector measure. *Bull. Amer. Math. Soc.*, **54**, 416-21.

Halmos, P. R. 1949.   2433
Measurable transformations. *Bull. Amer. Math. Soc.*, **55**, 1015-34.

Halmos, P. R. & Savage, L. J. 1949.   2434
Application of the Radon-Nikodym theorem to the theory of sufficient statistics. *Ann. Math. Statist.*, **20**, 225-41.

Halphen, É. 1949.   2435
Quelques remarques sur le problème de l'estimation. *Le calcul des probabilités et ses applications. Colloq. Int. Centre Nat. Rech. Sci., Paris*, **13**, 87-91.

Halton Thomson, D. *See* **Thomson, D. Halton.**

Halvorson, H. O. & Moeglein, A. 1940.   2436
Application of statistics to problems in bacteriology. V. The probability of occurrence of various experimental results. *Growth*, **4**, 157-68.

Hamaker, H. C. 1948.   2436ᵃ
Een systematische vergelijking van de statistische eigenschappen van hedendaagse steekproef-schema's. (A systematic comparison of the statistical properties of present-day sampling schemes.) (Dutch. English summary.) *Statistica Neerlandica*, **2**, 19-39.

Hamaker, H. C. 1948.   2437
Random sampling numbers. (Dutch. English summary.) *Statistica Neerlandica*, **2**, 97-106.

Hamaker, H. C. 1948.   2438
Foutentheorie en wiskundige statistiek. (Error theory and mathematical statistics.) (Dutch. English summary.) *Statistica Neerlandica*, **2**, 177-205.

Hamaker, H. C. 1948.   2438ᵃ
De invoering van moderne statistische methoden en opvattingen in het massaproducerend bedrijf. *Tijdschr. Effic. Docum.*, **18**, 266-8.

Hamaker, H. C. 1949.   2438ᵇ
De ruis in radiobuizen als statistisch verschijnsel. (Noise in radio valves as a statistical phenomenon.) (Dutch. English summary.) *Statistica Neerlandica*, **3**, 19-30.

Hamaker, H. C. 1949.   2438ᶜ
Critiek op de " Hyperbolische foutenwet ". Naschrift. *Statistica Neerlandica*, **3**, 140-3.

Hamaker, H. C. 1949.   2439
The industrial application of statistics in the Netherlands. *Bull. Int. Statist. Inst.*, (Publ. 1950) **32** (2), 76-98.

Hamaker, H. C. 1949.   2440
A simple technique for producing random sampling numbers. *Proc. Kon. Ned. Akad. Wetensch.*, **52**, 145-50.

Hamaker, H. C. 1949.   2441
Random sampling frequencies; an implement for rapidly constructing large-size artificial samples. *Proc. Kon. Ned. Akad. Wetensch.*, **52**, 432-9. (Also: *Statistica Neerlandica*, **2** (1948), 129-37.)

Hamaker, H. C. 1949.   2441ᵃ
Theorie van steekproefschema's. *Philips Technisch Tijdschr.*, **11**, 264-74.

Hamilton, E. L. 1949.   2441ᵇ
The problem of sampling rainfall in mountainous areas. *Proc. Berkeley Symp. Math. Statist. and Probab.*, 1945-6, pp. 469-75.

Hamilton, M. 1948.   2442
Nomogram for the tetrachoric correlation coefficient. *Psychometrika*, **13**, 259-70. (Also: *Nature*, **160**, 473-4.)

Hamilton, M. 1949. 2443
A simple diagram for obtaining tetrachoric correlation coefficients. *Brit. J. Psychol.*, **39**, 168-71.

Hammer, P. C. 1945. 2443[a]
Limits for control charts. *Industr. Qual. Contr.*, **2** (3), 9-11.

Hammersley, J. M. 1949. 2444
The unbiassed estimate and standard error of the interclass variance. *Metron*, **15**, 189-206.

Hamming, G. 1947. 2445
Graphic correction of a Fisher experiment. *Landbouwk. Tijdschr.*, *Wageningen*, **59**, 496-504.

Hammon, P. H. & Clarke, R. D. 1941. 2446
Some effects upon insurance problems of modern criticisms of the frequency theorem of probability. (German, French and Italian summaries.) *Trans. 12th Int. Congr. Actuar., Lucerne, 1940*, **1**, 207-24.

Hammond, W. H. 1944. 2447
Factor analysis as an aid to nutritional assessment. *J. Hyg., Camb.*, **43**, 395-9.

Hanks, J. H. & James, D. F. 1940. 2448
The enumeration of bacteria by the microscopic method. *J. Bact.*, **39**, 297-305.

Hannay, C. L. 1946. 2449
A control chart for bacterial colony counts. *Proc. Soc. Appl. Bact.*, **1946**, 85-8.

Hanner, O. 1949. 2450
Deterministic and non-deterministic stationary processes. *Ark. Mat.*, **1**, 161-77.

Hansen, C. W. 1944. 2451
Factors associated with successful achievement in problem solving in sixth grade arithmetic. *J. Educ. Res.*, **38**, 111-18.

Hansen, M. H. 1944. 2452
Census to sample population growth. *Domestic Commerce*, **32**, 6ff.

Hansen, M. H. 1947. 2453
Sampling of human populations. *Proc. 25th. Session Int. Statist. Inst. Conf., Washington, D.C., 1947* (Publ. 1951), **3A**, 113-28.

Hansen, M. H. & Deming, W. E. 1943. 2454
On some census aids to sampling. *J. Amer. Statist. Ass.*, **38**, 353-7.

Hansen, M. H. & Hauser, P. M. 1945. 2455
Area sampling—some principles of sampling design. *Public Opinion Quart.* **9**, 183-93.

Hansen, M. H. & Hurwitz, W. N. 1942. 2456
Relative efficiencies of various sampling units in population enquiries. *J. Amer. Statist. Ass.*, **37**, 89-94.

Hansen, M. H. & Hurwitz, W. N. 1943. 2457
On the theory of sampling from finite populations. *Ann. Math. Statist.*, **14**, 333-62.

Hansen, M. H. & Hurwitz, W. N. 1944. 2458
A new sample of the population. *Estadística*, **2**, 483-93.

Hansen, M. H. & Hurwitz, W. N. 1946. 2459
The problem of non-response in sample surveys. *J. Amer. Statist. Ass.*, **41**, 517-29.

Hansen, M. H. & Hurwitz, W. N. 1946. 2460
Sampling methods applied to census work. *Washington, D.C., United States Dept. of Commerce, Bureau of Census.*

Hansen, M. H. & Hurwitz, W. N. 1949. 2461
Dependable samples for market surveys. *J. Marketing*, **14**, 363-72.

Hansen, M. H. & Hurwitz, W. N. 1949. 2462
On the determination of optimum probabilities in sampling. *Ann. Math. Statist.*, **20**, 426-32.

Hansen, M. H., Hurwitz, W. N. & Gurney, M. 2463
1946. Problems and methods of the sample survey of business. *J. Amer. Statist. Ass.*, **41**, 173-89 (correction: 529). (Spanish version (1949): *Estadística*, **7**, 197-213.)

Hansen, M. H., Meir, N. C., 2463[a]
Warner, L. H. & Wilson, E. C. 1946.
Sampling problems. *Proc. Central City Conf. Public Opinion Res.*, 29-31 July 1946, pp. 53-63. (Nat. Opinion Res. Center, Univ. Denver.)

Hardin, G. 1945. 2464
A more meaningful form of the " logistic " equation. *Amer. Nat.*, **79**, 279-81.

Harding, E. W. 1944. 2464[a]
Quality control in the foundry. General principles and experience in high duty iron production. I, II. *Canadian Metals & Metall. Ind.*, **7**, (8), 39-44, 46; (9), 37-40.

Harding, E. W. 1944. 2464[b]
Quality control in high duty iron production. *Foundry Trade J.*, **72**, 219-23; 239-42; 265-70; 294-8.

Harding, E. W. 1946. 2465
Statistical control applied to high duty iron production. *J. R. Statist. Soc. Suppl.*, **8**, 233-43.

Hardy, J. I. & Wolf, H. W. 1947. 2466
Wool fibre density of Shropshire lambs. *J. Animal Sci.*, **6**, 72-82.

Harman, H. H. 1940. 2466[a]
Four aspects of factor analysis. *Proc. Educ. Res. Forum, Endicott, N.Y.*, pp. 60-8.

Harman, H. H. 1941. 2467
On the rectilinear prediction of oblique factors. *Psychometrika*, **6**, 29-35.

Harrington, J. B. 1941. 2468
The effect of having rows different distances apart in rod row plot tests of wheat, oats and barley. *Scientific Agric.*, **21**, 589-606.

Harris, C. W. 1948. 2468[a]
Direct notation to primary structure. *J. Exper. Psychol.*, **39**, 449-68.

Harris, C. W. & Knoell, D. M. 1948. 2469
The oblique solution in factor analysis. *J. Educ. Psychol.*, **39**, 385-403.

Harris, G. B. 1945. 2469[a]
Statistical method lowers inspection costs. *Die Casting*, **3**, 63-4.

Harris, H. 1946. 2470
Microspermia in an individual from a family of unusually high sex ratio and low fertility. *Ann. Eugen.*, **13**, 156-60.

Harris, H. 1946.   2471
The inheritance of premature baldness in man. *Ann. Eugen.*, **13**, 172-81.

Harris, H. & Smith, C. A. B. 1949.   2472
The sib-sib age of onset correlation among individuals suffering from a hereditary syndrome produced by more than one gene. *Ann. Eugen.*, **14**, 309-18.

Harris, M., Horvitz, D. G. & Mood, A. M. 1948.   2473
On the determination of sample sizes in designing experiments. *J. Amer. Statist. Ass.*, **43**, 391-402 (errata: **46**, 515).

Harris, T. E. 1947.   2474
Note on differentiation under the expectation sign in the fundamental identity of sequential analysis. *Ann. Math. Statist.*, **18**, 294-5.

Harris, T. E. 1948.   2475
Branching processes. *Ann. Math. Statist.*, **19**, 474-94.

Harris, T. E. 1949.   2475ᵃ
A model for the reliability of complex mechanisms. *RAND Corp. Res. Memo.*, 5 Dec. 1949, RM-302, 7 pp.

Harris, T. E. & Paxson, E. W. 1948.   2476
A differential equation with random shocks. *RAND Corp. Res. Memo*, 3 December 1948, RM-74, 7 pp.

Harrison, C. J. & Bose, S. S. 1942.   2477
Studies of the variations in value of tea and its chemical constituents. *Sankhyā*, **6**, 151-66.

Harrison, J. L. 1945.   2478
Stored products, and the insects infesting them as examples of the logarithmic series. *Ann. Eugen.*, **12**, 280-2.

Harsh, C. M. 1940.   2478ᵃ
Constancy and variation in patterns of factor loadings. *J. Exper. Psychol.*, **31**, 335-59.

Harshbarger, B. 1944-5.   2479
On the analysis of a certain six-by-six four-group lattice design using the recovery of interblock information. *Ann. Math. Statist.*, **15**, 307-20; **16**, 387-90.

Harshbarger, B. 1946.   2480
Preliminary report on the rectangular lattices. *Biometrics Bull.*, **2**, 115-19.

Harshbarger, B. 1947.   2481
Rectangular lattices. *Virginia Agric. Exper. Sta.*, Mem. no. 1, iii+26 pp.

Harshbarger, B. 1949.   2482
Triple rectangular lattices. *Biometrics*, **5**, 1-13.

Hart, A. G. 1942.   2483
Risk, uncertainty, and the unprofitability of compounding probabilities. *Studies in Mathematical Economics and Econometrics in Memory of Henry Schultz* (Univ. Chicago Press), pp. 110-18.

Hart, B. I. 1942.   2484
Significance levels for the ratio of the mean square successive difference to the variance. *Ann. Math. Statist.*, **13**, 445-7.

Hart, B. I. & von Neumann, J. 1942.   2485
Tabulation of the probabilities for the ratio of the mean square successive difference to the variance. *Ann. Math. Statist.*, **13**, 207-14.

Hart, H. 1945.   2486
Logistic social trends. *Amer. J. Sociol.*, **50**, 337-52.

Hart, H. 1946.   2487
Depression, war and logistic trends. *Amer. J. Sociol.*, **52**, 112-22.

Harte, C. 1948.   2488
Die Aufstellung von Koppelungsgruppen unter Verwendung der Korrelationsrechnung. *Zeit. Naturforsch.*, **3**, 99-105.

Harte, R. A. 1948.   2489
A simple graphical solution for potency calculations of multidose assays. *Science*, **107**, 401-2.

Hartkemeier, H. P. & Miller, H. E. 1942.   2490
Obtaining differences from punched cards. *J. Amer. Statist. Ass.*, **37**, 285-7.

Hartley, H. O. 1940.   2491
Bibliography of mathematical statistics. *J. R. Statist. Soc.*, **103**, 534-60.

Hartley, H. O. 1940.   2492
Testing the homogeneity of a set of variances. *Biometrika*, **31**, 249-55.

Hartley, H. O. 1941.   2492ᵃ
Tables of percentage points of the incomplete beta-function: Methods of interpolation. *Biometrika*, **32**, 161-7.

Hartley, H. O. 1942.   2493
The probability integral of the range in samples of *n* observations from a normal population. II. Numerical evaluation of the probability integral. *Biometrika*, **32**, 309-10.

Hartley, H. O. 1942.   2494
The range in random samples. *Biometrika*, **32**, 334-48.

Hartley, H. O. 1944.   2495
Studentization, or the elimination of the standard deviation of the parent population from the random sample-distribution of statistics. *Biometrika*, **33**, 173-80.

Hartley, H. O. 1945.   2496
Note on the calculation of the distribution of the estimate of mean deviation in normal samples. Tables of the probability integral of the mean deviation in normal samples. *Biometrika*, **33**, 257-65.

Hartley, H. O. 1946.   2497
The application of some commercial calculating machines to certain statistical calculations. *J. R. Statist. Soc. Suppl.*, **8**, 154-83.

Hartley, H. O. 1948.   2498
The estimation of non-linear parameters by 'internal least squares'. *Biometrika*, **35**, 32-45.

Hartley, H. O. 1948.   2499
Approximation errors in distributions of independent variates. *Biometrika*, **35**, 417-18.

Hartley, H. O. 1949.   2500
Tests of significance in harmonic analysis. *Biometrika*, **36**, 194-201.

Hartley, H. O. & Khamis, S. H. 1947.   2501
A numerical solution of the problem of moments. *Biometrika*, **34**, 340-51.

Hartley, H. O. & Pearson, E. S. 1946.   2501ᵃ
Prefatory note to tables for testing the homogeneity of a set of estimated variances. *Biometrika*, **33**, 296-301.

Hartman, J. D. & Stair, E. C. 1942.   2502
Field plot technique studies with tomatoes. *Proc. Amer. Soc. Hort. Sci.*, **41**, 315-20.

Hartman, J. D. & Stair, E. C. 1946.   2503
Correlation of means and standard deviations in tomato field experiments. *Proc. Amer. Soc. Hort. Sci.*, **48**, 337-40.

Hartman, P. 1941.   2504
Normal distributions and the law of the iterated logarithm. *Amer. J. Math.*, **63**, 584-8.

Hartman, P. & Wintner, A. 1940.   2504[a]
Statistical independence and statistical equilibrium. *Amer. J. Math.*, **62**, 646-54.

Hartman, P. & Wintner, A. 1940.   2505
On the standard deviations of additive arithmetical functions. *Amer. J. Math.*, **62**, 743-52.

Hartman, P. & Wintner, A. 1940.   2506
On the spherical approach to the normal distribution law. *Amer. J. Math.*, **62**, 759-79.

Hartman, P. & Wintner, A. 1941.   2507
On the law of the iterated logarithm. *Amer. J. Math.*, **63**, 169-76.

Hartman, P. & Wintner, A. 1941.   2508
On the needle problem of Laplace and its generalisations. *Bol. Mat.*, **14**, 260-3.

Hartman, P. & Wintner, A. 1942.   2509
On the infinitesimal generators of integral convolutions. *Amer. J. Math.*, **64**, 273-98.

Hartman, P. & Wintner, A. 1948.   2510
On the effect of decimal corrections on errors of observation. *Ann. Math. Statist.*, **19**, 389-93.

Hartman, S. 1948.   2511
Sur une généralisation de la notion d'indépendance stochastique. *Colloq. Math.*, **1**, 341-2.

Hartmann, G. 1946.   2511[a]
L'importance des enquêtes par sondages pour l'économie publique et privée. *Rev. Écon. Soc.*, **4**, 62-72.

Hartree, D. R. 1946.   2511[b]
The Eniac: an electronic computing machine. *Nature*, **158**, 500-6.

Hasel, A. A. 1941.   2512
Estimation of vegetation type areas by linear measurement. *J. Forestry*, **39**, 34-40.

Hasel, A. A. 1942.   2513
Estimation of volume in timber stands by strip sampling. *Ann. Math. Statist.*, **13**, 179-206.

Hasel, A. A. 1942.   2514
Sampling error of cruises in the California pine region. *J. Forestry*, **40**, 211-17.

Hasel, A. A. 1946.   2515
Logging cost as related to tree size and intensity of cutting in ponderosa pine. *J. Forestry*, **44**, 552-60.

Hasel, A. A. 1949.   2515[a]
Long-term silvicultural experiment on methods of cutting. *Proc. Berkeley Symp. Math. Statist. and Probab.*, 1945-6, pp. 477-9.

Hashizume, A., Midzuno, H. & Kimura, H.   2516
1949. On the amount of contribution. (Japanese.) *Res. Mem. Inst. Statist. Math., Tokyo*, **5**, 423-7.

Hasnain Jaffri, S. M. 1948.   2517
Note on "Calculation of cumulants". *Math. Student*, **16**, 37-8.

Hastings, C., Jr. 1947.   2517[a]
Maximization of a function $\phi (X, Y)$. *RAND Corp. Res. Memo.*, 31 Jan. 1947, RM-24, 5 pp.

Hastings, C., Jr. & Marcum, J. I. 1948.   2517[b]
Tables of integrals associated with the error function of a complex variable. *RAND Corp. Res. Memo.*, 1 August 1948, RM-50, 61 pp.

Hastings, C., Jr., Mosteller, F., Tukey, J. W.   2518
& Winsor, C. P. 1947.
Low moments for small samples: A comparative study of order statistics. *Ann. Math. Statist.*, **18**, 413-26.

Hatke, M. A. 1949.   2519
A certain cumulative probability function. *Ann. Math. Statist.*, **20**, 461-3.

Hauschild, J. 1947.   2520
Zur Beurteilung des Pflanzgutwertes von Saatkartoffelfeldern unter Berucksichtigung des Auftretens der Überträger der Kartoffelvirosen. Versuch einer rechnerischen Lösung des Problems. *Züchter*, **17/18**, 241-7.

Hauser, P. M. 1942.   2521
Proposed annual sample census of population. *J. Amer. Statist. Ass.*, **37**, 81-8.

Hauser, P. M. 1945.   2522
Wartime developments in census statistics. *Amer. Sociol. Rev.*, **10**, 160-9.

Hauser, P. M. & Hansen, M. H. 1944.   2523
On sampling in market surveys. *J. Marketing*, **9**, 26-31.

Hayashi, C. 1946.   2524
On some types of correlated chains. (Japanese.) *Res. Mem. Inst. Statist. Math., Tokyo*, **2**, 439-56.

Hayashi, C. 1946.   2525
On compound normal distribution. (Japanese.) *Res. Mem. Inst. Statist. Math., Tokyo*, **2**, 457-65.

Hayashi, C. 1949.   2526
Optimum sampling probabilities given to the elements of a universe. (Japanese.) *Res. Mem. Inst. Statist. Math., Tokyo*, **5**, 156-60.

Hayashi, C. 1949.   2527
Response errors. (Japanese.) *Res. Mem. Inst. Statist. Math., Tokyo*, **5**, 335-41.

Hayashi, C. & Maruyama, F. 1948.   2528
On a certain method of stratification. *Res. Mem. Inst. Statist. Math., Tokyo*, **4**, 399ff.

Hayashi, C., Isida, M., Maruyama, F.   2529
& Nisihira, S. 1949.
Some types of distribution functions in the literacy survey. (Japanese.) *Res. Mem. Inst. Statist. Math., Tokyo*, **5**, 328-34.

Haycocks, H. W. 1947.   2530
Probability. *J. Inst. Actuar. Students' Soc.*, **6**, 189-95.

Hayes, S. P., Jr. 1943.   2531
Tables of the standard error of tetrachoric correlation coefficient. *Psychometrika*, **8**, 193-203.

Hayes, S. P., Jr. 1946. 2532
Diagrams for computing tetrachoric correlation coefficients from percentage differences. *Psychometrika*, **11**, 163-72.

Hayes, S. P., Jr. 1948. 2533
Commercial surveys as an aid in the determination of public policy: a case study. *J. Marketing*, **12**, 475-82.

Hayne, D. W. 1949. 2534
Two methods for estimating populations from trapping records. *J. Mammalogy*, **30**, 399-411.

Haynes, A. & Rigdon, R. H. 1942. 2534ᵃ
Statistical study of the number of cells. *Anat. Rec.*, **83**, 587.

Hayward, J. F. 1943. 2535
An application of the principles of allometry to the study of English Senonian Echinocorys. *Nature*, **151**, 617.

Hayward, K. 1943. 2535ᵃ
Quality control-application to small-quantity output in the aircraft industry. *Aircraft Production*, **5**, 359-63.

Hazel, L. N. 1943. 2536
The genetic basis for constructing selection indices. *Genetics*, **28**, 476-90.

Hazel, L. N. 1946. 2537
The covariance analysis of multiple classification tables with unequal subclass numbers. *Biometrics Bull.*, **2**, 21-5.

Hazel, L. N. & Lush, J. L. 1942. 2538
The efficiency of three methods of selection. *J. Heredity*, **33**, 393-9.

Hazel, L. N. & Terrill, C. E. 1946. 2539
Heritability of weaning traits in range Colombia, Corriedale and Targhee lambs. *J. Animal Sci.*, **5**, 371-7.

Hazel, L. N., Baker, M. L. & Reinmiller, C. F. 2540
1943. Genetic and environmental correlations between the growth rates of pigs at different ages. *J. Animal Sci.*, **2**, 118-28.

Heady, E. O. 1946. 2541
Production functions from a random sample of farms. *J. Farm Econ.*, **28**, 989-1004.

Headley, F. B. 1945. 2542
Relation of production of dairy cows to the nutrients fed. *J. Animal Sci.*, **4**, 369-72.

Healy, M. J. R. 1949. 2543
Routine computation of biological assays involving a quantitative response. *Biometrics*, **5**, 330-4.

Hecht, B. 1947. 2543ᵃ
Process control methods. *Industr. Qual. Contr.*, **4** (1), 7-11.

Hecht, M. & Flaskämper, P. 1940. 2544
Bedeutung und Grenzen der Mathematik in der Statistik. (French summary.) *Bull. Int. Statist. Inst.*, **30** (3), 287-94.

Hedén, C. G. 1946. 2545
On the estimation of fifty per cent. end points in serological titrimetry. *J. Path. Bact.*, **58**, 477-81.

Heese, K. W. 1942. 2546
A general factor in improvement with practice. *Psychometrika*, **7**, 213-23.

Heiberg, P. 1940. 2547
Causerier over talmæssige Undersogelser. (Lectures on numerical analysis.) *Ugeskr. Laeg.*, **102**, 540-5.

Heiberg, P. & Petersen, H. 1946. 2548
The epidemic curve for mumps. *J. Hyg., Camb.*, **44**, 350-1.

Heim, A. W. & Wallace, J. G. 1949. 2549
The effects of repeatedly retesting the same group on the same intelligence test. *Quart. J. Exper. Psychol.*, **1**, 151-9.

Heitler, W. & Jánossy, L. 1949. 2550
On the absorption of meson-producing nucleons. *Proc. Phys. Soc. A*, **62**, 374-85.

Hekker, Th. 1947. 2551
Construction of chance ellipses in a correlation diagram. (Dutch. English summary.) *Statistica, Leiden*, **1**, 203-8.

Hekker, Th. 1949. 2552
Statistiek van lineaire macromoleculen. (Statistics of long-chain molecules: with a postscript by P. de Wolff.) (Dutch. English summary.) *Statistica Neerlandica*, **3**, 77-83.

Helmer, O. 1947. 2553
Randomness. *RAND Corp. Res. Memo.*, 24 March 1947, RM-5, 2 pp.

Helmer, O. 1947. 2553ᵃ
An experiment in estimation. *RAND Corp. Res. Memo.*, 21 July 1947, RM-10, 2 pp.

Helmer, O. & Oppenheim, P. 1945. 2554
A syntactical definition of probability and of degree of confirmation. *J. Symbolic Logic*, **10**, 25-60.

Helsen, H. 1947. 2555
Adaption-level as frame of reference for prediction of psychophysical data. *Amer. J. Psychol.*, **60**, 1-29.

Hemeirijk, J. 1949. 2556
Construction of a confidence region for a line. *Proc. Kon. Ned. Akad. Wetensch.*, **52**, 995-1005 (*Indag. Math.*, **11**, 374-84).

Hemelrijk, J. 1949. 2557
Construction of a confidence region for and estimation of the coefficients of a line from a number of points which have been observed with error in one or both directions. (Dutch.) *Math. Centrum Amsterdam, Mimeo Rep.*, S 28.

Hemelrijk, J. 1949. 2558
On the determination of confidence intervals and estimates for the coefficients of a straight line from a number of inaccurately observed points. (Dutch.) *Math. Centrum Amsterdam, Rep.* ZW-1949-013, 39 pp.

Hempel, C. G. & Oppenheim, P. 1945. 2558ᵃ
A definition of "degree of confirmation". *Philos. Sci.*, **12**, 98-115.

Henderson, C. R. & Riley, E. C. 1945. 2559
Certain statistical considerations in patch testing. *J. Invest. Dermat.*, **6**, 227-30.

Henderson, R. 1940. 2560
Actuarial notes on (i) Sheppard's corrections, (ii) χ^2 test, (iii) difference equation graduation. *Trans. Actuar. Soc. Amer.*, **41**, 480-6.

Hendricks, W. A. 1942. 2561
Theoretical aspects of the use of the crop meter. (No. 2 of a series of analyses of sample farm data.) *United States Dept. Agric., Agric. Marketing Service.*

Hendricks, W. A. 1942. 2562
The theory of sampling with special reference to the collection and interpretation of agricultural statistics. *North Carolina Inst. Statist., Mimeo. Ser.,* no. 1.

Hendricks, W. A. 1944. 2563
The relative efficiencies of groups of farms as sampling units. *J. Amer. Statist. Ass.,* **39,** 366-76.

Hendricks, W. A. 1944. 2564
Untangling figures in the statistical laboratory. *Res. & Farming,* 3, Progr. Rep. no. 1, 10 pp.

Hendricks, W. A. 1948. 2565
Mathematics of sampling. *Virginia Agric. Exper. Sta., Special Tech. Bull.,* 45 pp.

Hendricks, W. A. 1949. 2566
Adjustment for bias caused by non-response in mailed surveys. *Agric. Econ. Res.,* **1,** 52-6.

Hendricks, W. A. & Scholl, J. C. 1943. 2567
Techniques in measuring joint relationships. The joint effects of temperature and precipitation on corn yields. *North Carolina Agric. Exper. Sta. Tech. Bull.,* **74,** 1-34.

Hening, J. C. 1948. 2568
Flavour evaluation procedures. *New York Agric. Exper. Sta. Tech. Bull.,* **284,** 20 pp.

Hening, J. C. 1949. 2569
Operations of a routine testing group in a small laboratory. *Food Tech.,* **3,** 162-3.

Hénon, R. 1943. 2570
L'amortissement du matérial industriel. *J. Soc. Statist. Paris,* **84,** 119-55.

Henriksen, E. K. 1948. 2571
Simultaneous operation of several machines by one person. Application of a method of probability. *Nord. Tidsskr. Teknisk. Økonomi,* **37,** 133-40.

Henry, F. M. 1947. 2572
The theoretical efficiency of a test. *Res. Quart. Amer. Ass. Hlth.,* **18,** 90-103.

Henry, G. F., Down, E. E. & Baten, W. D. 2573
1942. An adequate sample of corn plots with reference to moisture and shelling percentages. *J. Amer. Soc. Agron.,* **34,** 777-81.

Henry, J. A. 1946. 2574
Quality control for the engineering student. *Industr. Qual. Contr.,* **3** (2), 28-9.

Henry, L. & Vincent, P. 1947. 2575
Rhythme maximum d'accroissement d'une population stable. *Population,* **2,** 663-80.

Herbach, L. H. 1948. 2576
Bounds for some functions used in sequentially testing the mean of a Poisson distribution. *Ann. Math. Statist.,* **19,** 400-5.

Herchenroder, M. V. M. 1943. 2577
A review of modern practical methods of analysis in statistics. *Rev. Agric. Île Maurice,* **22,** 51-68.

Herdan, G. 1943. 2578
Logical and analytical relationship between the theory of accidents and factor analysis. *J. R. Statist. Soc.,* **106,** 125-42.

Herdan, G. 1949. 2578a
Control charts for the standard mortality ratio. *Brit. J. Soc. Med.,* **3,** 69-76.

Herdan, G. 1949. 2578b
Estimation of polymer distribution on the basis of differences between the average molecular weights of different order. *Nature,* **163,** 139.

Herdan, G. 1949. 2578c
Inequalities between average molecular weights of polymers, and their relations to the distribution function. *Nature,* **164,** 502-4.

Herdan, G. 1949. 2578d
Interpretation of inequality between the comparative mortality figure (C.M.F.) and the standard mortality ratio (S.M.R.). *Statistica, Milano,* **9,** 465-74.

Herdan, G. 1949. 2579
Use of statistical inequalities in polymer research. *Research,* **2,** 235-7.

Herrey, E. M. J. & Herrey, H. 1945. 2580
Principles of physics applied to traffic movements and road conditions. *Amer. J. Phys.,* **13,** 1-14.

Herrick, A. M. 1944. 2581
Multiple correlation in predicting the growth of many-aged oak-hickory stands. *J. Forestry,* **42,** 812-17.

Herrick, A. M. 1945. 2582
A numerical evaluation of stand structure. *J. Forestry,* **43,** 891-9.

Herrold, G. V. 1944. 2582a
The introduction of quality control at Colonial Radio Corporation. *Industr. Qual. Contr.,* **1** (1), 4-9.

Hersch, L. 1940. 2583
De quelques potentiels-vie et de certaines variétés de vie moyenne. (English summary.) *Rev. Int. Statist. Inst.,* **8,** 128-62.

Hersch, L. 1942. 2584
La méthode des potentiels-vie appliquée à l'étude du mouvement naturel de la population. (English summary.) *Rev. Int. Statist. Inst.,* **10,** 152-83.

Hersch, L. 1944. 2585
De la démographie actuelle à la démographie potentielle. *Mélanges d'études écon. soc., offerts à W. E. Rappard (Geneva),* pp. 55-129.

Hersch, L. 1944. 2586
Quelques précisions sur la méthode des potentiels-vie et ses notions fondamentales. *Rev. Int. Statist. Inst.,* **12,** 23-35.

Hersh, A. H. 1942. 2587
Drosophila and the course of research. *Ohio J. Sci.,* **42,** 198-200.

Hersh, A. H. 1943. 2588
A further application of the allometric equation. *Anat. Rec.,* **87,** 19-20.

Herz, H. 1943. 2589
Methodische Fragen zur Bevölkerungsfortschreibung in den Grossstädten. *Dtsch. Statist. Zbl.,* **35** (3-4), 65-72.

Herzberger, M. & Morris, R. H. 1947.   2590
A contribution to the method of least squares. *Quart.*
Appl. Math., **5**, 354-7.

Herzog, F. 1947.   2591
Upper bound for terms of the binomial expansion.
Amer. Math. Monthly, **54**, 485-7.

Hetzer, H. O., Dickerson, G. E. & Zeller, J. H. 2592
1944. Heritability of type in Poland China swine as
evaluated by scoring. *J. Animal Sci.*, **3**, 390-8.

Hewlett, P. S. 1947.   2593
A direct-spray technique for the biological evaluation
of pyrethrum-in-oil insecticides for use against stored
product insects in warehouses. *Ann. Appl. Biol.*, **34**,
357-75.

Hiatt, C. W. 1947.   2594
Certain mathematical aspects of the susceptibility of
erythrocytes to lysis. *Proc. Soc. Exper. Biol.*, **66**,
279-81.

Hibbert, L. 1941.   2595
Les équations du problème des fluctuations écono-
miques et de l'interdépendance des marchés, d'après
M. B. Chait. *Bull. Soc. Math. France*, **69**, 1-22.

Hildebrand, F. C. & Koehn, R. C. 1944.   2596
Sources of error in the determination of the protein
content of bulk wheat. *Cereal Chem.*, **21**, 370-4.

Hilgard, E. R. & Payne, S. L. 1944.   2597
Those not at home: riddle for pollsters. *Public*
Opinion Quart., **8**, 254-61.

Hill, A. Bradford. 1947.   2598
Statistics in the medical curriculum? *Brit. Med. J.*, **2**,
366-8.

Hill, A. Bradford. 1947.   2599
Statistics in medicine. *Trans. Manchester Statist. Soc.*,
1946-7, 15 pp.

Hill, H. W. 1944-6.   2600
" Speed of reaction " hypothesis. I. Its numerical
foundation in respect to the tubercle bacillus. II.
Further numerical implications regarding tuberculosis.
Amer. Rev. Tuberc., **49**, 414-22; **53**, 1-33.

Hill, T. L. & Hill, L. E. 1945.   2601
Contribution to the theory of discrimination learning.
Bull. Math. Biophys., **7**, 107-14.

Hilmy, H. 1940.   2602
Sur la récurrence ergodique dans les systèmes dynamiques. (Russian.) *Mat. Sbornik*, **7** (49), 101-8.

Hinman, W. F., Tucker, R. E., Jans, L. M.   2603
& Halliday, E. G. 1946.
Excessively high riboflavin retention during braising of
beef. A comparison of methods of assay. *Industr.*
Engng. Chem. (*Anal. Ed.*), **18**, 296-301.

Hintzsche, E. 1946.   2604
Biologische Statistik durch materialgerechte Klas-
seneinteilung. *Schweiz. Zeit. Volkwirtsch. Statist.*, **82**,
433-43.

Hirschman, A. O. 1943.   2605
On measures of dispersion for a finite distribution.
J. Amer. Statist. Ass., **38**, 346-52.

Hitchcock, F. L. 1941.   2606
The distribution of a product from several sources to
numerous localities. *J. Math. Phys.*, **20**, 224-30.

Hitchcock, H. P. 1940.   2607
The estimation of the probable error from successive
and independent variances. *Ballistic Res. Lab.*,
Aberdeen Proving Ground, Md., *Rep.* no. 193, 23 pp.

Hitosi-Iyoï. 1940.   2608
Calcul explicite de la distance de deux lois de probabilités. *Ann. Univ. Lyon A*, (3) **3**, 55-63.

Hitt, H. L. 1940.   2609
A sampling technique for studying population changes
in rural areas. *Social Forces*, **19**, 208-13.

Hitt, H. L. 1947.   2610
The use of selected cartographic techniques in health
research. *Social Forces*, **26**, 189-96.

Hoblyn, T. N. 1945.   2611
The design of field experiments with cacao. *Rep.*
Cacao Res. Conf. London, May-June, 1945, pp. 164-8.

Hobson, L. S., Ingles, R. S. & McCantis, R. P.   2612
1945. Application of quality control to resistance
welding. *Trans. Amer. Inst. Elect. Engrs.*, **64**, 573-5.

Hochstim, J. R. & Smith, D. M. K. 1948.   2613
Area sampling or quota control? Three sampling
experiments. *Public Opinion Quart.*, **12**, 73-80.

Hocking, W. S. 1948.   2614
The balance of sexes in Great Britain. *J. Inst. Actuar.*,
74, 340-4.

Hodges, J. L., Jr. 1949.   2615
The choice of inspection stringency in acceptance
sampling by attributes. *Univ. Calif. Publ. Statist.*, **1**,
1-14.

Hoeffding, W. *See also* **Höffding, W.**

Hoeffding, W. 1948.   2616
A class of statistics with asymptotically normal
distribution. *Ann. Math. Statist.*, **19**, 293-325.

Hoeffding, W. 1948.   2617
A non-parametric test of independence. *Ann. Math.*
Statist., **19**, 546-57.

Hoeffding, W. & Robbins, H. E. 1948.   2618
The central limit theorem for dependent random
variables. *Duke Math. J.*, **15**, 773-80.

Hoel, P. G. 1940.   2619
The errors involved in evaluating correlation determinants. *Ann. Math. Statist.*, **11**, 58-65.

Hoel, P. G. 1941.   2620
On methods of solving normal equations. *Ann. Math.*
Statist., **12**, 354-9.

Hoel, P. G. 1943.   2621
On indices of dispersion. *Ann. Math. Statist.*, **14**,
155-62.

Hoel, P. G. 1943.   2622
The accuracy of sampling methods in ecology. *Ann.*
Math. Statist., **14**, 289-300.

Hoel, P. G. 1944.   2623
On statistical co-efficients of likeness. *Univ. Calif.*
Publ. Math. (N.S.), **2** (1), 1-8.

Hoel, P. G. 1945.   2624
Testing the homogeneity of Poisson frequencies. *Ann.*
Math. Statist., **16**, 362-8.

Hoel, P. G. 1946.   2625
The efficiency of the mean moving range. *Ann. Math.*
Statist., **17**, 475-82.

Hoel, P. G. 1947. 2626
On the choice of forecasting formulas. *J. Amer. Statist. Ass.*, **42**, 605-11.

Hoel, P. G. 1947. 2627
Discriminating between binomial distributions. *Ann. Math. Statist.*, **18**, 556-64.

Hoel, P. G. 1948. 2628
On the uniqueness of similar regions. *Ann. Math. Statist.*, **19**, 66-71.

Hoel, P. G. & Peterson, R. P. 1949. 2629
A solution to the problem of optimum classification. *Ann. Math. Statist.*, **20**, 433-8.

Höffding, W. *See also* **Hoeffding, W.**

Höffding, W. 1940. 2630
Maszstabinvariante Korrelationstheorie. *Univ. Berlin, Schr. Math. angew. Math.*, **5** (3), 181-233.

Höffding, W. 1941. 2631
Maszstabinvariante Korrelationsmasse für diskontinuierliche Verteilungen. *Arch. Math. Wirtsch.*, **7**, 49-70.

Höffding, W. 1942. 2632
Stochastische Abhängigkeit und funktionaler Zusammenhang. *Skand. Aktuartidskr.*, **25**, 200-27.

Höffding, W. 1947. 2633
On the distribution of the rank correlation coefficient τ, when the variates are not independent. *Biometrika*, **34**, 183-96.

Hoffman, C. A. & Ault, G. M. 1948. 2634
Application of statistical methods to study of gasturbine blade failure. *Technical Note* 1603 (Publ. by Nat. Advisory Comm. for Aeronautics).

Hogben, L. 1947. 2635
Risk of jaundice following transfusion with pooled plasma or serum. *Brit. J. Soc. Med.*, **1**, 209-11.

Hogben, L. & Cross, K. W. 1948. 2636
The statistical specificity of a code personnel cypher sequence. *Brit. J. Soc. Med.*, **2**, 149-52.

Hogben, L. & Johnstone, M. M. 1947. 2637
The relation of morbidity to age in an army population. *Brit. J. Soc. Med.*, **1**, 149-81.

Hohaus, R. 1940. 2638
Actuarial problems in social insurance. *J. Amer. Statist. Ass.*, **35**, 37-46.

Holck, H. G. O., Kimura, K. K. & Bartels, B. 2639
1946. Effect of the anaesthetic and the rate of injection of digitalis upon its lethal dose in cats. *J. Amer. Pharm. Ass.*, **35**, 366-70.

Holden, J. 1945. 2639[a]
Recorded tests prove effective in maintaining welding quality: Lockheed Aircraft Corporation. *Amer. Machinist*, **89**, 126-8.

Hole, N. 1946. 2640
On the statistical teatment of counting experiments in nuclear physics. *Ark. Mat. Astr. Fys.*, **33A** (11), 11 pp.

Hole, N. 1947. 2641
On the distribution of counts in a counting apparatus. *Ark. Mat. Astr. Fys.*, **33B** (8), 8 pp.

Hole, N. 1947. 2642
Note on the statistical analysis of counter data. *Ark. Mat. Astr. Fys.*, **34B** (12), 8 pp.

Hole, N. 1948. 2643
On the statistical treatment of counter data. *Ark. Mat. Astr. Fys.*, **34B** (20), 8 pp.

Holiday, E. R., Irwin, J. O. and others. 1946. 2644
The assay of crystalline preparations of aneurine by means of the ultra-violet absorption spectrum. *Quart. J. Pharm.*, **19**, 155-72.

Holland, B. 1943. 2644[a]
Quality control keeps product standards high. *Aviation*, **42**, 160-2.

Hollander, W. F. 1946. 2645
Notes on the graphic biometric comparisons of samples. *Amer. Nat.*, **80**, 494-6.

Holley, J. W. 1947. 2646
A note on the reflection of signs in the extraction of centroid factors. *Psychometrika*, **12**, 263-5.

Hollingsworth, C. A. 1948. 2647
The average boundaries of statistical chains. *J. Chem. Phys.*, **16**, 544-7.

Hollingsworth, C. A. 1949. 2648
The transverse boundary of the random coil. *J. Chem. Phys.*, **17**, 97-9.

Holloway, J. K. 1949. 2649
Biological association of insects: parasite and host populations. *Proc. Berkeley Symp. Math. Statist. and Probab.*, 1945-6, pp. 493-501.

Holmes, I. 1943. 2650
Some sampling uses of data from the census of agriculture. *J. Amer. Statist. Ass.*, **38**, 78-86.

Holmes, I. 1944. 2651
Value of farm products by colour and tenure of farm operator. *U.S. Bureau of census*, 291 pp.

Holmsgaard, E. 1945. 2652
Analysis of tree-ring data from Central Jutland. *Dansk. Skovforen. Tidsskr.*, **31**, 129-73.

Holt, S. B. 1948. 2653
The effect of maternal age on the manifestation of a polydactyl gene in mice. *Ann. Eugen.*, **14**, 144-57.

Holubar, J. & Kohlik, E. 1948. 2654
Tabulky k rychlému vypoctu smerodatné odchylky rozdílu procent. (Tables destinées au calcul rapide de la deviation-type des différences entre les pourcentages.) (Czech.) *Čas. Lék. čes.*, **87** (30), 855-6.

Holzinger, K. J. 1940. 2655
A synthetic approach to factor analysis. *Psychometrika*, **5**, 235-50.

Holzinger, K. J. 1942. 2656
Why do people factor? *Psychometrika*, **7**, 147-56.

Holzinger, K. J. 1944. 2657
Factoring test scores and implications for the method of averages. *Psychometrika*, **9**, 155-67.

Holzinger, K. J. 1944. 2658
A simple method of factor analysis. *Psychometrika*, **9**, 257-62.

Holzinger, K. J. 1945. 2659
Interpretation of second order factors. *Psychometrika*, **10**, 21-5.

Holzinger, K. J. 1946. 2660
A comparison of the principal axis and centroid factors. *J. Educ. Psychol.*, **37**, 449-72.

Holzinger, K. J. 1949. 2661
Applications of the simple method of factor analysis. *J. Educ. Psychol.*, **40**, 129-42.

Homeyer, P. G. & Black, C. A. 1947. 2662
Sampling replicated field experiments on oats for yield determinations. *Proc. Soil Sci. Soc. Amer.*, **11**, 341-4.

Homeyer, P. G., Clem, M. A. 2663
& Federer, W. T. 1947.
Punched card and calculating machine methods for analysing lattice experiments, including lattice squares and the cubic lattice. *Iowa Agric. Exper. Sta. Res. Bull.*, **347**, 31-171.

Honka, K. 1947. 2664
Eine statistische Untersuchung über die Anzahl der Krankentage bei den finnischen Betriebskrankenkassen. *Skand. Aktuartidskr.*, **30**, 191-9.

Hoogland, J. J. 1941. 2665
Note on the numerical calculation of the orthogonal polynomials. *Ann. Eugen.*, **11**, 77-9.

Hopf, E. 1949. 2666
Ergodic theory. (Russian.) *Usp. Mat. Nauk (N.S.)*, **4**, 1(29), 113-82.

Hopf, E. 1949. 2667
Statistics of geodesic lines on manifolds of negative curvature. (Russian.) *Usp. Mat. Nauk (N.S.)*, **4**, 2(30), 129-70. (Also (1939), *Ber. Verh. Sächs. Akad. Wiss. Leipzig*, **91**, 261-304.)

Hopkins, J. A. 1942. 2668
Statistical comparisons of record-keeping farms and a random sample of Iowa farms for 1939. *Iowa Agric. Exper. Sta. Res. Bull.*, **308**, 265-87.

Hopkins, J. W. 1946. 2669
Precision of assessment of palatability of foodstuffs by laboratory panels. *Canadian J. Res. F*, **24**, 203-14.

Hopkins, J. W. 1946. 2670
Statistical design of experiments. *Canadian Chemistry & Process Industries*, **30**, (5), 113-16.

Hopkins, J. W. 1947. 2671
Height and weight of Ottawa elementary school children of two socioeconomic strata. *Hum. Biol.*, **19**, 68-72.

Hopkins, J. W. & Weatherburn, M. W. 1947. 2672
Precision of laboratory measurements of breaking strength of textiles. *Canadian J. Res. F*, **25**, 264-72.

Hopp, H. 1947. 2673
Statistics is no mystery. (How you can use statistical analysis in agricultural research.) *U.S. Soil Conservation Service*, 55 pp.

Horn, D. 1942. 2674
A correction for the effect of tied ranks on the value of the rank difference correlation coefficient. *J. Educ. Psychol.*, **33**, 686-90.

Horn, D. 1947. 2675
A study of pilots with repeated accidents. *J. Aviat. Med.*, **18**, 440-9.

Horner, F. 1946. 2676
A problem on the summation of simple harmonic functions of the same amplitude and frequency but of random phase. *Phil. Mag.*, (7) **37**, 145-62.

Hornich, H. 1941. 2677
Zur Theorie des Risikos. *Monatsh. Math. Phys.*, **50**, 142-50.

Horrocks, S. W., Dickerson, P. M., 2678
Dodge, H. F., Ott, E. R., Romig, H. G., Rupp, W. B., Steen, J. R., Wareham, R. E. & Wright, A. K. (Joint Electron Tube Engineering Council.) 1946.
A sampling procedure for design tests of electron tube. *Industr. Qual. Contr.*, **3** (3), 19-24.

Horst, P. 1941. 2679
Mathematical Contributions. *Bull. Soc. Sci. Res. Council*, no. 48, pp. 403-47.

Horst, P. 1941. 2680
A non-graphical method for transforming an arbitrary factor matrix into a simple structure factor matrix. *Psychometrika*, **6**, 79-99.

Horst, P. 1948. 2681
Regression weights as a function of test length. *Psychometrika*, **13**, 125-34.

Horst, P. 1949. 2682
Determination of the optimal test length to maximize the multiple correlation. *Psychometrika*, **14**, 79-88.

Horton, H. B. 1948. 2683
A method for obtaining random numbers. *Ann. Math. Statist.*, **19**, 81-5.

Horton, H. B. & Smith, R. T., III. 1949. 2684
A direct method for producing random digits in any number system. *Ann. Math. Statist.*, **20**, 82-90.

Horton, J. S. 1941. 2685
The sample plot as a method of quantitative analysis of chaparral vegetation in southern California. *Ecology*, **22**, 457-68.

Hosemann, H. 1941. 2686
Eine neue Methode zur Bestimmung der Fruchtbarkeit eines Volkes. (Berechnung nach geometrischen Reihen.) *Zbl. Gynäk*, **65** (39), 1726-41.

Hoskins, J. K. 1940. 2687
Most probable numbers for evaluation of coliaerozenes tests by fermentation tube method. *U.K. Ministry of Health Rep. Publ. Health* no. 1621.

Hostelet, G. 1949. 2688
L'importance de la méthodologie de l'analyse expérimentale pour l'investigation des faits sociaux statistiques. *Bull. Int. Statist. Inst.*, **32** (2), 309-14.

Hostinský, B. 1940. 2689
Sur le coefficient de corrélation. *Memorial vol. dedicated to D. A. Grave, Moscow*, pp. 48-51.

Hostinský, B. 1940. 2690
On the probability of changes in a system which evolves in the course of time. (Czech.) *Rozpravy II, Třídy České Akad.*, **50** (26), 9 pp.

Hostinský, B. 1941. 2691
Stacionární poloupnosti velicin závislych na náhod a Slutského veta o limitnim rozdeleni podle sinusiody. (Suites stationnaires de quantités aléatoires et la loi sinusoïdale limite de Slutsky.) (Czech. French and German summaries.) *Statist. Obzor*, **22**, 141-60.

Hostinský, B. 1949.   2692
Sur le calcul des probabilités relatives à l'évolution d'un système. (Czech. French summary.) *Aktuárske Vědy*, **8** (2), 61-7.

Hotelling, H. 1940.   2693
The selection of variates for use in prediction with some comments on the general problem of nuisance parameters. *Ann. Math. Statist.*, **11**, 271-83.

Hotelling, H. 1940.   2694
The teaching of statistics. *Ann. Math. Statist.*, **11**, 457-71.

Hotelling, H. 1941.   2695
Experimental determination of the maximum of a function. *Ann. Math. Statist.*, **12**, 20-45.

Hotelling, H. 1942.   2696
Problems of prediction. *Amer. J. Sociol.*, **48**, 61-76.

Hotelling, H. 1942.   2697
Rotations in psychology and the statistical revolution. *Science*, **95**, 504-7.

Hotelling, H. 1943.   2698
Some new methods in matrix calculation. *Ann. Math. Statist.*, **14**, 1-34.

Hotelling, H. 1943.   2699
Further points on matrix calculation and simultaneous equations. *Ann. Math. Statist.*, **14**, 440-1.

Hotelling, H. 1943.   2700
Dr. Peters' criticisms of Fisher's statistics. *J. Educ. Res.*, **36**, 707-11.

Hotelling, H. 1944.   2701
Some improvements in weighing and other experimental techniques. *Ann. Math. Statist.*, **15**, 297-306.

Hotelling, H. 1944.   2702
Note on a matric theorem of A. T. Craig. *Ann. Math. Statist.*, **15**, 427-9.

Hotelling, H. 1949.   2703
The place of statistics in the university. *Proc. Berkeley Symp. Math. Statist. and Probab.*, 1945-6, pp. 21-49.

Hotelling, H. 1949.   2704
Practical problems of matrix calculations. *Proc. Berkeley Symp. Math. Statist. and Probab.*, 1945-6, pp. 275-93.

Hotelling, H. 1949.   2705
Stochastic processes: historical summary of the problem. *Econometrica*, **17**, 66-8.

Hough, L. F. & Welker, E. L. 1943.   2706
Combining genetically different samples for correlation analysis. *Proc. Amer. Soc. Hort. Sci.*, **43**, 155-9.

Householder, A. S. & Landahl, H. D. 1944.   2707
Mathematical biophysics of the central nervous system. *Math. Biophys. Monogr.* no. 1, ix+124 pp.

Houseman, E. E. 1943.   2708
Methods of computing a regression of yield on weather. *Iowa Agric. Exper. Sta. Res. Bull.*, **302**, 863-904.

Houseman, E. E. 1947.   2709
Application of area sampling. *U.S. Bureau Agric. Econ.*, 7 pp.

Houseman, E. E. 1947.   2710
The sample design for a national survey by the Bureau of Agricultural Economics. *J. Farm Econ.*, **29**, 241-5.

Houseman, E. E. 1948.   2711
Outline of some methods for selecting samples of households. *Proc. New England Res. Council Marketing and Food Supply*, 1948, pp. 71-4.

Houseman, E. E. 1949.   2712
Design of samples for surveys. *Agric. Econ. Res.*, **1**, 3-10. (Also: *Proc. Auburn Conf. Statist. Appl. Res. Social Sci., Plant Sci. & Animal Sci.*, 1948, pp. 3-14.)

Housner, G. W. & Brennan, J. F. 1948.   2713
The estimation of linear trends. *Ann. Math. Statist.*, **19**, 380-8.

Hovanitz, W. 1948.   2714
A graphical method of illustrating ecological and geographical distributions. *Ecology*, **29**, 121.

Howell, H. 1943.   2714[a]
Stabilized quality control. *Aircraft Production*, **5**, 579-84.

Howell, H. 1944-5.   2714[b]
Quality control: a review of three common misapplications of the system. With discussion. *Aircraft Production*, **6**, 198-201; 290-1; **7**, 33-6; 65-9.

Howell, J. M. 1945.   2714[c]
Statistical quality control: some American views on its fundamental concepts. *Aircraft Production*, **7**, 475-7.

Howell, H. 1945.   2714[d]
Quality control: a comparison of compressed limit gauging methods with measurement check in dimensional quality control practice. *Aircraft Production*, **7**, 539-43.

Howell, H. 1945.   2714[e]
Significance of accurate fine measurement in the statistical prediction of quality in engineering component manufacture. *Engng. Insp.*, **10** (1), 4-16.

Howell, J. M. 1949.   2715
Control chart for largest and smallest values. *Ann. Math. Statist.*, **20**, 305-9 (errata: **21**, 615-16).

Hoyt, C. J. 1941.   2716
Note on a simplified method of computing test reliability. *Educ. and Psychol. Measurement*, **1**, 93-5.

Hoyt, C. J. 1941.   2717
Test reliability estimated by analysis of variance. *Psychometrika*, **6**, 153-60.

Hoyt, C. J. 1945.   2718
The principle of likelihood as a basis for tests of significance. *J. Exper. Educ.*, **13**, 136-44.

Hoyt, C. J. 1945.   2719
Testing linear hypotheses illustrated by a simple example in correlation. *Psychometrika*, **10**, 199-204.

Hoyt, R. S. 1947.   2720
Probability functions for the modulus and angle of the normal complex variate. *Bell Syst. Tech. J.*, **26**, 318-59.

Hrabak, M. 1946.   2721
Pouzitelnost mechanickych vyrovnavacich method. (L'applicabilité des méthodes mécaniques d'ajustement.) (Czech. Russian, English and French summaries.) *Statist. Obzor*, **26**, 91-105.

Hsu, C. T. 1940.   2722
On samples from a normal bivariate population. *Ann. Math. Statist.*, **11**, 410-26.

Hsu, C. T. 1941. 2723
Samples from two bivariate normal populations. *Ann. Math. Statist.*, **12**, 279-92.

Hsu, C. T. & Lawley, D. N. 1940. 2724
The derivation of the fifth and sixth moments of the distribution of b_2 in samples from a normal population. *Biometrika*, **31**, 238-48.

Hsü, E. H. 1946. 2725
On the correlation between a variable and its super-factor. *J. Psychol.*, **22**, 89-92.

Hsü, E. H. & Sherman, M. 1946. 2726
The factorial analysis of the electro-encephalogram. *J. Psychol.*, **21**, 189-96.

Hsu, L. C. 1944. 2727
Some combinatorial formulas with applications to probable values of a polynomial-product and to differences of zero. *Ann. Math. Statist.*, **15**, 399-413.

Hsu, L. C. 1945. 2728
Some combinatorial formulas on mathematical expectation. *Ann. Math. Statist.*, **16**, 369-80.

Hsu, L. C. 1948. 2729
Approximations to a class of double integrals of functions of large numbers. *Amer. J. Math.*, **70**, 698-708.

Hsu, L. C. 1948. 2730
Note on an asymptotic expansion of the nth difference of zero. *Ann. Math. Statist.*, **19**, 273-7.

Hsu, P. L. 1940. 2731
An algebraic derivation of the distribution of rect-angular coordinates. *Proc. Edin. Math. Soc.*, **6**, 185-9.

Hsu, P. L. 1940. 2732
On generalised analysis of variance. I. *Biometrika*, **31**, 221-37.

Hsu, P. L. 1941. 2733
On the limiting distributions of the canonical correla-tions. *Biometrika*, **32**, 38-45.

Hsu, P. L. 1941. 2734
Analysis of variance from the power function stand-point. *Biometrika*, **32**, 62-9.

Hsu, P. L. 1941. 2735
On the limiting distribution of roots of a determinantal equation. *J. Lond. Math. Soc.*, **16**, 183-94.

Hsu, P. L. 1941. 2736
On the problem of rank and the limiting distribution of Fisher's test function. *Ann. Eugen.*, **11**, 39-41.

Hsu, P. L. 1941. 2737
Canonical reduction of the general regression problem. *Ann. Eugen.*, **11**, 42-6.

Hsu, P. L. 1942. 2738
The limiting distribution of a general class of statistics. *Acad. Sinica Sci. Rec.*, **1**, 37-41.

Hsu, P. L. 1943. 2739
Some simple facts about the separation of degrees of freedom in factorial experiments. *Sankhyā*, **6**, 253-4.

Hsu, P. L. 1945. 2740
The approximate distributions of the mean and variance of a sample of independent variables. *Ann. Math. Statist.*, **16**, 1-29.

Hsu, P. L. 1945. 2741
On the approximate distribution of ratios. *Ann. Math. Statist.*, **16**, 204-10.

Hsu, P. L. 1945. 2742
On the power functions for the E^2-test and the T^2-test. *Ann. Math. Statist.*, **16**, 278-86.

Hsu, P. L. 1946. 2743
On the asymptotic distributions of certain statistics used in testing the independence between successive observations from a normal population. *Ann. Math. Statist.*, **17**, 350-4.

Hsu, P. L. 1949. 2744
The limiting distribution of functions of sample means and application to testing hypotheses. *Proc. Berkeley Symp. Math. Statist. and Probab.*, 1945-6, pp. 359-402.

Hsu, P. L. & Chung, K. L. 1946. 2745
Sur un théorème de probabilités dénombrables. *C. R. Acad. Sci., Paris*, **223**, 467-9.

Hsu, P. L. & Robbins, H. E. 1947. 2746
Complete convergence and the law of large numbers. *Proc. Nat. Acad. Sci. U.S.A.*, **33**, 25-31.

Hubback, J. A. 1946. 2747
Sampling for rice yield in Bihar and Orissa. *Sankhyā*, **7**, 281-94.

Hubbs, C. L. & Perlmutter, A. 1942. 2748
Biometric comparison of several samples, with particular reference to racial investigations. *Amer. Nat.*, **76**, 582-92.

Hugas, A. 1946-7. 2749
Het object van het opinie-onderzoek. (Selection of subjects in public opinion research.) (Dutch. English summary.) *Statistica, Leiden*, **1**, 115-18.

Hughes, H. M. 1949. 2750
Estimation of the variance of the bivariate normal distribution. *Univ. Calif. Publ. Statist.*, **1** (4), 37-52.

Hull, F. C. 1947. 2751
A new method for making rapid and accurate estimates of grain size. *Metals Tech.*, **14** (4), 1-13.

Hulme, H. R. 1940. 2752
Statistical theory of errors. *Monthly Not. Roy. Astron. Soc.*, **100**, 303-14.

Hultman, K. 1942. 2753
Einige numerische Untersuchungen auf Grund der kollektiven Risiko theorie. I, II. *Skand. Aktuartidskr.*, **25**, 84-119; 169-99.

Humm, D. G. 1942. 2754
Note on the product-moment correlation of non-rectilinear data. *Amer. J. Psychol.*, **55**, 127-30.

Hummel, F. C. 1947. 2755
The Bowmont Norway Spruce sample plots (1930-45) (*Picea abies, Karst*). *Forestry*, **21**, 30-42.

Hunt, I. A. 1942. 2756
Some potshots at this relative thing called precision. *Instruments*, **15**, 506-9.

Hunter, E. 1944. 2756a
The making of high duty castings in specification. *Engng. Insp.*, **9** (2), 23-30.

Huntington, E. V. 1940. 2757
Stirling's formula with remainder. *Biometrika*, **31**, 390.

Hurtado, A. 1945. 2758
Métodos estadísticos. *An. Fac. Med., Lima*, **28**, 125-306.

Hurwicz, L. 1944. 2759
Stochastic models of economic fluctuations. *Econometrica*, **12**, 114-24.

Hurwicz, L. 1947. 2760
Some problems arising in estimating economic relations. *Econometrica*, **15**, 236-40.

Hurwitz, A. & Mann, F. C. 1946. 2761
The membership of the American Statistical Association —an analysis. *J. Amer. Statist. Ass.*, **41**, 155-70.

Hurwitz, H. & Kac, M. 1944. 2762
Statistical analysis of certain types of random functions. *Ann. Math. Statist.*, **15**, 173-81.

Hussain, Q. M. 1941. 2763
Standardisation of examination marks. *Sankhyā*, **5**, 295-300.

Hussain, Q. M. 1943. 2764
A note on interaction. *Sankhyā*, **6**, 321-2.

Hussain, Q. M. 1945. 2765
Symmetrical incomplete block designs with $\lambda = 2$, $k = 8$ or 9. *Bull. Calcutta Math. Soc.*, **37**, 115-23.

Hussain, Q. M. 1945. 2766
On the totality of the solutions for the symmetrical incomplete block designs $\lambda = 2$, $k = 5$ or 6. *Sankhyā*, **7**, 204-8.

Hussain, Q. M. 1946. 2767
Impossibility of the symmetrical incomplete block design with $\lambda = 2$, $k = 7$. *Sankhyā*, **7**, 317-22.

Hussain, Q. M. 1948. 2768
Structure of some incomplete block designs. *Sankhyā*, **8**, 381-3.

Hussain, Q. M. 1948. 2769
Alternative proof of the impossibility of the symmetrical design with $\lambda = 2$, $k = 7$. *Sankhyā*, **8**, 384.

Hutchinson, A. H. & Knapp, F. M. 1946. 2770
Random sampling, planned sampling, and selective sampling: as applied to forest ecology and silviculture. *Trans. Roy. Soc. Canada*, **40** (5), 77-9.

Hutchinson, G. E. 1947. 2771
A note on the competition between two social species. *Ecology*, **28**, 319-21.

Hutt, F. B. & Bozivich, H. 1946. 2772
On the supposed matroclinous inheritance of egg size in fowl. *Poultry Sci.*, **25**, 554-61.

Huzurbazar, V. S. 1948. 2773
The likelihood equation, consistency and the maxima of the likelihood function. *Ann. Eugen.*, **14**, 185-200.

Huzurbazar, V. S. 1949. 2774
Inverse probability and sufficient statistics. *Proc. Phil. Soc.*, **45**, 225-9.

Huzurbazar, V. S. 1949. 2775
On a property of distributions admitting sufficient statistics. *Biometrika*, **36**, 71-4.

Hvidsten, H. 1940. 2776
Berefning av vekta hos storfe etter mal. (Calculations of the weight of cattle by measuring.) *Norg. Landbrukshögsk. ForForsök. Beretn.*, **49**, 1-39.

Hynes, M. 1947. 2776[a]
The distribution of leucocytes on the counting chamber. *J. Clin. Path.*, **1**, 25-9.

Hyrenius, H. 1949. 2777
Användnung ov samplingmetodik i den Svenska statistiken. (The application of the sampling method in Swedish statistics.) *Statsvetenskaplig Tidskr.*, **52** (2), 105-12.

Hyrenius, H. 1949. 2778
" The qualified lie." Comments on what agricultural statistics are and might be. (Swedish.) *Jordbruk. För. Uppl. A, Östra Medd.*, **19** (43), 1, 3.

Hyrenius, H. 1949. 2779
Sampling distributions from a compound normal parent population. *Skand. Aktuartidskr.*, **32**, 180-7.

Hyrenius, H. 1949. 2780
Summary indices of the age distribution of a population. *Population Stud.*, **2**, 454-60.

I

Ibsen, J. & Toft, H. I. 1946. 2781
Biological assay of strychnine in young mice using death time and convulsion time as biometrical scores. *Acta Pharmocol. Scand.*, **2**, 167-84.

Idelson, N. 1943. 2782
On the computation of the weights of the unknowns in the method of least squares. *Astr. J. Moscow*, **20**, 11-13.

Idenburg, P. J. 1949. 2783
De waardering van de statistiek. (The valuation of statistics.) (Dutch. English and French summaries.) *Econ.-statist. Berichten.*, **34**, no. 1625, 7-8.

Immer, F. R. 1945. 2784
Some uses of statistical methods in plant breeding. *Biometrics Bull.*, **1**, 13-15, 28.

Insolera, F. 1948. 2784[a]
A proposito di tavole selazionate. *Riv. Ital. Demogr. Statist.*, **2**, 495-503.

Insolera, F. 1949. 2784[b]
Sulla mortalità come fenomeno ereditario nel senso Volterra. *Atti 9ma Riun., Soc. Ital. Demogr. Statist.*, pp. 259-63.

Invrea, R. 1941. 2785
Il rischio medio di un' operazione assicurativa e l'applicazione di un teorema del Cantelli. *G. Ist. Ital. Attuari*, **12**, 167-90.

Invrea, R. 1942. 2786
Ancora a proposito di rischio medio. *G. Ist. Ital. Attuari*, **13**, 54-6.

Ionescu Tulcea, C. T. & Marinescu, G. 1948. 2787
Sur certaines chaînes à liaisons complètes. *C. R. Acad. Sci., Paris*, **227**, 667-9 (errata: 1119).

Ipsen, J. 1942. 2788
Systematische und zufällige Fehlerquellen bei Messung kleiner Antitoxinmengen. *Zeit. Immun.Forsch.*, **102**, 347-68.

Ipsen, J. 1949. 2789
A practical method of estimating the mean and standard deviation of truncated normal distributions. *Hum. Biol.*, **21**, 1-16.

Ipsen, J., Jr. 1949. 2790
Biometric analysis of graded response with incomplete measurements in assays of analgesic drugs. Appendix: The estimate of the mean and standard deviation in distributions with incomplete measurements. *Acta Pharm. Toxicol.*, **5**, 321-46.

Ipsen, J. & Jerne, N. K. 1944. 2791
Graphical evaluation of the distribution of small experimental series. *Acta Path. Microbiol. Scand.*, **21**, 343-61.

Irwin, J. O. 1941. 2791a
The analysis of variance of the results. *Quart. J. Pharm.*, **14**, 334-6.

Irwin, J. O. 1942. 2792
The distribution of the logarithms of survival times when the true law is exponential. *J. Hyg., Camb.*, **42**, 328-33.

Irwin, J. O. 1942. 2793
On the distribution of a weighted estimate of variance and on analysis of variance in certain cases of unequal weighting. *J. R. Statist. Soc.*, **105**, 115-18.

Irwin, J. O. 1943. 2794
On the calculation of the error of biological assays. *J. Hyg., Camb.*, **43**, 121-8.

Irwin, J. O. 1943. 2795
The error of the biological assay of insulin by the mouse-convulsion test. *Quart. J. Pharm.*, **16**, 352-62.

Irwin, J. O. 1943. 2796
Table of variance of $\sqrt{x}$ when x has a Poisson distribution. *J. R. Statist. Soc.*, **106**, 143-4.

Irwin, J. O. 1944. 2797
A statistical examination of the accuracy of vitamin A assays. An analysis of three co-operative experiments designed to ascertain the value of the conversion factor for transforming spectrophotometric values into international units. *J. Hyg., Camb.*, **43**, 291-314.

Irwin, J. O. 1946. 2798
On the characteristic function of the distribution of the product of two normal variates. *Proc. Camb. Phil. Soc.*, **42**, 82-4.

Irwin, J. O. 1946. 2799
On the interpretation of within and between class analysis of variance when the intra class correlation is negative. *J. R. Statist. Soc.*, **109**, 157-8.

Irwin, J. O. 1949. 2800
A note on the subdivision of χ^2 into components. *Biometrika*, **36**, 130-4.

Irwin, J. O. 1949. 2801
The standard error of an estimate of expectation of life, with special reference to expectation of tumourless life in experiments with mice. *J. Hyg., Camb.*, **47**, 188-9.

Irwin, J. O. & Goodman, N. 1946. 2802
The statistical treatment of measurements of the carcinogenic properties of tars and mineral oils. *J. Hyg., Camb.*, **44**, 362-420.

Irwin, J. O. & Kendall, M. G. 1944. 2803
Sampling moments of moments for a finite population. *Ann. Eugen.*, **12**, 138-42.

Irwin, J. O., Armitage, P. & Davies, C. N. 1949. 2804
Overlapping of dust particles on a sampling plate. *Nature*, **163**, 809.

Itô, Kiyosi. 1940-1. 2805
On the probability distribution on a compact group. I, II. *Proc. Physico-Math. Soc. Japan*, (3) **22**, 997-8; **23**, 512-27.

Itô, Kiyosi. 1942. 2806
On stochastic processes. I. (Infinitely divisible laws of probability.) *Jap. J. Math.*, **18**, 261-301.

Itô, Kiyosi. 1944. 2807
On the ergodicity of a certain stationary process. *Proc. Imp. Acad., Tokyo*, **20**, 54-5.

Itô, Kiyosi. 1944. 2808
A kinematic theory of turbulence. *Proc. Imp. Acad., Tokyo*, **20**, 120-2.

Itô, Kiyosi. 1944. 2809
On the normal stationary process with no hysteresis. *Proc. Imp. Acad., Tokyo*, **20**, 199-202.

Itô, Kiyosi. 1944. 2810
A screw line in Hilbert space and its application to the probability theory. *Proc. Imp. Acad., Tokyo*, **20**, 203-9.

Itô, Kiyosi. 1944. 2811
Stochastic integral. *Proc. Imp. Acad., Tokyo*, **20**, 519-24. (Japanese version (1948): *Sûgaku*, **1**, 172-7.)

Itô, Kiyosi. 1944. 2812
On Student's test. *Proc. Imp. Acad., Tokyo*, **20**, 694-700.

Itô, Kiyosi. 1946. 2813
On a stochastic integral equation. *Proc. Japan Acad.*, **22** (1-4), 32-5. (Japanese version: (1948) *Sûgaku*, **1**, 172-7.)

Itô, Kiyosi. 1947. 2814
On the amount of information. (Japanese.) *Res. Mem. Inst. Statist. Math., Tokyo*, **3**, 170-82.

Ito, P. K. 1942. 2815
Comparative biometrical study of physique of Japanese women born and reared under different environments. *Hum. Biol.*, **14**, 279-351.

Iwasawa, K. 1943. 2816
One parameter family of probability laws. (Japanese summary.) *Nippon Sûgaku Buturi gakwai-Kizi* (*Proc. Phys.-math. Soc. Japan*), **17**, 217-20.

Iyengar, R. 1944. 2817
Variation of fibre length in a bulk sample of cotton and in a single seed of the bulk. *Technol. Leafl. Indian Cott. Comm. Technol. Lab.*, **6**, 3.

Iyer, P. V. K. 1940. 2818
The analysis of asymmetrical experiments with special reference to the partition of treatment sum of squares. *Proc. Indian Acad. Sci. A*, **11**, 369-75.

Iyer, P. V. K. 1941. 2819
Standard error of the difference between two estimates for incomplete block experiments. *Current Science*, **10**, 165.

Iyer, P. V. K. 1945.　　　　　　　　　2820
The distribution of the mean of samples from a rectangular population. *Current Science*, **14**, 18-19.

Iyer, P. V. K. 1945.　　　　　　　　　2820ª
A note on Hotelling's T^2. *Current Science*, **14**, 173-5.

Iyer, P. V. K. 1945.　　　　　　　　　2820ᵇ
Tests of significance by analysis of covariance in multivariate populations. *Current Science*, **14**, 297.

Iyer, P. V. K. 1945.　　　　　　　　　2821
The use of generalized Dirichlet's integral in solving some distribution problems of statistics. *Proc. Indian Acad. Sci. A*, **22**, 75-83.

Iyer, P. V. K. 1947-8.　　　　　　　　2822
Random association of points on a lattice. *Nature*, **160**, 714; **162**, 333.

Iyer, P. V. K. 1948.　　　　　　　　　2823
The theory of probability distributions of points on a line. *J. Indian Soc. Agric. Statist.*, **1**, 173-95.

Iyer, P. V. K. 1949.　　　　　　　　　2824
Calculation of factorial moments of certain probability distributions. *Nature*, **164**, 282.

Iyer, P. V. K. 1949.　　　　　　　　　2825
The first and second moments of some probability distributions arising from points on a lattice and their application. *Biometrika*, **36**, 135-41.

Iyer, P. V. K. & Sukhatme, B. V. 1949.　　2826
Probability distribution of points on a line. *Science & Culture*, **15**, 200.

J

Jackson, C. H. N. 1940-8.　　　　　　　2827
The analysis of a tsetse-fly population. I, II, III. *Ann. Eugen.*, **10**, 332-69; **12**, 176-205; **14**, 91-108.

Jackson, C. H. N. 1941.　　　　　　　　2828
The economy of a tsetse population. *Bull. Ent. Res.*, **32**, 53-5.

Jackson, H. H. 1944.　　　　　　　　　2829
Recent developments in inspection methods. *Engng. Insp.*, **9** (2), 30-5.

Jackson, R. W. B. 1940.　　　　　　　　2830
Application of the analysis of variance and covariance method to educational problems. *Univ. Toronto, Dep. Educ. Res. Bull.* no. 11.

Jackson, R. W. B. 1940.　　　　　　　　2831
Some pitfalls in the statistical analysis of data expressed in the form of IQ scores. *J. Educ. Psychol.*, **31**, 677-85.

Jackson, R. W. B. 1941.　　　　　　　　2832
Some difficulties in the application of the analysis of covariance method to educational problems. *J. Educ. Psychol.*, **32**, 414-22.

Jackson, R. W. B. 1942.　　　　　　　　2833
Note on the relationship between internal consistency and test-retest estimates of the reliability of a test. *Psychometrika*, **7**, 157-64.

Jackson, R. W. B. 1943.　　　　　　　　2834
Approximate multiple regression weights. *J. Exper. Educ.*, **11**, 221-5.

Jackson, R. W. B. & Ferguson, G. A. 1941.　2835
Studies on the reliability of tests. *Univ. Toronto, Dep. Educ. Res. Bull.*, no. 12, 132 pp.

Jackson, R. W. B. & Ferguson, G. A. 1943.　2836
A functional approach in test construction. *Educ. and Psychol. Measurement*, **3**, 23-8.

Jackson, R. W. B. & Phillips, A. J. 1945.　　2837
Prediction efficiences by deciles for various degrees of relationship. *Univ. Toronto Dept. Educ. Res., Educ. Res. Ser.* no. 11, 18 pp.

Jacob, M. 1941.　　　　　　　　　　　2838
Su di un metodo d'approssimazione per il calcolo del rischio quadratio medio. (German, French and English summaries.) *Trans. 12th. Int. Congr. Actuar.*, *Lucerne*, 1940, **1**, 285-307.

Jacob, W. C. 1944.　　　　　　　　　　2839
Statistical analysis of factorial experiments. *Bol. Minist. Agric., Rio de Janeiro*, **33**, 41-56.

Jacob, W. C., White-Stevens, R. H. & Wessels, P. H. 1949.　　　　　　　　2840
The influence of irrigation on the nitrogen, phosphorus and potash requirements of different potato varieties. *Amer. Potato J.*, **26**, 241-55.

Jacobaeus, C. 1947.　　　　　　　　　　2841
Influence of the size of selectors on the number of selectors in telephone plants. *Ericsson Rev.*, **24**, 2-9.

Jacobs, A. 1942.　　　　　　　　　　　2842
Zur Frage der Gruppenbildung und Repräsentation in der Wirtschaftsstatistik. *Vierteljh. Wirtsch.*, **16** (1-2), 75-94.

Jacobs, W. W. & Broida, S. F. 1949.　　　2843
Current inventory development. *Survey of Current Business*, **29** (4), 14 pp.

Jacobsen, H. 1947.　　　　　　　　　　2844
Use of statistical methods in research. (Danish.) *Lin. Dansk-Svensk Hørtidsskr.*, **1**, 48-52.

Jacobson, P. H. 1947.　　　　　　　　　2845
The relative power of three statistics for small sample destructive tests. *J. Amer. Statist. Ass.*, **42**, 575-84.

Jahn, J., Schmid, C. F. & Schrag, C. 1947.　2846
The measurement of ecological segregation. *Amer. Sociol. Rev.*, **12**, 293-303.

James, E. 1947.　　　　　　　　　　　2847
A modification of the formulae for regression. *J. Amer. Soc. Agron.*, **39**, 545-6.

James, H. M. 1947.　　　　　　　　　　2848
Statistical properties of networks of flexible chains. *J. Chem. Phys.*, **15**, 651-68.

James, H. M. & Guth, E. 1949.　　　　　2849
Simple presentation of network theory of rubber, with a discussion of other theories. *J. Polymer Sci.*, **4**, 153-82.

James, S. F. 1949.　　　　　　　　　　2850
A note on Carnap's theory of probability. *J. R. Statist. Soc. A*, **112**, 309-15.

Janardana Aiyer, S. *See* **Aiyer, S. J.**

Janardan Poti, S. *See* **Poti, S. J.**

Janer, J. L. 1945.　　　　　　　　　　2851
Population growth in Puerto Rico and its relation to time changes in vital statistics. *Hum. Biol.*, **17**, 267-313.

Janis, I. L. & Fadner, R. H. 1943.   2852
A coefficient of inbalance for content analysis. *Psychometrika*, **8**, 105-19.

Janko, J. 1940.   2853
Homogenita statistického souboru. (Homogenity of a statistical population.) (Czech. French and English summaries.) *Statist. Obzor*, **21**, 239-63.

Janko, J. 1940.   2854
Ověřovaní statistických hypothes. (Testing statistical hypotheses.) *Rozpravy jednoty pro vědy pojistné*, **21**.

Janko, J. 1946.   2855
Statistika v. planovanem hospodárstivi. (Statistique et économie dirigée.) (Czech. English, French and Russian summaries.) *Statist. Obzor*, **26**, 9-19.

Janko, J. 1947.   2856
Studium statistiky. (Les études statistiques.) (Czech. English, French and Russian summaries.) *Statist. Obzor*, **27**, 1-7.

Jánossy, L. 1944.   2857
Rate of n-fold accidental coincidences. *Nature*, **153**, 165.

Jarcho, S. 1945.   2858
Equal-area projections and the azimuthal equidistant projection in maps of disease. *Amer. J. Publ. Health*, **35**, 1005-13.

Jardin, A. 1949.   2859
Instruction et formation des statisticiens. *Bull. Statist., Inst. Nat. Statist., Belg.*, **35**, 1494-503.

Jarrett, R. F. 1945.   2860
On the permissible coarseness of grouping. *J. Educ. Psychol.*, **36**, 385-95.

Jarvik, M. E. 1946.   2861
Probability discrimination and the gambler's fallacy in guessing. *Amer. Psychologist*, **1**, 453-4.

Jaspen, N. 1946.   2862
Serial correlation. *Psychometrika*, **11**, 23-30.

Jebe, E. & King, A. J. 1940.   2863
An experiment in pre-harvest sampling of wheat fields. *Iowa Agric. Exper. Sta. Res. Bull.*, **273**, 624-9.

Jecklin, H. 1941.   2864
The theory of probability in insurance. (German. French, Italian and English summaries.) *Trans. 12th. Int. Congr. Actuar.*, *Lucerne*, 1940, **1**, 71-115.

Jecklin, H. 1941.   2865
Ist die Anwendbarkeit der Wahrscheinlichkeitstheorie in der Lebensversicherung besser fundiert als in der Sachversicherung? (French, Italian and English summaries.) *Trans. 12th Int. Congr. Actuar.*, *Lucerne*, 1940, **1**, 377-93.

Jecklin, H. 1941.   2866
Die Wahrscheinlichkeitstheorie in Versicherungswesen. *Mitt. Ver. Schweiz. Versich.-Math.*, **41**, 39-66.

Jecklin, H. 1944.   2867
Über den Zusammenhang zwischen gewissen Zusatzversicherungen, Prämienzerlegungen und Approximationen in der Lebensversicherungstechnik. *Mitt. Ver. Schweiz. Versich.-Math.*, **44**, 221-32.

Jecklin, H. 1947.   2868
Zur Systematik der statistischen Mittelwerte. *Schweiz. Zeit. Volkwirtsch. Statist.*, **83**, 340-7.

Jecklin, H. 1948.   2869
La notion de vie moyenne et sa portée pratique. *Bull. Ass. Actuair. Belg.*, **54**, 23-39.

Jecklin, H. 1949.   2870
Grundsätzliche Bemerkungen zur t-Methode. *Mitt. Ver. Schweiz. Versich.-Math.*, **49**, 170-8.

Jecklin, H. 1949.   2871
La notion de moyenne. *Metron*, **15**, 3-12.

Jecklin, H. & Zimmermann, H. 1948.   2872
Eine praktische Interpolationsformel. *Mitt. Ver. Schweiz. Versich.-Math.*, **48**, 126-44.

Jeffreys, H. 1940.   2873
Note on the Behrens-Fisher formula. *Ann. Eugen.*, **10**, 48-51.

Jeffreys, H. 1941.   2874
Some applications of the method of minimum χ'^2. *Ann. Eugen.*, **11**, 108-14.

Jeffreys, H. 1942.   2875
Probability and quantum theory. *Phil. Mag.*, (7) **33**, 815-31.

Jeffreys, H. 1942.   2876
On the significance tests for the introduction of new functions to represent measures. *Proc. Roy. Soc. A*, **180**, 256-68.

Jeffreys, H. 1946.   2877
An invariant form for the prior probability in estimation problems. *Proc. Roy. Soc. A*, **186**, 453-61.

Jellinek, E. M. 1946.   2878
Clinical tests on comparative effectiveness of analgesic drugs. *Biometrics Bull.*, **2**, 87-91.

Jelonek, Z., Fitch, E. & Chalk, J. H. H. 1947.   2879
Diversity reception; statistical evaluation of possible gain. *Wireless Engr.*, **24** (281), 54-62.

Jeming, J. 1943.   2880
Estimates of average service life and life expectancies and the standard deviation of such estimates. *Econometrica*, **11**, 141-50.

Jenkins, R. L. & Gwin, J. 1940.   2881
Twin and triplet birth ratios. Rigorous analysis of the interrelations of the frequencies of plural births. *J. Heredity*, **31**, 243-8.

Jenkins, W. L. 1946.   2881[a]
A quick method for multiple R and partial r's. *Educ. and Psychol. Measurement*, **6**, 274-82.

Jenkins, W. L. 1946.   2882
A short-cut method for σ and r. *Educ. and Psychol. Measurement*, **6**, 533-6.

Jennison, M. W. & Wadsworth, G. P. 1940.   2883
Evaluation of the errors involved in estimating bacterial numbers by the plating method. *J. Bact.*, **39**, 389-97.

Jennison, R. F., Penfold, J. B. &   2884
Roberts, J. A. Fraser. 1948.
An application to a laboratory problem of discriminant function analysis involving more than two groups. *Brit. J. Soc. Med.*, **2**, 139-48.

Jensen, A. 1948.   2885
An elucidation of A. K. Erlang's statistical works through the theory of stochastic processes. *Trans. Danish Acad. Sci.*, **2**, The life and works of A. K. Erlang, pp. 23-100.

Jensen, A. 1948. 2886
Stochastic processes applied in a simple problem of administrative economy. *Nord. Tidskr. Teknisk. Økonomi.*, **37**, 151-5.

Jensen, H. 1944. 2887
An attempt at a systematic classification of some methods for the solution of normal equations. *Geodætisk Inst. Medd., Copenhagen*, no. 18.

Jenss, R. M. 1943. 2888
An inquiry into methods of studying the sex ratio at birth for the United States during war and post-war years. *Hum. Biol.*, **15**, 255-66.

Jenss, R. M. 1945. 2889
Statistical methods in anthropometric studies in the field of nutritional research. *Amer. J. Publ. Health*, **35**, 1053-6.

Jerne, N. K. & Wood, E. C. 1949. 2890
The validity and meaning of the results of biological assays. *Biometrics*, **5**, 273-99.

Jessen, A. 1945. 2891
Et kombinatorisk problem. *Mat. Tidsskr. B*, **1945**, 58.

Jessen, B. 1943. 2892
A problem in geometrical probability. (Danish.) *Festskr. J. F. Steffensen*, pp. 72-5.

Jessen, B. 1947. 2893
Abstract maal-og integralteori. (Abstract measure and integral calculus.) *Mat. Tidsskr.*, **1947**, 1-31.

Jessen, R. J. 1942. 2894
Methods of obtaining representative samples of farm management data. *Illinois Univ. Dept. Agric. Econ. and Agric. Exper. Sta., Rep.* AE-1837.

Jessen, R. J. 1942. 2895
Statistical investigation of a sample survey for obtaining farm facts. *Iowa Agric. Exper. Sta. Res. Bull.*, **304**, 1-104.

Jessen, R. J. 1945. 2896
The master sample of agriculture. II. Design. *J. Amer. Statist. Ass.*, **40**, 46-56.

Jessen, R. J. 1947. 2897
The master sample project and its use in agricultural economics. *J. Farm Econ.*, **29**, 531-40.

Jessen, R. J. 1949. 2898
Some inadequacies of the federal censuses of agriculture. *J. Amer. Statist. Ass.*, **44**, 279-92.

Jessen, R. J. & Houseman, E. E. 1944. 2899
Statistical investigations of farm sample surveys in Iowa, Florida and California. *Iowa Agric. Exper. Sta. Res. Bull.*, **329**, 261-338.

Jessen, R. J., Blythe, R. H., Kempthorne, O. & Deming, W. E. 1947. 2900
On a population sample for Greece. *J. Amer. Statist. Ass.*, **42**, 357-84.

Jiménez, J. H. 1948. 2901
El " test " de secuencia. *Agros, Cochabamba*, **1**, 61-6.

Johansen, N. P. 1944. 2902
Free functions. (Danish.) *Geodaetisk Inst. Skr., Danemark*, (3) **4**, 30 pp.

Johnson, A. P. 1947. 2903
An index of item validity providing a correction for chance success. *Psychometrika*, **12**, 81-8.

Johnson, D. A. 1949. 2904
An experimental study of the effectiveness of films and film strips in teaching geometry. *J. Exper. Educ.*, **17**, 363-72.

Johnson, D. M. & Reynolds, F. 1941. 2905
A factor analysis of verbal ability. *Psychol. Rev.*, **4**, 183-95.

Johnson, E., Jr. 1940. 2906
Estimates of parameters by means of least squares. *Ann. Math. Statist.*, **11**, 453-6.

Johnson, F. A. 1943. 2907
A statistical study of sampling methods for tree nursery inventories. *J. Forestry*, **41**, 674-9.

Johnson, F. A. 1949. 2908
Statistical aspects of timber volume sampling in the Pacific North West. *J. Forestry*, **47**, 292-5.

Johnson, H. A. & Paarlberg, D. 1948. 2909
A method of predicting numbers of hens and pullets on Indiana farms, January 1. *J. Farm Econ.*, **30**, 756-61.

Johnson, H. C. 1944. 2910
The effect of instruction in mathematical vocabulary upon problem solving in arithmetic. *J. Educ. Res.*, **38**, 97-110.

Johnson, H. G. 1944. 2911
An empirical study of the influence of errors of measurement upon correlation. *Amer. J. Psychol.*, **57**, 521-36.

Johnson, H. G. 1946. 2912
Certain properties of the correlation coefficient. *J. Exper. Educ.*, **14**, 263-6.

Johnson, H. M. 1940. 2913
Pre-experimental assumptions as determiners of experimental results. *Psychol. Rev.*, **47**, 338-46.

Johnson, H. M. 1942. 2914
General rules for predicting the selectivity of a test (when the standardizing population and the parent population are not necessarily homogeneous). *Amer. J. Psychol.*, **55**, 436-42.

Johnson, H. M. 1943. 2915
Index-numerology and measures of impairment. *Amer. J. Psychol.*, **56**, 551-8.

Johnson, H. M. 1944. 2916
A useful interpretation of Pearsonian r in 2×2 contingency tables. *Amer. J. Psychol.*, **57**, 236-42.

Johnson, H. M. 1945. 2917
Maximal selectivity, correctivity and correlation obtainable in 2×2 contingency tables. *Amer. J. Psychol.*, **58**, 65-8.

Johnson, H. M. 1946. 2918
The detection and treatment of accident-prone drivers. *Psychol. Bull.*, **43**, 489-532.

Johnson, I. J. & Murphy, H. C. 1943. 2919
Lattice and lattice square designs without uniformity data and in variety trials. *J. Amer. Soc. Agron.*, **35**, 291-305.

Johnson, N. L. 1940. 2920
Parabolic test for linkage. *Ann. Math. Statist.*, **11**, 227-53.

Johnson, N. L. 1948. 2921
Alternative systems in the analysis of variance. *Biometrika*, **35**, 80-7.

Johnson, N. L. 1948. 2922
Tests of significance in the variance difference method. *Biometrika*, **35**, 206-9.

Johnson, N. L. 1949. 2923
Systems of frequency curves generated by methods of translation. *Biometrika*, **36**, 149-76.

Johnson, N. L. 1949. 2924
Bivariate distributions based on simple translation systems. *Biometrika*, **36**, 297-304.

Johnson, N. L. & Welch, B. L. 1940. 2925
Applications of the non-central *t*-distribution. *Biometrika*, **31**, 362-89.

Johnson, P. O. 1944. 2926
The increase in precision in educational and psychological experimentation through statistical controls. *J. Educ. Res.*, **38**, 149-52.

Johnson, P. O. & Hoyt, C. J. 1947. 2927
On determining three-dimensional regions of significance. *J. Exper. Educ.*, **15**, 203-12. (Reprinted: 342-53.)

Johnson, P. O. & Tsao, F. 1944. 2928
Factorial design in the determination of differential limen values. *Psychometrika*, **9**, 107-44.

Johnson, P. O. & Tsao, F. 1945. 2929
Factorial design and covariance in the study of individual educational development. *Psychometrika*, **10**, 133-62.

Johnson, P. O. & Tsao, F. 1945. 2930
Testing a certain hypothesis regarding variances affected by means. *J. Exper. Educ.*, **13**, 145-8.

Johnson, R. H. 1946. 2931
Variations in department store sales-expense ratios. *Survey of Current Business*, **26** (9), 18-24.

Johnston, J. P., Longuet-Higgins, H. C. 2932
& Ogston, A. G. 1945.
On the distribution of the molecular weights of proteins. *Trans. Faraday Soc.*, **41**, 588-93.

Joint Electron Tube Engng. Council. *See* **Horrocks, S. W. and others.**

Jolliffe, E. T. 1941. 2933
Fundamental principles in tabulating machine methods of statistical analysis. *J. Exper. Educ.*, **9**, 254-74.

Jolly, A. L. 1942. 2934
Uniformity trials on estate cacao fields in Grenada, B.W.I. *Trop. Agriculturist*, **19**, 167-74.

Jones, A. E. 1946. 2935
A useful method for the routine estimation of dispersion from large samples. *Biometrika*, **33**, 274-82.

Jones, A. E. 1948. 2936
Systematic sampling of continuous parameter populations. *Biometrika*, **35**, 283-90.

Jones, D. Caradog. 1941. 2937
Evolution of the Social Survey in England since Booth. *Amer. J. Sociol.*, **46**, 818-26.

Jones, E. W. 1945. 2938
Index of diversity as applied to ecological problems. *Nature*, **155**, 390.

Jones, F. G. W. 1945. 2939
Soil populations of beet eelworm (*Heterodera schachtii*, Schm.) in relation to cropping. *Ann. Appl. Biol.*, **32**, 351-80.

Jones, H. L. 1941. 2940
The use of grouped measurements. *J. Amer. Statist. Ass.*, **36**, 525-9.

Jones, H. L. 1943. 2941
Fitting polynominal trends to seasonal data by the method of least squares. *J. Amer. Statist. Ass.*, **38**, 453-65.

Jones, H. L. 1946. 2942
Linear regression functions with neglected variables. *J. Amer. Statist. Ass.*, **41**, 356-69.

Jones, H. L. 1946. 2943
Note on square-root charts. *Econometrica*, **14**, 313-15.

Jones, H. L. 1947. 2944
Sampling plans for verifying clerical work. *Industr. Qual. Contr.*, **3** (4), 5-11.

Jones, H. L. 1948. 2945
Exact lower moments of order statistics in small samples from a normal distribution. *Ann. Math. Statist.*, **19**, 270-3.

Jones, J. I. M. 1945. 2946
The biological estimation of vitamin D. *Quart. J. Pharm.*, **18**, 92-108.

Jones, P. C. T. & Mollison, J. E. 1948. 2947
A technique for the quantitative estimation of soil micro-organisms. *J. Gen. Microbiol.*, **2**, 54-65.

Jones, W. D. 1946. 2948
A simple way to figure machine downtime. *Fact. Magmt.*, **104**, 118-21.

Jones, W. D. 1949. 2949
Machine interference. *J. Industr. Engng.*, **1**, 10-11; 19.

Jonsson, B. 1942. 2950
Einige Formeln der mittleren Fehler der aus den Blutgruppenfrequenzen hergeleiteten Funktionen. *Acta Path. Microbiol. Scand.*, **19**, 321-6.

Jordan, K. 1941. 2951
A korreláció számitása. I. *Magyar Statisztikai Szemle*, **1**, 47ff.

Jordan, K. 1941. 2952
Remarques sur la loi des erreurs. *Acta Univ. Szeged, Sci. Math.*, **10**, 112-33.

Jordan, K. 1946. 2953
Complément au théorème de Simmons sur les probabilités. *Acta Univ. Szeged, Sci. Math.*, **11**, 19-27.

Jordan, K. 1949. 2954
Approximation, conformément, au principe des moindres carrés, des observations présentant une tendance périodique. (Hungarian. French summary.) *Időjárás*, **53**, 226-31; 274.

Jordan, K. 1949. 2955
Note on approximation and graduation by orthogonal moments. *Acta Math. Acad. Sci. Hung.*, **1** (4), 4-9.

Jordan, R. C. & Jacobs, S. E. 1944-6. 2956
Studies in the dynamics of disinfection. I-VII. *J. Hyg., Camb.*, **43**, 275-89; 363-9; **44**, 210-20; *Ann. Appl. Biol.*, **32**, 221-9; *J. Hyg., Camb.*, **44**, 243-55; 421-9.

Jordan, R. C., Jacobs, S. E. & Davies, H. E. F. 2957
1947. Studies in the dynamics of disinfection. VIII-XI. *J. Hyg., Camb.*, **45**, 136-48; 333-53.

Joseph, A. W. 1946. 2958
The valuation of whole-life assurances by the use of moments. *J. Inst. Actuar.*, **72**, 498-515.

Joseph, A. W. 1947. 2959
Third-order moments of a bivariate frequency distribution. *J. Inst. Actuar.*, **73**, 427-9.

Joseph, A. W. 1948. 2960
A comment on interpolation in two variables. *J. Inst. Actuar.*, **74**, 82-5.

Josephs, H. J. 1945. 2961
Fixing of confidence limits to measurements. *J. Inst. Elect. Engrs.*, **92** (2), 194-213.

Jost, R. 1947. 2962
Bemerkungen zur mathematischen Theorie der Zähler. *Helvetica Phys. Acta*, **20**, 173-82.

Jourdan, C. & Nogueira, R. 1948. 2963
Sôbre uma aplicação da teoria das equações de diferenças finitas ao problema da capitalização com sorteio de títulos. *Bol. Inst. Brasil. Atuár.*, **4**, 54-69.

Jowett, G. H. 1949. 2964
Calculation of sums of squares and products on a desk calculating machine. *J. R. Statist. Soc. B*, **11**, 89-90.

Jowett, G. H. & Sarjant, R. J. 1949. 2965
Statistical methods in fuel technology. *J. Inst. Fuel*, **22**, 238-50; 374-5.

Jowett, G. H. & Scurfield, G. 1949. 2966
Statistical test for optimal conditions: note on a paper of Emmett and Ashby. *J. Ecology*, **37**, 65-7.

Jowett, G. H. & Scurfield, G. 1949. 2967
A statistical investigation into the distribution of *Holcus mollis L.* and *Deschampsia flexuosa (L.) Trin. J. Ecology*, **37**, 68-81.

Julin, A. 1940. 2968
Sur le taux d'accroissement de la population dans un territoire déterminé. *Bull. Acad. Roy. Belg., Cl. Lettres Sci. Morales et Pol.*, (5) **26**, 310-38.

Juncosa, M. L. 1949. 2969
The asymptotic behaviour of the minimum in a sequence of random variables. *Duke Math. J.*, **16**, 609-18.

Juran, J. M. 1943. 2969a
Management problems in judging quality conformance in the inspection function. *Mech. Engng.*, **65**, 805-8.

Juran, J. M. 1943. 2969b
Management problems of measurement in the inspection function. *Advanced Mgmt.*, **8**, 86-91.

Juran, J. M. 1944. 2969c
A.B.C. of quality control. *Mech. Engng.*, **66**, 529-35. (Also: *Glass Industry*, **25**, 358-60; 407-8.)

Juran, J. M. 1949. 2970
Application of statistics to the science of management. *Mech. Engng.*, pp. 321-4. (Also: *Mech. World and Engng. Record*, **125** (3252), 541-4.)

Juran, J. M. 1949. 2971
The role of statistics as a tool of management. *Bull. Int. Statist. Inst.*, **32** (2), 30-8.

Jurgenson, C. E. 1943. 2972
A nomograph for rapid determination of medians. *Psychometrika*, **8**, 265-9.

Jurgensen, C. E. 1947. 2973
Table for determining phi coefficients. *Psychometrika*, **12**, 17-29.

Jurkat, E. H. 1946. 2974
Statistical analysis and interpretation of chemical market research data. *Chemical Industry*, **59**, 1021-4.

K

Kac, M. 1940. 2975
On a problem concerning probability and its connection with the theory of diffusion. *Bull. Amer. Math. Soc.*, **46**, 534-7.

Kac, M. 1941. 2975a
Note on the distribution of values of the arithmetic function $d(m)$. *Bull. Amer. Math. Soc.*, **47**, 815-17.

Kac, M. 1942. 2976
Note on the partial sums of the exponential series. *Rev. Cienc. Tucumán A*, **3**, 151-3.

Kac, M. 1943. 2977
On the average number of real roots of a random algebraic equation. *Bull. Amer. Math. Soc.*, **49**, 314-20 (correction: 938).

Kac, M. 1945. 2978
Random walk in the presence of absorbing barriers. *Ann. Math. Statist.*, **16**, 62-7.

Kac, M. 1945. 2979
A remark on independence of linear and quadratic forms involving independent Gaussian variables. *Ann. Math. Statist.*, **16**, 400-1.

Kac, M. 1946. 2980
On the average of a certain Wiener functional and a related limit theorem in calculus of probability. *Trans. Amer. Math. Soc.*, **59**, 401-14.

Kac, M. 1946. 2980a
On the distribution of values of sums of the type $\Sigma f(2^k t)$. *Ann. Math.*, (2) **47**, 33-49.

Kac, M. 1947. 2981
On the notion of recurrence in discrete stochastic processes. *Bull. Amer. Math. Soc.*, **53**, 1002-10.

Kac, M. 1947. 2982
Random walk and the theory of Brownian motion. *Amer. Math. Monthly*, **54**, 369-91.

Kac, M. 1948. 2983
On the characteristic functions of the distributions of estimates of various deviations in samples from a normal population. *Ann. Math. Statist.*, **19**, 257-61.

Kac, M. 1949. 2984
On the average number of real roots of a random algebraic equation. II. *Proc. Lond. Math. Soc.*, **50**, 390-408.

Kac, M. 1949. 2985
On deviations between theoretical and empirical distributions. *Proc. Nat. Acad. Sci. U.S.A.*, **35**, 252-7.

Kac, M. 1949. 2986
On distributions of certain Wiener functionals. *Trans. Amer. Math. Soc.*, **65**, 1-13.

Kac, M. 1949. 2986ᵃ
Probability methods in some problems of analysis and number theory. *Bull. Amer. Math. Soc.*, **55**, 641-65.

Kac, M. & Siegert, A. J. F. 1947. 2987
An explicit representation of a stationary Gaussian process. *Ann. Math. Statist.*, **18**, 438-42.

Kac, M. & Siegert, A. J. F. 1947. 2988
On the theory of noise in radio receivers with square law detectors. *J. Appl. Phys.*, **18**, 383-97.

Kac, M., Salem, R. & Zygmund, A. 1948. 2988ᵃ
A gap theorem. *Trans. Amer. Math. Soc.*, **63**, 235-43.

Kafuri, J. F. 1945. 2989
A cooperaçao da estatística com a economia. *Rev. Brasil Estatíst.*, **6**, 393-410.

Kahn, H. 1949. 2990
Modification of the Monte Carlo method. *Proc. Seminar Sci. Computation, I.B.M. Corp., New York.* (Also: *RAND Corp. Paper*, 14 November 1949, P-132, 18 pp.)

Kahn, H. 1949. 2991
Stochastic (Monte Carlo) attenuation analysis. *RAND Corp. Paper*, 14 July 1949, P-88, 21 pp. (Also: *Symp. Monte Carlo Methods, Univ. Calif.*, 30 June 1949.)

Kaitz, H. B. A. 1945. 2992
A comment on the correction of reliability coefficients for restriction of range. *J. Educ. Psychol.*, **36**, 510-12.

Kaitz, H. B. A. 1945. 2993
A note on reliability. *Psychometrika*, **10**, 127-31.

Kakehashi, T. 1949. 2994
On the density of Lissajous' figures. *J. Osaka Inst. Sci. Tech.*, I, **1**, 87-8.

Kakeya, S. 1940. 2995
On selections with probabilities. (Japanese.) *Tokyo Buturi Gakko Zassi*, **49**, 169-78.

Kakeya, S. 1941. 2996
The problem of final vote. (Japanese.) *Tokyo Buturi Gakko Zassi*, **50**, 167-71.

Kakeya, S. 1941. 2997
On the uniform distribution. (Japanese.) *Tokyo Buturi Gakko Zassi*, **50**, 340-2.

Kakeya, S. 1947. 2998
On the problem of election. (Japanese.) *Res. Mem. Inst. Statist. Math., Tokyo*, **3**, 1-6.

Kakeya, S. 1947. 2999
On the restrictive cumulative voting. (Japanese.) *Res. Mem. Inst. Statist. Math., Tokyo*, **3**, 7-16.

Kakeya, S. 1947. 3000
On the transportation problem. (Japanese.) *Res. Mem. Inst. Statist. Math., Tokyo*, **3**, 17-22.

Kakutani, S. 1940. 3001
Ergodic theorems and the Markoff process with a stable distribution. *Proc. Imp. Acad. Tokyo*, **16**, 49-54.

Kakutani, S. 1941. 3002
Concrete representation of abstract (*L*) spaces and the mean ergodic theorem. *Ann. Math.*, (2) **42**, 523-37.

Kakutani, S. 1944. 3003
On Brownian motions in *n*-space. *Proc. Imp. Acad. Tokyo*, **20**, 648-52.

Kakutani, S. 1944. 3004
Two-dimensional Brownian motion and harmonic functions. *Proc. Imp. Acad. Tokyo*, **20**, 706-14.

Kakutani, S. 1945. 3005
On Brownian motion. I. (Japanese.) *Res. Mem. Inst. Statist. Math., Tokyo*, **1**, 34-45.

Kakutani, S. 1949. 3006
Two-dimensional Brownian motion and the type problem of Riemann surfaces. *Proc. Japan Acad.*, **21**, 138-40.

Kakutani, S. 1949. 3007
Markoff process and the Dirichlet problem. *Proc. Japan Acad.*, **21**, 227-33.

Kalamkar, R. J. & Dhannalal. 1940. 3007ᵃ
Sampling studies in cotton varietal trial. *Sankhyā*, **4**, 567-76.

Kalamkar, R. J. & Satakopan, V. 1940. 3008
The influence of the rainfall distribution on the cotton yields at the governmental experimental farms at Akola and Jalgaon. *Indian J. Agric. Sci.*, **10**, 960-74.

Kalecki, M. 1945. 3009
On the Gibrat distribution. *Econometrica*, **13**, 161-70.

Kalecki, M. & Tew, B. 1940. 3010
A new method of trend elimination. *Econometrica*, **8**, 117-29 (correction: **9**, 93-4).

Kalkanis, J. Ph. 1940. 3011
Über eine Formel der Versicherungsmathematik. (Greek.) *Bull. Soc. Math. Grèce*, **20**, 66-78.

Kalmus, H. & Smith, C. A. B. 1947. 3012
The incidence of placenta praevia and antepartum haemorrhage according to maternal age and parity. (With a note on the mathematical treatment by Smith.) *Ann. Eugen.*, **13**, 283-90. (Errata (1947): **14**, 1.)

Kaloujnine, L. 1949. 3013
Quelques idées au sujet du mémoire de M. G. Neymann " L'estimation statistique traitée comme un problème classique de probabilité ". *Publ. Math., Debrecen*, **1**, 101-3.

Kamalamma, K. N. 1941. 3014
A statistical analysis of medical examination reports of university students, Mysore. *Sankhyā*, **5**, 269-78.

Kamke, E. 1940. 3015
Zu meinem Aufsatz " Kritische Bemerkungen zu K. Marbe, Grundfragen der angewandten Wahrscheinlichkeitsrechnung und theoretischen Statistik ". *Jber. Dtsch. Mathver.*, **49**, 255-6.

Kampé de Fériet, J. 1946. 3016
Sur la moyenne des mesures, dans un écoulement turbulent, des anémomètres dont les indications sont indépendantes de la direction de la vitesse. *La Météorologie*, (4) **1**, 133-43.

Kampé de Fériet, J. 1947. 3017
Sur une représentation des fonctions aléatoires. *C. R. Acad. Sci., Paris*, **225**, 37-8.

Kampé de Fériet, J. 1947. 3018
Fonctions aléatoires définies sur un groupe abstrait. *C. R. Acad. Sci., Paris*, **225**, 428-9.

Kampé de Fériet, J. 1947. 3019
Analyse harmonique des fonctions aléatoires strictement stationnaires. *C. R. Acad. Sci., Paris*, **225**, 623-4.

Kampé de Fériet, J. 1948. 3020
Analyse harmonique des fonctions aléatoires stationnaires d'ordre 2 définies sur un groupe abelien localement compact. *C. R. Acad. Sci., Paris*, **226**, 868-70.

Kampé de Fériet, J. 1948. 3021
Le tenseur spectral de la turbulence homogène non
isotrope. *Proc. 7th. Int. Congr. Appl. Maths.*, pp. 6-26.

Kampé de Fériet, J. 1948. 3022
Le tenseur spectral de la turbulence homogène non
isotrope dans un fluide incompressible. *C. R. Acad.
Sci., Paris*, **227**, 760-1.

Kampé de Fériet, J. 1949. 3023
Fonctions aléatoires stationnaires et groupes de
transformations dans un espace abstrait. *Le calcul
des probabilités et ses applications. Colloq. Int.
Centre Nat. Rech. Sci., Paris*, **13**, 67-73.

Kampé de Fériet, J. 1949. 3024
Sur un problème d'algèbre abstraite posé par la
définition de la moyenne dans la théorie de la
turbulence. *Ann. Soc. Sci. Bruxelles*, I, **63**, 165-80.

Kanellos, S. G. 1940. 3025
Étude des répétitions dans une suite infinie de tirages.
Loi des répétitions. *Bull. Soc. Math. Grèce*, **20**,
79-84.

Kanellos, S. G. 1948. 3026
Statistical test of an observation on logarithmic tables
by a method of Pearson. (Greek. English summary.)
Bull. Soc. Math. Grèce, **23**, 127-31.

Kanellos, S. G. 1948. 3027
Two problems of the calculus of probability. (Greek.
English summary.) *Bull. Soc. Math. Grèce*, **23**,
132-42.

Kanellos, S. G. 1949. 3028
On the independence of two events and the regulariza-
tion of a random variable. (Greek. English summary.)
Bull. Soc. Math. Grèce, **24**, 85-102.

Kant, E. 1949. 3029
Quelques problèmes concernant la représentation de
la densité des habitation rurales. Exemples pris en
Estonie. *Soc. Litt. Estonica in Suecia, Stockh.*,
pp. 453-61.

Kaplan, E. L. 1949. 3030
Distribution generated by the randomization of a
fixed sample. Preliminary report. *Princeton Univ.
Statist. Res. Group, Memo. Rep.* no. 44.

Kaplansky, I. 1943. 3031
A characterization of the normal distribution. *Ann.
Math. Statist.*, **14**, 197-8.

Kaplansky, I. 1943. 3032
Solution of the " problème des ménages ". *Bull.
Amer. Math. Soc.*, **49**, 784-5.

Kaplansky, I. 1944. 3033
Symbolic solution of certain problems in permutations.
Bull. Amer. Math. Soc., **50**, 906-14.

Kaplansky, I. 1945. 3034
The asymptotic distribution of runs of consecutive
elements. *Ann. Math. Statist.*, **16**, 200-3.

Kaplansky, I. 1945. 3035
A common error concerning kurtosis. *J. Amer.
Statist. Ass.*, **40**, 259.

Kaplansky, I. 1945. 3035a
A contribution to von Neumann's theory of games.
Ann. Math. (2), **46**, 474-9.

Kaplansky, I. & Riordan, J. 1945. 3036
Multiple matching and runs by the symbolic method.
Ann. Math. Statist., **16**, 272-7.

Kaplansky, I. & Riordan, J. 1946. 3037
The " problème des ménages ". *Scripta Math.*, **12**,
113-24.

Kaplansky, I. & Riordan, J. 1946. 3038
The problem of the rooks and its applications. *Duke
Math. J.*, **13**, 259-68.

Kappos, D. A. 1949. 3039
Zur mathematischen Begründung der Wahrscheinlich-
keitstheorie. *Sitzung.-Ber. Math.-Nat. Kl. Bayer.
Akad. Wiss.*, **1948**, 309-20.

Kaprocki, S. 1943. 3040
Le problème de la corrélation. *Samml. Wissensch.
Arbeiten Schweiz internierten Polen*, **1** (1), 54-71.

Karhunen, K. 1946. 3041
Zur Spektraltheorie stochastischer Prozesse. *Ann.
Acad. Sci. Fenn. A.I*, **34**, 7 pp. (Translated by **I.
Selin**: *RAND Corp. Transl.*, 11 August 1960, T-129,
12 pp.)

Karhunen, K. 1947. 3042
Lineare Transformationen stationärer stochastischer
Prozesse. *Proc. 10th Skand. Mat. Kongr. København*,
1946, pp. 320-4.

Karhunen, K. 1947. 3043
Über lineare Methoden in der Wahrscheinlichkeitsrechnung. *Ann. Acad. Sci. Fenn. A.I.*, **37**, 3-79. (Spanish
version (1952): *Trab. Estadist.*, **3**, 59-137.) (Translated by **I. Selin**: *RAND Corp. Transl.*, 11 August
1960, T-131, 101 pp.)

Karmel, P. H. 1947. 3044
The relations between male and female reproduction
rates. *Population Stud.*, **1**, 249-74.

Karmel, P. H. 1948. 3045
The relations between male and female nuptiality in
a stable population. *Population Stud.*, **1**, 353-87.

Karmel, P. H. 1948. 3046
An analysis of the sources and magnitude of incon-
sistencies between male and female net reproduction
rates in actual populations. *Population Stud.*, **2**,
240-73.

Karmel, P. H. 1948. 3047
A rejoinder to Mr. Hajnal's comments. *Population
Stud.*, **2**, 361-72.

Karn, M. N. 1947. 3048
Length of human gestation with special reference to
prematurity. *Ann. Eugen.*, **14**, 44-59.

Karpinos, B. D. 1941. 3049
Towards determining the true rate of growth of the
Negro population. *Amer. J. Hyg.*, **34**, 24-7.

Karpinos, B. D. 1946. 3050
Use of life table death rates for comparative mortality.
Hum. Biol., **18**, 127-31.

Kärsna, A. 1940. 3051
Über das System der einmodigen Häufigkeitskurven. *Acta Comment. Univ. Tartuensis. A,* **35** (1), 65 pp.

Karsten, K. & Brooks, E. 1943. 3052
" Retro " charts. *J. Amer. Statist. Ass.,* **38,** 302-10.

Kašanin, R. 1947. 3053
Le coefficient d'approximation moyenne et le coefficient de corrélation. *Acad. Serbe. Sci. Publ. Inst. Math.,* **1,** 71-87.

Katzell, R. A. & Cureton, E. E. 1947. 3054
Biserial correlation and prediction. *J. Psychol.,* **24,** 273-8.

Katzoff, E. T. 1942. 3055
The measurement of conformity. *Psychometrika,* **7,** 31-42.

Kaufmann, F. 1945. 3056
Scientific procedure and probability. *Phil. Phenom. Res.,* **6,** 47-66.

Kaufmann, F. 1946. 3056[a]
On the nature of inductive inference. *Phil. Phenom. Res.,* **6,** 602-9; 609-11; 614-15; 649.

Kavanagh, A. J. 1941. 3057
Note on the adjustment of observations. *Ann. Math. Statist.,* **12,** 111-14.

Kavanagh, A. J. & Richards, O. W. 1942. 3058
Mathematical analysis of the relative growth of organisms. *Proc. Rochester Acad. Sci.,* **8,** 150-74.

Kawada, Y. 1941. 3059
On the measurable stochastic process. *Proc. Phys.-Math. Soc. Japan,* (3) **23,** 512-27.

Kawada, Y. 1943. 3060
Über eine verbandstheoretische Begründung der Wahrscheinlichkeitsrechnung. *Japanese J. Math.,* **18,** 887-972.

Kawada, Y. 1944. 3061
On normal stochastic processes. (Japanese.) *Res. Mem. Inst. Statist. Math., Tokyo,* **1,** 121-57.

Kawada, Y. 1946. 3062
On random ergodic theorems. (Japanese.) *Res. Mem. Inst. Statist. Math., Tokyo,* **2,** 400-17.

Kawada, Y. 1949. 3063
On a characterization of multiple normal distributions. *Kōdai, Tokyo Inst. Tech.,* **3,** 1-2.

Kawada, Y. & Kiyosi, I. 1940. 3064
On the probability distribution on a compact group. I. *Proc. Phys.-Math. Soc. Jap.,* (3) **22,** 977-98.

Kawata, T. 1940. 3065
The Fourier series of the characteristic function of a probability distribution. *Tôhoku Math. J.,* **47,** 121-5.

Kawata, T. 1940. 3066
On the strong law of large numbers. *Proc. Imp. Acad. Tokyo,* **16,** 109-12.

Kawata, T. 1940. 3067
On the division of a probability law. *Proc. Imp. Acad. Tokyo,* **16,** 249-54.

Kawata, T. 1941. 3068
The characteristic function of a probability distribution. *Tôhoku Math. J.,* **48,** 245-52.

Kawata, T. 1941. 3069
The function of mean concentration of a chance variable. *Duke Math. J.,* **8,** 666-77.

Kawata, T. 1944. 3070
The distribution of grouped moments in large samples. *Proc. Imp. Acad. Tokyo,* **20,** 337-9.

Kawata, T. 1946. 3071
On the convergence problem of the series of independent random variables. (Japanese.) *Res. Mem. Inst. Statist. Math., Tokyo,* **2,** 418-31.

Kawata, T. 1948. 3072
On the relative stability of sums of positive random variables. (Japanese.) *Sûgaku,* **1,** 121-3.

Kawata, T. & Sakamoto, H. 1949. 3073
On the characterisation of the normal population by the independence of the sample mean and the sample variance. *J. Math. Soc. Japan,* **1,** 111-15.

Kawata, T. & Udagawa, M. 1949. 3073[a]
On infinite convolutions. *Kōdai Math. Sem.,* **1,** 55-62.

Keeling, D. B. & Cisne, L. E. 1942. 3074
Using double sampling inspection in a manufacturing plant. *Bell Syst. Tech. J.,* **21,** 37-50.

Keeping, E. S. 1946. 3075
Estimation and confidence. *Proc. 1st. Canadian Math. Congr., Montreal,* 1946, pp. 36-44.

Keir, G. 1949. 3076
The progressive matrices as applied to school children. *Brit. J. Psychol (Statist. Sec.),* **2,** 140-50.

Kelker, G. H. 1947. 3077
Computing the rate of increase for deer. *J. Wildlife Management,* **11,** 177-83.

Keller, J. D. 1946. 3078
Growth curves of nations. *Hum. Biol.,* **18,** 204-20.

Keller, W. 1946. 3078[a]
Designs and technic for the adaptation of controlled competition to forage plant breeding. *J. Amer. Soc. Agron.,* **38,** 580-8.

Kellerer, H. 1949. 3079
Elementare Ausführungen zur Theorie und Technik des Stichprobenverfahrens. *Mitt. Math. Statist.,* **1,** 96-114; 203-18.

Kellerer, H. 1949. 3080
Neuere Stichprobenverfahren in der amtlichen Statistik unter besonderer Berücksichtigung amerikanischer Erfahrungen. *Allg. Statist. Arch.,* **33,** 83-112.

Kelley, T. L. 1940. 3081
Comment on Wilson and Worcester's " Note on factor analysis ". *Psychometrika,* **5,** 117-20.

Kelley, T. L. 1942. 3082
The reliability coefficient. *Psychometrika,* **7,** 75-83.

Kelley, T. L. 1943. 3083
The evidence for periodicity in short time series. *J. Amer. Statist. Ass.,* **38,** 319-26.

Kelley, T. L. 1944. 3084
A variance-ratio test of the uniqueness of principal-axis components as they exist at any stage of the Kelley iterative process for their determination. *Psychometrika,* **9,** 199-200.

Kemble, E. C. 1941. 3085
The probability concept. *Philos. Sci.,* **8,** 204-32.

Kemble, E. C. 1942. 3086
Is the frequency theory of probability adequate for all scientific purposes? *Amer. J. Phys.*, **10**, 6-16.

Kemperman, J. H. B. 1949. 3087
Some methods from sequential analysis. (Dutch.) *Math. Centrum Amsterdam Rap.* ZW-1949-009, 9 pp.

Kempthorne, O. 1944. 3088
Simpson's theorem concerning sampling. *J. R. Statist. Soc.*, **107**, 58.

Kempthorne, O. 1946. 3089
Analysis of a series of experiments by the use of punched cards. *J. R. Statist. Soc. Suppl.*, **8**, 118-27.

Kempthorne, O. 1946. 3090
Use of a punched-card system for the analysis of survey data, with special reference to the analysis of the National Farm Survey. *J. R. Statist. Soc.*, **109**, 284-95.

Kempthorne, O. 1947. 3091
A simple approach to confounding and fractional replication in factorial experiments. *Biometrika*, **34**, 255-72.

Kempthorne, O. 1947. 3092
Recent developments in the design of field experiments. IV. Lattice squares with split-plots. *J. Agric. Sci.*, **37**, 156-62.

Kempthorne, O. 1947. 3093
A note on differential responses in blocks. *J. Agric. Sci.*, **37**, 245-8.

Kempthorne, O. 1948. 3094
The factorial approach to the weighing problem. *Ann. Math. Statist.*, **19**, 238-45.

Kempthorne, O. & Federer, W. T. 1948. 3095
The general theory of prime-power lattice designs. I. Introduction and designs for p^n varieties in blocks of p plots. II. Designs for p^n varieties in blocks of p^s plots, and in squares. *Biometrics*, **4**, 54-79; 109-21.

Kendall, D. G. 1946. 3096
Fisher's " Problem of the Nile ". *Nature*, **158**, 452.

Kendall, D. G. 1947. 3097
A review of some recent work on discontinuous Markoff processes with applications to biology, physics and actuarial science. *J. R. Statist. Soc.*, **110**, 130-7.

Kendall, D. G. 1948. 3098
A form of wave propagation associated with the equation of heat conduction. *Proc. Camb. Phil. Soc.*, **44**, 591-4.

Kendall, D. G. 1948. 3099
On the generalized " Birth-and-Death " process. *Ann. Math. Statist.*, **19**, 1-15.

Kendall, D. G. 1948. 3100
On some modes of population growth leading to R. A. Fisher's logarithmic series distribution. *Biometrika*, **35**, 6-15.

Kendall, D. G. 1948. 3101
On the number of lattice points inside a random oval. *Quart. J. Math.*, **19**, 1-26.

Kendall, D. G. 1948. 3102
On the role of variable generation time in the development of a stochastic birth process. *Biometrika*, **35**, 316-30

Kendall, D. G. 1949. 3103
Stochastic processes and population growth. *J. R. Statist. Soc. B*, **11**, 230-64.

Kendall, D. G. & Rankin, R. A. 1947. 3104
On the number of Abelian groups of a given order. *Quart. J. Math.*, (1) **18**, 197-208.

Kendall, M. G. 1940. 3105
Conditions for uniqueness in the problem of moments. *Ann. Math. Statist.*, **11**, 402-9 (correction: **12**, 464).

Kendall, M. G. 1940. 3106
Note on the distribution of quantiles for large samples. *J. R. Statist. Soc. Suppl.*, **7**, 83-5.

Kendall, M. G. 1940. 3107
On the method of maximum likelihood. *J. R. Statist. Soc.*, **103**, 388-99.

Kendall, M. G. 1940. 3108
Some properties of k-statistics. *Ann. Eugen.*, **10**, 106-11.

Kendall, M. G. 1940. 3109
Proof of Fisher's rules for ascertaining the sampling semi-invariants of k-statistics. *Ann. Eugen.*, **10**, 215-22.

Kendall, M. G. 1940. 3110
The derivation of multivariate sampling formulae from univariate formulae by symbolic operation. *Ann. Eugen.*, **10**, 392-402.

Kendall, M. G. 1941. 3111
Effect of the elimination of trend on oscillations in time-series. *J. R. Statist. Soc.*, **104**, 43-52.

Kendall, M. G. 1941. 3112
Relationship between correlation formulae and elliptic functions. *J. R. Statist. Soc.*, **104**, 281-3.

Kendall, M. G. 1941. 3113
A theory of randomness. *Biometrika*, **32**, 1-15.

Kendall, M. G. 1941. 3114
A recurrence relation for the semi-invariants of Pearson curves. *Biometrika*, **32**, 81-2.

Kendall, M. G. 1941. 3115
Proof of relations connected with the tetrachoric series and its generalization. *Biometrika*, **32**, 196-8.

Kendall, M. G. 1942. 3116
On the future of statistics. *J. R. Statist. Soc.*, **105**, 69-80.

Kendall, M. G. 1942. 3117
Note on the estimation of a ranking. *J. R. Statist. Soc.*, **105**, 119-21.

Kendall, M. G. 1942. 3118
Partial rank correlation. *Biometrika*, **32**, 277-83.

Kendall, M. G. 1942. 3119
On seminvariant statistics. *Ann. Eugen.*, **11**, 300-5.

Kendall, M. G. 1943. 3120
Oscillatory movements in English agriculture. *J. R. Statist. Soc.*, **106**, 91-124.

Kendall, M. G. 1944. 3121
On autoregressive time series. *Biometrika*, **33**, 105-22.

Kendall, M. G. 1945. 3122
On the analysis of oscillatory time-series. *J. R. Statist. Soc.*, **108**, 93-141.

Kendall, M. G. 1945.   3123
Note on Yule's paper on studying time-series based
on their internal correlations. *J. R. Statist. Soc.*, **108**,
226-30.

Kendall, M. G. 1945.   3124
The treatment of ties in ranking problems. *Biometrika*,
33, 239-51.

Kendall, M. G. 1946.   3124a
Contributions to the study of oscillatory time-series.
Nat. Inst. Econ. Soc. Res. Occasional Papers IX,
76 pp. (Cambridge Univ. Press.)

Kendall, M. G. 1947.   3125
Variance of τ when both rankings contain ties.
Biometrika, **34**, 297-8.

Kendall, M. G. 1948.   3126
Systematic sampling of continuous parameter popula-
tions. *Biometrika*, **35**, 291-6.

Kendall, M. G. 1949.   3127
The estimation of parameters in linear autoregressive
time series. *Econometrica Suppl.*, **17**, 44-57. (Also:
*Proc. 25th Session Int. Statist. Inst. Conf. Washington,
D.C.*, 1947 (Publ. 1951), **5**, 44-57.)

Kendall, M. G. 1949.   3128
On the reconciliation of theories of probability.
Biometrika, **36**, 101-16.

Kendall, M. G. 1949.   3129
Rank and product-moment correlation. *Biometrika*,
36, 177-93.

Kendall, M. G. 1949.   3130
Tables of autoregressive series. *Biometrika*, **36**, 267-89.

Kendall, M. G. & Smith, B. Babington. 1940.   3131
On the method of paired comparisons. *Biometrika*,
31, 324-45.

Kennedy, C. W. 1946.   3131a
Statistical control cuts scrap cost 88 per cent. *Factory
Mgmt.*, **104**, 102-5.

Kenney, J. F. 1942.   3132
Characteristic functions in statistics. *Nat. Math. Mag.*,
17, 51-67; 99-114.

Kent, J. F., Bukantz, C. S. & Rein, C. R. 1946.   3133
Studies in complement fixation. I. Spectophotometric
titration of complement: construction of graphs for
direct determination of the 50 per cent. hemolytic
unit. *J. Immunol.*, **53**, 37-50.

Kent, R. H. & von Neumann, J. 1940.   3134
The estimation of the probable error from successive
differences. *Ballistic Res. Lab. Rep.* no. 175, February
1940.

Kent-Jones, D. W. & Meiklejohn, M. 1944.   3134a
Some experiences of microbiological assay of ribo-
flavin, nicotinic acid and other nutrient factors.
Analyst, **69**, 330-6.

Kerawala, S. M. 1941.   3135
The enumeration of the Latin rectangle of depth three
by means of a difference equation. *Bull. Calcutta
Math. Soc.*, **33**, 119-27.

Kerawala, S. M. 1941.   3136
A rapid method for calculating the least squares solu-
tion of a polynomial of degree not exceeding the fifth.
Indian J. Phys., **15**, 241-76.

Kerawala, S. M. 1946.   3137
Note on symmetrical incomplete block designs; $\lambda = 2$,
$k = 6$ or 7. *Bull. Calcutta Math. Soc.*, **38**, 190-2.

Kerawala, S. M. 1947.   3137a
A note on self-conjugate Latin squares of prime
degree. *Math. Student*, **15**, 16.

Kerawala, S. M. 1948.   3138
On bounds of skewness and kurtosis. *Bull. Calcutta
Math. Soc.*, **40**, 41-4.

Kerawala, S. M. & Hanafi, A. R. 1941.   3139
The table of symmetric functions of weight 10. *Proc.
Nat. Acad. Sci. India*, **11** (3), 56-63.

Kerawala, S. M. & Hanafi, A. R. 1942.   3140
Table of monomial symmetric functions of weight 11.
Proc. Nat. Acad. Sci. India, **12** (2), 81-96.

Kerawala, S. M. & Hanafi, A. R. 1947.   3141
Table of monomial symmetric functions of weight 12
in terms of power sums. *Sankhyā*, **8**, 345-59.

Kermack, W. O. & McKendrick, A. G. 1940.   3142
The design and interpretation of experiments based
on a fourfold table: the statistical assessment of
the effect of treatment. *Proc. Roy. Soc. Edin.*, **60**,
362-75.

Kern, E. M. & Alper, C. 1945.   3143
Multi-dimensional graphical representation for analyz-
ing variation in quantitative characters. *Ann. Missouri
Bot. Gdn.*, **32**, 279-81.

Kerr, W. A. 1944.   3143a
Some axioms of quality control. *Industr. Qual.
Contr.*, **1** (1), 3.

Kerrich, J. E. 1949.   3144
Normalization of frequency functions. *Nature*, **164**,
1089.

Kesteven, G. L. 1946.   3144a
The coefficient of variation. *Nature*, **158**, 520-1.

Keyfitz, N. 1945.   3145
The sampling approach to economic data. *Canadian
J. Econ. Polit. Sci.*, **11**, 467-77.

Khan, A. R. & Dalal, J. R. 1943.   3146
Optimum size and shape of plots for Brassica experiments in the Punjab. *Sankhyā*, **6**, 317-20.

Khargonkar, S. A. 1948.   3147
The estimation of missing plot value in split-plot
and strip trials. *J. Indian Soc. Agric. Statist.*, **1**,
147-61.

Khinchin, A. 1941.   3148
Sur les méthodes analytiques de la mécanique statistique.
C. R. (Dokl.) Acad. Sci. URSS, **33**, 438-41.

Khinchin, A. 1941.   3149
Valeurs moyennes des fonctions sommatoires dans la
mécanique statistique. *C. R. (Dokl.) Acad. Sci.
URSS*, **33**, 442-5.

Khinchin, A. 1941.   3150
Sur la corrélation intermoléculaire. *C. R. (Dokl.)
Acad. Sci. URSS*, **33**, 482-4.

Khinchin, A. 1943.   3151
Les fonctions convexes et les théorèmes d'évolution
de la mécanique statistique. (Russian. French
summary.) *Izv. Akad. Nauk SSSR, Ser. Mat.*, **7**,
111-22.

Khinchin, A. 1943. 3152
Sur le problème ergodique de la mécanique quantique. (Russian. French summary.) *Izv. Akad. Nauk SSSR, Ser. Mat.*, **7**, 167-84.

Khinchin, A. 1943. 3153
Sur un cas de corrélation à posteriori. (French. Russian summary.) *Mat. Sbornik*, **12** (54), 185-96.

Kibble, W. F. 1941. 3154
A two-variate gamma type distribution. *Sankhyā*, **5**, 137-50.

Kibble, W. F. 1941. 3154a
Note on Mr. Rajabhusanam's paper. *Sankhyā*, **5**, 177-8.

Kibble, W. F. 1945. 3154b
An extension of a theorem of Mehler on Hermite polynomials. *Proc. Camb. Phil. Soc.*, **41**, 12-15.

Kimball, B. F. 1940. 3155
Orthogonal polynomials applied to least square fitting of weighted observations. *Ann. Math. Statist.*, **11**, 348-52.

Kimball, B. F. 1942. 3156
Limited type of primary probability distribution applied to annual maximum flood flows. *Ann. Math. Statist.*, **13**, 318-25.

Kimball, B. F. 1943. 3157
General theory of plant account subject to constant mortality law of retirements. *Econometrica*, **11**, 61-82.

Kimball, B. F. 1944. 3158
Note on asymptotic value of probability distribution of sum of random variables which are greater than a set of arbitrarily chosen numbers. *Ann. Math. Statist.*, **15**, 423-7.

Kimball, B. F. 1945. 3159
The failure of the unit-summation procedure as a group method of estimating depreciation. *Econometrica*, **13**, 225-44.

Kimball, B. F. 1946. 3160
Sufficient statistical estimation functions for the parameters of the distribution of maximum values. *Ann. Math. Statist.*, **17**, 299-309 (correction: *J. Amer. Statist. Ass.*, **50**, 578).

Kimball, B. F. 1946-7. 3161
Assignment of frequencies to a completely ordered set of sample data. *Trans. Amer. Geophys. Un.*, **27**, 843-6; **28**, 952.

Kimball, B. F. 1947. 3162
Some basic theorems for developing tests of fit for the case of the non-parametric probability distribution function. I. *Ann. Math. Statist.*, **18**, 540-8.

Kimball, B. F. 1947. 3163
A system of life tables for physical property based on the truncated normal distribution. *Econometrica*, **15**, 342-60.

Kimball, B. F. 1949. 3164
An approximation to the sampling variance of an estimated maximum value of given frequency based on fit of double exponential distribution of maximum values. *Ann. Math. Statist.*, **20**, 110-13.

Kincaid, C. M., Litton, G. W. & Hunt, R. E. 3165
1945. Some factors that influence the production of steers from pasture. *J. Animal Sci.*, **4**, 164-73.

Kincaid, W. M. 1948. 3166
Note on the error in interpolation of a function of two independent variables. *Ann. Math. Statist.*, **19**, 85-8.

Kincaid, W. M. 1948. 3167
Solution of equations by interpolation. *Ann. Math. Statist.*, **19**, 207-19.

Kincaid, W. M., Scott, W. R., Chover, J. 3168
& Copeland, A. H. 1949.
Analysis of a one-person game. *Univ. Mich. Eng. Res. Inst. Rep.* nos. M.720-1, R.21, R.22.

King, A. J. 1945. 3169
The master sample of agriculture. I. Development and use. *J. Amer. Statist. Ass.*, **40**, 38-45.

King, A. J. 1946. 3170
Some recent developments in sampling. *U.S. Quartermaster Corps Comm. Food Res. Conf. Food Acceptance Res.*, pp. 43-5.

King, A. J. & Houseman, E. E. 1942. 3171
Determination of sample sizes. *Illinois Univ. Dept. Agric. Econ. and Agric. Exper. Sta.*, *Rep.* AE-1837.

King, A. J. & McCarty, D. E. 1941. 3172
Application of sampling to agricultural statistics with emphasis on stratified samples. *J. Marketing*, **5**, 462-74.

King, A. J. & Simpson, G. D. 1940. 3173
New developments in agricultural sampling. *J. Farm. Econ.*, **22**, 341-9.

King, A. J., McCarty, D. E. & McPeek, M. 3174
1942. An objective method of sampling wheat fields to estimate production and quality of wheat. *U.S. Dept. Agric. Tech. Bull.*, no. 814, 1-87.

King, G. W. 1948. 3175
Dependence of physical properties of high polymers on molecular structure; statistical investigations with the aid of punched card methods. *Office Naval Res. Tech. Rep.* no. 1.

King, G. W. 1949. 3176
New methods in the statistical mechanics of high polymers. *Office Naval Res. Tech. Rep.* no. 2.

Kingston, J. 1944. 3177
Dimensionamento de amostras. (Sample sizes.) (Portuguese.) *Rev. Brasil. Estatíst.*, **5**, 299-304.

Kingston, J. 1944. 3178
Reparos sobre certas condiçòes estatísticas. (Portuguese.) *Rev. Brasil. Estatíst.*, **5**, 519-28.

Kingston, J. 1945. 3179
Sôbre um novo método de ajustamento pelos mínimos quadrados. (Portuguese.) *Rev. Brasil. Estatíst.*, **6**, 11-16.

Kingston, J. 1946. 3180
Sôbre a aplicaçào do critério dos mínimos quadrados às distribuiçòes contínuas. (Portuguese.) *Rev. Brasil. Estatíst.*, **7**, 775-80.

Kingston, J. 1947. 3181
Principios basicos do ajustamento estatístico. (Portuguese.) *Rev. Brasil. Estatíst.*, **8**, 43-56.

Kiranoff, P. 1947. 3182
Statistique et économie. (Bulgarian. English, French and Russian summaries.) *Statistika, Sofia*, **8** (1), 3-17.

Kiranoff, P. 1947. 3183
Le plan et la statistique. (Bulgarian. French, English and Russian summaries.) *Statistika, Sofia*, **8** (2-3), 3-28.

Kirchen, C. J. 1948. 3184
Levels of significance for variance ratio of two samples of equal size. *J. Amer. Statist. Ass.*, **43**, 564-5.

Kirkwood, J. G. 1946. 3185
The statistical mechanical theory of transport processes. *J. Chem. Phys.*, **14**, 180-201.

Kirkwood, J. G. & Boggs, E. M. 1942. 3186
The radial distribution function in liquids. *J. Chem. Phys.*, **10**, 394.

Kish, L. 1949. 3187
A procedure for objective respondent selection within the household. *J. Amer. Statist. Ass.*, **44**, 380-7.

Kishen, K. 1940. 3188
On a simplified method of expressing the components of the second-order interaction in a 3^3 factorial design. *Sankhyā*, **4**, 577-80.

Kishen, K. 1941. 3189
Symmetrical unequal block arrangements. *Sankhyā*, **5**, 329-44.

Kishen, K. 1942. 3190
On expressing any single degree of freedom for treatments in an s^m factorial arrangement in terms of its sets for main effects and interactions. *Sankhyā*, **6**, 133-40.

Kishen, K. 1942. 3191
On Latin and Hyper-Graeco-Latin cubes and hyper-cubes. *Current Science*, **11**, 98-9.

Kishen, K. 1945. 3192
On the design of experiments for weighing and making other types of measurements. *Ann. Math. Statist.*, **16**, 294-300. (Also: *Current Science*, **14**, 194-5.)

Kishen, K. 1948. 3193
On fractional replication of the general symmetrical factorial design. *J. Indian Soc. Agric. Statist.*, **1**, 91-106. (Also (1947): *Current Science*, **16**, 138-9.)

Kishen, K. 1949. 3194
On the construction of Latin and Hyper-Graeco-Latin cubes and hyper-cubes. *J. Indian Soc. Agric. Statist.*, **2**, 20-48.

Kitagawa, T. 1940. 3195
Independent random variables. I, II. (Japanese.) *Nippon Sûgaku-buturi-gakukai-si*, **14**, 236-54; 255-95.

Kitagawa, T. 1940. 3196
The limit-theorems of the stochastic contagious processes. *Mem. Fac. Sci. A, Kyusyu*, **1**, 167-94.

Kitagawa, T. 1941. 3197
The weakly contagious discrete stochastic process. *Mem. Fac. Sci. A, Kyusyu*, **2**, 37-65.

Kitagawa, T. & Huruya, S. 1941. 3198
The application of the limit theorem of the contagious stochastic process to the contagious diseases. *Mem. Fac. Sci. A, Kyusyu*, **1**, 195-207.

Kitagawa, T., Huruya, S. & Yazima, T. 1947. 3199
The probabilistic analysis of the time-series of rare events. I. *Mem. Fac. Sci. A, Kyusyu*, **2**, 151-204.

Kivikoski, E. 1948. 3200
Über die Konvergenz des Iterationsverfahrens bei der Berechnung des effektiven Zinsfusses der Anleihen. *Skand. Aktuartidskr.*, **31**, 135-56.

Klauber, L. M. 1941. 3201
The frequency distribution of certain herpetological variables. *Bull. Zool. Soc., San Diego*, **17**, 5-31.

Klauber, L. M. 1941. 3202
Illustrations of the relationship between populations and samples. *Bull. Zool. Soc., San Diego*, **17**, 33-71.

Klauber, L. M. 1945. 3203
Herpetological correlations. I. Correlations in homogeneous populations, *Bull. Zool. Soc., San Diego*, **21**, 1-101.

Klein, L. R. 1943. 3204
Pitfalls in the statistical determination of the investment schedule. *Econometrica*, **11**, 246-58.

Klelzkowski, A. 1949. 3205
The transformation of local lesion counts for statistical analysis. *Ann. Appl. Biol.*, **36**, 139-52.

Klemens, P. G. 1948. 3206
Resolution of devices actuated by random events. *Phil. Mag.*, (7) **39**, 656-60.

Kloepfer, H. W. 1946. 3207
An investigation of 171 possible linkage relationships in man. *Ann. Eugen.*, **13**, 35-71.

Knapp, B., Jr. & Nordskog, A. W. 1946. 3208
Heritability of growth and efficiency in beef cattle. *J. Animal Sci.*, **5**, 62-70.

Knobloch, H. 1941. 3209
Funktionsgewichte in der Ausgleichsrechnung. *Zeit. angew. Math. Mech.*, **21**, 315-16.

Knoll, F. 1942. 3210
Zur Grosszahlforschung: Über die Zerspaltung einer Mischverteilung in Normalverteilungen. *Arch. Math. Wirtsch.*, **8**, 36-49.

Knoll, F. 1943. 3211
Über Näherungsverfahren bei empirisch gegebenen Verteilungsfunktionen und damit verbundene Korrekturformeln. *Deutsche Math.*, **7**, 187-94.

Knopp, K. 1943. 3212
Über eine Erweiterung des Äquivalenzsatzes der *C*- and *H*-Verfahren und eine Klasse regulär wachsender Funktionen. *Math. Zeit.*, **49**, 219-55.

Knowler, L. A. 1946. 3213
Fundamentals of quality control. *Industr. Qual. Contr.*, **3** (1), 7-18.

Knowler, L. A. 1947. 3214
Some industrial effects of quality control by statistical methods. *Sch. Sci. Math.*, **47**, 207-11.

Knudsen, L. F. 1940. 3215
Interdependence in a series. *J. Amer. Statist. Ass.*, **35**, 507-14.

Knudsen, L. F. 1942. 3216
A punched card technique to obtain coefficients of orthogonal polynomials. *J. Amer. Statist. Ass.*, **37**, 496-506.

Knudsen, L. F. 1943. 3217
A method for determining the significance of a shortage. *J. Amer. Statist. Ass.*, **38**, 466-70.

Knudsen, L. F. 1944.   3218
The value of statistics in the formulation of chemical methods. *J. Ass. Off. Agric. Chem.*, **27**, 145-
53.

Knudsen, L. F. 1945.   3219
Note on statistical probabilities of finding hyper-
sensitive subjects in random samples. *J. Invest.
Dermat.*, **6**, 231-2.

Knudsen, L. F. 1945.   3220
The use of statistics in biological experimentation
and assay. *J. Ass. Off. Agric. Chem.*, **28**, 806-
13.

Knudsen, L. F. & Curtis, J. M. 1947.   3221
The use of angular transformation in biological assay.
J. Amer. Statist. Ass., **42**, 282-96.

Knudsen, L. F. & Randall, W. A. 1945.   3222
Penicillin assay and its control chart analysis. *J. Bact.*,
50, 187-200.

Knudsen, L. F., Smith, R. B., Vos, B. J. &   3223
McClosky, W. T. 1946.
The biological assay of epinephrine. *J. Pharmacol.*,
86, 339-43.

Kobbernagel, P. 1943.   3224
Über einen allgemein vorkommenden Mangel bei
statistischem Material. (Danish.) *Festkr. J. F.
Steffensen*, pp. 82-4.

Koch, A. 1943.   3225
Das Dualkreuzungsverfahren zur Verminderung der
Nebensprechkopplung in Fernmeldekablen. *Elektr.
Nachr. Techn.*, **20**, 259-63.

Koenker, R. H. & Hansen, C. W. 1942.   3226
Steps for the application of the Johnson-Neyman
technique—a sample analysis. *J. Exper. Educ.*, **10**,
164-73.

Kogan, L. S. 1948.   3227
Analysis of variance—repeated measurements. *Psychol. Bull.*, **45**, 131-43.

Koller, S. 1941.   3228
Über die Anwendbarkeit und Verbesserung der
Probandenmethode. *Zeit. Vererbungs.-Konst.lehre*,
25, 375-90.

Koller, S. 1942.   3229
Methodische Bemerkungen zur Frage des Männer oder
Frauenüberschusses und zum Problem der Heiratswahr-
scheinlichkeit. *Arch. Bevölkerungswissensch. und
Bevolkerungspol.*, **12** (1-2), 85-97.

Kolmogorov, A. N. 1940.   3230
On a new confirmation of Mendel's laws. *C. R.
(Dokl.) Acad. Sci. URSS*, **27**, 37-41.

Kolmogorov, A. N. 1941.   3231
Confidence limits for an unknown distribution
function. *Ann. Math. Statist.*, **12**, 461-3.

Kolmogorov, A. N. 1941.   3232
Interpolation und Extrapolation von stationaren
zufälligen Folgen. (Russian. German summary.)
Izv. Akad. Nauk SSSR, Ser. Mat., **5**, 3-14.

Kolmogorov, A. N. 1941.   3233
Über das logarithmisch normale Verteilungsgesetz der
Dimensionen der Teilchen bei Zerstückelung. *C. R.
(Dokl.) Acad. Sci. URSS*, **31**, 99-101.

Kolmogorov, A. N. 1941.   3234
Stationary sequences in Hilbert space. (Russian.)
Byull. Moskov. Gos. Univ., **2** (6), 1-40. (Spanish
version (1953): *Trab. Estadíst.*, **4**, 55-73; 243-70.)

Kolmogorov, A. N. 1942.   3235
Sur l'estimation statistique des paramètres de la loi
de Gauss. (Russian. French summary.) *Izv. Akad.
Nauk SSSR, Ser. Mat.*, **6**, 3-32.

Kolmogorov, A. N. (Editor). 1945.   3236
Collection of papers on the theory of artillery fire. I.
(Russian.) *Trudy Inst. Math. Steklov.*, **12**, 106 pp.
(Translated by E. Hewitt, *RAND Corp. Trans.*, 13
October 1948, T-14, 132 pp.)

Kolmogorov, A. N. 1946.   3237
On the proof of the method of least squares. (Russian.)
Usp. Mat. Nauk (N.S.), **1**, 1 (11), 57-70.

Kolmogorov, A. N. 1947.   3238
The role of Russian science in the development of the
theory of probability. (Russian.) *Uch. Zap. Moskov.
Gos. Univ.*, **91**, 53-64.

Kolmogorov, A. N. 1947.   3239
Statistical theory of oscillations with a continuous
spectrum. (Russian.) *Yubileinye Sb. Akad. Nauk
SSSR*, **1**, 242-51. (*30th anniversary of the October
Revolution.*) (Transl. by M. D. Friedman, Newtonville,
Mass., 1956, 12 pp.)

Kolmogorov, A. N. 1949.   3240
A local limit theorem for classical Markov chains.
(Russian.) *Izv. Akad. Nauk SSSR, Ser. Mat.*, **13**,
281-300.

Kolmogorov, A. N. 1949.   3241
The real meaning of the results of dispersion analysis.
(Russian.) *Trudy Utor. Uses. Sov. Mat. Statist.
Uzbek.*, 27 Sept.-2 Okt. 1948, pp. 240-68.

Kolmogorov, A. N. 1949.   3242
The solution of a problem in the theory of probability,
connected with the question of the mechanism of
the formation of strata. (Russian.) *Dokl. Akad. Nauk
SSSR*, **65**, 793-6. (Transl. (1951): *Amer. Math. Soc.
Translation*, **53**, 8 pp.)

Kolmogorov, A. N. & Dmitriev, N. A. 1947.   3243
Branching stochastic processes. (Russian.) *Dokl.
Akad. Nauk SSSR*, **56**, 7-10.

Kolmogorov, A. N. & Prokhorov, Yu. V. 1949.   3244
On sums of a random number of random variables.
(Russian.) *Usp. Mat. Nauk (N.S.)*, **4**, 4(32), 168-
72.

Kolmogorov, A. N. & Sevastyanov, B. A. 1947.   3245
The calculation of final probabilities for branching
random processes. (Russian.) *Dokl. Akad. Nauk
SSSR*, **56**, 783-6.

Kolmogorov, A. N., Petrov, A. A.   3246
& Smirnov, Yu. M. 1947.
On a Gaussian formula from the theory of the method
of least squares. (Russian.) *Izv. Akad. Nauk SSSR,
Ser. Mat.*, **11**, 561-6.

Kolodziejczyk, S. 1941.   3247
Sur les événements à probabilité élevée. (German,
Italian and English summaries.) *Trans. 12th Int. Congr.
Actuar.*, Lucerne, 1940, **1**, 309-19.

Koopman, B. O. 1940. 3248
The axioms and algebra of intuitive probability. *Ann. Math.*, (2) **41**, 269-92.

Koopman, B. O. 1940. 3249
The bases of probability. *Bull. Amer. Math. Soc.*, **46**, 763-74.

Koopman, B. O. 1941. 3250
Intuitive probabilities and sequences. *Ann. Math.*, (2) **42**, 169-87.

Koopmans, T. C. 1940. 3251
The degree of damping in business cycles. *Econometrica*, **8**, 79-89.

Koopmans, T. C. 1941. 3252
Distributed lags in dynamic economics. *Econometrica*, **9**, 128-34.

Koopmans, T. C. 1942. 3253
Serial correlation and quadratic forms in normal variables. *Ann. Math. Statist.*, **13**, 14-33.

Koopmans, T. C. 1945. 3254
Statistical estimation of simultaneous economic relations. *J. Amer. Statist. Ass.*, **40**, 448-66.

Koopmans, T. C. 1947. 3255
Measurement without theory. *Rev. Econ. Statist.*, **29**, 161-72. (Also: *Cowles Commission Paper New Series*, no. 25.)

Koopmans, T. C. 1947. 3256
Statistical methods of measuring economic relationships. *Cowles Commission Discussion paper* no. 310, 126 pp. (mimeo).

Koopmans, T. C. 1949. 3257
Identification problems in economic model construction. *Econometrica*, **17**, 125-43.

Korčak, J. 1940. 3258
Les deux types fondamentaux de distribution statistiques. *Bull. Int. Statist. Inst.*, **30** (3), 295-9.

Korčak, J. 1941. 3259
Prírodní dualita statistického rozlození (La dualité de la distribution statistique dans la nature). *Statist. Obzor*, **22**, 171-222.

Korenistov, D. V. 1948. 3260
The skew distribution of S. N. Kritskii and M. F. Menkel in probability calculations of river flow. (Russian.) *Hydrotekh. Stroit.*, no. 6.

Kormes, M. 1940. 3261
Statistical methods as applied to casualty insurance. *J. Amer. Statist. Ass.*, **35**, 47-54.

Kosambi, D. D. 1941. 3262
A bivariate extension of Fisher's *z* test. *Current Science*, **10**, 191-3.

Kosambi, D. D. 1941. 3263
Correlation and time series. *Current Science*, **10**, 372-4.

Kosambi, D. D. 1942. 3264
A test of significance for multiple observations. *Current Science*, **11**, 271-4.

Kosambi, D. D. 1942. 3265
On valid tests of linguistic hypotheses. *New Indian Antiquary*, **5**, 21-4.

Kosambi, D. D. 1943. 3266
Statistics in function space. *J. Indian Math. Soc.* (*N.S.*), **7**, 76-88.

Kosambi, D. D. 1944. 3267
The estimation of map distances from recombination values. *Ann. Eugen.*, **12**, 172-5.

Kosambi, D. D. 1944. 3268
The geometric method in mathematical statistics. *Amer. Math. Monthly*, **51**, 382-9.

Kosambi, D. D. 1946. 3269
The law of large numbers. *Math. Student*, **14**, 14-19.

Kosambi, D. D. 1947. 3270
An extension of the least-squares method for statistical estimation. *Ann. Eugen.*, **13**, 257-61.

Kosambi, D. D. 1949. 3271
Characteristic properties of series distributions. *Proc. Nat. Inst. Sci., India*, **15**, 109-13.

Kossak, C. F. 1945. 3272
On the mechanics of classification. *Ann. Math. Statist.*, **16**, 95-8.

Kossack, C. F. 1947. 3273
The existence of collectives in abstract space. *Sankhyā*, **8**, 219-34.

Kossack, C. F. 1948. 3274
On the computation of zero-order correlation coefficients. *Psychometrika*, **13**, 91-3.

Kossack, C. F. 1949. 3275
Some techniques for simple classification. *Proc. Berkeley Symp. Math. Statist. and Probab.*, 1945-6, pp. 345-52.

Kosten, L. 1943. 3276
On the frequency distribution of the number of discharges counted by a Geiger-Müller counter in a constant interval. *Physica*, **10**, 749-56.

Kosten, L. 1947. 3277
On the influence of repeated calls in the theory of probabilities of blocking. (Dutch.) *De Ingenieur*, **59**, 1-25.

Kosten, L. 1948. 3278
On the measurement of congestion quantities by means of fictitious traffic. *Het P.T.T. Bedrijf*, **2**, 15-25.

Kosten, L. 1948. 3279
On the validity of the Erlang and Engset loss formulae. *Het P.T.T. Bedrijf*, **2**, 42-5.

Kosten, L. Manning, J. R. & Garwood, F. 1949. 3280
Accuracy of measurements of probabilities of loss in telephone systems. *J. R. Statist. Soc. B*, **11**, 54-67.

Kostitzin, V. A. 1940. 3281
Sur la loi logistique et ses généralizations. *Acta Biotheor. A*, **5**, 155-9.

Kostitzin, V. A. 1940. 3282
Sur la ségrégation physiologique et la variation des espèces. *Acta Biotheor. A*, **5**, 160-8.

Kostitzin, V. A. 1942. 3283
Evolution. (Spanish.) *Rev. Acad. Colomb. Cienc. Exact. Fis. Nat.*, **5**, 241-5.

Kotzig, A. 1948. 3284
Použiti zobecněnej Póly-ovej schémy pre výskum chýb v psychologii. (Application of the Pólya scheme in ascertaining mistakes in psychological research. *Statist. Obzor*, **28**, 135-44.

Kotzig, A. 1949. 3285
The weights of the results of partial tests for determining the total result of the test. *Aktuarské Vědy*, **8** (4), 129-37.

Koyenuma, N. 1941. 3286
Zur Theorie der biologischen Strahlenwirkung. I, II. *Zeit. Physik*, **117**, 510-14; *Phys. Zeit.*, **42**, 213-17.

Koyenuma, N. 1942. 3287
Trefferwahrscheinlichkeit und Variabilität. Bermerkungen zur Arbeit von H. v. Schelling in *Naturwiss.*, 30, 306. *Naturwiss*, **30**, 732-3.

Koyenuma, N. 1943. 3288
Beiträge zur Theorie der biologischen Strahlenwirkung. *Zeit. Phys.*, **120**, 185-211.

Kozakiewicz, W. 1940. 3289
Sur la convergence presque certaine. *Bull. Sci. Math.*, (2) **64**, 121-8.

Kozakiewicz, W. 1947. 3290
On the convergence of sequences of moment generating functions. *Ann. Math. Statist.*, **18**, 61-9.

Kozlik, A. 1941. 3291
The use of per capita figures for demand curves. *J. Amer. Statist. Ass.*, **36**, 417-22.

Kozulyaev, P. A. 1941. 3292
Sur les problèmes d'interpolation et d'extrapolation des suites stationnaires. *C. R. (Dokl.) Acad. Sci. URSS*, **30**, 13-17.

Kozulyaev, P. A. 1947. 3293
On a question of extrapolation of stationary random processes. (Russian.) *Dokl. Akad. Nauk SSSR*, **56**, 903-5.

Kozulyaev, P. A. 1949. 3294
On the theory of extrapolation of stationary sequences. (Russian.) *Uch. Zap. Moskov. Gos. Univ.*, **145**, Mat. 3, 59-91.

Kramer, H. H. & Burnham, C. R. 1947. 3295
Methods of combining linkage intensity values from backcross F_2 and F_3 genetic data. *Genetics*, **32**, 379-90.

Kramer, M. 1940. 3296
Frequency surfaces in two variables each of which is uniformly distributed. *Amer. J. Hyg.*, **32**, 45-65.

Kramer, P. R. & Sturgeon, E. E. 1942. 3297
Transect method of estimating forest area from aerial photograph index sheets. *J. Forestry*, **40**, 693-6.

Kreis, H. 1941. 3298
Zerfällung einer Gesamtheit in Aktiven- und Invalidengruppen. *Mitt. Ver. Schweiz. Versich.-Math.*, **41**, 205-9.

Kreis, H. 1945. 3299
Beitrag zur Theorie der Häufigkeitsfunktionen. *Mitt. Ver. Schweiz. Versich.-Math.*, **45**, 239-56.

Kreis, H. 1946. 3300
Lineare Abhängigkeit und Äquivalenz von Punktsystemen. *Mitt. Ver. Schweiz. Versich.-Math.*, **46**, 169-86.

Krishna Iyer, P. V. *See* **Iyer, P. V. K.**

Krishna Sastry, K. V. *See* **Sastry, K. V. K.**

Krishnamurthy, T. & Krishnamurthy, R. S. 1941. 3301
An estimate of the population of India for the year 1941. *Sankhyā*, **5**, 279-83.

Krishnaswami Ayyangar, A. A. *See* **Ayyangar, A. A. K.**

Krishnan Nair, A. N. *See* **Nair, A. N. K.**

Kritskii, S. N. & Menkel, M. F. 1948. 3302
On the correspondence of theoretical skew probability distributions to given observations on river flow. (Russian.) *Problems of Regulating River Flow, Bull.* 3, *Izv. Akad. Nauk SSSR.*

Krizenecky, J. & Kudlicka, K. 1949. 3303
Effect of length of dry period on the birthweight of calves. *Zeit. Tierz. Zücht Biol.*, **56**, 299-320.

Krochmal, S. 1941. 3304
Einige Untersuchungen auf dem Gebiete der Theorie der kleinsten Quadrate. (Russian. German summary.) *Ucherye Zap. Leningrad Gos. Univ., Ser. Mat.*, **12**, 150-98.

Kroll, A. 1940. 3305
Item validity as a factor in test validity. *J. Educ. Psychol.*, **31**, 425-36.

Kronig, R. 1943. 3306
On time losses in machinery undergoing interruptions. I. *Physica*, **10**, 215-24.

Kronig, R. & Mondria, H. 1943. 3307
On time losses in machinery undergoing interruptions. II. *Physica*, **10**, 331-6.

Kruithof, I. J. 1946. 3308
Rotary traffic machine. *Elect. Commun.*, **23**, 192-211.

Krumbein, W. C. 1941. 3308[a]
The effects of abrasion on the size, shape and roundness of rock fragments. *J. Geology*, **49**, 482-520.

Kruskal, W. H. 1946. 3309
Helmert's distribution. *Amer. Math. Monthly*, **53**, 435-8.

Krzyżanski, M. 1945. 3310
Sur les solutions de l'équation linéaire du type parabolique déterminées par les conditions initiales. *Ann. Pol. Math.*, **18**, 145-56.

Kucera, E. 1945. 3311
Náhodnost v rade císlic (Le rôle du hasard dans une série numérique). (Czech. summary.) *Prumyslovíj Vestník*, **32** (5), 85-7.

Kull, W. 1946. 3312
Das Harmoniegesetz der Statistik. Eine Buchbesprechung. *Schweiz. Zeit. Volkwirtsch. Statist.*, **82**, 414-32.

Kullback, S. 1947. 3313
On the Charlier type B series. *Ann. Math. Statist.*, **18**, 574-81 (correction: **19**, 427).

Kullback, S. & Frankel, A. 1940. 3314
A simple sampling experiment on confidence intervals. *Ann. Math. Statist.*, **11**, 209-13.

Kunisawa, K. 1942. 3315
On the power set of a probability law. I. *Proc. Phys.-Math. Soc. Japan*, **24**, 681-95.

Kunisawa, K. 1944. 3316
Mean concentration function and the law of large numbers. *Proc. Imp. Acad. Japan*, **20**, 627-30.

Kunisawa, K. 1946. 3317
On the mean concentration and typical function. (Japanese.) *Res. Mem. Inst. Statist. Math., Tokyo*, **2**, 422-9.

Kunisawa, K. 1946.   3318
On a theorem concerning the sums of positive independent random variables. *Res. Mem. Inst. Statist. Math., Tokyo*, **2**, 163-9.

Kunisawa, K. 1946-7.   3319
On the mean concentration function and quasi mean concentration function. I-VI. (Japanese.) *Res. Mem. Inst. Statist. Math., Tokyo*, **2**, 79-88, 112-21, 136-45, 233-44, 422-9; **3**, 43-7.

Kunisawa, K. 1948.   3320
Some problems on infinitely subdivisible laws. (Japanese.) *Sûgaku*, **1**, 117-19.

Kunisawa, K. 1948.   3321
On the strong law of large numbers. (Japanese.) *Sûgaku*, **1**, 214-16.

Kunisawa, K. 1949.   3322
On an analytical method in the theory of independent random variables. *Ann. Inst. Statist. Math., Tokyo*, **1**, 1-77.

Kunisawa, K. 1949.   3323
On the mixed Markoff process. *Kōdai, Tokyo Inst. Tech.*, **3**, 28-32.

Kurbatov, J. D. & Mann, H. B. 1945.   3324
Correction of G-M counter data. *Phys. Rev.*, (2) **68**, 40-3.

Kurita, S. 1948.   3325
A theoretical consideration on the method for estimating the yearly survival rate of fish stock by using the age of difference between the oldest and the average. I. *Bull. Jap. Soc. Sci. Fish.*, **14**, 1-12.

Kurtz, A. K. 1946.   3326
Scoring rating scales after the responses are punched on I.B.M. cards. *Proc. Res. Forum, IBM Corp., New York*, 26-30 August 1946, pp. 28-34.

Kuvin, L. 1945.   3326ª
How statistics will help in postwar textile problems. *Industr. Standardization*, **16**, 103-4.

Kuzmin, R. O. 1941.   3327
The mathematical works of S. N. Bernstein. (Russian.) *Usp. Mat. Nauk*, (8), 3-7.

Kuznets, G. M. & Klein, L. R. 1943.   3328
A statistical analysis of the domestic demand for lemons, 1921-41. *California Agric. Exper. Sta. Mimeo. Rep.* no. 84, 112 pp.

Ky Fan. *See under* **Fan.**

L

Labutin, D. N. 1940.   3329
On a generating function. (Russian.) *Uch. Zap. Leningrad Gos. Univ., Ser. Mat.*, **10**, 139-47.

Lacey, A. H. 1946.   3330
Further observations on the rabbit method of insulin assay. *Endocrinology*, **39**, 344-57.

Lacroix, H. 1942.   3331
Méthodes de mesure quantitative d'un ensemble hétérogène. *Bull. Statist. Gen. France*, **30** (2), 95-109.

Lah, I. 1941.   3332
Wahrscheinlichkeitsrechnung und Versicherungswesen. (French, Italian and English summaries.) *Trans. 12th. Int. Congr. Actuar., Lucerne*, 1940, **1**, 409-34.

Lakshmanamurti, M. 1945.   3333
Coefficient of association between two attributes in statistics. *Proc. Indian Acad. Sci. A*, **22**, 123-33.

Laloni, N. 1942.   3334
Einführung in das Studium der Eisenbahnstatistik. *Zeit. Ver. Mitteleurop. Eisenbahnverwaltungen*, **82** (26), 349-52.

Lamas, P. J. A. 1944.   3335
The number of frequencies and accuracy in field trials. *Granos*, **8**, 3-16.

Lancaster, H. O. 1949.   3336
The combination of probabilities arising from data in discrete distributions. *Biometrika*, **36**, 370-82 (correction: **37**, 452).

Lancaster, H. O. 1949.   3337
The derivation and partition of χ^2 in certain discrete distributions. *Biometrika*, **36**, 117-29 (correction: **37**, 452).

Lancaster, O. E. 1942.   3338
Machine method for the extraction of cube root. *J. Amer. Statist. Ass.*, **37**, 112-15.

Landahl, H. D. 1941.   3339
Studies in the mathematical biophysics of discrimination and conditioning. II. Special case. Errors, trials, and number of possible responses. *Bull. Math. Biophys.*, **3**, 71-7.

Landahl, H. D. 1945.   3340
A note on the mathematical biophysics of central excitation and inhibition. *Bull. Math. Biophys.*, **7**, 219-21.

Landahl, H. D. 1940.   3340ª
Time scores and factor analysis. *Psychometrika*, **5**, 67-74.

Landahl, H. D., McCulloch, W. S.   3341
& Pitts, W. 1943.
A statistical consequence of the logical calculus of nervous nets. *Bull. Math. Biophys.*, **5**, 135-7.

Landau, H. G. 1944.   3342
Note on the variance and best estimates. *Ann. Math. Statist.*, **15**, 219-21.

Landauer, W. & Bliss, C. I. 1946.   3343
Insulin-induced rumplessness of chickens. III. The relationship of dosage and of developmental stage at time of injection to response. *J. Exper. Zool.*, **102**, 1-22.

Landon, V. 1941-2.   3344
The distribution of amplitude with time in fluctuation noise. *Proc. Inst. Radio Engrs.*, **29**, 50-5; **30**, 425-9 (correction: 526).

Landry, B. A. 1945.   3344ª
Missing data on coal sampling. *Trans. Amer. Soc. Mech. Engrs.*, **67**, 69-79.

Lang, K. 1942-3.   3345
Analysis of net premium formulas for the income endowment policy. *Rec. Amer. Inst. Actuar.*, **31**, 398-405; **32**, 156-70.

Langer, H. 1942.   3346
Die Masszahlen in der Fremdenverkehrsstatistik.
Dtsch. Statist. Zbl., **34** (3-4), 45-52.

Laplume, J. 1948.   3347
Sur le nombre de signaux discernables en présence du
bruit erratique dans un système de transmission à
bande passante limitée. *C. R. Acad. Sci., Paris*, **226**,
1348-9.

Larsen, H. D. 1947.   3348
On the graphical approximations to the mode. *Math.
Mag.*, **21**, 35-9.

LaSalle, J. P. 1949.   3348a
Solutions of a class of continuous games. *RAND
Corp. Res. Memo.*, 19 Aug. 1949, RM-215, 11 pp.

Lasch, C. H. 1940.   3349
Krebskrankenstatistik. Beginn und Aussicht. *Zeit.
Krebsforsch.*, **50**, 245-98.

Latané, H. A. 1942.   3350
Seasonal factors determined by difference from
average of adjacent months. *J. Amer. Statist. Ass.*, **37**,
517-22.

Lathrop, F. H. & Plummer, B. E. 1942.   3351
A simplified method of sampling known areas of apple
leaves for chemical analysis. *J. Econ. Ent.*, **35**, 961.

Latimer, H. B. 1947.   3352
Correlations of organ weights with body weight,
body length and with other weights in the adult cat.
Growth, **11**, 61-75.

Lavergne, G.-H. 1944.   3352a
Numération des hématies; concordance et discordance
des résultats fournis par différents types d'hémati-
mètres. *Sang*, **16**, 204-10.

Lavin, M. 1946.   3353
Inspection efficiency and sampling inspection plans.
J. Amer. Statist. Ass., **41**, 432-8.

Lawley, D. N. 1940.   3354
The estimation of factor loadings by the method of
maximum likelihood. *Proc. Roy. Soc. Edin.*, **60**,
64-82.

Lawley, D. N. 1942.   3355
Further investigations in factor estimation. *Proc.
Roy. Soc. Edin. A*, **61**, 176-85.

Lawley, D. N. 1943.   3356
The application of the maximum likelihood method to
factor analysis. *Brit. J. Psychol.*, **33**, 172-5.

Lawley, D. N. 1943.   3357
A note on Karl Pearsons' selection formulae. *Proc.
Roy. Soc. Edin. A*, **62**, 28-30.

Lawley, D. N. 1943.   3358
On problems connected with item selection and test
construction. *Proc. Roy. Soc. Edin. A*, **61**, 273-87.

Lawley, D. N. 1944.   3359
The factorial analysis of multiple item tests. *Proc.
Roy. Soc. Edin. A*, **62**, 74-82.

Lawley, D. N. 1949.   3360
Problems in factor analysis. *Proc. Roy. Soc. Edin. A*,
62, 394-9 (correction: *A*, **63**, 93-4).

Lawrence, H. 1941.   3361
Graphic records for quality control in welding. *Steel*,
109 (22), 76-82.

Lawshe, C. H. 1942.   3362
A nomograph for estimating the validity of test items.
J. Appl. Psychol., **26**, 846-9.

Lazarfeld, P. F. 1942.   3363
The statistical analysis of reasons as research operation.
Sociometry, **5**, 29-47.

Lea, D. E. 1945.   3364
The biological assay of carcinogens. *Cancer Res.*, **5**,
633-40.

Lea, D. E. & Coulson, C. A. 1949.   3365
The distribution of the numbers of mutants in bacterial
populations. *J. Genet.*, **49**, 264-84.

Leavens, D. H. 1947.   3366
Accuracy in the Doolittle solution. *Econometrica*, **15**,
45-50.

Lebedeff, G. M. & Goode, H. P. 1946.   3367
P charts for quality control. *Fact. Mgmt.*, **104** (9),
129-36.

LeCam, L. 1947.   3368
Un instrument d'étude des fonctions aléatoires: la
fonctionelle caractéristique. *C. R. Acad. Sci., Paris*,
224, 710-11.

Leclerg, E. L. 1942.   3369
Relation of field plot design to seed-source tests of
Irish potatoes in the south. *Amer. Potato J.*, **19**,
75-9.

Leclerg, E. L. & Henderson, M. T. 1940.   3370
Relative efficiency of the two-dimensional quasifactorial
design as compared with a randomized-block arrangement when concerned with yields of Irish potatoes.
Amer. Potato J., **17**, 279-82.

Ledermann, W. 1940.   3371
On a problem concerning matrices with variable
diagonal elements. *Proc. Roy. Soc. Edin.*, **60**, 1-17.

Leggatt, C. W. 1941.   3372
A study of the relative efficiency of seed sampling
methods. *Canadian. J. Res. C*, **19**, 156-62.

Le Grand, Y. 1949.   3373
Sur l'emploi de la formule de Poisson dans les
statistiques du seuil absolu de vision. *C. R. Acad.
Sci., Paris*, **229**, 1089-91.

Legras, P. 1942.   3374
Über das asymptotische Verhalten der Erneuerungsfunktion. *Mitt. Ver. Schweitz. Versich.-Math.*, **42**,
183-204.

Le Heux, J. W. N. 1947.   3375
The growth-curve. *Proc. Kon. Ned. Akad. Wetensch.*,
50, 1201-13.

Lehmann, E. 1946.   3376
Une propriété optimale de certains ensembles critiques
du type *A*. *C. R. Acad. Sci., Paris*, **223**, 567-9.

Lehmann, E. L. 1947.   3377
On families of admissible tests. *Ann. Math. Statist.*,
18, 97-104.

Lehmann, E. L. 1947.   3378
On optimum tests of composite hypotheses with one
constraint. *Ann. Math. Statist.*, **18**, 473-93.

Lehmann, E. L. 1949.   3379
Some comments on large sample tests. *Proc. Berkeley
Symp. Math. Statist. and Probab.*, 1945-6, pp. 451-7.

Lehmann, E. L. & Scheffé, H. 1947.   3380
On the problem of similar regions. *Proc. Nat. Acad. Sci. U.S.A.*, **33**, 382-6.

Lehmann, E. L. & Stein, C. 1948.   3381
Most powerful tests of composite hypotheses. I. Normal distributions. *Ann. Math. Statist.*, **19**, 495-516.

Lehmann, E. L. & Stein, C. 1949.   3382
On the theory of some non-parametric hypotheses. *Ann. Math. Statist.*, **20**, 28-45.

Lehmer, E. 1942.   3382[a]
Solution of a mathematical problem connected with the theory of heredity. (Translation of **Bernstein, S. N.** (1924).) *Ann. Math. Statist.*, **13**, 53-61. (Also: *C.R. Acad. Sci., Paris*, **177**, 528-31, 581-4.)

Lehmer, E. 1944.   3383
Inverse tables of probabilities of errors of the second kind. *Ann. Math. Statist.*, **15**, 388-98.

Leipnik, R. B. 1947.   3384
Distribution of the serial correlation coefficient in a circularly correlated universe. *Ann. Math. Statist.*, **18**, 80-7.

Lembke, B. 1942.   3385
Statistische Modelle einer Schiefen. *Quote, Danzig*, **15**.

Lenzen, V. F. 1949.   3386
Statistical mechanics and its application to physics. *Proc. Berkeley Symp. Math. Statist. and Probab.* 1945-6, pp. 125-42

Leontief, W. 1947.   3387
Introduction to a theory of the internal structure of functional relationships. *Econometrica*, **15**, 361-73.

Leontief, W. 1949.   3388
Structural matrices of national economies. *Econometrica Suppl.*, **17**, 273-82.

Leopold, L. 1941.   3389
De standardafwijking van het eenvoudige monster. (Standard-deviation of simple sampling.) (Dutch.) *Tijdschr. Soc. Geneesk.*, **19**, 157-62.

Lerner, I. M. 1945.   3390
Nicking in relation to sexual maturity of S.C.W. Leghorns. *Amer. Nat.*, **79**, 152-9.

Lerner, I. M. & Taylor, L. W. 1944.   3391
Early recognition of superior families. *Poultry Sci.*, **23**, 413-17.

Le Roy, R. & Vaulot, É. 1945.   3392
Sur la proportion d'appels perdus dans certains systèmes de téléphonie automatique ne permettant dans un groupe d'organes qu'une seule exploration simultanée. *C. R. Acad. Sci., Paris*, **220**, 84-5.

Leser, G. E. V. 1942.   3393
Inequalities for Multivariate Frequency Distributions. *Biometrika*, **32**, 284-93.

Leslie, P. H. 1945.   3394
On the use of matrices in certain population mathematics. *Biometrika*, **33**, 183-212.

Leslie, P. H. 1948.   3395
On the distribution in time of the births in successive generations. *J. R. Statist. Soc. A*, **111**, 44-53.

Leslie, P. H. 1948.   3396
Some further notes on the use of matrices in population mathematics. *Biometrika*, **35**, 213-45.

Leslie, P. H., Perry, J. S. & Watson, J. S. 1945.   3397
The determination of the median bodyweight at which female rats reach maturity. *Proc. Zool. Soc. London*, **115**, 473-88.

Lesser, A., Jr. 1946.   3397[a]
The statistical approach in industrial research. *Iron Age*, **158**, 50-8.

Lester, A. M. 1949.   3398
The edge marking of statistical cards. *J. Amer. Statist. Ass.*, **44**, 293-4.

Letestu, S. 1948.   3399
Note on discriminating analysis. *Experientia*, **4**, 22-3.

Lettvin, J. Y. & Pitts, W. 1943.   3400
A mathematical theory of the affective psychoses. *Bull. Math. Biophys.*, **5**, 139-48.

Lev, J. 1949.   3401
The point biserial coefficient of correlation. *Ann. Math. Statist.*, **20**, 125-6.

Levenberg, K. 1944.   3402
A method for the solution of certain non-linear problems in least squares. *Quart. Appl. Math.*, **2**, 164-8.

Levene, H. & Dobzhansky, T. 1945.   3403
Experiments on sexual isolation in *Drosophila*. V. The effect of varying proportions of *D. pseudo-obscura* and *D. persimilis* on the frequency of isolation. *Proc. Nat. Acad. Sci. U.S.A.*, **31**, 274-81.

Levene, H. & Wolfowitz, J. 1944.   3404
The covariance matrix of runs up and down. *Ann. Math. Statist.*, **15**, 58-69.

Levene, H. & Wolfowitz, J. 1949.   3405
On a matching problem arising in genetics. *Ann. Math. Statist.*, **20**, 91-4.

Le Veque, W. J. 1949.   3406
On the size of certain number-theoretic functions. *Trans. Amer. Math. Soc.*, **66**, 440-63.

Leverett, H. M. 1947.   3406[a]
Notes on the use of the normal distribution in psychometrics. *J. Educ. Psychol.*, **38**, 283-9.

Leverett, H. M. 1947.   3407
Table of mean deviates for various portions of the unit normal distribution. *Psychometrika*, **12**, 141-52.

Levert, C. 1948.   3408
Een statistisch probleem in de klimatologie. (Dutch. English summary.) *Statistica Neerlandica*, **2**, 107-19.

Levert, C. & Scheen, W. L. 1943.   3409
Probability fluctuations of discharges in a Geiger-Müller counter produced by cosmic radiation. *Physica*, **10**, 225-38.

Levi, E. 1949.   3410
Acerca del empleo de la formula de mitscherlich en la interpretación de ciertos fenómenos de les arrollo vegetal. *Rev. Agr. Cochabamba*, **6** (5), 57-65.

Levi, F. 1946.   3411
Graphical solutions of statistical problems. *Engineer, London*, **182**, 338-40; 362-4.

Levi, F. W. 1940.   3412
Remarks on Mr. V. Narasimha Murthi's paper: On a problem of arrangements. I. *J. Indian Math. Soc.*, *N.S.*, **4**, 45-6.

Levin, M. L. & Goldstein, H. 1945.   3413
Significance of negative results in small samples. *Science*, **102**, 407.

Levinson, N. 1947.   3414
The Wiener RMS (root mean square) error criterion in filter design and prediction. *J. Math. Phys.*, **25**, 261-78.

Levinson, N. 1947.   3415
A heuristic exposition of Wiener's mathematical theory of prediction and filtering. *J. Math. Phys.*, **26**, 110-19.

Lévy, P. 1940.   3416
Le mouvement brownien plan. *Amer. J. Math.*, **62**, 487-550.

Lévy, P. 1941.   3417
Intégrales stochastiques. *C. R. Acad. Sci., Paris*, **212**, 1066-8.

Lévy, P. 1941.   3418
Intégrales stochastiques. *Ann. Univ. Lyon A*, (3) **4**, 67-74.

Lévy, P. 1942.   3419
Sur la détermination expérimentale de la loi des erreurs. *Enseign. Math.*, **38**, 227-31.

Lévy, P. 1944.   3420
Une propriété d'invariance projective dans le mouvement brownien. *C. R. Acad. Sci., Paris*, **219**, 378-9.

Lévy, P. 1944.   3421
Dérivation, intégration et équations différentielles stochastiques. *C. R. Acad. Sci., Paris*, **219**, 602-3.

Lévy, P. 1944.   3422
Un théorème d'invariance projective relatif au mouvement brownien. *Comment. Math. Helvetia*, **16**, 242-8.

Lévy, P. 1945.   3423
Sur le mouvement brownien dépendant de plusieurs paramètres. *C. R. Acad. Sci., Paris*, **220**, 420-2.

Lévy, P. 1946.   3424
Les processus fortement continus et la loi de Laplace. *C. R. Acad. Sci., Paris*, **222**, 839-41.

Lévy, P. 1947.   3425
Remarques sur un théorème de M. Émile Borel. *C. R. Acad. Sci., Paris*, **225**, 918-19.

Lévy, P. 1948.   3426
The arithmetical character of the Wishart distribution. *Proc. Camb. Phil. Soc.*, **44**, 295-7.

Lévy, P. 1948.   3427
Chaînes doubles de Markoff et fonctions aléatoires de deux variables. *C. R. Acad. Sci., Paris*, **226**, 53-5.

Lévy, P. 1948.   3428
Exemples de processus doubles de Markoff. *C. R. Acad. Sci., Paris*, **226**, 307-8.

Lévy, P. 1948.   3429
Étude d'une nouvelle classe de permutations. *C. R. Acad. Sci., Paris*, **227**, 578-9.

Lévy, P. 1949.   3430
Processus doubles de Markoff. *Le Calcul des Probabilités et ses Applications. Colloq. Int. Centre Nat. Rech. Sci., Paris*, **13**, 53-9.

Lévy, P. 1949.   3431
L'analyse harmonique des fonctions aléatoires stationnaires. *Analyse harmonique. Colloq. Int. Centre Nat. Rech. Sci., Paris*, **15**, 111-20.

Lévy, P. 1949.   3432
Arithmétique et calcul des probabilités. *Congr. Int. Phil. Sci., Paris*, **IV**. *Calcul des probabilités*, pp. 125-33.

Lévy, P. 1949.   3433
Exemples de processus pseudo-markoviens. *C. R. Acad. Sci., Paris*, **228**, 2004-6.

Lévy, P. 1949.   3434
Fonctions aléatoires laplaciennes. *C. R. Acad. Sci., Paris*, **229**, 1057-8.

Lévy, P. 1949.   3435
Les fondements du calcul des probabilités. *Dialectica*, **3**, 55-64.

Lévy, P. 1949.   3436
Les paradoxes de l'infini et le calcul des probabilités. *Bull. Sci. Math.*, **73** (2), 186-92.

Levy, S. 1940.   3437
A correlation method for the elimination of errors due to unstable excitation conditions in quantitative spectrum analysis. *J. Appl. Phys.*, **11**, 480-7.

Lewis, D. & Burke, C. J. 1949.   3438
The use and misuse of the chi-square test. *Psychol. Bull.*, **46**, 433-89.

Lewis, E. G. 1942.   3439
On the generation and growth of a population. *Sankhyā*, **6**, 93-6.

Lewis, H. 1941.   3440
On the distribution of the partial elasticity coefficient. *J. Amer. Statist. Ass.*, **36**, 413-16.

Lewis, N. W. 1948.   3441
Note on the exponential distribution in statistics. *J. Post Office Elect. Engrs.*, **41**, 10-12.

Lexen, B. 1941.   3442
The application of sampling to log scaling. *J. Forestry*, **39**, 624-31.

Lexen, B. 1947.   3443
The determination of net volume by sample-tree measuring. *J. Forestry*, **45**, 21-32.

L'Homme, J. 1947.   3444
Deux expressions statistiques de la réalité sociale, le total et la moyenne. *Rev. Écon. Pol., Paris*, **57** (1), 112-32.

Li, J. C. R. 1944.   3445
Design and statistical analysis of some confounded factorial experiments. *Iowa Agric. Exper. Sta. Res. Bull.*, **333**, 453-92.

Licklider, J. C. R. & Dzendolet, E. 1948.   3446
Oscillographic scatterplots illustrating various degrees of correlation. *Science*, **107**, 121-4.

Lidstone, G. J. 1941.   3447
Laplace's antecedent-probability function. *Math. Gaz.*, **25**, 162.

Lidstone, G. J. 1943.   3448
Notes on the Poisson frequency distribution. *J. Inst. Actuar.*, **71**, 284-91.

Lidwell, O. M. 1944.   3449
A particle size distribution function for air-borne ducts. *Nature*, **158**, 61-2.

Lienau, C. C. 1941. 3450
Discrete bivariate distribution in certain problems of statistical order. *Amer. J. Hyg.*, **33**, 65-85.

Lienau, C. C. 1947. 3451
Quantitative aspects of organization. *Hum. Biol.*, **19**, 163-216,

Lindblom, S. G. 1946. 3452
On the connection between tests of significance for correlation coefficients and for differences between means. *Skand. Aktuartidskr.*, **29**, 12-29.

Linder, A. 1943. 3453
Statistische Methoden in der Industrie. *Industrielle Organization*, **12** (1), 1-4.

Linder, A. 1946. 3454
Sur la manière d'organiser les expériences afin d'obtenir un rendement maximum. *Arch. Sci. Phys. Nat. Geneva*, (5) **28**, 181-91.

Lindley, D. V. 1946. 3455
Distribution of the variance and variance-ratio in samples from a grouped Gaussian population. *U.K. Min. Supply Advisory Service Statist. Method. & Qual. Contr.* no. ASSM. TH-33, 8 April 1946, 20 pp.

Lindley, D. V. 1946. 3455[a]
Linear " curves of best fit " and regression lines. *Nature*, **158**, 272-3.

Lindley, D. V. 1946. 3456
On the solution of some equations in least squares. *Biometrika*, **33**, 326-7.

Lindley, D. V. 1947. 3457
Regression lines and the linear functional relationship. *J. R. Statist. Soc. Suppl.*, **9**, 218-44.

Lindman, E. L. 1940. 3458
The adequacy of follow-up samplings. *Occupations*, **19**, 33-5.

Lindquist, E. F. 1940. 3459
Sampling in educational research. *J. Educ. Psychol.*, **31**, 561-74.

Lindquist, E. F. 1947. 3460
Goodness of fit of trend curves and significance of trend differences. *Psychometrika*, **12**, 65-78.

Linés Escardó, E. 1941. 3461
Un teorema sobre la frecuencia de los puntos de una red que estan sobre una franja interior a otra, ambas de amplitud conocida. *Rev. Mat. Hisp.-Amer.*, (4) **1**, 75-81.

Linés Escardó, E. 1941-4. 3462
El problema de las coincidencias. II. Los problemas de coincidencias. *Rev. Mat. Hisp.-Amer.*, (4) **1**, 292-314; **4**, 188-205.

Linés Escardó, E. 1945. 3463
El método de la función arbitraria del Cálculo de Probabilidades. *Rev. Mat. Hisp.-Amer.*, (4) **5**, 3-26; 63-72.

Linnik, Yu. V. 1947. 3464
On the accuracy of the approximation to the Gaussian distribution by sums of independent random variables. *C. R. (Dokl.) Acad. Sci. URSS*, **55**, 571-3.

Linnik, Yu. V. 1947. 3465
On the accuracy of the approximation to the Gauss distribution by sums of independent variables.

(Russian. English summary.) *Izv. Akad. Nauk SSSR, Ser. Mat.*, **11**, 111-38.

Linnik, Yu. V. 1948. 3466
On non-stationary Markov chains. (Russian.) *Dokl. Akad. Nauk SSSR*, **60**, 21-4.

Linnik, Yu. V. 1949. 3467
On the theory of non-uniform Markov chains. (Russian.) *Izv. Akad. Nauk SSSR, Ser. Mat.*, **13**, 65-94.

Linnik, Yu. V. & Sapogov, N. A. 1949. 3468
Multiple integrals and local laws for inhomogeneous Markov chains. (Russian.) *Izv. Akad. Nauk SSSR, Ser. Mat.*, **13**, 533-66.

Lins Martins, O. A. 1946. 3469
Sôbre o coeficiente de correlação bisserial; estudo experimental de distribução de seus valores obtidos em pequenas amostras. (Portuguese.) *Rev. Brasil. Estatíst.*, **7**, 713-62.

Lins Martins, O. A. 1946. 3469[a]
Note on a comment on the " correction " of reliability co-efficients for restriction of range. *J. Educ. Psychol.*, **37**, 182-3.

Lins Martins, O. A. 1947. 3469[b]
O método factorial de investigação das faculdades mentais; análise de resultados experimentais obtidos em Sao Paulo em 1944. (Portuguese.) *Rev. Brasil. Estatíst.*, **8**, 303-38.

Lisman, J. H. C. 1946-7. 3470
Verklaring van het verloop van een verschijnsel uit den toestand op één oofenblik, toegepast op het giroverkeer. *Statistica, Rijswijk*, **1**, 55-63.

Lisman, J. H. C. 1948. 3471
Enige frequentieverschijnselen in het gelverkeer. *De Economist*, **96**, 293-7.

Lisman, J. H. C. 1948. 3472
Enkele frequentieverdelingen in de muziek. (Some frequency distributions in music.) (Dutch. English summary.) *Statistica Neerlandica*, **2**, 120-3.

Lison, L. 1940. 3473
Analyse quantitative des facteurs de la morphogénèse des formes spirales logarithmiques biologiques. *Bull. Acad. R. Belg. Cl. Sci.*, (5) **26**, 64-82.

Lissdaniels, O. M. 1947. 3474
The size and spacing of sample plots in strip surveys. *Svenska Skogsforen, Tidskr.*, **45**, 217-45.

Litchfield, J. T., Jr. 1949. 3475
A method for rapid graphic solution of time percent effect curves. *J. Pharmacol.*, **97**, 399-408.

Litchfield, J. T., Jr. & Fertig, J. W. 1941. 3476
On a graphic solution of the dosage effect curve. *Bull. Johns Hopkins Hosp.*, **69**, 276-86.

Litchfield, J. T., Jr. & Wilcoxon, F. 1949. 3477
A simplified method of evaluating dose-effect experiments. *J. Pharmacol. Exptl. Therap.*, **96** (2), 99-113.

Little, K. L. 1943. 3478
A study of a series of human skulls from Castle Hill, Scarborough. *Biometrika*, **33**, 25-35.

Littlewood, J. E. & Offord, A. C. 1943. 3479
On the number of real roots of a random algebraic equation. III. (English. Russian summary.) *Mat. Sbornik*, **12** (54), 277-86.

Liu, N.-M. 1947. 3480
Calcul de la différence moyenne. *Proc. 25th. Session Int. Statist. Inst. Conf., Washington, D.C.*, 1947 (Publ. 1951), **3B**, 781-93.

Liu, Y. C. 1948. 3481
On the study of approximate numbers. (Chinese. English summary.) *Fukien Agr. J.*, **10**, 69-74.

Livada, G. 1942. 3482
Su alcune ordinate caratteristiche della curva di concentrazione. *Atti 3za Riun. Sci., Soc. Ital. Statist.*, pp. 25-34.

Livada, G. 1942. 3483
Un procedimento grafico per il calcolo dello scostamento medio. *Atti 3za Riun. Sci., Soc. Ital. Statist.*, pp. 35-9.

Livada, G. 1943. 3484
Sulle curve logistiche. *Atti 5ta Riun. Sci., Soc. Ital. Statist.*, pp. 202-14.

Livada, G. 1945. 3485
Procedimento per il calcolo della intensità di transvarizione. *Atti 6ta Riun. Sci., Soc. Ital. Statist.*, pp. 63-73.

Livermore, J. R. 1940. 3486
Report of the committee on standardization of field plot technique. *Amer. Potato J.*, **17**, 114-23.

Livi, L. 1949. 3486[a]
Considérations théoriques et pratiques sur le concept de " minimum de population ". *Population*, **4**, 754-6.

Ljunggren, W. 1947. 3486[b]
An elementary proof of a formula of A. C. Dixon. (Norwegian.) *Norsk. Mat. Tidsskr.*, **29**, 35-8.

Loève, M. 1940. 3487
Nouvelles classes de lois limites. *C. R. Acad. Sci., Paris*, **210**, 202-4.

Loève, M. 1941. 3488
Sur les systèmes d'événements; application à deux théorèmes classiques. *C. R. Acad. Sci., Paris*, **212**, 261-3.

Loève, M. 1941. 3489
La loi des grands nombres pour des variables aléatoires liées et des événements liés. *C. R. Acad. Sci., Paris*, **212**, 840-3.

Loève, M. 1941. 3490
La loi forte des grands nombres pour des variables aléatoires liées. *C. R. Acad. Sci., Paris*, **212**, 1121-3.

Loève, M. 1941. 3491
La tendance centrale des sommes de variables aléatoires liées. *C. R. Acad. Sci., Paris*, **213**, 9-11.

Loève, M. 1942. 3492
Systèmes d'événements en nombre fini. *Ann. Univ. Lyon A*, (3) **5**, 55-74.

Loève, M. 1945. 3493
Sur la covariance d'une fonction aléatoire. *C. R. Acad. Sci., Paris*, **220**, 295-6.

Loève, M. 1945. 3494
Analyse harmonique générale d'une fonction aléatoire. *C. R. Acad. Sci., Paris*, **220**, 380-2.

Loève, M. 1945. 3495
Nouvelles classes de lois limites. *Bull. Soc. Math. France*, **73**, 107-26.

Loève, M. 1945. 3496
Sur les fonctions aléatoires stationnaires de second ordre. *Rev. Sci., Paris*, **83**, 297-303.

Loève, M. 1946. 3497
I. Étude asymptotique des sommes de variables aléatoires liées. II. Espaces compacts et localement compact. Thesis, Faculty of Sci., Univ. of Paris. (Part I also published (1945): *J. Math. Pures Appl.*, **24**, 249-318.)

Loève, M. 1946. 3498
Fonctions aléatoires à décomposition orthogonale exponentielle. *Rev. Sci., Paris*, **84**, 159-62.

Loève, M. 1946. 3499
Fonctions aléatoires de second ordre. *Rev. Sci., Paris*, **84**, 195-206.

Loève, M. 1946. 3500
Quelques propriétés des fonctions aléatoires de second ordre. *C. R. Acad. Sci., Paris*, **222**, 469-70.

Loève, M. 1946. 3501
Remarques sur les ensembles de lois. *C. R. Acad. Sci., Paris*, **222**, 628-30.

Loève, M. 1946. 3502
Sur les fonctions aléatoires vectorielles de second ordre. *C. R. Acad. Sci., Paris*, **222**, 942-4.

Loève, M. 1948. 3503
Sur l'équivalence asymptotique des lois. *C. R. Acad. Sci., Paris*, **227**, 1335-7.

Loève, M. 1949. 3504
On the "central" probability problem. *Proc. Nat. Acad. Sci. U.S.A.*, **35**, 328-32.

Loève, M. 1949. 3505
Indicateurs abstraits et champs stochastiques. *C. R. Acad. Sci. Paris*, **228**, 1561-4.

Loevinger, J. 1947. 3506
A systematic approach to the construction and evaluation of tests of ability. *Psychol. Monogr.*, **61** (285), 49 pp.

Loevinger, J. 1948. 3507
The technic of homogeneous tests compared with some aspects of " scale analysis " and factor analysis. *Psychol. Bull.*, **45**, 507-29.

Loewe, S. 1947. 3508
Bio-assay by direct potency estimation. *Science*, **106**, 89-91.

Lombard, H. L. & Doering, C. R. 1947. 3509
Treatment of the fourfold table by partial correlation as it relates to public health problems. *Biometrics*, **3**, 123-8.

Long, W. F. & Burr, I. W. 1949. 3510
Development of a method for increasing the utility of multiple correlations by considering both testing time and test validity. *Psychometrika*, **14**, 137-61.

Lonseth, A. T. 1942. 3511
Systems of linear equations with coefficients subject to error. *Ann. Math. Statist.*, **13**, 332-7.

Lonseth, A. T. 1944. 3512
On relative errors in systems of linear equations. *Ann. Math. Statist.*, **15**, 323-5.

Lonseth, A. T. 1947. 3513
The propagation of errors in linear problems. *Trans. Amer. Math. Soc.*, **62**, 193-212.

Lonseth, A. T. 1949. 3514
An extension of an algorithm of Hotelling. *Proc. Berkeley Symp. Math. Statist. and Probab.*, 1945-6, pp. 353-8.

Loomis, C. P. & Pepinsky, H. B. 1948. 3515
Sociometry 1937-47: theory and methods. *Sociometry*, **11**, 262-86.

Loomis, L. H. 1946. 3516
On a theorem of von Neumann. *Proc. Nat. Acad. Sci. U.S.A.*, **32**, 213-15.

Loomis, R. D. 1946. 3517
Accuracy in timber estimating. *For. Chron.*, **22**, 201-2.

Lord, E. 1947. 3518
The use of range in place of standard deviation in the *t* test. *Biometrika*, **34**, 41-67 (correction: **39**, 442).

Lord, F. M. 1944. 3519
Alignment chart for calculating the fourfold point correlation coefficient. *Psychometrika*, **9**, 41-2.

Lord, F. M. 1944. 3520
Reliability of multiple-choice tests as a function of number of choices per item. *J. Educ. Psychol.*, **35**, 175-80.

Lord, R. D. 1948. 3521
A problem on random vectors. *Phil. Mag.*, (7) **39**, 66-71.

Lorenz, P. 1940. 3522
Darstellung statistischer Übersichten mit zwei Eingängen durch orthogonale ganze rationale Funktionen (Flächendarstellung). *Arch. math. Wirtsch.*, **6**, 57-70.

Lorenz, P. 1949. 3523
Herleitung der Näherungsformel von Laplace für die Binomialverteilung, ohne Grenzübergang. *Zeit. angew. Math. Mech.*, **29**, 368-74.

Lorenz, P. 1949. 3524
Über Wahrscheinlichkeitsnetze und Wahrscheinlichkeitstafeln. *Mitt. Math. Statist.*, **1**, 21-36.

Lorge, I. 1940. 3525
The computation of Hotelling canonical correlations. *Proc. Educ. Res. Forum, I.B.M. Corp. New York*, 1940, pp. 68-74.

Lorge, I. 1940. 3526
Two-group comparisons by multivariate analysis. *Amer. Educ. Res. Ass.*, **1940**, 1-4.

Lorge, I. 1945. 3527
Computational technics. *Rev. Educ. Res.*, **15**, 441-6.

Lorr, M. 1944. 3528
Interrelationships of number-correct and limen scores for an amount-limit test. *Psychometrika*, **9**, 17-30.

Lotka, A. J. 1940. 3529
Sur une équation intégrale de l'analyse démographique et industrielle. *Mitt. Ver. Schweiz. Versich.-Math.*, **40**, 1-16.

Lotka, A. J. 1940. 3529a
The place of the intrinsic rate of natural increase in population analysis. *Proc. 8th. Amer. Sci. Congr.*, **8**, 297-313.

Lotka, A. J. 1940. 3530
The theory of industrial replacement. A commentary. *Skand. Aktuartidskr.*, **23**, 1-14.

Lotka, A. J. 1942. 3531
The progeny of an entire population. *Ann. Math. Statist.*, **13**, 115-26.

Lotka, A. J. 1943. 3532
Some reflections—statistical and other—on a non-material universe. *J. Amer. Statist. Ass.*, **38**, 1-15.

Lotka, A. J. 1945. 3533
Population analysis as a chapter in the mathematical theory of evolution. *Essays on Growth and Form, presented to D'Arcy Wentworth Thompson*, pp. 355-85.

Lotka, A. J. 1947. 3534
Evaluation of some methods of measuring net fertility with special regard to recent developments. *Proc. 25th. Session Int. Statist. Inst. Conf. Washington, D.C.*, 1947 (Publ. 1951), **3B**, 715-32.

Lotka, A. J. 1948. 3535
Application of recurrent series in renewal theory. *Ann. Math. Statist.*, **19**, 190-206.

Lott, E. 1945. 3536
Quality control. *Engng. Insp.*, **10** (1), 36-9.

Love, A. & Love, D. 1943. 3537
The significance of differences in the distribution of diploids and polyploids. *Hereditas, Lund.*, **29**, 145-61.

Lovera, G. 1942. 3538
Un'applicazione del coefficiente de correlazione alle medie statistiche. *Atti Accad. Sci. Torino, Sci. Fis. Mat. Nat.*, **77**, 341-6.

Lovera, G. 1945. 3539
Metodo abbreviato di calcolo delle caratteristiche di una correlazione multipla. *Atti Accad. Sci. Torino, Sci. Fis. Mat. Nat.*, **80**, 194-8.

Lovera, G. 1946. 3540
Sulle coincidenze triple accidentali. *Accad. Lincei. R. C. Sci. Fis. Mat. Nat.*, (8) **1**, 964-9.

Lovera, G. 1947. 3541
Sullo scarto quadratico medio nei conteggi con i contatori. *Ric. Sci.*, **17**, 223-8.

Lovera, G. 1947. 3542
Questioni statistiche sulla distribuzione temporale degli eventi casuali. *Ric. Sci.*, **17**, 2042-4.

Lublin, M. 1943. 3543
Das Gesetz der Gleichaltrigkeit und die Formel von Makeham. (Danish.) *Festskr. Prof. J. F. Steffensen*, pp. 100-08.

Luce, R. D. & Perry, A. D. 1949. 3544
A method of matrix analysis of group structure. *Psychometrika*, **14**, 95-116.

Lüders, R. 1947. 3545
Eine Verallgemeinerung der Formel von Pollaczek-Geiringer und ihre Anwendung auf die Verteilungsfunktion der Hagelschäden. *Zeit. angew. Math. Mech.*, **25/27**, 21-8.

Ludwig, W. 1942. 3546
Notiz zu der unternormalen Streuung in den Moewusschen Chlamydomonas-Versuchen. *Zeit. Indukt. Abstamm. VererbLehre*, **80**, 612-15.

Lukacs, E. 1941. 3547
Wahrscheinlichkeitstheoretischer Aufbau der Theorie des mittleren Risikos. (French, Italian and English summaries.) *Trans. 12th. Int. Congr. Actuar., Lucerne,* 1940, **1**, 171-205.

Lukacs, E. 1942. 3548
A characterization of the normal distribution. *Ann. Math. Statist.*, **13**, 91-3.

Lukacs, E. 1948. 3549
On the mathematical theory of risk. *J. Inst. Actuar. Students' Soc.*, **8**, 20-37.

Lundberg, G. A. 1940. 3550
Some problems of group classification and measurement. *Amer. Sociol. Rev.*, **5**, 351-60.

Lundberg, O. 1940. 3551
On random processes and their application to sickness and accident statistics. *Univ. of Stockholm thesis,* viii+172 pp. (Almqvist and Wiksells).

Lundberg, O. 1941. 3552
On the importance of regarding risk premiums in voluntary sickness and accident insurance. A theoretical basis for regrading. (German, French and Italian summaries.) *Trans. 12th Congr. Actuar., Lucerne,* 1940, **2**, 543-60.

Lunt, T. J. 1944. 3552[a]
Estimation of batch quality. *Aircraft Engng.*, **16**, 305.

Lure, A. L. 1945. 3553
La loi directe, inverse et absolue des grands nombres. *C. R. (Dokl.) Acad. Sci. URSS,* **49**, 546-9.

Lure, A. L. 1945. 3554
On an inverse Bernoulli theorem. *C. R. (Dokl.) Acad. Sci. URSS,* **50**, 45-8.

Luria, S. 1940. 3555
Méthodes statistiques appliquées à l'étude des ultravirus. *Ann. Inst. Pasteur*, **64**, 415-38.

Luria, S. E. & Delbrück, M. 1943. 3556
Mutations of bacteria from virus sensitivity to virus resistance. *Genetics,* **28**, 491-511.

Lush, J. L. 1940. 3557
Intra-sire correlations or regression of offspring on dam as a method of estimating heritability of characteristics. *Proc. 33rd Ann. Meeting Amer. Soc. Anim. Prod.*, pp. 459-76.

Lush, J. L. 1944. 3558
The optimum emphasis on dams' record when proving dairy sires. *J. Dairy Sci.*, **27**, 937-51.

Lush, J. L. 1947. 3559
Family merit and individual merit as bases for selection. *Amer. Nat.*, **81**, 241-61; 362-79.

Luxenburger, H. 1940. 3560
Die Bedeutung des Masses der Stichprobenauslese für die Berechnung der Manifestationswahrscheinlichkeit erblicher Merkmale. (Zur Methodik der Zwillingsforschung.) *Zeit. KonstLehre,* **24**, 309-12.

Luykx, H. M. C. 1944-5. 3561
Biostatistics in medical research. I. Significant differences. II. Probabilities in small samples. III. Samples which are 100 per cent positive. *Nav. Med. Bull. Wash.*, **43**, 1208-15; **44**, 125-33; 370-4.

Luykx, H. M. C. 1949. 3561[a]
Teaching statistical methods in medicine. *J. Ass. Amer. Med. Coll.*, **24**, 208-13.

Luzzato-Fegiz, P. 1942. 3562
Sondaggi statistici dell' opinione pubblica. *Statistica, Ferrara,* **2**, 25-40.

Lynch, D. W. & Schumacher, F. X. 1941. 3563
Concerning the dispersion of natural regeneration, *J. Forestry,* **39**, 49-51.

Lynch, P. B. 1940. 3564
Sampling methods for the estimation of grain yields in cereal trials. *New Zealand J. Sci. Tech.*, **22**, 151a-7a.

Lyons, W. J. 1946. 3565
An approximate function for testing the significance of differences according to the " Student "-Fisher *t*-test. *Textile Res. J.*, **16**, 438-40.

M

Ma, R. H. & Harrington, J. B. 1948. 3565[a]
Standard errors of different designs of field experiments at the University of Saskatchewan. *Scient. Agric.*, **28**, 461-74.

Ma, R. H. & Harrington, J. B. 1949. 3565[b]
A study on field experiments of semi-Latin square design. *Scient. Agric.*, **29**, 241-51.

Ma, R. H. & Kao, L. H. 1940. 3566
A factorial experiment on rice culture. *Empire J. Exper. Agric.*, **8**, 23-33.

Maccaferri, E. 1947. 3567
Un'osservazione sullo scarto medio di una variablile casuale. *Statistica, Milano,* **7**, 96-9.

McCallan, S. E. A. & Wellman, R. H. 1943. 3568
Cumulative error terms for comparing fungicides by established laboratory and greenhouse methods. *Contr. Boyce Thompson Inst.*, **13**, 135-41.

McCallan, S. E. A., Wellman, R. H. & Wilcoxon, F. 1941. 3569
An anlaysis of factors causing variations in spore germination tests of fungicides. III. Slope of toxicity curves, replicate tests and fungi. *Contr. Boyce Thompson Inst.*, **12**, 49-78.

McCandliss, D. A. 1941. 3570
Objective sampling in estimating southern crops. *J. Farm Econ.*, **23**, 246-55.

McCarroll, R. H. & McCloud, J. L. 1944. 3570[a]
Quality control of engineering materials during manufacturing and processing. *J. Soc. Automotive Engrs.*, **52**, 337-47.

McCarthy, P. J. 1947. 3571
Approximate solutions for means and variances in a certain class of box problems. *Ann. Math. Statist.*, **18**, 349-83.

McCarthy, P. J., Toner, R. K. & Whitwell, J. C. 1946. 3571[a]
Statistical methods for equilibrium moisture correlation. *Textile Res. J.*, **16**, 307-17.

McCloy, C. H. 1941. 3572
The factor analysis as a research technique. *Res. Quart. Amer. Ass. Health Phys. Educ.*, **12**, 22-33.

MacColl, H. G. 1944. 3573
The statistical control of accuracy in routine analysis. *Chem. & Industry*, **49**, 418-21.

McCormick, T. C. 1943. 3574
An approach to the measurement of farm population pressure in Wisconsin. *J. Amer. Statist. Ass.*, **38**, 165-77.

McCormick, T. C. 1945. 3575
Note on the validity of mathematical probability in sociological research. *Amer. Sociol. Rev.*, **10**, 626-31.

McCormick, T. C. 1946. 3576
A note on the correlation of attributes. *Social Forces*, **25**, 166-7.

McCrea, W. H. & Whipple, F. J. W. 1940. 3577
Random paths in two and three dimensions. *Proc. Roy. Soc. Edin.*, **60**, 281-98.

McCulloch, W. S. 1945. 3578
A heterarchy of values determined by the topology of nervous nets. *Bull. Math. Biophys.*, **7**, 89-93.

McCulloch, W. S. & Pitts, W. 1948. 3579
The statistical organization of nervous activity. *Biometrics*, **4**, 91-9.

MacDonald, D. K. C. 1949. 3580
Spontaneous fluctuations. *Rep. Progress Phys.*, **12**, 56-81.

MacDonald, D. K. C. 1949. 3581
Some statistical properties of random noise. *Proc. Camb. Phil. Soc.*, **45**, 368-72.

Maceda, E. C. *See* **Cansado Maceda, E.**

McEwen, G. F. 1949. 3582
The reality of regularities indicated in sequences of observations. *Proc. Berkeley Symp. Math. Statist. and Probab.*, 1945-6, pp. 229-38.

MacFarlane, G. G. 1947. 3583
A theory of flicker noise in valves and impurity semi-conductors. *Proc. Phys. Soc.*, **59**, 366-75.

Mack, C. 1948. 3584
An exact formula for $Q_k(n)$, the probable number of k-aggregates in a random distribution of n points. *Phil. Mag.*, (7) **39**, 778-90.

Mack, C. 1949. 3584a
The expected number of aggregates in a random distribution of points. *Proc. Camb. Phil. Soc.*, **46**, 285-92.

McKendrick, A. G. 1940. 3584b
The dynamics of crowd infection. *Edin. Med. J.*, **47**, 117-36.

McKittrick, D. S. 1947. 3585
The selection of chicks for growth experiments and the evaluation of growth. *Growth*, **11**, 89-99.

Maclaury, D. 1942. 3586
A " slide-rule " for determining time intervals. *Poultry Sci.*, **21**, 462-3.

McLean, G. O. 1944. 3586a
Consumer sampling: applying statistical theory to domestic supplies. *Elect. Rev.*, **134**, 589-92.

McMillan, B. 1941. 3587
On two problems of sampling. *Ann. Math.*, (2) **42**, 437-45.

McMillan, B. 1949. 3588
Spread of minima in large samples. *Ann. Math. Statist.*, **20**, 444-7.

McNemar, Q. 1940. 3589
Sampling in psychological research. *Psychol. Bull.*, **37**, 331-65.

McNemar, Q. 1941. 3590
On the sampling errors of factor loadings. *Psychometrika*, **6**, 141-52.

McNemar, Q. 1942. 3591
On the number of factors. *Psychometrika*, **7**, 9-18.

McNemar, Q. 1942. 3592
In reply to Garrett. *Amer. J. Psychol.*, **55**, 581-2.

McNemar, Q. 1945. 3593
The mode of operation of suppressant variables. *Amer. J. Psychol.*, **58**, 554-5.

McNemar, Q. 1947. 3594
Note on the sampling error of the difference between correlated proportions or percentages. *Psychometrika*, **12**, 153-7.

McNish, A. G. & Lincoln, J. V. 1949. 3595
Prediction of sunspot numbers. *Trans. Amer. Geophys. Un.*, **30**, 673-85.

McPherson, J. C. 1941. 3596
On mechanical tabulation of polynomials. *Ann. Math. Statist.*, **12**, 317-27.

McPherson, J. C. 1942. 3597
Mathematical operations with punched cards. *J. Amer. Statist. Ass.*, **37**, 275-81.

McQuitty, J. V. 1946. 3598
Maximum use of mechanical aid in handling test results. *Proc. Res. Forum, IBM Corp. New York*, 26-30 August 1946, pp. 52-5.

MacStewart, W. 1941. 3599
A note on the power of the sign test. *Ann. Math. Statist.*, **12**, 236-9.

McVay, F. E. 1947. 3600
Sampling methods applied to estimating numbers of commercial orchards in a commercial peach area. *J. Amer. Statist. Ass.*, **42**, 533-40.

Madeira, J. L. 1947. 3601
A logística e o cálculo das suas constantes características. *Bol. Inst. Brasil. Atuár.*, **3**, 7-87.

Madhava, K. B. 1940. 3601a
Technique of random sampling. *Sankhyā*, **4**, 532-4. (Also: *Proc. 2nd. Indian Statist. Conf.*)

Madow, L. H. 1946. 3602
Systematic sampling and its relation to other sampling designs. *J. Amer. Statist. Ass.*, **41**, 204-17.

Madow, W. G. 1940. 3603
The distribution of quadratic forms in non-central normal random variables. *Ann. Math. Statist.*, **11**, 100-03.

Madow, W. G. 1940. 3604
Limiting distributions of quadratic and bilinear forms. *Ann. Math. Statist.*, **11**, 125-46.

Madow, W. G. 1940.   3605
Note on tests of departure from normality. *J. Amer. Statist. Ass.*, **35**, 515-17.

Madow, W. G. 1945.   3606
Note on the distribution of the serial correlation coefficient. *Ann. Math. Statist.*, **16**, 308-10.

Madow, W. G. 1946.   3607
Por que usamos amostras. (Why we use samples.) (Portuguese.) *Rev. Brasil. Estatíst.*, **7**, 489-502.

Madow, W. G. 1948.   3608
On a source of downward bias in the analysis of variance and covariance. *Ann. Math. Statist.*, **19**, 351-9.

Madow, W. G. 1948.   3609
On the limiting distributions of estimates based on samples from finite universes. *Ann. Math. Statist.*, **19**, 535-45.

Madow, W. G. 1949.   3610
On the theory of systematic sampling. II. *Ann. Math. Statist.*, **20**, 333-54.

Madow, W. G. & Madow, L. H. 1944.   3611
On the theory of systematic sampling. I. *Ann. Math. Statist.*, **15**, 1-24.

Mahalanobis, P. C. 1940.   3612
Anthropological observations on the Anglo-Indians of Calcutta. III. Statistical analysis of measurements of seven characters. *Rec. Indian Museum*, **23**, 151-87.

Mahalanobis, P. C. 1940.   3613
Errors of observation in physical measurements. *Science & Culture*, **5**, 443.

Mahalanobis, P. C. 1940.   3614
Report on the sample census of the area under jute in Bengal in 1940 (submitted to the Indian Central Jute Committee). *Proc. 2nd. Indian Statist. Conf.*

Mahalanobis, P. C. 1940.   3615
A review of the application of statistical theory to agricultural field experiments in India. *Indian J. Agric. Sci.*, **10**, 192-212.

Mahalanobis, P. C. 1940.   3616
A sample survey of the acreage under jute in Bengal. *Sankhyā*, **4**, 511-31. (Also: *Proc. 2nd. Indian Statist. Conf.*)

Mahalanobis, P. C. 1941.   3617
A note on random fields. *Science & Culture*, **7**, 54.

Mahalanobis, P. C. 1941.   3618
A statistical report on the rupee census. Mathematical appendix. *Rep. Currency & Finance* 1940-1, *Reserve Bank of India*, p. 54.

Mahalanobis, P. C. 1941.   3619
Statistical survey of "Public Opinion". *Modern Review*, **1941**, 393-7.

Mahalanobis, P. C. 1942.   3620
Mathematics and statistics. Sample surveys. *Science & Culture*, Suppl., **7**, 1-2.

Mahalanobis, P. C. 1942.   3621
Sample surveys. *Proc. 29th. Indian Sci. Congr.*, II, 25-46.

Mahalanobis, P. C. 1942.   3622
Statistical definition of Standard Yield Crops. *Sankhyā*, **6**, 97-8.

Mahalanobis, P. C. 1944.   3623
On large-scale sample surveys. *Phil. Trans. B*, **231**, 329-451.

Mahalanobis, P. C. 1946.   3624
Recent experiments in statistical sampling in the Indian Statistical Institute. *J. R. Statist. Soc.*, **109**, 326-78.

Mahalanobis, P. C. 1946.   3625
Sample surveys of crop yield in India. *Sankhyā*, **7**, 269-80.

Mahalanobis, P. C. 1946.   3626
Use of small-size plots in sample surveys for crop yields. *Nature*, **158**, 798-9.

Mahalanobis, P. C. 1948.   3627
Walter A. Shewhart and statistical quality control in India. *Sankhyā*, **9**, 51-60.

Mahalanobis, P. C. 1949.   3628
Anthropometric survey of the United Provinces, 1941: A statistical study. III. Anthropological observations. *Sankhyā*, **9**, 181-236.

Mahalanobis, P. C. 1949.   3629
Anthropometric survey of the United Provinces, 1941: A statistical study. Appendix 1. Historical note on the D^2 statistic. *Sankhyā*, **9**, 237-40.

Mahalanobis, P. C. 1949.   3630
Statistical tools in resource appraisal and utilization. *Proc. U.N. Sci. Conf. Conservation and Utilization of Resources*, **1**, 196-200.

Mahalanobis, P. C. & Bose, C. 1941.   3631
Correlation between anthropometric characters in some Bengal castes and tribes. *Sankhyā*, **5**, 249-60.

Mahalanobis, P. C. & Ghosh, B. N. 1943.   3632
Statistical analysis of data relating to incidence of pests and diseases on different varieties of sugarcane. *Proc. Indian Statist. Conf.*

Mahalanobis, P. C. & Nair, K. R. 1941.   3633
Statistical analysis of experiments on differential limen values for lifted weights. *Sankhyā*, **5**, 285-94.

Mahalanobis, P. C. & Rao, C. R. 1949.   3634
Anthropometric survey of the United Provinces, 1941: A statistical study. II. Statistical analysis. *Sankhyā*, **9**, 111-80.

Mahalanobis, P. C. & Rao, C. R. 1949.   3635
Anthropometric survey of the United Provinces, 1941: A statistical study. Appendix 2. A note on the use of indices. *Sankhyā*, **9**, 240-6.

Mahalanobis, P. C., Mukherjea, R. K.   3636
& Ghosh, A. 1946.
A sample survey of after-effects of the Bengal famine of 1943. *Sankhyā*, **7**, 337-40.

Maier-Leibnitz, M. 1942.   3637
Die Koinzidenzmethode und ihre Anwendung auf Kernphysicalische probleme. *Phys. Zeit.*, **43**, 333-62.

Mainguy, Y. & Guilbaud, G.-Th. 1947.   3638
Les différents comportements du consommateur et leur détermination statistique. *Inst. Sci. Écon. Appl. Cahiers. (B) annexes*, **4**, 1-63.

Mainland, D. 1948.   3639
Statistical methods in medical research. *Canadian J. Res. E*, **26**, 1-166.

Majorana, E. 1942. 3640
Il valore delle leggi statistiche nella fisica e nelle scienze sociali. *Scientia*, **71** (2-3), 58-66.

Makski, U. K. 1949. 3641
A note on interpenetrating samples. *J. Indian Soc. Agric. Statist.*, **2**, 189-95.

Malécot, G. 1940. 3642
Le calcul des probabilités et les problèmes de l'hérédité. *Ann. Univ. Lyon A*, (3) **2**, 25-37.

Malécot, G. 1941. 3643
Étude mathématique des populations " mendéliennes ". I. Consanguinité pure. *Ann. Univ. Lyon A*, (3) **4**, 45-60.

Malécot, G. 1942. 3644
Mendélisme et consanguinité. *C. R. Acad. Sci., Paris*, **215**, 313-14.

Malécot, G. 1944. 3645
Sur un problème de probabilités en chaîne que pose la génétique. *C. R. Acad. Sci., Paris*, **219**, 379-81.

Malécot, G. 1945. 3646
La diffusion des gènes dans une population mendélienne. *C. R. Acad. Sci., Paris*, **221**, 340-2.

Malécot, G. 1946. 3647
La consanguinité dans une population limitée. *C. R. Acad. Sci., Paris*, **222**, 841-3.

Malécot, G. 1947. 3648
Les critères statistique et la subjectivité de la connaissance scientifique. *Ann. Univ. Lyon A*, (3) **10**, 43-74.

Malécot, G. 1948. 3649
Le regroupement des classes d'une table de contingence et ses applications à la génétique. *C. R. Acad. Sci., Paris*, **226**, 1682-3.

Malécot, G. 1949. 3650
Les processus stochastiques de la génétique. *Le calcul des probabilités et ses applications. Colloq. Int. Centre Nat. Rech. Sci., Paris*, **13**, 121-6.

Malkin, I. G. 1944. 3651
On stability with constantly acting disturbances. (Russian.) *Prikl. Mat. i Mekh.*, **8**, 241-5.

Mallik, A. D., Satakopan, V. & Rao, S. G. 1945. 3652
A study of the estimation of the yield of wheat by sampling. *Indian J. Agric. Sci.*, **15**, 219-25.

Malmquist, F. 1941. 3653
Abfindung beim Rucktritt vom Lebensversicherungsvertrag. *Skand. Aktuartidskr.*, **24**, 70-6.

Malmquist, K. G. 1941. 3654
The elimination of the effects of accidental errors of measurement in statistical investigations. *Ark. Mat. Astr. Fys.*, **27A** (24), 13 pp.

Malmquist, K. G. 1943. 3655
On some formulas for the computation of space densities. *Ark. Mat. Astr. Fys.*, **29B** (8), 7 pp.

Malmquist, S. 1947. 3656
A statistical problem connected with the counting of radioactive particles. *Ann. Math. Statist.*, **18**, 255-64.

Maloney, C. J. 1948. 3657
Stratification in survey sampling. *Iowa State Coll. J. Sci.*, **23**, 53-4.

Maltaner, F. & Thompson, W. R. 1943. 3657a
Chemical analyses of the blood plasma of chicks deficient in vitamin *K*. *Arch. Biochem.*, **2**, 49-54.

Maltsev, A. I. 1947. 3658
Note on the paper of A. N. Kolmogorov, A. A. Petrov, and Yu. M. Smirnov " On a Gaussian formula from the theory of the method of least squares ". (Russian.) *Izv. Akad. Nauk SSSR, Ser. Mat.*, **11**, 567-8.

Mandel, J. 1945. 3659
Efficient statistical methods in chemistry. *Industr. Engng. Chem.*, **17**, 201-6.

Mandelbrojt, S. 1948. 3660
Quelques considérations sur le problème des moments. *C. R. Acad. Sci., Paris*, **226**, 862-4.

Mandelbrojt, S. 1948. 3661
Sur une égalité fondamentale. *Ann. École Norm. Supér.*, (3) **63** (4), 357-78.

Mandelson, J. 1946. 3661a
Estimation of optimum sample size in destructive testing by attributes. *Industr. Qual. Contr.*, **3** (3), 24-6.

Mandeville, J. P. 1946. 3662
Improvements in methods of census and survey analysis. *J. R. Statist. Soc.*, **109**, 111-29.

Mandeville, L. C. 1949. 3663
Congenital absence of permanent maxillary lateral incisor teeth: a preliminary investigation. *Ann. Eugen.*, **15**, 1-10.

Manheimer, D. & Hyman, H. 1949. 3663a
Interviewer performance in area sampling. *Public Opinion Quart.*, **13**, 83-92.

Maniya, G. M. 1949. 3664
Generalization of the criterion of A. N. Kolmogorov for an estimate for the law of distribution for empirical data. (Russian.) *Dokl. Akad. Nauk SSSR*, **69**, 495-7.

Mann, H. B. 1942. 3665
The construction of orthogonal Latin squares. *Ann. Math. Statist.*, **13**, 418-23.

Mann, H. B. 1943. 3666
On the construction of sets of orthogonal Latin squares. *Ann. Math. Statist.*, **14**, 401-14.

Mann, H. B. 1943. 3667
Quadratic forms with linear constraints. *Amer. Math. Monthly*, **50**, 430-3.

Mann, H. B. 1944. 3668
On orthogonal Latin squares. *Bull. Amer. Math. Soc.*, **50**, 249-57.

Mann, H. B. 1945. 3669
Nonparametric tests against trend. *Econometrica*, **13**, 245-59.

Mann, H. B. 1945. 3670
Note on a paper by C. W. Cotterman and L. H. Snyder. *Ann. Math. Statist.*, **16**, 311-12.

Mann, H. B. 1945. 3671
On a problem of estimation occurring in public opinion polls. *Ann. Math. Statist.*, **16**, 85-90 (errata: **17**, 87-8).

Mann, H. B. 1945. 3672
On a test for randomness based on signs of differences. *Ann. Math. Statist.*, **16**, 193-9.

Mann, H. B. 1946. 3673
A note on the correction of Geiger-Müller counter data. *Quart. Appl. Math.*, **4**, 307-9.

Mann, H. B. & Wald, A. 1942. 3674
On the choice of the number of class intervals in the application of the chi square test. *Ann. Math. Statist.*, **13**, 306-17.

Mann, H. B. & Wald, A. 1943. 3675
On the statistical treatment of linear stochastic difference equations. *Econometrica*, **11**, 173-220.

Mann, H. B. & Wald, A. 1943. 3676
On stochastic limit and order relationships. *Ann. Math. Statist.*, **14**, 217-26.

Mann, H. B. & Whitney, D. R. 1947. 3677
On a test of whether one of two random variables is stochastically larger than the other. *Ann. Math. Statist.*, **18**, 50-60.

Manuele, J. 1944. 3677a
Elementary principles of controlling quality of product during manufacturing. *Glass Industry*, **25**, 450-4.

Manuele, J. 1944. 3677b
A new way of controlling the quality of your product. *Ceramic Industry*, **43**, 47-9. (Also: *Brick and Clay Record*, **106**, 39-41).

Manuele, J. 1945. 3677c
Control chart for determining tool wear. *Industr. Qual. Contr.*, **1** (6), 7-10.

Manuele, J. 1945. 3677d
Controlling quality of products by statistical methods. *Steel*, **116** (24), 123-4; 164-70.

Manuele, J. & Goffman, C. 1945. 3677e
Statistical tools for controlling quality. *Elect. Engng.*, New York, **64**, 524-8.

Manuele, J., Dodge, H. F., Peterson, A. I. 3677f
& Wareham, R. E. 1945-6.
Statistical methods in quality control. I-IX. *Elect. Engng.*, New York, **64**, 181-2; 249-50; 299; 328-9; 363-4; 401-2; 448-60; **65**, 23-4; 81-3.

Manuila, A. 1945. 3678
Contributions aux études séro-anthropologique. 1. Quel est le nombre nécessaire et suffisant d'examens dans les recherches biologiques? *Arch. suisses Anthrop. gén. Suppl.*, **11**, 1-46.

Marbre, K. 1942. 3679
Zur Bedeutung der Psychologie für die Statistik (zur Frage des Wochentages bei der Geburtenstatistik). *Zeit. angew. Psychol.*, **63**, 328-46.

Marcantoni, A. 1941. 3680
Pesi e correlazioni per misure dirette condizionate. *R. C. Atti Accad. Ital.*, **3** (7), 23-32.

Marcantoni, A. 1942. 3681
Pesi e correlazioni per misure indirette e condizionate. *R. C. Ist. Lombardo sci. Lett. Sci. Mat. Nat.*, (3) **6** (75), 37-46.

Marcantoni, A. 1942. 3682
Il principio dei minimi quadrati. *Univ. Roma, Ist. Naz. Alta Mat., R. C. Mat. Appl.*, (5) **3**, 192-202.

Marcantoni, A. 1946. 3683
Saggio di un'applicazione del calcolo delle matrici alla teoria degli errori. *Univ. Roma, Ist. Naz. Alta Mat., R. C. Mat. Appl.*, (5) **5**, 252-70.

Marchal, A. 1948. 3684
De la théorie à la prévision par la méthode des modèles. *Rev. Écon. Pol.*, **58**, 481-512.

Marcinkiewicz, J. 1940. 3684a
Un théorème sur les fonctions caractéristiques. *Bull. Acad. Pol. Sci. Lett.*, **1**.

Marcum, J. I. 1947-8. 3685
A statistical theory of target detection by pulsed radar. *RAND Corp. Res. Memos.*, 1 December 1947, RM-754, 81 pp; 1 July 1948, RM-753, 113 pp.

Marcum, J. I. 1948. 3685a
Tables of Hermite polynomials and the derivatives of the error function. *RAND Corp. Paper*, 29 Dec. 1948, P-90, 241 pp. (Also: *Math. Tables Aids Comp.*, **3**, 521.)

Marcuse, S. 1945. 3686
An application of the control chart method to the testing and marketing of foods. *J. Amer. Statist. Ass.*, **40**, 214-22.

Marcuse, S. 1947. 3687
Applying control chart methods to tasting. *Food Industr.*, **19**, 316-18.

Marcuse, S. 1949. 3688
Optimum allocation and variance components in nested sampling with an application to chemical analysis. *Biometrics*, **5**, 189-205.

Marczewski, E. 1947-48. 3688a
Indépendance d'ensembles et prolongement de mesures. *Colloq. Math.*, **1**, 122-32.

Maret, A. 1941. 3689
Direkte Berechnung der Vorgangsfunktionen einer offenen Gesamtheit. (German, Italian and English summaries.) *Trans. 12th. Int. Congr. Actuar.*, Lucerne, 1940, **3**, 387-93.

Maret, A. 1947. 3690
De la fonction d'événement d'un ensemble ouvert variable. *Mitt. Ver. Schweiz. Versich.-Math.*, **47**, 321-7.

Margenau, H. 1945. 3691
On the frequency theory of probability. (English. Spanish summary.) *Phil. Phenom. Res.*, **6**, 11-25.

Marino, A. E. 1940. 3692
Efficiencia de ensayos planeados por el metodo de las parcelas divididas. (Efficiency (or accuracy) of trials calculated by the divided-plot method.) *Rev. Argent. Agron.*, **7**, 69-88.

Marino, A. E. 1943. 3693
Relation between the number of leaves and earliness in maize under different times of sowing. *Rev. Argent. Agron.*, **10**, 239-43.

Marino, A. E. 1947. 3694
Statistical study of the correlation between rainfall and maize yield. *Rev. Argent. Agron.*, **14**, 189-209.

Marino, A. E. & Luna, J. T. 1941. 3695
Planeos de ensayos en blocks incompletos (lattice y lattice balanceado). Analisis de resultados en ensayos con maices. (Methods of experiments in incomplete blocks—lattice and balanced lattice. Analyses of results in experiments with corn.) *Rev. Argent. Agron.*, **8**, 281-316.

Mark, A. M. 1949. 3696
Some probability limit theorems. *Bull. Amer. Math. Soc.*, **55**, 885-900.

Marks, E. S. 1947. 3696[a]
Selective sampling in psychological research. *Psychol. Bull.*, **44**, 267-75.

Marks, E. S. 1948. 3697
A lower bound for the expected travel among *m* random points. *Ann. Math. Statist.*, **19**, 419-22.

Marks, H. P. 1940. 3698
The mouse method for the assay of insulin. *Quart. J. Pharm.*, **13**, 344-8.

Marrama, V. 1949. 3699
La teoria della crisi alla luce dei recenti documenti. *G. Economisti*, **8**, 502-20.

Marschak, J. 1942. 3699[a]
Economic interdependence and statistical analysis. *Studies in Mathematical Economics and Econometrics in Memory of Henry Schultz*, Univ. of Chicago Press, pp. 135-50.

Marschak, J. 1947. 3700
Statistical inference from non-experimental observation: an economic example. (French summary.) *Proc. 25th. Session Int. Statist. Inst. Conf., Washington, D.C.*, 1947 (Publ. 1951), **3A**, 289-301.

Marschak, J. 1949. 3701
Role of liquidity with complete and incomplete information. *Amer. Econ. Rev.*, **39**, 182-95.

Marschak, J. & Andrews, W. H., Jr. 1944. 3702
Random simultaneous equations and the theory of production. *Econometrica*, **12**, 143-205.

Marseguerra, V. 1949. 3703
Un'applicazione del calcolo delle probabilità. *Archimede*, **1**, 59-61.

Marseguerra, E. 1949. 3704
Su alcuni valori caratteristici delle serie cicliche trattate con metodo continuo. *Metron*, **15**, 71-115.

Marsh, J. F. 1947. 3705
The use of " adjusted condition " for estimating yield per acre. *J. Farm Econ.*, **29**, 541-6.

Marshall, A. W. 1949. 3706
A note on the power function of the Wald-Wolfowitz tolerance limits for a normal distribution. *RAND Corp. Res. Memo.*, 21 Oct. 1949, RM-271, 6 pp.

Marshall, E. W. 1945. 3707
Principles underlying exposed-to-risk formulae. *Trans. Actuar. Soc. Amer.*, **46**, 10-50.

Marsili, L. M. 1941. 3708
La variabilità nelle serie storiche. *Economia, Roma*, **19** (27), 118-24.

Martin, D. 1946. 3709
On the radial error in a Gaussian elliptical scatter. *Phil. Mag.*, (7) **37**, 636-9.

Martin, H. 1943. 3710
The evaluation of fungicides: A study of quantitative toxicology. *J. Soc. Chem. Industr.*, **62**, 67-71, 112.

Martin, J. T. 1940-2. 3711
The problem of the evaluation of rotenone-containing plants. V. The relative toxicities of different species of derris. VI. The toxicity of *l*-elliptone and of poisons applied jointly, with further observations on the rotenone equivalent method of assessing the toxicity of derris root. *Ann. Appl. Biol.*, **27**, 274-94; **29**, 69-81.

Martin, L. 1949. 3712
Évolution de la biométrie, de Quetelet au 2me congrès international de biométrie (Genève, 1949). *Bull. Inst. Agron. Gembloux*, **17**, 43-66.

Martindale, J. G. 1941. 3713
A correlation periodograph for the measurement of periods in disturbed wave-forms. *J. Textile Inst.*, **32**, 71-82.

Martinez-Fortun, O. 1946. 3714
Importancia de la estadística en epidemiología. *Rev. Med. Cirug. Habana*, **51**, 228-42.

Martinotti, P. 1940. 3715
Misura dell'approssimazione interpolatoria. *Atti 1ma Riun. Sci., Soc. Ital. Statist.*, pp. 75-9.

Martinotti, P. 1941. 3716
Il metodo di traslazione nell'interpolazione. *Statistica, Ferrara*, **1**, 205-20.

Martinotti, P. 1941. 3717
Di alcune recenti medie. *Acta Pontif. Acad. Sci.*, **5**, 113-21.

Martinotti, P. 1942. 3718
Proprietà teoriche dell'interpolazione. *Statistica, Ferrara*, **2**, 137-42.

Martins, O. A. L. *See* **Lins Martins, O. A.**

Martins, R. G. 1945. 3719
Agricultural experimentation. *Bol. Minist. Agric., Rio de Janeiro*, **34**, 1-14.

Maruyama, G. 1947. 3720
On the integral representation of normal stochastic processes. (Japanese.) *Res. Mem. Inst. Statist. Math., Tokyo*, **3**, 55-60.

Maruyama, G. 1948. 3721
On stationary processes. (Japanese.) *Sûgaku*, **1**, 120-3.

Maruyama, G. 1949. 3722
The harmonic analysis of stationary stochastic processes. *Mem. Fac. Sci. A, Kyusyu*, **4**, 45-106.

Maruyama, G. & Onoyama, T. 1948. 3723
(Japanese.) *Res. Mem. Inst. Statist. Math., Tokyo*, **4**, 71-4.

Marzolf, S. S. 1945. 3724
Symptom and syndrome statistically interpreted. *Psychol. Bull.*, **42**, 162-76.

Masciotti, R. 1941. 3725
Un teorema fondamentale e le sue applicazioni alla determinaẑione dei valori di riscatto. (English, French and German summaries.) *Trans. 12th. Int. Congr. Actuar., Lucerne.* 1940, **2**, 291-309.

Massé, M. 1949. 3726
Les choix économiques dans un monde aléatoire et la notion d'espérance marginale. *Econometrica* **17**, *Suppl.*, 192-4.

Massé, P. 1944. 3727
Application des probabilités en chaîne à l'hydrologie statistique et au jeu des réservoirs. *J. Soc. Statist. Paris*, **85**, 204-19.

Massé, P. 1944. 3728
Sur les principes de la régulation d'un débit aléatoire par un réservoir. *C. R. Acad. Sci., Paris*, **219**, 19-21.

Massé, P. 1944. 3729
Sur les effets de la régulation d'un débit aléatoire par un réservoir. *C. R. Acad. Sci., Paris*, **219**, 150-1.

Massé, P. 1944. 3730
Sur un cas particulier remarquable de la régulation d'un débit aléatoire par un réservoir. *C. R. Acad. Sci., Paris*, **219**, 173-5.

Masuyama, M. 1940. 3731
On the meaning of the symmetric correlation coefficient between vector sets. *Proc. Phys.-Math. Soc. Japan*, (3) **22**, 579-85.

Masuyama, M. 1940. 3732
On the subdependency. *Proc. Phys.-Math. Soc. Japan*, (3) **22**, 855-8.

Masuyama, M. 1940. 3733
The variance tensor of vector set and a nature of the symmetric correlation coefficient. *Proc. Phys.-Math. Soc. Japan*, (3) **22**, 858-61.

Masuyama, M. 1941. 3734
The standard error of the mean vector. *Proc. Phys.-Math. Soc. Japan*, (3) **23**, 194-5.

Masuyama, M. 1941. 3735
The normal law of frequency for vector quantities. *Proc. Phys.-Math. Soc. Japan*, (3) **23**, 196-9.

Masuyama, M. 1941. 3736
On the characteristic values of the correlation tensor and a new measure of correlation between vector quantities. *Proc. Phys.-Math. Soc. Japan*, (3) **23**, 199-204.

Masuyama, M. 1941. 3737
The totally orthonormalised vector set and the normal form of correlation tensor. *Proc. Phys.-Math. Soc. Japan*, (3) **23**, 346-51.

Masuyama, M. 1941. 3738
The mean angle between two vector sets. *Proc. Phys.-Math. Soc. Japan*, (3) **23**, 351-5.

Masuyama, M. 1941. 3739
Correlation coefficient between two sets of complex vectors. *Proc. Phys.-Math. Soc. Japan*, (3) **23**, 918-24.

Masuyama, M. 1941. 3740
On the significance test of the additive correlation coefficient. *Proc. Phys.-Math. Soc. Japan*, (3) **23**, 1016-19.

Masuyama, M. 1942. 3741
The Bienaymé-Tchebycheff inequality for Hermitic tensors. *Proc. Phys.-Math. Soc. Japan*, (3) **24**, 409-11.

Masuyama, M. 1944. 3742
Stochastic studies on sedimentation rate and on brain waves. *Medicine & Biology*, **5**, 483ff.

Masuyama, M. 1946. 3743
A formula for assaying Penicillin. *Res. Mem. Inst. Statist. Math., Tokyo*, **2**, 466.

Masuyama, M. 1947. 3744
Superposition method of assaying antibiotic substances and its fundamental formula. *Res. Mem. Inst. Statist. Math., Tokyo*, **3**, 48.

Masuyama, M. 1947. 3745
Method of estimating the minimum effective dose pooling the results of replicated experiments. *Res. Mem. Inst. Statist. Math., Tokyo*, **3**, 129.

Masuyama, M. 1948. 3746
Some measures of variability in sampling from finite multivariate population. *Bull. Math. Statist.*, **3** (3), 53.

Masuyama, M. 1949. 3747
A method of estimating parameters in duration curve. *Res. Mem. Inst. Statist. Math., Tokyo*, **5**, 58.

Masuyama, M. 1949. 3748
On a one-dimensional diffusion method of assaying antibiotic substances and its fundamental formulas. *Biometrics*, **5**, 317-29.

Masuyama, M. 1949. 3749
Zigzag sampling and its application. *Res. Mem. Inst. Statist. Math., Tokyo*, **5**, 75ff.

Matern, B. 1947. 3750
Metoder att uppskatta noggraunheten vid linjeoch provytetaxering. (Methods of estimating the accuracy of line and sample plot surveys.) (Swedish. English summary.) *Medd. Skogsforskningsinst.*, **36** (1), 1-138.

Matern, B. 1949. 3751
Independence of non-negative quadratic forms in normally correlated variables. *Ann. Math. Statist.*, **20**, 119-20.

Mateur, A. 1945. 3752
A simple test of significance. *Engineering, London*, **160**, 452.

Mathen, K. K. 1946. 3753
A criterion for testing whether two samples have come from the same population without assuming the nature of the population. *Sankhyā*, **7**, 329.

Mathen, K. K. 1948. 3754
Studies on the sampling procedure for a general health survey. *Bull. Calcutta Statist. Ass.*, **1**, 106-13.

Mather, K. 1940. 3755
The design and significance of synergic action tests. *J. Hyg., Camb.*, **40**, 513-31.

Mather, K. 1942. 3756
The balance of polygenic combinations. *J. Genet.*, **43**, 309-36.

Mather, K. 1943. 3757
Polygenic inheritance and natural selection. *Biol. Rev. Camb. Phil. Soc.*, **18**, 32-64.

Mather, K. 1944. 3758
The calculation of sister-reunion frequency. *J. Genet.*, **46**, 252-63.

Mather, K. 1946. 3759
The genetical requirements of bio-assays with higher organisms. *Analyst*, **71**, 407-11.

Mather, K. 1949. 3760
The analysis of extinction time data in bioassay. *Biometrics*, **5**, 127-43.

Mather, K. 1949. 3761
The genetical theory of continuous variation. *Proc. 8th Int. Congr. Genetics, Hereditas*, **35**, *Suppl.*, 376-401.

Mather, K. & Beale, G. H. 1942. 3762
The calculation and precision of linkage values from tetrad analysis. *J. Genet.*, **43**, 1-30.

Mather, K. & Philip, U. 1940. 3763
The inheritance of hare lip and cleft palate in man. *Ann. Eugen.*, **10**, 403-16.

Mather, K., Bowler, R. G., Crooke, A. C. 3764
& Morris, C. J. O. R. 1947.
The precision of plasma volume determinations by the Evans Blue Method. *Brit. J. Exper. Path.*, **28**, 12-24.

Mathew, N. T. 1941. 3765
The influence of seasons on human reproduction. *Sankhyā*, **5**, 261-8.

Mathew, N. T. 1947. 3766
Factors influencing the relative proportion at birth of the two sexes. *Sankhyā*, **8**, 277-81.

Mathisen, H. C. 1943. 3767
A method of testing the hypothesis that two samples are from the same population. *Ann. Math. Statist.*, **14**, 188-94.

Matusita, K. 1949. 3768
Note on the independence of certain statistics. *Ann. Inst. Statist. Math., Tokyo*, **1**, 79-82.

Mauchly, J. W. 1940. 3769
A significance-test for ellipticity in the harmonic dial. *Terrestr. Magnet. Atmos. Electr.*, **45**, 145-8.

Mauchly, J. W. 1940. 3770
Significance test for sphericity of a normal *n*-variate distribution. *Ann. Math. Statist.*, **11**, 204-9.

Maung, K. 1941. 3771
Discriminant analysis of Tocher's eye-colour data for Scottish school children. *Ann. Eugen.*, **11**, 64-76.

Maung, K. 1942. 3772
Measurement of association in a contingency table with special reference to the pigmentation of hair and eye colours of Scottish school children. *Ann. Eugen.*, **11**, 189-223.

Maurin, J. 1947. 3773
Un mode de calcul général de la fonction de probabilité de moyennes. *C. R. Acad. Sci., Paris*, **225**, 1268-9.

Maurin, J. 1948. 3774
Extension analytique d'un calcul de la fonction de probabilité de moyennes correspondant à une probabilité négative. *C. R. Acad. Sci., Paris*, **226**, 51-3.

Mautz, R. K. 1945. 3775
Accounting and statistics. *Accounting Rev.*, **20**, 399-410.

May, K. 1948. 3776
Probabilities of certain election results. *Amer. Math. Monthly*, **55**, 203-9.

Mayhew, W. L. & Vajda, S. 1946. 3777
An application of the theory of probability to the examinations of the Institute of Actuaries. *J. Inst. Actuar. Students' Soc.*, **6**, 67-75.

Mayot, M. 1946. 3778
Sur la détermination statistique des composantes cycliques d'un phénomène; application aux étoiles variables. *C. R. Acad. Sci., Paris*, **223**, 125-7.

Mays, W. J. 1945. 3779
The valuation of risks. *Amer. Math. Monthly*, **52**, 138-48.

Mazurkiewicz, S. 1948. 3780
Un théorème sur les fonctions caractéristiques. *Bull. Acad. Polon. Sci. III Cl. Sci. Math.*, **1940-1946**, 1-3.

Mazurkiewicz, S. 1949. 3781
Sur les espaces de variables aléatoires. *Fundam. Math.*, **36**, 288-302.

Meacham, A. D. 1940. 3782
The value of the collator in using prepunched cards for obtaining moments and product moments. *Proc. Educ. Res. Forum, IBM Corp., New York.*

Medawar, P. B. 1944. 3783
The shape of the human being as a function of time. *Proc. Roy. Soc. B*, **132**, 133-41.

Medland, F. F. 1947. 3784
An empirical comparison of methods of communality estimation. *Psychometrika*, **12**, 101-9.

Meehl, P. E. 1945. 3785
A simple algebraic development of Horst's suppressor variables. *Amer. J. Psychol.*, **58**, 550-4.

Meerwarth, R. 1947. 3786
Missbrauchte Statistik. *Statist. Praxis.*, **2**, 91.

Mehta, N. C. 1945. 3787
Statistics and social values. *Sankhyā*, **7**, 167-72.

Meier, J. 1940. 3788
Zur Theorie der unabhängigen Wahrscheinlichkeiten. *Mitt. Ver. Schweiz. Versich.-Math.*, **39**, 53-74.

Meier, N. C. & Burke, C. J. 1947-8. 3789
Laboratory tests of sampling technique. *Public Opinion Quart.*, **11**, 586-93.

Meili, R. 1949. 3790
Sur la nature des facteurs de l'intelligence. *Arch. Psychol.*, **34**, 33-47.

Meizler, D. G. 1949. 3791
On a problem of B. V. Gnedenko. (Russian.) *Ukrain. Mat. Zh.*, **1** (2), 67-84.

Meizler, D. G., Parasyuk, O. S. 3792
& Rvacheva, E. L. 1948.
A multidimensional local limit theorem of the theory of probability. (Russian.) *Dokl. Akad. Nauk SSSR*, **60**, 1127-8.

Meizler, D. G., Parasyuk, O. S. 3793
& Rvacheva, E. L. 1949.
On a many-dimensional local limit theorem of the theory of probability. (Russian.) *Ukrain. Mat. Zh.*, **1** (1), 9-20.

Mellor, S. D. 1942. 3794
Delayed call formulae when calls are served in random order. *Post Office Elect. Engrs.' J.*, **35**, 53-6.

Memored, J. M. P. 1948. 3795
Considerations on statistical tests. (Portuguese.) *Rev. Ceres*, **8**, 58-65.

Mendonca, P. de Varennese. 1942. 3796
Orthogonality and analysis of variance. *Portug. Math.*, **3**, 234-52.

Menger, K. 1942. 3797
Statistical metrics. *Proc. Nat. Acad. Sci. U.S.A.*, **28**, 535-7.

Menger, K. 1944. 3798
On the relation between calculus of probability and statistics. *Univ. Notre Dame, Indiana, Notre Dame Math. Lect.* no. 4, pp. 44-53.

Merli, L. 1940.   3799
Recenti risultati sulla convergenza dei polinomi di interpolazione di Langrane e di Hermite. *G. Ist. Ital. Attuari*, **11**, 107-18.

Merli, L. 1941.   3800
Sulla convergenza in media della formula di interpolazione di Lagrange. *G. Ist. Ital. Attuari*, **12**, 34-42.

Merrell, M. 1947.   3801
Time-specific life tables contrasted with observed survivorship. *Biometrics Bull.*, **3**, 129-136.

Merrill, A. A. 1947.   3802
A tailored logarithmic scale. *Gen. Elect. Rev.*, **50**, 45-7.

Merrington, M. 1941.   3803
Numerical approximations to percentage points of the χ^2 distribution. *Biometrika*, **32**, 200-2.

Merrington, M. 1942.   3804
Tables of percentage points of the *t*-distribution. *Biometrika*, **32**, 300.

Merrington, M. & Thompson, C. M. 1943.   3805
Tables of percentage points of the inverted beta (*F*) distribution. *Biometrika*, **33**, 73-88.

Metfessel, M. 1947.   3806
A proposal for quantitative reporting of comparative judgement. *J. Psychol.*, **24**, 229-35.

Metropolis, N. & Ulam, S. 1949.   3807
The Monte Carlo method. *J. Amer. Statist. Ass.*, **44**, 335-41.

Meurers, J. 1948.   3808
Fehlertrennung durch Wahrscheinlichteitsbetrachtung. *Zeit. angew. Math. Mech.*, **28**, 183-6.

Meyer, H. A. 1940.   3809
A mathematical expression for height curves. *J. Forestry*, **38**, 415-20.

Meyer, H. A. 1943.   3810
Accuracy of growth prediction for short periods. *J. Forestry*, **41**, 376-80.

Meyer, S. N. 1946.   3811
Some theoretical views on the shape of the tubercular infection curve and its dependence on infection risk. *Skand. Aktuartidskr.*, **29**, 1-11.

Meyer, S. N. 1947.   3812
Statistic problems regarding tuberculosis infection and morbidity of tuberculosis. *Skand. Aktuartidskr.*, **30**, 130-50.

Meyer, W. 1943.   3813
De actuarielle behandeling van subnormale risico's. *Verzekerings-archief*, **24**, 214-26.

Meyer, W. H. 1945.   3814
Volume-diameter ratios as a general basis for board-foot volume tables. *J. Forestry*, **43**, 49-55.

Meyrich, C. 1943.   3815
Ein Beitrag zum Problem des Gesetzes in der Statistik. *Dtsch. Statist. Zbl.*, **35** (3-4), 49-55.

Miani-Calabrese, D. 1945.   3815a
Coefficienti sintetici di correlazione di serie di indici di prezzi al minuto. *Atti 7ma Riun. Sci., Soc. Ital. Statist.*, pp. 503-30.

Miani-Calabrese, D. 1949.   3815b
Criteri metodologici per lo studio di gruppi soggetti ad interventi riparatori. *Statistica, Milano*, **9**, 491-7.

Michael, W. B. 1949.   3816
Factor analysis of tests and criteria: a comparative study of two AAF pilot populations. *Psychol. Monogr.*, **63** (298), 55 pp.

Michailoff, I. 1943.   3817
Zahlenmässiges Verfahren für die Ausführung der Bestandeshöhenkurven. *Forstwissen. Zbl.*, **65**, 273-9.

Michailoff, I. 1944.   3818
Über die Genauigkeit der Formeln für Sektionsweise-stammkubierüng. *Forstwissen. Zbl.*, **66**, 120-5.

Michalup, E. 1944.   3819
Nota acerca del ajustamiento mecanica. (English summary.) *Estadística*, **2** (6), 208-22.

Michalup, E. 1946.   3820
Über den Begriff " Exzess " in der mathematischen Statistik. *Mitt. Ver. Schweiz. Versich.-Math.*, **46**, 231-6.

Michalup, E. 1946.   3821
El promedio de la duracion de la vida y la function de Prym. *Estadística*, **4**, 252-9.

Michalup, E. 1948.   3822
The characteristics. (Spanish.) *Estados. Unidos de Venezuela, Bol. Acad. Cienc. Fis. Mat. Nat.*, **11**, 448-78.

Michalup, E. 1949.   3823
Über die Stirlingsche Fakultätenformel. *Statist. Vierteljschr.*, **2**, 117-19.

Michel, J. G. L. 1946.   3824
Central difference formulae obtained by means of operator expansions. *J. Inst. Actuar.*, **72**, 470-80.

Michelsen, O., Caster, O. W. & Keys, A. 1947.   3825
A statistical evaluation of the thiamine and pyramin excretions of normal young men on controlled intake of thiamine. *J. Biol. Chem.*, **168**, 415-31.

Middleton, D. 1946.   3826
The response of biased, saturated linear and quadratic rectifiers to random noise. *J. Appl. Phys.*, **17**, 778-801.

Middleton, D. 1948.   3827
Some general results in the theory of noise through non-linear devices. *Quart. Appl. Math.*, **5**, 445-98.

Middleton, D. 1948.   3828
Spurious signals caused by noise in triggered circuits. *J. Appl. Phys.*, **19**, 817-30.

Middleton, D. 1949.   3829
The spectrum of frequency-modulated waves after reception in random noise. I. *Quart. Appl. Math.*, **7**, 129-73.

Migliorini, E. 1940.   3830
Note metodiche sui sistemi usati per rappresentare la distribuzione della popolazione. *Boll. Soc. Geografica Ital.*, **7** (5) 5, 262-74.

Mihoc, G. 1943.   3831
Sur le problème des itérations dans une suite d'épreuves. *Bull. Math. Soc. Roumaine Sci.*, **45**, 81-95.

Mihoc, G. 1949.   3832
La loi limite de la probabilité des nombres des itérations de longueur donné. (Romanian. Russian and French summaries.) *An. Acad. R. P. Romîne. Secţ. Şti. Mat. Fiz. Chim. A*, **2**, 213-27.

Mikhlin, S. G. 1948.   3833
On the convergence of the method of least squares.
(Russian.) *Dokl. Akad. Nauk SSSR*, **59**, 1245-7.

Milatz, J. M. W. 1941.   3834
Brownian motion. (Dutch.) *Ned. Tijdschr. Natuurk.*,
8, 19-36.

Miles, A. A. 1946.   3835
The frequencies of bacterial subtypes in a carrier
community and their significance. *J. Path. Bact.*, **58**,
269-73.

Milicer-Gruzewska, H. 1946.   3836
The coefficient of correlation *a posteriori* of equivalent
variables. (English. Polish summary.) *Soc. Sci.
Lett. Varsovie C. R. Cl. III, Sci. Math. Phys.*, **39**,
3-17.

Milicer-Gruzewska, H. 1948.   3837
Sulla legge limite delle variabili casuali equivalenti.
Atti Accad. Lincei. Mem. Sci. Fis. Mat. Nat., (8) **2**,
25-33.

Milicer-Gruzewska, H. 1949.   3838
On the law of probability and the characteristic function
of the standardized sum of equivalent variables.
(English. Polish summary.) *Soc. Sci. Lett. Varsovie,
C. R. III Sci. Math. Phys.*, **42**, 99-143.

Millan, G. A. & Sprague, G. F. 1940.   3839
The use of punched card equipment in predicting the
performance of corn double crosses. *J. Amer. Soc.
Agron.*, **32**, 815-16.

Miller, G. A. & Frick, F. C. 1949.   3840
Statistical behavioristics and sequences of responses.
Psychol. Rev., **56**, 311-24.

Miller, G. A. & Gerner, W. R. 1944.   3841
Effect of random presentation on the psychometric
function: implications for a quantal theory of discrimination. *Amer. J. Psychol.*, **57**, 451-67.

Miller, L. C. & Tainter, M. L. 1944.   3842
Estimation of the ED_{50} and its error by means of
logarithmic-probit graph paper. *Proc. Soc. Exper.
Biol.*, **57**, 261-4.

Miller, L. P. 1946.   3843
Particle size distribution in cocoa powders. *Contrib.
Boyce Thompson Inst.*, **14**, 325-34.

Miller, R. B. 1949.   3844
Problems of the optimum catch in small whitefish
lakes. *Biometrics*, **5**, 14-26.

Miller, R. S. 1944.   3845
An attempted simplification of the mathematical
method of sub-specific differentiation and identification. *Emu*, **43**, 253-8.

Mills, F. C. 1946.   3846
Elasticity of physical quantities and flexibility of unit
prices in the dimension of time. *J. Amer. Statist. Ass.*,
41, 439-67.

Milne, A. 1943.   3847
The comparison of sheep-tick populations (*Ixodes
ricinus L.*). *Ann. Appl. Biol.*, **30**, 240-50.

Miner, J. R. 1945.   3848
Some uses of statistical methods in medicine.
Biometrics Bull., **1**, 3-5.

Mineur, H. 1944.   3849
Sur la meilleure représentation d'une variable aléatoire
par fonction linéaire des variables à choisir parmi des
variables aléatoires données. *Ann. Astrophys.*, **7**,
17-30.

Mineur, H. 1944.   3850
Extension de la méthode des moindres carrés. Appli-
cation à la détermination de l'apex au moyen des
mouvements propres. *Ann. Astrophys.*, **7**, 121-
32.

Mintz, A. & Blum, M. L. 1949.   3851
A re-examination of the accident proneness concept.
J. Appl. Psychol., **33**, 195-211.

Mitropolskii, A. K. 1940.   3852
On the calculation of ordinary correlation equations.
(Russian.) *Zh. Tekh. Fiz. Akad. Nauk SSSR*, **10**,
1227-41.

Mitropolskii, A. K. 1947.   3853
On the calculation of correlation equations by a
summation method. (Russian.) *Trudy Lesotekh.
Akad. S. M. Kirova*, **60**, 63-72.

Mitropolskii, A. K. 1949.   3854
Ordinary correlation equations. (Russian.) *Usp.
Mat. Nauk (N.S.)*, **4**, 5(33), 142-75.

Mitscherlich, E. A. 1947.   3855
A method for eliminating the systematic error due to
soil heterogeneity in drainage and irrigation experiments. *Zeit. Pfl.-Ernähr. Düng.*, **37**, 259-64.

Mittmann, O. M. J. 1940.   3856
Theoretische Erbprognose und Gattenwahl. *Deutsche
Math.*, **5**, 328-37.

Mittmann, O. M. J. 1940.   3857
Funktionale Zusammenhänge in erbbiologischen
Gesamtheiten. *Arch. math. Wirtsch.*, **6**, 70-80. (Also:
(1941), *Deutsche Math.*, **5**, 563-70.)

Mogno, R. 1940.   3858
Su una formula approssimata per il calcolo di $n!$ e le
sue applicazione. *Metron*, **14**, 67-78.

Mogno, R. 1941.   3859
Nota su una formula approssimata per il calcolo di $n!$
Metron, **14**, 409-11.

Mohr, E. 1941.   3860
Bemerkungen zu Mises' Behandlung des Nadel-
problems von Buffon. *Deutsche Math.*, **6**, 108-13.

Mohr, E. 1942.   3861
Bemerkung zum Buffonschen Nadelproblem. *Zeit.
angew. Math. Mech.*, **22**, 170-1.

Molina, E. C. 1946.   3862
Fermat's theorem as a problem in probability. *Amer.
Math. Monthly* **53**, 525.

Molina, E. C. 1946.   3863
Some fundamental curves for the solution of sampling
problems. *Ann. Math. Statist.*, **17**, 325-35.

Mollenkopf, W. G. 1949.   3864
Variation of the standard error of measurement.
Psychometrika, **14**, 189-229.

Montel, P. 1942.   3865
Sur les combinaisons avec répétitions limitées. *Bull.
Sci. Math.*, (2) **66**, 86-103.

Montello, J. 1945.   3866
Do ajustamento das distributioçòes de frequencia pelo criterio dos mínimos quadrados. (Portuguese.) *Rev. Brasil. Estatíst.*, **6**, 411-18.

Montoya, H. 1946.   3867
Metodología en estadísticas agrícolas de las Américas. I, II. Sistemas estadísticos agrícolas en algunos países, latinoaméricanos. *Estadística*, **4**, 3-69; 172-232.

Montroll, E. W. 1947.   3868
On the theory of Markoff chains. *Ann. Math. Statist.* **18**, 18-36.

Mood, A. M. 1940.   3869
The distribution theory of runs. *Ann. Math. Statist.*, **11**, 367-92.

Mood, A. M. 1941.   3870
On the joint distribution of the medians in samples from a multivariate population. *Ann. Math. Statist.*, **12**, 268-78.

Mood, A. M. 1943.   3871
On the dependence of sampling inspection plans upon population distributions. *Ann. Math. Statist.*, **14**, 415-25.

Mood, A. M. 1946.   3872
On Hotelling's weighing problem. *Ann. Math. Statist.*, **17**, 432-46.

Mood, A. M. 1946.   3873
Statistical control of the production process. *Food Industries, New York*, **18**, 1189-91.

Mood, A. M. 1949.   3874
An asymptotic distribution for a mortality problem. *RAND Corp. Res. Memo.*, 28 February 1948, RM-111, 9 pp.

Mood, A. M. 1949.   3875
Tests of independence in contingency tables as unconditional tests. *Ann. Math. Statist.*, **20**, 114-16.

Moore, G. H. 1947.   3876
Accuracy of government statistics. *Harvard Busin. Rev.*, **25** (3), 306-17.

Moore, G. H. & Wallis, W. A. 1943.   3877
Time series significance tests based on signs of differences. *J. Amer. Statist. Ass.*, **38**, 153-64.

Moore, P. G. 1949.   3878
A test for randomness in a sequence of two alternatives involving a 2×2 table. *Biometrika*, **36**, 305-16.

Moore, T. V. & Hsu, E. H. 1946.   3879
Factorial analysis of anthropological measurements in psychotic patients. *Hum. Biol.*, **18**, 133-57.

Moore, W. & Bliss, C. I. 1942.   3880
A method for determining insecticidal effectiveness using " *aphis rumicis* " and certain organic compounds. *J. Econ. Ent.*, **35**, 544-53.

Moran, P. A. P. 1946.   3881
Random associations on a lattice. *Nature*, **158**, 521.

Moran, P. A. P. 1947.   3882
On the method of paired comparisons. *Biometrika*, **34**, 363-5.

Moran, P. A. P. 1947.   3883
Random associations on a lattice. *Proc. Camb. Phil. Soc.*, **43**, 321-8.

Moran, P. A. P. 1947.   3884
The random division of an interval. I. *J. R. Statist. Soc. Suppl.*, **9**, 92-8.

Moran, P. A. P. 1947-8.   3885
Some theorems on time series. I, II. The significance of the serial correlation coefficient. *Biometrika*, **34**, 281-91; **35**, 255-60.

Moran, P. A. P. 1948.   3886
A class of complex Markov chains. *Quart. J. Math.*, **19**, 140-9.

Moran, P. A. P. 1948.   3887
The interpretation of statistical maps. *J. R. Statist. Soc. B*, **10**, 243-51.

Moran, P. A. P. 1948.   3888
Rank correlation and permutation distributions. *Proc. Camb. Phil. Soc.*, **44**, 142-4.

Moran, P. A. P. 1948.   3889
Rank correlation and product moment correlation. *Biometrika*, **35**, 203-6.

Moran, P. A. P. 1948.   3890
The statistical distribution of the length of a rubber molecule. *Proc. Camb. Phil. Soc.*, **44**, 342-4.

Moran, P. A. P. 1949.   3891
The spectral theory of discrete stochastic processes. *Biometrika*, **36**, 63-70.

Moran, P. A. P. 1949.   3892
Statistical analysis of the sunspot and lynx cycles. *J. Animal Ecology*, **18**, 115-16.

Morant, G. M. 1948.   3893
Comparisons of heights and weights of German civilians recorded in 1946-7 and Royal Air Force and other British series. *Biometrika*, **35**, 368-96.

Moreno, J. L. & Jennings, H. H. 1945.   3894
Sociometric measurement of social configurations, based on deviations from chance. *Sociometry Monogr.* no. 3, 35 pp.

Morgan, C. T. 1945.   3895
The statistical treatment of hoarding data. *J. Comp. Psychol.*, **38**, 247-56.

Morin, F. & Monod, J. 1942.   3896
Sur l'expression analytique de la croissance des populations bactériennes. *Rev. Sci., Paris*, **80**, 227-9.

Moriyama, I. M. 1945.   3896a
A method for indexing statistical tabulations. *Estadística*, **3**, 391-4.

Morrell, A. J. H. 1944.   3897
Note on Wilson and Hilferty's approximation to the χ^2 distribution. *J. R. Statist. Soc.*, **107**, 59.

Morrell, C. A. 1942.   3898
The application of statistical analysis with special reference to the assay of vitamins. *Chem. & Industry*, **61**, 35-9.

Morris, J. 1942.   3899
Frequency equations. *Aircraft Engng.*, **14**, 108-10.

Morris, J. & Head, J. W. 1942.   3900
Lagrangian frequency equations. An "escalator" method for numerical solution. *Aircraft Engng.*, **14**, 312-14, 316.

Morris, J. & Head, J. W. 1944.   3901
The " escalator " process for the solution of Lagrangian frequency equations. *Phil. Mag.*, (7) **35**, 735-59.

Morrison, A. W. 1942.   3902
A graphical device for comparing the form of a given distribution of test scores with the form of the standard distribution for the test. *J. Educ. Res.*, **36**, 218-20.

Morrow, E. B., Darrow, G. M.   3903
& Rigney, J. A. 1949.
A rating system for the evaluation of horticultural material. *Proc. Amer. Soc. Hort. Sci.*, **53**, 276-80.

Morse, A. P. & Grubbs, F. E. 1947.   3904
The estimation of dispersion from differences. *Ann. Math. Statist.*, **18**, 194-214. (Based on: *Ballistic Res. Lab. Rep.*, 557, July 1945 by **A. P. Morse.**)

Mortara, G. 1943.   3904a
Nota acêrca do aproveitamento do censo demográfico para a determinação da freqüência das variações de estado civil em função da Idade. *Rev. Brazil. Estatíst.*, **4**, 435-8.

Moser, C. A. 1949.   3905
The use of sampling in Great Britain. *J. Amer. Statist. Ass.*, **44**, 231-59.

Mosier, C. I. 1940.   3906
A modification of the method of successive intervals. *Psychometrika*, **5**, 101-7.

Mosier, C. I. 1940-1.   3907
Psychophysics and mental test theory: I. Fundamental postulates and elementary theorems. II. The constant process. *Psychol. Rev.*, **47**, 355-66; **48**, 235-49.

Mosier, C. I. 1941.   3908
A short cut in the estimation of the split-halves coefficients. *Educ. and Psychol. Measurement*, **1**, 407-8.

Mosier, C. I. 1943.   3909
On the reliability of a weighted composite. *Psychometrika*, **8**, 161-8.

Mosier, C. I. 1946.   3910
Machine methods in scaling by reciprocal averages. *Proc. Res. Forum. IBM Corp. New York*, 26-30 August 1946, pp. 35-9.

Mosier, C. I. & McQuitty, J. V. 1940.   3911
Methods of item validation and the Abacs for item-test correlation and critical ratio of upper-lower difference. *Psychometrika*, **5**, 57-65.

Mosteller, F. 1940.   3912
Some miscellaneous contributions to scale theory: Remarks on the method of paired comparisons. *Cambridge: Harvard Univ. Lab. Soc. Relations, Rep.* no. 10, chap. III.

Mosteller, F. 1941.   3913
Note on an application of runs to quality control charts. *Ann. Math. Statist.*, **12**, 228-32.

Mosteller, F. 1946.   3914
On some useful " inefficient " statistics. *Ann. Math. Statist.*, **17**, 377-408.

Mosteller, F. 1947.   3914a
Equality of margins. *Amer. Statistician*, **1** (2), 12.

Mosteller, F. 1948.   3915
A *k*-sample slippage test for an extreme population. *Ann. Math. Statist.*, **19**, 58-65.

Mosteller, F. 1948.   3916
On pooling data. *J. Amer. Statist. Ass.*, **43**, 231-42.

Mosteller, F. & Tukey, J. W. 1949.   3916a
Practical applications of new theory: a review. I. Location and scale: tables. II. Counted data—graphical methods. *Industr. Qual. Contr.*, **6** (2), 5-8; (3), 5-7.

Mosteller, F. & Tukey, J. W. 1949.   3917
The uses and usefulness of binomial probability paper. *J. Amer. Statist. Ass.*, **44**, 174-212.

Motokawa, K. 1943.   3918
Eine Statistisch-mechanische Theorie über das Elektroenkephalogramm. *Tôhoku J. Exper. Med.*, **45**, 278-96.

Motokawa, K. & Mita, T. 1942-3.   3919
Das Wahrscheinlichkeitsprinzip über die geheimelektrischen Erscheinungen des Menschen. *Jap. J. Med. Sci.*, **8**, 63-77.

Mottley, C. M. 1945.   3919a
The application of statistical methods to the development and quality control of high tensile steel. *J. Amer. Soc. Naval Engrs.*, **57**, 21-55.

Mottley, C. McC. 1942.   3920
Experimental designs for developing and testing a stocking policy. *Trans. North Amer. Wildlife Conf.*, **7**, 224-38.

Mottley, C. McC. 1943.   3921
Modern methods of studying fish populations. *Trans. North Amer. Wildlife Conf.*, **7**, 356-60.

Mottley, C. McC. & Embody, D. R. 1942.   3922
The effect of the full moon on trout fishing. *J. Amer. Statist. Ass.*, **37**, 41-7.

Mou, T. C. 1944.   3923
Some mathematical considerations which play a role in diffusion problems. (Dutch, English, French and German summaries.) *Ned. Akad. Wetensch. Verslagen. Afd. Natuurk.*, **53**, 400-10.

Mountain, H. S. 1949.   3924
Determining the solid wood volume of four foot pulpwood stacks. *J. Forestry*, **47**, 627-31.

Mourier, É. 1946.   3925
Étude de choix entre deux lois de probabilité. *C. R. Acad. Sci., Paris*, **223**, 712-14.

Mourier, É. 1949.   3926
Sur l'espérance mathématique d'un élément aléatoire dans un espace de Banach. *C. R. Acad. Sci., Paris*, **229**, 1300-1.

Mowbray, A. H. 1941.   3927
Observation on correlation analysis. *J. Amer. Statist. Ass.*, **36**, 248-52.

Moyal, J. E. 1942.   3928
Approximate probability distribution functions for the sum of two independent variates. *J. R. Statist. Soc.*, **105**, 42-3.

Moyal, J. E. 1949.   3929
Causality, determinism and probability. *Philosophy*, **24**, 310-17.

Moyal, J. E. 1949.   3930
Comments on Richardson's paper on the distribution of wars in time. *J. R. Statist. Soc. A*, **112**, 446-9.

Moyal, J. E. 1949.   3931
Quantum mechanics as a statistical theory. *Proc. Camb. Phil Soc.*, **45**, 99-124.

Moyal, J. E. 1949.   3932
Stochastic processes and statistical physics. *J. R. Statist. Soc. B*, **11**, 150-210; 265-82.

Mrugowsky, J. 1941.   3932a
Die Analyse von Seuchenkurven. *Zeit. Hyg. Infekt.Kr.*, **123**, 361-73.

Mueller, C. G. 1949.   3933
Numerical transformations in the analysis of experimental data. *Psychol. Bull.*, **46**, 198-223.

Muench, H. 1945.   3934
Experiments and the statistician. *Nutr. Rev.*, **3**, 321-2.

Muench, H. 1947.   3935
Statistics in the planning and evaluation of health practices. *Amer. J. Publ. Health*, **37**, 1273-6.

Muhsam, H. V. 1946.   3935a
Representation of relative variability on a semi-logarithmic grid. *Nature*, **158**, 453.

Muhsam, H. V. 1947.   3936
Correlation in growth. *Hum. Biol.*, **19**, 260-9.

Muirhead, D. P. 1944.   3936a
The industrial application of mechanical engineering inspection. *Engng. Insp.*, **9** (3), 6-18.

Mukherjea, R. K. & Mukherjee, M. M. 1946.   3937
A note on concentration of income in Bengal villages. *Sankhyā*, **7**, 327-8.

Mukherjee, M. M. 1946.   3938
A note on concordance. *Sankhyā*, **7**, 441.

Mukherji, N. P. 1942.   3939
Why and what in factors. *Indian J. Psychol.*, **17**, 41-7.

Mullemeister, H. 1945.   3940
Mean lengths of line segments. *Amer. Math. Monthly*, **52**, 250-2.

Müller, E. 1942.   3940a
Genauigkeit der bei Reduktion von Fehlergleichungen eliminierten Unbekannten. *Zeit. Vermessungs.*, **71**, 186-90.

Muller, H. J. 1941.   3941
On judging the significance of a difference obtained by averaging essentially different series. *Amer. Nat.*, **75**, 264-71.

Müller, M. 1943.   3942
Note sur le produit de plusieurs probabilités d'extinction appliquées à des groupes de valides ou d'invalides. *Mitt. Ver. Schweiz. Versich.-Math.*, **43**, 89-97.

Muller, R. H. 1944.   3943
Verification of short range weather forecasts. (A survey of the literature.) *Bull. Amer. Met. Soc.*, **25**, 18-25, 47-53, 88-95.

Munger, J. H. 1944.   3943a
Statistical quality control at Bell Aircraft Corporation. *Industr. Qual. Contr.*, **1** (2), 3-9.

Munger, T. T. 1945.   3944
Sample scaling by trees. *For. Res. Note Pac. N.W. For. Exper. Sta.*, **33**, 12-13.

Münzner, H. 1947.   3945
Eine wahrscheinlichkeitstheoretische Behandlung der Jokereigenschaft. (German. Russian summary.) *Zeit. angew. Math. Mech.*, **25/27**, 119-22.

Münzner, H. 1947.   3946
Ein Kriterium für den Vergleich zweier Häufigkeiten. *Zeit. angew. Math Mech.*, **25/27**, 138-9.

Münzner, H. 1949.   3947
Die typischen Schlussweisen der mathematischen Statistik. *Mitt. Math. Statist.*, **1**, 5-20, 69-80, 185-202.

Münzner, H. 1949-50.   3948
Über die Verteilungszahl. *Arch. Math., Karlsruhe*, **2**, 42-8.

Münzner, H. & Schwarz, H. 1940.   3949
Ein Zuzammenhang zwischen Erneuerungszahlen und dem Moivre'schen Problem. *Arch. Math. Wirtsch.*, **6**, 46-9.

Murphy, R. B. 1948.   3950
Non-parametric tolerance limits. *Ann. Math. Statist.*, **19**, 581-9.

Murti, V. N. 1940.   3951
On a problem of arrangements. I. *J. Indian Math. Soc. (N.S.)*, **4**, 39-43.

Murti, V. N. 1942.   3952
A problem in combinations. *Math. Student*, **10**, 85-6.

Musham, M. V. 1947.   3953
Sur l'interprétation du coefficient de corrélation. *J. Soc. Statist. Paris*, **88**, 134-8.

Myers, R. J. 1941.   3953a
The validity and significance of male net reproduction rates. *J. Amer. Statist. Ass.*, **36**, 275-82.

Myers, R. J. 1943.   3954
A note on the variance of sex ratios. *Hum. Biol.*, **15**, 267-70.

Myers, R. J. 1947.   3955
Laymen don't have logarithmic eyes; The case against the casual use of semilog charts. *Amer. Statistician*, **1** (2), 17.

Myers, R. J. 1947.   3956
Shuffle along to better hands. *Bridge World*, **18**, 22-4.

Myers, R. J. & Ober, H. 1943.   3957
Statistics of wage stabilization. *J. Amer. Statist. Ass.*, **38**, 425-37.

Myers, W. M. 1943.   3958
Analysis of variance and covariance of chromosomal association and behaviour during the meiosis in clones of *Dactylis glomerata*. *Bot. Gaz.*, **104**, 541-52.

N

Nabeya, S. 1948.   3959
On the sampling distribution of the multiple correlation coefficient. (Japanese.) *Res. Mem. Inst. Statist. Math., Tokyo*, **4**, 381-5.

Nag, A. C. 1942.   3960
A study in the area distribution of infantile mortality in Calcutta during 1905-1935. *Sankhyā*, **6**, 193-4.

Nag, A. C. 1949.   3961
Some features of graduation. *Bull. Calcutta Statist. Ass.*, **2**, 120-5.

Nagel, E. 1945.   3962
Probability and non-demonstrative inference. *Phil. Phenom. Res.*, **5**, 485-507.

Nagel, E. 1946.   3963
Is the Laplaceian theory of probability tenable? *Phil. Phenom. Res.*, **6**, 614-18.

Nair, A. N. K. 1941.   3964
A statistical analysis of the family expenditure of a sample of working class families in Madras City. *Sankhyā*, **5**, 201-8.

Nair, A. N. K. 1941.   3965
On the distribution of Student's " t " and the correlation coefficient in samples from non-normal populations. *Sankhyā*, **5**, 383-400.

Nair, A. N. K. 1942.   3966
On the probability of obtaining k sets of consecutive successes in n trials. *Math. Student*, **10**, 83-4.

Nair, K. R. 1940.   3967
The median in tests by randomization. *Sankhyā*, **4**, 543-50.

Nair, K. R. 1940.   3968
Table of confidence interval for the median in samples from any continuous population. *Sankhyā*, **4**, 551-8.

Nair, K. R. 1940.   3969
The application of the technique of analysis of covariance to field experiments with several missing or mixed-up plots. *Sankhyā*, **4**, 581-8.

Nair, K. R. 1941.   3970
Balanced confounded arrangements for the 5^n type of experiment. *Sankyhā*, **5**, 57-70.

Nair, K. R. 1941.   3971
A note on the method of " fitting constants " for analysis of non-orthogonal data arranged in double classification. *Sankhyā*, **5**, 317-28.

Nair, K. R. 1942.   3972
Efficiency of the adjustment for concomitant characters in biological experiments. *Sankhyā*, **6**, 167-74.

Nair, K. R. 1943.   3973
Certain inequality relationships among the combinatorial parameters of incomplete block designs. *Sankhyā*, **6**, 255-9.

Nair, K. R. 1943.   3974
A note on the problem of k samples. *Current Science*, **12**, 112-13.

Nair, K. R. 1944.   3975
Calculation of standard errors and tests of significance of different types of treatment comparisons in split-plot and strip arrangements of field experiments. *Indian J. Agric. Sci.*, **14**, 315-19.

Nair, K. R. 1944.   3976
The recovery of inter-block information in incomplete block designs. *Sankhyā*, **6**, 383-90.

Nair, K. R. 1947.   3977
A note on the mean deviation from the median. *Biometrika*, **34**, 360-2.

Nair, K. R. 1948.   3978
The distribution of the extreme deviate from the sample mean and its Studentized form. *Biometrika*, **35**, 118-44.

Nair, K. R. 1948.   3979
Statistical methods and experimental design. *Indian Forester*, **74**, 247-50.

Nair, K. R. 1948.   3980
The Studentized form of the extreme mean square test in the analysis of variance. *Biometrika*, **35**, 16-31.

Nair, K. R. 1948.   3981
Certain symmetrical properties of unbiased estimates of variance and covariance. *J. Indian Soc. Agric. Statist.*, **1**, 162-72.

Nair, K. R. 1949.   3982
On the application of statistical quality control methods in wood-based industries. *Indian Forest Leaflet (Statistical)*, no. 109.

Nair, K. R. 1949.   3983
The efficiency of Gini's mean difference. *Bull. Calcutta Statist. Ass.*, **2**, 129-30.

Nair, K. R. 1949.   3984
Modern inventory methods. *Agric. Situation in India*, **4**, 178-81.

Nair, K. R. 1949.   3985
A further note on the mean deviation from the median. *Biometrika*, **36**, 234-5.

Nair, K. R. & Banerjee, K. S. 1943.   3986
A note on the fitting of straight lines if both the variables are subject to error. *Sankhyā*, **6**, 331.

Nair, K. R. & Bose, P. K. 1945.   3987
Influence of humidity and temperature on the yield of cotton. *Sankhyā*, **7**, 213-16.

Nair, K. R. & Mahalanobis, P. C. 1940.   3988
A simplified method of analysis of quasi-factorial experiments in square lattice with a preliminary note on joint analysis of yield of paddy and straw. *Indian J. Agric. Sci.*, **10**, 663-85.

Nair, K. R. & Rao, C. R. 1941.   3989
Confounded designs for asymmetrical factorial experiments. *Science & Culture*, **7**, 313-14.

Nair, K. R. & Rao, C. R. 1942.   3990
Confounded designs for the $k \times p^m \times q^n$... type of factorial experiments. *Science & Culture*, **7**, 361-2.

Nair, K. R. & Rao, C. R. 1942.   3991
A general class of quasi-factorial designs leading to confounded designs for factorial experiments. *Science & Culture*, **7**, 457-8.

Nair, K. R. & Rao, C. R. 1942.   3992
A note on partially balanced incomplete block designs. *Science & Culture*, **7**, 568-9.

Nair, K. R. & Rao, C. R. 1942.   3993
Incomplete block designs for experiments involving several groups of varieties. *Science & Culture*, **7**, 615-16.

Nair, K. R. & Rao, C. R. 1948.   3994
Confounding in asymmetrical factorial experiments. *J. R. Statist. Soc. B*, **10**, 109-31.

Nair, K. R. & Shrivastava, M. P. 1942.   3995
On a simple method of curve fitting. *Sankhyā*, **6**, 121-32.

Nair, K. R., Hedayetullah, S. & Sen, S. 1944.   3996
Influence of dates of planting and spacings on some winter varieties of rice. *Indian J. Agric. Sci.*, **14**, 248-59.

Nair, U. S. 1941.   3997
Probability statements regarding the ratio of standard deviations and correlation coefficient in a bivariate normal population. *Sankhyā*, **5**, 151-6.

Nair, U. S. 1941.   3998
A comparison of tests for the significance of the difference between two variances. *Sankhyā*, **5**, 157-64.

Nair, U. S. & Sastry, S. 1948.   3999
Tests of statistical hypotheses. *Math. Student*, **16**, 80-6.

Nakagami, M. 1940.   4000
A method of calculating probability by means of differential operator. *Nippon Elect. Commun. Engng.*, **21**, 28-34.

Nakagami, M. 1940.   4001
Study on the resultant amplitude of many vibrations whose phases and amplitudes are at random. *Nippon Elec. Commun. Engng.*, **22**, 69-92.

Nakagami, M. & Ohno, M. 1940.   4002
On the resultant intensity of a number of vibrations whose phase are at random. *Nippon Elect. Commun. Engng.*, **19**, 129-37.

Nakano, H. 1944.   4003
Über stochastischen Prozess. I. *Proc. Imp. Acad. Tokyo*, **20**, 513-18.

Nanda, D. N. 1948.   4004
Distribution of a root of a determinantal equation. *Ann. Math. Statist.*, **19**, 47-57.

Nanda, D. N. 1948.   4005
Limiting distribution of a root of a determinantal equation. *Ann. Math. Statist.*, **19**, 340-50.

Nanda, D. N. 1949.   4006
Efficiency of the application of discriminant function in plant-selection. *J. Indian Soc. Agric. Statist.*, **2**, 8-19.

Nanda, D. N. 1949.   4007
The standard errors of discriminant function coefficients in plant-breeding experiments. *J. R. Statist. Soc. B*, **11**, 283-90.

Nanda, D. N., Afzal, M. & Panse, V. G. 1944.   4008
A statistical study of flower production in cotton. *Indian J. Agric. Sci.*, **14**, 78-88.

Nandi, H. K. 1945.   4009
On the relation between certain types of tactical configurations. *Bull. Calcutta Math. Soc.*, **37**, 92-4.

Nandi, H. K. 1946.   4010
Enumeration of non-isomorphic solutions of balanced incomplete block designs. *Sankhyā*, **7**, 305-12. (Also: *Proc. Indian Sci. Congr.*, 1945.)

Nandi, H. K. 1946.   4011
A further note on non-isomorphic solutions of incomplete block designs. *Sankhyā*, **7**, 313-16.

Nandi, H. K. 1946.   4012
Note on tests applied to samples from normal bivariate population. *Science & Culture*, **12**, 249.

Nandi, H. K. 1946.   4013
On the power function of Studentised D^2-statistic. *Bull. Calcutta Math. Soc.*, **38**, 79-84.

Nandi, H. K. 1946.   4014
On the average power of test criteria. *Sankhyā*, **8**, 67-72. (Also: *Proc. Indian Sci. Congr.*, 1945.)

Nandi, H. K. 1947.   4015
A mathematical set-up leading to analysis of a class of designs. *Sankhyā*, **8**, 172-6.

Nandi, H. K. 1947.   4016
A note on the Student's t for paired samples. *Bull. Calcutta Math. Soc.*, **39**, 61-4.

Nandi, H. K. 1947.   4017
Misuse of statistics. *Bull. Calcutta Statist. Ass.*, **1**, 16-19.

Nandi, H. K. 1947.   4018
Tests of significance on multivariate samples. *Bull. Calcutta Statist. Ass.*, **1**, 42-3.

Nandi, H. K. 1948.   4190
Choosing a random sample. *Bull. Calcutta Statist. Ass.*, **1**, 143-52.

Nandi, H. K. 1948.   4020
Use of well-known statistics in sequential analysis. *Sankhyā*, **8**, 339-44.

Nandi, H. K. 1949.   4021
" t " test on non-normal populations. *Bull. Calcutta Statist. Ass.*, **2**, 32-7.

Nandi, H. K. 1949.   4022
A critique of U.P. Anthropometric survey. *Bull. Calcutta Statist. Ass.*, **2**, 95-107.

Nandi, H. K. 1949.   4023
Indian national sample survey. *Bull. Calcutta Statist. Ass.*, **3**, 11-20.

Nandi, H. K. 1949.   4024
A note on conditional tests of significance. *Bull. Calcutta Math. Soc.*, **41**, 121-4.

Narain, R. D. 1946.   4025
Frequency distribution of χ^2 constituents under a linear constraint. *Proc. Benares Math. Soc. (N.S.)*, **8** (1), 33-9.

Narain, R. D. 1948.   4026
A new approach to sampling distributions of the multivariate normal theory. I, II. *J. Indian Soc. Agric. Statist.*, **1**, 59-69; 137-46.

Narain, R. D. 1948.   4027
On the distribution of estimated error components in analysis of variance and covariance. *J. Indian Soc. Agric. Statist.*, **1**, 70-9.

Narain, R. D. 1949.   4027[a]
On the completely unbiased character of tests of independence in multivariate normal systems. *Current Science*, **18**, 41-2.

Narain, R. D. 1949. 4028
Some results on discriminant functions. *J. Indian Soc. Agric. Statist.*, **2**, 49-59.

Näslund, M. 1945. 4029
The number of sample trees and the accuracy of the cubic volume in forest estimation by stem counting. *Medd. Skogsförsöksanst.*, **34**, 285-308.

Nass, C. A. G. 1946-7. 4030
Het quantitatieve verband tussen dosering en letaliteit bij proefdieren. (On the quantal response of animals to drugs.) *Statistica Neerlandica*, **1**, 257-66.

Nass, C. A. G. 1948. 4031
De grondslagen der regressieanalyse, met een toepassing op een doseringsletalitetproef. (The principles of the analysis of regression with an application to dosage mortality.) *Statistica Neerlandica*, **2**, 74-94.

Nass, C. A. G. 1949. 4032
Ein statistisches Verfahren zur qualitativen Bestimmung der Immunität mittels Hautreaktionen. (German. English summary.) *Statistica Neerlandica*, **3**, 31-41.

Nataf, A. & Roy, R. 1948. 4033
Remarques et suggestions relatives aux nombres-indices. *Econometrica*, **16**, 330-46.

Nath, P. 1948. 4034
Percentage inspection. *J. R. Statist. Soc. A*, **111**, 235-7.

Natta, G. 1945. 4035
Leggi di ripartizione delle singole specie molecolari nei prodotti di una catena di reazioni successive. *R. C. 1st Lombardo sci. Lett. Cl. Sci. Mat. Nat.*, (3) **9(78)**, 307-20.

Naylor, G. F. K. 1945. 4036
Estimation of multiple correlation by means of stereographic projection. *Nature*, **156**, 58-9.

Neal, N. R. 1945. 4037
The application of statistical methods to the control of industrial costs. *Proc. Inst. Mech. Engrs.*, **152**, 76-81.

Neel, J. V., Kodani, M., Brewer, R. & Anderson, R. C. 1949. 4038
The incidence of consanguineous matings in Japan, with remarks on the estimation of comparative gene frequencies and the expected rate of appearance of induced recessive mutations. *Amer. J. Hum. Genet.*, **1**, 156-78.

Neiswanger, W. A. & Allen, H. K. 1947. 4038[a]
A well-rounded curriculum in statistics. *Amer. Statistician*, **1** (1), 16-19.

Neuberger, H. 1945. 4039
A simple mechanical aid in the statistical analysis of climatic data. *Trans. Amer. Geophys. Un.* (*Sect. Meteorol.*), **36**, 443-5.

Nevens, W. B. 1945. 4039[a]
A comparison of sampling procedures in making pasture yield determinations. *J. Dairy Sci.*, **28**, 171-85.

Newcombe, H. E. 1948. 4039[b]
Delayed phenotypic expression of spontaneous mutations in *Escherichia coli*. *Genetics*, **33**, 447-76.

Newton, R. G. 1945. 4040
A simplified method of calculating standard errors. *Chemistry & Industry*, **1945**, 322-3.

Neyman, J. 1941. 4041
Fiducial argument and the theory of confidence intervals. *Biometrika*, **32**, 128-50.

Neyman, J. 1941. 4042
On a statistical problem arising in routine analyses and in sampling inspections of mass production. *Ann. Math. Statist.*, **12**, 46-76.

Neyman, J. 1942. 4043
Basic ideas and some recent results of the theory of testing statistical hypotheses. *J. R. Statist. Soc.*, **105**, 292-327.

Neyman, J. 1944. 4044
Probabilities of errors of the second kind in testing linear hypotheses. *Yearbook Amer. Philos. Soc.*, **1944**, 141-4.

Neyman, J. 1946. 4045
Un théorème d'existence. *C. R. Acad. Sci., Paris*, **222**, 843-5.

Neyman, J. 1947. 4046
Outline of statistical treatment of problems of diagnosis. *Publ. Health Rep.*, **62**, 1449-56.

Neyman, J. 1947. 4047
Raisonnement inductif ou comportement inductif? Les conceptions modernes de la statistique mathématique. *Proc. 25th. Session Int. Statist. Inst. Conf. Washington, D.C.*, 1947 (Publ. 1951), **3A**, 423-33.

Neyman, J. 1949. 4048
Contribution to the theory of the χ^2 test. *Proc. Berkeley Symp. Math. Statist. and Probab.*, 1945-6, pp. 239-73.

Neyman, J. 1949. 4049
On the problem of estimating the number of schools of fish. *Univ. Calif. Pub. Statist.*, **1** (3), 21-36.

Neyman, J. & Scott, E. L. 1948. 4050
Consistent estimates based on partially consistent observations. *Econometrica*, **16**, 1-32.

Nichol, A. J. 1941. 4051
Probability analysis in the theory of demand, net revenue and price. *J. Polit. Econ.*, **49**, 637-61.

Nicholson, C. 1941. 4052
A geometrical analysis of the frequency-distribution of the ratio between two variables. *Biometrika*, **32**, 16-28.

Nicholson, C. 1943. 4053
Probability integral for two variables. *Biometrika*, **33**, 59-72.

Nicholson, J. L. 1949. 4054
Variations in working class expenditure. *J. R. Statist. Soc. A*, **112**, 359-418.

Nicolas, M. 1948. 4055
Kenn- oder Messziffern? *Statist. Praxis*, **3**, 69-70.

Nicolas, M. 1949. 4056
Mathem... und Statistik. *Statist. Praxis*, **4**, 17-20.

Nicolas, M. 1949. 4057
Grundbegriffe der allgemeinen Statistik. *Statist. Praxis*, **4**, 57-8.

Nicolini, T. 1945. 4058
Un tipo di curva a curvatura distribuita come la densità della probabilità nella legge normale. *R. C. Accad. Sci. Fis. Mat. Napoli*, (4) **13**, 109-15.

Niedermann, H. 1946. 4059
Untersuchungen über den Wahrscheinlichkeitscharakter der Sterblichkeit. *Mitt. Ver. Schweiz. Versich.-Math.*, **46**, 131-68.

Nielsen, E. L. 1944. 4060
Analysis of variation in *Panicum virgatum*. *J. Agric. Res.*, **69**, 327-53.

Nielsen, K. L. & Goldstein, L. 1947. 4061
An algorithm for least squares. *J. Math. Phys.*, **26**, 120-32.

Niessen, A. M. 1945. 4062
On the summation of certain progressions useful in time series analysis. *J. Amer. Statist. Ass.*, **40**, 98-100.

Niessen, A. M. 1948. 4063
Actuarial estimates for public sickness insurance plans. *J. Amer. Statist. Ass.*, **43**, 61-73.

Nilssen, B. 1945. 4064
Some remarks on counting. (Norwegian.) *Nord. Mat. Tidskr.*, **27**, 106-11.

Nissen, Ø. 1947. 4065
The interaction between neighbouring plots in root experiments. *Meld. Norg. LandbrHøjsk.*, **27**, 155-64.

Nissen, Ø. & Ottestad, P. 1943. 4066
On the analysis of variance and the effect of non-normality. *Meld. Norg. LandbrHøgsk.*, **23**, 475-96.

Nixon, H. K. 1946. 4067
Internal evidence of validity of a rating scale. *J. Psychol.*, **22**, 97-115.

Noether, G. E. 1948. 4068
On confidence limits for quantiles. *Ann. Math. Statist.*, **19**, 416-19.

Noether, G. E. 1949. 4069
Confidence limits in the non-parametric case. *J. Amer. Statist. Ass.*, **44**, 89-100.

Noether, G. E. 1949. 4070
On a theorem by Wald and Wolfowitz. *Ann. Math. Statist.*, **20**, 455-8.

Nogueira, R. 1947. 4071
Sobre um sistema de equações algébricao e sua aplicação ao ajuestamento das leis de sobrevivência. *Bol. Inst. Brasil. Atuár.*, **3**, 88-147.

Noland, E. W. 1945. 4072
Worker attitude and industrial absenteeism: a statistical appraisal. *Amer. Sociol. Rev.*, **10**, 503-10.

Nolfi, P. 1941. 4073
Die jährlichen Sterblichkeitsschwankungen und ihre wahrscheinlichkeitstheoretische Erfassung. (French, English and Italian summaries.) *Trans. 12th. Int. Congr. Actuar.*, *Lucerne*, 1940, **1**, 395-408.

Nolfi, P. 1942. 4074
Die Darstellung stochastischer Vorgänge mit Hilfe der Wahrscheinlichkeitstheorie. *Verh. Schweiz. natur. Ges.*, **1942**, 77.

Nolfi, P. 1943. 4075
Wahrscheinlichkeit unstetiger Vorgänge bei kontinuierlich wirkenden Ursachen. *Comment. Math. Helvetia*, **15**, 36-44.

Nolfi, P. 1944. 4076
Zur Bestimmung der Rückschlusswahrscheinlichkeit einer geschlossenen Gesamtheit. *Mitt. Ver. Schweiz. Versich.-Math.*, **44**, 217-20.

Nolfi, P. 1945. 4077
Zur mathematischen Darstellung wachsender Gesamtheiten. *Mitt. Ver. Schweiz. Versich.-Math.*, **45**, 311-21.

Nordberg, S. 1947. 4078
Ein Vergleich zwischen Probeflächenmethode und Linientaxierungsmethode bei quantitativen Aufnahmen des Vogelbestandes. *Ornis Fennica*, **24**, 87-92.

Nordin, J. A. 1944. 4079
Determining sample size. *J. Amer. Statist. Ass.*, **39**, 497-506.

Nordskog, A. W. & Crump, S. L. 1948. 4080
Systematic and random sampling for estimated egg production in poultry. *Biometrics*, **4**, 223-33.

Nordskog, A. W., Clark, R. T. & Van Horn, L. 4081
1945. Sampling wool clips for clean yield by the core boring method. *J. Animal Sci.*, **4**, 113-21.

Nørlund, N. E. 1940. 4082
Ausgleichung nach der Methode der kleinsten Quadrate bei gruppenweiser Anordnung der Beobachtungen. *Acta Math.*, **72**, 283-353.

Nørlund, N. E. 1943. 4083
Determination of the weights for the unknowns in the graduation of elements. (Danish.) *Festskr. Prof. J. F. Steffensen*, pp. 126-8.

Norman, O. K. 1942. 4084
Results of highway capacity studies. *Public Roads*, **23**, 57-81.

Norman, O. K. 1949. 4085
Fundamentals of highway capacity. *Public Roads*, **25**, 215-34.

Norman, O. K. 1949. 4086
Relating hourly capacities to annual average volumes and peak flows. *Public Roads*, **25**, 268-77.

Norris, N. 1940. 4087
The standard errors of the geometric and harmonic means and their application to index numbers. *Ann. Math. Statist.*, **11**, 445-8.

North, D. D. 1943. 4088
Analysis of the factors which determine signal noise discrimination. *R.C.A. Lab. Rep.* PTR-6C.

North, J. D. 1947. 4089
The probability approach to manual tracking. *Boulton Paul Aircraft Ltd., Wolverhampton, Tech. Rep. no. 50.*

Norton, H. W. 1945. 4090
Calculation of the chi-square for complex contingency tables. *J. Amer. Statist. Ass.*, **40**, 251-8.

Norton, H. W. 1946. 4091
Estimating the correlation coefficient. *Bull. Amer. Met. Soc.*, **27**, 589-90.

Norton, H. W. 1949. 4092
Estimation of linkage in Ruckers' pedigree of nystagmus and colour-blindness. *Amer. J. Hum. Genet.,* **1**, 55-65.

Numata, M. 1949. 4093
The basis of sampling in the statistics of plant communities. *Bot. Mag., Tokyo,* **62**, 35-8.

Núñez Bazalar, T. 1945. 4094
On the law of large numbers of the theory of probability. (Spanish.) *Rev. Cienc., Lima,* **47**, 601-43.

Nuyens, M. & Grosjean, C. 1949. 4095
Sur la diffusion des neutrons thermiques. *C. R. Acad. Sci., Paris,* **228**, 245-6.

Nybølle, H. C. 1943. 4096
Das Preisniveau als statistische Variable. (Danish.) *Festskr. Prof. J. F. Steffensen,* pp. 113-25.

O

Oberg, E. N. 1947. 4097
Approximate formulas for the radii of circles which include a specified fraction of a normal bivariate distribution. *Ann. Math. Statist.,* **18**, 442-7.

Obrechkoff, N. 1947. 4098
Sur quelques lois asymptotiques de probabilités et sur les solutions bornées de quelques équations intégrales singulières et des équations linéaires à un nombre infini des inconnues. (Bulgarian. French summary.) *Annu. Fac. Sci. Phys. Math. Univ. Sofia,* I, **43**, 269-349.

Obrechkoff, N. 1948. 4099
Sur quelques lois asymptotiques de probabilités. (Bulgarian. French summary.) *Annu. Fac. Sci. Phys. Math. Univ. Sofia,* I, **44**, 201-33.

Obukhov, A. M. 1940. 4100
Eine Korrelationstheorie der Vektoren. (Russian. German summary.) *Uch. Zap. Moskov. Gos. Univ., Ser. Mat.,* **45**, 73-92.

Obukhov, A. M. 1946. 4101
The statistics of turbulence. *Trudy Inst. Theor. Geofiz. Akad. Nauk SSSR,* **1**.

Obukhov, A. M. 1947. 4102
Applicability of test figures. (Russian. English summary.) *Zh. Prikl. Mat. Mekh. Akad. Nauk SSSR,* **11**, 485-8.

Occhialini, G. & de Souza Santos, M. D. 1941. 4103
On a method of recording random events. *Ann. Acad. Brasil. Sci.,* **13**, 57-62.

O'Dea, W. T. 1940. 4103ᵃ
Statistical methods and factors of safety: an argument for the revision of existing standards. *J. Inst. Elect. Engrs.,* **87**, 22-32. (Also: *Mech. World,* **107**, 539-40.)

Odhnoff, W. 1946. 4104
Some studies of the characteristic functions and the semi-ínvariants of Pearson's frequency-functions. *Förs.-mat. Stud. Filip Lundberg,* pp. 168-79 (Stockholm).

Odone, V. 1942. 4105
Il collaudo di prodotti in serie ed il calcolo delle probabilità. *Atti Accad. Sci. Torino, Sci. Fis. Mat. Nat.,* **77**, 407-30.

Offord, A. C. 1945. 4106
An inequality for sums of independent random variables. *Proc. Lond. Math. Soc.,* (2) **48**, 467-77.

Ogawa, J. 1949. 4107
On the independence of bilinear and quadratic forms of a random sample from a normal population. *Ann. Inst. Statist. Math., Tokyo,* **1**, 83-108.

Ogawa, J. & Nabeya, S. 1949. 4108
On the independence of statistics. (Japanese.) *Sûgaku,* **2**, 69-73.

Ogawara, M. 1946. 4109
On the normal stationary Markov process of higher order. *Bull. Math. Statist.,* **2**, 101-19.

Ogawara, M. 1948. 4110
Note on Brownian motions. (Japanese.) *Sûgaku,* **1**, 123-4.

Ogawara, M. 1948. 4111
On correlation functions of random vector in different dimensions. (Japanese.) *Sûgaku,* **1**, 216-19.

O'Hanlon, G. S. A. 1940. 4111ᵃ
An investigation into the relationship between fertility and intelligence. *Brit. J. Educ. Psychol.,* **10**, 196-211.

Okaya, T. 1941. 4112
Numerical integration by Tchebychef's q-functions. *Proc. Phys.-Math. Soc. Japan,* (3) **19**, 273-82.

Okrouhly, J. 1947. 4113
Statistické metody uzité v regionalnim plánováni. (Statistical methods employed in regional planning.) (Czech. English, French and Russian summaries.) *Statist. Obzor,* **27**, 232-7.

Olbrycht, T. M. 1941. 4114
Statistical analysis of black colour in Wessex saddleback breed. *Ann. Eugen.,* **11**, 80-8.

Olbrycht, T. M. 1943. 4115
The statistical basis of selection in animal husbandry: studies on life performance of brood sows. I. An analysis of variance and covariance of progeny born and reared. II. The judging of brood sows by their number of offspring born and reared in earliest litters. *J. Agric. Sci.,* **33**, 28-43; 74-84.

Olbrycht, T. 1948. 4116
Significance of statistical methods in the experimental work. (Polish. English summary.) *Przegl. Hodowl.,* **16** (1-3), 12-13.

Olds, E. B. 1949. 4117
The city block as a unit for recording and analysing urban data. *J. Amer. Statist. Ass.* **44**, 485-500.

Olds, E. G. 1940. 4118
On a method of sampling. *Ann. Math. Statist.,* **11**, 355-8.

Olds, E. G. 1942. 4118ᵃ
On some of the essentials of control chart analysis. *Trans. Amer. Soc. Mech. Engrs.,* **64**, 521-7.

Olds, E. G. 1945. 4118[b]
Statistical quality control of methods and materials. *Materials & Methods*, **22**, 1097-1101.

Olds, E. G. 1949. 4119
The 5 per cent. significance levels for sums of squares of rank differences and a correction. *Ann. Math. Statist.*, **20**, 117-18.

Olds, E. G. & Wells, C. 1949. 4119[a]
Statistical methods for evaluating the quality of certain wrought steel products. *Amer. Soc. Metals*, no. 16, 46 pp.

Olekiewicz, M. 1949. 4120
On the efficiency of biased estimates. (English. Polish summary.) *Ann. Univ. Mariae Curie-Sklodowska A*, **3**, 103-40.

Olifiers, E. 1947-9. 4121
Uma simbologia racional das fórmulas dos " expostos ao risco ". *Bol. Inst. Brasil. Atuár.*, **3**, 148-82; **5**, 38-59.

Olmstead, P. S. 1940. 4122
Note on theoretical and observed distributions of repetitive occurrences. *Ann. Math. Statist.*, **11**, 363-6.

Olmstead, P. S. 1946. 4123
Distribution of sample arrangements for runs up and down. *Ann. Math. Statist.*, **17**, 24-33.

Olmstead, P. S. & Tukey, J. W. 1947. 4124
A corner test for association. *Ann. Math. Statist.*, **18**, 495-513.

Olmstead, P. S. & Walker, A. C. 1945. 4124[a]
Textile yarn abrasion test. *Textile Res. J.*, **15**, 201-22.

Olshevsky, L. 1940. 4125
Two properties of sufficient statistics. *Ann. Math. Statist.*, **11**, 104-6.

O'Neil, J. B. 1942. 4126
The analysis of covariance by the method of individual comparisons. *Scientific Agric.*, **22**, 721-4.

O'Neil, J. B. & Gutteridge, H. S. 1941. 4127
A note on the calculation of standard errors for treatment means after adjustment for regression. *Scientific Agric.*, **21**, 358-9.

Onicescu, O. 1940. 4128
La probabilité d'un événement isolé. *Bull. Sect. Sci. Acad. Roum.*, **22**, 280-6.

Onicescu, O. 1943. 4129
Les structures planes. *Bull. Math. Soc. Roum. Sci.*, **45**, 63-76.

Onicescu, O. 1946. 4130
Les séries de structures. *Bull. Sect. Sci. Acad. Roum.*, **26**, 503-10.

Onicescu, O. & Mihoc, G. 1940. 4131
Comportement asymptotique des chaînes à liaisons complètes. *Disquisit. Math. Phys.*, **1**, 61-2.

Onicescu, O. & Mihoc, G. 1940. 4132
Propriétés asymptotiques des chaînes de Markoff étudiées à l'aide de la fonction caractéristique. *Mathematica, Cluj*, **16**, 13-43.

Onicescu, O. & Mihoc, G. 1940. 4133
Sur les sommes de variables enchaînées dans le cas d'un ensemble numérable de valeurs. *Bull. Sect. Sci. Acad. Roum.*, **22**, 231-6.

Onicescu, O. & Mihoc, G. 1943. 4134
Un cas d'exception dans la théorie des chaînes de Markoff. *Bull. Sect. Sci. Acad. Roum.*, **24**, 401-8.

Onicescu, O. & Mihoc, G. 1943. 4135
Les chaînes de variables aléatoires. Problèmes asymptotiques. *Étud. Acad. Roum.*, **14**, 167 pp.

Onicescu, O. & Mihoc, G. 1944. 4136
Le coefficient de dispersion et la dépendance des épreuves. *Bull. Math. Soc. Roum. Sci.*, **46**, 77-80.

Onicescu, O. & Mihoc, G. 1947. 4137
Chaînes de mouvements discontinus et changements d'état. *Bull. Math. Soc. Roum. Sci.*, **48**, 32-42.

Ono, K. 1940. 4138
Eine Ausgleichungsmethode der statistischen Reihen. *Jap. J. Math.*, **17**, 117-26.

Ono, K. 1941. 4139
Über eine Art der Ausgleichung der statistischen Reihen. *Jap. J. Math.*, **17**, 513-15.

Onoyama, T. 1949. 4140
On the linear translatable stochastic functional equation. *Kōdai, Tokyo Inst. Tech.*, **3**, 33-6.

Onsager, L. 1944. 4141
Crystal statistics. I. A two-dimensional model with an order-disorder transition. *Phys. Rev.*, **65**, 117-149.

Opatowski, I. 1942. 4142
An inverse problem concerning a chain process. *Proc. Nat. Acad. Sci. U.S.A.*, **28**, 83-8.

Opatowski, I. 1945. 4143
Markoff chains with reverse transitions. *Proc. Nat. Acad. Sci. U.S.A.*, **31**, 411-14.

Opatowski, I. 1945-6. 4144
Chain processes and their biophysical applications. I, II. The effect of recovery. *Bull. Math. Biophys.*, **7**, 161-80; **8**, 7-15.

Opatowski, I. 1946. 4145
The probabilistic approach to the effects of radiations and variability of sensitivity. *Bull. Math. Biophys.*, **8**, 101-19.

Opatowski, I. 1947. 4146
Simple Markoff chains with reverse transitions: The time moments. *Bull. Amer. Math. Soc.*, **53**, 68-9.

Orcutt, G. H. 1948. 4147
A new regression analyser. *J. R. Statist. Soc. A*, **111**, 54-70.

Orcutt, G. H. 1948. 4148
A study of the autoregressive nature of the time-series used for Tinbergen's model of the economic system of the United States, 1919-1932. *J. R. Statist. Soc. B*, **10**, 1-53.

Orcutt, G. H. & Cochrane, D. 1949. 4149
A sampling study of the merits of autoregressive and reduced form transformations in regression analysis. *J. Amer. Statist. Ass.*, **44**, 356-72.

Orcutt, G. H. & James, S. F. 1948. 4150
Testing the significance of correlation between time series. *Biometrika*, **35**, 397-413.

Ording, A. 1941. 4151
Annual ring analyses of spruce and pine. *Medd. Skogforsöksvesen*, **7**, 101-354.

Ornstein, L. S. & Milatz, J. M. W. 1941.　　4152
The analogy between the statistics of numbers and
statistical mechanics. *Proc. Kon. Ned. Akad. Wetensch.*,
44, 163-72.

Orts Aracil, J. M. 1941.　　4153
Estabilidad de la leg normal de probabilidad depen-
diente de dos variables aleatorias. (The stability of
the normal probability distribution for two random
variables.) (Spanish.) *Rev. Mat. Hisp.-Amer.*, (4) **1**,
34-6.

Orts Aracil, J. M. 1941.　　4154
Los polinomios de Legendre y el esquema de las
pruebas repetidas. (The Legendre polynomials and
the scheme of repeated trials.) (Spanish.) *Rev. Mat.
Hisp.-Amer.*, (4) **1**, 198-201.

Orts Aracil, J. M. 1943.　　4155
Sobre el comportamiento de ciertas probabilidades.
(On the behaviour of certain probabilities.) (Spanish.)
Rev. Mat. Hisp.-Amer., (4) **3**, 157-63.

Orts Aracil, J. M. 1944.　　4156
Convergencia de algunos valores medios. (Con-
vergence of some mean values.) (Spanish.) *Rev.
Mat. Hisp-Amer.*, (4) **4**, 127-30.

Orts Aracil, J. M. 1944.　　4157
Sobre ciertas probabilidades iteradas. (On certain
iterated probabilities.) (Spanish.) *Rev. Mat. Hisp.-
Amer.*, (4) **4**, 153-8.

Orts Aracil, J. M. 1945.　　4158
Sobre alguras sucesiones de variables aleatorias.
(On some sequences of random variables.) (Spanish.)
Rev. Mat. Hisp.-Amer., (4) **5**, 53-7.

Orts Aracil, J. M. 1946.　　4159
Una propiedad de reciprocidad de la función característica. (A reciprocity property of the characteristic
function.) (Spanish.) *Rev. Mat. Hisp.-Amer.*, (4)
6, 43-7.

Osborne, J. G. 1941.　　4160
On the precision of estimates from systematic versus
random samples. *Science*, **94**, 584-5.

Osborne, J. G. 1942.　　4161
Sampling errors of systematic and random surveys of
cover-type areas. *J. Amer. Statist. Ass.*, **37**, 256-64.

Osgood, O. T. 1949.　　4162
Results of two sampling methods used in farm management research. *J. Farm Econ.*, **31**, 157-68.

Osida, I. 1942.　　4163
On the harmonic analysis of random functions. *Proc.
Phys.-Math. Soc. Japan*, (3) **24**, 292-6.

Osida, I. 1942.　　4164
Brownian motion in a plasto-elastic medium. *Proc.
Phys.-Math. Soc. Japan*, (3) **24**, 599-601.

Osida, I. 1943.　　4165
Statistical theory of transport phenomena. *Proc.
Phys.-Math. Soc. Japan*, (3) **25**, 590-4.

Ostrowski, A. 1940.　　4166
Sur la convergence et l'estimation des erreurs dans
quelques procédés de résolution des équations
numériques. *Memorial vol. dedicated to D. A. Grave,
Moscow*, pp. 213-34.

Ostrowski, A. 1946.　　4167
Sur la formule de Moivre-Laplace. *C. R. Acad. Sci.,
Paris*, **223**, 1090-2.

Ott, E. R. 1944.　　4168
Difference equations in average value problems. *Amer.
Math. Monthly*, **51**, 570-8.

Ott, E. R. 1947.　　4168[a]
Indirect calibration of an electronic test-set. *Industr.
Qual. Contr.*, **3** (4), 11-14.

Ottaviani, G. 1940.　　4169
Sullo scarto quadratico medio della frequenza di
transvariazione. *Atti 1ma Riun. Sci. Soc. Ital. Statist.*,
pp. 93-4.

Ottaviani, G. 1940.　　4170
La teoria del rischio del Lundberg e il suo legame con
la teoria classica del rischio. *G. Ist. Ital. Attuari*, **11**,
163-89.

Ottaviani, G. 1940.　　4171
Sulle funzioni indipendenti. *G. Ist. Ital. Attuari*, **11**,
270-82.

Ottaviani, G. 1941.　　4172
Sulle formule de contribuzione e sulla partecipazione
degli assicurati agli utili. *G. Ist. Ital. Attuari*, **12**,
191-207.

Ottaviani, G. 1942.　　4173
Sulle tavole di mortalità. *G. Ist. Ital. Attuari*, **13**, 66-76.

Ottaviani, G. 1947.　　4174
Su una equazione integrale della statistica matematica.
Atti Accad. Lincei, R. C. Sci. Fis. Mat. Nat., (8) **3**,
59-63.

Ottaviani, G. 1949.　　4175
Intorno alle probabilità di Karup e legame con la
teoria dei capitali accumulati. *Atti Accad. Lincei,
R. C. Sci. Fis. Mat.*, (8) **6**, 679-85.

Ottaviani, G. 1949.　　4176
La loi uniforme des grands nombres dans l'esprit de
la théorie classique des probabilités. Considérations
relatives au concept de nombre et aux liens avec la
théorie de M. de Misès. *Le Calcul des Probabilités et
ses Applications. Colloq. Int. Centre Nat. Rech. Sci.,
Paris*, **13**, 11-17.

Otter, R. 1949.　　4177
The multiplicative process. *Ann. Math. Statist.*, **20**,
206-24.

Ottestad, P. 1942.　　4177[a]
On periodical variations in the yield of the great sea
fisheries and the possibility of establishing yield
prognoses. *Rep. Norwegian Fishery & Marine Investigations*, **7** (5), 11 pp.

Ottestad, P. 1943.　　4178
On Bernoullian, Lexis, Poisson and Poisson-Lexis
series. *Skand. Aktuartidskr.*, **26**, 15-67.

Ottestad, P. 1944.　　4179
On certain compound frequency distributions. *Skand.
Aktuartidskr.*, **27**, 32-42.

Ottestad, P. 1948.　　4179[a]
Note on the χ^2 test. *Medd. Norg. LandbrHøgs.*, **6**, 1-4.

Ottestad, P. 1948.　　4180
On some discrete frequency functions. *Skand.
Aktuartidskr.*, **31**, 1-13.

Overman, A. & Li, J. C. R. 1948.   4181
Dependability of food judges as indicated by analysis
of scores of food testing panels. *Food Res.*, **13**, 441-9.

Overton, R. S. 1949.   4182
Use of semi-controlled mail surveys for initiating new
statistical series. *Agric. Econ. Res.*, **1**, 87-92.

Owen, A. R. G. 1948.   4183
Ancillary statistics and fiducial distributions. *Sankhyā*,
9, 1-18.

Owen, A. R. G. 1949.   4184
The theory of genetical recombination. I. Long-
chromosome arms. *Proc. Roy. Soc. B*, **136**, 67-94.

P

Pabst, W. R., Jr. 1947.   4184[a]
Statistical quality control in American industry.
*Proc. 25th. Session Int. Statist. Conf., Washington,
D.C.*, 1947 (Publ. 1951), 3A, 319-29.

Paddock, H. E. 1945.   4184[b]
The quality habit. *Industr. Qual. Contr.*, **1** (4), 3-5; 17.

Page, L. F. 1940.   4185
An example of periodic analysis of a persistent series.
Bull. Amer. Met. Soc., **21**, 196-9.

Paglino, F. 1941.   4186
Su la distribuzione dei guadagni degli assicurati.
Assicurazioni, **8** (4).

Paglino, F. 1941.   4187
Su la misura della fecondità matrimoniale della donna.
Metron, **14**, 287-408.

Paglino, F. 1942.   4188
Ulteriori contributi alla ricerca sperimentale sull'inter-
polazione di serie statistiche. *Atti 3za Riun. Sci.,
Soc. Ital. Statist.*, pp. 89-92.

Paglino, F. 1942.   4189
Su la concentrazione dei guadagni. *Atti 3za Riun.
Sci., Soc. Ital. Statist.*, pp. 298-314.

Pailloux, H. 1945.   4190
Sur un problème de répartition. *Ann. Univ. Grenoble,
Sci. Math. Phys.* (N.S.), **21**, 123-5.

Palacios, A. R. 1947.   4191
Eficiencia del diseño experimental lattice. *Chapingo*,
no. 15, 5-16.

Pall, G. 1945.   4192
The arithmetical invariants of quadratic forms. *Bull.
Amer. Math. Soc.*, **51**, 185-97.

Pallez, C. 1949.   4193
Normes de la statistique, du calcul des probabilités et
des erreurs de mesure. *J. Soc. Statist., Paris*, **90**,
125-33.

Palm, C. 1941.   4194
Mätnoggrannhet vid bestämning av trafikmängd
enligt genomsökningsförfarandet. (Swedish.) *Tekn.
Medd. Från. Kungl. Tele.*, nos. 7-9.

Palm, C. 1943.   4195
En formfaktor för bedömning av väntetidsfördelningar.
(Swedish.) *Tekn. Medd. Från. Kungl. Tele.*, no.
1-3.

Palm, C. 1943.   4196
Intensitätsschwankungen im Fernsprechverkehr. *Ericsson Technics*, **44**, 1-189.

Palm, C. 1946.   4197
Några Anmarkningar över de Erlang' ska Formlerna
for Upptaget system. (Swedish.) *Specialnummer for
Teletrafikteknik. Tekn. Medd. Från. Kungl. Tele*,
pp. 110.

Palm, C. 1947.   4198
The distribution of repairmen in servicing automatic
machines. (Swedish.) *Industritidningen Norden*, **75**,
75-80, 90-4, 119-23.

Palm, C. 1947.   4199
Waiting times when traffic has variable mean intensity.
Ericsson Rev., **24**, 102-7.

Palmer, G. L. 1943.   4200
Factors in the variability of response in enumerative
studies. *J. Amer. Statist. Ass.*, **38**, 143-52.

Palomba, G. 1947.   4201
Criteica delle osservazioni macroscopiche. *Riv. Ital.
Demogr. Statist.*, **1**, 23-33.

Palumbo, F. A. & Strugala, E. S. 1945.   4201[a]
Fraction defective of battery adapter used in Handie-
Talkie. *Industr. Qual. Contr.*, **2** (3), 6-8; 14.

Panraz, O. 1940.   4202
Sur la notion de probabilité. (Czech.) *Čas mat. fys.*,
69 (2), 73-81.

Panse, V. G. 1940.   4203
A statistical study of quantitative inheritance. *Ann.
Eugen.*, **10**, 76-105.

Panse, V. G. 1941.   4204
Studies in the technique of field experiments. V. Size
and shape of blocks and arrangement of plots in
cotton trials. *Indian J. Agric. Sci.*, **11**, 850-65.

Panse, V. G. 1942.   4205
Methods in plant breeding. *Indian J. Genet. and Plant
Breeding*, **2**, 151-8.

Panse, V. G. 1946.   4206
An application for the discriminant function for
selection in poultry. *J. Genet.*, **47**, 242-8.

Panse, V. G. 1946.   4207
Plot-size in yield surveys on cotton. *Current Science*,
15, 218-19.

Panse, V. G. 1947.   4208
Plot-size in yield surveys. *Nature*, **159**, 820.

Panse, V. G. & Ayachit, G. R. 1944.   4209
Ten per cent probability of z and the variance ratio.
Indian J. Agric. Sci., **14**, 244-7.

Panse, V. G. & Boktil, S. D. 1948.   4210
Estimation of genetic variability in plants. *J. Indian
Soc. Agric. Statist.*, **1**, 80-90.

Panse, V. G. & Kalamkar, R. J. 1944.   4211
Forecasting and estimation of crop yields. *Current
Science*, **13**, 120-4.

Panse, V. G. & Kalamkar, R. J. 1944.   4212
A further note on the estimation of crop yields. *Current
Science*, **13**, 223-5.

Panse, V. G. & Kalamkar, R. J. 1945.   4213
A large-scale yield survey on cotton. *Current Science*,
14, 287-91.

Panse, V. G. & Sahasrabudhe, V. B. 1943. 4214
A rapid method of sampling for fibre weight determination in cotton. *Indian J. Genet.*, 3, 28-44.

Panse, V. G. & Shaligram, G. C. 1947. 4215
Improvement of statistics of cotton production in India. *Indian Cotton Growing Rev.*, 1, 119-42.

Panse, V. G. & Sukhatme, P. V. 1948. 4216
Crop surveys in India. I. *J. Indian Soc. Agric. Statist.*, 1, 34-58.

Papadakis, J. S. 1940. 4217
A comparison of different methods of phytotechnical experimentation. *Rev. Argent. Agron.*, 7 297-362.

Parenti, G. 1941. 4218
Su un'estensione del coefficiente di correlazione. *Statistica, Ferrara*, 1, 382-400.

Parenti, G. 1941. 4219
Estensione di una relazione del Fréchet al coefficiente di correlazione parabolica di ordine *k*. *G. Economisti*, 3, 319-24.

Parenti, G. 1943. 4220
Sul rapporto di correlazione del Pearson e sulla misura della " strettezza " delle relazioni statistiche. *Statistica, Bologna*, 3, 217-42.

Parenti, G. 1946. 4221
Sull'errore medio del coefficiente di variabilità relativa *Arch. Antrop. Etnologia*, 76.

Park, B. C. & Day, B. B. 1942. 4221[a]
A simplified method for determining the condition of white-tailed deer in relation to available forage. *U.S. Dept. Agric., Washington D.C., Tech. Bull.* no. 840, 60 pp.

Park, T. 1945. 4222
Life tables for the black flour beetle, *Tribolium Madens* Charp. *Amer. Nat.*, 79, 436-44.

Park, T. 1948. 4223
Experimental studies of interspecies competition. I. *Ecol. Monogr.*, 18, 265-308.

Parker, E. R. 1942. 4224
Adjustment of yields in an experiment with orange trees. *Proc. Amer. Soc. Hort. Sci.*, 41, 23-33.

Parker, J. B. 1947. 4225
The accumulation of chance effects and the Gaussian frequency distribution. *Phil. Mag.*, (7) 38, 681-2.

Parker-Rhodes, A. F. 1942. 4226
Studies in the mechanism of fungicidal action. II. elements of the theory of variability. *Ann. Appl. Biol.*, 29, 126-35.

Parkin, E. A. & Green, A. A. 1943. 4227
A film technique for the biological evaluation of pyrethrum—in oil insecticides for use against stored product insects in warehouses. *Ann. Appl. Biol.*, 30, 279-92.

Parle, H. V. 1945. 4227[a]
Practical uses of probabilities. *Nebraska Blue Print*, 45, 8-10.

Parsons, R. H. 1942. 4227[b]
Size of samples. *Engineering, London*, 154, 294-5.

Parsons, R. H. 1942. 4227[c]
Sampling and probability. *Engineer, London*, 173, 528-9.

Paschal, F. C. 1942. 4228
On the weighting of broad categories. *Psychol. Bull.*, 39, 576-7.

Patau, K. 1942. 4229
Eine neue χ^2 Tafel. *Zeit. Indukt. Abstamm. VererbLehre*, 80, 558-64.

Patau, K. & Timoféeff-Ressovsky, N. W. 4230
1943. Statistical testing of the difference in the temperature coefficients of high and normal mutation rates, together with an example for the planning of temperature experiments. *Zeit. Indukt. Abstamm. VererbLehre*, 81, 62-71.

Patnaik, P. B. 1948. 4231
The power function of the test for the difference between two proportions in a 2×2 table. *Biometrika*, 35, 157-75.

Patnaik, P. B. 1949. 4232
The non-central χ^2 and *F* distributions and their applications. *Biometrika*, 36, 202-32.

Patte, W. E. 1944. 4232[a]
Nomograph for analysing percentage tolerances. *Chem. & Metall. Engng.*, 51 (3), 117.

Patterson, R. E. 1946. 4233
The use of adjusting factors in the analysis of data with disproportionate subclass numbers. *J. Amer. Statist. Ass.*, 41, 334-46.

Paulson, E. 1941. 4234
On certain likelihood-ratio tests associated with the exponential distribution. *Ann. Math. Statist.*, 12, 301-6.

Paulson, E. 1942. 4235
An approximate normalization of the analysis of variance distribution. *Ann. Math. Statist.*, 13, 233-5.

Paulson, E. 1942. 4236
A note on the estimation of some mean values for a bivariate distribution. *Ann. Math. Statist.*, 13, 440-5.

Paulson, E. 1943. 4237
A note on tolerance limits. *Ann. Math. Statist.*, 14, 90-3.

Paulson, E. 1947. 4238
A note on the efficiency of the Wald sequential test. *Ann. Math. Statist.*, 18, 447-50.

Paulson, E. 1949. 4239
A multiple decision procedure for certain problems in the analysis of variance. *Ann. Math. Statist.*, 20, 95-8.

Peach, P. 1943. 4240
Introduction of statistical quality control into factory practice. *United States, War Prod. Board Publication*.

Peach, P. 1945. 4241
A comparison of acceptance inspection plans. *Industr. Qual. Contr.*, 1 (6), 11-14.

Peach, P. 1946. 4241[a]
The use of statistics in the design of experiments. *Industr. Qual. Contr.*, 3(3), 15-17.

Peach, P. 1949. 4242
Applications of statistics to complex engineering problems. *Proc. Conf. Qual. Contr., Amer. Soc. for Qual. Contr.*

Peach, P. & Littauer, S. B. 1946.   4243
A note on sampling inspection. *Ann. Math. Statist.*, **17**, 81-4.

Pearce, S. C. 1943.   4244
An investigation into means of reducing the labour needed for recording crops. *Annu. Rep. East Malling Res. Sta.*, 1942, pp. 36-40.

Pearce, S. C. 1944.   4245
Sampling methods for the measurement of fruit crops. *J. R. Statist. Soc.*, **107**, 117-26.

Pearce, S. C. 1946.   4246
The measurement of fruit crops by sampling. *Annu. Rep. East Malling Res. Sta.*, 1946, pp. 77-82.

Pearce, S. C. 1948.   4247
Randomized blocks with interchanged and substituted plots. *J. R. Statist. Soc. B*, **10**, 252-6.

Pearce, S. C. 1949-50.   4248
The interpretation of uniformity trials. *Annu. Rep. East Malling Res. Sta.*, 1949-1950, pp. 91-2.

Pearce, S. C. & Hoblyn, T. N. 1947.   4249
A review of experimental design at East Malling. (1919-47.) *Annu Rep. East Malling Res. Sta.*, 1947, pp. 88-100.

Pearce, S. C. & Taylor, J. 1948.   4250
The changing of treatments in a long-term trial. *J. Agric. Sci.*, **38**, 402-10.

Pearcey. T. 1948.   4251
Delays in landing of air traffic. *J. Roy. Aero Soc.*, **52**, 799-812.

Pearl, E., Park, T. & Miner, J. R. 1941.   4252
Experimental studies on the duration of life. XVI. Life tables for the flour beetle *tribolium confusum* Duval. *Amer. Nat.*, **75**, 5-19.

Pearl, R. 1940.   4253
The aging of populations. *J. Amer. Statist. Ass.*, **35**, 277-97.

Pearl, R., Reed, L. J. & Kish, J. F. 1940.   4254
The logistic curve and the census count of 1940. *Science* (*N. S.*), **92**, 486-8.

Pearson, E. S. 1941.   4255
A note on further properties of statistical tests. *Biometrika*, **32**, 59-61.

Pearson, E. S. 1941.   4256
Prefatory note to tables of percentage points of the incomplete beta-function. *Biometrika*, **32**, 151-3.

Pearson, E. S. 1942.   4257
The probability integral of the range in samples of *n* observations from a normal population. I. Foreword and tables. *Biometrika*, **32**, 301-8.

Pearson, E. S. 1942.   4258
Notes on testing statistical hypotheses. *Biometrika*, **32**, 311-16.

Pearson, E. S. 1943.   4259
Prefatory note to percentage points of *F* distribution. *Biometrika*, **33**, 73-88.

Pearson, E. S. 1945.   4260
The application of the theory of probability to industrial problems. *L'application du calcul des probabilités*, Colloquium held at Geneva, 12-15 July 1939, pp. 161-81. (Inst. Int. de Coopération Intellectuelle.)

Pearson, E. S. 1945.   4261
Note on the probability integral of the mean deviation. *Biometrika*, **33**, 252-3 (correction: **35**, 424).

Pearson, E. S. 1947.   4262
The choice of statistical tests illustrated on the interpretation of data classed in a 2×2 table. *Biometrika*, **34**, 139-67.

Pearson, E. S. 1948.   4263
Note on J. B. S. Haldane's paper regarding the treatment of rare events. *Biometrika*, **35**, 301-3.

Pearson, E. S. & Hartley, H. O. 1943.   4264
Tables of the probability integral of the Studentized range. *Biometrika*, **33**, 89-99.

Pearson, E. S. & Merrington, M. 1948.   4265
2×2 tables, the power function of the test on a randomized experiment. *Biometrika*, **35**, 331-45.

Pearson, K. 1941.   4266
The laws of chance in relation to thought and conduct. Gresham Lecture Delivered in 1892. *Biometrika*, **32**, 89-100.

Pease, Joyce. 1940.   4267
Analysis of petal size in an Oenothera hybrid. *Ann. Eugen.*, **10**, 144-59.

Peatman, J. G. & Schafer, R. 1942.   4268
A table of random numbers from selective service numbers. *J. Psychol.*, **14**, 295-305.

Pechanec, J. F. 1941.   4269
Application of analysis of covariance to range research data. *U.S. Forest Serv., Inter-mountain Forest and Range Exp. Sta. Tech. Note*, **1**, 1-21.

Pechanec, J. 1941.   4270
Sampling error in range surveys of sagebrush grass vegetation. *J. Forestry*, **39**, 52-4.

Pechanec, J. F. & Stewart, G. 1941.   4271
Sagebrush-grass range sampling studies: variability of native vegetation and sampling error. *J. Amer. Soc. Agron.*, **33**, 1057-71.

Pedroni, F. 1949.   4272
Osservazioni sulle rappresentazioni a co-ordinate ortogonali e sulla loro comparabilità. *Statistica, Milano*, **9**, 57-71.

Pedroni, F. 1949.   4273
Rappresentazioni statistiche a coordinate ortogonali, diagrammi cartesiani e geometria anamorfica. *Atti 8va Riun. Sci., Soc. Ital. Statist.* (publ. 1951), pp. 63-76.

Peel, E. A. 1946.   4274
A new method for analysing aesthetic preferences: some theoretical considerations. *Psychometrika*, **11**, 129-37.

Peel, E. A. 1947.   4275
A short method of calculating maximum battery reliability. *Nature*, **159**, 816-17.

Peel, E. A. 1948.   4276
Prediction of a complex criterion and battery reliability. *Brit. J. Psychol.* (*Statist. Sec.*), **1**, 84-94.

Peel, E. A. 1949.   4277
Item difficulty as the measuring device in objective mental test. *Brit. J. Psychol.* (*Statist. Sec.*), **2**, 69-75.

Peiser, A. M. 1943.   4278
Asymptotic formulas for significance levels of certain distributions. *Ann. Math. Statist.*, **14**, 56-62 (correction: **20**, 128-9).

Peller, S. 1946.   4278[a]
A new rule for predicting the occurrence of multiple births. *Amer. J. Phys. Anthrop.*, **4**, 99-106.

Pendharkar, V. G. & Mathur, G. D. 1943.   4279
Monthly fluctuations in raw jute prices. *Sankhyā*, **6**, 265-70.

Penglaou, C. 1946.   4280
Le champ d'application de la méthode statistique. *J. Soc. Statist. Paris*, **87**, 146-62.

Penrose, L. S. 1942.   4281
On the assignment of precise normal scale values to frequency distributions. *Bull. Canadian Psychol. Ass.*, **2**, 1-2.

Penrose, L. S. 1945.   4282
Discrimination between normal and psychotic subjects by revised examination. *Bull. Canadian Psychol. Ass.*, **5**, 37-40.

Penrose, L. S. 1946.   4283
Elementary statistics of majority voting. *J. R. Statist. Soc.*, **109**, 53-7.

Penrose, L. S. 1946.   4284
A further note on the sib-pair linkage method. *Ann. Eugen.*, **13**, 25-9.

Penrose, L. S. 1946.   4284[a]
Familial data on 144 cases of anencephaly, spina bifida and congenital hydrocephaly. *Ann. Eugen.*, **13**, 73-98.

Penrose, L. S. 1946.   4285
On the familial appearances of maternal and foetal incompatability. *Ann. Eugen.*, **13**, 141-5. (Errata (1947): **14**, 1.)

Penrose, L. S. 1946.   4286
Social aspects of psychiatry: The importance of statistics. *J. Mental Sci.*, **92** (389), 713-18.

Penrose, L. S. 1947.   4287
Some notes on discrimination. *Ann. Eugen.*, **13**, 228-37.

Penrose, L. S. 1949.   4288
The meaning of "Fitness" in human populations. *Ann. Eugen.*, **14**, 301-4.

Penteado Rocha, H. A. 1943.   4289
A moderna teoria matematica da correlaçao entre duas variaveis. *Rev. Brasil. Estatíst.*, **4**, 37-78.

Pentikainen, T. 1947.   4290
Einige numerische Untersuchungen über das risiko-theoretische Verhalten von Sterbekassen. *Skand. Aktuartidskr.*, **30**, 75-87.

Pérez Calvet, R. 1945.   4291
A study on uniformity experiments and their use in the choice of replication plots. *Bol. Inst. Invest. Exper. Agron. For.*, *Madrid*, **12**, 329-48.

Pérez Calvet, R. & de Zulueta, M. M. 1946.   4292
Statistical methods for comparing a large number of varieties. *Bol. Inst. Invest. Exper. Agron. For.*, *Madrid*, **14**, 29-62.

Perks, W. 1946.   4293
Two-variable developments of the *n*-ages method. *J. Inst. Actuar.*, **72**, 377-414.

Perks, W. 1947.   4294
Some observations on inverse probability including a new indifference rule. *J. Inst. Actuar.*, **73**, 285-334.

Perks, W. 1947.   4295
A simple proof of Gauss's inequality. *J. Inst. Actuar. Students' Soc.*, **7**, 38-41.

Perrone, R. 1949.   4295[a]
Sul fattore riduzione nell'assicurazione malattie. *Riv. Ital. Econ. Demogr. Statist.*, **3** (3-4), 134-8.

Persegani, I. 1942.   4296
La "scala prospettica", le sue proprietá e le sue applicazioni. *Statistica, Ferrara*, **2**, 143-56.

Persico, E. 1941.   4297
L'idea di probabilità nella fisica classica. *R. C. Semin. Mat. Fis. Torino*, **7**, 25-35. (Also (1940): *Questioni di matematica applicata*, Bologna.)

Persico, E. 1942.   4298
Sul concetto di probabilità. Una proposta. *Statistica, Ferrara*, **2**, 65-7.

Peters, B. G. 1941.   4299
Dilution egg-counts and the Poisson series. *J. Helminthol.*, **19**, 59-62.

Peters, C. C. 1941.   4300
A method of matching groups for experiment with no loss of population. *J. Educ. Res.*, **34**, 606-12.

Peters, C. C. 1941.   4301
A technique for correlating measurable traits with freely observed social behaviours. *Psychometrika*, **6**, 209-19.

Peters, C. C. 1943.   4301[a]
Misuses of Fisher statistics. *J. Educ. Res.*, **36**, 546-9.

Peters, C. C. 1944.   4302
Interaction in analysis of variance interpreted as intercorrelation. *Psychol. Bull.*, **41**, 287-99.

Peters, C. C. 1946.   4303
A new descriptive statistic: the parabolic correlation coefficient. *Psychometrika*, **11**, 57-69.

Peters, C. C., Townsend, A. &   4303[a]
Traxler, A. E. 1945.
Research methods and designs. *Rev. Educ. Res.*, **15**, 377-93.

Peterson, A. I. 1944.   4303[b]
Applied quality control. *Industr. Qual. Contr.*, **1** (3), 3-4.

Petrescu, T. 1940-1.   4304
Teoria erorilor si verificarea ei asupra fenomenelor silvice. (The theory of errors as applied to forestry phenomena.) *Rev. Padurilor, Bucharest*, **52**, 433-42, 693-7; **53**, 1-5.

Petrov, A. P. 1942.   4305
An investigation into the phytocoenose of deciduous woodlands. *Soviet Bot.*, **4 & 5**, 15-30.

Petrovitch, M. 1941.   4306
Figures d'équilibre de deux événements ayant la même probabilité. *Acad. Serbe Bull. Acad. Sci. Mat. Nat. A*, **7**, 55-9.

Petterson, H. 1943.   4307
Plant breeding and forestry. *Skogen*, **30**, 31-7.

Philip, U. 1944.   4308
An analysis of chromosomal polymorphism in two species of Chironomus. *J. Genet.*, **44**, 129-42.

Phillips, R. C. & Weiss, P. R. 1944.   4309
Theoretical calculation on best smoothing of position data for gunnery prediction. *Mass. Inst. Tech. Radio Lab. Rep.* no. 532.

Phillips, R. H. S. 1944.   4309ᵃ
Quality control and industrial development. *Aircraft Engng.*, **16**, 265-7.

Phillips, R. H. S. 1945.   4309ᵇ
Quality control; some advantages of a system of fixed period renewal. *Aircraft Engng.*, **17**, 179-82.

Phillips, R. W. & Stoehr, J. A. 1945.   4310
The accuracy of measurements and weights of sheep. *J. Animal Sci.*, **4**, 311-16.

Phipp, M. 1944.   4310ᵃ
Statistical control in the inspection of materials. *Aircraft Engng.*, **16**, 119.

Phipps, I. F., Pugsley, A. T., Hockley, S. R.   4311
& Cornish, E. A. 1944.
The analysis of cubic lattice designs in varietal trials. *Bull. C.S.I.R. Aust.*, **176**, 41 pp.

Piaget, J. 1943.   4312
Interprétation probabiliste de la loi de Weber et de celle des centrations relatives. *C. R. Soc. Phys. Hist. Nat. Genève*, **60**, 200-4.

Picard, H. C. 1949.   4313
Het verband tussen werkelijke verdeling, fouten-verdeling en waarneembare verdeling. (The relation between the true distribution, the error distribution and the observable distribution.) *Statistica Neer-landica*, **3**, 101-7.

Pierce, J. A. 1940.   4314
A study of a universe of *n* finite populations with application to moment-function adjustments for grouped data. *Ann. Math. Statist.*, **11**, 311-34.

Pierce, J. A. 1943.   4315
Correction formulas for moments of a grouped-distribution of discrete variates. *J. Amer. Statist. Ass.*, **38**, 57-62.

Pierce, J. A. 1944.   4316
On the summation of progressions useful in time series analysis. *J. Amer. Statist. Ass.*, **39**, 387-9 (errata: 521).

Pietra, G. 1940.   4317
Sur la statistique méthodologique italienne. *Rev. Int. Statist. Inst.*, **8**, 163-94.

Pietra, G. 1941.   4318
Delle curve di concentrazione. *Statistica, Ferrara*, **1**, 185-94.

Pietra, G. 1942.   4319
Intorno alla misura della connessione e della concordanza. *Statistica, Ferrara*, **2**, 59-64.

Pietra, G. 1944.   4320
La statistique méthodologique italienne de 1939 à 1942. *Rev. Int. Statist. Inst.*, **12**, 36-45.

Pilé, G. 1947.   4320ᵃ
Le statistique appliquée au contrôle de fabrication. *J. Soc. Statist. Paris*, **88**, 421-36.

Pillai, K. C. S. 1943.   4321
Trend analyser. *Proc. Indian Acad. Sci. A*, **17**, 187-94.

Pillai, K. C. S. 1943.   4322
A note on Poisson distribution. *Proc. Indian Acad. Sci. A*, **18**, 179-89.

Pillai, K. C. S. 1946.   4323
Confidence interval for the correlation coefficient. *Sankhyā*, **7**, 415-22.

Pillai, K. C. S. 1948.   4324
A note on ordered samples. *Sankhyā*, **8**, 375-80.

Pinel, E. 1948.   4325
Essai d'interprétation cinématique des courbes en cloche de Gauss. *C. R. Acad. Sci., Paris*, **227**, 236-8.

Pinney, E. 1947.   4326
Fitting curves with zero or infinite end points. *Ann. Math. Statist.*, **18**, 127-31.

Pinto, E. A. 1943.   4326ᵃ
Statistical quality control in the aircraft industry. *Aero Digest*, **43**, 313-15.

Piotrowski, S. L. 1948.   4327
Some remarks on the weights of unknowns as determined by the method of differential corrections. *Proc. Nat. Acad. Sci. U.S.A.*, **34**, 23-6.

Pistolesi, E. 1943.   4328
Criteri statistici per il proporzio namento delle strutture dei velivoli. *Statistica, Ferrara*, **3**, 3-10.

Pitt, H. R. 1940.   4329
General Tauberian theorems. II. *J. Lond. Math. Soc.*, **15**, 97-112.

Pitt, H. R. 1940.   4330
A special class of homogeneous random processes. *J. Lond. Math. Soc.*, **15**, 247-57.

Pitt, H. R. 1942.   4331
Some generalizations of the ergodic theorem. *Proc. Camb. Phil. Soc.*, **38**, 325-43.

Pitt, H. R. 1946.   4332
A theorem on random functions with applications to a theory of provisioning. *J. Lond. Math. Soc.*, **21**, 16-22.

Pitt, H. R. 1947.   4333
On a class of linear integro-differential equations. *Proc. Camb. Phil. Soc.*, **43**, 153-63.

Pitt, H. R. 1949.   4334
On the theory of statistical procedures. *Proc. Camb. Phil. Soc.*, **45**, 354-9.

Pittman, M. & Lieberman, J. E. 1948.   4335
An analysis of the Wilson-Worcester method of determining media effective dose of pertussis vaccine. *Amer. J. Publ. Health*, **38**, 15-21.

Pitts, W. 1943.   4336
A general theory of learning and conditioning. I, II. *Psychometrika*, **8**, 1-18, 131-40.

Pizzetti, E. 1940.   4337
Betrachtungen über die Messung der Variabilität vermittels der mittleren Differenz nach Gini. *Arch. Rass. Ges. Biol.*, **34**, 321-8.

Pizzetti, E. 1940.   4338
Medie ascendenti e medie discendenti. *Metron*, **14**, 55-66. (Also: *Atti 1ma Riun. Sci., Soc. Ital. Statist.*)

Pizzetti, E. 1941.   4339
Un nuovo aspetto nella misura della variabilità. *Statistica, Ferrara*, **1**, 315-25.

Pizzetti, E. 1941. 4340
Relazione fra il rapporto di concentrazione e l'indice di concentrazione del Gini. *Atti 2da Riun. Sci., Soc. Ital. Statist.*, pp. 11-24.

Pizzetti, E. 1947. 4341
Sul concetto di variabilità. *Statistica, Milano,* **7,** 227-36.

Pizzetti, E. 1948. 4342
Sensibilità degli indici di concentrazione. *G. Economisti,* **7,** 101-6.

Plackett, R. L. 1944. 4342[a]
Progressive sampling inspection. *U.K. Min. Supply Advisory Service Statist. Method & Qual. Contr. Tech. Rep. Ser. R,* no. QC/R/7 (II), 1 January 1944, 12 pp.

Plackett, R. L. 1944. 4342[b]
Distribution of the variance and the variance-ratio in samples from a rectangular population. *U.K. Min. Supply Advisory Service Statist. Method & Qual. Contr. Tech. Rep. Ser. R,* no. QC/R/9, 5 February 1944, 13 pp.

Plackett, R. L. 1944. 4342[c]
The mean range and its relation to the median ordinate and the standard deviation. *U.K. Min. Supply Advisory Service Statist. Method & Qual. Contr. Tech. Rep. Ser. R,* no QC/R/22, 22 March 1944, 4 pp.

Plackett, R. L. 1946. 4343
Some generalizations in the multifactorial design. *Biometrika,* **33,** 328-32.

Plackett, R. L. 1946. 4344
Literature on testing the equality of variances and covariances in normal populations. *J. R. Statist. Soc.,* **109,** 457-68.

Plackett, R. L. 1947. 4345
Cyclic intra-block subgroups and allied designs. *Sankhyā,* **8,** 275-6.

Plackett, R. L. 1947. 4346
Limits of the ratio of mean range to standard deviation. *Biometrika,* **34,** 120-2.

Plackett, R. L. 1947. 4347
An exact test for the equality of variances. *Biometrika,* **34,** 311-19.

Plackett, R. L. 1948. 4348
Boundaries of minimum size in binomial sampling. *Ann. Math. Statist.,* **19,** 575-80.

Plackett, R. L. 1949. 4349
A historical note on the method of least squares. *Biometrika,* **36,** 458-60.

Plackett, R. L. & Bates, C. D. 1944. 4349[a]
The distribution of the range in samples from a rectangular population. *U.K. Min. Supply Advisory Service Statist. Method & Qual. Contr. Tech. Rep. Ser. R,* no. QC/R/10, 5 February 1944, 5 pp.

Plackett, R. L. & Burman, J. P. 1946. 4350
The design of optimum multifactorial experiments. *Biometrika,* **33,** 305-25.

Plackett, R. L. & Hewlett, P. S. 1948. 4350[a]
Statistical aspects of the independent joint action of poisons, particularly insecticides. *Ann. Appl. Biol.,* **35,** 347-58.

Platt, J. R. 1943. 4351
A mechanical determination of correlation coefficients and standard deviations. *J. Amer. Statist. Ass.,* **38,** 311-18.

Platzer, H. 1940. 4352
Die Statistik und die Kalender-reform. (French summary.) *Bull. Int. Statist. Inst.,* **30** (3), 284-6.

Plesner, A. I. & Rokhlin, V. A. 1946. 4353
Spectral theory of linear operators. (Russian.) *Usp. Mat. Nauk (N.S.)* **1,** 1(11), 71-193.

Plessing, H. C. 1948. 4354
Problems of telephone economy as seen from a statistical point of view. *Nord. Tidskr. Teknisk. Økonomi,* **12,** 201-13.

Ploeg, A. G. 1944. 4355
Verzekeringswezen en statistiek. (Insurance and statistics.) (Dutch.) *Verzekeringsbode, Utrecht,* **63** (8), 29-30.

Ploeg, A. G. 1949. 4356
Lebensversicherungsmathematik. (Dutch.) *Euclides, Groningen,* **24,** 156-68.

Plymen, J. 1948. 4357
Operational research. *Proc. Cent. Ass. Inst. Actuar.,* **3,** 313-28.

Pohle, E. M., Hazel, L. N. & Keller, H. R. 1944. 4358
Sampling and measuring methods for determining fineness and uniformity in wool. *Circ. U.S. Dep. Agric.,* no. 704, 15 pp.

Politz, A. & Simmons, W. 1949. 4359
An attempt to get the "notat homes" into the sample without callbacks. *J. Amer. Statist. Ass.,* **44,** 9-31 (addendum: **45,** 136-7).

Pollaczek, F. 1942. 4360
Sur quelques lois asymptotiques de la théorie de l'encombrement des réseaux téléphoniques. *Ann. Univ. Lyon A,* **5,** 21-35.

Pollaczek, F. 1945. 4361
Résolution de certaines équations intégrales de deuxième espèce. *J. Math. Pures Appl.,* **24,** 73-93.

Pollaczek, F. 1946. 4362
La loi d'attente des appels téléphoniques. *C. R. Acad. Sci., Paris,* **222,** 353-5.

Pollaczek, F. 1946. 4363
Sur un problème du calcul des probabilités qui se rapporte à la téléphonie. *J. Math. Pures Appl.,* **25,** 307-34.

Pollaczek, F. 1948. 4364
Sur l'application de la théorie des fonctions au calcul de certaines probabilités continues utilisées dans la théorie des réseaux téléphoniques. *Ann. Inst. H. Poincaré,* **10,** 1-56.

Pollaczek, F. 1948. 4365
Sur la probabilité de perte d'un appel téléphonique dans le cas d'un seul groupe de lignes avec blocage temporaire. *C. R. Acad. Sci., Paris,* **226,** 2045-7.

Pollaczek, F. 1949. 4366
Application d'opérateurs intégrocombinatoires dans la théorie des intégrales multiples de Dirichlet. *Ann. Inst. H. Poincaré,* **11,** 113-33.

Pollaczek, F. 1949. 4367
Réductions de différents problèmes concernant la probabilité d'attente au téléphone à la résolution de systèmes d'équations intégrales. *Ann. Inst. H. Poincaré*, **11**, 135-73.

Pollak Ried, E. 1948. 4368
La estadística y su aplicacion a la biologia social. *Horizontes Econ.*, January 1948, 29-38.

Pollard, A. H. 1947. 4369
A note concerning published annual vital statistics. *Trans. Actuar. Soc. Aust.*, **6**, 192-3.

Pollard, A. H. 1948. 4370
The measurement of reproductivity. *J. Inst. Actuar.*, **74**, 288-337.

Pollard, A. H. 1949. 4371
Methods of forecasting mortality using Australian data. *J. Inst. Actuar.*, **75**, 151-82.

Pólya, G. 1941. 4372
Heuristic reasoning and the theory of probability. *Amer. Math. Monthly*, **48**, 450-65.

Pólya, G. 1946. 4373
Sur une généralisation d'un problème élémentaire classique, importante dans l'inspection des produits industriels. *C. R. Acad. Sci., Paris*, **222**, 1422-4.

Pólya, G. 1948. 4374
Exact formulas in the sequential analysis of attributes. *Univ. Calif. Publ. Statist.*, **1**, 229-39.

Pólya, G. 1949. 4375
Preliminary remarks on a logic of plausible inference, *Dialectica*, **3**, 28-35.

Pólya, G. 1949. 4376
Remarks on characteristic functions. *Proc. Berkeley Symp. Math. Statist. and Probab.*, 1945-6, pp. 115-23.

Pólya, G. 1949. 4377
Remarks on computing the probability integral in one and two dimensions. *Proc. Berkeley Symp. Math. Statist. and Probab.*, 1945-6, pp. 63-78.

Pomnitz, C. E. 1940. 4377[a]
Quality control. *Tool Engr.*, **9** (6), 24-8.

Pompilj, G. 1946. 4378
Sulla regressione. *R. C. Mat. Univ. Roma, Ist. Naz. Alta. Mat.*, (5) **5**, 186-219.

Pompilj, G. 1947. 4379
Sulla media di una distribuzione normale. *Statistica, Bologna*, **7**, 89-95.

Pompilj, G. 1947. 4380
Sulla media geometrica e sopra un indice di mutabilità calcolati mediante un campione. *Mem. Soc. Ital. Sci.*, (3) **26**, 299-339.

Pompilj, G. 1948. 4381
Teorie statistiche della significatività e conformità dei risultati sperimentali agli schemi teorici. *Statistica, Milano*, **8**, 7-42.

Pompilj, G. 1949. 4382
Per la caratterizzazione delle curve di diramazione dei piani quadrupli. *R. C. Mat. Applic.*, (5) **8**, 77-93.

Pompilj, G. 1949. 4383
Sulla frequenza di trasmissione dei caratteri. *Atti 8va Riun. Sci., Soc. Ital. Statist.*, (publ. 1951), pp. 77-101.

Pompilj, G. 1949. 4384
Sulle medie combinatorie potenziate dei campioni. *R. C. Mat. Univ. Padova*, **18**, 181-96.

Pompilj, G. 1949. 4385
Sulla significatività della costanti statistiche. *Boll. Un. Mat. Ital.*, (3) **4**, 112-17.

Pompilj, G. 1949. 4386
Statistica pura. *Atti 8va Riun. Sci., Soc. Ital. Statist.*, (publ. 1951), pp. 1-20.

Pontecorvo, G. 1946. 4387
The genetical aspects of bio-assays with micro-organisms. *Analyst*, **71**, 411-13.

Popescu-Zeletin, I. 1947. 4388
Procedeul de inventariere cu benzi de proba. (Das Probestreifenverfahren.) (German summary.) *Rev. Padicrilor, Bucharest*, **62**, 65-75.

Popoff, K. 1942. 4389
Observations sur la théorie des probabilités en chaîne de Markoff. Cas d'une suite continue d'épreuves. (Bulgarian. French summary.) *Annu. Fac. Phys. Math., Univ. Sofia, I*, **38**, 319-30.

Popoff, K. 1942. 4390
Osservazioni sulla teoria delle probabilità concatenate di Markoff. Caso di una successione continua de prove. *R. C. Mat. Univ. Roma, Ist. Naz. Alta Mat.*, (5) **3**, 282-92.

Pôrto Carreiro, O. 1948. 4390[a]
A estatística e a atuária. (Portuguese.) *Rev. Brasil Estatíst.*, **9**, 357-72.

Pôrto Carreiro, O. & Nogueira, R. 1947. 4391
A representaçâo abstrata do acaso como fundamento do câlculo das probabilidades. *Rev. Brasil. Estatíst.*, **8**, 210-48.

Post, J. J. 1947. 4391[a]
Blanco proeven. (Uniformity trials.) (Dutch. English summary.) *Statistica Neerlandica*, **1**, 317-21.

Posthumus, G. 1947. 4391[b]
De bepaling van de nauwkeurigheid, waarmede metingen of beoordelingen worden verricht. (Determination of the accuracy with which measurements and judgments are made.) (Dutch. English summary.) *Statistica Neerlandica*, **1**, 240-8.

Postman, L. & Bruner, J. S. 1946. 4392
The reliability of constant errors in psychophysical measurements. *J. Psychol.*, **21**, 293-9.

Poti, S. J. 1946. 4393
A study of expenditure pattern of Calcutta middle class family budgets. *Sankhyā*, **7**, 425-8.

Poti, S. J. 1948. 4394
Splitting mixed-up populations. *Bull. Calcutta Statist. Ass.*, **1**, 183-6.

Potter, F. M. 1944. 4394[a]
Aids of quality control in the manufacture of aircraft generators. *Elect. Engng.*, **63**, 525-9.

Potter, W. D. 1949. 4395
Normalcy tests of precipitation and frequency studies of runoff on small watersheds. *U.S. Dept. Agric. Soil Conservation Service, Tech. Bull.* no. 985, 24 pp.

Potter, W. D. 1949. 4396
Simplification of the Gumbel method for computing probability curves. *U.S. Dept. Agric. Soil Conservation Service, Tech. Paper* no. 78, 22 pp.

Powell, R. W. 1943. 4396[a]
A simple method of estimating flood frequency. *Civil Engng.*, 13, 105-7.

Powers, L. 1944. 4397
Meiotic studies of crosses between *Fragaria ovalis* and × *F. ananassa. J. Agric. Res.*, 69, 435-48.

Prabhu, S. S. & Amble, V. N. 1946. 4398
Weaned versus unweaned—a statistical study of an experiment on goats. *Indian J. Vet. Sci.*, 16, 212-22.

Prakash, O. 1947. 4399
The mean deviation in grouped data. *J. Inst. Actuar. Students' Soc.*, 7, 52-3.

Pratelli, A. 1940. 4400
Sulle medie trigonometriche. *Atti 1ma Riun. Sci., Soc. Ital. Statist.*, pp. 99-104.

Pratt, D. M. 1943. 4401
Analysis of population development in *Daphnia* at different temperatures. *Biol. Bull., Woods Hole*, 85, 116-40.

Prebble, M. L. 1943. 4402
Sampling methods in population studies of the European spruce sawfly, *Gilpinia Hercyniae* (Hartig) in eastern Canada. *Trans. Roy. Soc. Canada*, (5) 37, 93-126.

Preinreich, G. A. D. 1940. 4403
The economic life of industrial equipment. *Econometrica*, 8, 12-44.

Presburger, M. 1941. 4404
Sur l'étude générale des collectivités de personnes. (German, Italian and English summaries.) *Trans. 12th. Int. Congr Actuar, Lucerne*, 1940, 3, 353-67.

Preston, F. W. 1948. 4405
The commonness, and rarity of species. *Ecology*, 29, 254-83.

Preston, M. G. 1940. 4406
Concerning the determination of trait variability, *Psychometrika*, 5, 275-81.

Preston, M. G. & Zeid, P. M. 1943. 4407
Observations on sequences of choices made at five successive choice points. *J. Exper. Psychol.*, 32, 275-90.

Price, D. O. 1947. 4408
A check on underenumeration in the 1940 census. *Amer. Sociol. Rev.*, 12, 44-9.

Price, G. B. 1946. 4409
Distributions derived from the multinomial expansion. *Amre. Math. Monthly*, 53, 59-74.

Price, W. A. & Vaughan, E. C. 1940-1. 4409[a]
An experiment in mixing and sampling Kentucky Bluegrass. *Proc. Ass. Offic. Seed Analysts N. Amer.*, 32, 77-80.

Price, W. C. 1946. 4410
Measurement of virus activity in plants. *Biometrics Bull.*, 2, 81-6.

Price, W. C. & Spencer, E. L. 1943. 4411
Accuracy of the local-lesion method for measuring virus activity. I. Tobacco-mosaic virus. II. Tobacco-necrosis, alfalfa-mosaic, and tobacco-ringspot. III. The standard deviation of the log-ratio of potencies as a measure of the accuracy of measurement. *Amer. J. Bot.*, 30, 280-90; 340-6; 720-35. (Part III also in *J. Amer. Pharm. Ass.*, 28, 644-57.)

Pridmore, W. A. 1944. 4412
An application of statistical methods to presswork operation (aircraft stringers). *U.K. Min. Supply Advisory Service Statist. Method & Qual. Contr. Tech. Rep.* no. QC/E/8, 13 June 1944.

Probst, A. H. 1943. 4413
Border effect in soya bean nursery plots. *J. Amer. Soc. Agron.*, 35, 662-6.

Prodan, M. 1949. 4414
Näherungsverfahren zur Bestimmung einiger höherer statistischer Masszahlen der statistischen Kollektive. *Mitt. Math. Statist.*, 1, 53-63.

Proebsting, E. L. 1942. 4415
The relative yield of border fruit trees. *Proc. Amer. Soc. Hort. Sci.*, 41, 34-6.

Prokhorov, Yu. V. 1949. 4416
On the strong law of large numbers. (Russian.) *Dokl. Akad. Nauk SSSR*, 69, 607-10.

Prot, M. 1943. 4417
Réflexions psychologiques sur les notions de probabilité et de hasard et sur quelques notions connexes. *J. Soc. Statist. Paris*, 84, 23-34.

Prot, M. 1948. 4418
Une nouvelle technique d'essai des matériaux. L'essai de fatigue sous charge progressive. *Mem. Ann. Ponts Chauss.*, 118, 441-64.

Proudfoot, M. J. 1942. 4419
Sampling with transverse traverse lines. *J. Amer. Statist. Ass.*, 37, 265-70.

Prytz, K. 1948. 4420
Landbrugsmeteorologiske Korrelationsundersøgelsen. (Correlation theory and its application to meteorological problems in agriculture.) *Ingeniørvidensk. Skrift.*, 4, 1-124.

Przyborowski, J. & Wilenski, H. 1940. 4421
Homogeneity of results in testing samples from Poisson series with an application to testing clover seed for dodder. *Biometrika*, 31, 313-23.

Pugsley, L. I. 1946. 4422
The application of the principles of statistical analysis to the biological assay of hormones. *Endocrinology*, 39, 161-76.

Pugsley, L. I. & Morrell, C. A. 1943. 4423
Variables affecting the biological assay of estrogens. *Endocrinology*, 33, 48-61.

Puig Adam, P. 1941. 4424
Ensayo de una teoría matemática de escalafones cerrados y sus aplicaciones a problemas de hacienda y previsión. *Rev. Mat. Hisp.-Amer.*, (4) 1 (2), 82-103.

Purcell, W. R. 1949. 4425
Capillary pressures—their measurement using mercury and the calculation of permeability therefrom. *Trans. Amer. Inst. Mining Met. Engrs.*, 186, 39-48.

Purcell, W. R. 1949.   4426
Saving time in testing life of incandescent lamps. *Elect. Engng. New York*, **68**, 617-20.

Q

Quenouille, M. H. 1947.   4427
Notes on the calculation of autocorrelations of linear autoregressive schemes. *Biometrika*, **34**, 365-7.

Quenouille, M. H. 1947.   4428
A large-sample test for the goodness of fit of autoregressive schemes. *J. R. Statist. Soc.*, **110**, 123-9.

Quenouille, M. H. 1947.   4429
On the problem of random flights. *Proc. Camb. Phil. Soc.*, **43**, 581-2.

Quenouille, M. H. 1948.   4430
The analysis of covariance and non-orthogonal comparisons. *Biometrics*, **4**, 240-6.

Quenouille, M. H. 1948.   4430ª
Distribution of colonies per field—Poisson Series. *J. Gen. Microbiol.*, **2**, 65-9.

Quenouille, M. H. 1948.   4431
Some results in the testing of serial correlation coefficients. *Biometrika*, **35**, 261-7.

Quenouille, M. H. 1949.   4432
Approximate tests of correlation in time-series. *J. R. Statist. Soc. B*, **11**, 68-84.

Quenouille, M. H. 1949.   4433
Approximate tests of correlation in time-series 3. *Proc. Camb. Phil. Soc.*, **45**, 483-4.

Quenouille, M. H. 1949.   4434
A further note on discriminatory analysis. *Ann. Eugen.*, **15**, 11-14.

Quenouille, M. H. 1949.   4435
Note on the elimination of insignificant variates in discriminatory analysis. *Ann. Eugen.*, **14**, 305-8.

Quenouille, M. H. 1949.   4436
The evaluation of probabilities in a normal multivariate distribution, with special reference to the correlation ratio. *Proc. Edin. Math. Soc.*, (2) **8**, 95-100.

Quenouille, M. H. 1949.   4437
A method of trend elimination. *Biometrika*, **36**, 75-91.

Quenouille, M. H. 1949.   4438
Problems in plane sampling. *Ann. Math. Statist.*, **20**, 355-75.

Quenouille, M. H. 1949.   4439
The joint distribution of serial correlation coefficients. *Ann. Math. Statist.*, **20**, 561-71.

Quenouille, M. H. 1949.   4440
A relation between the logarithmic, Poisson and negative binomial series. *Biometrics*, **5**, 162-4.

Quensel, C.-E. 1940.   4441
Truncated normal curves and correlation distributions. *Lunds Univ. Årsskrift (N.F.)*, **36** (15), 1-17. (*Fysiogr. Sallskapets Handl.* (*N.F.*) **51** (15), 17 pp.)

Quensel, C.-E. 1943.   4442
An extension of the validity of Student-Fisher's law of distribution. *Skand. Aktuartidskr.*, **26**, 210-19.

Quensel, C.-E. 1945.   4443
Den nya inkomstatistiken. *Ekon. Tidskr.*, **47**, 346-52.

Quensel, C.-E. 1945.   4444
Studies of the logarithmic normal curve. *Skand. Aktuartidskr.*, **28**, 141-53.

Quensel, C.-E. 1947.   4445
The validity of the z-criterion when the variates are taken from different normal populations. *Skand. Aktuartidskr.*, **30**, 44-55.

Quensel, C.-E. 1948.   4446
En utvidgad inkomstatistik. *Ekon. Tidskr.*, **50**, 1-9.

R

Rabe, F. W. 1946.   4447
Considerations on the correctness of the Erlang formula for automatic telephone traffic. *De Ingenieur*, **58**, 12.

Rabe, F. W. 1949.   4448
Variations of telephone traffic. *Elect. Commun.*, **26**, 243-8.

Race, R. R., Ikin, E. W., Taylor, G. L.   4449
& Prior, A. M. 1942.
A second series of families examined in England for the A_1A_2BO and MN blood group factors. *Ann. Eugen.*, **11**, 385-94.

Rader, L. T. 1943.   4450
Putting quality into quantity: quality control based on rules of probability. *Amer. Machinist*, **87**, 92-3.

Radhakrishna Rao, C. *See* Rao, C. R.

Raff, M. A. 1949.   4451
Space-time relationships at "stop" intersections. *Proc. Inst. Traff. Engrs.*, pp. 42-9.

Ragazzini, J. R. & Zadeh, L. A. 1949.   4452
Probability criterion for the design of servomechanisms. *J. Appl. Phys.*, **20**, 141-4.

Raiford, T. E. 1942.   4453
Skewness of combined distributions. *J. Amer. Statist. Ass.*, **37**, 391-3.

Raimondi, E. R. 1942.   4454
On a problem of geometric probabilities on the sets of triangles. (Spanish.) *Rev. Union Mat. Argent.*, **8**, 1-16. (Also: (1940) *Union Mat. Argent. Publ.* no 25, 18 pp.)

Rainwater, L. J. 1948.   4455
Application of probability theory to nuclear particle detection. *Nucleonics*, **1** (2), 60-9; **2** (1), 42-9.

Rajabhusanam, D. S. 1941.   4456
An unconventional approach to frequency distribution. *Sankhyā*, **5**, 176.

Rajalakshman, D. V. 1941.   4457
On the extreme values of samples taken from a rectangular population. *Math. Student*, **9**, 103-11.

Rajalakshman, D. V. 1943.   4458
On the interval between the ranked individuals of samples taken from a rectangular population. *J. Madras Univ. B*, **15**, 31-44.

Ramamurti, B. & Sitaraman, B. 1942.   4459
On maximal sets of confounded interactions in a
(2^n, 2^k) confounded design. *Sankhyā*, **6**, 183-8.

Ramaswamy, V. & Rao, K. S. 1945.   4460
On the probability that two kth power-free integers
belonging to an assigned arithmetic progression should
be prime to one another. *J. Indian Math. Soc.*, **9**
(3-4), 88-92.

Ramzy, I. & Pickard, P. 1949.   4461
The reliability of Rorschach scoring. *J. Gen. Psychol.*,
40, 3-10.

Rantz, S. F. & Riggs, H. C. 1949.   4462
Magnitude and frequency of floods in the Columbia
river basin. *United States Geol. Survey, Water Supply
Paper* no. 1080.

Rao, C. R. 1942.   4463
On the sum of n observations from different gamma
type populations. *Science & Culture*, **7**, 614-15.

Rao, C. R. 1942.   4464
On bivariate correlation surfaces. *Science & Culture*,
8, 236-7.

Rao, C. R. 1942.   4465
On the volume of a prismoid in n-space and some
problems in continuous probability. *Math. Student*,
10, 68-74.

Rao, C. R. 1943.   4466
Quasi-Latin squares in experimental arrangements.
Current Science, **12**, 322-3.

Rao, C. R. 1944.   4467
On balancing parameters. *Science & Culture*, **9**, 554-5.

Rao, C. R. 1944.   4468
Extension of the theorems of Singer and Bose. *Science
& Culture*, **10**, 57.

Rao, C. R. 1944.   4469
On linear estimation and testing of hypotheses.
Current Science, **13**, 154-5.

Rao, C. R. 1944.   4470
On the linear set-up leading to intra- and inter-block
informations. *Science & Culture*, **10**, 259-60.

Rao, C. R. 1945.   4471
Familial correlations or the multivariate generalizations of the intraclass correlation. *Current Science*,
14, 66-7.

Rao, C. R. 1945.   4472
On the generalisation of Markoff's theorem and tests
of linear hypotheses. *Sankhyā*, **7**, 9-16.

Rao, C. R. 1945.   4473
Information and the accuracy attainable in the estima-
tion of statistical parameters. *Bull. Calcutta Math.
Soc.*, **37**, 81-91.

Rao, C. R. 1945.   4474
Markoff's theorem with linear restrictions on parameters. *Sankhyā*, **7**, 16-19.

Rao, C. R. 1945.   4475
Studentised tests of linear hypotheses. *Science &
Culture*, **11**, 202-3.

Rao, C. R. 1946.   4476
On the linear combination of observations and the
general theory of least squares. *Sankhyā*, **7**, 237-
56.

Rao, C. R. 1946.   4477
Confounded factorial designs in quasi-Latin squares.
Sankhyā, **7**, 295-304.

Rao, C. R. 1946.   4478
Difference sets and combinatorial arrangements deriv-
able from finite geometries. *Proc. Nat. Inst. Sci.
India*, **12**, 123-35.

Rao, C. R. 1946.   4479
Hypercubes of strength " d " leading to confounded
designs in factorial experiments. *Bull. Calcutta Math.
Soc.*, **38**, 67-78.

Rao, C. R. 1946.   4480
On the mean conserving property. *Proc. Indian Acad.
Sci. A*, **23** (4), 165-73.

Rao, C. R. 1946.   4481
Tests with discriminant functions in multivariate
analysis. *Sankhyā*, **7**, 407-14.

Rao, C. R. 1946.   4482
On the most efficient designs in weighing. *Sankhyā*, **7**
440.

Rao, C. R. 1947.   4483
Factorial experiments derivable from combinatorial
arrangements of arrays. *J. R. Statist. Soc. Suppl.*, **9**,
128-39.

Rao, C. R. 1947.   4484
General methods of analysis for incomplete block
designs. *J. Amer. Statist. Ass.*, **42**, 541-61.

Rao, C. R. 1947.   4485
Minimum variance and the estimation of several
parameters. *Proc. Camb. Phil. Soc.*, **43**, 280-3.

Rao, C. R. 1947.   4486
The problem of classification and distance between
two populations. *Nature*, **159**, 30-1.

Rao, C. R. 1947.   4487
Note on a problem of Ragnar Frisch. *Econometrica*,
15, 245-9 (correction: **17**, 212).

Rao, C. R. 1947.   4488
On the significance of the additional information
obtained by the inclusion of some extra variables in
the discrimination of populations. *Current Science*,
16, 216-17.

Rao, C. R. 1947.   4489
A statistical criterion to determine the group to which
an individual belongs. *Nature*, **160**, 835-6.

Rao, C. R. 1948.   4490
Large sample tests of statistical hypotheses concerning
several parameters with applications to problems of
estimation. *Proc. Camb. Phil. Soc.*, **44**, 50-7.

Rao, C. R. 1948.   4491
Tests of significance in multivariate analysis.
Biometrika, **35**, 58-79.

Rao, C. R. 1948.   4492
The utilization of multiple measurements in problems
of biological classification. *J. R. Statist. Soc. B*, **10**,
159-203.

Rao, C. R. 1949.   4493
Anthropometric survey of the United Provinces,
1941: A statistical study. Appendix 3. On the
distance between two populations. *Sankhyā*, **9**,
246-8.

Rao, C. R. 1949.   4494
Anthropometric survey of the United Provinces, 1941:
A statistical study. Appendix 4. Representation of
" p " dimensional data in lower dimensions. *Sankyhā*,
9, 248-51.

Rao, C. R. 1949.   4495
Anthropometric survey of the United Provinces, 1941:
A statistical study. Appendix 5. On a transformation
useful in multivariate analysis computations. *Sankhyā*,
9, 251-3.

Rao, C. R. 1949.   4496
On a class of arrangements. *Proc. Edin. Math. Soc.*,
8, 119-25.

Rao, C. R. 1949.   4497
On some problems arising out of discrimination with
multiple characters. *Sankhyā*, **9**, 343-66.

Rao, C. R. 1949.   4498
Sufficient statistics and minimum variance estimates.
Proc. Camb. Phil. Soc., **45**, 213-18.

Rao, C. R. & Poti, S. J. 1946.   4499
On locally most powerful tests when alternatives are
one sided. *Sankhyā*, **7**, 439.

Rao, C. R. & Shaw, D. C. 1948.   4500
On a formula for the prediction of cranial capacity.
Biometrics, **4**, 247-53.

Rao, C. R. & Slater, P. 1949.   4501
Multivariate analysis applied to differences between
neurotic groups. *Brit. J. Psychol. (Statist. Sec.)*, **2**,
17-29.

Rao, M. V. S. 1946.   4502
A statistical study of labour in the Assam tea planta-
tion. *Sankhyā*, **7**, 445-8.

Rao, W. V. B. S., Desai, S. V.   4503
& Reddy, M. K. 1945-8.
Studies in the methods of estimating total bacterial
counts in the soil. *Indian J. Agric. Sci.*, **15**, 111-15.

Rapoport, A. 1948.   4504
Steady states in random nets. II. *Bull. Math.
Biophys.*, **10**, 221-6.

Rapoport, A. 1949.   4505
Outline of a probabilistic approach to animal sociology.
I, II. *Bull. Math. Biophys.*, **11**, 183-96; 273-81.

Rapoport, A. & Shimbel, A. 1948.   4506
Steady states in random nets. I. *Bull. Math. Biophys.*,
10, 211-20.

Rappleye, S. C. 1946.   4507
A study of the delays encountered by toll operators in
obtaining an idle trunk. *Bell Syst. Tech. J.*, **25**,
539-62.

Rasch, G. 1947.   4508
Recent biometric developments in Denmark.
Biometrics, **3**, 172-5.

Rasch, G. 1948.   4509
A functional equation for Wishart's distribution.
Ann. Math. Statist., **19**, 262-6.

Rashevsky, N. 1945.   4510
A reinterpretation of the mathematical biophysics of
the central nervous system in the light of neuro-
physiological findings. *Bull. Math. Biophys.*, **7**, 151-
60.

Rashevsky, N. 1945.   4511
Some remarks on the Boolean algebra of nervous nets
in mathematical biophysics. *Bull. Math. Biophys.*, **7**,
203-11.

Rashevsky, N. 1945.   4512
A suggestion for another statistical interpretation of
the fundamental equations of the mathematical
biophysics of the central nervous system. *Bull. Math.
Biophys.*, **7**, 223-6.

Rashevsky, N. 1946.   4513
Further contributions to a probabilistic interpretation
of the mathematical biophysics of the central nervous
system. *Bull. Math. Biophys.*, **8**, 51-7.

Rasmussen, P. N. 1948.   4514
Some remarks on the joint effects of simultaneous
relations between economic variables. *Nord. Tidskr.
Teknisk Økonomi*, **12**, 215-22.

Rasmussen, P. N. 1949.   4515
Om estimeringsproblemer for macromodeller. (On
problems of estimation in macromodels.) *National-
økono. Tidskr.*, **87**, 59-69.

Rasor, E. A. 1949.   4516
The fitting of logistic curves by means of a nomograph.
J. Amer. Statist. Ass., **44**, 548-53.

Raven, J. C. 1941.   4517
Standardization of progressive matrices test. *Brit. J.
Med. Psychol.*, **19**, 137-50.

Raven, J. C. 1948.   4518
The comparative assessment of intellectual ability.
Brit. J. Psychol., **39**, 12-19.

Read, D. R. 1949.   4519
A study of the accuracy of simple sampling methods for
the estimation of egg production and mean egg weight.
J. Agric. Sci., **39**, 259-64.

Reboul, G. 1941.   4520
Sur la compressibilité des solides ou des liquides
considerée du point de vue des théories de probabilité.
C. R. Acad. Sci., Paris, **212**, 149-51.

Reboul, G. 1946.   4521
Relations de probabilités dans les cas d'interdépen-
dance. Applications à la chimie. *C. R. Acad. Sci.,
Paris*, **222**, 1320-2.

Reboul, G. 1947.   4522
Probabilités physiques et principes de la thermo-
dynamique. *C. R. Acad. Sci., Paris*, **224**, 314-
16.

Reboul, G. 1948.   4523
Sur les divers modes d'application des relations de
probabilité. *C. R. Acad. Sci., Paris*, **226**, 33-5.

Reboul, G. & Reboul, J.-A. 1944.   4524
Probabilités mathématiques et probabilités physiques.
Applications. *J. Phys. Radium*, (8) **5**, 108-16.

Reboul, G. & Reboul, J.-A. 1946.   4525
Applications des relations de probabilités aux équilibres
physiques et biologiques. *C. R. Acad. Sci., Paris*, **222**,
1063-6.

Reboul, G. & Reboul, J.-A. 1948.   4526
Applications des relations de probabilité aux statistiques
de contamination tuberculeuse. *C. R. Acad. Sci.,
Paris*, **226**, 1653-5.

Reboul, J.-A. 1941. 4527
Facteurs de probabilité et constantes physiques. *C. R. Acad. Sci., Paris,* **212,** 222-4.

Redington, F. M. & Michaelson, R. L. 1941. 4528
An aspect of the " a priori " probability theory of mortality. (German, French and Italian summaries.) *Trans. 12th Int. Congr. Actuar., Lucerne,* 1940, **1,** 225-39.

Reed, J. F & Rigney, J. A.. 1947. 4529
Soil sampling from fields of uniform and non-uniform appearance and soil types. *J. Amer. Soc. Agron.,* **39,** 26-40.

Reed, V. D. 1942. 4530
Business uses of data by census tracts and blocks. *J. Amer. Statist. Ass.,* **37,** 238-46.

Reich, E. 1949. 4531
On the convergence of the classical iterative method of solving linear simultaneous equations. *Ann. Math. Statist.,* **20,** 448-51.

Reichenbach, H. 1941. 4532
Note on probability implication. *Bull. Amer. Math. Soc.,* **47,** 265-7.

Reichenbach, H. 1945. 4533
Reply to Donald C. Williams' criticism of the frequency theory of probability. *Phil. Phenom. Res.,* **5,** 508-12.

Reichenbach, H. 1949. 4534
Philosophical foundations of probability. *Proc. Berkeley Symp. Math. Statist. and Probab.,* 1945-6, pp. 1-20.

Reiersøl, O. 1940. 4535
A method for recurrent computation of all the principal minors of a determinant and its application in confluence analysis. *Ann. Math. Statist.,* **11,** 193-8.

Reiersøl, O. 1941. 4536
Confluence analysis by means of lag moments and other methods of confluence analysis. *Econometrica,* **9,** 1-24.

Reiersøl, O. 1944. 4537
Measures of departure from symmetry. *Skand. Aktuartidskr.,* **27,** 229-34.

Reiersøl, O. 1945. 4538
Confluence analysis by means of instrumental sets of variables. *Ark. Mat. Astr. Fys.,* **32A** (4), 119 pp.

Reiersøl, O. 1945. 4539
Residual variables in regression and confluence analysis. *Skand. Aktuartidskr.,* **28,** 201-17.

Reiersøl, O. 1949. 4540
Identifiability of a linear relation between variables which are subject to error. *Cowles Commission Discussion Papers, Statistics* no. 337.

Reinhardt, H. & Benson, E. D. 1944. 4540[a]
A simplified method of computing control limits for per cent defective. *Industr. Qual. Contr.,* **1** (3), 13-16.

Rémèz, E. J. 1940. 4541
Principe des moindres puissances, $2k$-ièmes et principe des moindres carrés dans les problèmes d'approximation. *C. R. (Dokl.) Acad. Sci. URSS,* **28,** 396-9.

Remmers, H. H. & Akdins, R. M. 1942. 4542
Reliability of multiple-choice measuring instruments as a function of the Spearman-Brown prophecy formula. VI. *J. Educ. Psychol.,* **33,** 385-90.

Remmers, H. H. & Ewart, E. 1941. 4543
Reliability of multiple-choice measuring instruments as a function of the Spearman-Brown prophecy formula. III. *J. Educ. Psychol.,* **32,** 61-6.

Remmers, H. H. & House, J. M. 1941. 4544
Reliability of multiple-choice measuring instruments as a function of the Spearman-Brown prophecy formula. IV. *J. Educ. Psychol.,* **32,** 372-6.

Remmers, H. H. & Sageser, H. W. 1941. 4545
Reliability of multiple-choice measuring instruments as a function of the Spearman-Brown prophecy formula. V. *J. Educ. Psychol.,* **32,** 445-51.

Remmers, H. H., Karslake, R. 4546
& Gage, N. L. 1940.
Reliability of multiple-choice measuring instruments as a function of the Spearman-Brown prophecy formula. I. *J. Educ. Psychol.,* **31,** 583-90.

Renbourn, E. T. & Bonsall, F. F. 1946. 4547
Observations on normal body temperatures in N. India. *Brit. Med. J.,* 909-14.

Rendel, J. M. 1943. 4548
Variations in the weights of hatched and unhatched ducks' eggs. *Biometrika,* **33,** 48-58.

Rényi, A. 1946. 4548[a]
On a Tauberian theorem of O. Szász. *Acta Sci. Math.,* **11,** 119-23.

Rényi, A. 1948. 4549
Simple proof of a theorem of Borel and of the law of the iterated logarithm. *Mat. Tidsskr. B,* **1948,** 41-8.

Rényi, A. 1949. 4550
Un nouveau théorème concernant les fonctions indépendantes et ses applications à la théorie des nombres. *J. Math. Pures Appl.,* (9) **28,** 137-49.

Rényi, A. 1949. 4551
Some remarks on independent random variables. *Acta Math. Acad. Sci. Hung.,* **1** (4), 17-20.

Rényi, A. 1949. 4552
Sur un théorème général de probabilité. *Ann. Inst. Fourier,* **1,** 43-52.

Rényi, A. 1949. 4553
30 years of mathematics in the Soviet Union. I. On the foundation of probability theory. (Hungarian. Russian and English summaries.) *Mat. Lapok.,* **1,** 27-64.

Rényi, A. & Varga, O. 1949. 4554
On the coefficients of Schlicht functions. *Publ. Math., Debrecen,* **1,** 18-23.

Resta, P. 1948. 4555
Scarto quadratico medio e valori potiori. *Riv. Ital. Demogr. Statist.,* **2,** 184-9.

Resta, P. 1949. 4556
Possibilità di abbassare in alcuni casi il limite superiore indicato da Bienaymé-Tchebychef, delle frequenze degli scarti superiori ad un dato limite. *Atti 9ma Riun., Soc. Ital. Demogr. Statist.,* **1947,** pp. 249-56.

Reyburn, H. A. & Raath, M. J. 1949. 4556[a]
Simple structure: a critical examination. *Brit. J. Psychol. (Statist. Sec.),* **2,** 125-33.

Reyburn, H. A. & Taylor, J. G. 1941.   4557
Factorial analysis and school subjects. A criticism.
Trans. Roy. Soc. South Africa, **28**, 168-85.

Reyburn, H. A. & Taylor, J. G. 1941.   4558
Factors in introversion and extroversion. *British J.
Psychol.*, **31**, 335-40.

Reyburn, H. A. & Taylor, J. G. 1943.   4559
On the interpretation of common factors: a criticism
and a statement. *Psychometrika*, **8**, 53-64.

Reynolds, M. M. 1945.   4559a
Process economic analysis aided by new graphic
method. *Chem. Metall. Engng.*, **52**, 104-6.

Reynolds, W. A. 1946.   4560
A prepunched master deck for the computation of
square roots on IBM electrical accounting equipment.
Psychometrika, **11**, 223-38.

Rhodes, E. C. 1940.   4561
Population mathematics. I, II, III. *J. R. Statist. Soc.*,
103, 61-89; 218-45; 362-87.

Rhodes, E. C. 1941.   4562
Secular changes in death rates. *J. R. Statist. Soc.*,
104, 15-42.

Rhodes, F. 1946.   4563
Percentage table for the estimation of sickness rates
for special periods of sickness. *J. Inst. Actuar.*, **72**,
455-69.

Ribeiro, H. 1940.   4564
On a problem of Tchebycheff. *Rev. Fac. Cienc.
Lisboa A*, **2**, 89-92.

Rice, S. O. 1943.   4565
Filtered thermal noise—fluctuation of energy as a
function of internal length. *J. Acoust. Soc. Amer.*, **14**,
216-27.

Rice, S. O. 1944-5.   4566
Mathematical analysis of random noise. *Bell Syst.
Tech. J.*, **23**, 282-332; **24**, 46-156.

Rice, S. O. 1948.   4567
Statistical properties of a sine wave plus random noise.
Bell Syst. Tech. J., **27**, 109-57.

Rice, W. A. 1944.   4568
Setting tolerances scientifically. *Mech. Engng.*, **66**,
801-3.

Rice, W. B. 1943.   4568a
Quality control applied to business administration.
J. Amer. Statist. Ass., **38**, 228-32.

Rice, W. B. 1943-4.   4568b
Quality control through statistics. *Western Industry*,
8, 32; **9**, 36.

Rice, W. B. 1944.   4568c
Statistical uses of accounting data. *Accounting Rev.*,
19, 260-6.

Rice, W. B. 1945.   4568d
Maintaining scientific tolerances by inspection. *Mech.
Engng.*, **67**, 168-70.

Rice, W. B. 1946.   4568e
Statistical quality control: what it is and what it does.
Industr. Qual., Contr., **2** (4), 6-10.

Rich, C. D. 1940.   4569
A general theory of mortality. *J. Inst. Actuar.*, **70**,
364-79.

Rich, C. D. 1948.   4570
The rationale of the use of the geometric average as an
investment index. *J. Inst. Actuar.*, **74**, 338-9.

Rich, W. H. 1943.   4571
An application of the control chart method to the
analysis of fisheries data. *Science*, **97**, 269-70.

Rich, W. H. & Terry, M. C. 1946.   4572
Industrial " control chart " applied to study of epidemics. *Publ. Health Rep.*, **61**, 1501-11.

Richards, P. I. 1948.   4573
Probability of coincidence for two periodically
recurring events. *Ann. Math. Statist.*, **19**, 16-29.

Richardson, J. T. 1946.   4574
Table of Lagrangian coefficients for logarithmic interpolation of standard statistical tables to obtain other
probability levels. *J. R. Statist. Soc. Suppl.* **8**, 212-15.

Richardson, L. F. 1944.   4575
Distribution of wars in time. *J. R. Statist. Soc.*, **107**,
242-50.

Richardson, L. F. 1946.   4576
The number of nations on each side of a war. *J. R.
Statist. Soc.*, **109**, 130-56.

Richardson, L. F. 1946.   4577
The probability of encounters between gas molecules.
Proc. Roy. Soc. A, **186**, 422-31.

Richardson, L. F. 1948.   4578
Variation of the frequency of fatal quarrels with
magnitude. *J. Amer. Statist. Ass.*, **43**, 523-44.

Richardson, M. W. 1940.   4579
Possible applications of factor analysis to public
personnel work. *Publ. Person. Rev.*, **1**, 18-22.

Richardson, M. W. 1941.   4580
The combination of measures. *Bull. Soc. Sci. Res.
Council*, no. 48, pp. 377-402.

Richmond, H. A. & Lejeune, R. R. 1945.   4581
The deterioration of fire-killed spruce by wood-boring
insects in northern Saskatchewan. *For. Chron.*, **21**,
168-92.

Richter, H. 1940.   4582
Eine Bemerkung zum Erneuerungsproblem. *Arch.
Math. Wirtsch.*, **6** (3), 135-6.

Richter, H. 1940.   4583
Die Konvergenz der Erneuerungsfunktion. *Blä.
Versich.-math.*, **5**, 21-35.

Richter, H. 1941.   4584
Untersuchungen zum Erneuerungsproblem. *Math.
Ann.*, **118**, 145-94.

Richter, H. 1949.   4585
Zur Maximalkorrelation. *Zeit. angew. Math. Mech.*,
29, 127-8.

Richter, H. 1949.   4586
Zur Gaussischen Verteilung im *n*-dimensionalen
Raume. (German. Russian summary.) *Zeit.
angew. Math. Mech.*, **29**, 161-4.

Ricker, W. E. 1944.   4587
Further notes on fishing mortality and effort. *Copeia*,
1944, 23-44.

Ricker, W. E. 1945.   4588
Some applications of statistical methods to fishery
problems. *Biometrics Bull.*, **1**, 73-8.

Ricker, W. E. 1948.   4589
Methods of estimating vital statistics of fish populations. *Indiana Univ. Publ. Sci. Series*, no. 15.

Riddell, W. J. B. 1942.   4590
Studies in the classification of eye colour. *Ann. Eugen.*,
11, 245-60.

Riddell, W. J. B. 1945.   4591
Studies in the classification of eye colour. II, III.
Ann. Eugen., **12**, 24-30; 226-73.

Riddell, W. J. B. 1945.   4592
The relationship between the number of speakers and
the number of contributions to the Transactions of the
Ophthalmological Society of the United Kingdom
between 1881 and 1890. *Ann. Eugen.*, **12**, 274-9.

Riddle, O. C. & Baker, G. A. 1944.   4593
Biases encountered in large-scale yield tests. *Hilgardia*,
16, 1-14.

Riebesell, P. 1940.   4594
Einige grundsätzliche Bermerkungen zur Frage des mittleren Fehlers. *Mitt. Math. Ges. Hamburg*, **8** (2), 31-3.

Riebesell, P. 1940.   4595
Neue deutsche Forschungen über das Gesetz der grossen
Zahl. *Blä. Versich.-math.*, **5**, 68-75.

Riebesell, P. 1941.   4596
Die mathematischen Grundlagen der Sachversicherung.
(French, Italian and English summaries.) *Trans. 12th
Int. Congr. Actuar., Lucerne*, 1940, **4**, 27-36.

Riebesell, P. 1948.   4597
Kritische Betrachtungen zur sogenannten Grosszahlforschung in der Technik und zur Anwendung
mathematischstatistischer Methoden in der Biologie
und Medizin. *Zeit. angew. Math. Mech.*, **28**, 226-34.

Riebesell, P. 1949.   4598
Ein einfaches Stabilitätsmess und seine Anwendung in
der Versicherung. *Mitt. Math. Arch.*, **1**, 181-4.

Rife, D. C. 1940.   4599
Handedness with special reference to twins. I, II, III.
Genetics, **25**, 178-86.

Rife, D. C. & Kloepfer, H. W. 1943.   4600
An investigation of the linkage relationships of the
blood groups and types with hand patterns and
handedness. *Ohio J. Sci.*, **43**, 182-5.

Rigg, F. A. 1944.   4601
A method of combining two frequency distributions.
*U.K. Min. Supply Advisory Service Statist. Method
& Qual. Contr. Tech. Rep. Ser. R*, no. QC/R/8, 17
January 1944, 4 pp.

Rigg, F. A. 1946.   4602
Recent advances in mathematical statistics. *J. R.
Statist. Soc.*, **109**, 395-450.

Rigney, J. A. 1946.   4603
Good experiments are not accidental. *Res. & Farming*,
5, Progress Rep. no. 1, 10, 12.

Rigney, J. A. 1946.   4604
Some statistical problems confronting horticultural
investigators. *Proc. Amer. Soc. Hort. Sci.*, **48**, 351-7.

Rigney, J. A. 1949.   4605
Techniques in field plot experimentation. *Proc.
Auburn Conf. Statist. Appl. Res. Social Sci., Plant. Sci.
and Animal Sci.*, 1948, pp. 39-44.

Rigney, J. A. & Blaser, R. E. 1948.   4606
Sampling alyce clover for chemical analyses.
Biometrics, **4**, 234-9.

Rigney, J. A. & Reed, J. F. 1945.   4607
Some factors affecting the accuracy of soil sampling.
Proc. Soil Sci. Soc. Amer., **10**, 257-9.

Rigney, J. A. & Wakeley, J. T. 1947.   4608
The use of frequency distributions of weather factors
in agronomic practices. *J. Amer. Soc. Agron.*, **39**,
1088-93.

Rigney, J. A., Morrow, E. B.   4609
& Lott, W. L. 1949.
A method of controlling experimental error for
perennial horticultural crops. *Proc. Amer. Soc. Hort.
Sci.*, **54**, 209-12.

Rimmer, F. & Henderson, M. T. 1943.   4610
Linkage studies in barley. *Genetics*, **28**, 419-40.

Riordan, J. 1944.   4611
Three-line Latin rectangles. I, II. *Amer. Math.
Monthly*, **51**, 450-2; **53**, 18-20.

Riordan, J. 1949.   4612
Inversion formulas in normal variable mapping. *Ann.
Math. Statist.*, **20**, 417-25.

Rios, S. 1946.   4613
Sobre la probabilidad de que una serie de Taylor
admita prolongacion analitica. *Rev. Mat. Hisp.-Amer.*,
(4) **6**, 174-6.

Risser, R. 1944.   4614
Sur les courbes de distribution statistique. *C. R.
Acad. Sci., Paris*, **219**, 505-7.

Risser, R. 1944.   4615
Étude spéciale du type de tirages de boules d'une urne,
renfermant des boules de deux couleurs, dans l'hypothèse de non remise des boules après tirage. *C. R.
Acad. Sci., Paris*, **219**, 541-2.

Risser, R. 1945.   4616
Sur l'équation caractéristique des surfaces de probabilités. *C. R. Acad. Sci., Paris*, **220**, 31-2.

Risser, R. 1945.   4617
Sur le mode de tirages contagieux. *C. R. Acad. Sci.,
Paris*, **220**, 210-12.

Risser, R. 1947.   4618
D'un certain mode de recherche des surfaces
de probabilités. *C. R. Acad. Sci., Paris*, **225**,
1266-8.

Risser, R. 1948.   4619
Note relative aux surfaces de probabilités. *Bull. Ass.
Actuair. Belg.*, **53**, 5-48. (Also: *J. Soc. Statist. Paris*,
89, 381-409.)

Risser, R. 1948.   4620
Essai sur les courbes de distribution statistique. *Bull.
Ass. Actuair. Belg.*, **54**, 41-72. (Also: *J. Soc. Statist.
Paris*, **89**, 288-306.)

Risser, R. 1949.   4621
Solution de la question relative au calcul des
probabilités. *Bull. Trim. Inst. Actuair. Français*, **60**,
43-5.

Rissik, H. 1940.   4621ª
Statistical methods in engineering practice. *Engineer,
London*, **170**, 341-2; 357-9; 372-3; 389-90; 404-6.

Rissik, H. 1941.   4621ᵇ
Probability graph paper and its engineering applications. I, II. *Engineer, London*, **172**, 276-8; 296-8.

Rissik, H. 1942.   4621ᶜ
Model quality control charts. I, II, III. *Engineer, London*, **174**, 64-5; 86-9; 106-8.

Rissik, H. 1942.   4622
Quality control in production engineering. *Machinery, London*, **60**, 257-60; 291-5. (Also (1943): *Aircraft Engng.*, **15**, 55-8; 85-90; 115-19; 121.)

Rissik, H. 1942.   4622ᵃ
Pioneering achievement in quality control. *Machinery, London*, **61**, 169-72.

Rissik, H. 1943.   4622ᵇ
Quality assurance through sampling inspection. *Engng. Insp.*, **8** (2), 12-29. (Also: *Engineer, London*, **175**, 334-5; 346-7.)

Rissik, H. 1943.   4622ᶜ
Recent developments in quality control. *Machinery, London*, **63**, 10-16.

Rissik, H. 1943.   4622ᵈ
Sampling inspection and quality determination. *Aircraft Engng.*, **15**, 149-51; 179-82.

Rivlin, R. S. 1945.   4623
An extension of Campbell's theorem of random fluctuations. *Phil. Mag.*, (7) **36**, 688-93.

Robbins, H. E. 1944.   4624
On the measure of a random set. *Ann. Math. Statist.*, **15**, 70-4.

Robbins, H. E. 1944.   4625
On distribution-free tolerance limits in random sampling. *Ann. Math. Statist.*, **15**, 214-16.

Robbins, H. E. 1944.   4626
On the expected values of two statistics. *Ann. Math. Statist.*, **15**, 321-3.

Robbins, H. E. 1945.   4627
On the measure of a random set. II. *Ann. Math. Statist.*, **16**, 342-7 (addendum: **18**, 297).

Robbins, H. E. 1946.   4628
On the (*C*, 1) summability of certain random sequences. *Bull. Amer. Math. Soc.*, **52**, 699-703.

Robbins, H. E. 1948.   4629
On the asymptotic distribution of the sum of a random number of random variables. *Bull. Amer. Math. Soc.*, **54**, 1151-1161. (Also: *Proc. Nat. Acad. Sci. U.S.A.*, **34**, 162-3.)

Robbins, H. E. 1948.   4630
Convergence of distributions. *Ann. Math. Statist.*, **19**, 72-6.

Robbins, H. E. 1948.   4631
The distribution of a definite quadratic form. *Ann. Math. Statist.*, **19**, 266-70.

Robbins, H. E. 1948.   4632
Mixture of distributions. *Ann. Math. Statist.*, **19**, 360-9.

Robbins, H. E. 1948.   4633
The distribution of Student's *t* when the population means are unequal. *Ann. Math. Statist.*, **19**, 406-10.

Robbins, H. E. 1948.   4634
Some remarks on the inequality of Tchebychef. *Studies and Essays presented to R. Courant*, pp. 345-50.

Robbins, H. & Pitman, E. J. G. 1949.   4635
Application of the method of mixtures to quadratic forms in normal variates. *Ann. Math. Statist.*, **20**, 552-60.

Roberts, A. 1941.   4636
The interval selector: a device for measuring time distribution of pulses. *Rev. Sci. Instru.*, **12**, 71-6.

Roberts, F. L. 1941.   4636ᵃ
Teaching of statistical analysis in medical schools. *J. Ass. Amer. Med. Coll.*, **16**, 45-8.

Roberts, W. J. 1945.   4637
How quality control can improve batch production. *Industr. Power & Production*, **21**, 47-8.

Robertson, A. & Lerner, I. M. 1949.   4638
The heritability of all-or-none traits: viability in poultry. *Genetics*, **34**, 395-411.

Robertson, F. W. & Sang, J. H. 1944.   4639
The ecological determinants of population growth in a *drosophila* culture. I. Fecundity of adult flies. II. Circumstances affecting egg viability. *Proc. Roy. Soc. B*, **132**, 258-91.

Robertson, W. M. & Mulloy, G. A. 1946.   4640
Sample plot methods. *Dominion Forest Service, Ottawa*.

Robinson, H. 1945.   4640ᵃ
Determination by statistical analysis of process minimums for spot welding. *Welding J., Easton*, **24**, 455-61.

Robinson, H. F. 1947.   4641
How do experimental statistics fit into agricultural research? *Res. & Farming*, **5**, Progress Rep. no 2, 7 pp.

Robinson, H. F. & Watson, G. S. 1949.   4641ᵃ
An analysis of simple and triple rectangular lattice designs. *North Carolina Agric. Exper. Sta. Tech. Bull.* no. 88, 56 pp.

Robinson, H. F., Comstock, R. E.   4642
& Harvey, P. H. 1949.
Estimates of heritability and the degree of dominance in corn. *Agron. J.*, **41**, 353-59.

Robinson, H. F., Rigney, J. A.   4643
& Harvey, P. H. 1948.
Investigations in peanut plot technique. *North Carolina Agric. Exper. Sta. Tech. Bull.*, **36**, 19 pp.

Robinson, J. 1948.   4644
A note on exact sequential analysis. *Univ. Calif. Publ. Statist.*, **1**, 241-6.

Robinson, J. L. & Reiss, F. 1944.   4645
The 1943 Iowa corn yield test. *Iowa Agric. Exper. Sta. Res. Bull.*, **358**, 852-903.

Rocard, Y. 1948.   4646
Quelques faits mathématiques fondamentaux en économétrie. *Rev. Sci., Paris*, **86**, 199-207.

Rocard, Y. 1949.   4647
Les modèles économiques dynamiques. *Econometrica Suppl.*, **17**, 328-9.

Rochlitz, J. 1943.   4648
Forditasi problémák a statisztikai irodalom köréböl. (Problems of translation in statistics) *Magyar Statist. Szemle, Budapest*, **21**, (2-3), 102-12.

Rockwood, N. C. 1940. 4649
Sampling cement materials. *Rock Products*, **43**, 47-8.

Roddam, T. 1945. 4650
What is quality control. Background for wireless technicians. *Wireless World*, **51**, 243-5.

Rodgers, E. 1940. 4651
Probable errors for Poisson distributions. *Phys. Rev.*, (2) **57**, 735-7.

Rodrigues, M. da S. 1943. 4652
Sistemas de atributos. (Portuguese.) *Rev. Brasil. Estatíst.*, **4**, 3-10.

Rodrigues, M. da S. 1945. 4653
On an extension of the concept of moment with applications to measures of variability, general similarity and overlapping. *Ann. Math. Statist.*, **16**, 74-84.

Rodrigues, M. da S. 1945. 4654
Note on a general expression of the means. *Estadística, Mexico*, **3**, 538-9.

Rodrigues, M. da S. 1945. 4655
On the training of statisticians. *J. Amer. Statist. Ass.*, **40**, 172-4. (Also (1946): A formaçào do estatístico. *Rev. Brasil. Estatíst.*, **7**, 245-54.)

Roessler, E. B. 1943. 4656
Valid estimates of variance in the analysis of pooled data. *Proc. Amer. Soc. Hort. Sci.*, **42**, 481-3.

Roessler, E. B. 1946. 4657
Testing the significance of observations compared with a control. *Proc. Amer. Soc. Hort. Sci.*, **47**, 249-51.

Roessler, E. B. & Leach, L. D. 1944. 4658
Analysis of combined data for identical replicated experiments. *Proc. Amer. Soc. Hort. Sci.*, **44**, 323-8.

Roff, M. 1940. 4659
Linear dependence in multiple correlation work. *Psychometrika*, **5**, 295-8.

Roff, M. & Roff, C. 1940. 4660
An analysis of the variance of conflict behaviour in pre-school children. *Child Development*, **11**, 43-60.

Rogers, W. T. 1946. 4661
Practical application of statistical methods in a quality control program. *Blast Furnace & Steel Plant*, **34**, 233-5. (Also (1946): *Trans. Amer. Soc. Metals*, **36**, 361-88.)

Rogers, W. T. 1946. 4662
Statistical methods of quality control. *Purchasing*, **20**, 122-3.

Rojas, G. C. 1942. 4663
Formula para el error standard de una razón. *Bol. Soc. Venezolana Cienc. Nat.*, **7**, 229-31.

Romanovskii, V. I. 1940. 4664
Connected series and tests of randomness. (Russian.) *Izv. Akad. Nauk Uzbek. SSR, Ser. Fiz.*, **7**, 38-50.

Romanovskii, V. I. 1940. 4665
On inductive conclusions in statistics. *C. R. (Dokl.) Acad. Sci. URSS*, **27**, 419-21.

Romanovskii, V. I. 1940. 4666
Statistical problems connected with Markov chains. (Russian.) *Trudy Fiz. Uzbek. Akad. Nauk SSR.*

Romanovskii, V. I. 1941. 4667
Bicyclic sequences. (Russian.) *Trudy Fiz. Uzbek. Akad. Nauk SSR, Ser. Mat.*, **1**.

Romanovskii, V. I. 1941. 4668
Fundamental concepts and problems of mathematical statistics. (Russian.) *Trudy Uzbek. Fiz. Akad. Nauk SSR, Ser. Mat.*, **2**.

Romanovskii, V. I. 1941. 4669
Markov's method of deriving the limit distribution for events connected in chains. (Russian.) *Izv. Uzbek. Fiz. Akad. Nauk SSR*, **3**, 3-8.

Romanovskii, V. I. 1942. 4670
On inductive deduction in statistics. (Russian.) *Trudy Uzbek. Fiz. Akad. Nauk SSR, Ser. Mat.*, **3**.

Romanovskii, V. I. 1943. 4671
On fundamental problems in the theory of errors. (Russian.) *Trudy Uzbek. Fiz. Akad. Nauk SSR, Ser. Mat.*, **4**.

Romanovskii, V. I. 1945. 4672
Fundamental properties of polycyclic chains (Russian.) *Byull. Sred. Asia. Gos. Univ.*, **23**, 22ff.

Romanovskii, V. I. 1945. 4673
On limiting distributions for stochastic processes with discrete time parameter. (Russian.) *Trudy Sred. Asia. Gos. Univ.*, **4**, 25 pp.

Romanovskii, V. I. 1945. 4674
On Markov-Bruns chains. (Russian.) *Byull. Sred. Asia. Gos. Univ.*, **23**.

Romanovskii, V. I. 1945. 4675
On a random series of correlated events. (Russian.) *Byull. Sred. Asia. Gos. Univ.*, **23**, 17-19.

Romanovskii, V. I. 1945. 4676
On sampling characteristics of a limit distribution. (Russian.) *Byull. Sred. Asia Gos. Univ.*, **23**.

Romanovskii, V. I. 1946. 4677
On Pearson's curves. (Russian.) *Trudy Inst. Mat. Mekh. Akad. Nauk Uzbek. SSR.*

Romanovskii, V. I. 1946. 4678
On the probabilities of the recurrence of cycles in polycyclic chains. (Russian.) *Trudy Sred. Asia. Gos. Univ.*, **7**, 20 pp. (Also (1945): *Byull. Sred. Asia. Gos. Univ.*, **23**.)

Romanovskii, V. I. 1946. 4679
Sur certains théorèmes concernant la méthode des moindres carrés. *C. R. (Dokl.) Acad. Sci. URSS*, **51**, 263-5.

Romanovskii, V. I. 1947. 4680
Estimating the quality of production by small samples selected at frequent intervals. (Russian.) *Trudy Inst. Mat. Mekh. Akad. Nauk Uzbek. SSR.*

Romanovskii, V. I. 1947. 4681
On estimating the location of a target using results classified by sign. (Russian.) *Trudy Inst. Mat. Mekh. Akad. Nauk Uzbek. SSR*, **2**.

Romanovskii, V. I. 1947. 4682
On some problems of mass production. (Russian.) *Trudy Inst. Mat. Mekh. Akad. Nauk Uzbek, SSR*, **2**.

Romanovskii, V. I. 1948. 4683
On estimating a successful outcome. (Russian.) *Dokl. Akad. Nauk Uzbek. SSR*, **8**.

Romanovskii, V. I. 1949. 4684
On an implicit lemma of Markov and lemmas similar to it. (Russian.) *Dokl. Akad. Nauk Uzbek. SSR*, **1949** (4), 3-5.

Romanovskii, V. I. 1949. 4685
On a limit distribution of extreme values of samples drawn from a continuous distribution. (Russian.) *Jubilee Publ., 25th Anniv. Uzbek. SSR.*

Romanovskii, V. I. 1949. 4686
On ordered samples drawn from the same continuous population. (Russian.) *Trudy Inst. Mat. Mekh. Akad. Nauk Uzbek. SSR,* **7.**

Romer, B. 1947. 4687
Die Bestimmung von durchschnittlichen Krankenkosten an Stichproben. *Mitt. Ver. Schweiz. Versich.-Math.,* **47,** 249-71.

Roop, W. P. 1947. 4688
Transitional evaluations and treatment of experimental data subject to very wide scatter. *Bull. Amer. Soc. Test. Mat.,* **147,** 73-6.

Roper, E. 1940. 4689
Sampling public opinion. *J. Amer. Statist. Ass.,* **35,** 325-34.

Ros, J. J. 1945. 4690
Medidas de variación, oscilación y permanencia. *Bol. Estadíst. Dir. Gen. Estadíst., Madrid,* **28,** 358-66.

Rosander, A. C. 1942. 4691
The use of inversions as a test of random order. *J. Amer. Statist. Ass.,* **37,** 352-8.

Rose Jibaja, J. 1946. 4692
Aplicabilidad en la agricultura peruana del método estadístico de los " ejemplares-tipo ". *Estadíst. Peruana,* **2** (4), 27-49.

Rosenblatt, A. 1940. 4693
On the law of large numbers in the theory of probability. (Spanish.) *Univ. Nac. Litoral, Publ. Inst. Mat.,* **2,** 141-6.

Rosenblatt, A. 1940. 4694
Sur les théorèmes des grands nombres dans la théorie de la probabilité. *Actas Acad. Cient., Lima,* **3,** 152-9.

Rosenblatt, A. 1940. 4695
Sur les théorèmes des petits nombres de Poisson, de Bortkiewicz et G. Pólya. Application aux phénomènes rares. I. Propagation des maladies contagieuses: peste bubonique au Brésil. *Actas Acad. Cient., Lima,* **3,** 160-7.

Rosenblatt, A. 1940. 4696
Sur le concept de contagion de M. G. Pólya dans le calcul des probabilités. Divers schèmes. Application à la peste bubonique au Pérou. *Actas Acad. Cient., Lima,* **3,** 186-204.

Rosenblatt, A. 1944. 4697
On the application of mathematical statistics to bacteriology. I. Method of dilution of Louis Pasteur. Case of a single dilution. Application of the second law of P. S. Laplace. (Spanish.) *Rev. Univ. Nac. Tucumán A,* **4,** 217-34.

Rosenblatt, A. 1945. 4698
On the strong law of large numbers. (Spanish.) *Actas Acad. Cient., Lima,* **8,** 7-26.

Rosenblatt, A. 1946. 4699
On the theory of the X chromosomes in genetics. *Rev. Cient., Lima,* **48,** 3-17.

Rosi, M. 1949. 4700
More on the sampling method in agricultural statistics and its application to agriculture in the Province of Milan. (Italian.) *Riv. Econ. Agron.,* **4,** 118-26.

Rosner, B. S. 1948. 4701
An algebraic solution for the communalities. *Psychometrika,* **13,** 181-4.

Ross, K. E. & Summers, C. M. 1944. 4702
The application of statistics to dielectrics. *Elect. Engng., New York,* **63,** 405.

Rossi, B. & Greisen, K. 1941. 4703
Cosmic-ray theory. *Rev. Mod. Phys.,* **13,** 240-309.

Rothschild, C. & Mourier, É. 1947. 4704
Sur les lois de probabilité à régression linéaire et écart type lié constant. *C. R. Acad. Sci., Paris,* **225,** 1117-19.

Rott, N. 1946. 4705
Über Wahrscheinlichkeitsprobleme der Garnfestigkeitsprüfung. *Schweiz. Arch. Angew. Wiss. Tech.,* **12,** 93-5.

Rounsefell, G. A. 1949. 4706
Methods of estimating total runs and escapements of salmon. *Biometrics,* **5,** 115-26.

Rouquet la Carrigue, V. 1949. 4707
Fluctuations longues et oscillations cycliques. *J. Soc. Statist. Paris,* **90,** 298-313.

Roy, G. C. 1944. 4708
On the application of time-series analysis to the data relating to the Indian Posts and Telegraphs Department. *Sankhyā,* **6,** 391-8.

Roy, R. 1944. 4709
Théorie des choix. *J. Soc. Statist. Paris,* **85,** 134-8.

Roy, R. 1949. 4710
Les nombres indices. *J. Soc. Statist. Paris,* **90,** 15-34.

Roy, R. 1949. 4711
De la théorie des choix aux budgets de familles. *Economtrica Suppl.,* **17,** 179-91.

Roy, S. N. 1940. 4712
On the distribution of certain symmetric functions of p-statistics on the null hypothesis. Distributions of p-statistics on the non-null hypothesis. *Science & Culture,* **5,** 562-3.

Roy, S. N. 1941. 4713
The distribution on the non-null hypothesis of the statistic, the ratio of " between standard deviation " and " within standard deviation ". *Science & Culture,* **6,** 552.

Roy, S. N. 1942. 4714
The sampling distribution of p-statistics and certain allied statistics on the non-null hypothesis. *Sankhyā,* **6,** 15-34.

Roy, S. N. 1942. 4715
Analysis of variance for multivariate normal populations: the sampling distribution of the requisite p-statistics on the null and non-null hypotheses. *Sankhyā,* **6,** 35-50.

Roy, S. N. 1945. 4716
On a certain class of multiple integrals. *Bull. Calcutta Math. Soc.,* **37,** 69-77.

Roy, S. N. 1945.   4717
The individual sampling distribution of the maximum, the minimum and any intermediate of the p-statistics on the null-hypothesis. *Sankhyā*, **7**, 133-58.

Roy, S. N. 1946.   4718
Multivariate analysis of variance: the sampling distribution of the numerically largest of the p-statistics on the non-null hypothesis. *Sankhyā*, **8**, 15-52.

Roy, S. N. 1946.   4719
A note on multivariate analysis of variance when the number of variates is greater than the number of linear hypotheses per character. *Sankhyā*, **8**, 53-66.

Roy, S. N. 1947.   4720
A note on critical angles between two flats in hyperspace with certain statistical applications. *Sankhyā*, **8**, 177-94.

Roy, S. N. 1947.   4721
A note on the relation between testing of hypotheses and estimation by confidence interval. *Bull. Calcutta Statist. Ass.*, **1**, 89-91.

Roy, S. N. 1947-8.   4722
Notes on testing of composite hypotheses. I, II. *Sankhyā*, **8**, 257-70; **9**, 19-38.

Roy, S. N. 1948.   4723
An outline of some modern theories of statistical inference. *Proc. 35th Indian Sci. Congr.*, II, 177-202.

Roy, S. N. & Banerjee, K. 1940.   4724
On hierarchical sampling, hierarchical variances and their connexion with other aspects of statistical theory. *Science & Culture*, **6**, 189.

Roy, S. N. & Bose, P. K. 1940.   4725
On the reduction formulae for the incomplete probability integral of the Studentized D^2-statistic. *Science & Culture*, **5**, 773-5.

Roy, S. N. & Bose, P. K. 1940.   4726
The distribution of the root-mean square of the second type of the multiple correlation coefficient. *Science & Culture*, **6**, 59.

Roy, S. N. & Bose, P. K. 1945.   4727
Bernoulli's theorem and Tshebycheff's analogue. *Sankhyā*, **7**, 209-10.

Roy, S. N. & Bose, P. K. 1948.   4728
On the construction of unbiassed and most powerful critical region out of any given statistic. *Bull. Calcutta Statist. Ass.*, **1**, 177-82.

Roy, S. N. & Bose, R. C. 1940.   4729
The use and distribution of the Studentized D^2-statistic when the variances and covariances are based on k samples. *Sankhyā*, **4**, 535-42.

Royan, R. 1945.   4730
Comment on post-war quality control of commercial products. *Engng. Insp.*, **10** (1), 39.

Royan, R. & Rissik, H. 1942.   4731
Statistical control of quality in production engineering. *Engng. Insp.*, **7** (1), 4-19.

Royer, E. B. 1941.   4732
A machine method for computing the biserial correlation coefficient in item validation. *Psychometrika*, **6**, 55-9.

Ruark, A. E. 1944.   4733
Differential equations for the probability distribution of events. *Phys. Rev.*, (2) **65**, 88-90.

Rubbert, F. K. 1948.   4734
Praktische Interpolation höherer Ordnung. *Zeit. angew. Math. Mech.*, **28**, 122-4.

Rubin, H. 1945.   4735
On the distribution of the serial correlation coefficient. *Ann. Math. Statist.*, **16**, 211-15.

Ruch, H. 1949.   4736
Die Gewinnbeteiligung bei hohen Versicherungssummen. *Skand. Aktuartidskr.*, **32**, 74-81.

Ruch, H. 1949.   4737
Eine Variation der t-Methode. *Mitt. Ver. Schweiz. Versich.-Math.*, **49**, 165-9.

Ruhland, G. C., Gillick, F. C.   4738
& Chinn, B. D. 1945.
The possibility of predicting the future needs in venereal disease control. *J. Venereal Disease Inform.*, **26**, 222-9.

Ruist, E. 1946.   4739
Standard errors of the tilling coefficients used in confluence analysis. *Econometrica*, **14**, 235-41.

Ruiz Almansa, J. 1944.   4740
Tecnica y technologia en estadística. Sus fundamentos racionales. *Bol. Estadíst. Dir. Gen. Estadíst. Madrid*, **22**, 273-306.

Rulon, P. J. 1949.   4741
Matrix representation of models for the analysis of variance and covariance. *Psychometrika*, **14**, 259-78.

Rusam, F. 1941.   4742
Grundzuge der Mathematik der privaten Krankheitkostenversicherung. *Trans. 12th Int. Congr. Actuar.*, *Lucerne*, 1940, **4**, 147-67.

Russell, C. Scott. 1945.   4743
Errors in the routine daily measurement of the puerperal uterus. *Biometrika*, **33**, 213-21.

Rutherford, C. D. 1946.   4744
Actuarial mathematics and statistics. *Proc. 1st Canadian Math. Congr.*, *Montreal*, 1945, pp. 25-30.

Rutman, M. A. 1946.   4745
Concerning a paper by T. A. Sarymsakov. *C. R. (Dokl.) Acad. Sci. URSS*, **52**, 567-8.

Rybarz, J. 1949.   4746
Zum Hattendorffschen Satz. *Statist. Viertjschr.*, **2**, 32-6.

S

Sabin, A. R. 1940.   4747
A new technique for the estimation of changes in farm employment (No. 1 of a series of analyses of sample farm data). *United States Dept. Agric., Agric. Marketing Service.*

Sacchetti, A. 1941.   4748
Sulla misura della variabilità dei caratieri lineari in antropometria. *Atti 2da Riun. Sci., Soc. Ital. Statist.*, pp. 40-51.

Sadowsky, M. A. 1944.   4749
Mathematical analysis in psychology of education: computation of stimulation, rapport, and instructor's driving power. *Psychometrika*, **9**, 249-56.

Safford, H. F. 1946.   4749a
The U.S. Army Ordnance Department's use of quality control. *Indu str. Qual. Contr.*, **2** (4a), 4.

Sagoroff, S. 1949.   4750
Die Berechnung des Volkseinkommens als statistisches Problem. *Allg. Statist. Arch.*, **33**, 171-90.

Saibel, E. 1944.   4751
A rapid method of inversion of certain types of matrices. *J. Franklin Inst.*, **237**, 197-201.

Sakamoto, H. 1943.   4752
On the distributions of the product and the quotient of the independent and uniformly distributed random variables. *Tôhoku Math. J.*, **49**, 243-60.

Sakamoto, H. 1944.   4753
On the independence of two statistics. *Res. Mem. Inst. Statist. Math., Tokyo*, **1**, 1-25.

Sakamoto, H. 1949.   4754
On the criteria of the independence and the degrees of freedom of statistics and their applications to the analysis of variance. *Ann. Inst. Statist. Math., Tokyo*, **1**, 109-22.

Sakamoto, H. 1949.   4755
On independence of statistical quantities. (Japanese.) *Sûgaku*, **1**, 263-74.

Sala, E. 1949.   4756
Studio statistico di una equazione stocastica particolare. *Riv. Ital. Econ. Demogr. Statist.*, **3** (3-4), 223-9.

Sala, F. 1947.   4757
Sur une méthode approximative pour le calcul des primes pures pour quelque position caractéristique, sans connaître autre que les probabilités annuelles de survie pour les âges de 1 en 10 ans. *Verzekerings-archief.*, **27**, 128-34.

Sales Valles, F. de A. 1947.   4758
Some considerations on the foundations of the theory of errors. (Spanish.) *Rev. Mat. Hisp.-Amer.*, (4) **7**, 165-72.

Sales Valles, F. de A. 1948.   4759
Sobre la primera ley de errores de Laplace. *Coll. Mat.*, **1** (2), 85-135.

Salmon, S. C. 1940.   4760
The use of modern statistical methods in field experiments. *J. Amer. Soc. Agron.*, **32**, 308-20.

Salter, L. A. 1942.   4761
A comment on Deming's classification of problems of inference. *J. Amer. Statist. Ass.*, **37**, 540-2.

Salvekar, P. M. 1945.   4761a
Minimum size of the sample required for experimental work to estimate the population mean with a specified degree of accuracy for a specified level of reliability. *J. Univ. Bombay*, A, **13** (5), 2-6.

Salvemini, T. 1942.   4762
Gli indici semplici di omofilia e di correlazione tra classi di valori equispaziati. *Atti 3za Riun. Sci., Soc. Ital. Statist.*, pp. 62-75.

Salvemini, T. 1942.   4763
Di uno scarto trigonometrico medio, nel caso delle serie cicliche. *Atti 2do Congr. Un. Mat. Ital., Bologna*, 1940, pp.657-71.

Salvemini, T. 1943.   4764
La revisione critica del Gini ai fondamenti della metodologia statistica. *Statistica, Ferrara*, **3** (1), 46-59.

Salvemini, T. 1943.   4765
Sullo scarto trigonometrico medio. *Atti 5ta Riun. Sci., Soc. Ital. Statist.*, pp. 215-27.

Salvemini, T. 1945.   4766
Sul calcolo degli indici di concordanza tra due caratteri quantitativi. *Atti 6ta Riun. Sci., Soc. Ital. Statist.*, pp. 117-43.

Salvemini, T. 1945-6.   4767
Sulla misura della strettezza o rigore di una relazione statistica. *Statistica. Milano*, **5-6**, 291-315.

Salvemini, T. 1947.   4768
Su alcuni indici usati per la misura delle relazioni, statistiche. *Statistica, Milano*, **7**, 200-18.

Salvemini, T. 1947.   4769
Su un nuovo indice proposto da Fréchet per la misura della dipendenza statistica. *Statistica, Milano*, **7**, 219-26.

Salvemini, T. 1948.   4770
Aspetti della correlazione. *Atti 3to Congr. Un. Mat. Ital., Pisa*, pp. 1-5.

Salvemini, T. 1948.   4771
Sulla variabilità relativa. *Statistica, Milano*, **8**, 240-79.

Salvemini, T. 1948.   4772
Recenti contributi alla teoria della transvariazione. *Statistica, Milano*, **8**, 356-60.

Salvemini, T. 1949.   4773
Contributo allo studio della mutabilità delle serie cicliche. *Metron*, **15**, 29-70.

Salvemini, T. 1949.   4774
Nuovi procedimenti di calcolo degli indici di dissomiglianza e di connessione. *Statistica, Milano*, **9**, 3-26.

Salvi, F. 1949.   4775
Estensione di alcuni teoremi classici del calcolo delle probabilitá. *R. C. Mat. Univ. Roma, Ist. Naz. Alta Mat.*, (5) **8**, 282-308.

Samuelson, P. A. 1941.   4776
Conditions that the roots of a polynomial be less than unity in absolute value. *Ann. Math. Statist.*, **12**, 360-4.

Samuelson, P. A. 1942.   4777
A method of determining explicitly the coefficients of the characteristic equation. *Ann. Math. Statist.*, **13**, 424-9.

Samuelson, P. A. 1942.   4778
The stability of equilibrium. Linear and nonlinear systems. *Econometrica*, **10**, 1-25.

Samuelson, P. A. 1942.   4779
A note on alternative regressions. *Econometrica*, **10**, 80-3.

Samuelson, P. A. 1943.   4780
Fitting general Gram-Charlier series. *Ann. Math. Statist.*, **14**, 179-87.

Samuelson, P. A. 1948.   4781
Exact distribution of continuous variables in sequential analysis. *Econometrica*, **16**, 191-8.

Sandler, J. 1949.   4782
The reciprocity principle as an aid to factor analysis. *Brit. J. Psychol. (Statist. Sec.)*, **2**, 177-84.

Sandomire, M. M. 1941.   4783
Accumulating cubes with punch cards. *J. Amer. Statist. Ass.*, **36**, 507-14.

Sandon, F. 1943.   4784
Control charts in script assessment in large written examinations. *J. R. Statist. Soc.*, **106**, 343-8.

Sandon, F. 1946.   4785
Scores for ranked data in school examination practice. *Ann. Eugen.*, **13**, 118-21.

Santa da Costa, A. M. 1948.   4786
Classificaca estatistica. *Rev. Economia Lisboa*, **1** (1), 26-8.

Santaló, L. A. 1940.   4787
On mean values and geometrical probabilities. *Abh. Math. Sem. Hansischen Univ.*, **13**, 284-94.

Santaló, L. A. 1940.   4787[a]
Sur quelques problèmes de probabilités géométriques. *Tôhoku Math. J.*, **47**, 159-71.

Santaló, L. A. 1941.   4787[b]
Generalisation of a problem of geometrical probabilities. *Rev. Union Mat. Argent.*, **7**, 129-32.

Santaló, L. A. 1941.   4788
A system of mean values in the theory of geometric probabilities. (Spanish.) *Rev. Cient., Lima*, **43**, 147-54.

Santaló, L. A. 1943.   4789
On the probable distribution of corpuscles in a body, derived from their distribution in its cross-sections, and similar problems. (Spanish.) *Rev. Union Mat. Argent.*, **9**, 145-64.

Santaló, L. A. 1945.   4789[a]
Mean value of the number of regions into which a body is divided by *n* arbitrary planes. *Rev. Union Mat. Argent.*, **10**, 101-8.

Santaló, L. A. 1945.   4789[b]
Las probabilidades geometricas y la geometria integral. *Bol. Fac. Ingeniera Montevideo*, **3** (1), 91-113.

Santaló, L. A. 1946.   4789[c]
On the length of a space curve as a mean value of the length of its orthogonal projection. (Spanish.) *Math. Notae*, **6**, 158-66.

Santaló, L. A. 1947.   4790
On the first two moments of the measure of a random set. *Ann. Math. Statist.*, **18**, 37-49.

Sapogov, N. A. 1947.   4791
On singular Markov chains. (Russian.) *Dokl. Akad. Nauk SSSR*, **58**, 193-6.

Sapogov, N. A. 1947.   4792
The Laplace-Lyapunov limit theorem for singular Markov chains. (Russian.) *Dokl. Akad. Nauk SSSR*, **58**, 1905-8.

Sapogov, N. A. 1948.   4793
On sums of dependent random variables. (Russian.) *Dokl. Akad. Nauk SSSR*, **63**, 353-6.

Sapogov, N. A. 1948.   4794
On the law of the iterated logarithm for dependent variables. (Russian.) *Dokl. Akad. Nauk SSSR*, **63**, 487-90.

Sapogov, N. A. 1949.   4795
An integral limit theorem for multidimensional Markov chains. (Russian.) *Usp. Mat. Nauk (N.S.)*, **4**, 4(32), 190-2.

Sapogov, N. A. 1949.   4796
On the strong law of large numbers. (Russian.) *Usp. Mat. Nauk (N.S.)*, **4**, 4(32), 194-5.

Sapogov, N. A. 1949.   4797
On the law of the iterated logarithm for Markov chains. (Russian.) *Usp. Mat. Nauk (N.S.)*, **4**, 4(32), 195-6.

Sapogov, N. A. 1949.   4798
On a limit theorem. (Russian.) *Dokl. Akad. Nauk SSSR*, **69**, 15-18.

Sapogov, N. A. 1949.   4799
On multidimensional inhomogeneous Markov chains. (Russian.) *Dokl. Akad. Nauk SSSR*, **69**, 133-5.

Sapogov, N. A. 1949.   4800
A two-dimensional limit theorem for two-dimensional chains. (Russian.) *Izv. Akad. Nauk SSSR, Ser. Mat.*, **13**, 301-14.

Sappenfield, B. R. 1947.   4801
A rapid method of computing standard scores. *J. Appl. Psychol.*, **31**, 638-9.

Sard, A. 1949.   4802
Smoothest approximation formulas. *Ann. Math. Statist.*, **20**, 612-15.

Sargent, H. 1945.   4803
Projective methods: their origin, theory and application in personality research. *Psychol. Bull.*, **42**, 257-93.

Sarle, C. F. 1940.   4804
The possibilities and limitations of objective sampling in strengthening agricultural statistics. *Econometrica*, **8**, 45-61.

Sarle, C. F. 1949.   4805
Need for special-purpose sampling in estimating agricultural production. *Agric. Econ. Res.*, **1**, 134-8.

Sarle, C. F. & Callander, W. F. 1948.   4806
How some of the needs for agricultural statistics can be met by sampling. *United States Bur. Agric. Econ., Washington, D.C.*, 11 pp.

Sarmanov, O. V. 1941.   4807
Sur la corrélation isogène. *C. R. (Dokl.) Acad. Sci. URSS*, **32**, 28-30.

Sarmanov, O. V. 1945.   4808
On isogeneous correlation. (Russian. English summary.) *Izv. Akad. Nauk SSSR, Ser. Mat.*, **9**, 169-200.

Sarmanov, O. V. 1946.   4809
Sur les solutions monotones des équations intégrales de corrélation. *C. R. (Dokl.) Acad. Sci. URSS*, **53**, 773-6.

Sarmanov, O. V. 1947.   4810
Generalization of a limit theorem of the theory of probability to sums of almost independent variables satisfying Lindeberg's condition. (Russian.) *Izv. Akad. Nauk SSSR, Ser. Mat.*, **11**, 569-75.

Sarmanov, O. V. 1947. 4811
On the rectification of a symmetrical correlation. (Russian.) *Dokl. Akad. Nauk SSSR*, **58**, 745-7.

Sarmanov, O. V. 1948. 4812
On the rectification of an asymmetrical correlation. (Russian.) *Dokl. Akad. Nauk SSSR*, **59**, 861-3.

Sarmanov, O. V. 1948. 4813
On the order of magnitude of a line of regression. I, II. (Russian.) *Dokl. Akad. Nauk SSSR*, **59**, 1061-4; **60**, 545-8.

Sarmanov, O. V. 1948. 4813ª
On the rectification of correlation. (Russian.) *Uspehi Mat. Nauk*, **3** (5), 190-2.

Sarymsakov, T. A. 1945. 4814
The law of the iterated logarithm for Markov schemes. (Russian.) *Trudy Sred. Asia. Gos. Univ.*, **5**, 2-16.

Sarymsakov, T. A. 1945. 4815
Sur les suites des matrices stochastiques. *C. R. (Dokl.) Acad. Sci. URSS*, **47**, 326-8.

Sarymsakov, T. A. 1945. 4816
Sur les chaînes de Markoff à une infinité dénombrable d'états possibles. *C. R. (Dokl.) Acad. Sci. URSS*, **47**, 617-19.

Sarymsakov, T. A. 1945. 4817
Sur une synthèse des deux méthodes d'exposer la théorie des chaînes discrètes de Markoff. *C. R. (Dokl.) Acad. Sci. URSS*, **48**, 159-61.

Sarymsakov, T. A. 1945. 4818
Un nouveau critère nécessaire et suffisant pour la régularité des chaînes de Markoff dont l'ensemble des états possibles est continu. *C. R. (Dokl.) Acad. Sci. URSS*, **49**, 85-8.

Sarymsakov, T. A. 1945. 4819
Sur les chaînes de Bruns. *C. R. (Dokl.) Acad. Sci. URSS*, **49**, 241-3.

Sarymsakov, T. A. 1949. 4820
On the theory of stationary stochastic processes without after effect. (Differential equations for characteristic functions.) (Russian.) *Trudy Inst. Mat. Mekh., Akad. Nauk Uzbek. SSR*, **5**, 61-9.

Sarymsakov, T. A. & Sultanova, M. 1948. 4821
The law of the iterated logarithm for Markov chains. (Russian.) *Dokl. Akad. Nauk SSSR*, **59**, 1249-52.

Sastry, K. V. K. 1946. 4822
On a certain distribution in the theory of sampling. *Proc. Nat. Inst. Sci. India*, **12**, 427-8.

Sastry, K. V. K. 1948. 4823
On a Bessel function of the second kind and Wilks' Z-distribution. *Proc. Indian Acad. Sci. A*, **28**, 532-6.

Sastry, N. S. N. 1941. 4824
Can there be a factor-analysis of aesthetic judgment? *Sankhyā*, **5**, 313-16.

Sastry, N. S. 1942. 4825
Systems of weights for an index of industrial production. *Sankhyā*, **6**, 141-4.

Sastry, N. S. R. 1947. 4826
The methods of enquiry by sample. *Indian J. Agric. Econ.*, **2**, 61-6.

Sasuly, M. 1947. 4827
Irving Fisher and Social Science. *Econometrica*, **15**, 255-73.

Sato, K. 1949. 4828
On general probability functions of square amplitudes in electroencephalogram. *Folia Psychiat. Neur. Jap.*, **3**, 227-33.

Sato, K. & Nakane, K. 1948. 4829
Note on the general probability function of the alpha wave amplitudes in electroencephalogram. *Folia Psychiat. Neur. Jap.*, **2**, 3-14.

Sato, R. 1941. 4830
On the binomial distribution function, Poisson's law and Pólya-Eggenberger's law. (Japanese.) *Tokei Sûri Kenyu (Study of Math. Statist.)*, **1**.

Sato, R. 1941. 4831
A contribution to the theory of testing statistical composite hypotheses. (Japanese.) *Tokei Sûri Kenkyu (Study of Math. Statist.)*, **1**.

Satterthwaite, F. E. 1941. 4832
A concise analysis of certain algebraic forms. *Ann. Math. Statist.*, **12**, 77-83.

Satterthwaite, F. E. 1941. 4833
Synthesis of variance. *Psychometrika*, **6**, 309-16.

Satterthwaite, F. E. 1942. 4834
A generalized analysis of variance. *Ann. Math. Statist.*, **13**, 34-41.

Satterthwaite, F. E. 1942. 4835
Linear restrictions on chi-square. *Ann. Math. Statist.*, **13**, 326-31.

Satterthwaite, F. E. 1942. 4836
Generalized Poisson distribution. *Ann. Math. Statist.*, **13**, 410-17.

Satterthwaite, F. E. 1944. 4837
Error control in matrix calculation. *Ann. Math. Statist.*, **15**, 373-87.

Satterthwaite, F. E. 1946. 4838
An approximate distribution of estimates of variance components. *Biometrics Bull.*, **2**, 110-14.

Satterthwaite, F. E. 1949. 4839
A new continuous sampling inspection plan based on an analysis of costs. *General Electric Co., Bridgeport Conn., Rep.* no. 130.

Satterthwaite, F. E. & Grad, B. 1949. 4840
The choice of lot inspection plans on the basis of cost. *General Electric Co. Bridgeport Conn., Rep.* no. 135.

Sauer, L. 1946. 4841
Statistika a ucetnictvi (La statistique et la comptabilité). *Podrikové Hospodárstvi, Praha*, **1** (5-6), 233-40.

Saunders, A. R. 1944. 4842
Efficiency of design in field experiment at Potchefstroom, S. Africa. *Emp. J. Exper. Agric.*, **12**, 157-62.

Saunders, D. R. 1948-9. 4843
Factor analysis. I. Some effects of chance error. II. A note concerning rotation of axes to simple structure. *Psychometrika*, **13**, 251-7; *Educ. and Psychol. Measurement*, **9**, 753-6.

Savage, G. M. & Halvorson, H. O. 1941. 4844
The effect of culture environment on results obtained with the dilution method of determining bacterial population. *J. Bact.*, **41**, 355-62.

Savage, L. J. 1947. 4845
A uniqueness theorem for unbiased sequential binomial estimation. *Ann. Math. Statist.*, **18**, 295-7.

Savage, L. J. 1949. 4845ª
An apparent ambiguity in the interpretation of minimum risk. *RAND Corp. Res. Memo.*, 13 July 1949, RM-184, 3 pp.

Savkevich, V. P. 1940. 4846
Sur le schéma des urnes à composition variable. *C. R. (Dokl.) Acad. Sci. URSS*, **28**, 8-12.

Savkevich, V. P. 1941. 4847
Schéma de l'urne aux boules surajoutées. (Russian. French summary.) *Uch. Zap. Leningrad Gos. Univ.*, **83**, *Mat. Ser.* **12**, 129-49.

Savoor, R. R. 1948. 4848
The scope and limitations of the application of statistical methods. *Bansilal Amritlal Agric. Coll. Mag.*, **1** (1), 15-17; **1** (2), 8-11; **2**, 10-13.

Savorgnan, F. 1940. 4849
Studi di microstatistica. *Ann. Statist.*, *Roma*, **7** (6), 45 pp.

Savur, S. R. 1942. 4850
A test of significance in approximate periodogram analysis. *Sankhyā*, **6**, 77-84.

Sawitz, W. G. & Faust, E. C. 1942. 4851
The probability of detecting intestinal protozoa by successive stool examinations. *Amer. J. Trop. Med.*, **22**, 131-6.

Sawitz, W. G. & Hammerstrom, R. J. 1943. 4852
The statistical significance of a negative stool examination in the diagnosis of amebiasis. *Amer. J. Hyg.*, **38**, 1-7.

Sawitz, W. & Karpinos, B. D. 1942. 4853
Statistical problem involved in the application of the N.I.H. swab for the diagnosis of ozyurisses. *Amer. J. Hyg.*, **35**, 15-26.

Sawkins, D. T. 1940. 4853ª
Elementary presentation of the frequency distribution of certain statistical populations associated with the normal population. *Proc. Roy. Soc. N.S.W.*, **74**, 209-39.

Sawkins, D. T. 1941. 4854
Remarks on goodness of fit of hypotheses and on Pearson's χ^2 test. *Proc. Roy. Soc. N.S.W.*, **75**, 85-95.

Sawkins, D. T. 1944. 4855
Simple regression and correlation. *Proc. Roy. Soc. N.S.W.*, **77**, 85-95.

Sawkins, D. T. 1947. 4856
A new method of approximating the binomial and hypergeometric probabilities. *Proc. Roy. Soc. N.S.W.*, **81**, 38-47.

Saxén, T. 1948. 4857
On the probability of ruin in the collective risk theory for insurance enterprises with only negative risk sums. *Skand. Aktuartidskr.*, **31**, 199-228.

Schack, H. 1947. 4858
Zahl oder Anzahl? *Statist. Praxis*, **2**, 117-18.

Schack, H. 1948. 4859
Die " Ratio " in der Statistik. *Statist. Praxis*, **3**, 171-2.

Schärf, H. 1941. 4860
Über einige Variationsprobleme der Versicherungsmathematik. *Mitt. Ver. Schweiz. Versich.-Math.*, **41**, 163-96.

Schärf, H. 1944. 4861
Über partielle Bestandsänderungen und eine Klasse neuer Integrationsprozesse. *Mitt. Ver. Schweiz. Versich.-Math.*, **44**, 233-49.

Scheffé, H. 1942. 4862
An inverse problem in correlation theory. *Amer. Math. Monthly*, **49**, 99-104.

Scheffé, H. 1942. 4863
On the theory of testing composite hypotheses with one constraint. *Ann. Math. Statist.*, **13**, 280-93.

Scheffé, H. 1942. 4864
On the ratio of the variances of two normal populations. *Ann. Math. Statist.*, **13**, 371-88.

Scheffé, H. 1943. 4865
On solutions of the Behrens-Fisher problem, based on the *t*-distribution. *Ann. Math. Statist.*, **14**, 35-44.

Scheffé, H. 1943. 4866
On a measure problem arising in the theory of non-parametric tests. *Ann. Math. Statist.*, **14**, 227-33.

Scheffé, H. 1943. 4867
Statistical inference in the non-parametric case. *Ann. Math. Statist.*, **14**, 305-32.

Scheffé, H. 1944. 4868
A note on the Behrens-Fisher problem. *Ann. Math. Statist.*, **15**, 430-2.

Scheffé, H. 1944. 4869
Note on the use of the tables of percentage points of the incomplete beta function to calculate small sample confidence intervals for a binomial *p*. *Biometrika*, **33**, 181.

Scheffé, H. 1947. 4870
The relation of control charts to analysis of variance and chi-square tests. *J. Amer. Statist. Ass.*, **42**, 425-31 (correction: 634).

Scheffé, H. 1947. 4871
A useful convergence theorem for probability distributions. *Ann. Math. Statist.*, **18**, 434-8.

Scheffé, H. 1949. 4872
Operating characteristics of average and range charts. *Industr. Qual. Contr.*, **5** (1), 13-18.

Scheffé, H. & Tukey, J. W. 1944. 4873
A formula for sample sizes for population tolerance limits. *Ann. Math. Statist.*, **15**, 217.

Scheffé, H. & Tukey, J. W. 1945. 4874
Non-parametric estimation. I. Validation of order statistics. *Ann. Math. Statist.*, **16**, 187-92.

Schepis, G. 1949. 4874ª
Un nuovo campo di applicazione del metodo statistico; lo studio dell'effecto detto di " percezione extra-sensoriale " (Esp). *Atti 9ma Riun., Soc. Ital. Demogr. Statist.*, 1947, pp. 186-97.

Scheurer, F. 1943. 4875
La détermination des objets à soumettre à la statistique dans l'entreprise. *Bull. Verband Schweiz. Bücherexp.*, **17** (1), 1-6.

Schild, H. D. 1942. 4876
A method of conducting a biological assay on a preparation giving repeated graded responses. *J. Physiol.*, **101**, 115-30.

Schiller, P. 1948. 4877
The application of statistical methods to electricity supply problems. *J. Inst. Elect. Engrs.*, **95**, 161-74.

Schilling, W. 1944. 4878
Analysis of the data of a public health organization by the control chart method. *J. Amer. Statist. Ass.*, **39**, 311-24.

Schilling, W. 1947. 4879
A frequency distribution represented as the sum of two Poisson distributions. *J. Amer. Statist. Ass.*, **42**, 407-24.

Schlamowitz, I. 1946. 4880
An analysis of the time relationships within the cardiac cycle in electro-cardiograms of normal men. *Amer. Heart J.*, **31**, 329-42; 464-76.

Schmetterer, L. 1949. 4881
Einführung in die Sequential Analysis. *Statist. Vierteljschr.*, **2**, 101-5.

Schmid, J., Jr. 1947. 4882
The relationship between the coefficient of correlation and the angle included between regression lines. *J. Educ. Res.*, **41**, 311-13.

Schmidt, R. J. 1941. 4883
On the numerical solution of linear simultaneous equations by an iterative method. *Phil. Mag.*, (7) **32**, 369-83.

Schmidtmayer, I. 1947. 4884
Trendy ve statistice (General trends in statistics). *Rozhledy mat.-prirodov., Praha*, **24** (2), 10-19, 73-5.

Schneider, O. 1942. 4885
On a parameter used to characterize bivariate statistical distributions. (Spanish.) *An. Soc. Cient. Argent.*, **133**, 397-401.

Schneider, S. 1948. 4886
Sur l'ajustement des courbes à branches limitées. *J. Soc. Statist. Paris*, **89**, 218-27.

Schobe, W. 1943. 4887
Das Lucassche Ehepaarproblem. *Math. Zeit.*, **48**, 781-4.

Schoenberg, I. J. 1948. 4888
Some analytical aspects of the problem of smoothing. *Studies and Essays presented to R. Courant*, pp. 351-70.

Scholl, J. C. & Burkhead, C. E. 1949. 4889
Interviewing non-respondents to a mail survey: an experiment in connection with April 1948 farm stocks report. *Agric. Econ. Res.*, **1**, 16-23.

Scholz, E. 1941. 4890
Ein methodischer Beitrag zur Berechnung des Erbgefüges. *Deutsche Math.*, **6**, 100-4.

Scholz, E. 1941. 4891
Die Auflösung eines gewissen linear homogenen Systems von Rückschlussformeln und ihre Anwendung auf Probleme der Inzucht. *Deutsche Math.*, **6**, 104-7.

Schorer, E. 1941. 4892
Zur Frage der Korrelation. *Schweiz. Zeit. Volkwirtsch. Statist.*, **77**, 376-97.

Schorer, E. 1942-3. 4893
Statistik und medizinische Forschungsarbeit. *Allg. Statist. Arch.*, **31**, 206-28.

Schouten, J. P. & Giltay, J. 1940. 4894
Oplossing van een problem uit di waarschijnlijkheidsrekening van belan vaar de automatische telephonie. *De Ingenieur*, **55**, 67-75.

Schrader, W. A. B. 1940. 4895
Analysis of variance applied to liberalism scores. *J. Exper. Educ.*, **8**, 267-70.

Schreiner, A. 1940. 4896
Certain projective depth and breadth measurements of the facial skeleton in man. *Biometrika*, **31**, 272-86.

Schrek, R. 1942. 4897
Logarithmic correlation coefficients and regression equations. *Hum. Biol.*, **14**, 95-103.

Schrek, R. & Lipson, H. I. 1941. 4898
Logarithmic frequency distributions. *Hum. Biol.*, **13**, 1-22.

Schrock, E. M. 1944. 4899
Matters of misconception concerning the quality control chart. *J. Amer. Statist. Ass.*, **39**, 325-34.

Schrödinger, E. 1944. 4900
The statistical law in nature. *Nature*, **153**, 704-6.

Schrödinger, E. 1945. 4901
Probability problems in nuclear chemistry. *Proc. Roy. Irish Acad. A*, **51**, 1-8.

Schrödinger, E. 1947. 4902
The foundation of the theory of probability. I, II. *Proc. Roy. Irish Acad. A*, **51**, 51-66; 141-6.

Schuck, H. A. 1949. 4903
Relationships of catch to changes in population size of New England Haddock. *Biometrics*, **5**, 213-31.

Schulte, A. 1942. 4904
Leitsatze für die Einleitung und Durchführung statistischer Erhebungen. *Sestfallische*, **6** (4), 106-8.

Schultz, F. G. 1945. 4905
Recent developments in the statistical analysis of ranked data adapted to educational research. *J. Exper. Educ.*, **13**, 149-52.

Schultz, T. W. & Brownlee, O. H. 1942. 4906
Two trials to determine expectation models applicable to agriculture. *Quart. J. Econ.*, **56**, 487-96.

Schulz, G. 1940. 4907
Über eine für die Statistik wichtige Verallgemeinerung des Rencontrespiels. *Sitzungs-Ber. Berlin Math. Ges.*, **38-9**, 73-83.

Schulz, G. 1942. 4908
Über die Häufigkeit der Iterationenen in einer Beobachtungsfolge. *Deutsche Math.*, **7**, 22-38.

Schulz, G. 1947. 4909
Das Summenproblem bei mehrdimensionalen arithmetischen Wahrscheinlichkeitsverteilungen. *Ber. Math.-Tagung Tübingen*, 1946, pp. 131-4.

Schumacher, F. X. 1945. 4910
Statistical methods in forestry. *Biometrics Bull.*, **1**, 29-32.

Schumacher, F. X. 1946. 4911
Stacked and solid volume of south-eastern pulpwood. *J. Forestry*, **44**, 579-82.

Schumacher, F. X. 1946. 4912
Volume-weight ratios of pine logs in the Virginia-North Carolina Coastal Plain. *J. Forestry*, **44**, 583-6.

Schumacher, F. X. & Chapman, R. A. 1942. 4913
Sampling methods in forestry and range management. *Duke Univ. Sch. Forest. Bull.*, no. 7, pp. 1-213.

Schumacher, F. X. & Eschmeyer, R. W. 1943. 4914
The estimate of fish populations in lakes or ponds. *J. Tennessee Acad. Sci.*, **18**, 228-49.

Schumacher, F. X. & Young, H. E. 1943. 4915
Empirical log rules according to species, groups and lumber grades. *J. Forestry*, **41**, 511-18.

Schumann, T. E. W. 1940. 4916
The principles of a mechanical method for calculating regression equations and multiple correlation co-efficients and for the solution of simultaneous linear equations. *Phil. Mag.*, (7) **29**, 258-73.

Schumann, T. E. W. 1940. 4917
A mechanical appliance for the smoothing of time series. *Phil. Mag.*, (7) **30**, 39-48.

Schumann, T. E. W. 1940. 4918
Theoretical aspects of the size distribution of fog particles. *Quart. J. R. Met. Soc.*, **66**, 195-207.

Schumann, T. E. W. 1942. 4919
On Yule's method of investigating periodicities of disturbed series. The motion of a pendulum in a turbulent fluid. *Phil. Mag.*, (7) **33**, 138-50.

Schumann, T. E. W. 1946. 4920
Statistical weather forecasting. *Nature*, **158**, 551-2.

Schumann, T. E. W. & Hofmeyer, W. L. 1942. 4921
The problem of auto-correlation of meteorological time-series. *Quart. J. R. Met. Soc.*, **68**, 177-88.

Schützenberger, M.-P. 1947. 4922
Remarques sur des relations d'ordre entre variables aléatoires indépendantes. *C. R. Acad. Sci., Paris*, **224**, 878-80.

Schützenberger, M.-P. 1947. 4923
Sur certains paramètres caractéristiques des systèmes d'événements compatibles et dépendants et leur application au calcul des cumulants de la répétition. *C. R. Acad. Sci., Paris*, **225**, 277-8.

Schützenberger, M.-P. 1948. 4924
An Abac for the sample range. *Psychometrika*, **13**, 95-7.

Schützenberger, M.-P. 1948. 4925
Étude statistique d'un problème de sociométrie. *Gallica Biol. Acta*, **1**, 9 pp.

Schützenberger, M.-P. 1948. 4926
Valeurs caractéristiques du coefficient de correlation par rang de Kendall dans le cas général. *C. R. Acad. Sci., Paris*, **226**, 2122-3.

Schützenberger, M.-P. 1949. 4927
A non-existence theorem for an infinite family of symmetrical block designs. *Ann. Eugen.*, **14**, 286-7.

Schuyler, L. G. 1948. 4928
The ordering of n items assigned to k rank categories by votes of m individuals. *J. Amer. Statist. Ass.*, **43**, 559-63.

Schwartz, D. H. 1947. 4928a
Statistical " sleuthing " to detect bias in visual inspection. *Industr. Qual. Contr.*, **3** (6), 14-17.

Schwartz, E. R. & Fox, K. R. 1942. 4928b
Application of rank correlation to the development of testing methods. *Bull. Amer. Soc. Test. Mat.*, **119**, 21-4.

Schwartz, L. 1941. 4929
Sur la module de la fonction caractéristique du calcul des probabilités. *C. R. Acad. Sci., Paris*, **212**, 418-21.

Schwarz, A. 1945. 4930
Über Begriffsbestimmungen in Nationalökonomie und Statistik. *Schweiz. Zeit. Volkwirtsch. Statist.*, **81**, 302-7.

Schwarz, H. 1943. 4931
Zur " wahrscheinlichkeitstheoretischen Stabilisierung " beim Erneuerungsproblem. *Math. Ann.*, **118**, 771-9.

Schwarz, N. 1946-7. 4932
Drie soorten statistiek in de natuurkunde? (Three kinds of statistics in physics?) *Statistica Neerlandica*, **1**, 304-16.

Scossiroli, R. 1949. 4933
Sur certaines recherches méthodologiques concernant la statistique agricole. *Inst. Nat. Statist. Études Écon., Bull. Statist. Gén. France*, **37**, 234-50; 346-61.

Scossiroli, R. 1949. 4934
Experimental designs and statistical methods for agricultural tests. (Italian. English summary.) *Ann. Sper. Agron., N.S.*, **3**, 547-84.

Scott, A. D. 1951.
Bibliography of applications of mathematical statistics to economics, 1943-1949. *J. R. Statist. Soc. A*, **114**, 372-93.

Scott, C. R., Jr. 1945. 4934a
Quality control in the manufacture of ball bearings. *Industr. Qual. Contr.*, **2** (3), 3-6.

Scott, E. L. 1949. 4935
Distribution of the longitude of periastron of spectroscopic binaries. *Astrophys. J.*, **109**, 194-207; 446-51.

Scott Blair, G. W. *See* **Blair, G. W. Scott.**

Scott, J. A. 1942. 4936
The natural pattern of dilution counts of helminth eggs. *Amer. J. Trop. Med.*, **22**, 647-54.

Scott Russell, C. *See* **Russell, C. Scott.**

Scott, T. G. 1941. 4937
A method of estimating the red fox population. *Iowa State Coll. J. Sci.*, **15**, 155-9.

Seal, H. L. 1943. 4938
Tests of a mortality table graduation. *J. Inst. Actuar.*, **71**, 5-67.

Seal, H. L. 1945. 4939
The mathematics of a population composed of k stationary strata each recruited from the stratum below and supported at the lowest level by a uniform annual number of entrants. *Biometrika*, **33**, 226-30.

Seal, H. L. 1947. 4940
A historical note on the use of χ^2 to test the adequacy of a mortality table graduation. *J. Inst. Actuar. Students' Soc.*, **6**, 185-7.

Seal, H. L. 1947.   4941
Multiple decrement tables and the force of mortality—
a historical note. *J. Inst. Actuar. Students' Soc.*, **6**,
197-9.

Seal, H. L. 1947.   4942
A probability distribution of deaths at age x when
policies are counted instead of lives. *Skand. Aktuartidskr.*, **30**, 18-43.

Seal, H. L. 1948.   4943
A note on the χ^2 smooth test. *Biometrika*, **35**, 202.

Seal, H. L. 1948.   4944
The probability of decrements from a population. A
study in discrete random processes. *Skand. Aktuartidskr.*, **31**, 14-45 (correction: **39**, 38).

Seal, H. L. 1949.   4945
Discrete random processes. *J. Inst. Actuar. Students'
Soc.*, **8**, 204-9.

Seal, H. L. 1949.   4946
The historical development of the use of generating
functions in probability theory. *Mitt. Ver. Schweiz.
Versich.-Math.*, **49**, 209-28.

Seal, H. L. 1949.   4947
Mortality data and the binomial probability law.
Skand. Aktuartidskr., **32**, 188-216.

Sealy, E. H. 1943.   4948
Specification of tolerances on components and final
assembly. Methods of tightening tolerances on
final assembly. *U.K. Min. Supply Advisory Service
Statist. Method & Qual. Contr. Tech. Rep. Ser. R*,
no. QC/R/3 (II), 19 May 1943, 8 pp.

Sealy, E. H. 1943.   4949
The probability integral of the mean deviation.
*U.K. Min. Supply Advisory Service Statist. Method
& Qual. Contr. Tech. Rep. Ser. R*, no. QC/R/1, 28
April 1943, 5 pp.

Sealy, E. H. 1943.   4949[a]
The effect of a varying mean on the production charact-
eristic of a machine. *U.K. Min. Supply Advisory
Service Statist. Method & Qual. Contr. Tech. Rep.
Ser. R*, no. QC/R/5, 9 November 1943, 19 pp.

Seares, F. H. 1944.   4950
Regressions lines and the functional relation. *Astrophys. J.*, **100**, 255-63.

Seares, F. H. 1945.   4951
Regression lines and the functional relation. II.
Charlier's formulae for a moving cluster. *Astrophys.
J.*, **102**, 366-76.

Seath, D. M. 1944.   4952
A 2×2 factorial design for double reversal feeding
experiments. *J. Dairy Sci.*, **27**, 159-64.

Segerdahl, C.-O. 1942.   4953
Über einige risikotheoretische Fragestellungen. *Skand.
Aktuartidskr.*, **25**, 43-83.

Segerdahl, C.-O. 1948.   4954
Some properties of the ruin function in the collective
theory of risk. *Skand. Aktuartidskr.*, **31**, 46-87.

Seitz, B. 1940.   4955
Sur une équation diophantienne en rapport avec le
calcul des probabilités. *Comment. Math. Helvetia*, **12**,
323-5.

Seitz, J. 1949.   4956
Poznámka ke zobecněnému Pólyovu urnovému
schematu. (A note on generalized Pólya's schema.)
Trans. Fac. Spec. Instruction Tech. Univ., Prague.

Seiwell, H. R. 1949.   4957
The principles of time series analysis applied to ocean
wave data. *Proc. Nat. Acad. Sci. U.S.A.*, **35**, 518-28.

Selberg, H. L. 1940.   4958
Über eine Ungleichung der mathematischen Statistik.
Skand. Aktuartidskr., **23**, 114-20.

Selberg, H. L. 1940.   4959
Zwei Ungleichungen zur Ergänzung des Tchebycheffschen Lemmas. *Skand. Aktuartidskr.*, **23**, 121-5.

Selberg, H. L. 1940.   4960
Über eine Verschärfung der Tchebycheffschen
Ungleichung. *Arch. Mat. Naturv.*, **43**, 30-2.

Selberg, H. L. 1942.   4961
Über die Darstellung willkürlicher Funktionen durch
Charliersche Differenzreihen. *Skand. Aktuartidskr.*,
25, 228-46.

Selberg, H. L. 1942.   4962
On an inequality in mathematical statistics. (Norwegian.) *Nord. Mat. Tidskr.*, **24**, 1-12.

Selberg, H. L. 1943.   4963
Über die Darstellung der Dichtefunktion einer Ver-
teilung durch eine Charliersche B-Reihe. *Arch. Mat.
Naturv.*, **46**, 127-38.

Selberg, H. L. 1947.   4964
On the corrections for grouping. *Skand. Aktuartidskr.*,
30, 179-90.

Senevet, G. 1942.   4964[a]
Quelques notions pratiques de statistique médicale.
Arch. Inst. Pasteur, Algér., **20**, 172-97.

Senf, C. 1948.   4965
Sampling error in the estimated proportion of farms
having a characteristic. *U.S. Bur. Agric. Econ.
C.R.P.*, **22**, 7 pp.

Seng, Y. P. 1949.   4966
Practical problems in sampling for social and demo-
graphic inquiries in undeveloped countries. *Population
Stud.*, **3**, 170-91.

Sen Gupta, J. M. 1944.   4967
A note on adjustments for first and second moments in
a grouped frequency distribution split-up into sub-
sections. *Sankhyā*, **6**, 413-14.

Sensini, G. 1948.   4968
La numerosità delle popolazioni animali. *Riv. Ital.
Demogr. Statist.*, **2**, 317-33.

Servien, P. 1949.   4969
Probabilités, erreurs, quanta. *Proc. 10th. Int. Congr.
Philos., Amsterdam*, 11-18 August 1948, **1**, pp. 797-9.

Seth, G. R. 1949.   4970
On the variance of estimates. *Ann. Math. Statist.*, **20**,
1-27.

Seutemann, K. 1949.   4971
Wahrscheinlichkeit und Statistik. *Allg. Statist.
Arch.*, **33**, 224-43.

Sevastyanov, B. A. 1948.   4972
Branching random processes. *Vestnik Moskov. Gos.
Univ.*, **3**, 13-34.

Sevastyanov, B. A. 1948.   4973
On the theory of branching random processes.
(Russian.) *Dokl. Akad. Nauk SSSR*, **59**, 1407-10.

Shafer, J. L. 1946.   4974
Sampling incoming material. *Industr. Qual. Contr.*,
3 (2), 16-20.

Shannon, C. E. 1948.   4975
A mathematical theory of communication. *Bell Syst.
Tech. J.*, **27**, 379-423; 623-56.

Shannon, C. E. 1949.   4976
Communication in the presence of noise. *Proc. Inst.
Radio Engrs.*, **37**, 10-21.

Shannon, C. E. 1949.   4977
Communication theory of secrecy systems. *Bell Syst.
Tech. J.*, **28**, 656-715.

Shannon, S. 1941.   4978
Some assumptions and hypotheses underlying actuarial
calculations. (German, French and Italian summaries.)
Trans. 12th. Int. Congr. Actuar., Lucerne, 1940, **1**,
137-58.

Shannon, S. 1942.   4979
Comparative aspects of the point binomial polygon and
its associated normal curve of error. *Rec. Amer. Inst.
Actuar.*, **31**, 208-26.

Shannon, S. 1943.   4980
A theory of automatic premium-loan approximations:
Formulas derived and compared. *Rec. Amer. Inst.
Actuar.*, **32**, 74-82.

Shapiro, A. 1946.   4981
The kinetics of growth and mutation in bacteria.
Cold Spring Harbour Symp. Quant. Biol., **11**, 228-34.

Shapiro, H. L. 1942.   4982
Variations in samples of identical populations. *Anthrop. Briefs*, **1** (2), 16-28.

Shapiro, S. 1943.   4983
The distribution of deposits and currency in the
United States, 1929-39. *J. Amer. Statist. Ass.*, **38**,
438-44.

Shaul, J. R. H. 1943.   4984
Maize forecasts in Mazoe district of Southern Rhod-
esia, 1920-42. *South African J. Econ.*, **11**, 294-6.

Shaul, J. R. H. 1946.   4985
Derivation of total fertility, gross and net reproduction
rates from census statistics of marriage fertility. *J. R.
Statist. Soc.*, **109**, 278-83.

Shaul, J. R. H. 1947.   4986
Sampling surveys in Central Africa. *J. Amer. Statist.
Ass.*, **47**, 239-54.

Shea, H. G. 1945.   4987
Meeting specifications in U. H. F. *Electronic Ind.*, **4**,
84-5.

Shen, E. 1940.   4988
Experimental design and statistical treatment in
educational research. *J. Exper. Educ.*, **8**, 346-53.

Shen, E. 1940.   4988a
A generalized formula for testing the significance of
experimental treatments. *Harvard Educ. Rev.*, **10**, 70-4.

Shenton, L. R. 1949.   4989
On the efficiency of the method of moments and
Neyman's type *A* distribution. *Biometrika*, **36**, 450-4.

Sherwood, M. B. 1947.   4990
Simple formulas for calculating percentage potency in
three- and four-dose assay procedures. *Science*, **106**,
152-3.

Sherwood, M. B., Falco, E. A. & de Beer, E. J.   4991
1944. A rapid quantitative method for the determination of penicillin. *Science*, **99**, 247-8.

Shewhart, W. A. 1941.   4992
Contribution of statistics to the science of engineer-
ing. *Bell Syst. Monogr.*, B-1319. (Also: *Univ.
Penn. Bicent. Conf., Fluid Mech. Statist. Meth.
Engng.*, pp. 97-124 and (1942) *Metal Progr.*, **41**,
854-8.)

Shewhart, W. A. 1943.   4992a
Ten years progress in management: Statistical control
in applied science. *Trans. Amer. Soc. Mech. Engrs.*,
65, 222-5.

Shewhart, W. A. 1946.   4993
The advancing statistical front. *J. Amer. Statist. Ass.*,
41, 1-15.

Shimbel, A. & Rapoport, A. 1948.   4994
A statistical approach to the theory of the central
nervous system. *Bull. Math. Biophys.*, **10**, 41-55.

Shock, N. W. & Morales, M. F. 1942.   4995
A fundamental form for the differential equation of
colonial and organism growth. *Bull. Math. Biophys.*,
4, 63-71.

Shock, N. W. & Sebrell, W. H. 1946.   4996
The effect of different concentrations of pyridoxine
hydrochloride on the work output of perfused frog
muscles. *Amer. J. Physiol.*, **146**, 399-402.

Shohat, J. A. & Tamarkin, J. D. 1943.   4996a
The problem of moments. *Amer. Math. Soc. Math.
Surveys*, no. 1, xiv+140 pp.

Shone, K. J. 1949.   4997
Relations between the standard deviation and the
distribution of range in non-normal populations.
J. R. Statist. Soc. B, **11**, 85-8.

Shourie, K. L. 1946.   4998
Fluorine and dental caries in India. *Indian J. Med.
Res.*, **34**, 97-104.

Shrimpton, E. A. G. 1940.   4999
The error of vitamin D assay by the ash content of
bone method. *Quart. J. Pharm.*, **13**, 97-108.

Shrimpton, E. A. G. 1943.   5000
The biological assay of crystalline vitamin B_1, aneurine
hydrochloride, by the rat growth method. *Quart. J.
Pharm.*, **16**, 86-101.

Shrivastava, M. P. 1940.   5001
The distribution of the mean for certain Bessel function
populations. *Science & Culture*, **6**, 244-5.

Shrivastava, M. P. 1941.   5002
Bivariate correlation surfaces. *Science & Culture*, **6**,
615-16.

Shrivastava, M. P. 1941.   5003
On the D^2-statistic. *Bull. Calcutta Math. Soc.*, **33**,
71-85.

Shryock, H. S., Jr. 1941.   5004
General population statistics. *J. Amer. Statist. Ass.*,
36, 376-80.

Shukla, P. D. & Narain, R. 1943.   5005
Standardisation of marking and its effects on the results of the Indian Civil Service Examination. *Sankhyā*, **6**, 260-4.

Shyü, K. 1944.   5005a
Two theorems concerning combinations. *Duke Math. J.*, **11**, 293-9.

Sibagaki, W. 1949.   5006
On the theory of statistical adjustment of data. I. Conditions containing parameters. *J. Phys. Soc. Japan*, **4**, 216-21.

Sibirani, F. 1942.   5007
Esperienze sul comportamento delle frequenze in eventi di probabilità costante ma ignota. *Mem. Accad. Sci. Ist. Bologna, Sci. Fis.*, (9) **9**, 167-74.

Sibirani, F. 1944.   5008
Alcune probabilità geometriche. *Mem. Accad. Sci. Ist. Bologna, Sci. Fis.*, (10) **1**, 113-23.

Sichel, H. S. 1947.   5009
An experimental and theoretical investigation of bias error in mine sampling with special reference to narrow gold reefs. *Bull. Inst. Mining Metall.*, **483**, 1-41.

Sichel, H. S. 1947.   5010
Fitting growth and frequency curves by the method of frequency moments. *J. R. Statist. Soc.*, **110**, 337-47.

Sichel, H. S. 1949.   5011
The method of frequency moments and its application to type VII populations. *Biometrika*, **36**, 404-25.

Siegel, I. H. 1941.   5012
The difference between the Paasche and Laspeyres index-number formulas. *J. Amer. Statist. Ass.*, **36**, 343-50.

Siegel, I. H. 1941.   5013
Further notes on the difference between index-number formulas. *J. Amer. Statist. Ass.*, **36**, 519-24.

Siegel, I. H. 1942.   5014
Index-number differences: Geometric means. *J. Amer. Statist. Ass.*, **37**, 271-4.

Siegel, I. H. 1943.   5015
Note on a common statistical inequality. *J. Amer. Statist. Ass.*, **38**, 217-22.

Siegert, A. J. F. 1949.   5015a
On the approach to statistical equilibrium. *Phys. Rev.*, **76**, 1708-14.

Sievert, R. M. 1941.   5016
Zur theoretischer-mathematischen Behandlung des Problems der biologischen Strahlenwirkung. *Acta Radiologica*, **22**, 237-51.

Silber, J. 1948.   5017
Multiple sampling for variables. *Ann. Math. Statist.*, **19**, 246-56.

Silberstein, L. 1940.   5018
On a hystero-differential equation arising in a probability problem. *Phil. Mag.*, (7) **29**, 75-84.

Silberstein, L. 1944.   5019
The accumulation of chance effects and the Gaussian frequency distribution. *Phil. Mag.*, (7) **35**, 395-404.

Silberstein, L. 1944.   5020
Solution of the restricted problem of the random walk. *Phil. Mag.*, (7) **35**, 538-43.

Silberstein, L. 1945.   5021
The probable number of aggregates in random distributions of points. *Phil. Mag.*, (7) **36**, 319-36.

Silberstein, L. 1946.   5022
On two accessories of three-dimensional colorimetry. I. The probable error of colorimetric tensor components as derived from a number of color matchings. II. The determination of the principal colorimetric axes at any point of the color threefold. *J. Opt. Soc. Amer.*, **36**, 464-8.

Sillitto, G. P. 1947.   5023
The distribution of Kendall's τ coefficient of rank correlation in rankings containing ties. *Biometrika* **34**, 36-40.

Sillitto, G. P. 1948.   5024
The numbers of observations needed in experiments leading to a t-test of significance of a mean or the difference of two means. *Research*, **1**, 520-5.

Sillitto, G. P. 1949.   5025
Note on approximations to the power function of the " 2×2 " comparative trial. *Biometrika*, **36**, 347-52.

Silva, G. 1941.   5026
Una generalizzazione del problema delle concordanze. *Ist. R. Veneto, Sci. Mat. Nat.*, II, **100**, 689-709.

Silvey, R. J. E. 1944.   5027
Methods of listener research employed by the British Broadcasting Corporation. *J. R. Statist. Soc.*, **107**, 190-230.

Simaika, J. B. 1941.   5028
On an optimum property of two important statistical tests. *Biometrika*, **32**, 70-80.

Simaika, J. B. 1942.   5029
Interpolation for fresh probability levels between standard table levels of a function. *Biometrika*, **32**, 263-76.

Simaika, J. B. 1946.   5030
Note on M. Fréchet index of correlation. *Proc. Math. Phys. Soc. Egypt*, **3**, 21-2.

Simaika, J. B. 1947.   5031
On the significance of a typical value in the renewal theory. *Skand. Aktuartidskr.*, **30**, 121-9.

Simaika, J. B. 1949.   5032
On the problem of over-year storage. *Proc. Egypt Acad. Sci.*, **5**, 43-51.

Simmons, R. T., Graydon, J. J.   5033
& Avias, J. 1949.
Blood group M-N Type and Rh Type frequencies in New Caledonians and the Loyalty and Pine Islanders. *Med. J. Aust.*, **1949** (1), 733-8.

Simon, H. A. 1943.   5034
Symmetric tests of the hypothesis that the mean of one normal population exceeds that of another. *Ann. Math. Statist.*, **14**, 149-54.

Simon, H. A. 1945.   5035
Statistical tests as a basis for " Yes-no " choices. *J. Amer. Statist. Ass.*, **40**, 80-4.

Simon, L. E. 1941.   5036
On the initiation of statistical methods for quality control in industry. *J. Amer. Statist. Ass.*, **36**, 53-60.

Simon, L. E. 1941.   5036ª
Statistical methods and quality. *Army Ordnance*, 22, 489-92.

Simon, L. E. 1942.   5037
Application of statistical methods to ordnance engineering. *J. Amer. Statist. Ass.*, 37, 313-24.

Simon, L. E. 1942.   5037ª
Quality control and the war: experience of U.S. Army Ordnance Department in applying quality control in production of munitions. *Elect. Engng.*, 61, 449-52.

Simon, L. E. 1944.   5038
The industrial lot and its sampling implications. *J. Franklin Inst.*, 237, 359-70.

Simon, L. E. 1946.   5038ª
On teaching of quality control to engineers. *J. Engng. Educ.*, 37, 111-16.

Simonsen, W. 1944-5.   5039
On distributions of functions of samples from a normally distributed infinite population. *Skand. Aktuartidskr.*, 27, 235-61; 28, 20-43.

Simonsen, W. 1946.   5040
On the foundation of the collective risk theory. (Danish.) *Förs.mat. Stud. Filip Lundberg*, pp. 246-64.

Simonsen, W. 1948.   5041
On divided differences and osculatory interpolation. *Skand. Aktuartidskr.*, 31, 157-64.

Simpson, E. H. 1949.   5042
The measurement of diversity. *Nature*, 163, 688-91.

Simpson, G. G. 1945.   5043
Note on the graphic biometric comparison of samples. *Amer. Nat.*, 79, 95-6.

Simpson, G. G. 1947.   5044
Note on the measurement of variability and on relative variability of teeth of fossil mammals. *Amer. J. Sci.*, 245, 522-5.

Simpson, G. G. & Roe, A. 1942.   5045
A standard frequency distribution method. *Amer. Mus. Novit.*, 1190, 1-19.

Simpson, H. 1943.   5046
On a theorem concerning sampling. *J. R. Statist. Soc.*, 106, 266-7.

Singh, J. 1943.   5047
A study on the secular trend and seasonal fluctuations of passenger traffic on the East Indian Railway. *Sankhyā*, 6, 315-16.

Singh, J. 1945.   5048
Incidence of ticketless travelling on the Lucknow-Cawnpore section of the East Indian Railway. *Sankhyā*, 7, 211-12.

Singh, J. G. 1946.   5049
Theories of probability. *Sankhyā*, 7, 257-62.

Singh, J. 1948.   5050
A note on the selection of a site for a Ganges bridge in Bihar. *Sankhyā*, 8, 385-8.

Singleton, R. R. 1940.   5051
A method for minimizing the sum of absolute values of deviations. *Ann. Math. Statist.*, 11, 301-10.

Sinha, A. R. 1941.   5052
A preliminary note on the effect of price on the future supply of raw jute. *Sankhyā*, 5, 413-16.

Sinha, G. 1949.   5053
A note on the expression for the sample estimate of the coefficient of partial correlation. *Bull. Calcutta Math. Soc.*, 41, 159-61.

Sinha, H. 1940.   5054
Role of mathematics in economic statistics. *Science & Culture*, 6, 255-8.

Sirazhdinov, S. Kh. 1949.   5055
Trudy Sred. Asia Gos. Univ.

Sitaraman, B. 1940.   5056
On correlation constants in mingled records. *Math. Student*, 8, 73-5.

Sittig, J. 1946.   5057
Nomogram van de χ^2 test of goodness of fit. *Statistica Neerlandica*, 1, 107-11.

Sittig, J. 1946-7.   5058
Eenige statistische opmerkingen over verpakkings-en doseeringsproblemen. (Some statistical observations on packing problems in mass production.) (Dutch. English summary.) *Statistica Neerlandica*, 1, 131-5.

Sittig, J. 1948.   5058ª
Normaliseren van de kwaliteit. *Tijdschr. Effic. Docum.*, 18, 241-5.

Sittig, J. 1948.   5059
Superposition of two frequency distributions. (Dutch. English summary.) *Statistica Neerlandica*, 2, 206-27.

Sittig, J. 1949.   5060
Het probleem der waarnemingsfouten bij een massaal onderzoek. (Errors of observations in large-scale statistical research.) *Statistica Neerlandica*, 3, 49-68.

Skalicky, V. 1941.   5061
Methodik der Mathematik der Kollektiverscheinungen. (Czech.) *Čas. pěst. mat.*, 70, 186-209.

Skellam, J. G. 1946.   5062
Frequency distribution of the difference between two Poisson variates belonging to different populations. *J. R. Statist. Soc.*, 109, 296.

Skellam, J. G. 1948.   5063
A probability distribution derived from the binomial distribution by regarding the probability of success as variable between the sets of trials. *J. R. Statist. Soc. B*, 10, 257-61.

Skellam, J. G. 1949.   5064
Distribution of moment statistics of samples drawn without replacement from a finite population. *J. R. Statist. Soc. B*, 11, 291-6.

Skellam, J. G. 1949.   5065
The probability distribution of gene-differences in relation to selection mutation and random extinction. *Proc. Camb. Phil. Soc.*, 45, 364-7.

Slack, M. 1946.   5066
The probability distributions of sinusoidal oscillations combined in random phase. *J. Inst. Elect. Engrs.*, 93, 76-86.

Slack, M. 1947. 5067
A problem on the summation of simple harmonic functions of the same amplitude and frequency but of random phase, and the probability distributions of sinusoidal oscillations combined in random phase. *Phil. Mag.*, (7) **38**, 297-8.

Slater, P. 1947. 5068
Factor analysis of a matrix of 2×2 tables. *J. R. Statist. Soc. Suppl.*, **9**, 114-27.

Slater, P. 1948. 5069
Comment on " The comparative assessment of intellectual ability ". *Brit. J. Psychol.*, **39**, 20-1.

Slutsky, E. 1941. 5069[a]
On the table of chi-square (incomplete gamma function). *Izv. Akad. Nauk SSSR, Ser. Mat.*, **5**, 183-4.

Smallwood, H. M. 1946. 5070
Statistical methods in research. *J. Chem. Educ.*, **23**, 352-6.

Smeed, R. J. 1949. 5071
Statistical aspects of road safety research. *J. R. Statist. Soc. A*, **112**, 1-34.

Smeed, R. J. & Bennett, G. 1949. 5072
Research on road safety and traffic flow. *Inst. Civ. Engrs., Road paper* no. 29.

Smirnov, N. V. 1941. 5073
On the estimation of the maximum term in a series of observations. *C. R. (Dokl.) Acad. Sci. URSS*, **33**, 346-50.

Smirnov, N. V. 1944. 5074
Approximate laws of distribution of random variables from empirical data. (Russian.) *Usp. Mat. Nauk*, (10), 179-206.

Smirnov, N. V. 1947. 5075
Sur un critère de symétrie de la loi de distribution d'une variable aléatoire. (Russian.) *Dokl. Akad. Nauk SSSR*, **56**, 13-16.

Smirnov, N. V. 1948. 5076
Table for estimating the goodness of fit of empirical distributions. *Ann. Math. Statist.*, **19**, 279-81.

Smirnov, N. V. 1949. 5077
On the distribution of the number of cycles in cyclic systems. (Russian.) *Usp. Mat. Nauk (N.S.)*, **4**, 4(32), 192-3.

Smirnov, N. V. 1949. 5078
On the Cramér-Mises criterion. (Russian.) *Usp. Mat. Nauk (N.S.)*, **4**, 4(32), 196-7.

Smirnov, N. V. 1949. 5079
Limit distribution for the terms of a variational series. (Russian.) *Trudy Mat. Inst. Steklov*, **25**, 60 pp. (English transl. (1952): *Amer. Math. Soc. Transl.*, **67**, 64 pp.)

Smith, B. Babington. 1941. 5080
Note on an alternant suggested by statistical theory. *Edinb. Math. Notes*, **32**, 19-22.

Smith, C. A. B. 1947. 5081
Some examples of discrimination. *Ann. Eugen.*, **13**, 272-82 (errata: **14**, opp. p. 279).

Smith, C. A. B. & Hartley, H. O. 1948. 5082
Construction of Youden squares. *J. R. Statist. Soc. B*, **10**, 262-3.

Smith, F. C. 1948. 5083
The force of mortality function. *Amer. Math. Monthly*, **55**, 277-84.

Smith, G. C., Jr. 1947. 5084
Lorenz curve analysis of industrial decentralization. *J. Amer. Statist. Ass.*, **42**, 591-6.

Smith, G. S. 1949. 5085
Rapid calculation of standard deviations. *Nature*, **164**, 718.

Smith, H. Fairfield. 1947. 5086
Use of hydrometers to estimate dry rubber content of latex. *J. Rubber Res. Inst., Malaya*, **12**, 47-61.

Smith, H. Fairfield. 1947. 5087
Standard errors of means in sampling surveys with two-stage sampling. *J. R. Statist. Soc.*, **110**, 257-9.

Smith, H. Fairfield. 1948. 5088
Sample survey of tappings on small holdings, 1939-40. *J. Rubber Res. Inst., Malaya*, **12**, 78-125.

Smith, H. G. 1941. 5089
Some practical uses for hyperbolic grids. *J. Amer. Statist. Ass.*, **36**, 293-8.

Smith, H. G. 1943. 5090
Utility of statistical method in aerodynamics. *J. Amer. Statist. Ass.*, **38**, 341-5.

Smith, J. C. 1945. 5091
Asymptotic distribution of sums of Rademacher functions. *Bull. Amer. Math. Soc.*, **51**, 941-4.

Smith, J. H. 1942. 5091[a]
Weighted regressions in the analysis of economic series. *Studies in Mathematical Economics and Econometrics in Memory of Henry Schultz*, Univ. of Chicago Press, pp. 151-64.

Smith, J. H. 1946. 5092
Constant-amplitude scales for plotting stock prices. *Econometrica*, **14**, 316-19.

Smith, J. H. 1947. 5093
Estimation of linear functions of cell proportions. *Ann. Math. Statist.*, **18**, 231-54.

Smith, J. L. S. 1944. 5094
Specification of disturbed periodic time-series of the type of Wolfer's annual sunspot numbers. *J. R. Statist. Soc.*, **107**, 231-41.

Smith, K. W., Marks, H. P., Fieller, E. C. 5095
& Broom, W. A. 1944.
An extended cross-over design and its use in insulin assay. *Quart. J. Pharm.*, **17**, 108-17.

Smith, O. S. 1946. 5096
We recommend the teaching of statistics in high school. *Math. Teacher*, **39**, 182-3.

Smith, V. E. 1945. 5097
The statistical production function. *Quart. J. Econ.*, **59**, 543-62.

Smythe, V. R. 1945. 5098
Studies on the effects of transport and storage on the bacteriological quality of raw milk. I. The reduction of methylene blue by raw milk as influenced by time and temperature of storage. *Quart. J. Agric. Sci.*, **2**, 128-56.

Snedecor, G. W. 1941. 5099
Non-agricultural applications of analysis of variance. *Statist. J., City College, New York*, **4**, 9-13.

Snedecor, G. W. 1942.   5100
The use of tests of significance in an agricultural experiment station. *J. Amer. Statist. Ass.*, **37**, 383-6.

Snedecor, G. W. 1947.   5101
Application of the theory of experimental design in biology: the utilization of experimental data for improving design. (French summary.) *Proc. 25th. Session Int. Statist. Inst. Conf. Washington, D.C.*, 1947 (Publ. 1951), **3A**, 440-52.

Snedecor, G. W. 1947.   5102
An experiment in the collection of morbidity and mortality data on farm animals. *Proc. U.S. Livestock Sanitary Ass.*, pp. 218-25.

Snedecor, G. W. 1948.   5103
On the design of sampling investigations. *Amer. Statistician*, **2** (6), 6-9, 13.

Snedecor, G. W. 1948.   5104
A proposed basic course in statistics. *J. Amer. Statist. Ass.*, **43**, 53-60.

Snedecor, G. W. 1949.   5105
Some principles of experimental design. *Proc. Auburn Conf. Statist. Appl. Res. Social Sci., Plant Sci. and Animal Sci.*, 1948, pp. 47-51.

Snedecor, G. W. 1949.   5106
On a unique feature of statistics. *J. Amer. Statist. Ass.*, **44**, 1-8.

Snedecor, G. W. & Breneman, W. R. 1945.   5107
A factorial experiment to learn the effects of four androgens injected into male chicks. *Iowa State Coll. J. Sci.*, **19**, 333-42.

Snedecor, G. W. & Brown, G. W. 1947.   5108
Curve fitting: An art or a science? *Iowa State Coll. J. Sci.*, **21**, 245-50.

Snedecor, G. W. & Haber, E. S. 1946.   5109
Statistical methods for an incomplete experiment on a perennial crop. *Biometrics Bull.*, **2**, 61-7.

Snedecor, G. W. & King, A. J. 1942.   5110
Recent developments in sampling for agricultural statistics. *J. Amer. Statist. Ass.*, **37**, 95-102.

Snider, O. J. 1943.   5110a
Progress in precision; inspection methods used in manufacturing airplane engine crankshafts. *J. Soc. Automotive Engrs.*, **51**, 421-31.

Snyder, L. H. 1941.   5111
Studies in human inheritance. XX. Four sets of alleles tested for incomplete sex linkage. *Ohio J. Sci.*, **41**, 89-92.

Snyder, L. H. 1947.   5111a
A statement of general principles and concepts of population genetics. *Milbank Mem. Fund Quart.*, **25**, 367-72. (Correction (1948): **26**, 328-9.)

Snyder, L. H., Baxter, R. C. &   5112
Knisely, A. W. 1941.
Studies in human inheritance. XIX. The linkage relations of the blood groups, the blood types, and taste deficiency to P.T.C. *J. Heredity*, **32**, 22-5.

Sobel, M. & Wald, A. 1949.   5113
A sequential decision procedure for choosing one of three hypotheses concerning the unknown mean of a normal distribution. *Ann. Math. Statist.*, **20**, 502-22.

Sofia, A. 1948.   5113a
Su un nuovo metodo di calcolo dello scostamento semplice medio. *Statistica, Milano*, **8**, 78-88.

Solandt, D. Y., de Lury, D. B. & Hunter, J.   5114
1943. Effect of electrical stimulation on atrophy of denervated muscle. *Arch. Neurol. Psychiat. Chicago*, **49**, 802-7.

Solomon, L. 1947.   5115
Integral equations: some applications to statistical science. *Trans. Fac. Actuar. Edin.*, **18**, 139-65.

Solomon, L. 1948.   5116
The analysis of heterogeneous mortality data. *J. Inst. Actuar.*, **74**, 94-112.

Solomon, L. 1948.   5117
Statistical estimation. *J. Inst. Actuar. Students' Soc.*, **7**, 144-73; 213-34.

Solterer, J. 1941.   5118
A sequence of historical random events: Do Jesuits die in threes? *J. Amer. Statist. Ass.*, **36**, 477-84.

Somermeyer, W. N. 1947.   5118a
De betrouwbaarheid van controleurs. (With reply by **J. H. Enters**.) (Dutch. English summary.) *Statistica Neerlandica*, **1**, 231-9.

Somers, R. H. 1942.   5118b
Ordnance inspection. *Industr. Standardization*, **13**, 155-7.

Sonnino, G. 1949.   5119
Sulle progressioni aritmetiche e geometriche di ordine superiore e i loro valori medi. *Atti 8va Riun. Sci., Soc. Ital. Statist.* (publ. 1951), pp. 102-49.

Souloumiac. 1947.   5120
The application of statistical methods to the construction of a volume table. *Rev. Eaux Forêts*, **85**, 649-67.

Špaček, A. 1949.   5121
Note on successive cumulative sums of independent random variables. (English. Czech summary.) *Čas pěst. mat.*, **74**, 41-5.

Sparre Andersen, E. *See* **Andersen, E. S.**

Spearman, C. 1946.   5122
Theory of general factor. *Brit. J. Psychol.*, **36**, 117-31.

Spencer-Smith, J. L. 1947.   5123
Oscillatory properties of the moving average. *J. R. Statist. Soc. Suppl.*, **9**, 104-13.

Spencer-Smith, J. L. & Todd, H. A. C. 1941.   5124
Time-series met with in textile research. *J. R. Statist. Soc. Suppl.*, **7**, 131-45.

Spicer, C. C. 1947.   5125
The estimation of tumour susceptibility in pure lines. *Brit. J. Cancer*, **1**, 298.

Spiegelman, S. 1946.   5126
The constants in the logistic equation. *Amer. Nat.*, **80**, 186-8.

Spiegelman, S. & Reiner, J. M. 1945.   5127
A note on steady states and the Weber-Fechner Law. *Psychometrika*, **10**, 27-35.

Spielmans, J. V. 1948.   5128
Profile graphs. *J. Amer. Statist. Ass.*, **43**, 96-108.

Spiller, D. 1948. 5129
Truncated log-normal and root-normal frequency distributions of insect populations. *Nature,* 162, 530-1.

Spitzbart, A. 1946. 5130
Approximation in the sense of least *p*th powers with a single auxiliary condition of interpolation. *Bull. Amer. Math. Soc.,* 52, 338-46.

Spoerl, C. A. 1941-2. 5131
The Whittaker-Henderson graduation formula *A.* The mixed difference case. *Trans. Actuar. Soc. Amer.,* 42, 292-313; 43, 68-80.

Spoerl, C. A. 1943. 5132
A fundamental proposition in the solution of simultaneous linear equations. *Trans. Actuar. Soc. Amer.,* 44, 276-88.

Spoerl, C. A. 1944. 5133
On solving simultaneous linear equations. *Trans. Actuar. Soc. Amer.,* 45, 18-32.

Spurr, W. A. 1940. 5134
A graphic short cut to the moving average method of measuring seasonality. *J. Amer. Statist. Ass.,* 35, 667-70.

Spurr, W. A. & Arnold, D. R. 1948. 5135
A short cut method of fitting a logistic curve. *J. Amer. Statist. Ass.,* 43, 127-34.

Spurway, H. 1945. 5136
The genetics and Cytology of *Drosophila subobscura.* I. Element A. Sex-linked mutants and their standard order. *J. Genet.,* 46, 268-86.

Spurway, H. 1945. 5137
Sex determination in *Triturus vulgaris* Linn. (*taeniatus schneid*). *Amer. Nat.,* 79, 377-80.

Spurway, H. 1949. 5138
Remarks on Vavilov's law of homologous variation. *Ric. Sci., Suppl., Symp. Fatt. Ecol. Genet. Spec. Animali.*

Spurway, H. & Mandeville, L. C. 1949. 5139
The development of hybrids between *Ranaosculenta* and *Rana ridibunda. Brit. J. Herpet.,* 1, 39-50.

Spurway, H., Philip, U., Rendel, J. M. & Haldane, J. B. S. 1944. 5140
Genetics and karyology of *Drosophila subobscura. Nature,* 154, 260.

Sreedharan, P. K. C. 1943. 5141
Trend analyser. *Proc. Indian Acad. Sci. A,* 17, 187-94.

Sreenivasan, P. S. 1943. 5142
Studies on the estimation of growth and yield of jowar by sampling. *Indian J. Agric. Sci.,* 13, 399-412.

Stadtman, E. R., Barker, H. A., Haas, V. & Mrak, E. M. 1946. 5143
Storage of dried fruit. Influence of temperature on deterioration of apricots. *Industr. Engng. Chem.,* 38, 541-3.

Staller, K. 1947. 5144
Matematicky rozbor zásady hospodárnosti. (Analyse mathématique du principe d'économie.) (Czech.) *Strojn. Obzor,* 27, 203-11.

Stanford, E. H. 1941. 5144a
A new factor for resistance to bunt, *Tilletia tritici,*

linked with the Martin and Turkey factors. *Amer. Soc. Agron.,* 33, 559-68.

Stange, K. 1948. 5145
Über die Verteilungsdichte der Mess- oder Beobachtungsfehler eines dreidimensionalen Punktraumes. (German. Russian summary.) *Zeit. angew. Math. Mech.,* 28, 235-43.

Stange, K. 1948. 5146
Die zweckmässige Auswertung von punktweise aufgenommenen Zeit-Weglinien. *Ingenieur-Arch.,* 16, 384-402.

Stange, K. 1949. 5147
Mehrfaches Ausgleichen einer fehlerhaften Punktreihe. *Zeit. angew. Math. Mech.,* 29, 114-26.

Stange, K. 1949. 5148
Das Bildungsgesetz für die Fehlerformeln beim Ausgleichen von fehlerhaften Messreihen mit Hilfe ganzer rationaler Funktionen wachsender Ordnung. *Zeit. angew. Math. Mech.,* 29, 225-38.

Stansfield, R. G. 1947. 5149
Statistical theory of d.f. fixing. *J. Inst. Elect. Engrs., III A,* 94, 762-70.

Stansly, P. G. & Schlosser, M. E. 1947. 5150
Studies in polymyxin: An agar diffusion method of assay. *J. Bact.,* 54, 585-97.

Stanton, F. 1941. 5151
Problems of sampling in market research. *J. Consult. Psychol.,* 5, 149-53.

Stanton, R. G. 1946. 5152
Filial and fraternal correlations in successive generations. *Ann. Eugen.,* 13, 18-24. (Errata (1947): 14, 1.)

Starke, L. G. K. 1949. 5153
Some thoughts on the analysis of numerical data. *J. Inst. Actuar.,* 75, 183-231.

Starr, D. F. 1944. 5154
The theory of probits at high mortalities. *J. Econ. Ent.,* 37, 850.

Steadman, F. M. 1944. 5155
Quality control posts mill-production odds. *Textile World,* 94, 63.

Steen, J. R. 1945. 5156
Analysis of double sampling plans. *Industr. Qual. Contr.,* 1 (6), 3-6; 10; 20.

Steffenson, J. F. 1941. 5157
On the coefficient of correlation for continuous distributions. *Skand. Aktuartidskr.,* 24, 1-12 (correction: 232).

Steffenson, J. F. 1941. 5158
On the ω test of dependence between statistical variables. *Skand. Aktuartidskr.,* 24, 13-33.

Steggerda, F. R. & Mitchell, H. H. 1946. 5159
Variability in the calcium metabolism and calcium requirements of adult human subjects. *J. Nutrit.,* 31, 407-22.

Stein, A. & Shaw, L. W. 1943. 5160
Some methods of reducing the amount of inspection in the application of double sampling inspection procedures. *Aberdeen Proving Ground Ballistic Res. Lab. Rep.* no. 248.

Stein, C. 1945.   5161
A two-sample test for a linear hypothesis whose power is independent of the variance. *Ann. Math. Statist.*, **16**, 243-58.

Stein, C. 1946.   5162
A note on cumulative sums. *Ann. Math. Statist.*, **17**, 498-9.

Stein, C. & Wald, A. 1947.   5163
Sequential confidence intervals for the mean of a normal distribution with known variance. *Ann. Math. Statist.*, **18**, 427-33.

Steindler, A. 1949.   5164
Su alcune curve statistiche. *Riv. Ital. Econ. Demogr. Statist.*, **3**, 230-3.

Steiner, E. H. 1948.   5165
Application of statistical methods in calculating proportions of ingredients in certain food products: the application of statistical methods to food problems. *Analyst*, **73**, 15-29.

Steinhaus, H. 1940.   5166
Sur les fonctions indépendantes. VI. Équipartition. (French. Ukrainian summary.) *Studia Math.*, **9**, 121-32.

Steinhaus, H. 1948.   5167
Elementary inequalities between the expected values of current estimates of variance. *Colloq. Math.*, **1**, 312-21.

Steinhaus, H. 1948.   5168
Sur les fonctions indépendantes. VII. Un essaim de points à l'intérieur d'un cube. *Studia Math.*, **10**, 1-20.

Steinhaus, H. 1948.   5169
Sur l'interprétation des résultats statistiques. *Colloq. Math.*, **1**, 232-8.

Steinhaus, H. 1949.   5170
Sur la division pragmatique. *Econometrica Suppl.*, **17**, 315-19.

Steinhaus, H. 1949.   5171
Sur les fonctions indépendantes. VIII. *Studia Math.*, **11**, 133-44.

Steinhaus, H. 1949.   5172
The so-called Petersburg paradox. *Colloq. Math.*, **2**, 56-8.

Stephan, F. F. 1941.   5173
Stratification in representative sampling. *J. Marketing*, **6**, 38-46.

Stephan, F. F. 1942.   5174
An iterative method of adjusting sample frequency tables when expected marginal totals are known. *Ann. Math. Statist.*, **13**, 166-78.

Stephan, F. F. 1945.   5175
The expected value and variance of the reciprocal and other negative powers of a positive Bernoullian variate. *Ann. Math. Statist.*, **16**, 50-61.

Stephan, F. F. 1948.   5176
History of the uses of modern sampling procedures. *J. Amer. Statist. Ass.*, **43**, 12-39. (Also: *Proc. 25th. Session Int. Statist. Inst. Conf. Washington, D.C.*, 1947 (Publ. 1951), **3A**, 81-112.)

Stephan, F. F. & McCarthy, P. J. 1947.   5177
Sampling opinion attitudes, and consumer wants. *Amer. Statistician*, **1** (3), 6-7.

Stephan, F. F., Deming, W. E.   5178
& Hansen, M. H. 1940.
The sampling procedure of the 1940 population census. *J. Amer. Statist. Ass.*, **35**, 615-30.

Stephenson, W. 1940.   5179
Two contributions to the theory of mental testing. II. A statistical regard of performance. *Brit. J. Psychol.*, **30**, 230-47.

Stern, C. 1943.   5180
The Hardy-Weinberg Law. *Science*, **97**, 137-8.

Stern, E. 1941.   5181
Leibrenten und veränderliche Todesfallversicherungen. *Verzekerings-archief*, **22**, 285-318.

Sternberg, W. 1940.   5182
The general limit theorem in the theory of probability. *Bull. Amer. Math. Soc.*, **46**, 292-8.

Stevens, N. E. 1947.   5183
The anecdote as an antidote to statistical analysis. *Chron. Bot.*, **11**, 188-90.

Stevens, S. S. 1946.   5184
On the theory of scales of measurement. *Science*, **103**, 677-80.

Stevens, W. L. 1940.   5184[a]
On the interpretation of the data of certain experiments in paranormal cognition. *Proc. Soc. Psych. Res.*, **46**, 256-60.

Stevens, W. L. 1940.   5185
The standardization of rubber flexing test. *India Rubber World*, 1 August 1940.

Stevens, W. L. 1942.   5186
Accuracy of mutation rates. *J. Genet.*, **43**, 301-7.

Stevens, W. L. 1942-3.   5187
Mathematical theory of some distributions used in statistics. (Portuguese.) *Rev. Fac. Cienc. Coimbra*, **10**, 247-88; **11**, 85-102.

Stevens, W. L. 1944.   5188
Statistical estimation. Theory of the estimation of two or more parameters, illustrated by the problem of the estimation of the frequencies of the genes of blood groups. (Portuguese.) *Rev. Fac. Cienc. Coimbra*, **12**, 23-104; 175-221.

Stevens, W. L. 1945.   5189
Análise discriminante. *Inst. Antrop. Coimbra*.

Stevens, W. L. 1945.   5190
Application of the χ^2 test to the analysis of variance. (Portuguese.) *Rev. Fac. Cienc. Coimbra*, **13**, 4-17.

Stevens, W. L. 1948.   5191
Control by gauging. *J. R. Statist. Soc. B*, **10**, 54-108.

Stevens, W. L. 1948.   5192
Statistical analysis of a non-orthogonal tri-factorial experiment. *Biometrika*, **35**, 346-67.

Stewart, A. B. 1947.   5193
Memoranda on colonial fertilizer experiments. II. Planning and conduct of fertilizer experiments. *Colon. Office Memo.* no. 214, pp. 3-9.

Stewart, D. C. 1945.   5194
Significance tests for industrial injury rates. *Edison Elect. Inst. Bull.*, **13**, 361-3.

Stewart, J. Q. 1947. 5195
Empirical mathematical rules concerning the distribution and equilibrium of population. *Geogr. Rev.*, **37**, 461-85.

Stewart, O. F. 1945. 5195ª
The philosophy of the statistical approach to quality control. *Industr. Engr.*, **5**, 19-22.

Stewart, W. M. 1941. 5196
A note on the power of the sign test. *Ann. Math. Statist.*, **12**, 236-9.

Stihi, E. E. 1940. 5197
Sur la valeur réelle de la mesure d'une grandeur. *Ann. Sci. Univ. Jassy*, I, **26**, 528-30.

Stirewalt, C. & Bordeaux, J. 1944. 5197ª
Statistical methods of quality control. *Iron Age*, **153**, 56-60.

Stock, J. S. & Hochstim, J. R. 1947. 5198
Commercial uses of sampling. *Proc. 25th. Session Int. Statist. Inst. Conf. Washington, D.C.*, 1947 (Publ. 1951), **3A**, 129-60.

Stockman, C. M. 1944. 5199
A method of obtaining an approximation for the operating characteristic of a Wald sequential probability ratio test applied to a binomial distribution. *U.K. Min. Supply Advisory Service Statist. Method & Qual. Contr. Ser. R*, no. QC/R/19, 10 March 1944, 7 pp.

Stockman, C. M. & Armitage, P. 1946. 5200
Some properties of closed sequential schemes. *J. R. Statist. Soc. Suppl.*, **8**, 104-12.

Stocks, P. 1941. 5201
Diphtheria and scarlet fever incidence during the dispersal of 1939-40. *J. R. Statist. Soc.*, **104**, 311-45.

Stocks, P. 1942. 5202
Measles and whooping-cough incidence before and during the dispersal of 1939-41. *J. R. Statist. Soc.*, **105**, 259-91.

Stoffels, A. 1940. 5203
De berekening van middelbare fouten by niet homogene proef velden. (Calculating standard errors in connection with non-homogeneous experimental fields.) *Landbouwk Tijdschr., Wageningen*, **52**, 165-74.

Stoffels, A. 1944. 5204
The accuracy of measurements with Weise's hypsometer. *Ned. Boschb. Tijdschr.*, **17**, 201-5.

Stoffels, A. 1947. 5205
Determination of stand volume by measurement of two sample trees. *Ned. Boschb. Tijdschr.*, **19**, 228-35.

Stoffels, A. 1947. 5206
The treatment of field experiments by Knut Vik's method. (Dutch. English summary.) *Statistica Neerlandica*, **1**, 209-18.

Stoffels, A. 1949. 5207
The treatment of the results of field experiments by reducing the yields in two directions. (Dutch. English summary.) *Statistica Neerlandica*, **2**, 242-9.

Stol, J. J. Dijkveld. 1942. 5208
Het uitschakelen van systematische fouten bij proefvelden in vierkantsvorm. (Ausschaltung der systematischen Fehler bei Versuchfelder in Quadratform.)

(Dutch. German summary.) *Landbouwk Tijdschr., Wageningen*, **54**, 185-202.

Stoll, A. 1947. 5209
Das Proportionalwahlsystem als diophantische Näherungsaufgabe. *Vjschr.naturf. Ges. Zürich*, **92**, 204-12.

Stommel, H. 1947. 5210
Note on the use of the T-S correlation for dynamic height anomaly computations. *J. Marine Res.*, **6** (2), 85-92.

Stonaker, H. H. & Lush, J. L. 1942. 5211
Heritability of conformation in Poland-China swine as evaluated by scoring. *J. Animal Sci.*, **1**, 99-105.

Stone, C. P. 1947. 5212
Methodological resources for the experimental study of innate behaviour as related to environmental facts. *Psychol. Rev.*, **44**, 342-7.

Stone, J. R. N. 1945. 5213
The analysis of market demand. *J. R. Statist. Soc.*, **108**, 186-391.

Stone, J. R. N. 1947. 5214
On the interdependence of blocks of transactions. *J. R. Statist. Soc. Suppl.*, **9**, 1-45.

Stone, J. R. N. 1947. 5215
Prediction from autoregressive schemes and linear stochastic difference systems. (French summary.) *Proc. 25th. Session Int. Statist. Inst. Conf., Washington, D.C.*, 1947 (Publ. 1951), **5**, 29-38. (Also: *Econometrica*, **17**, *Suppl.*, 29-38.)

Stone, J. R. N. 1948. 5216
The analysis of market demand. An outline of methods and results. *Rev. Int. Statist. Inst.*, **16**, 23-35.

Stoner, P. M. 1941. 5217
Fitting the exponential function and the Gompertz function by the method of least squares. *J. Amer. Statist. Ass.*, **36**, 515-18.

Strand, N. V. & Jessen, R. J. 1943. 5218
Some investigations on the suitability of the township as a unit for sampling Iowa agriculture. *Iowa Agric. Exper. Sta. Res. Bull.*, **315**, 613-50.

Strandskov, H. H. 1942. 5219
On the variance of human live birth sex ratios. *Hum. Biol.*, **14**, 85-94.

Strandskov, H. H. 1945. 5220
Plural birth frequencies in the total, the " white " and the " coloured " U.S. populations. *Amer. J. Phys. Anthrop.* (*N.S.*), **3**, 49-55.

Strandskov, H. H. & Edelen, E. W. 1946. 5220ª
Monozygotic and dizygotic twin birth frequencies in the " white " and the " coloured " U.S. populations. *Genetics*, **31**, 438-46.

Strandskov, H. H. & Siemens, G. J. 1946. 5220ᵇ
An analysis of the sex ratio among single and plural births in the total, the " white " and the " coloured " U.S. populations. *Amer. J. Phys. Anthrop.* (N.S.), **4**, 491-501.

Stratton, F. 1945. 5221
The inheritance of the allelomorphs of the *Rh* gene with special reference to the *Rh'* and *Rh″* genes. *Ann. Eugen.*, **12**, 250-60.

Strecker, H. 1949.   5222
Die Quotientenmethode, eine Variante der " Variate Difference " Methode. *Mitt. Math. Statist.*, **1**, 115-30; 218.

Strutt, M. J. O. 1943.   5223
Bounds for the characteristic parameter-values corresponding to problems of Hill. I. Characteristic values of smallest moduli. II. Characteristic values of any order. (Dutch.) *Proc. Kon. Ned. Akad. Wetensch.*, **52**, 83-90; 97-104.

Strutt, M. J. O. 1943.   5224
Curves of characteristic parameter-values corresponding to problems of Hill. I. General character of the curves. II. Asymptotic character of the curves. (Dutch.) *Proc. Kon. Ned. Akad. Wetensch.*, **52**, 153-62; 212-22.

Strutt, M. J. O. 1943.   5225
Characteristic functions corresponding to problems of Hill. I. Completeness of the sets of periodic and of almost-periodic characteristic functions. II. Expansion formulae in series of periodic and of almost-periodic characteristic functions. (Dutch.) *Proc. Kon. Ned. Akad. Wetensch.*, **52**, 488-96; 584-91.

Strutt, M. J. O. 1944.   5226
Real eigen-values of Hill's problems of the second order. (German.) *Math. Zeit.*, **49**, 593-643.

Strutt, M. J. O. 1948.   5227
On Hill's problems with complex parameters and a real periodic function. *Proc. Roy. Soc. Edin.* A, **62**, 278-96.

Stumpers, F. L. H. M. 1947.   5228
On a non-linear noise problem. *Philips Research Rep.*, **2**, 241-59.

Subramanian, S. 1940.   5229
Compatibility of Fisher's tests for index number formulae. *Math. Student*, **8**, 124-7.

Sugawara, M. 1949.   5230
On the test for the hypothesis given by an inequality $\sigma \leq f(\mu)$. (Japanese.) *Res. Mem. Inst. Stat. Math., Tokyo*, **5**, 62-74.

Sukhatme, B. V. 1949.   5230[a]
Random association of points on a lattice. *J. Indian Soc. Agric. Statist.*, **2**, 60-85.

Sukhatme, B. V. 1949.   5231
Variance of triplets. *Nature*, **164**, 841.

Sukhatme, P. V. 1942.   5232
On Bernstein's improved method of estimating blood-group gene frequencies. *Sankhyā*, **6**, 85-92.

Sukhatme, P. V. 1944.   5233
Moments and product moments of moment-statistics for samples of finite and infinite populations. *Sankhyā*, **6**, 363-82.

Sukhatme, P. V. 1944.   5233[a]
Note on the method of calculating sire index for milk production in cattle. *Indian J. Vet. Sci. & Animal Husb.*, **14**, 114-23.

Sukhatme, P. V. 1944.   5233[b]
Statistical study of a breeding experiment with goats. *Indian J. Vet. Sci. & Animal Husb.*, **14**, 167-76.

Sukhatme, P. V. 1945.   5234
Random sampling for estimating rice yield in Madras province. *Indian J. Agric. Sci.*, **15**, 308-18.

Sukhatme, P. V. 1946.   5235
Bias in the use of small-size plots in sample surveys for yield. *Current Science*, **15**, 119-20. (Also: *Nature*, **157**, 630.)

Sukhatme, P. V. 1946.   5236
Size of sampling unit in yield surveys. *Nature*, **158**, 345.

Sukhatme, P. V. 1947.   5237
The problem of plot size in large-scale yield surveys. *J. Amer. Statist. Ass.*, **42**, 297-310; 460.

Sukhatme, P. V. 1947.   5238
Report on random sample survey for estimating the out-turn of paddy in Central Province and Berar 1945-6. *Indian Coun. Agric. Res.*, 59ff.

Sukhatme, P. V. 1947.   5239
Report on random sample survey for estimating the out-turn of paddy in Madras, 1945-6. *Indian Coun. Agric. Res.*, 66ff.

Sukhatme, P. V. 1947.   5240
Use of small-size plots in yield surveys. *Nature*, **160**, 542.

Sukhatme, P. V. 1949.   5240[a]
Sample surveys in agriculture. *Proc. Indian Sci. Congr.*, **37** (11), 51-73.

Sukhatme, P. V. & Aggarwal, O. P. 1949.   5241
Report on random sample surveys for estimating yield of wheat in Delhi Province. *Indian Coun. Agric. Res.*

Sukhatme, P. V. & Koshal, R. S. 1947.   5242
Report of the scheme for crop cutting: experimental survey on paddy in the Bombay Province, 1945-6. *Indian Coun. Agric. Res.*, 40ff.

Sukhatme, P. V. & Panse, V. G. 1942.   5242[a]
Size of experiments for testing sera or vaccines. *Indian J. Vet. Sci. & Animal Husb.*, **13**, 75-82.

Sukhatme, P. V., Pendharkar, V. G.   5242[b]
& Sankaran, A. N. 1948.
The composition of milk. II. Statistical Study. *Indian Coun. Agric. Res. Misc. Bull.*, no. 61, pp. 11-81.

Sukhatme, P. V., Prabhu, S. S.   5243
& Amble, V. N. 1948.
On a method of estimating nutrient requirement in metabolism studies on animals. *J. Indian Soc. Agric. Statist.*, **1**, 117-36.

Suleimanova, Kh. R. 1949.   5244
Stochastic matrices with real characteristic numbers. (Russian.) *Dokl. Akad. Nauk SSSR*, **66**, 343-5.

Sumner, F. C. & Dehaney, K. G. 1943.   5245
Size and placement of intervals as influencing a Pearson product-moment correlation coefficient obtained by the scatter-diagram procedure. *J. Psychol.*, **15**, 27-30.

Sun, Shu Peng. 1945.   5246
On the successive approximation to the distribution of the third moment about the mean of independent variates. *Acad. Sinica Sci. Rec.*, **1**, 351-4.

Sun, Shu Peng. 1948.   5247
The approximate distribution of the kth moment about the mean of large samples. *Acad. Sinica Sci. Rec.*, **2**.

Sun, Y.-P. & Shepard, H. H. 1947. 5248
Methods of calculating and correcting the mortality of insects. *J. Econ. Ent.*, **40**, 710-15.

Sundström, M. 1944. 5249
Untersuchung über die Kränklichkeit in den staatlich unterstützten krankenkassen Schwedens. *Skand. Aktuartidskr.*, **27**, 177-228.

Surdin, M. 1943. 5250
Distribution in time of spontaneous fluctuation voltage. *Phil. Mag.*, (7), **34**, 716-22.

Sutherland, J. 1942. 5251
An investigation into some aspects of problem solving in arithmetic. *Brit. J. Educ. Psychol.*, **12**, 35-46.

Sverdrup, E. 1947. 5252
Derivation of the Wishart distribution of the second order sample moments by straightforward integration of a multiple integral. *Skand. Aktuartidskr.*, **30**, 151-66.

Swan, A. W. 1945. 5253
Sampling schemes for qualitative inspection. *Proc. Inst. Mech. Engrs.*, **152**, 81-92.

Swan, A. W. 1948. 5253a
The χ^2 significance test—expected vs. observed results. *Engineer, London*, **186**, 679.

Swanson, C. O. 1945. 5254
Probabilities in estimating the grade of gold deposits. *Trans. Canadian Min. Inst.*, **48**, 323-50.

Swaroop, S. A. 1941. 5255
A modification of the routine dilution tests and tables showing the most probable number of organisms and the standard error of this number. *Indian J. Med. Res.*, **29**, 499-510.

Swaroop, S. A. 1941. 5256
A consideration of the accuracy of estimation of the most probable number of organisms by dilution tests. *Indian J. Med. Res.*, **29**, 511-22.

Swartout, H. O. & Webster, R. G. 1940. 5257
To what degree are mortality statistics dependable? *Amer. J. Publ. Health*, **30**, 811-15.

Swed, F. S. & Eisenhart, C. 1943. 5258
Tables for testing randomness of grouping in a sequence of alternatives. *Ann. Math. Statist.*, **14**, 66-87.

Swineford, F. 1941. 5259
Analysis of a personality trait. *J. Educ. Psychol.*, **32**, 438-44.

Swineford, F. 1941. 5260
Some comparisons of the multi-factor and the bi-factor methods of analysis. *Psychometrika*, **6**, 375-82.

Swineford, F. 1946. 5261
Graphical and tabular aids for determining sample size when planning experiments which involve comparisons of percentages. *Psychometrika*, **11**, 43-9.

Swineford, F. 1948. 5262
A table for estimating the significance of the difference between correlated percentages. *Psychometrika*, **13**, 23-5.

Swineford, F. 1949. 5263
Further notes on differences between percentages. *Psychometrika*, **14**, 183-7.

Swineford, F. & Holzinger, K. J. 1940-2. 5264
Selected references on statistics, the theory of test construction and factor analysis. *School Rev.*, **48**, 460-6; **49**, 461-7; **50**, 456-65.

Swyer, G. I. M. & Emmens, C. W. 1947. 5265
A modified method for the viscosimetric assay of hyaluronidase. *Bio-Chem. J.*, **41**, 29-34.

Syzrantzev, P. I. 1941. 5266
Basic coefficients for mathematical treatment of experimental data by the method of averages. *Dokl. Vses. Akad. S.-KH. Nauk*, **1941**, 45-8.

Szatrowski, Z. 1945. 5267
The relationship between price change and price level for common stocks. *J. Amer. Statist. Ass.*, **40**, 467-83.

Szatrowski, Z. 1945. 5268
Time series correlated with the beef-pork consumption ratio. *Econometrica*, **13**, 60-78.

Szatrowski, Z. 1946. 5269
Calculating the geometric mean from a large amount of data. *J. Amer. Statist. Ass.*, **41**, 218-20.

T

Täcklind, S. 1942. 5270
Sur le risque de ruine dans des jeux inéquitables. *Skand. Aktuartidskr.*, **25**, 1-42.

Täcklind, S. 1944. 5271
Elementare Behandlung vom Erneuerungsproblem für den stationären Fall. *Skand. Aktuartidskr.*, **27**, 1-15.

Täcklind, S. 1945. 5272
Fourieranalytische Behandlung vom Erneuerungsproblem. *Skand. Aktuartidskr.*, **28**, 68-105.

Tager, P. G. 1947. 5273
The frequency spectrum in phase-pulse modulation. (Russian.) *Avtomat. i Telemekh.*, **8**, 117-35.

Tagliacarne, G. 1947. 5274
Note di statistica economica. *G. Economisti*, **6**, 61-8.

Tagliacarne, G. 1949. 5275
Delle stime quantitative e del tipo di medie che ad esse si conviene. *Riv. Ital. Econ. Demogr. Statist.*, **3**, 234-44. (Also: *Ann. Univ. Macerata*, **17**.)

Talacko, J. 1949. 5276
Mathematical theory of growth with special regard to population problems. *Aktuárské Vědy*, **8**, 21-34.

Talekar, V. L. 1947. 5277
New methods of obtaining squares of numbers. *Current Science*, **16**, 337-8.

Tanner, L. & Deming, W. E. 1949. 5278
Some problems in the sampling of bulk materials. *Proc. Amer. Soc. Test. Mat.*, **49**, 1181-8.

Tarjan, R. 1941. 5279
Untersuchungen über den Kapitalbedarf des Lebens-versicherungsgeschäftes. (French, Italian and English summaries.) *Trans. 12th Int. Congr. Actuar., Lucerne, 1940*, **3**, 335-51.

Tarjan, R. 1944. 5280
Untersuchungen zum Erneuerungsproblem nichtkonstanter Gesamtheiten. *Mitt. Ver. Schweiz. Versich.-Math.*, **44**, 95-105.

Tate, M. W. 1948. 5281
Individual differences in speed of response in mental test materials of varying degrees of difficulty. *Educ. and Psychol. Measurement*, **8**, 353-74.

Tavares, H. 1945. 5282
Confidence in experimental results. *Bol. Sec. Agric. Industr. Comm., Pernambuco*, **12**, 293-8.

Taylor, A. J. 1942. 5283
Grading and sampling of wattle bark. *J. South African Forest Ass.*, **8**, 103-11.

Taylor, E. 1946. 5284
The use of a single card column for recording variables with a range of 30 or fewer units. *Proc. Res. Forum, I.B.M. Corp., New York*, pp. 62-8.

Taylor, E. K. 1947. 5285
Tables for the determination of the significance of skewness and of the significance of the difference in the skewness of two independent distributions. *Psychometrika*, **12**, 111-25.

Taylor, E. K. & Gaylord, R. H. 1947. 5286
Table for use in the computation of statistics of dichotomous and truncated distributions. *Educ. and Psychol. Measurement*, **7**, 441-56.

Taylor, J. 1948. 5287
Errors of treatment comparisons when observations are missing. *Nature*, **162**, 262-3.

Taylor, J. 1949. 5288
A valid restriction of randomization for certain field experiments. *J. Agric. Sci.*, **39**, 303-8.

Taylor, J. J. 1945. 5289
Statistical methods applied to insulator development and manufacture. *Trans. Amer. Inst. Elect. Engrs.*, **64**, 495-9.

Taylor, W. J. 1945. 5290
Method of Lagrangian curvilinear interpolation. *J. Res., Nat. Bur. Stand.*, **35**, 151-5.

Taylor, W. S. 1942. 5291
The use of interactions in analysing psychological data. *Brit. J. Psychol.*, **32**, 248-58.

Taylor, W. S. 1942. 5292
Partialling out sums of squares and products in calculating correlations with non-homogeneous data. *Brit. J. Psychol.*, **32**, 318-23.

Tchen, Chan-Mou. 1947. 5293
Mean value and correlation problems connected with the motion of small particles suspended in a turbulent fluid. (English. Dutch summary.) *Martinus Nijhoff., The Hague*, **7**, 125 pp.

Teatini, U. 1948. 5294
Interpolazione di serie cicliche. *Statistica, Milano*, **8**, 125-40.

Tedin, O. 1945. 5295
Small samples of Poisson series. *Hereditas, Lund.*, **31**, 238-40.

Teissier, G. 1946. 5296
Mathématiques et biologie. *Rev. Gén. Sci. Pures Appl.*, **53**, 92-9.

Teissier, G. 1948. 5297
La relation d'allométrie, sa signification statistique et biologique. *Biometrics*, **4**, 14-53.

Telang, D. M. & Bhagwat, G. A. 1941. 5298
Studies in the vital capacity of Bombay medical students. I. Statistical correlation with physical measurements. *Indian J. Med. Res.*, **29**, 723-50.

Telegdy-Kovats, L. 1943. 5299
The principles of modern field experimentation technique. *Rep. Hung. Agric. Exper. Sta.*, **46**, 183-95.

ten Pas, W. G. J. 1941. 5300
Wahrscheinlichkeitsrechnung und Statistik in der Versicherungsmathematik. (French, Italian and English summaries.) *Trans. 12th Int. Congr. Actuar., Lucerne*, 1940, **1**, 263-83.

Tepping, B. J., Hurwitz, W. N. & Deming, W. E. 1943. 5301
On the efficiency of deep stratification in block sampling. *J. Amer. Statist. Ass.*, **38**, 93-100.

Terrill, C. E., Pohle, E. M., Emik, L. O. & Hazel, L. N. 1945. 5302
Estimation of clean fleece weight from grease-fleece weight and staple length. *J. Agric. Res.*, **70**, 1-10.

Tharp, W. H., Wadleigh, C. H. & Barker, H. D. 1941. 5303
Some problems in handling and interpreting plant disease data in complex factorial design. *Phytopath.*, **31**, 26-48.

Thawani, V. D. 1949. 5304
A note on a property of the median. *Math. Student*, **16**, 35-6.

Theil, H. 1949. 5305
A note on the inequality of Camp and Meidell. (Dutch. English summary.) *Statistica Neerlandica*, **3**, 201-8.

Theiss, E. 1948. 5306
Tervgazdasag es statisztika. (L'économie planifiée et la statistique.) (Hungarian. French summary.) *Statist. Szemle*, **26**, 69-78.

Théodorescu, N. 1941. 5307
Un problème de loterie. *Disquisit. Math. Phys.*, **1**, 339-56.

Thesen, G. 1940. 5308
Über periodische Funktionen, ihre Observation und Ausgleichung. *Skand. Aktuartidskr.*, **23**, 168-95.

Thionet, P. 1945. 5309
Essai de détermination mathématique du stock optimum. *J. Soc. Statist. Paris*, **86**, 99-121. (Addendum (1947): **88**, 203-8.)

Thionet, P. 1945. 5310
L'école moderne de statisticiens italiens. *J. Soc. Statist. Paris*, **86**, 245-55.

Thionet, P. 1948. 5311
Le problème théorique du plan d'échantillonnage. *J. Soc. Statist. Paris*, **89**, 136-54.

Thom, H. C. S. 1940. 5312
On statistical analysis of rainfall data. *Trans. Amer. Geophys. Un.*, **21**, 490-9.

Thomas, H. A., Jr. 1948. 5313
Frequency of minor floods. *J. Boston Soc. Civil Engrs.*, 35, 425-42.

Thomas, M. 1949. 5314
A generalization of Poisson's binomial limit for use in ecology. *Biometrika*, 36, 18-25.

Thompson, A. P. 1945. 5315
A sampling approach to New Zealand timber cruising problems. *New Zealand J. Forestry*, 5, 103-17.

Thompson, C. M. 1941. 5316
Tables of percentage points of the incomplete beta-function. *Biometrika*, 32, 151-81.

Thompson, C. M. 1941. 5317
Tables of percentage points of the χ^2 distribution. *Biometrika*, 32, 187-91.

Thompson, C. M. & Merrington, M. 1946. 5318
Tables for testing the homogeneity of a set of estimated variances. *Biometrika*, 33, 302-4.

Thompson, W. R. 1947. 5319
Use of moving averages and interpolation to estimate median-effective dose. I. Fundamental formulas, estimation of error, and relation to other methods. *Bact. Rev.*, 11, 115-45.

Thompson, W. R. 1948. 5320
Direct probability sequential analysis, preliminary report. *Bull. Amer. Math. Soc.*, 54, 288-9.

Thompson, W. R. 1948. 5321
On the use of parallel or non-parallel systems of transformed curves in bio-assay: illustration in the quantitative complement-fixation test. *Biometrics*, 4, 197-208.

Thompson, W. R. 1949. 5322
Statistical methods for evaluation of diagnostic and other procedures: An objective weeding-out process applicable to material used in surveys of diagnostic variability. *Hum. Biol.*, 21, 17-34.

Thompson, W. R. & Maltaner, F. 1940. 5323
On the construction of graphs and tables for evaluation of the quantitative complement-fixation reactions, and reaction ratios. *J. Immunol.*, 38, 147-57.

Thomson, D. Halton 1947. 5324
Approximate formulae for the percentage points of the incomplete beta function and of the χ^2 distribution. *Biometrika*, 34, 368-72.

Thomson, G. H. 1940. 5325
Weighting for battery reliability and prediction. *Brit. J. Psychol.*, 30, 357-66.

Thomson, G. H. 1941. 5326
The use of the Latin square in designing educational experiments. *Brit. J. Educ. Psychol.*, 11, 135-7.

Thomson, G. H. 1942. 5327
Following up individual items in a group intelligence test. *Brit. J. Psychol.*, 32, 310-17.

Thomson, G. H. 1944. 5328
The applicability of Karl Pearson's selection formulae in follow-up experiments. *Brit. J. Psychol.*, 34, 105.

Thomson, G. H. 1947. 5329
The maximum correlation of two weighted batteries. (Hotelling's " most predictable criterion.") *Brit. J. Psychol. (Statist. Sec.)*, 1, 27-34.

Thomson, G. H. 1949. 5330
On estimating oblique factors. *Brit. J. Psychol. (Statist. Sec.)*, 2, 1-2.

Thorndike, R. L. 1942. 5331
Regression fallacies in the matched groups experiment. *Psychometrika*, 7, 85-102.

Thornton, G. R. 1943. 5332
The significance of rank difference coefficients of correlation. *Psychometrika*, 8, 211-22.

Thorold, C. A. 1947. 5333
A study of yield, preparation out-turns, and quality in Arabica coffee. I. Yields. *Emp. J. Exper. Agric.*, 15, 96-106.

Thurstone, L. L. 1940. 5333a
Current issues in factor analysis. *Psychol. Bull.*, 37, 189-236.

Thurstone, L. L. 1940. 5334
Experimental study of simple structure. *Psychometrika*, 5, 153-68.

Thurstone, L. L. 1944. 5335
Graphical method of factoring the correlation matrix. *Proc. Nat. Acad. Sci. U.S.A.*, 30, 129-34.

Thurstone, L. L. 1944. 5336
Second-order factors. *Psychometrika*, 9, 71-100.

Thurstone, L. L. 1945. 5337
A multiple group method of factoring the correlation matrix. *Psychometrika*, 10, 73-8.

Thurstone, L. L. 1945. 5338
The effects of selection in factor analysis. *Psychometrika*, 10, 165-98.

Thurstone, L. L. 1945. 5339
The prediction of choice. *Psychometrika*, 10, 237-53.

Thurstone, L. L. 1946. 5340
A single plane method of rotation. *Psychometrika*, 11, 71-9.

Thurstone, L. L. 1947. 5341
The calibration of test items. *Amer. Psychologist*, 2, 103-4.

Thurstone, L. L. 1947. 5342
Factorial analysis of body measurements. *Amer. J. Phys. Anthrop.*, 5, 15-28.

Thurstone, L. L. 1949. 5343
Note about the multiple group method. *Psychometrika*, 14, 43-5.

Tietze, H. 1947. 5344
Würfelspiel und Integralgeometrie. *Sitzungs Ber. Math.-Nat. Abt. Bayer. Akad. Wissen.*, 1945-6, 131-58.

Tildesley, M. L. 1940. 5345
Extent to which the grouping of the data effects the accuracy of mean value. *Man*, 40, 132-6.

Tildesley, M. L. 1940. 5346
Sources and extent of errors in estimating standard deviations of normally distributed populations. *Man*, 40, 146-55.

Tillman, J. R., Reynolds, F. H. & Hilton, P. J. 1948. 5347
A method for producing a random sequence of numbers. *Phil. Mag.*, (7), 39, 807-20.

Tinbergen, J. 1940. 5348
Econometric business-cycle research. *Rev. Econ. Stud.*, 7, 73-90.

Tinbergen, J. 1943. 5349
Ligevaegtstyper og konjunkturbevaegelse. *Nord. Tidskr. Teknisk. Økonomi*, 32, 45-63.

Tinbergen, J. 1947. 5350
The use of correlation analysis in economic research. *Ekon. Tidskr.*, 49, 173-92.

Tintner, G. 1940. 5351
The analysis of economic time series. *J. Amer. Statist. Ass.*, 35, 93-100.

Tintner, G. 1940. 5352
The variate difference method. *Cowles Commission Monogr.*, no. 5, xiii+175 pp.

Tintner, G. 1941. 5353
The variate difference method: a reply. *Econometrica*, 9, 163-4.

Tintner, G. 1941. 5354
The theory of choice under subjective risk and uncertainty. *Econometrica*, 9, 298-304.

Tintner, G. 1941. 5355
The pure theory of production under technological risk and uncertainty. *Econometrica*, 9, 305-11.

Tintner, G. 1942. 5356
A contribution to the non-static theory of choice. *Quart. J. Econ.*, 56, 274-306.

Tintner, G. 1942. 5357
A contribution to the non-static theory of production. *Studies in Mathematical Economics and Econometrics in Memory of Henry Schultz* (Univ. Chicago Press), pp. 92-109.

Tintner, G. 1944. 5358
A note on the derivation of production functions from farm records. *Econometrica*, 12, 26-34.

Tintner, G. 1944. 5359
An application of the variate difference method to multiple regression. *Econometrica*, 12, 97-113.

Tintner, G. 1945. 5360
A note on rank, multicollinearity and multiple regression. *Ann. Math. Statist.*, 16, 304-8.

Tintner, G. 1946. 5361
Some applications of multivariate analysis to economic data. *J. Amer. Statist. Ass.*, 41, 472-500.

Tintner, G. 1946. 5362
Multiple regression for systems of equations. *Econometrica*, 14, 5-36.

Tintner, G. 1947. 5363
Une théorie " simple " des fluctuations économiques. *Rev. Écon. Pol.*, 57, 209-15.

Tintner, G. 1948. 5364
Homogeneous systems in mathematical economics. *Econometrica*, 16, 273-94.

Tintner, G. 1949. 5365
Foundations of probability and statistical inference. *J. R. Statist. Soc. A*, 112, 251-86.

Tintner, G. 1949. 5366
La position de l'économétrie dans la hierarchie des sciences sociales. *Rev. Écon. Pol.*, 59, 634-41.

Tintner, G. 1949. 5367
Scope and method of econometrics. *J. Statist. Social Inquiry Soc. Ireland*, 21, 1-15.

Tintner, G. 1949. 5368
Static macro-economic models and their econometric verifications. *Metroeconomica*, 1, 48-52.

Tintner, G. & Brownlee, O. H. 1944. 5369
Production functions derived from farm records. *J. Farm Econ.*, 26, 566-71.

Tippett, L. H. C. 1944. 5370
The control of industrial processes subject to trends in quality. *Biometrika*, 33, 163-72.

Tippett, L. H. C. 1944. 5371
The efficient use of gauges in quality control. *Engineer, London*, 177, 481.

Tippett, L. H. C. 1947. 5372
Quality control in the textile industry. *Textile Inst. J.*, 38, 594-600.

Tippett, L. H. C. 1947. 5373
The study of industrial efficiency, with special reference to the cotton industry. *J. R. Statist. Soc.*, 110, 108-22.

Tippett, L. H. C. 1949. 5374
Applications of statistical methods to problems of production in industry. *Bull. Int. Statist. Inst.*, 32 (2), 30-9.

Țițeica, Ș. 1940. 5375
Sur un problème de probabilités. *Bull. Math. Phys. Éc. Polytech. Bucarest*, 10 (1938-39), 57-64.

Tocher, K. D. 1949. 5376
A note on the analysis of grouped probit data. *Biometrika*, 36, 9-17.

Todd, H. 1940. 5377
A note on random associations in a square point lattice. *J. R. Statist. Soc. Suppl.*, 7, 78-82.

Todd, H. A. C. 1941. 5378
A note on systematic coding for card sorting systems. *J. R. Statist. Soc. Suppl.*, 7, 151-4.

Toledo Piza, A. P. de. *See* de Toledo Piza, A. P.

Tolman, B. 1942. 5379
Multiple versus single-factor experiments. *Proc. Amer. Soc. Sugar Beet Technol.*, 1942, 170-80.

Toman, W. 1949. 5379[a]
Die Faktorenanalyse in der Psychologie. *Statist. Viertel.schr.*, 2, 57-68.

Tombesi, L. 1947. 5380
Modifiche alla legge fisiologicamatematica di Mitscherlich. *Prog. Vinic. Aleario*, 23 (2), 15-17.

Tompkins, H. M. 1946. 5381
Statistics: an engineering tool. *Chem. & Engng. News*, 24, 2774-5.

Tonini, A. 1945. 5382
Sulla ricerca di un anno tipico per le elaborazioni idrologiche. *Atti 7ma Riun. Sci., Soc. Ital. Statist.*, pp. 385-414.

Toops, H. A. 1941. 5383
The *L*-method. *Psychometrika*, 6, 249-66.

Toops, H. A. 1943. 5384
Some possibilities of statistical analysis rendered possible by recent applications of punched card and sorting equipment. *Ohio Coll. Ass. Bull.*, 131, 2508-14.

Toranzos, F. I. 1949.   5385
Elements of a definition of probability. (Spanish.)
Rev. Fac. Ci. Econ. Univ. Cuyo, **1,** 6 pp.

Toranzos, F. I. 1949.   5386
A system of frequency curves which generalizes that
of Pearson. *Rev. Fac. Ci. Econ. Univ. Cuyo,* **1,** 7 pp.

Törnqvist, L. 1945.   5387
On the economic theory of lottery gambles. *Skand.
Aktuartidskr.,* **28,** 228-46.

Törnqvist, L. 1946.   5388
On the distribution function for a function of n statistic
variables and the central limit theorem in the mathematical theory of probability. *Skand. Aktuartidskr.,*
29, 206-29.

Törnqvist, L. 1948.   5389
An attempt to analyse the problem of an economical
production of statistical data. *Nord. Tidskr. Teknisk.
Økonomi,* **37,** 265-74.

Torrie, J. H. & Dickson, J. G. 1943.   5390
The use of statistical methods in quality evaluation of
barley and malt data. *Cereal Chem.,* **20,** 579-94.

Torrie, J. H., Sands, H. L. & Leith, B. D. 1943.   5391
Efficiency studies of types of design with small grain
yield trials. *J. Amer. Soc. Agron.,* **35,** 645-61.

Tortrat, A. 1949.   5392
Sur les fonctions de corrélation des processus de
Markoff. *C. R. Acad. Sci., Paris,* **228,** 1559-61.

Toscano, R. 1943.   5393
El problema del muestre en estadística. *Proc. 8th
Amer. Sci. Congr., Washington, D.C.,* 1940, **8,** 341-2.

Toschi, U. 1947.   5394
Statistica e geografia. *Riv. Ital. Demogr. Statist.,*
1, 167-74.

Toteff, A. U. 1947.   5395
The analysis of time series: measurement of the
secular trend. (Bulgarian. English, French and
Russian summaries.) *Statistika Sofia,* **8** (1), 18-40.

Travers, R. M. W. 1947.   5396
Statistical methods related to test construction and
evaluation. *Rev. Educ. Research,* **17,** 110-26.

Treloar, L. R. G. 1946.   5397
The statistical length of long-chain molecules. *Trans.
Faraday Soc.,* **42,** 77-82.

Tříska, V. 1947.   5398
O měření spolehivosti testů. (Measuring test reliability.) *Statist. Obzor,* **27,** 199-215.

Truesdell, L. E. 1941.   5399
New features of the 1940 population census. *J. Amer.
Statist. Ass.,* **36,** 361-8.

Truesdell, C. 1947.   5400
A note on the Poisson Charlier functions. *Ann. Math.
Statist.,* **18,** 450-4.

Truksa, L. 1940.   5401
The simultaneous distribution in samples of mean and
standard deviation, and of mean and variance.
Biometrika, **31,** 256-71.

Trumpler, R. J. 1949.   5402
The statistical study of the galactic star system. *Proc.
Berkeley Symp. Math. Statist. and Probab.,* 1945-6,
pp. 295-302.

Tsai, H. & Chow, C. Y. 1943.   5403
Studies on field plot technique in wheat. *Chinese J.
Sci. Agric.,* **1,** 117-18.

Tsao, F. 1942.   5404
Tests of statistical hypotheses in the case of unequal
or disproportionate numbers of observations in the
subclasses. *Psychometrika,* **7,** 195-212.

Tsao, F. 1946.   5405
General solution of the analysis of variance and
covariance in the case of unequal or disproportionate
numbers of observations in the subclasses. *Psychometrika,* **11,** 107-28.

Tsao, F. & Johnson, P. O. 1946.   5406
A note on solutions of analysis of variance for the
problem of unequal or disproportionate subclass
numbers. *J. Exper. Educ.,* **14,** 253-62.

Tucker, L. R. 1940.   5407
The role of correlated factors in factor analysis.
Psychometrika, **5,** 141-52.

Tucker, L. R. 1940.   5408
A matrix multiplier. *Psychometrika,* **5,** 289-94.

Tucker, L. R. 1944.   5409
A semi-analytical method of factorial rotation to
simple structure. *Psychometrika,* **9,** 43-68.

Tucker, L. R. 1944.   5410
The determination of successive principal components
without computation of tables of residual correlation
coefficients. *Psychometrika,* **9,** 149-53.

Tucker, L. R. 1946.   5411
Maximum validity of a test with equivalent items.
Psychometrika, **11,** 1-13.

Tucker, L. R. 1946.   5412
Simplified punched-card methods in factor analysis.
Proc. Res. Forum, I.B.M. Corp., New York, pp.
9-19.

Tucker, L. R. 1948.   5413
A note on the computation of a table of inter-correlations. *Psychometrika,* **13,** 245-50.

Tucker, L. R. 1949.   5414
A note on the estimation of test reliability by the
Kuder-Richardson formula (20). *Psychometrika,* **14,**
117-19.

Tuckerman, L. B. 1941.   5415
On the mathematically significant figures in the solution
of simultaneous linear equations. *Ann. Math. Statist.,*
12, 307-16.

Tukey, J. W. 1946.   5416
An inequality for deviations from medians. *Ann.
Math. Statist.,* **17,** 75-8.

Tukey, J. W. 1947-8.   5417
Non-parametric estimation. II. Statistically equivalent
blocks and tolerance regions—the continuous case.
III. Statistically equivalent blocks and multivariate
tolerance regions—the discontinuous case. *Ann. Math.
Statist.,* **18,** 529-39; **19,** 30-9.

Tukey, J. W. 1948.   5418
Approximate weights. *Ann. Math. Statist.,* **19,** 91-2.

Tukey, J. W. 1948.   5419
Some elementary problems of importance in small
sample practice. *Hum. Biol.,* **20,** 205-14.

Tukey, J. W. 1949. 5420
Comparing individual means in the analysis of variance. *Biometrics*, **5**, 99-114. (Also: *Princeton Univ. Statist. Res. Group, Memo. Rep.*, 6.)

Tukey, J. W. 1949. 5421
One degree of freedom for non-additivity. *Biometrics*, **5**, 232-42.

Tukey, J. W. 1949. 5422
Dyadic anova, an analysis of variance for vectors. *Hum. Biol.*, **21**, 65-110.

Tukey, J. W. 1949. 5423
The simplest signed-rank tests. *Princeton Univ. Statist. Res. Group Memo. Rep.*, 17.

Tukey, J. W. 1949. 5424
Interaction in a row-by-column design. *Princeton Univ. Statist. Res. Group Memo. Rep.*, 18.

Tukey, J. W. 1949. 5425
A problem in the distribution of rankings. *Princeton Univ. Statist. Res. Group Memo Rep.*, 40.

Tukey, J. W. 1949. 5426
The sampling theory of power spectrum estimates. *Symp. Applications of Autocorrelation Analysis to Physical Problems, Woods Hole Mass.*, 13-14 June 1949, pp. 47-67.

Tukey, J. W. 1949. 5427
Sufficiency, truncation and selection. *Ann. Math. Statist.*, **20**, 309-11.

Tukey, J. W. 1949. 5428
Moments of random group size distributions. *Ann. Math. Statist.*, **20**, 523-39.

Tukey, J. W. & Wilks, S. S. 1946. 5429
Approximation of the distribution of the product of beta variables by a single beta variable. *Ann. Math. Statist.*, **17**, 318-24.

Tuller, W. G. 1949. 5430
Theoretical limitations on the rate of transmission of information. *Proc. Inst. Radio Engrs.*, **31**, 468-78.

Turing, A. M. 1947. 5431
Rounding off errors in matrix processes. *Quart. J. Mech. & Appl. Math.*, **1**, 287-308.

Turner, F. C. 1944. 5432
A model for quantitative statistical experiments. *Engineer, London*, **178**, 26-7.

Turner, W. D. 1940. 5433
A method for the analysis and interpretation of intra-group changes in measurements. *J. Gen. Psychol.*, **23**, 343-65.

Tweedie, M. C. K. 1945. 5434
Inverse statistical variates. *Nature*, **155**, 453.

Tweedie, M. C. K. 1946. 5435
The regression of the sample variance on the sample mean. *J. Lond. Math. Soc.*, **21**, 22-8.

Tweedie, M. C. K. 1947. 5436
Functions of a statistical variate with given means, with special reference to Laplacian distributions. *Proc. Camb. Phil. Soc.*, **43**, 41-9.

Tyler, W. J., Chapman, A. B. & Dickerson, G. E. 1947. 5437
Sources of variation in the birth weight of Holstein-Friesian calves. *J. Dairy Sci.*, **30**, 483-98.

U

Uchytil, J. 1945. 5438
Vyrovnáni jednoduchych volnych závislosti pomeri orthogonalnich polynomu. (L'ajustement des dépendances libres simples à l'aide des polynômes orthogonaux.) (Czech.) *Elektrotech. Obzor*, **34**, 54-60.

Uchytil, J. 1946. 5439
Zjistováni a adrzováni nejvyhodnejsich podmínek ve vyrobním procesu. (Investigation and control of the most advantageous conditions in manufacturing processes.) (Czech.) *Strojnicky Obzor*, **26**, 267-72.

Uchytil, J. 1946. 5440
Vyrovnáni obecnych stochastickych závislostí. (Ajustement des dépendances stochastiques générales.) (Czech. Russian, English and French summaries.) *Statist. Obzor*, **26**, 428-37.

Ugaheri, T. 1949. 5441
On a certain sequence of chance variables. *Kōdai, Tokyo Inst. Tech.*, **3**, 25-7.

Uggé, A. 1941. 5442
Sul metodo di eliminazione nella costruzione dei numeri indici dei prezzi. *Acta Pontif. Acad. Sci.*, **5**, 67-71.

Uggé, A. 1942. 5443
Considerazioni sugli indici di normalità ricavati dal confronto fra momenti. *Statistica, Ferrara*, **2**, 157-62.

Uggé, A. 1942. 5444
Di alcune proprietà dei momenti della curva di probabilità e degli indici di normalità. *Acta Pontif. Acad. Sci.*, **6**, 229-35.

Ullman, J. 1944. 5445
The probability of convergence of an iterative process of inverting a matrix. *Ann. Math. Statist.*, **15**, 205-13.

Ulmer, M. J. 1946. 5446
On the economic theory of cost of living index numbers. *J. Amer. Statist. Ass.*, **41**, 530-42.

United Nations Economic and Social Council Sub-Commission on Statistical Sampling. 1949. 5447
Report to the Statistical Commission on the second session of the Sub-Commission on statistical sampling held from 30 August to 11 September 1948. *Sankhyā*, **9**, 377-91.

United Nations Economical and Social Council Sub-Commission on Statistical Sampling. 1949. 5448
Recommendations concerning the preparation of reports of Sampling Surveys. *Sankhyā*, **9**, 392-98.

United Nations Statistical Commission Sub-Commission on Statistical Sampling. 1949. 5449
Report to the Statistical Commission on the third session of the Sub-Commission on statistical sampling held September 1949. *Geneva*, E/CN, 3/38, E/CN. 3/SUB. 1/20.

United States Army Air Forces. 1944. 5450
Critique of verification of weather forecasts. *Weather Division USAAF, Washington, D.C.*, 39 pp.

United States Army Air Forces. 1944. 5451
Short range forecast verification program. *Weather Information Bureau USAAF, Rep. no. 602.*

United States Bureau of Census. 1943.   5452
A revised sample for current surveys. *Washington, D.C., United States Dept. of Commerce, Bureau of Census.*

Upholt, W. M. 1942.   5453
The use of the square root transformation and analysis of variance with contagious distributions. *J. Econ. Ent.*, **35**, 536-43.

Upholt, W. M. 1945.   5454
Observations on wartime biometrics. *Biometrics Bull.*, **1**, 47-52.

Upholt, W. M. & Graig, R. A. 1940.   5455
A note on the frequency distribution of black scale insects. *J. Econ. Ent.*, **33**, 113-14.

Usai, G. 1940.   5456
Proprietà combinatoria di certe medie. *Scritti Mat. Circ. Mat. Catania*, **12**.

Usai, G. 1940.   5457
Alcune considerazioni sulle medie. *Boll. Accad. Gioenia, Catania*, 1940.

Uspensky, J. V. 1945.   5458
On the problem of the ruin of gamblers. (Spanish.) *Univ. Nac. Litoral, Publ. Inst. Mat.*, **7**, 155-86.

Utting, J. E. G. 1949.   5459
Social accounting—some first results of the enquiry. *Local Govt. Finance*, **53**, 9-13.

Utting, J. E. G. 1949.   5460
The social accounting inquiry for 1947-8. *Local Govt. Finance*, **53**, 289-90.

V

Vagholkar, B. P., Apte, V. N. & Iyer, S. S. 1940. 5461
A study on plot size and shape technique for field experiments on sugarcane. *Indian J. Agric. Sci.*, **10**, 388-403.

Vaidyanathan, M. & Iyer, S. S. 1940.   5462
A note on the analysis of 3^3 and 3^4 designs (with three factor interactions confounded) in field experiments in agriculture. *Indian J. Agric. Sci.*, **10**, 213-36.

Vajda, S. 1941.   5463
Die erweiterte Sterbetafel und ihre wahrscheinlich-keitstheoretische Verwendung. (French, Italian and English summaries.) *Trans. 12th Int. Congr. Actuar., Lucerne*, 1940, **1**, 241-51.

Vajda, S. 1943.   5464
Algebraic analysis of contingency tables. *J. R. Statist. Soc.*, **106**, 333-42.

Vajda, S. 1945.   5465
The analysis of variance of mortality rates. *J. Inst. Actuar.*, **72**, 240-5.

Vajda, S. 1945.   5466
On the constituent items of the reduction and the remainder in the method of least squares. *Ann. Math. Statist.*, **16**, 381-6.

Vajda, S. 1946.   5467
Average sampling numbers from finite lots. *J. R. Statist. Soc. Suppl.*, **8**, 198-201.

Vajda, S. 1947.   5468
Statistical investigation of casualties suffered by certain types of vessels. *J. R. Statist. Soc. Suppl.*, **9**, 141-75.

Vajda, S. 1947.   5469
The stratified semistationary population. *Biometrika*, **34**, 243-54.

Vajda, S. 1947.   5470
Technique of the analysis of variance. *Nature*, **160**, 27.

Vajda, S. 1948.   5471
Introduction to a mathematical theory of the graded stationary population. *Mitt. Ver. Schweiz. Versich.-Math.*, **48**, 251-73.

Vajda, S. 1948.   5472
A note on the use of weighted orthogonal functions in statistical analysis. *Proc. Camb. Phil. Soc.*, **44**, 588-90.

Vajda, S. 1948.   5473
An outline of the theory of the " analysis of variance ". *J. Inst. Actuar. Students' Soc.*, **7**, 235-52.

Vali, M. A. 1942.   5474
On the sampling distribution of harmonic means. *Bull. Calcutta Math. Soc.*, **34**, 87-91.

Van Boven, A. 1947.   5475
A modified Aitken pivotal condensation method for partial regression and multiple correlation. *Psychometrika*, **12**, 127-33.

van Braam, A. 1948.   5476
Over de methode in de survey ten behoeve van een stedelijk uitbreidings-plan-in-hoofdzaak. (Méthodologie du " survey " en vue d'un plan global d'extension urbaine.) *Tijdschr. Volkshuisv.*, **29** (11), 165-9.

van Dantzig, D. 1941.   5477
Mathematical and empirical foundations of the calculus of probability. (Dutch. English summary.) *Nederl. Tijdschr. Natuurkunde*, **8**, 70-93.

van Dantzig, D. 1948.   5477ª
On the inversion of k-dimensional Fourier-Stieltjes-integrals. *Proc. Kon. Ned. Akad. Wetensch. A*, **51**, 858-67 (*Indag. Math.*, **10**, 286-95).

van Dantzig, D. 1949.   5478
Sur l'analyse logique des relations entre le calcul des probabilités et ses applications. *Congr. Int. Phil. Sci.* (Actualités Scient. Industr., no. 1146).

van Dantzig, D. 1949.   5479
Sur la méthode des fonctions génératrices. *Le calcul des probabilités et ses applications. Colloq. Int. Centre Nat. Rech. Sci. Paris*, **13**, 29-45.

van de Hulst, H. C. 1948.   5480
Scattering in a planetary atmosphere. *Astrophys. J.*, **107**, 220-46.

van der Laan, E. 1943.   5481
Proceedings of the study circle for experimental methods. *Landbouwk. Tijdschr., Wageningen*, **55**, 621.

van der Laan, E. & Ignatius, J. G. W. 1947.   5482
Evaluation of a regression by means of orthogonal polynomials. (Dutch. English summary.) *Statistica Neerlandica*, **1**, 219-30.

van der Maen, W. J. 1943. 5483
Het berekenen van sterftekansen. *Verzekerings-archief*, 24, 281-300.

Van der Plank, J. E. 1947. 5484
A method for estimating the number of random groups of adjacent diseased plants in a homogeneous field. *Trans. Roy. Soc. South Africa*, 31, 269-78.

van der Velden, H. A. & Endt, P. M. 1942. 5485
On some fluctuation problems connected with the counting of impulses produced by a Geiger-Müller counter or ionisation chamber. *Physica*, 9, 641-57.

van der Waerden, B. L. 1940. 5486
Biologische Konzentrationsauswertung. *Ber. Verh. Sächs. Akad. Leipzig*, 92, 41-4.

van der Werff, J. T. 1942. 5487
Die mathematische Theorie der biologischen Reaktionserscheinungen, besonders nach Roentgenbestrahlung. *Acta Radiologica*, 23, 603-21.

van Dobben de Bruyn, M. 1947. 5488
The condition for equilibrium in automatic telephone traffic. *De Ingenieur*, 59, 1-12.

van Ebbenhorst-Tensbergen, C. 1941. 5489
Verschiedene Methoden für die Berechnung der Forderungen und Verpflichtungen einer Sozialversicherungskasse. (Dutch.) *Verzekerings-archief*, 22, 453-70.

van Ettinger, J. 1947. 5490
Het begrip " Universum " in de statistica. (The meaning of " population " in statistics.) (Dutch. English summary.) *Statistica Neerlandica*, 1, 171-5.

van Kreveld, A. 1941. 5491
Dispersion of the distribution in space of particles of different classes. *Physica*, 8, 1045-58.

van Olst, H. R. 1948. 5492
Differentievergelijkingen als uitdrukkinswijze voor de stabiliteit van het economische leven. *Statist. Econ. Onderzoek.*, 3, 12-25.

van Olst, H. R. & Ignatius, J. G. W. 1948. 5493
De prijsvorming van aadbeien. *Statist. Econ. Onderzoek.*, 3, 84-91.

van Rest, E. D. 1946-7. 5494
Applied statistics in England. *Statistica Neerlandica*, 1, 5-11.

van Rooijen, J. P. 1943. 5495
De berekening der periodieke sterftekansen. (Le calcul des quotients périodiques de mortalité.) *Verzekerings-archief*, 24, 176-87.

van Rooijen, J. P. 1944. 5496
De logistische functie in de Nederlandsche sterftestatistiek. *Verzekerings-archief*, 25, 1-32.

van Tulder, J. J. M. 1949. 5497
Statistisch onderzoek in de verzekeringswetenschappen. (Dutch. English summary.) *Statistica Neerlandica*, 3, 8-18.

van Uven, M. J. 1941. 5498
Likelihood as conditioned probability. *Proc. Kon. Ned. Akad. Wetensch. A*, 44, 947-55.

van Uven, M. J. 1943. 5499
Correlation. I, II. *Landbouwk. Tijdschr., Wageningen*, 55, 622-38.

van Uven, M. J. 1946-7. 5500
Scheefheid en exces bij frequentie- en kansverdeelingen. (Skewness and excess in frequency and probability distributions.) (Dutch. English summary.) *Statistica Neerlandica*, 1, 145-55.

van Uven, M. J. 1947-8. 5501
Extension of Pearson's probability distributions to two variables. I, II, III, IV. *Proc. Kon. Ned. Akad. Wetensch. A*, 50, 1063-70; 1252-64; 51, 41-52; 191-6. (*Indag. Math.*, 9, 477-84; 578-90; 10, 12-23; 62-7.)

Varangot, V. 1948. 5502
Over correlatierekening en de herleiding van klimatologische reeksen. (A useful climatological application of regression theory.) *Statistica Neerlandica*, 2, 250-2.

Vargas, L. 1941. 5503
Aplicación taxónomica de un método estadístico. *Rev. Inst. Salub. Inferm. Trop.*, 2, 123-28.

Varley, G. C. 1947. 5504
The natural control of population balance in the knapweed gall-fly (*Urophora jaceara*). *J. Animal Ecol.*, 16, 139-87.

Varoli, G. 1948. 5505
Alcune probabilità relative al trinomio ax^2+bx+c. *R. C. Mat. Univ. Roma, Ist. Naz. Alta Mat.*, (5) 7, 72-90.

Varoli, G. 1949. 5506
Probabilità. *Period. Mat.*, (4) 27, 1-29.

Vasilevskis, S. 1940. 5507
Scheme for the solution of normal equations on the calculating machine. (English. Latvian summary.) *Acta Univ. Latv.*, (3) 11, 3-12. *Publ. Observ. Astr. Univ. Lett.*, no. 4.)

Vaswani, S. P. 1947. 5508
A pitfall in correlation theory. *Nature*, 160, 405-6.

Vatnsdal, J. R. 1946. 5509
Minimal variance and its relation to efficient moment tests. *Ann. Math. Statist.*, 17, 198-207.

Vaughan, H. 1946. 5510
Some notes on interpolation. *J. Inst. Actuar.*, 72, 482-97.

Vaulot, É. 1946. 5511
Délais d'attente des appels téléphoniques traités au hasard. *C. R. Acad. Sci., Paris*, 222, 268-9.

Vaulot, É. 1947. 5512
Application du calcul des probabilités à la téléphonie. *École Nat. Sup. Télécommun.*

Vaulot, É. 1947. 5513
Sur la proportion d'appels perdus dans la système de téléphonie automatique où chaque organe de contrôle est commun à tous les appareils d'un groupe. *Admin. Française des P.T.T., Étude 9RS, Service des recherches et du contrôle techniques*, Nov. 1947.

Vaulot, É. 1947-9. 5514
Sur les formules d'Erlang et leurs expressions asymptotiques. *Admin. Française des P.T.T., Étude 31RS, Service de recherches et du contrôle techniques*, 17 pp.

Vaulot, É. & Chauveau, J. 1949. 5515
Extension de la formule d'Erlang au cas où le trafic est fonction du nombre d'abonnés occupés. (Notamment en raison du nombre limité d'abonnés.) *Ann. Télécommun.*, 4, 319-24.

Venema, W. 1944. 5516
De integraalvergelijkingen voor de premiereserve van de spaarverzekering. *Verzekerings-archief.*, **25**, 53-61.

Vercelli, F. 1940. 5517
Per equazione e analysi delle curve oscillanti. *Atti 2do Congr. Un. Mat. Ital.*, 672ff.

Verhulst, M. J. J. 1948. 5518
The pure theory of production applied to the French gas industry. *Econometrica*, **16**, 295-308.

Verma, O. P., Dilwali, C. K. & Thomson, A. M. 5519
1947. A feeding experiment on Indian army pioneer recruits with special reference to the relative value of meat and milk in rations. *Indian J. Med. Res.*, **35**, 41-57.

Vernon, P. E. 1946. 5520
Statistical methods in the selection of Navy and Army personnel. *J. R. Statist. Soc. Suppl.*, **8**, 139-53.

Vernon, P. E. 1948. 5521
Indices of item consistency and validity. *Brit. J. Psychol. (Statist. Sec.)*, **1**, 152-66.

Vernotte, P. 1940. 5522
Détermination de la courbe passant aux mieux à travers des points expérimentaux. Mise en formule d'une loi expérimentale. Dérivation d'une loi expérimentale. *C. R. Acad. Sci., Paris*, **210**, 329-31.

Vernotte, P. 1940. 5523
Mise en formule d'une loi expérimentale: calcul des coefficients de la formule; détermination de la valeur moyenne de la fonction expérimentale. Régularité d'une suite de valeurs expérimentales. *C. R. Acad. Sci., Paris*, **210**, 475-7.

Vernotte, P. 1940. 5524
Mise en formule d'une loi expérimentale, par la méthode des valeurs moyennes; généralisation; raccord de deux formules; partage optimum de l'intervalle expérimental. La méthode des moindres carrées continue. *C. R. Acad. Sci., Paris*, **210**, 565-7.

Vernotte, P. 1943. 5525
Détermination, par la méthode de moindre imprécision, des coefficients d'une formule représentant une courbe expérimentale, où ils figurent linéairement. *C. R. Acad. Sci., Paris*, **215**, 568-70.

Vernotte, P. 1943. 5526
Détermination, par la condition de moindre imprécision, d'une formule dépendant linéairement de paramètres, destinée à la représentation d'une courbe expérimentale. *C. R. Acad. Sci., Paris*, **216**, 33-5.

Vernotte, P. 1943. 5527
Représentation d'une courbe expérimentale dans un cas général, par la condition de moindre imprécision. *C. R. Acad. Sci., Paris*, **216**, 148-50.

Vernotte, P. 1943. 5528
Sur les systèmes d'équations auxquels conduit la méthode de la moindre imprécision. *C. R. Acad. Sci., Paris*, **216**, 289-91.

Vernotte, P. 1945. 5529
Détermination, par la condition de moindre imprécision, du polynôme du second degré représentant au mieux l'ensemble d'une courbe expérimentale. *C. R. Acad. Sci., Paris*, **221**, 609-11.

Vervelde, G. J. 1948. 5530
Lattice squares—mathematically applied. (Dutch.) *Neder. Landb.-dienst. Maandbl.*, **5**, 117-21.

Vescan, T. 1940. 5531
Introduction à l'étude statistique des équations du mouvement des fluides. *Bull. Sci. École Polytech. Timişoara*, **9**, 287-308.

Vessereau, A. 1949. 5532
À propos de la méthodologie des recherches agronomiques. *Rev. Gén. Sci. Pures Appl.*, **56**, 145-7.

Vestal, A. G. 1943. 5533
Unequal scales for rating species in communities. *Amer. J. Bot.*, **30**, 305-10.

Vianelli, S. 1943. 5534
Sulle cosidette perequazioni meccaniche. Combinazioni lineari empiriche e schemi generali. *Statistica, Bologna*, **3**, 113-42.

Vianelli, S. 1943. 5535
Sulle cosidette perequazioni meccaniche. Un nuovo schema empirico e la perequazioni razionale delle serie storiche. *Statistica, Bologna*, **3**, 286-310.

Vianelli, S. 1948. 5536
Schemi teorici e nuovi orientamenti nello studio delle distribuzioni difrequenze. *Ann. Fac. Econ. Com., Palermo*, **1**, 21-30.

Vianelli, S. 1948. 5537
Di alcune costanti caratteristiche nell'analisi delle serie storiche. *Ann. Fac. Econ. Com., Palermo*, **2**, 93-138.

Vianelli, S. 1948. 5538
Sulle trasformazioni di alcune variabili statistiche. *Ann. Fac. Econ. Com., Palermo*, **2**, 121-47.

Vianelli, S. 1948. 5539
Di alcuni criteri statistici per l'analisi economica delle serie storiche. *Riv. Ital. Demogr. Statist.*, **2**, 90-106.

Vianelli, S. 1948. 5540
Aspetti statistici di una particolare distribuzione di probabilità. *Ann. Fac. Econ. Com., Palermo*, **2**, 198-212.

Vianelli, S. 1949. 5541
Ancora sugli aspetti statistici di una particolare distribuzione di probabilità. *Ann. Fac. Econ. Com., Palermo*, **3**, 163-90.

Vianelli, S. 1949. 5542
Introduzione ad una teoria statistica delle combinazioni ereditarie per l'analisi economica delle serie storiche. *Ann. Fac. Econ. Com., Palermo*, **3**, 185-218.

Vianelli, S. 1949. 5543
Orientamenti attuali nello studio delle distribuzioni di frequenze. *Atti 9ma Riun. Soc. Ital. Demogr. & Statist.*, 1947, pp. 173-80.

Vianelli, S. 1949. 5544
A proposito di asimmetria statistica. *Statistica, Milano*, **9**, 218-34.

Vianelli, S. 1949. 5545
Premessa ad una teoria statistica delle combinazioni storiche ereditorie. *Statistica, Milano*, **9**, 476-90.

Vianelli, S. 1949. 5546
La statistica per controllo dei prodotti industriali. *Industria, Milano*, **1949**, 210-23.

Vickery, C. W. 1944. 5547
Cyclically invariant graduation. *Econometrica*, **12**, 19-25.

Vila, G. R. & Gross, M. D. 1945. 5547a
Application of statistical methods to the production of synthetic rubber. *Rubber Age*, **57**, 551-8.

Villars, D. S. 1947. 5548
A significance test and estimation in the case of exponential regression. *Ann. Math. Statist.*, **18**, 596-600.

Villars, D. S. & Anderson, T. W. 1943. 5549
Some significance tests for normal bivariate distributions. *Ann. Math. Statist.*, **14**, 141-8.

Ville, J. 1942. 5550
Sur un problème de géométrie suggéré par l'étude du mouvement brownien. *C. R. Acad. Sci., Paris*, **215**, 51-2.

Ville, J. 1943. 5551
Sur un critère d'indépendance. *C. R. Acad. Sci., Paris*, **216**, 552-3.

Ville, J. 1943. 5552
Sur l'application, à un critère d'indépendance, du dénombrement des inversions présentées par une permutation. *C. R. Acad. Sci., Paris*, **217**, 41-2.

Ville, J. 1943. 5553
Sur les processus stochastiques stationnaires analytiques. *C. R. Acad. Sci., Paris*, **217**, 101-3.

Ville, J. 1944. 5554
Statistical study of irregularities in co-axial cables. Echoes and after effects. *Bull. Soc. Française Elect.*, **4**, 253.

Ville, J. 1944. 5555
Sur la théorie invariante de l'estimation statistique. *Bull. Sci. Math.*, (2) **68**, 95-108.

Ville, J. 1944. 5556
Sur la transitivité d'une méthode d'estimation. *Ann. Univ. Lyon A*, (3) **7**, 14-20.

Ville, J. 1945. 5557
Sur l'opérateur $\exp\{x+(d/dx)\}$. *C. R. Acad. Sci., Paris*, **221**, 529-30.

Ville, J. 1946. 5558
Sur les conditions d'existence d'une ophélimité totale et d'un indice du niveau des prix. *Ann. Univ. Lyon.* (3) A, **9**, 32-9.

Ville, J. 1948. 5559
Théorie et applications de la notion de signal analytique. *Cables et Transmissions*, **2**, 61 ff. (Translated by I. Selin: *RAND Corp. Transl.*, 1 August 1958, T-92, 34 pp.)

Ville, J. 1949. 5560
Fonctions aléatoires et transmission de l'information. *Le Calcul des Probabilités et ses Applications. Colloq. Int. Centre Nat. Rech. Sci., Paris*, **13**, 115-19.

Vincent, P. E. 1945. 5560a
Potentiel d'accroissement d'une population. *J. Soc. Statist. Paris*, **86**, 16-39.

Vincent, P. E. 1946. 5561
De la mesure du taux intrinsèque d'accroissement naturel dans les populations monogames. *Population*, **1**, 699-712.

Vincent, P. E. 1947. 5562
French Demography in the Eighteenth century. *Population Stud.*, **1**, 44-71.

Vincent, P. E. 1947. 5563
Nomogrammes pour la détermination des différences significatives entre deux taux. *Population*, **2**, 313-22.

Vinci, F. 1945. 5564
Le distribuzione statistiche degli errori sperimentali. *Studi. Ist. Sci. Econ. Statist. Univ. Milano*, **1**, 99-121.

Vining, R. 1945. 5565
Regional variation in cyclical fluctuation viewed as a frequency distribution. *Econometrica*, **13**, 183-213.

Virgilii, F. 1940. 5566
Le cause di errore nell'osservazione dei fatti. *Scientia, Milano*, **67**, 188-92.

Visman, J. 1948. 5566a
Enige toepassingen van de wiskundige statistiek in de mijnbouw. (Mathematical statistics for some problems in the mining industry.) (Dutch. English summary.) *Ingenieur*, **60**, 53-7.

Visser, S. W. 1946-7. 5567
Weersverwachting op lange termijn. (The long term weather forecast.) (Dutch. English summary.) *Statistica Neerlandica*, **1**, 98-101.

Vlach, V. 1947. 5568
Testování rozdilu mezi relativnimi cetnostmi. (Testing of differences between relative frequencies.) (Czech. English and French summaries.) *Statist. Obzor*, **27**, 427-56.

Vlach, V. 1949. 5569
Hlavni zasady representationiho setreni. (Les principes fondamentaux du sampling.) (Czech. French summary.) *Statist. zpravodaj*, **12**, 225-8.

Vlach, V. 1949. 5569a
Pouziti vyberovych method v setrení obyvatelstva. (L'application des méthodes de sondage dans les statistiques démographiques.) (Czech. French summary.) *Statist. zpravodaj.*, **12**, 435-8.

Vladimirsky, V. & Terletsky, J. 1945. 5570
Hydrodynamical theory of translational Brownian motion. (Russian. English summary.) *Zh. Eksper. Teor. Fiz. Akad. Nauk SSSR*, **15**, 258-63.

Vlček, I. 1948. 5571
Extrapolace růstovýych křivek. (The extrapolation of growth curves.) (Czech. Russian and English summaries.) *Statist. Obzor*, **28**, 33-44.

Vodička, V. 1947. 5572
Fonctions symétriques et leur application dans la statistique mathématique. (Czech and French.) *Acta Fac. Nat. Univ. Carol., Prague*, **174**, 17-19. (Also: *Electrotech. Obzor.*)

von Hentig, H. 1940. 5572a
A statistical test of causal significance. *Amer. Sociol. Rev.*, **5**, 930-6.

von Klezl-Norberg, F. 1943-4. 5573
Das Doppelgesicht der Statistik. (Erkenntnistheoretische Einführung in die Theorie der Statistik.) *Allg. Statist. Arch.*, **32**, 23-33.

von Mises, R. 1941.   5574
On the foundations of probability and statistics. *Ann. Math. Statist.*, **12**, 191-205; 215-17.

von Mises, R. 1942.   5575
On the correct use of Bayes' formula. *Ann. Math. Statist.*, **13**, 156-65.

von Mises, R. 1943.   5576
On the problem of testing hypotheses. *Ann. Math. Statist.*, **14**, 238-52.

von Mises, R. 1945.   5577
On the classification of observation data into distinct groups. *Ann. Math. Statist.*, **16**, 68-73.

von Mises, R. 1945.   5578
Comments on Donald Williams' paper. *Phil. Phenom. Res.*, **6**, 45-6.

von Mises, R. 1945.   5579
On the probabilities in a set of games and the foundation of probability theory. *Rev. Cienc. Lima*, **47**, 435-56.

von Mises, R. 1947.   5580
On the asymptotic distribution of differentiable statistical functions. *Ann. Math. Statist.*, **18**, 309-48.

von Mises, R. & Doob, J. L. 1941.   5581
Discussion of papers on probability theory. *Ann. Math. Statist.*, **12**, 215-17.

von Neumann, J. 1941.   5582
Distribution of the ratio of the mean square successive difference to the variance. *Ann. Math. Statist.*, **12**, 367-95.

von Neumann, J. 1942.   5583
A further remark concerning the distribution of the ratio of the mean square successive difference to the variance. *Ann. Math. Statist.*, **13**, 86-8.

von Neumann, J. & Goldstine, H. H. 1947.   5583ᵃ
Numerical inverting of matrices of high order. *Bull. Amer. Math. Soc.*, **53**, 1021-99.

von Neumann, J., Kent, R. H., Bellinson, H. R. 5584
& Hart, B. I. 1941.
The mean square successive difference. *Ann. Math. Statist.*, **12**, 153-62.

von Schelling, H. 1940.   5585
Zur Beurteilung einer alternativen Stichprobe von *n* Beobachtungen. *Deutsche Math.*, **5**, 107-15.

von Schelling, H. 1940.   5586
Über die exacte Behandlung des Zusammenhanges zwischen biologischen Merkmalsreichen. *Arb. Staatl.-Inst. exper. Ther. Frankf.H.*, **39**, 35-71.

von Schelling, H. 1940.   5587
Fehlerrechnung bei biologischen Messungen. *Naturwiss.*, **28**, 430-1, 765-6. (Also: (1941) *Klin. Wschr.*, **20**, 741-3.)

von Schelling, H. 1940.   5588
Zur Statistik seltener Ereignisse. *Astr. Nachr.*, **270**, 189-92.

von Schelling, H. 1941.   5589
Die Bedeutung der statistischen Methodik für die Biologie. *Ergeb. Hyg. Bakter. Immun. Exper. Therapie*, **24**, 87-149.

von Schelling, H. 1941.   5590
Bemerkungen zur Geschwistermethode. *Zeit. Konst-Lehre*, **25**, 391-7.

von Schelling, H. 1941.   5591
Bemerkungen zur Verteilung von Pascal. *Naturwiss.*, **29**, 517-18.

von Schelling, H. 1941.   5592
Statistische Schätzungen auf kombinatorischer Grundlage. *Zeit. angew. Math. Mech.*, **21**, 52-8.

von Schelling, H. 1942.   5593
Mutungsgrenzen für den Ausfall einer geplanten Versuchsreihe beschränkten Umfangs. *Naturwiss.*, **30**, 64-5.

von Schelling, H. 1942.   5594
Trefferwahrscheinlichkeit und Variabilität. Ein Versuch zur Deutung der Wirksamkeit von Antigenen. *Naturwiss.*, **30**, 306-12.

von Schelling, H. 1942.   5595
Eine Formel für die Teilsummen gewisser hypergeometrischer Reihen und deren Bedeutung für die Wahrscheinlichkeitstheorie. *Naturwiss.*, **30**, 757-8.

von Schelling, H. 1943.   5596
Über die Verteilung der Kopplungswerte in gekreuzten Fernmeldekabeln grosser Länge. *Elektr. Nachr. Techn.*, **20**, 251-9.

von Schelling, H. 1944.   5597
Gedanken zum Weber-Fechnerschen Gesetz. *Abh. Preuss. Akad. Wiss. Math.-Nat. Kl.*, **1944** (5), 12 pp.

von Schelling, H. 1944.   5598
Das Alles-oder-Nichts-Gesetz, gedeutet als Endergebnis einer Auslösungsfolge. *Abh. Preuss. Akad. Wiss. Math.-Nat. Kl.*, **1944**, (6), 25 pp.

von Schelling, H. 1945.   5599
Ma non può dopo tutto essere un caso? *Atti 7ma Riun. Sci., Soc. Ital. Statist.*, pp. 307-14.

von Schelling, H. 1949.   5600
Erste Ergebnisse einer Aufgliederung der Sterblichkeit nach Geburtsjahrgängen und Kalenderjahren. *Metron*, **15**, 359-74.

von Schelling, H. 1949.   5601
A formula for the partial sums of some hypergeometric series. *Ann. Math. Statist.*, **20**, 120-2.

von Schrutka, L. 1941.   5602
Eine neue Einteilung der Permutationen. *Math. Ann.*, **118**, 246-50.

Vonsovskii, S. 1946.   5603
Derivation of fundamental kinetic equation in quantum mechanics. (English.) *J. Phys. Acad. Sci. USSR*, **10**, 367-76. (Russian version: *Zh. Eksper. Teoret. Fiz. Akad. Nauk SSSR*, **16**, 908-18.)

von Wright, G. H. 1945.   5604
Über Wahrscheinlichkeit. Eine logische und philosophische Untersuchung. *Acta Soc. Sci. Fenn. Nova. A*, (3) **11**, 66ff.

Voss, H. A. 1947.   5605
Analysis in terms of frequencies of differences. *Psychometrika*, **12**, 43-9.

Votaw, D. F., Jr. 1946.   5606
The probability distribution of the measure of a random linear set. *Ann. Math. Statist.*, **17**, 240-4.

Votaw, D. F., Jr. 1948.   5607
Testing compound symmetry in a normal multivariate distribution. *Ann. Math. Statist.*, **19**, 447-73.

Vroom, H. H. 1943. 5608
The statistical control of quality: Application of statistical inspection in the telephone industry. *Engng. J., Canada*, **26**, 398-400.

W

Waddell, J. & Kennedy, G. H. 1947. 5609
The antirachitic potency of pure crystalline vitamin D_3—in comparison with the U.S.P. reference cod liver oil when assayed by the chick method. *J. Ass. Off. Agric. Chem., Wash.*, **30**, 190-206.

Wadleigh, C. H. & Tharp, W. H. 1940. 5610
Factorial design in plant nutrition experiments in the greenhouse. *Arkansas Agric. Exper. Sta. Bull.*, **401**, 1-67.

Wadley, F. M. 1945. 5611
An application of the Poisson series to some problems of enumerations. *J. Amer. Statist. Ass.*, **40**, 85-92.

Wadley, F. M. 1945. 5612
Incomplete block experimental designs in insect population problems. *J. Econ. Ent.*, **38**, 651-4.

Wadley, F. M. 1946. 5613
Incomplete block design adapted to paired tests of mosquito repellents. *Biometrics Bull.*, **2**, 30-2.

Wadley, F. M. 1948. 5614
Experimental design in comparisons of allergens in cattle. *Biometrics*, **4**, 100-8.

Wadley, F. M. & Sullivan, W. N. 1943. 5615
A study of the dosage mortality curve. *J. Econ. Ent.*, **36**, 367-72.

Wadley, F. M. & Wolfenbarger, D. O. 1944. 5616
Regression of insect density on distance from centre of dispersion as shown by a study of the smaller European elm bark beetle. *J. Agric. Res.*, **69**, 299-308.

Wagenführ, R. 1943-4. 5617
Die Gentt'sche Graphik—eine einfache Form der graphischen Plankontrolle. *Hefte Wirtsch.forsch., Hamburg*, **1-2**, 81-6.

Wahlund, S. G. W. 1949. 5618
Stickprovsmetodikens användning inom svensk officiell statistik. *Förh. Nord. Statist. Helsingfors.*, **1949**, 17-27.

Wake, W. C. 1948. 5619
The authenticity of the Pauline epistles: a contribution from statistical analysis. *Hibbert J.*, **47**, 50-5.

Wakeley, P. C. 1944. 5620
Geographic source of loblolly pine seed. *J. Forestry*, **42**, 23-32.

Wald, A. 1940. 5621
The approximate determination of indifference surfaces by means of Engel curves. *Econometrica*, **8**, 144-75.

Wald, A. 1940. 5622
The fitting of straight lines if both variables are subject to error. *Ann. Math. Statist.*, **11**, 284-300.

Wald, A. 1940. 5623
A new foundation of the method of maximum likelihood in statistical theory. *Cowles Comm. Res. Econ., Rep. 6th Ann. Res. Conf. Econ. & Statist.*, pp. 33-5.

Wald, A. 1940. 5624
A note on the analysis of variance with unequal class frequencies. *Ann. Math. Statist.*, **11**, 96-100.

Wald, A. 1941. 5625
Asymptotically most powerful tests of statistical hypotheses. *Ann. Math. Statist.*, **12**, 1-19.

Wald, A. 1941. 5626
On the analysis of variance in case of multiple classifications with unequal class frequencies. *Ann. Math. Statist.*, **12**, 346-50.

Wald, A. 1941. 5627
Some examples of asymptotically most powerful tests. *Ann. Math. Statist.*, **12**, 396-408.

Wald, A. 1942. 5628
Asymptotically shortest confidence intervals. *Ann. Math. Statist.*, **13**, 127-37.

Wald, A. 1942. 5629
Setting of tolerance limits when the sample is large. *Ann. Math. Statist.*, **13**, 389-99.

Wald, A. 1942. 5630
On the power function of the analysis of variance test. *Ann. Math. Statist.*, **13**, 434-9 (correction: **15**, 330-3).

Wald, A. 1942. 5631
On the principles of statistical inference. *Univ. Notre Dame, Indiana, Math. Lectures*, **1**, 50 pp. (Spanish version (1951): *Trab. Estadíst.*, **2**, 113-48.)

Wald, A. 1943. 5632
An extension of Wilks' method of setting tolerance limits. *Ann. Math. Statist.*, **14**, 45-55.

Wald, A. 1943. 5633
On the efficient design of statistical investigations. *Ann. Math. Statist.*, **14**, 134-40.

Wald, A. 1943. 5634
Sequential analysis of statistical data: Theory. *Rep. Statist. Res. Group Columb. Univ. Applied Maths. Panel. Nat. Defence Res. Commun.*

Wald, A. 1943. 5635
On a statistical generalization of metric spaces. *Proc. Nat. Acad. Sci. U.S.A.*, **29**, 196-7.

Wald, A. 1943. 5636
Tests of statistical hypotheses concerning several parameters when the number of observations is large. *Trans. Amer. Math. Soc.*, **54**, 426-82.

Wald, A. 1944. 5637
A general method of deriving the operating characteristics of any sequential probability Ratio test. *Columbia Univ. Statist. Res. Group Memo. Rep.*

Wald, A. 1944. 5638
On a statistical problem arising in the classification of an individual into one of two groups. *Ann. Math. Statist.*, **15**, 145-62.

Wald, A. 1944. 5639
On cumulative sums of random variables. *Ann. Math. Statist.*, **15**, 283-96.

Wald, A. 1944. 5640
Note on a lemma. *Ann. Math. Statist.*, **15**, 330-3.

Wald, A. 1944. 5641
On a statistical generalization of metric spaces. *Rep. Math. Colloq. Notre Dame*, (2) **5-6**, 76-9.

Wald, A. 1945. 5642
Sequential tests of statistical hypotheses. *Ann. Math. Statist.*, **16**, 117-86.

Wald, A. 1945. 5643
Some generalizations of the theory of cumulative sums of random variables. *Ann. Math. Statist.*, **16**, 287-93.

Wald, A. 1945. 5644
Sequential method of sampling for deciding between two alternative courses of action. *J. Amer. Statist. Ass.*, **40**, 277-306.

Wald, A. 1945. 5645
Statistical decision functions which minimize the maximum risk. *Ann. Math.*, (2) **46**, 265-80.

Wald, A. 1945. 5645a
Generalization of a theorem by v. Neumann concerning zero sum two person games. *Ann. Math.*, (2) **46**, 281-6.

Wald, A. 1946. 5646
Some improvements in setting limits for the expected number of observations required by a sequential probability ratio test. *Ann. Math. Statist.*, **17**, 466-74.

Wald, A. 1946. 5647
Differentiation under the expectation sign in the fundamental identity of sequential analysis. *Ann. Math. Statist.*, **17**, 493-7.

Wald, A. 1947. 5648
An essentially complete class of admissible decision functions. *Ann. Math. Statist.*, **18**, 549-55.

Wald, A. 1947. 5649
Foundations of a general theory of sequential decision functions. *Econometrica*, **15**, 279-313.

Wald, A. 1947. 5650
Limit distribution of the maximum and minimum of successive cumulative sums of random variables. *Bull. Amer. Math. Soc.*, **53**, 142-53.

Wald, A. 1947. 5651
A note on regression analysis. *Ann. Math. Statist.*, **18**, 586-9.

Wald, A. 1947. 5652
Sequential analysis. *Proc. 25th. Session Int. Statist. Inst. Conf. Washington, D.C.*, 1947 (Publ. 1951), **3A**, pp. 67-73; 74-80.

Wald, A. 1948. 5653
Asymptotic properties of the maximum likelihood estimate of an unknown parameter of a discrete stochastic process. *Ann. Math. Statist.*, **19**, 40-6.

Wald, A. 1948. 5654
On the distribution of the maximum of successive cumulative sums of independently but not identically distributed chance variables. *Bull. Amer. Math. Soc.*, **54**, 422-30.

Wald, A. 1948. 5655
Estimation of a parameter when the number of unknown parameters increases indefinitely with the number of observations. *Ann. Math. Statist.*, **19**, 220-7.

Wald, A. 1949. 5656
Statistical decision functions. *Ann. Math. Statist.*, **20**, 165-205.

Wald, A. 1949. 5657
Note on the consistency of the maximum likelihood estimate. *Ann. Math. Statist.*, **20**, 595-601.

Wald, A. & Brookner, R. J. 1941. 5658
On the distribution of Wilks' statistic for testing the independence of several groups of variates. *Ann. Math. Statist.*, **12**, 137-52.

Wald, A. & Wolfowitz, J. 1940. 5659
On a test whether two samples are from the same population. *Ann. Math. Statist.*, **11**, 147-62.

Wald, A. & Wolfowitz, J. 1941. 5660
Note on confidence limits for continuous distribution functions. *Ann. Math. Statist.*, **12**, 118-19.

Wald, A. & Wolfowitz, J. 1943. 5661
An exact test for randomness in the non-parametric case based on serial correlation. *Ann. Math. Statist.*, **14**, 378-88.

Wald, A. & Wolfowitz, J. 1944. 5662
Statistical tests based on permutations of the observations. *Ann. Math. Statist.*, **15**, 358-72.

Wald, A. & Wolfowitz, J. 1945. 5663
Sampling inspection plans for continuous production which insure a prescribed limit on the out-going quality. *Ann. Math. Statist.*, **16**, 30-49.

Wald, A. & Wolfowitz, J. 1946. 5664
Tolerance limits for a normal distribution. *Ann. Math. Statist.*, **17**, 208-15.

Wald, A. & Wolfowitz, J. 1948. 5665
Optimum character of the sequential probability ratio test. *Ann. Math. Statist.*, **19**, 326-39.

Wald, A. & Wolfowitz, J. 1949. 5666
Bayes solutions of sequential decision problems. *Proc. Nat. Acad. Sci. U.S.A.*, **35**, 99-102.

Waldapfel, L. 1943. 5667
Über das Profil der Permutationen. (Hungarian. German summary.) *Mat. Fiz. Lapok*, **50**, 257-61.

Waldford, L. A. 1946. 5668
A new graphic method of describing the growth of animals. *Biol. Bull.*, **90**, 141-7.

Walker, A. C. 1940. 5668a
Some thoughts on the scientific approach to textile problems. *Amer. Dyestuff Reporter*, **29**, 217-20.

Walker, A. M. 1943. 5668b
On the effect of a changing mean on the criterion for a machine to be capable of meeting its tolerances. *U.K. Min. Supply Advisory Service Statist. Method & Qual. Contr. Tech. Rep. Ser. R*, no. QC/R/6, 10 November 1943, 5 pp.

Walker, D. A. 1940. 5669
Answer pattern and score scatter in tests and examinations. *Brit. J. Psychol.*, **30**, 248-60.

Walker, G. 1941. 5670
Selection of factors in statistical investigations. *Quart. J. R. Met. Soc.*, **67**, 261-2.

Walker, G. 1946. 5671
On periods and symmetry points in pressure as aids to forecasting. *Quart. J. R. Met. Soc.*, **72**, 265-83.

Walker, H. M. 1940. 5672
Degrees of freedom. *J. Educ. Psychol.*, **31**, 253-69.

Walker, H. M. 1945. 5673
The role of the American Statistical Association. *J. Amer. Statist. Ass.*, **40**, 1-10.

Walker, H. M. 1947. 5673[a]
Certain unsolved statistical problems of importance in psychological research. *Harvard Educ. Rev.*, **17**, 297-304.

Walker, M. G. 1942. 5674
A mathematical analysis of the distribution in maize of *Heliothis armigera*, Hb.(*Obsoleta F.*). *Canadian J. Res. D*, **20**, 235-61.

Wallis, W. A. 1942. 5675
Compounding probabilities from independent significance tests. *Econometrica*, **10**, 229-48.

Wallis, W. A. 1947. 5676
Standard sampling-inspection procedures. (French summary.) *Proc. 25th. Session Int. Statist. Inst. Conf., Washington, D.C.*, 1947 (Publ. 1951), **3A**, 331-50.

Wallis, W. A. & Moore, G. H. 1941. 5677
A significance test for time series analysis. *J. Amer. Statist. Ass.*, **36**, 401-9. (Also: *Nat. Bur. Econ. Res., New York Technical paper*, no. 1, 59 pp.)

Walsh, J. E. 1946. 5678
On the power function of a sign test formed by using subsamples. *Douglas Aircraft Co. Inc., Santa Monica, Calif., Mimeo. Rep.*

Walsh, J. E. 1946. 5679
Some significance tests based on order statistics. *Ann. Math. Statist.*, **17**, 44-52.

Walsh, J. E. 1946. 5680
Some order statistic distributions for samples of size four. *Ann. Math. Statist.*, **17**, 246-8.

Walsh, J. E. 1946. 5681
On the power function of the sign test for slippage of means. *Ann. Math. Statist.*, **17**, 358-62.

Walsh, J. E. 1947. 5682
Concerning the effect of intraclass correlation on certain significance tests. *Ann. Math. Statist.*, **18**, 88-96.

Walsh, J. E. 1947. 5683
An extension to two populations of an analogue of Student's *t*-test using the sample range. *Ann. Math. Statist.*, **18**, 280-5.

Walsh, J. E. 1947. 5684
On the power efficiency of a *t*-test formed by pairing sample values. *Ann. Math. Statist.*, **18**, 601-4.

Walsh, J. E. 1947. 5685
Some significance tests for the mean using the sample range and midrange. *Douglas Aircraft Co. Inc., Santa Monica, Calif., Mimeo. Rep.*

Walsh, J. E. 1948. 5686
On the power function of a sign test formed by using sub-samples. *RAND Corp. Paper*, 7 January 1948, RAOP-7, 13 pp.

Walsh, J. E. 1948. 5687
On the use of the non-central *t*-distribution for comparing percentage points of normal populations. *Ann. Math. Statist.*, **19**, 93-4.

Walsh, J. E. 1949. 5688
On the "information" lost by using a *t*-test when the population variance is known. *J. Amer. Statist. Ass.*, **44**, 122-5.

Walsh, J. E. 1949. 5689
Applications of some significance tests for the median which are valid under very general conditions. *J. Amer. Statist. Ass.*, **44**, 342-55.

Walsh, J. E. 1949. 5690
On the best choice of sample sizes for a *t*-test when the ratio of variances is known. *J. Amer. Statist. Ass.*, **44**, 554-8 (correction: **45**, 111).

Walsh, J. E. 1949. 5691
Some comments on the efficiency of significance tests. *Hum. Biol.*, **21**, 205-17.

Walsh, J. E. 1949. 5691[a]
Some comments on an estimation problem for contaminated populations. *RAND Corp. Res. Memo.*, 28 April 1949, RM-148, 5 pp.

Walsh, J. E. 1949. 5691[b]
On the usefulness of artificial dispersion for a certain bombing problem. *RAND Corp. Res. Memo.*, 28 June 1949, RM-177, 4 pp.

Walsh, J. E. 1949. 5692
On the power function of tests of percentage points based on the non-central *t*-statistics. *RAND Corp. Paper*, 8 November 1949, P-91, 3 pp.

Walsh, J. E. 1949. 5693
Some significance tests for the median which are valid under very general conditions. *Ann. Math. Statist.*, **20**, 64-81.

Walsh, J. E. 1949. 5694
On the range-midrange test and some tests with bounded significance levels. *Ann. Math. Statist.*, **20**, 257-67.

Walsh, J. E. 1949. 5695
Concerning compound randomization in the binary system. *Ann. Math. Statist.*, **20**, 580-9.

Walsh, J. E. 1949. 5696
On the power function of the "best" *t*-test solution of the Behrens-Fisher problem. *Ann. Math. Statist.*, **20**, 616-18.

Walters, A. G. 1947. 5697
The distribution of projected areas of fragments. *Proc. Camb. Phil. Soc.*, **43**, 342-7.

Wang, C. M. 1947. 5698
Methods of determining the degrees of freedom for errors. *Mem. Fac. Agric., Nat. Univ. Taiwan*, **1** (5), 20 pp.

Wang, C. M. 1949. 5699
Application of maximum likelihoods methods to agriculture. (Chinese. English summary.) *Sun Yat-Sen Univ., Coll. Agric.*, **232**, 44-60.

Wang, M. C. & Uhlenbeck, G. E. 1945. 5700
On the theory of the Brownian motion. II. *Rev. Mod. Phys.*, **17**, 323-42.

Wannier, G. H. 1945. 5701
The statistical problem in cooperative phenomena. *Rev. Mod. Phys.*, **17**, 50-60.

Ward, A. G. 1942. 5702
A new method of determining half-value periods from observations with a single Geiger counter. *Proc. Roy. Soc. A*, **181**, 183-97.

Ward, D. F. 1942. 5703
Formulae for work curves. *Brit. J. Psychol.*, **33**, 130-7.

Ward, D. H. 1944. 5704
The distribution of the range in samples drawn from a grouped normal population. *U.K. Min. Supply Advisory Service Statist. Method Qual. Contr. Tech. Rep. Ser. R*, no. QC/R/25, 31 August 1944, 13 pp.

Warner, L. 1947. 5705
Estimating the character of unsampled segments of a universe. *J. Marketing*, **12**, 186-92.

Warren, S. W. 1942. 5706
Techniques of analyzing farm records. *Illinois Univ. Dept. Agric. Econ. and Agric. Exper. Sta., Rep.* AE-1837.

Waters, N. F. & Bywaters, J. H. 1943. 5707
A study of body weights in nine different strains of white Leghorns. *Poultry Sci.*, **22**, 178-87.

Watson, A. N. 1942. 5708
Use of small area census data in marketing analysis. *J. Marketing*, **6**, 42-7.

Waugh, F. V. 1942. 5709
Regressions between sets of variables. *Econometrica*, **10**, 290-310.

Waugh, F. V. 1943. 5710
Choice of the dependent variable in regression analysis. *J. Amer. Statist. Ass.*, **38**, 210-14.

Waugh, F. V. 1945. 5711
A note concerning Hotelling's method of inverting a partitioned matrix. *Ann. Math. Statist.*, **16**, 216-17.

Waugh, F. V. 1946. 5712
The computation of partial correlation coefficients. *J. Amer. Statist. Ass.*, **41**, 543-6.

Waugh, F. V. & Dwyer, P. S. 1945. 5713
Compact computation of the inverse of a matrix. *Ann. Math. Statist.*, **16**, 259-71.

Weaver, C. L. 1943. 5714
Modification of working formulas in Whittaker-Henderson A graduation method to produce the moments automatically. *Trans. Actuar. Soc. Amer.*, **44**, 27-30.

Weaver, C. L. 1947. 5715
A simple analytic proof of a general χ^2 theorem. *Amer. Math. Monthly*, **54**, 529-33.

Weaver, W. 1948. 5716
Probability, rarity, interest, and surprise. *Scientific Monthly*, **67**, 390-2.

Weaver, W. 1949. 5717
The mathematics of communication. *Scientific Amer.*, **181** (1), 11-16.

Webb, J. N., Northrop, M. S. & Payne, S. L. 5718
1943. Practical applications of theoretical sampling methods. *J. Amer. Statist. Ass.*, **38**, 69-77.

Weber, A. & Linder, A. 1949. 5719
Emploi d'une méthode statistique pour étudier les dépenses d'une famille. *Schweiz. Zeit. Volkwirtsch. Statist.*, **85**, 389-97.

Weck, F. A. 1947. 5720
The mortality rate and its derivation from actual experience. *Rec. Amer. Inst. Actuar.*, **36**, 23-54.

Wegener, K. 1942. 5721
Die statistische Prognose (des Wetters). *Ann. Hydrogr., Berlin*, **70** (9), 291-3.

Wei, D. S. 1943. 5722
Necessary and sufficient conditions that regression systems of sums with elements in common be linear. *Nat. Math. Mag.*, **17**, 151-8.

Weibull, W. 1949. 5723
A statistical representation of fatique failure in solids. *Kungl. Tekn. Högskolans. Handl.*, no. 27.

Weichelt, J. A. 1946. 5724
A first-order method for estimating correlation coefficients. *Psychometrika*, **11**, 215-21.

Weidhaas, H. 1942. 5725
Experimentelle Studien an Gemüse über die Entnahme von Durchschnittsproben zur chemischen Qualitätsbestimmung unter Anwendung statistischer Methoden. *Bodenk. Pflanzenernähr.*, **30**, 1-35.

Weil, A. 1940. 5726
Calcul des probabilités, méthode axiomatique, intégration. *Rev. Sci., Paris*, **78**, 201-8.

Weil, C. S. 1947. 5727
Statistical evaluation of growth curves. *Proc. Soc. Exper. Biol.*, **64**, 468-70.

Weiler, H. 1948. 5728
Mean charts of constant false alarm risk for non-normal distributions. *Aust. J. Appl. Sci.*, **9**, 326-31.

Weinberg, A. M. & Householder, A. S. 1941. 5729
Statistical distribution of impedance elements in biological systems. *Bull. Math. Biophys.*, **3**, 129-35.

Weinberg, D. 1945. 5730
Une expérience de contrôle des méthodes d'analyse factorielle. *C. R. Acad. Sci., Paris*, **220**, 214-16.

Weir, W. F. 1944. 5731
Figuring most economical machine assignment. *Fact. Mgmt.*, **102**, 100-2.

Weiss, E. S. 1948. 5731ᵃ
An abridged table of probits for use in the graphic solution of the dosage-effect curve. *Amer. J. Publ. Hlth*, **38**, 22-4.

Weiss, E. S. & Kendrick, P. L. 1943. 5732
The effectiveness of pertussis vaccine: An application of Sargent and Merrell's method of measurement. *Amer. J. Hyg.*, **38**, 306-9.

Welch, B. L. 1947. 5733
The generalization of 'Student's' problem when several different population variances are involved. *Biometrika*, **34**, 28-35.

Welch, B. L. 1947. 5734
On the Studentization of several variances. *Ann. Math. Statist.*, **18**, 118-22.

Welch, B. L. 1949. 5735
Further note on Mrs. Aspin's tables and on certain approximations to the tabled function. (Appendix to " Tables for use in comparisons whose accuracy involves two variances, separately estimated ".) *Biometrika*, **36**, 293-6.

Welhausen, E. J. 1943. 5736
The accuracy of incomplete block designs in varietal trials in West Virginia. *J. Amer. Soc. Agron.*, **35**, 66-76.

Welker, E. L. 1947. 5737
The distribution of the mean. *Ann. Math. Statist.*, **18**, 111-17.

Welker, E. L. & Wynd, F. L. 1943. 5738
Influence of unknown factors on the validity of mathematical correlations of biological data. *Plant Physiol.*, **18**, 498-507.

Wellman, R. H. & McCallan, S. E. A. 1943. 5739
Correlation within and between laboratory slide-germination, greenhouse tomato foliage disease, and wheat smut methods of testing fungicides. *Contr. Boyce Thompson Inst.*, **13**, 143-69.

Wentworth, C. K. 1947. 5740
Cycles in rainfall and validity in prediction of rainfall in Hawaii. *Pacific Sci.*, **1**, 215-20.

Wenzl, H. 1949. 5741
Zur Anwendung der Varianzanalyse in der Biologie. *Statist. Vierteljschr.*, **2**, 106-12.

Wernimont, G. 1946. 5742
Use of control charts in the analytical laboratory. *Industr. and Engng. Chem. (Anal. Ed.)*, **18**, 587-92.

Westcott, C. H. 1948. 5743
A study of expected loss rates in the counting of particles from pulsed sources. *Proc. Roy. Soc. A*, **194**, 508-26.

Westenberg, J. 1947. 5744
Mathematics of pollen diagrams. I, II. *Proc. Kon. Ned. Akad. Wetensch. A*, **50**, 509-20; 640-8.

Westenberg, J. 1948. 5745
Significance test for median and inter-quartile range in samples from continuous populations of any form. *Proc. Kon. Ned. Akad. Wetensch. A*, **51**, 252-61.

Western, D. W. 1948. 5746
Inequalities of the Markov and Bernstein type for integral norms. *Duke Math. J.*, **15**, 839-69.

Westman, A. E. R. 1945. 5746a
Statistical quality control. *Mfg. & Industr. Engng.*, **23**, 46-7.

Westman, A. E. R. 1947. 5746b
Statistical and quality control methods in industrial chemistry. *Canad. Chem. and Process Industries*, **31**, 716-25.

Weston, J. D. 1949. 5747
A note on the theory of communication. *Phil. Mag.*, (7) **40**, 449-53.

Weydanz, W. 1949. 5748
Der mittlere Fehler bei der Mittelwertbildung aus Wertgruppen. *Zeit. angew. Math. Mech.*, **29**, 188-90.

Wharton, A. S. 1943. 5748a
A brief summary of some simple methods of quality control. *Engng. Insp.*, **8** (1), 29-36.

Whelpton, P. K. 1946. 5749
Reproduction rates adjusted for age, parity, fecundity, and marriage. *J. Amer. Statist. Ass.*, **41**, 501-16.

Whelpton, P. K. 1947. 5749a
The fertility of successive cohorts of women in the United States. *Proc. 25th. Session Int. Statist. Inst. Conf., Washington, D.C.*, 1947 (Publ. 1951), **3B**, 631-59.

Whelpton, P. K. 1949. 5749b
Cohort analysis of fertility. *Amer. Sociol. Rev.*, **14**, 735-49.

Whelpton, P. K. & Kiser, C. V. 1946. 5749c
The sampling plan, selection and representativeness of couples in the inflated sample. *Milbank Mem. Fund Quart.*, **24**, 49-93.

Wherry, R. J. 1940. 5750
An approximation method for obtaining a maximized multiple criterion. *Psychometrika*, **5**, 109-15.

Wherry, R. J. 1941. 5751
An extension of the Doolittle method to simple regression problems. *J. Educ. Psychol.*, **32**, 459-64.

Wherry, R. J. 1944. 5752
Maximal weighting of qualitative data. *Psychometrika*, **9**, 263-6.

Wherry, R. J. 1946. 5753
Test selection and suppressor variables. *Psychometrika*, **11**, 239-47.

Wherry, R. J. 1947. 5754
Multiple bi-serial and multiple point bi-serial correlation. *Psychometrika*, **12**, 189-95.

Wherry, R. J. 1949. 5755
A new iterative method for correcting erroneous communality estimates in factor analysis. *Psychometrika*, **14**, 231-41.

Wherry, R. J. & Gaylord, R. H. 1943. 5756
The concept of test and item reliability in relation to factor pattern. *Psychometrika*, **8**, 247-64.

Wherry, R. J. & Gaylord, R. H. 1944. 5757
Factor pattern of test items and tests as a function of the correlation coefficient: content, difficulty, and constant error factors. *Psychometrika*, **9**, 237-44.

Wherry, R. J. & Taylor, E. K. 1946. 5758
The relation of multi-serial eta to other measures of correlation. *Psychometrika*, **11**, 155-61.

White, J. W. 1942. 5758a
Dimensional tolerances and quality control. *Product Engng.*, **13**, 634-6.

White, T. 1940. 5759
Linkage and crossing-over in the human sex chromosomes. *J. Genet.*, **40**, 403-37.

Whitehead, S. 1943. 5759a
A tentative statistical study of domestic radio interference. *J. Inst. Elect. Engrs.*, **90**, 181-92.

Whitfield, J. W. 1947. 5760
Rank correlation between two variables, one of which is ranked, the other dichotomous. *Biometrika*, **34**, 292-6.

Whitfield, J. W. 1949. 5761
Intra-class rank correlation. *Biometrika*, **36**, 463-7.

Whitlock, J. H. 1943. 5762
Characteristics of the population available for bio-assay of anthelmintics in *Nippostrongylus muris* infection in albino rats. *J. Parasit.*, **29**, 42-7.

Whitlock, J. H. & Bliss, C. I. 1943. 5763
A bio-assay technique for anthelmintics. *J. Parasit.*, **29**, 48-58.

Wick, G. G. 1940. 5764
L'idea di probabilità nella fisica dei quanti. *Questioni mat. appl., Bologna.*

Wien, R. & Phillips, G. E. 1945. 5765
The control of mercurochrome by toxicity tests. *Quart. J. Pharm.*, **18**, 35-40.

Wiener, A. S. & Irving, L. L. 1940. 5766
Chances of establishing the non-identity of biovular twins, with special reference to individuality tests of the blood. *Genetics*, **25**, 187-96.

Wiener, N. 1945. 5767
The theory of statistical extrapolation. (Spanish.) *Bol. Soc. Mat. Mexicana*, **2**, 37-42.

Wiener, N. 1948. 5768
Time, communication, and the nervous system. *Ann. N.Y. Acad. Sci.*, **50**, 197-220.

Wiener, N. 1949. 5769
Sur la théorie de la prévision statistique et du filtrage des ondes. *Analyse Harmonique. Colloq. Int. Cent. Nat. Rech. Sci., Paris*, **15**, 67-74.

Wiener, N. & Rosenblueth, A. 1946. 5770
The mathematical formulation of the problem of conduction of impulses in a network of connected excitable elements, specifically in cardiac muscle. (English. Spanish summary.) *Arch. Inst. Cardiol. Mexico*, **16**, 205-65.

Wiener, N. & Wintner, A. 1941. 5771
Harmonic analysis and ergodic theory. *Amer. J. Math.*, **63**, 415-26.

Wiener, N. & Wintner, A. 1941. 5772
On the ergodic dynamics of almost periodic systems. *Amer. J. Math.*, **63**, 794-824.

Wiener, N. & Wintner, A. 1943. 5773
The discrete chaos. *Amer. J. Math.*, **65**, 279-98.

Wiesler, H. 1944. 5774
Über die Grundlagen der Lebensversicherungs-Mathematik. *Mitt. Ver. Schweiz. Versich.-Math.*, **44**, 151-4.

Wiesler, H. 1946. 5775
Der Begriff der Wahrscheinlichkeit in Mathematik und Statistik. *Schweiz. Zeit. Volkwirtsch. Statist.*, **82**, 139-50.

Wiesler, H. 1949. 5776
Eine Darstellung der Wahrscheinlichkeiten $P(\chi^2, n)$ und ein Diagram für die χ^2 Verteilung. *Schweiz. Zeit. Volkwirtsch. Statist.*, **85**, 165-71.

Wigan, L. G. & Mather, K. 1942. 5777
Correlated response to the selection of polygenic characters. *Ann. Eugen.*, **11**, 354-64.

Wilcox, O. W. 1941. 5778
A critique of field experiments with plant nutrients. *Amer. Fertilizer*, **95**, 8-11, 24, 25.

Wilcoxen, L. C. 1942. 5779
The market forecasting significance of marketing movements. *J. Amer. Statist. Ass.*, **37**, 343-51.

Wilcoxon, F. 1945. 5780
Individual comparisons by ranking methods. *Biometrics Bull.*, **1**, 80-3.

Wilcoxon, F. 1946. 5781
Individual comparisons of grouped data by ranking methods. *J. Econ. Ent.*, **39**, 269-70.

Wilcoxon, F. 1947. 5782
Probability tables for individual comparisons by ranking methods. *Biometrics*, **3**, 119-22.

Wilcoxon, F. 1949. 5783
Some rapid approximate statistical procedures. *American Cynamid Co., Standford Res. Lab.*, July 1949, 16 pp.

Wild, A. M. 1947. 5784
General equation for the serial dilution technique in microbiological assays. *Nature*, **160**, 57-8.

Wilkins, J. E., Jr. 1944. 5785
A note on skewness and kurtosis. *Ann. Math. Statist.*, **15**, 333-5.

Wilkins, J. E., Jr. 1945. 5786
The differential difference equation for epidemics. *Bull. Math. Biophys.*, **7**, 149-50.

Wilkinson, R. I. 1941. 5787
The reliability of holding-time measurements. *Bell Syst. Tech. J.*, **20**, 365-404.

Wilkinson, R. I. 1942. 5788
The combination of probability curves in engineering. *Trans. Amer. Inst. Elect. Engrs.*, **61**, 953-63.

Wilks, S. S. 1940. 5789
Representative sampling and poll reliability. *Public Opinion Quart.*, **4**, 261-9.

Wilks, S. S. 1940. 5790
Confidence limits and critical differences between percentages. *Public Opinion Quart.*, **4**, 332-8.

Wilks, S. S. 1941. 5791
On the determination of sample sizes for setting tolerance limits. *Ann. Math. Statist.*, **12**, 91-6.

Wilks, S. S. 1941. 5792
Karl Pearson: founder of the science of statistics. *Science*, **53**, 249-53.

Wilks, S. S. 1941. 5793
Statistical basis of the quality control program. *J. Engng. Educ.*, **32**, 328-34.

Wilks, S. S. 1942. 5794
Statistical prediction with special reference to the problem of tolerance limits. *Ann. Math. Statist.*, **13**, 400-9.

Wilks, S. S. 1946. 5795
Sample criteria for testing equality of means, equality of variances, and equality of covariances in a normal multivariate distribution. *Ann. Math. Statist.*, **17**, 257-81.

Wilks, S. S. 1947. 5796
Personnel and training problems in statistics. *Amer. Math. Monthly*, **54**, 525-8.

Wilks, S. S. 1947. 5797
Statistical training for industry. *Industr. Engng. Chem.* **19**, 953-5.

Wilks, S. S. 1948. 5798
Order statistics. *Bull. Amer. Math. Soc.*, **54**, 6-50.

Willcox, W. F. 1947. 5799
Methods of apportioning seats among the states in the American House of Representatives. *Proc. 25th. Session Int. Statist. Inst. Conf., Washington, D.C.*, 1947 (Publ. 1951), **3B**, 858-67.

Williams, C. B. 1940.   5800
An analysis of four years' captures of insects in a
light trap. II. The effect of weather conditions on
insect activity; and the estimation and forecasting of
changes in the insect population. *Trans. Roy. Ent.
Soc. Lond.*, **90**, 227-306.

Williams, C. B. 1940.   5801
A note on the statistical analysis of sentence length as
a criterion of literary style. *Biometrika*, **31**, 356-61.

Williams, C. B. 1943.   5802
Area and number of species. *Nature*, **152**, 264-7.

Williams, C. B. 1944.   5803
Some applications of the logarithmic series and the
index of diversity to ecological problems. *J. Ecology*,
32, 1-44.

Williams, C. B. 1944.   5804
The number of publications written by biologists.
Ann. Eugen., **12**, 143-6.

Williams, C. B. 1945.   5805
Index of diversity as applied to ecological problems.
Nature, **155**, 390-1.

Williams, C. B. 1945.   5806
Recent light trap catches of lepidoptera in U.S.A.
analysed in relation to the logarithmic series and the
index of diversity. *Ann. Ent. Soc. Amer.*, **38**, 357-64.

Williams, C. B. 1946.   5807
Yule's " characteristic " and the " index of diversity ".
Nature, **157**, 482.

Williams, C. B. 1947.   5808
The logarithmic series and its application to biological
problems. *J. Ecology*, **34**, 253-72.

Williams, D. C. 1945.   5809
On the derivation of probabilities from frequencies.
I. (English. Spanish summary.) *Phil. Phenom. Res.*,
5, 449-84.

Williams, D. C. 1945.   5810
The challenging situation in the philosophy of
probability. *Phil. Phenom. Res.*, **6**, 67-86.

Williams, D. C. 1946.   5811
The problem of probability. *Phil. Phenom. Res.*, **6**,
619-22.

Williams, E. J. 1949.   5812
Confounding and fractional replication in factorial
experiments. *J. Aust. Inst. Agric. Sci.*, **15**, 145-53.

Williams, E. J. 1949.   5813
Experimental designs balanced for the estimation of
residual effects of treatments. *Aust. J. Sci. Res. A*, **2**,
149-68.

Williams, E. J. 1949.   5814
Simplified calculations for the estimation of gene
frequencies for the Rhesus factor and an application
to partially classified data. *Med. J. Aust.*, **1949** (1),
739-40.

Williams, J. D. 1941.   5815
Moments of the ratio of the mean square successive
difference to the mean square difference in samples
from a normal universe. *Ann. Math. Statist.*, **12**, 239-41.

Williams, J. D. 1946.   5816
An approximation to the probability integral. *Ann.
Math. Statist.*, **17**, 363-5.

Williams, J. J. 1948.   5817
Another commentary on so-called segregation indices.
Amer. Sociol. Rev., **13**, 298-303.

Williams, K. 1948.   5818
The classical theory of risk—a statistical approach.
J. Inst. Actuar. Students' Soc., **7**, 126-43.

Wilm, H. G. 1943.   5819
Efficient sampling of climatic and related environmental factors. *Trans. Amer. Geophys. Un.*, **24**,
208-12.

Wilm, H. G. 1945.   5820
Notes on analysis of experiments replicated in time.
Biometrics Bull., **1**, 16-20.

Wilm, H. G. 1946.   5821
The design and analysis of methods for sampling
microclimatic factors. *J. Amer. Statist. Ass.*, **41**,
221-32.

Wilm, H. G., Costello, D. F. & Klipple, G. E.   5822
1944. Estimating forage yield by the double-sampling
method. *J. Amer. Soc. Agron.*, **36**, 194-203.

Wilsdon, B. H. 1943.   5822a
Postwar industry and quality control. *J. Soc. Dyers
& Colorists*, **58**, 161-4. (Also: *Textile Manufacturer*,
69, 520-1.)

Wilson, A. J. C. 1949.   5823
The probability distribution of *X*-ray intensities. I.
Acta Cryst., **2**, 318-21.

Wilson, E. 1941.   5824
A simple technique for laying out sample plots. *J.
Forestry*, **39**, 650-1.

Wilson, E. B. 1941.   5825
The controlled experiment and the four-fold table.
Science, **93**, 557-60.

Wilson, E. B. 1942.   5826
On confidence intervals. *Proc. Nat. Acad. Sci. U.S.A.*,
28, 88-93.

Wilson, E. B. 1942.   5827
On contingency tables. *Proc. Nat. Acad. Sci. U.S.A.*,
28, 94-100.

Wilson, E. B. 1944.   5828
Note on the *t*-test. *Amer. Math. Monthly*, **51**, 563-6.

Wilson, E. B. 1947.   5829
The spread of measles in the family. *Proc. Nat. Acad.
Sci. U.S.A.*, **33**, 68-72.

Wilson, E. B. & Burke, M. H. 1942-3.   5830
The epidemic curve. I, II. *Proc. Nat. Acad. Sci.
U.S.A.*, **28**, 361-7; **29**, 43-8.

Wilson, E. B. & Worcester, J. 1942.   5831
Note on the *t*-test. *Proc. Nat. Acad. Sci. U.S.A.*, **28**,
297-301.

Wilson, E. B. & Worcester, J. 1942.   5832
Contingency tables. *Proc. Nat. Acad. Sci. U.S.A.*,
28, 378-84.

Wilson, E. B. & Worcester, J. 1942.   5833
The association of three attributes. *Proc. Nat. Acad.
Sci. U.S.A.*, **28**, 384-90.

Wilson, E. B. & Worcester, J. 1943.   5834
The determination of L.D.50. and its sampling error
in bio-assay. *Proc. Nat. Acad. Sci. U.S.A.*, **29**, 79-85;
114-20; 257-62.

Wilson, E. B. & Worcester, J. 1943. 5835
Bio-assay on a general curve. *Proc. Nat. Acad. Sci. U.S.A.*, **29**, 150-4.

Wilson, E. B. & Worcester, J. 1944. 5836
Note on stability of incidence of the " common cold ". *Science*, **99**, 468-9.

Wilson, E. B. & Worcester, J. 1944. 5837
A second approximation to Soper's epidemic curve. *Proc. Nat. Acad. Sci. U.S.A.*, **30**, 37-44.

Wilson, E. B. & Worcester, J. 1944. 5838
The epidemic curve with no accession of susceptibles. *Proc. Nat. Acad. Sci. U.S.A.*, **30**, 264-9.

Wilson, E. B. & Worcester, J. 1945. 5839
The law of mass action in epidemiology. *Proc. Nat. Acad. Sci. U.S.A.*, **31**, 24-34; 109-16.

Wilson, E. B. & Worcester, J. 1945. 5840
The variation of infectivity. *Proc. Nat. Acad. Sci. U.S.A.*, **31**, 142-7; 203-8.

Wilson, E. B. & Worcester, J. 1945. 5841
Damping of epidemic waves. *Proc. Nat. Acad. Sci. U.S.A.*, **31**, 294-8.

Wilson, E. B. & Worcester, J. 1945. 5842
The normal logarithmic transform. *Rev. Econ. Statist.*, **27**, 17-22.

Wilson, E. B. & Worcester, J. 1945. 5843
The spread of an epidemic. *Proc. Nat. Acad. Sci. U.S.A.*, **31**, 327-33.

Wilson, M. R. 1945. 5844
Maintaining quality of small arms ammunition. *Canadian Metals and Met. Industr.*, **8** (4), 37-40.

Wilson, R. H. 1941. 5845
Stockroom purchasing. *Purchasing*, **10**, 47-50.

Wilson, R. H. 1941. 5846
A universal system of stock control. *Purchasing*, **11**, 80-8.

Wilson, R. H. 1947. 5847
Scientific control of stockroom inventories. *Proc. Midwest Qual. Contr. Conf.*, 1947.

Winder, C. V. 1947. 5848
Misuse of " deduced ratios " in the estimation of median effective doses. *Nature*, **159**, 883.

Wing, H. D. 1941. 5849
A factorial study of musical tests. *Brit. J. Psychol.*, **31**, 341-55.

Wing, H. D. 1948. 5850
Tests of musical ability and appreciation. *Brit. J. Psychol. Monogr. Suppl.*, no. 27, 88 pp.

Winkler, W. 1941-2. 5851
Grundsätzliches zur genealogischen Statistik. *Allg. Statist. Arch.*, **30**, 277-92.

Winkler, W. 1942. 5852
Die stationäre Bevölkerung. (French and English summaries.) *Rev. Int. Statist. Inst.*, **10**, 49-74.

Winkler, W. 1944. 5853
Die Lebensjahre einer Bevölkerung. *Rev. Int. Statist. Inst.*, **12**, 5-22.

Winkler, W. 1947. 5854
On random variations in statistical data. (French summary.) *Proc. 25th. Session Int. Statist. Inst. Conf., Washington, D.C.*, 1947 (Publ. 1951), **3A**, 272-83.

Winkler, W. 1947. 5855
Age distribution and its interrelation with the elements of natural increase. *Proc. 25th. Session Int. Statist. Inst. Conf. Washington, D.C.*, 1947 (Publ. 1951), **3B**, 683-703.

Winkler, W. 1948. 5856
Ein Mass der Seelischen Komponente des Geburtenrückganges. *Statist. Vierteljschr.*, **1**, 94-9.

Winkler, W. 1949. 5857
Das erweiterte " Paretosche Gesetz " und seine ökonomische Bedeutung. *Statist. Vierteljschr.*, **2**, 124-43.

Winkler, W. 1949. 5858
The " Expectation of life of the dead ". A contribution to classify some fundamental notions. *Bull. Int. Statist. Inst.*, **32** (2), 365-7.

Winkler, W. 1949. 5859
The corrected Pareto law and its economic meaning. *Bull. Int. Statist. Inst.*, **32** (2), 441-9.

Winkler, W. 1949. 5860
Statistik und Wirtschaftslehre. *Zeit. Nat. Ökon.*, **12**, 429-41.

Winsor, C. P. 1944. 5861
Biometry. *Mod. Phys.*, 89-110.

Winsor, C. P. 1946. 5862
Which regression? *Biometrics Bull.*, **2**, 101-9.

Winsor, C. P. 1947. 5862[a]
" Das Gesetz der kleinen Zahlen." *Hum. Biol.*, **19**, 154-61.

Winsor, C. P. 1948. 5862[b]
Probability and listerism. *Hum. Biol.*, **20**, 161-9.

Winsor, C. P. 1948. 5863
Factorial analysis of a multiple dichotomy. *Hum. Biol.*, **20**, 195-204.

Winsor, C. P. & Clarke, G. L. 1940. 5864
A statistical study of variation in the catch of plankton nets. *J. Marine Res.*, **3**, 1-34.

Winsten, C. B. 1946. 5865
Inequalities in terms of mean range. *Biometrika*, **33**, 283-95.

Winterhalter, A. J. 1945. 5865[a]
Development of reject limits for measurements. *Industr. Qual. Contr.*, **1** (4), 12-15; (5), 12-13.

Winters, L. M. & Green, W. W. 1944. 5866
A study of the predictive value of scores on body conformation of pigs taken previous to final score. *J. Animal Sci.*, **3**, 399-405.

Wintner, A. 1940. 5867
Spherical equidistributions and a statistic of polynomials which occur in the theory of perturbations. *Astr. Papers dedicated to Elis Strömgren*, pp. 287-97.

Wintner, A. 1941. 5867[a]
On the distribution function of the remainder term of the prime number theorem. *Amer. J. Math.*, **63**, 233-48.

Wintner, A. 1941. 5868
On the iteration of distribution functions in the calculus of probability. (English. Spanish translation.) *Union Mat. Argent. Publ.*, no. 18, 12 pp.

Wintner, A. 1941. 5869
The singularities of Cauchy's distributions. *Duke Math. J.*, **8**, 678-81.

Wintner, A. 1941. 5869a
Statistics and prime numbers. *Nature*, **147**, 208-9.

Wintner, A. 1942. 5870
The distribution of primes. *Duke Math. J.*, **9**, 425-30.

Wintner, A. 1942. 5871
On a family of Fourier transforms. *Bull. Amer. Math. Soc.*, **48**, 304-8.

Wintner, A. 1942. 5872
On a statistics of the Ramanujan sums. *Amer. J. Math.*, **64**, 106-14.

Wintner, A. 1944. 5872a
Random factorization and Riemann's hypothesis. *Duke Math. J.*, **11**, 267-75.

Wintner, A. 1945. 5873
Mean values of arithmetical representations. *Amer. J. Math.*, **67**, 481-5.

Wintner, A. 1945. 5874
The moment problem of enumerating distributions. *Duke Math. J.*, **12**, 23-5.

Wintner, A. 1947. 5875
On the shape of the angular case of Cauchy's distribution curves. *Ann. Math. Statist.*, **18**, 589-93.

Wintner, A. 1949. 5876
Factorial moments and enumerating distributions. *Skand. Aktuartidskr.*, **32**, 63-8.

Wise, M. E. 1946. 5877
The use of the negative binomial distribution in an industrial sampling problem. *J. R. Statist. Soc. Suppl.*, **8**, 202-11 (addition: *B* **10**, 264).

Wishart, J. 1940. 5878
Field trials: their lay-out and statistical analysis. *Imp. Bur. Plant Breeding and Genetics Tech. Commun.*, 1940, 1-36.

Wishart, J. 1947. 5879
The cumulants of the Z and of the logarithmic χ^2 and the t distributions. *Biometrika*, **34**, 170-8 (correction: 374).

Wishart, J. 1947. 5880
Note on the probability distribution arising in the study of the Institute's examinations. *J. Inst. Actuar. Students' Soc.*, **6**, 140-3.

Wishart, J. 1947. 5881
The variance ratio test in statistics. *J. Inst. Actuar. Students' Soc.*, **6**, 172-84.

Wishart, J. 1947. 5882
Proof of the distributions of χ^2, of the estimate of variance, and of the variance ratio. *J. Inst. Actuar. Students' Soc.*, **7**, 98-103.

Wishart, J. 1948. 5883
Proofs of the distribution law of second order moment statistics. *Biometrika*, **35**, 55-7 (note: 422).

Wishart, J. 1948. 5884
The teaching of statistics. *J. R. Statist. Soc. A*, **111**, 212-29.

Wishart, J. 1948. 5885
Tests of significance in the simple regression problem. *J. Inst. Actuar. Students' Soc.*, **8**, 38-43.

Wishart, J. 1949. 5885a
Analisis de la varianza y covarianza. *Inst. Nac. Invest. Agron., Madrid.*

Wishart, J. 1949. 5886
Cumulants of multivariate multinomial distributions. *Biometrika*, **36**, 47-58.

Wishart, J. 1949. 5887
Test of homogeneity of regression coefficients, and its application in the analysis of covariance. *Le calcul des probabilités et ses applications. Colloq. Int. Centre Nat. Rech. Sci., Paris*, **13**, 93-9.

Wisseroth, K. 1947. 5888
Die günstigste Verteilungsbreite, ein neues Streuungsmass. *Zeit. angew. Math. Mech.*, **25/27**, 126-7.

Withell, E. R. 1942. 5889
The significance of the variation in shape of time-survivor curves. *J. Hyg., Camb.*, **42**, 124-83.

Wold, H. O. A. 1941. 5889a
Fertility outside marriage and during the first months of marriage. (Swedish.) *Statsvetenskaplig Tidskr.*, **44**, 377-422.

Wold, H. O. A. 1941. 5889b
Statistical demand analysis. (Swedish. English summary.) *Kungl. Lantbruksademiens Tidskr.*, **80**, 63-79.

Wold, H. O. A. 1941. 5890
Eine schwedische Untersuchung über die Elastizität der Nachfrage. *Metron*, **14**, 263-86. (Swedish version (1942): *Sosialt Arbeid*, Oslo, **16**, 33-48.)

Wold, H. O. A. 1943. 5890a
On infinite, non-negative definite, Hermitian matrices, and corresponding linear equation systems. *Ark. Mat., Astr. Fys.*, **29A** (19), 13 pp.

Wold, H. O. A. 1943-4. 5891
A synthesis of pure demand analysis. I, II, III. *Skand. Aktuartidskr.*, **26**, 85-118; 220-63; **27**, 69-120.

Wold, H. O. A. 1945. 5892
A theorem on regression coefficients obtained from successively extended sets of variables. *Skand. Aktuartidskr.*, **28**, 181-200.

Wold, H. O. A. 1946. 5893
A comment on spurious correlation. *Försmat. Stud. Filip Lundberg*, pp. 278-85.

Wold, H. O. A. 1947. 5894
A short-cut method for distinguishing between rigid and disturbed periodicity. (French summary.) *Proc. 25th. Session Int. Statist. Inst. Conf., Washington, D.C.*, 1947 (Publ. 1951), 3A, 302-7.

Wold. H. O. A. 1948. 5895
On prediction in stationary time series. *Ann. Math. Statist.*, **19**, 558-67.

Wold, H. O. A. 1948. 5896
Random normal deviates. *Tracts for computers*, no. 25, xiii+51 pp. (Also: *Statist. Uppsala*, 3.)

Wold. H. O. A. 1948. 5897
On stationary point processes and Markov chains. *Skand. Aktuartidskr.*, **31**, 229-40.

Wold, H. O. A. 1949. 5898
A large-sample test for moving averages. *J. R. Statist. Soc. B*, **11**, 297-305.

Wold, H. O. A. 1949. 5899
Sur les processus stationnaires ponctuels. *Le calcul des probabilites et ses applications. Colloq. Int. Centre Nat. Rech. Sci., Paris*, **13**, 75-86.

Wold, H. O. A. 1949. 5900
Statistical estimation of economic relationship. *Econometrica Suppl.*, **17**, 1-22. (Also: *Proc. 25th Session Int. Statist. Inst. Conf., Washington D.C.*, 1947 (Publ. 1951), **5**, 1-22.)

Wold, H. O. A. & Bentzel, R. 1948. 5900[a]
Some traffic problems in the light of statistics. (Swedish.) *Stat. Offent. Utred.* no. 20 (F), 386-98.

Wold, H. O. A. & Westin, G. 1943. 5901
Tooth inspection of recruits of 1942. The mathematical-statistical methods. (Swedish.) *Odontologisk Tidskr.*, **51**, 617-39.

Wolfe, D. 1940. 5902
Factor analysis to 1940. *Psychometrica Monogr.*, no. 3, vii+69 pp.

Wolfenden, H. H. 1942. 5903
On the formulae for calculating the " exposed to risk " in constructing mortality and other tables from the individual records of insured lives. *Trans. Actuar. Soc. Amer.*, **43**, 234-77.

Wolfle, D. 1942. 5904
Factor analysis in the study of personality. *J. Abnorm. & Soc. Psychol.*, **37**, 393-7.

Wolfowitz, J. 1942. 5905
Additive partition functions and a class of statistical hypotheses. *Ann. Math. Statist.*, **13**, 247-79.

Wolfowitz, J. 1943. 5906
Asymptotic distributions of ascending and descending runs. *Bull. Amer. Math. Soc.*, **49**, 539-40.

Wolfowitz, J. 1943. 5907
On the theory of runs with some applications to quality control. *Ann. Math. Statist.*, **14**, 280-8.

Wolfowitz, J. 1944. 5908
Note on runs of consecutive elements. *Ann. Math. Statist.*, **15**, 97-8.

Wolfowitz, J. 1944. 5909
Asymptotic distributions of runs up and down. *Ann. Math. Statist.*, **15**, 163-72.

Wolfowitz, J. 1946. 5910
Confidence limits for the fraction of a normal population which lies between two given limits. *Ann. Math. Statist.*, **17**, 483-8.

Wolfowitz, J. 1946. 5911
On sequential binomial estimation. *Ann. Math. Statist.*, **17**, 489-93.

Wolfowitz, J. 1947. 5912
Consistency of sequential binomial estimates. *Ann. Math. Statist.*, **18**, 131-5.

Wolfowtiz, J. 1947. 5913
The efficiency of sequential estimates and Wald's equation for sequential processes. *Ann. Math. Statist.*, **18**, 215-30.

Wolfowitz, J. 1949. 5914
The distribution of plane angles of contact. *Quart. Appl. Math.*, **7**, 117-20.

Wolfowitz, J. 1949. 5915
Non-parametric statistical inference. *Proc. Berkeley Symp. Math. Statist. and Probab.*, 1945-6, pp. 93-113.

Wolfowitz, J. 1949. 5916
The power of the classical tests associated with the normal distribution. *Ann. Math. Statist.*, **20**, 540-51.

Wolfowitz, J. 1949. 5917
On Wald's proof of the consistency of the maximum likelihood estimate. *Ann. Math. Statist.*, **20**, 601-2.

Wolkowitsch, D. 1948. 5918
Ajustement d'une ligne polygonale. *J. Soc. Statist. Paris*, **89**, 409-11.

Wolkowitsch, D. 1949. 5919
La géométrie et les diagrammes de la statistique. *J. Soc. Statist. Paris*, **90**, 67-74.

Womersley, J. R. 1946. 5920
Scientific computing in Great Britain. *Math. Tab. Aids Comput.*, **2**, 110-17.

Wong, W. A. & Hobbs, G. E. 1949. 5921
Personal factors in industrial accidents. A study of accident proneness in an industrial group. *J. Industr. Med. Surgery of Trauma*, **18**, 7ff.

Woo, T. L. 1943. 5922
A study of the Chinese humerus. *Biometrika*, **33**, 36-47.

Wood, E. C. 1944. 5923
Mathematics of biological assay. *Nature*, **153**, 84-5; 680-1.

Wood, E. C. 1945. 5924
Calculation of the results of microbiological assays. *Nature*, **155**, 632.

Wood, E. C. 1946. 5925
Computation of biological assays. *Nature*, **158**, 835.

Wood, E. C. 1946. 5926
The theory of certain analytical procedure with particular reference to microbiological assays. *Analyst*, **71**, 1-14.

Wood, E. C. 1947. 5927
The computation of microbiological assays of amino-acids and other growth factors. *Analyst*, **72**, 84-90.

Wood, E. C. 1947. 5928
Short cuts to the estimation of standard errors, particularly in microbiological assays. *Chemistry & Industry*, **1947**, 334-6.

Wood, E. C. & Finney, D. J. 1946. 5929
The design and statistical analysis of microbiological assays. *Quart. J. Pharm.*, **19**, 112-27.

Wood, G. H. 1945. 5930
Cricket scores and geometrical progression. *J. R. Statist. Soc.*, **108**, 12-40.

Woodbury, M. A. 1940. 5931
Rank correlation when there are equal variates. *Ann. Math. Statist.*, **11**, 358-62.

Woodbury, M. A. 1949. 5932
On a probability distribution. *Ann. Math. Statist.*, **20**, 311-13.

Woodbury, R. M. 1949. 5933
The incidence of industrial disputes. *Int. Lab. Rev.*, **60**, 451-66.

Woodbury, W. 1949. 5934
Monte Carlo calculations. *Proc. Seminar Sci. Computation, IBM Corp., New York.*

Woodruff, N. H. 1940. 5935
Mathematics used in biology. *J. Tennessee Acad. Sci.,* **15**, 177-266.

Woods, A. P. & Tayler, C. R. 1946. 5935ᵃ
A statistical method and results of a study of factors affecting open hearth production rate. *Blast Furnace & Steel Pl.,* **34**, 847-54.

Woodward, P. M. 1947. 5936
A statistical theory of cascade multiplication. *Proc. Camb. Phil. Soc.,* **44**, 404-12.

Woofter, T. J. 1946. 5937
Probabilities of death in closed population groups. Illustrated by probabilities of death of white fathers after birth of children. *Hum. Biol.,* **18**, 158-70.

Woofter, T. J. 1947. 5937ᵃ
Completed generation reproduction rates. *Hum. Biol.,* **19**, 133-53.

Woofter, T. J. 1949. 5938
The relation of the net reproduction rate to other fertility measures. *J. Amer. Statist. Ass.,* **44**, 501-17.

Woolf, B. 1949. 5939
Rapid calculation of standard deviations. *Nature,* **164**, 360-1.

Woolf, B. & Waterhouse, J. 1945. 5940
Studies in infant mortality. I. Influence of social conditions in country boroughs of England and Wales. *J. Hyg., Camb.,* **44**, 67-98.

Woolley, E. B. 1941. 5941
The method of minimized areas as a basis for correlation analysis. *Econometrica,* **9**, 38-62.

Worcester, J. & Wilson, E. B. 1943. 5942
A table determining L.D.50 or the fifty per cent end-point. *Proc. Nat. Acad. Sci. U.S.A.,* **29**, 207-12.

Working, E. J. 1942. 5943
Reliability of averages. *Illinois Univ. Dept. Agric. Econ. and Agric. Exper. Sta., Rep.* AE-1837.

Working, H. 1942. 5944
Tools of science and the war industry: Stanford University course in statistical methods of quality control and improved methods of sampling. *Science,* **96**, 494-5.

Working, H. 1946. 5945
Note on sampling probabilities. *J. Amer. Statist. Ass.,* **41**, 238-9.

Wotta, H. 1941. 5946
Wahrscheinlichkeitsmathematische Grundlagen der Erfolgsstatistik. *Dtsch. Zeit. Chir.,* **255**, 49-73.

Woytinsky, W. S. 1946. 5947
Relationship between consumers' expenditures, savings, and disposable income. *Rev. Econ. Statist.,* **28**, 1-12.

Woytinsky, W. S. 1948. 5948
Consumption-saving function: its algebra and philosophy. *Rev. Econ. Statist.,* **30**, 45-55.

Wren, F. L. 1943. 5949
The calculation of statistical moments. *J. Tennessee Acad. Sci.,* **18**, 204-10.

Wright, E. P. 1947. 5950
Behaviour of telephone exchange traffic where non-equivalent choice outlets are commoned. *Elect. Commun.,* **24**, 42-54.

Wright, G. H. V. 1940. 5951
On probability. *Mind,* **49**, 265-83.

Wright, K. T. 1942. 5952
Use and limitations of the biased sample supplied by farm financial records. *Illinois Univ. Dept. Agric. Econ. and Agric. Exper. Sta., Rep.* AE-1837.

Wright, S. 1940. 5953
The statistical consequences of Mendelian heredity in relation to speciation. *The New Systematics,* pp. 161-82.

Wright, S. 1942. 5954
Statistical genetics and evolution. *Bull. Amer. Math. Soc.,* **48**, 223-46.

Wright, S. 1943. 5955
Isolation by distance. *Genetics,* **28**, 114-38.

Wright, S. 1943. 5956
An analysis of local variability of flower colour of *Linanthus parryae. Genetics,* **28**, 139-56.

Wright, S. 1945. 5957
The differential equation of the distribution of gene frequencies. *Proc. Nat. Acad. Sci. U.S.A.,* **31**, 382-9.

Wright, S. 1946. 5958
Isolation by distance under diverse systems of mating. *Genetics,* **31**, 39-59.

Wright, S. 1948. 5959
On the roles of diverted and random changes in gene frequency in the genetics of populations. *Evolution,* **2**, 279-94.

Wright, S. & Dobzhansky, T. 1946. 5960
Genetics of natural populations. XII. Experimental reproduction of some of the changes caused by natural selection in certain populations of *Drosophila pseudoobscura. Genetics,* **31**, 125-56.

Wright, S., Dobzhansky, T. & 5960ᵃ
Hovanitz, W. 1942.
Genetics of natural populations. VII. The allelism of lethals in the third chromosome of *Drosophila pseudoobscura. Genetics,* **27**, 363-94.

Wrinch, D. 1948. 5961
On the relation between certain distributions and their corresponding Patterson distributions. *Phil. Mag.,* (7) **39**, 692-6.

Wunschmann, R. 1949. 5962
Abschätzung von Zufallsschwankungen bei Verhältniszahlen. *Statist. Praxis,* **4**, 7-8.

Wurtele, M. 1944. 5963
On the application of the theory of probability to meteorological statistics. *Bull. Amer. Met. Soc.,* **25**, 338-40.

Wyss, H. 1948. 5964
Erwägungen über abhängige und unabhängige Wahrscheinlichkeiten. *Mitt. Ver. Schweiz. Versich.-Math.,* **48**, 171-205.

Y

Yaglom, A. M. 1947.   5965
The ergodic principle for Markov processes with stationary distributions. (Russian.) *Dokl. Akad. Nauk SSSR*, **56**, 347-9.

Yaglom, A. M. 1947.   5966
On the statistical treatment of Brownian motion. (Russian.) *Dokl. Akad. Nauk SSSR*, **56**, 691-4.

Yaglom, A. M. 1947.   5967
Certain limit theorems of the theory of branching random processes. (Russian.) *Dokl. Akad. Nauk SSSR*, **56**, 795-8.

Yaglom, A. M. 1949.   5968
On the statistical reversibility of Brownian motion. (Russian.) *Mat. Sbornik*, **24** (66), 457-92. (German version (1953): *Abh. Sowjetsch. Phys.*, **3**, 7-42.)

Yaglom, A. M. 1949.   5969
On problems about the linear interpolation of stationary random sequences and processes. (Russian.) *Usp. Mat. Nauk* (*N.S.*), **4**, 4(32), 173-8.

Yamanouchi, Z. 1949.   5970
Estimates of mean and standard deviation of a normal distribution from linear combinations of some chosen order statistics. (Japanese. English abstract.) *Bull. Math. Statist.*, **3**, 52-7.

Yardi, M. R. 1946.   5971
A statistical approach to the problem of chronology and Shakespeare's plays. *Sankhyā*, **7**, 263-8.

Yates, F. 1940.   5972
Lattice squares. *J. Agric. Sci.*, **30**, 672-87.

Yates, F. 1940.   5973
Modern experimental design and its function in plant selection. *Emp. J. Exper. Agric.*, **8**, 223-30.

Yates, F. 1940.   5974
The recovery of inter-block information in balanced incomplete block designs. *Ann. Eugen.*, **10**, 317-25.

Yates, F. 1943.   5975
Methods and purposes of agricultural surveys. *J. R. Soc. Arts*, **91**, 367-79.

Yates, F. 1946.   5976
A review of recent statistical developments in sampling and sampling surveys. *J. R. Statist. Soc.*, **109**, 12-43.

Yates, F. 1947.   5977
Analysis of data from all possible reciprocal crosses between a set of parental lines. *Heredity*, **1**, 287-301.

Yates, F. 1947.   5978
The influence of agricultural research statistics on the development of sampling theory. *Proc. 25th. Session Int. Statist. Inst. Conf., Washington, D.C.*, 1947 (Publ. 1951), **3A**, 27-39.

Yates, F. 1947.   5979
Technique of the analysis of variance. *Nature*, **160**, 472-3.

Yates, F. 1948.   5980
The analysis of contingency tables, with groupings based on quantitative characters. *Biometrika*, **35**, 176-81 (correction: 424).

Yates, F. 1948.   5981
Systematic sampling. *Phil. Trans. A*, **241**, 345-77.

Yates, F. 1949.   5982
Agriculture, sampling and operational research. *Bull. Int. Statist. Inst.*, **32** (2), 220-7.

Yates, F. 1949.   5983
The design of rotation experiments. *Commonwealth Bur. Soil. Sci. Tech. Commun.*, no. 46, 16 pp.

Yates, F. 1949.   5984
The place of experimental investigations in the planning of resource utilization. *Proc. U.N. Sci. Conf. Conservation and Utilization of Resources*, **1**, 192-6.

Yates, F. & Finney, D. J. 1942.   5985
Statistical problems in field sampling for wireworms. *Ann. Appl. Biol.*, **29**, 156-67.

Yates, F., Boyd, D. A. & Mathison, I. 1944.   5986
The manuring of farm crops, some results of a survey of fertilizer practice in England. *Emp. J. Exper. Agric.*, **12**, 163-76.

Yeatts, M. W. M. 1941.   5987
Indian Census. *Sankhyā*, **5**, 239-46.

Yerushalmy, J. 1943.   5988
The age-sex composition of the population resulting from natality and mortality conditions. *Milbank Memorial Fund Quart.*, **21** (1), 37-63.

Yerushalmy, J. 1945.   5988a
On the interval between successive births and its effect on survival of infants. I. An indirect method of study. *Hum. Biol.*, **17**, 65-106.

Yerushalmy, J. 1947.   5989
Recent developments in applications of statistics to tuberculosis control programs. (French summary.) *Proc. 25th Session Int. Statist. Inst. Conf., Washington, D.C.*, 1947 (Publ. 1951), **3A**, 576-94.

Yerushalmy, J. 1947.   5990
Statistical problems in assessing methods of medical diagnosis, with special reference to X-ray techniques. *Publ. Health Rep.*, **62**, 1432-49.

Yosida, K. 1940.   5991
The Markoff process with a stable distribution. *Proc. Imp. Acad. Tokyo*, **16**, 43-8.

Yosida, K. 1948.   5992
On the differentiability and the representation of a one-parameter semi-group of linear operators. *J. Math. Soc. Jap.*, **1**, 15-21.

Yosida, K. 1948.   5993
Simple Markoff process with a locally compact phase space. *Math. Japon.*, **1**, 99-103.

Yosida, K. 1949.   5994
Brownian motion on the surface of the 3-sphere. *Ann. Math. Statist.*, **20**, 292-6.

Yosida, K. 1949.   5995
An extension of Fokker-Planck's equation. *Proc. Japan Acad.*, **25** (9), 1-3.

Yosida, K. 1949.   5996
Integration of Fokker-Planck's equation in a compact Riemannian space. *Ark. Mat.*, **1**, 71-5.

Yosida, K. 1949.   5997
An operator-theoretical treatment of temporally homogeneous Markoff process. *J. Math. Soc. Jap.*, **1**, 244-53.

Yosida K. & Kakutani, S. 1941. 5998
Operator-theoretical treatment of Markoff's process and mean ergodic theorem. *Ann. Math.*, (2) **42**, 188-228.

Youden, W. J. 1940. 5999
Experimental designs to increase accuracy of greenhouse studies. *Contr. Boyce Thompson Inst.*, **11**, 219-28.

Youden, W. J. 1948. 6000
Multiple factor experiments in analytical chemistry. *Anal. Chem.*, **20**, 1136-40.

Youden, W. J. 1949. 6001
The fallacy of the best two out of three. *Nat. Bur. Stand. Tech. News Bull.*, **33** (7), 77-8.

Youden, W. J. & Cameron, J. M. 1949. 6002
Sampling plan reduces inspection costs. *Nat. Bur. Stand. Tech. News Bull.*, **33** (8), 92-3.

Young, D. M. & Romans, R. G. 1948. 6003
Assays of Insulin with one blood sample per rabbit per test day. *Biometrics*, **4**, 122-31.

Young, G. 1941. 6004
Maximum likelihood estimation and factor analysis. *Psychometrika*, **6**, 49-53.

Young, G. & Householder, A. S. 1940. 6004[a]
Factorial invariance and significance. *Psychometrika*, **5**, 47-56.

Young, L. C. 1940. 6005
Statistical method. *Mech. Engng.*, **62**, 475-6.

Young, L. C. 1941. 6006
On randomness in ordered sequences. *Ann. Math. Statist.*, **12**, 293-300.

Young, L. C. 1942. 6006[a]
Teaching quality control theory to engineers. *J. Engng. Educ.*, **32**, 667-72.

Young, L. E. & Merrell, M. 1943. 6007
The mouse-adapted Lansing strain of poliomyelitis virus. II. A quantitative study of certain factors affecting the reliability of the neutralization test. *Amer. J. Hyg.*, **37**, 80-92.

Yudin, M. I. 1946. 6008
Physical mean-forming and the laws of turbulent diffusion. *C. R. (Dokl.) Acad. Sci. URSS*, **51**, 103-6.

Yule, G. U. 1945. 6009
Method of studying time-series based on their internal correlations. *J. R. Statist. Soc.*, **108**, 208-25.

Yule, G. U. 1946. 6010
Cumulative sampling: a speculation as to what happens in copying manuscripts. *J. R. Statist. Soc.*, **109**, 44-52.

Yule, G. U. 1947. 6011
Puyol's Classes A and B of tests of the " De Imitatione Christi ". *Recherches de Théologie ancienne et médiévale*, **14**, 65-88.

Z

Zapff, J. 1940. 6012
Die Ausgleichung von Sterbetafeln unter besonderer Berücksichtigung der Gewichte der Einzelbeobachtungen. *Blä. Versich.-math*, **5**, 1-21; 49-68.

Zapp, J. A. 1947. 6013
Statistical approaches to some problems of industrial preventive medicine. *Hum. Biol.*, **19**, 27-52.

Zappa, G. 1940. 6014
Sulla maniere di colmare le lacune di una serie statistica. *Atti 2da Riun. Sci., Soc. Ital. Statist.*

Zappa, G. 1940. 6015
Osservazioni sopra le medie combinatorie. *Metron*, **14**, 31-53.

Zarapkin, S. R. 1945. 6016
Alcuni problemi della analisi biometrica di popolazioni naturali. *Mem. Ist Ital. Idrobiol.*, **2**, 301 ff.

Zasukhin, V. 1941. 6017
On the theory of multidimensional stationary random processes. *C. R. (Dokl.) Acad. Sci. URSS*, **33**, 435-7.

Zeisel, H. & Harper, V. E. 1948. 6018
The advertising value of different magazines. *J. Marketing*, **13**, 56-61.

Zia-ud-Din, M. 1940. 6018[a]
Tables of symmetric functions for statistical purposes. *Proc. Nat. Acad. Sci. India*, **10** (2), 53-60.

Ziebolz, H. 1943. 6019
Automatized statistical control. *Instruments*, **16**, 18-19.

Zieve, L. 1940. 6020
Note on the correlation of initial scores with gains. *J. Educ. Psychol.*, **31**, 391-4.

Ziezold, B. 1942. 6021
Weitere Ergebnisse der Analyse von Seuchenkurven. *Zeit. Hyg. Infektkr.*, **124**, 93-114.

Ziezold, B. 1943. 6022
Zur Seuchenvorhersage. *Zeit. Hyg. Infektkr.*, **124**, 704-29.

Zimmerman, W. S. 1946. 6023
A simple graphical method for orthogonal rotation of axes. *Psychometrika*, **11**, 51-5.

Zimmermann, G. 1945. 6024
Der " *t*-test ", ein Hilfsmittel für die statistische Bearbeitung von Ergebnissen biologischer Versuche. *Landw. Jb. Schweiz.*, **59**, 893-914.

Zipf, G. K. 1946. 6025
The $\frac{P_1 P_2}{D}$ hypothesis: the case of Railway Express. *J. Psychol.*, **22**, 3-8.

Zuber, M. S. 1942. 6026
Relative efficiency of incomplete block designs using corn uniformity trial data. *J. Amer. Soc. Agron.*, **34**, 30-47.

Zucker, L. M. 1947. 6027
Evaluation of slopes and intercepts of straight lines. *Hum. Biol.*, **19**, 231-59.

Zwinggi, E. 1941. 6028
Study of internal variation in groups of persons. (German, French, Italian and English.) *Trans. 12th Int. Congr. Actuar., Lucerne*, 1940, **3**, 263-303.

Zwinggi, E. 1942. 6029
Leben und Sterben in mathematischer Darstellung. (Über Sinn und Herkommen der " Sterblichkeitgesetze ".) *Mitt. Ver. Schweiz. Versich.-Math.*, **42**, 77-95.

Zwinggi, E. 1944. 6030
Über den Vergleich von Verhältniszahlen. Beispiele für die Anwendung neuerer statistischer Verfahren im Gebiete der Versicherung. *Mitt. Ver. Schweiz. Versich.-Math.*, **44**, 71-93.

Zwinggi, E. 1945. 6031
Über die Berechnung der unabhängigen Sterbe- und Stornowahrscheinlichkeiten im ersten Versicherungsjahr. *Mitt. Ver. Schweiz. Versich.-Math.*, **45**, 57-66.

Zwinggi, E. 1948. 6032
Eine Näherungsformel für die Prämie der Invalidenversicherung. *Experientia*, **4**, 218-19.

Zwinggi, E. 1948. 6033
Initiation of a formula for approximate valuation of premiums for disability benefits. *Skand. Aktuartidskr.*, **31**, 165-70.

Zwinggi, E. 1949. 6034
Berechnung und Darstellung der abhängigen und unabhängigen Wahrscheinlichkeiten. *Mitt. Ver. Schweiz. Versich.-Math.*, **49**, 179-93.

Zwinggi, E. 1949. 6034[a]
The calculation of reserves by means of samples. *Schweiz. Zeit. Volkwirtsch. Statist.*, **85**, 384-8.

Zwingli, U. 1949. 6035
Die Berechnung des schweizerischen Volkseinkommens und ihr Erkenntniswert. *Schweiz. Zeit. Volkwirtsch. Statist.*, **85**, 97-118.

Zygmund, A. 1947. 6036
A remark on characteristic functions. *Ann. Math. Statist.*, **18**, 272-6.